This is an important topic which has not received enough attention. The interim arrangements De Groof discusses are a key strategy for institutionalising transitions. De Groof's work is an important contribution to mapping their core components through a detailed and broad comparative lens. The book deserves to be read by students, practitioners, and policy-makers, interested in transitions from conflict or social crisis. The repository of comparative material forms an important resource in itself.

Christine Bell, Professor of Constitutional Law, The University of Edinburgh

De Groof confronts transitional governance as a practice and field of research of its own, extracting and detaching it from traditional research embedding transitional governance in specific contexts and narratives. The book's focus on international law as a tool for analysing transitional governance brings in an inspiring legal 'formalism' to the debate, with the necessary nuances and restraints. The book is without much doubt a welcome and thought-provoking contribution to literature on the topic. It is a must-read for international lawyers in the field.

Eric De Brabandere, Professor of International Dispute Settlement and Director, Grotius Centre for International Legal Studies, Leiden University

Traditionally institutional change within a State is seen as a matter for domestic constitutional law. De Groof's groundbreaking study of recent practice, however, demonstrates that international law plays a role in regulating this process. Today international principles such as self-determination and non-intervention provide a normative framework for governance in the process of achieving a just peace.

John Dugard, Emeritus Professor of law universities of Leiden and the Witwatersrand

In *State Renaissance for Peace*, De Groof makes the useful argument that even if not directly governed by international law, situations of transitional governance within states are nonetheless embedded within international law, in particular via the principles of self-determination and non-intervention. Dr De Groof has written a timely and thought-provoking study, illustrating that there is far more to international law than rules and compliance.

Jan Klabbers, Professor of Law, University of Helsinki

Transitional governance has played a crucial – if contested – role in societies grappling with a legacy of violent conflict and political instability, as well as other challenges. It poses difficult questions at the interface of international law, political ethics, and public policy. This fascinating volume provides a unique contribution – as perhaps the first in-depth analysis of transitional governance from an international law perspective – and it is also meticulously researched and presented.

Edward Newman, Professor of International Security,
University of Leeds

Emmanuel De Groof has undertaken a systematic and meticulous study of *ius in interregno*: the international law pertaining to an existing state's transition from one political order to another. He elucidates the existing and emerging norms that bridle both transitional governing arrangements and external involvement in transition processes. A must-read for scholars concerned with the intersection of international and domestic legal authority.

Brad R. Roth, Professor of Law, Wayne State University

It appears at first that De Groof's intrastate focus on transitional governance would be of comparative constitutional nature. But the author analytically, and very convincingly, leads his reader through the international legal framework of *ius in interregno*. The book is interdisciplinary, yet firmly grounded in public international law. A very valuable contribution to international law and related fields.

Jure Vidmar, Professor of Public International Law, Maastricht
University, The Netherlands

STATE RENAISSANCE FOR PEACE

After 1989, the function of transitional governance changed. It became a process whereby transitional authorities introduce a constitutional transformation on the basis of interim laws. In spite of its domestic nature, it also became an international project and one with formidable ambitions: ending war, conflict or crisis by reconfiguring the state order. This model attracted international attention, from the UN Security Council and several regional organisations, and became a playing field of choice in international politics and diplomacy. Also without recourse to armed force, international actors could impact a state apparatus – through state renaissance. This book zooms in on the non-forcible aspects of conflict-related transitional governance while focusing on the transition itself. This study shows that, both transitional actors and external actors must respect specific rules when realising or contributing to state renaissance. The legal limits to indirectly provoking regime change are also being unveiled.

Emmanuel H. D. De Groof works in diplomacy for the Belgian Ministry of Foreign Affairs. He is an Associate to the Political Settlements Research Programme (University of Edinburgh); a Visiting Lecturer at the University of Maastricht; a Visiting Professor at the University of Kigali; and a scholar in the fields of international law, diplomacy, mediation, and development cooperation. An alumnus of the European University Institute ('EUI', PhD 2016), Université libre de Bruxelles (LLM, 2008), Katholieke Universiteit Leuven (Master, 2006), Humboldt-Universität zu Berlin (2005), Université de Namur (2003), and formerly a Fulbright-Schuman scholar at NYU School of Law, Emmanuel has won various awards including at the Charles Rousseau and Manfred Lachs moot court competitions. He has worked at the European Centre for Development Policy Management ('Pelican House'), the EUI administration, Belgium's Permanent Representation to the EU, the Brussels Bar, and as a Law Clerk for Justice Albie Sachs at the South African Constitutional Court.

STATE RENAISSANCE FOR PEACE

Transitional Governance under International Law

EMMANUEL H. D. DE GROOF

CAMBRIDGE
UNIVERSITY PRESS

University Printing House, Cambridge CB2 8BS, United Kingdom

One Liberty Plaza, 20th Floor, New York, NY 10006, USA

477 Williamstown Road, Port Melbourne, VIC 3207, Australia

314–321, 3rd Floor, Plot 3, Splendor Forum, Jasola District Centre,
New Delhi – 110025, India

79 Anson Road, #06–04/06, Singapore 079906

Cambridge University Press is part of the University of Cambridge.

It furthers the University's mission by disseminating knowledge in the pursuit of
education, learning, and research at the highest international levels of excellence.

www.cambridge.org
Information on this title: www.cambridge.org/9781108499767
DOI: 10.1017/9781108589864

© Emmanuel H. D. De Groof 2020

This publication is in copyright. Subject to statutory exception
and to the provisions of relevant collective licensing agreements,
no reproduction of any part may take place without the written
permission of Cambridge University Press.

First published 2020

A catalogue record for this publication is available from the British Library.

Library of Congress Cataloging-in-Publication Data
Names: De Groof, Emmanuel, H. D., 1983– author.
Title: State renaissance for peace : transitional governance under international law /
Emmanuel H. D. De Groof.
Description: Cambridge, United Kingdom ; New York, NY, USA : Cambridge University
Press, 2020. | Based on author's thesis (doctoral – European University Institute, 2016)
issued under title: Domestic interim governance under international law : towards a ius in
interregno for regulating post-conflict transitions. | Includes bibliographical references and
index.
Identifiers: LCCN 2019040384 (print) | LCCN 2019040385 (ebook) | ISBN 9781108499767
(hardback) | ISBN 9781108589864 (epub)
Subjects: LCSH: Interim governments. | Peace-building – Law and legislation. | Transitional
justice. | International and municipal law.
Classification: LCC KZ4024 .D4 2020 (print) | LCC KZ4024 (ebook) | DDC 342/.04–dc23
LC record available at https://lccn.loc.gov/2019040384
LC ebook record available at https://lccn.loc.gov/2019040385

ISBN 978-1-108-49976-7 Hardback

Cambridge University Press has no responsibility for the persistence or accuracy of
URLs for external or third-party internet websites referred to in this publication
and does not guarantee that any content on such websites is, or will remain,
accurate or appropriate.

To Albie, Christine, Jan
Company, Friendship, Old and New
Potential Futures, Too

CONTENTS

List of Tables   xviii
Foreword   xix
JEAN D'ASPREMONT
Preface   xxi
Acknowledgements   xxiv
List of Abbreviations   xxvii

Introduction   Transitional Governance Today   1

Section A   Contemporary Transitional Governance   3
1   Peace through Transition   6
2   Self-Regulation and Temporality   9
3   Non-Constitutionality   11
4   Formal Domestic Nature   12
   4.1   Domestic Stakeholders   12
   4.2   No State Creation   13
5   A Contemporary Phenomenon   14

Section B   Scope of the Book   16
1   Non-Forcible Aspects of Conflict-Related TG   16
   1.1   Conflict-Related TG   16
   1.2   Non-Forcible Aspects   18
2   The Voyage Is the Destination   19
   2.1   Focus on Replacement and Transplacement   19
   2.2   Focus on States in Transition, Official Reactions and the UNSC   21

Section C   The Argument: No Absolute Freedom in Times of Transition   23
1   Partial Invalidation of Initial Hypothesis   23
2   Why Analyse Transitions under International Law?   26

ix

CONTENTS

PART I The Unchartered Territory of Transitional Governance 31

Chapter 1 The Rise and Internationalisation of Transitional Governance 33

Section A The Rise of Transitional Governance 33

1 The Turn to the 'Light Footprint' 33
2 Prima Facie Legal Reasons behind the Rise of Transitional Governance 36
  2.1 International Territorial Administration As a Last Resort: TG As the Alternative? 37
  2.2 Less Constraints under International (Humanitarian) Law? 38
  2.3 Primary Responsibility of Domestic Transitional Authorities? 39
    2.3.1 Insistence by UNSC, UNGA and PBC on Domestic Responsibility for TG 39
    2.3.2 Correction of ITA Accountability Gap? 41

Section B The Internationalisation of Transitional Governance 42

1 The Multitude of Actors Influencing Transitional Governance 44
  1.1 The UN 44
  1.2 Regional Organisations 47
  1.3 Contact Groups: A New International Coordination Mechanism? 48
  1.4 Individual States 56
2 Unravelling the Assistance Model 58
  2.1 Concurring Assistance 58
  2.2 Beyond Assistance 59
  2.3 Between Multilateral State Transformation and Unilateral Constitutional Geopolitics 61

Chapter 2 Limitations of Existing Literature 63

Section A Limitations Inherent to Transitional Justice and *Ius Post Bellum* Literature 63

1 Limitations to Transitional Justice 63
2 Limitations to *Ius Post Bellum* 65

CONTENTS

Section B Irrelevance of the Transition
Paradigm 67

1 The Legitimacy Controversy 68
2 The Democracy Controversy 71
  2.1 The Variety of Definitions of
      Democracy 72
  2.2 Inconsistent Practice and Uncertain Legal
      Status 74

Conclusion of Part I 76

PART II **Foundation and Actors of Transitional
Governance ∗ Sources of *Ius in
Interregno* 79**

Chapter 3 The Foundation of Transitional
Governance 81

Section A Origin or Context: Non-
Constitutionality 81

1 Definition of Non-Constitutionality 81
2 Non-Constitutionality under International Law and
  Regional Frameworks 89
  2.1 Non-Constitutionality on the Global Level:
      International Law's Neutrality 89
  2.2 Non-Constitutionality under Regional Frameworks:
      Incoherent Implementation 91

Section B Supraconstitutionality and Transformative
Constitutionalism 95

1 The Function of Transition Instruments:
  Supraconstitutionality 95
  a Domestic Intrastate Agreements 106
  b Domestic Transitional Instruments 107
  c International Agreements 108
2 The Purpose of Transition Instruments:
  Transformative Constitutionalism 109

Chapter 4 The Actors of the Interregnum 114

Section A Nature of Transitional Authorities: Domestic,
Provisional and Relative Legal
Personality 116

1 Domestic Nature 116
  1.1 No Foreign Administration 117
  1.2 No International Administration 117

CONTENTS

    1.3   Gradations of International Involvement   119

  2 Provisional Nature   122

    2.1   Pre-Transition   126

    2.2   Foundation of the Transition   127

    2.3   Interregnum   128

    2.4   End of the Transition   132

  3 Functional International Legal Personality   134

Section B Raison d'être of Transitional Authorities: State Renaissance in the Post-Colonisation Era   140

  1 State Transformation Aim: A Civilian/Political Purpose   140

    1.1   Separate Structure, Hierarchy or Recognised Status   140

    1.2   Focus on the Civilian/Political Portfolio   143

    1.3   Severability Civilian/Political Versus Forcible/Military Aspects of TG   144

  2 Historic and Conceptual Distinction from National Liberation Movements   145

    2.1   Historic Criteria for Recognising NLM   145

    2.2   Indirect Relevance for Transitional Governance   148

Chapter 5 The Sources of *Ius in Interregno*   150

Section A Existing Law as the Basis of *Ius in Interregno*   151

  1 International Law As Residual Law of the Interregnum   151

  2 International Law Principles   156

    2.1   Principle of Self-Determination   156

    2.2   Principle of Non-Intervention   159

Section B Nascent Custom   163

  1 The Peace-through-Transition Paradigm As the 'Ecosystem' for *Opinio Necessitatis*   163

  2 *Usus* and *Opinio Iuris*   169

    2.1   The Question of Attribution   170

    2.2   Transition Instruments as Evidence of Nascent Custom   171

CONTENTS

2.2.1 Domestic Intrastate Agreements as Evidence of Nascent Custom 172
2.2.2 Domestic Transitional Instruments as Evidence of Nascent Custom 174
2.2.3 International Agreements as Evidence of Nascent Custom 175
2.3 International Reactions Confirming Nascent Custom 176

3 *Coutume Sauvage*, Contested Utility and Non-Compliance 183
3.1 Avoiding *Coutume Sauvage* 183
3.2 Limited Impact of Contested Utility and Non-Compliance 185

Conclusion of Part II 187

PART III Self-Determination through Transitional Governance 191

Nascent Customary Rules 191

Self-Redetermination 193

Introductory Caveats: Transitional Governance Practices Are Rudimentary and Contested 195

Rudimentary Nature of Transitional Governance Practices 195

Transitional Governance Practices Are Contested on Extra-Legal Grounds 196

Chapter 6 Limits *Ratione Temporis* and *Materiae* to Transitional Governance 199

Section A Limits *Ratione Temporis* 199

Section B Limits *Ratione Materiae* 207

1 Administer the Country during the Transition, and Ensure Security 207
2 Respect the Past vis-à-vis Third States and Private Persons· 211
3 Prepare for the Future without Entrenching it 218

Section C Calibrating the Power of Modification and the Duty of Conservation 222

Chapter 7 The Practice and Discourse of Inclusion 224

CONTENTS

Section A Inclusive Transitional Governance through the Lens of Self-Determination   227

Section B Facets of Inclusivity   232

    1 Who? Plurality of Groups to Be Involved in Transitional Governance (Expansion *Ratione Personae*)   232

    2 How? Diversified but Limited Choice for Implementing Inclusive TG (Expansion *Ratione Materiae*)   236

       2.1 Transitional Constitution-Making   236

       2.2 Constitution-Making *Tout Court*   237

       2.3 The Exercise of Public Authority during the Interregnum (Inclusivity of the Interim Rule)   240

       2.4 Constitutional Referenda and General Elections   242

    3 When? Involving the People throughout the Interregnum (Expansion *Ratione Temporis*)   243

    4 Whither? Inclusivity Adding Detail to Self-Determination   244

       4.1 Criticism: Inclusivity in the Dock   244

          4.1.1 Positive Criticism   244

          4.1.2 Negative Criticism   245

          4.1.3 Relative Legal Impact of Extra-Legal Criticism   248

       4.2 How Inclusivity Details and Extends Self-Determination   249

          4.2.1 Expansion *Ratione Personae*   249

          4.2.2 Expansion *Ratione Materiae*   252

          4.2.3 Expansion *Ratione Temporis*   254

    5 A Revival of the Principle of Self-Determination   258

Section C Ownership of Transitional Justice   260

    1 The Transitional Justice Cascade   262

    2 Scope of Transitional Justice: No Blanket Amnesty and Domestic Ownership   264

       2.1 No Blanket Amnesty   265

       2.2 Domestic Ownership   267

Conclusion of Part III   269

PART IV Moderating External Influence on Transitional Governance   275

CONTENTS xv

Defining assistance 277

Defining consent 279

Chapter 8 Limits to External Involvement with Transitional Governance 283

Section A Prohibitions Applicable to External Actors 286

1 Prohibition on Externally Imposing (Consensual) TG 286

2 Prohibition on Violating Limits *Ratione Temporis* 292

3 Prohibition on Violating Limits *Ratione Materiae* 296

   3.1 Prohibition on Leaving Post-Transition Imprint through Transition Instruments 296

   3.2 Respect for State Continuity 298

4 Prohibition on Undermining Inclusivity 298

5 Prohibition on Externally Imposed Constitution-Making *'Tout Court'* 302

6 Respect for Domestic Ownership of Transitional Justice 306

   6.1 Respect for Domestic Transitional Justice Choice 306

   6.2 Complementarity and Independence of the ICC 308

      6.2.1 Ability and Willingness Test: Flexible Standards 308

      6.2.2 Avoiding the Politicisation of the ICC 310

Section B Legal Implications 311

1 Potential Engagement of International Responsibility 312

2 Permissible Pressure 313

Chapter 9 The Inducement of Oppositional Transitional Governance 315

Section A External Inducement of Oppositional Transitional Authorities 317

1 Observing a Practice: Contact Groups Empowering Oppositional Transitional Authorities 318

xvi CONTENTS

    1.1 The Creation and Endorsement of the Syrian Oppositional Transitional Authority   320

    1.2 The Creation and Endorsement of the Libyan Oppositional Transitional Authority   323

  2 Labelling a Practice: Inducing Oppositional Transitions   324

Section B Inducing Oppositional Transitions under International Law   326

  1 The Irrelevance of the Doctrine of Recognition   327

  2 The Relevance of the Principle of Non-Intervention   331

    2.1 Coercion   331

    2.2 *Domaine Réservé*   332

  3 The UNSC Inducing Oppositional Transitions   334

Chapter 10 Indirect Regime Change: A Response to *Ius Cogens* Violations?   337

Section A Obligations of Non-Recognition, Cooperation and Peaceful Settlement   340

Section B As a Last Resort, Inducing Oppositional Transitions As a Non-Forcible Countermeasure?   342

  1 Thin Theoretical Compatibility: Indirect Regime Change by Solidarity Countermeasure   346

    1.1 Prior Unlawfulness: Need for Substantiation   347

    1.2 The *De Iure* Injured State and Solidarity Countermeasures   349

      1.2.1 Solidarity Countermeasures   350

      1.2.2 Countermeasures in Case of *Ius Cogens* Violations   351

  2 Thin Practical Compatibility: Compliance with Stringent Conditions   353

    2.1 Procedural Prerequisites and Their Preponderance   353

    2.2 Substantive Prerequisites   358

      2.2.1 Non-Performance   358

CONTENTS xvii

2.2.2 Reversibility 360
2.2.3 Proportionality 361
2.2.4 Qualifying the Inducement of
Oppositional TG 362
3 Policy Implications: The Highly Restricted Possibility
of Inducing Oppositional TG 364

Conclusion of Part IV 367

General Conclusion 369

Section A Reservations 371

1 International Law's Role: A Common Frame for Debate
on Transitions 371
2 Issues of Ineffectiveness or Non-Compliance: Relative
Legal Impact 372
3 The Current Maturation of *Ius in Interregno*: *Quo
Vadis*? 374

Section B Marginal Scrutiny 376

1 Limits to Discretionary Powers of Transitional
Authorities 376
2 Limits to Discretionary Powers of External
Actors 378

Index 383

TABLES

1.1 The internationalised interregnum   49

3.1 Transition instruments and their non-constitutional origin   82

3.2 Legal nature of supraconstitutional transition instruments   96

4.1 Categories and degrees of external involvement   120

4.2 Four stages of a transition: concepts   124

4.3 Four stages of a transition: examples   125

4.4 Embryonic, inchoate, midway or completed transitions   129

4.5 Functional international legal personality   138

6.1 Overview limitations *ratione temporis* to interregnum   202

7.1 The relation between self-determination and inclusivity   250

7.2 Inclusivity deconstructed   256

7.3 Mutual relevance of self-determination and transitional governance   261

8.1 Prohibitions applicable to external actors (per stage)   287

10.1 Limits to the inducement of oppositional TG in response to a *ius cogens*-violating state   343

FOREWORD

International lawyers have long been aspiring to a legal framework that guides the birth and death of states. They cannot be blamed for that. Controlling through legal mechanisms the making and unmaking of one of the most central components of the international legal order can be experienced as a necessity, at least since modern legal thought has led international lawyers to think of international law in terms of totality and systematicity. For that reason, contemporary international lawyers may even find it surprising that a proper 'law of statehood' only came to existence belatedly, that is in the second half of the twentieth century. In this context, no wonder that phases of transitions – which Emmanuel De Groof calls phases of *interregnum* – have spawned a similar anxiety for a legal framework. International lawyers obviously do not like ruptures, discontinuities and, above all, disorders. They prefer to see the world – and especially the world of states – in linear terms, with which transitions rarely fit. No surprise that a formidable creativity has been versed over the last decades into the design of rules, principles and frameworks meant to subdue and smoothen ruptures, discontinuities, disorders and transitions that accompany the making and unmaking – or, as Emmanuel De Groof puts it, the '*re*-determination' – of states. In the world of diplomacy and interstate relations, a similar creativity has informed attempts to control constitutional transitions – what Emmanuel calls 'constitutional geopolitics'. Bringing the debate on the law applicable to situations of interregnum to a new level of sophistication, the book of Emmanuel De Groof can be read as part of the abovementioned scholarly modern enterprise. And yet, at the same time, Emmanuel De Groof aptly invites the reader to be suspicious towards legalistic attempts to control transitions and tame disorders and pay heed to the complex dynamics at work *behind* legal arguments made in relation to such transitions. Drawing on an impressive wealth of practice and multidisciplinary scholarship, Emmanuel De Groof's opus is a very welcome addition to the literature as it offers the reader both an unprecedented study of which legal constructions can be deployed to manage transitions as well as a new perspective to take a hard look at such constructions and their legalistic ambitions. Whether for its novel approach to the legalisation of the transformation – and what Emmanuel De Groof calls 'renaissance' – of states or its insights on the limitations of such modern constructions applicable to transitions, this book will undoubtedly nourish debates on law and statehood for decades to come.

Jean d'Aspremont

PREFACE

This study on *ius in interregno* – the law applicable to domestic transitional governance – focuses on international legal aspects surrounding 'transitions'. Transitional governance ('TG') has gained enormous traction after the Cold War, especially since the South African transition from apartheid.

While I was a law clerk to living legend Albie Sachs in 2008 in South Africa, I observed how in neighbouring Zimbabwe the Global Political Agreement of September 2008 triggered a power-sharing government and constitutional change. A couple of years later, in September 2011, after a first experience in diplomacy, I started a doctorate at the European University Institute which, as I first intended, was to focus on transitional justice. But I shifted the focus to transitions, generally, when I witnessed, from a distance, how transitional authorities ('TA') were set up purportedly to steer regime change in countries going through the 'Arab Spring'.

This combination of factors triggered my reflection on the topic of transitions under international law, especially when TA were also created in sub-Saharan Africa in the years 2012 to 2014 (in Mali, the Central African Republic and Burkina Faso), with some commentators spelling the arrival of a 'Black Spring'. In 2017, I visited the Great Lakes region and informally happened to meet members of the Burundi opposition trying to organise a legal and political transition in their country. At the time of writing, transitions in Syria and Yemen were still being discussed, yet with sensibly less enthusiasm than several years ago; Sudan, South Sudan and Venezuela then came on the radar.

My research first concentrated on transitional institutions with oppositional origins, but was then extended to consensus-based transitional institutions derived from an agreement between the incumbent and opposition powers. Regardless of their oppositional or consensual origins, 'transitions', like several other political realities, can be read through the lens of international law. This has become a necessity: in recent times the so-called international community has taken a keen interest in TG,

xxi

which has become a tool at the disposal of the international collective security system, especially the UN Security Council, but can also be instrumentalised by individual states.[1]

States in transition should therefore raise their awareness about what is legally expected from them. In addition, these states may wish to know how to defend themselves against undue external interference during the interregnum. This book explains what the red lines are in both respects. Some red lines are clearly defined already while others are still being traced. The book concludes that TG is increasingly subject to marginal yet meaningful legal scrutiny. The legal framework for analysis it proposes will hopefully be insightful for the community of practitioners – diplomats, constitutional experts and mediators – which is constantly growing although the epistemic community around TG remains relatively small.

The analysis carried out in this study is based on complex realities as described in the accompanying online report 'The Features of Transitional Governance Today'.[2] But a number of practices are increasingly common to transitions, and often are sanctioned, e.g. by the UN Security Council and regional organisations. Through progressive custom formation, such practices may well add body and nuance to the law applicable to TG. *Ius in interregno* today centres around well-known and firmly established legal frameworks and principles, and tomorrow may also cover currently germinating 'surrounding' norms, which then will add a layer to existing law.

If current trends continue, *ius in interregno* will increasingly discipline not only domestic TA but also external parties involved in TG: international law is progressively providing benchmarks other than the unhelpful 'legitimacy' or 'democracy' tests to assess the limits to TG. Unless future developments deviate from current trends, *ius in interregno*, based on existing law, and, where it is currently developing, already rooted in a significant body of practice, cannot lightly be ignored – simply disregarding this legal evolution actually carries risks. At the same time, I readily accept that several aspects of

---

[1] E. De Groof, 'Domestic Interim Governance: The New Center Piece of the International Collective Security System', *Journal of Business, Economics and Political Science*, Vol. 5, nr. 9, April 2016.

[2] E. De Groof, 'The Features of Transitional Governance Today', Political Settlements Research Programme, University of Edinburgh, 2019, first edition. This report is available on www.politicalsettlements.org/publications-database/features-of-transitional-governance-today.

transitions will never, and perhaps should not, be governed by international law.

This book is divided into four parts. After an introduction on contemporary TG, the first part explains the choice to analyse TG from an international legal perspective. The second part examines the foundation and actors of TG as well as the sources of *ius in interregno*. The third part unveils how customary rules applicable to transitions emerge around existing principles. The fourth part, finally, analyses the limits to external involvement in TG – and thus to indirect regime change.

ACKNOWLEDGEMENTS

This book builds on the inspiration I received from lawyers worldwide since I started studies in law, in 2001, at the *Facultés universitaires Notre-Dame de la Paix* in Namur. The warm welcome I received there encouraged me to continue in law, first at the University of Leuven, which I represented at the Manfred Lachs moot court competition, then at the *Université libre de Bruxelles* ('ULB'), where I was given another opportunity to plead in a moot court competition, the *Concours Charles Rousseau*. Professor Eric David was our team's spiritual coach; his wit and knowledge continue to inspire me. At the *Concours Charles Rousseau*, I met Professor Yves Daudet who facilitated my attendance to The Hague Academy, an important step in my curriculum.

In 2008, I was invited to clerk for Justice Albie Sachs who played a tremendous role, both as a freedom fighter and lawyer, in the South African transition. I am greatly indebted to Albie, on the intellectual level but also personally. Albie taught me how to remain calm and efficient in tense situations, a skill I extensively relied on to assist Christine and Jan when they were unjustly accused, in December 2008, for one of the most obscure politico-legal scandals my country has ever experienced[1]. Their complaint lodged with the European Court of Human Rights in June 2009 remains un*answered* to date. This book is dedicated with love to my parents, and to Albie.

The European University Institute ('EUI'), where I wrote the first words of this book in 2011, is a little paradise on earth. I am grateful to the EUI, to the magnificent city and country hosting it, to its staff and professors, and to my former peers. My Supervisor Professor Francesco Francioni, and also Professor Nehal Bhuta, were particularly supportive of my work. In 2013, I was admitted as a Visiting Researcher to the NYU Law School. The support of the Fulbright-Schuman

---

[1] Fortunately, the real story has been unveiled in W. Van den Eynde, *Fortisgate: een stresstest voor justitie*, Halewyck, 2016. French translation and publication pending.

Commission, Professor Philip Alston, and the wider JSD community is greatly acknowledged. Before and after my stay in New York, I had the opportunity to engage with several scholars among whom was Micha Wiebusch, my always constructive *compagnon de thèse*.

At the doctoral thesis defence in June 2016, Professor Anne Peters and Professor Jean d'Aspremont engaged with my work as external jury members. This book originates from the dissertation, which much benefitted from their insights. I thank them here again, and wholeheartedly. After the defence, I couldn't quite leave Florence, and found ways to continue working for the EUI, first with fantastic colleagues at the Academy of European Law, then as an Advisor to the regretted Secretary-General of the EUI, Ambassador Vincenzo Schioppa-Narrante, and finally at the EUI's Communications Service. If I could somewhat prolong my time on the Tuscan hills, where I stayed even longer thanks to Kardelen, I also owe this to the comradery, and sometimes patience, of all those colleagues and friends.

After spending a fascinating time at the European Centre for Development Policy Management (also known as the Pelican House) in Maastricht, where I am very much indebted to the extraordinary Andrew Sherriff, I recently joined the Belgian Diplomatic Service (the 2019 promotion named after Marie Popelin) where Hugues Chantry, Gert De Beleyr, Patrick De Beyter, Eddy Delbecque, Ivo Goemans, Sabrina Heyvaert, Pascal Heyman and many other open-minded colleagues, older and younger, are re-initiating me to the job and to the diplomat's duties (a topic itself meriting further theoretical reflection). Hopefully my first book constitutes a useful tool not only for academia and the think tank world but also for diplomats, lawyers, mediators and practitioners worldwide who are, directly or indirectly, knowingly or unknowingly, engaged with *state renaissance for peace*. Needless to say, all errors and omissions are my responsibility alone. The views expressed in this book are personal and should not be ascribed to any of the institutions with which I work. I am extremely grateful to all my mentors, to Jean d'Aspremont in particular, and to Cambridge University Press for believing in me. Dear reader, please join me in thanking them and enjoy the journey!

This book represents the author's views and not necessarily those of the institution(s) he is called on to represent.

ABBREVIATIONS

ADB	Asian Development Bank
AfDB	African Development Bank
ANC	African National Congress figures
ASEAN	Association of Southeast Asian Nations
AU	African Union
CAR	Central African Republic
CCP	Chinese Communist Party
CFP	Constitutional Focal Point
CIAT	Comité international d'accompagnement de la transition
CNDD	National Council for the Defense of Democracy
CPA	Coalition Provisional Authority
CPA	Comprehensive Peace Agreement
CPLP	Community of Portuguese-Language countries
DARIO	ILC Draft articles on the responsibility of international organisations
DASR	ILC Draft articles on state responsibility
DDR	Disarmament, demobilisation and reintegration
DRC	Democratic Republic of Congo
DRI	Democracy Reporting International
ECCAS	Economic Community of Central African States
ECHR	European Convention for the Protection of Human Rights and Fundamental Freedoms (1950)
ECOMIB	ECOWAS Mission in Guinea-Bissau
ECOWAS	Economic Community of West African States
ECtHR	European Court of Human Rights
EEAS	European External Action Service
EU	European Union
EUI	European University Institute
GCC	Gulf Cooperation Council
GCC Agreement	Gulf Cooperation Council Agreement for Yemen (2011)
ICC	International Criminal Court
ICCPR	International Covenant on Civil and Political Rights (1966)
ICESCR	International Covenant on Economic, Social and Cultural Rights (1966)

LIST OF ABBREVIATIONS

ICG	International Crisis Group
ICG-CAR	International Contact Group on the Central African Republic
ICGL	International Contact Group on Liberia
ICG-MRB	International Contact Group on the Mano River Basin
ICG-S	International Contact Group for Somalia
ICJ	International Court of Justice
ICRC	International Committee of the Red Cross
ICTY	International Criminal Tribunal for the former Yugoslavia
IDEA	Institute for Democracy and Electoral Assistance
IDI	Institut de droit international
IDLO	The International Development Law Organization
IFI	International Financial Institutions
IGAD	Intergovernmental Authority for Development
IGC	Iraqi Governing Council
IHT	International Herald Tribune
ILC	International Law Commission
IMF	International Monetary Fund
Inter-Am.Ct.H.R.	Inter-American Court on Human Rights
Int'l	International (only in the tables)
IO	International organisation(s)
ITA	International territorial administration
MERCOSUR	Mercado Común del Sur
MINUGUA	UN Verification Mission in Guatemala
MINURSO	Mission des Nations Unies pour l'Organisation d'un Référendum au Sahara Occidental / United Nations Mission for the organisation of a Referendum in Western Sahara
MINUSCA	United Nations Multidimensional Integrated Stabilization Mission in the Central African Republic
MINUSMA	United Nations Multidimensional Integrated Stabilization Mission in Mali
MONUC	United Nations Organisation Mission in the Democratic Republic of the Congo / Mission de l'Organisation des Nations Unies en République démocratique du Congo
MPEPIL	Max Planck Encyclopedia of Public International Law
MSU	Mediation Support Unit
NATO	North Atlantic Treaty Organization
NDI	National Democratic Institute
NLM	National liberation movement(s)
NTC	National Transitional Council
NYT	New York Times
OAS	Organisation of American States
OAU	Organisation of African Unity

LIST OF ABBREVIATIONS

OIC	Organisation of the Islamic Conference
ONUB	United Nations Operation in Burundi
ONUMOZ	United Nations Operation in Mozambique
OSCE	Organisation for Security and Cooperation in Europe
OTP	Office of the Prosecutor (ICC)
PBC	Peacebuilding Commission
PILPG	Public International Law & Policy Group
PSC	The Peace and Security Council of the African Union
PSRP	Political Settlements Research Programme
R2P	Responsibility to protect
SNC	Syrian National Council/Syrian National Coalition
SPLM/SPLA	Sudan People's Liberation Movement/Army
SSR	Security sector reform
TA	Transitional authority/transitional authorities
TAL	Law of Administration for the State of Iraq for the Transitional Period
TEU	Treaty on European Union
TG	Transitional governance
TI	Transition instrument(s)
TJ	Transitional justice
TNC	Transitional National Council
UDHR	Universal Declaration of Human Rights
UN	United Nations
UNAMA	UN Assistance Mission in Afghanistan
UNAMI	UN Assistance Mission for Iraq
UNAMIR	UN Assistance Mission for Rwanda
UNAMSIL	UN Mission in Sierra Leone
UNAVEM	UN Angola Verification Mission
UNCHR	UN Commission on Human Rights
UNDP	UN Development Programme
UNDPA	UN Department of Political Affairs
UNDPPA	UN Department of Political and Peacebuilding Affairs
UNESCO	UN Educational, Scientific and Cultural Organization
UNGA	UN General Assembly
UNHCR	UN High Commissioner for Refugees
UNFICYP	UN Peacekeeping Force in Cyprus
UNIOGBIS	UN Peacebuilding Support Office in Guinea-Bissau
UNMHA	UN Mission to support the Hudaydah Agreement
UNMIH	UN Mission in Haiti
UNMIK	UN Interim Administration Mission in Kosovo
UNMIL	UN Mission in Liberia
UNMIN	UN Mission in Nepal

UNMIS	UN Mission in the Sudan
UNMISS	UN Mission in South Sudan
UNMOT	UN Mission of Observers in Tajikistan
UNOCI	UN Operation in Côte d'Ivoire
UNOMIG	UN Observer Mission in Georgia
UNOMIL	UN Observer Mission in Liberia
UNOMSIL	UN Observer Mission in Sierra Leone
UNOSOM	UN Operation in Somalia
UNPROFOR	UN Protection Force
UNSC	UN Security Council
UNSG	UN Secretary-General
UNSMIL	UN Support Mission in Libya
UNSMIS	UN Supervision Mission in Syria
UNSOM	UN Assistance Mission in Somalia
UNTAC	UN Transitional Authority in Cambodia
UNTAES	UN Transitional Administration for Eastern Slavonia, Baranja and Western Sirmium
UNTAET	UN Transitional Administration in East Timor
UNTAG	UN Transition Assistance Group
US	United States of America
USIP	The United States Institute of Peace
USSR	Union of Soviet Socialist Republics
VCLT	Vienna Convention on the Law of Treaties
WB	World Bank Group

Introduction

Transitional Governance Today

Of regime transitions there is no end. Since time began, constitutions and institutions of states, empires or other political organisations have been profoundly modified. History and legends are replete with instances of interim governance, broadly understood.[1] These range, to give random examples spanning three continents and two millennia, from Numa Pompilius' one-year interregnum after Romulus' death in 717 BC, the Scythian interregnum in Median dynasty history between 653 to 625 BC bridging the reigns of Phraortes and Cyaxares in Persia, and the Ottoman Interregnum (1402–3), to the interregnum of the Kingdom of Loango in the basin of the Kouilou and Niari rivers (1786).

Historically, transitional governance ('TG') concentrated mainly on regime succession. During the twentieth century the function of interim governance diversified. Throughout that century, interim institutions were created to deal not only with matters of regime or personal succession[2] but also to overthrow or restore political regimes,[3] to resist foreign occupation[4] or protest against international border settlements,[5]

---

[1] Historically, interregnums have seldom been studied from an international legal perspective. In one paragraph entitled 'Ministers sent during an interregnum by the nation itself or by regents', Vattel briefly mentions that diplomats appointed during an interregnum have the same rights as those appointed outside of such context. E. de Vattel, *Le Droit Des Gens, Ou, Principes de La Loi Naturelle, Appliqués À La Conduite et Aux Affaires Des Nations et Des Souverains*, W. S. Hein, 1995, p. 62.

[2] 1917 Russian Provisional Government (Russian Republic as transition between Russian Empire and the Russian Federation); 1944–50 Regency Prince Karel of Belgium (legal impossibility of King Leopold III to rule); 1989–91 provisional governments in the context of the fall of communism.

[3] 1912 Chinese provisional government (Xinhai Revolution and overthrow imperial dynasty).

[4] 1919–48 Provisional Government of Republic of Korea (resistance against Japanese empire); 1944–6 Gouvernement provisoire de la République française (resistance against German occupation).

[5] 1913 Provisional Government of Western Thrace (protest against border settlement of the 1913 Treaties of Bucharest and Constantinople); 1914 Autonomous Republic of Northern Epirus (protest against Protocol of Florence to the 1913 Treaty of London).

2   TRANSITIONAL GOVERNANCE TODAY

to struggle against domestic repression,[6] to strive for independence[7] or to indirectly control foreign territory.[8]

After 1989, the context, nature and function of TG changed. It became increasingly dissociated from decolonisation, secession or dissolution processes, and emerged more frequently in the context of non-international armed conflicts.[9] It became a process whereby transitional authorities ('TA') introduce a constitutional transformation on the basis of interim laws. TG furthermore became an international project, and one with formidable ambitions: ending war, conflict or crisis by reconfiguring the state order. This model attracted international attention, notably from the UN Security Council, and became a playing field of choice in international politics. Also without recourse to armed force, international actors could impact a state apparatus – through state renaissance.

Against this background, this book analyses how international law – as it currently stands and develops – applies to TG. As Roscoe Pound famously said, *the law must be stable, and yet it cannot stand still.*[10] The law applicable to TG, too, stands on firm grounds, yet cannot stand still. For ease of reference, the words *ius in interregno* will refer to

---

[6] 1915–18 Armenian 'Republic of Van' (resistance against Ottoman rule during Russian occupation).

[7] 1915 Nationalist Provisional Government of India (independence from British rule); 1918 Estonian Provisional Government (independence from Russian Federation/ German occupation); 1918 Latvian Provisional Government (independence from Russian Federation/German occupation); 1922 Provisional Government of Ireland (transition towards independence from Great Britain after Anglo-Irish Treaty); 1946–7 Interim government of India (decolonisation); 1948–9 Provisional Government of Israel (proclamation new state); 1954–62 Provisional Government Algerian Republic (decolonisation); 1971–2 Provisional Government of the People's Republic of Bangladesh (independence from Pakistan).

[8] 1937–40 Provisional Government of the Republic of China (vassal government of Japanese Empire).

[9] 'Most civil wars today end in negotiated settlements, and in most instances an essential part of such agreements is agreement on a defined political pathway through which a transitional process to consolidate peace is to unfold. These transition paths often feature the formation of transitional governments, sometimes constitution-making processes, and, at some point, an electoral process and event to give post-war governance a new sense of legitimacy. The transition sequences and institutional choices made in war-settlement negotiations often determine the nature and timing of initial post-war elections; in turn, these electoral processes deeply affect the nature of the state that emerges for years to follow.' T. D. Sisk, 'Elections and Statebuilding after Civil War, Lurching toward Legitimacy' in D. Chandler, T. D. Sisk (eds.), *Routledge Handbook of International Statebuilding*, Routledge, 2013, p. 259.

[10] R. Pound, *Interpretations of Legal History*, Cambridge University Press, 1923, p. 1.

CONTEMPORARY TRANSITIONAL GOVERNANCE

international law, with both stable and evolving components, applicable to TG. TG is increasingly subject to regulation. This is undoubtedly so on the domestic legal level. Domestic laws provide much detail as to how TG must be executed. The objective of domestic laws and post-sovereign (staged) constitution-making[11] is to 'avoid the legal and institutional state of nature'[12] during transitions. I will argue that, for the better or for the worse, international law increasingly guides and complements domestic laws in this endeavour.

The portrayal of the interregnum as a legal and institutional vacuum has always been a misrepresentation. This is likely to be even more so in the future unless there will be a major reversal of the practices and beliefs increasingly associated to TG today. Absent such a reversal, the vision expressed in 1920, more than a century ago, by the International Committee of Jurists that the role of international law remains relative in times of state transformation,[13] will need to be strongly nuanced.

In the following lines, I will detail how post-Cold War TG differs from previous forms of TG (Section A), detail the scope of this book (Section B) and present its argument: there is no absolute freedom in times of transition (Section C).

A Contemporary Transitional Governance

This book focuses on the period during which a state's constitution and institutions are held in abeyance, especially in the context of an armed conflict, or of a threat to international peace and security. This period will be called the *transitional period* or *interregnum*.

A *transition*, generally, refers to the renaissance of a state when its constitution and institutions are overhauled. In more detail, it concerns (1) the transformation of a state's regime, understood as 'the institutional structure of the state and government'[14] (2) by non-constitutional means,

---

[11] A. Arato, *Constitution Making under Occupation*, Columbia University Press, 2009; A. Arato, 'Post-Sovereign Constitution-Making and Its Pathology in Iraq', *New York Law School Law Review*, Vol. 51, 2006–7, pp. 536–55.

[12] A. Arato, 'Post-Sovereign Constitution-Making and Its Pathology in Iraq', op. cit., p. 541.

[13] Report of the International Committee of Jurists entrusted by the Council of the League of Nations with the task of giving an advisory opinion upon the legal aspects of the Åland Islands Question, October, 1920.

[14] Cf. Arato's analytical distinction between regime and government: a regime is the institutional structure of the state. A government refers to the functional branches of political power and the persons who control them. A. Arato, *Constitution Making Under Occupation*, op. cit.

4 TRANSITIONAL GOVERNANCE TODAY

(3) on the basis of legal instruments or of texts aspiring to such status, (4) regardless of their form (international agreements,[15] domestic intra-state agreements,[16] interim or transitional constitutions,[17] domestic/unilateral acts or declarations[18] or a combination thereof), (5) and regardless of their consensual or oppositional origin.

In law, the word transition is frequently used in the field of transitional justice ('TJ'). TJ examines how society (best) deals with questions of individual and societal responsibility after widescale violent conflict. In this book, the term transition will be detached from the TJ literature. Furthermore, a transition does not specifically refer to a 'market transition', a 'security transition' or even to the democratic transition paradigm, which was declared moribund in the wake of the millennium turn.[19]

TG or interim rule refers to public authority exercised during the interregnum. More accurately, TG refers to the exercise of public powers *ad interim*, including in relation to staged constitution-making procedures.[20] Since the end of the Cold War, the international community increasingly supports TG, often with the declared intention to bring peace and security in conflict-riven states. This model has become particularly popular after the acclaimed South African two-staged transition from apartheid to post-apartheid (1994–7), based on the 1994 interim constitution.[21]

---

[15] E.g. the Sun City Agreement of 19 April 2002 and the Pretoria Agreement of 16 December 2002 regarding the transition in the DRC.

[16] E.g. the Bonn Agreement of 5 December 2001 for Afghanistan, the Arusha agreement of 28 August 2000 for Burundi, but also the Accra Accord of 17 June 2003 for Liberia, the Lomé Accord of 7 July 1999 for Sierra Leone, and the Abuja Accord of 1 November 1998 for Guinea-Bissau. About the domestic nature of these accords, cf. J. I. Levitt, *Illegal Peace in Africa – An Inquiry into the Legality of Power Sharing with Warlords, Rebels, and Junta*, Cambridge University Press, 2012, p. 5.

[17] E.g. the Charte de la Transition of 13 November 2014 for Burkina Faso or the Interim Constitution of 27 April 1994 for South Africa.

[18] E.g. the Constitutional Declaration of 3 August 2011 for Libya.

[19] T. Carothers, 'The End of the Transition Paradigm', *Journal of Democracy* 13, no. 1, 2002, pp. 5–21.

[20] IDEA, 'Constitutionbuilding after Conflict: External Support to a Sovereign process', Policy Paper, May 2011, p. 11: 'constitution building is often *one element in a larger process of change* that affects the constitution'. Own emphasis.

[21] The intellectual ownership of this model can probably be attributed to the Constitutional Committee of the African National Conference, and to Suzuki Yasuzo. See A. Sachs, 'South Africa's Unconstitutional Constitution: the Transition from Power to Lawful Power', *Saint Louis University Law Journal*, Vol. 41, 1996–7, pp. 1249–58, and p. 1255. See, for the Japanese origin, S. B. Hamano, 'Incomplete Revolutions and Not so Alien

CONTEMPORARY TRANSITIONAL GOVERNANCE 5

Considering TG to be fruitful or not depends of course on the yardsticks used to measure success.[22] In several cases, TG has failed under any standards. At the time of writing, the disillusioning situation in Afghanistan, DRC, Iraq, Libya, South Sudan, and Yemen are self-explanatory. TA are often set up in so-called anocracies, that is countries where power is not firmly vested in institutions but spread among competing elite groups.[23] The result is that 'transitions are often more unstable and insecure than even the preceding periods of conflict'.[24] The combination of fragile TA and competition for power can be a recipe for failure. In spite of past failures, at the time of writing some commentators (and plenty of citizens) were calling for transitions in Algeria, Sudan and Venezuela. The conviction that TG can bring peace and stability has received a blow in expert circles but remains nevertheless deeply entrenched in legal culture, and is now being mainstreamed. This is what I will call the 'peace-through-transition paradigm'.

Since 1994, international assistance to TG has been deployed in various states. After the turn of the millennium, we are witnessing a sharp increase of internationally assisted TG. In its basic structure, TG was replicated *inter alia* in Afghanistan (2001); Burkina Faso (2014); Burundi (1998); Cambodia (1991); Central African Republic (2013); Comoros (2001); Côte d'Ivoire (2007); the DRC (2002); Guinea (2010); Guinea-Bissau (2012); Iraq (2004); Kyrgyzstan (2010); Liberia (2003); Libya (2011); Mali (2012); Nepal (2006); Rwanda (1994); Sierra Leone (1999); Somalia (2004); Sudan (2005); and Ukraine (2014).[25] At the time of writing, a transition was still being considered for war-shattered

---

Transplants: the Japanese Constitution and Human Rights', *University of Pennsylvania Journal of Constitutional Law*, Vol. 1, no. 3, 1998–9, p. 428.

[22] For a discussion, see also H. Ludsin, 'Peacemaking and Constitution-Drafting: A Dysfunctional Marriage', *University of Penssylvania Journal of International Law*, Vol. 33, 2011, p. 252.

[23] This is the definition by Systemic Peace: '[a]lso included in the anocracy category in this treatment are countries that are administered by transitional governments'; 'Research indicates that anocracies have been *highly unstable and transitory regimes*, with over fifty percent experiencing a major regime change within five years and over seventy percent within ten years'. M. G. Marshall, B. R. Cole, Center for Systemic Peace, 'Global Report 2014, Conflict, Governance, and State Fragility', p. 21. Own emphasis. In the same sense, K. Guttieri, J. Piombo (eds.), *Interim Governments – Institutional Bridges to Peace and Democracy?*, United States Institute of Peace Press, 2007, p. 4.

[24] C. L. Sriram, M.-J. Zahar, 'The Perils of Power-Sharing: Africa and Beyond', *Africa Spectrum*, Vol. 44, no. 3, 2009, pp. 11–39.

[25] See Table 3.1.

6   TRANSITIONAL GOVERNANCE TODAY

Syria.[26] Since 2015, opposition leaders in Burundi have regarded TG as a way out of the lingering crisis caused by the President's third term in office. In Venezuela, the opposition leader tried to trigger a transition during Spring 2019 to radically change the political landscape, and to end a socioeconomic crisis. In Sudan, the military and the opposition reached an agreement about a transition early July 2019 after widespread protests about the political and socioeconomic situation there.

Contemporary TG mostly exhibits four characteristics which we shall discuss in turn. First, its perceived instrumentality builds on the widespread peace-through-transition paradigm: TG copes with a situation of armed conflict, threat against international peace and security or serious crisis (1). TG is furthermore self-regulated and provisional: the interregnum is guided by a set of domestically valid secondary norms and institutions (2). Also, TG is non-constitutional as it contradicts, sidesteps or (partly) overrules existing constitutional rules and procedures (3). Finally, it is domestic as it primarily befalls on national actors to pursue TG (4). These characteristics distinguish contemporary TG from prior forms of interim governance (5).

1   *Peace through Transition*

In our day and age, armed conflicts or threats to peace and security are commonly addressed – successfully or in vain – by the triggering of a domestic transition resulting in the wholesale constitutional and institutional reconfiguration of a country, that is a state *renaissance* in the literal sense of a *rebirth*. The peace-through-transition paradigm posits that state reconfiguration is a means of coping with violent conflict. It is nurtured by a socialised discursive practice according to which the redefinition of the social contract is an effective conflict resolution mechanism. Consolidated after the South African transition, this conviction appears for example from official statements with regard to Syria,[27]

---

[26] Cf. the Statement of the International Syria Support Group of 17 May 2016, especially the last part on 'advancing a political transition', with reference to the Mediator's Summary of the 13–27 April Round of UN Facilitated Intra-Syrian Talks and to S/RES/2254 of 18 December 2015.

[27] In August 2015, the UNSC demanded that all parties in the Syrian conflict 'work urgently towards . . . launching of a Syrian-led political process leading to a political transition' so as to enable the Syrian people to determine their future 'through the establishment of an inclusive transitional governing body' (S/PRST/2015/15 of 17 August 2015, § 9). This call was repeated in December 2015 (S/RES/2254 of 18 December 2015) and May 2016 (cf. the Statement of the International Syria Support Group of 17 May 2016).

CONTEMPORARY TRANSITIONAL GOVERNANCE

Guinea-Bissau,[28] Yemen[29] and Libya,[30] which illustrate how deeply it is ingrained in international diplomatic culture. The 2015 Review of the UN Peacebuilding Architecture seems to suggest that this is a naive

[28] In December 2013, the UNSC President affirmed that 'the consolidation of peace and stability in Guinea-Bissau can *only* result from a consensual, inclusive and nationally owned transition process' (S/PRST/2013/19, Statement by the President of the UNSC of 9 December 2013. Own emphasis). After determining that the situation in Guinea-Bissau constituted a potential threat to international peace and security, the UNSC actively monitored the transition. See also S/RES/2048 of 18 May 2012, Preamble. On that date, the UNSC, '[m]indful of its primary responsibility for the maintenance of international peace and security under the Charter of the United Nations', seized itself of the matter. See furthermore S/RES/2103 of 22 May 2013, S/RES/2157 of 29 may 2014, S/RES/2186 of 25 November 2014, and S/RES/2203 of 18 February 2015.

[29] From late 2011 onwards, the UNSC followed the transition in Yemen, indicating that it did so 'mindful of its primary responsibility for the maintenance of international peace and security' (S/RES/2051 of 12 June 2012, Preamble). See also S/RES/2140 of 26 February 2014, in which the UNSC 'determin[ed] that the situation in Yemen constitutes a threat to international peace and security in the region', '[w]elcomes the recent progress made in the political transition of Yemen and expresses strong support for completing the next steps of the transition'. Acting under Chapter VII of the UN Charter, the UNSC insisted in February 2015 on 'the full and timely implementation of the political transition' (S/RES/2204 of 24 February 2015, § 1).

[30] After the uprisings in Libya in early 2011, the UNSC and, shortly after, the AU observed that the situation posed a threat to international peace and security. Indeed, the UNSC determined in its resolution 1973 that the situation in the Libyan Arab Jamahiriya continues to constitute a threat to international peace and security (S/RES/1973 of 17 March 2011, Preamble). On 26 April 2011, The AU Ad-Hoc High-Level Committee on Libya 'stressed the serious *threat that this situation poses for peace, security and stability in the region as a whole*, and reaffirmed AU's conviction on the need for an urgent African action'. Own emphasis. See 'Report of the chairperson of the commission on the activities of the AU High Level Ad Hoc Committee on the situation in Libya', 26 April 2011, § 15. Both at the global and regional level, detailed transitions were proposed to address this threat. Although differing on various points, fundamentally both the UNSC and the AU committed to the peace-through-transition paradigm, convinced that TG was the only way to remedy the threat to international peace and security. On 16 September 2011, the UNSC looked forward to the establishment of a transitional Government of Libya, and communicated a number of guidelines that were to be followed by the National Transitional Council. In so acting, the UNSC seconded the basic idea underpinning the proposals and exhortations previously made by the AU (cf. S/RES/2009 of 16 September 2011, §§ 2 a.f.). Indeed, on 26 April 2011 the AU Ad-Hoc High-Level Committee on Libya had 'reaffirmed the relevance of the elements of the Roadmap articulated by the Transitional National Council ('TNC'). It invited the Libyan authorities and the TNC to a meeting . . . *to discuss this Roadmap, in particular the establishment and the management of an inclusive transitional period* that would lead to political reforms meeting the aspirations of the Libyan people' ('Report of the chairperson of the commission on the activities of the AU High Level Ad Hoc Committee on the situation in Libya', op. cit., § 17.2. Own emphasis). On 25 May 2011, the Assembly of the AU again 'stressed that the ceasefire should lead to *the establishment of a consensual and inclusive*

8   TRANSITIONAL GOVERNANCE TODAY

stance,[31] and some authors harshly criticise the idea of linking peace-making to state renaissance.[32] The paradigm is nevertheless widespread. Sometimes diplomatic actors even consider TG as a *preventive* measure.[33]

Both state actors and international commentators believe in a causality between TG and peace. The peace-through-transition discourse is appropriated to remedy or anticipate a threat to international peace and security. Comforted by the conceptual expansion of the definition of threats to international peace and security,[34] United Nations Security Council ('UNSC') resolutions provide in detail how transitions must respond to such threats; or endorse transition agendas defined elsewhere.[35] The UNSC has adopted resolutions under Chapter VII of the UN Charter with regard to transitions in South Sudan,[36] Somalia,[37] Libya,[38] Mali,[39] Côte d'Ivoire,[40] Central African Republic ('CAR'),[41] Yemen,[42] Guinea-Bissau,[43] Libya,[44]

---

transitional period during which the necessary reforms to meet the legitimate aspirations of the Libyan people would be carried out, culminating in elections' ('African Union Decision on the Peaceful Resolution of the Libyan Crisis' of 25 May 2011, under reference EXT/ASSEMBLY/AU/DEC(01.2011)). As a result, Libya swiftly received UNSC-mandated constitutional assistance (V. Sripati, 'United Nations Constitutional Assistance in Statebuilding' in D. Chandler, T. D. Sisk (eds.), *Routledge Handbook of International Statebuilding*, Routledge, 2013, p. 143).

[31] 2015 Review of the UN Peacebuilding Architecture of 30 June 2015, A/69/967-S/2015/490, §§ 31, 32 and 33.

[32] H. Ludsin, 'Peacemaking and Constitution-Drafting: A Dysfunctional Marriage', op. cit.

[33] The fragile contexts of apparent calm but with a risk of renewed violence – as in Côte d'Ivoire anno 2015 – would justify a transition to 'prioritise the birth of a new [social] contract' as a preventive measure. See 'Côte d'Ivoire: Ivory Coast Needs a Transition Phase', AllAfrica, 24 March 2015.

[34] 2005 World Summit Outcome, UNGA Res. 60/1 (24 October 2005), §§ 6 and 69. See also 'In Larger Freedom: Towards Development, Security and Human Rights for All', UN Doc/59/2005, 24–5.

[35] See for example S/RES/2118 of 27 September 2013 in which the UNSC endorses the transition agenda of the Geneva Communiqué of 30 June 2012.

[36] S/RES/2187 of 25 November 2014.

[37] S/RES/2182 of 24 October 2014.

[38] S/RES/2174 of 27 August 2014.

[39] S/RES/2164 of 25 June 2014.

[40] S/RES/2153 of 29 April 2014 in which the UNSC refers to the Ouagadougou Agreement and '[d]ecides that the Ivoirian authorities shall submit biannual reports to [a] Committee . . . on progress achieved in relation to DDR and SSR'.

[41] S/RES/2149 of 10 April 2014.

[42] S/RES/2140 of 26 February 2014.

[43] S/RES/2048 of 18 May 2012.

[44] S/RES/2009 of 16 September 2011 in which the UNSC directly addressed itself to the National Transitional Council on the topic of the transition.

CONTEMPORARY TRANSITIONAL GOVERNANCE 9

Haiti[45] and Afghanistan[46] (reverse chronological order). The UNSC furthermore reserves the power to take sanctions against 'spoilers' impeding transitions.[47] Individual states also insist on TG.[48] Instruments triggering TG are often explicit about the peace-through-transition paradigm. Transition instruments ('TI') in Burundi,[49] Côte d'Ivoire,[50] DRC[51] and Nepal,[52] for instance, enshrine it explicitly. The peace-through-transition paradigm has become common currency. The emphasis hereby lies on the constitutional and procedural aspects of conflict-related transitions,[53] and TG is presented as an alternative to direct international territorial administration or forcible intervention, confirming a 'greater reliance on a legal-regulatory approach' in international cooperation.[54]

2 Self-Regulation and Temporality

The peace-through-transition paradigm relies on the self-regulatory and provisional nature of TG. Interim rule is generally self-constrained in two regards. TI not only 'proclaim themselves to be transitional or interim in

---

[45] S/RES/1529 of 29 February 2004 § 1.

[46] S/RES/1386 of 20 December 2001 in which the UNSC refers to the Bonn Agreement, which regulates the transition in Afghanistan. This agreement refers to S/RES/1378. For a discussion, cf. T. Marauhn, 'Konfliktbewältigung in Afghanistan zwischen Utopie und Pragmatismus', *Archiv des Völkerrechts*, Bd. 40, 2002, p. 496.

[47] Chapter 5, Section B.2.3, *in fine*.

[48] 'Thousands gather in Burkina Faso to denounce "military coup"', The Guardian, 2 November 2014: in November 2014, for example, 'the presidents of Ghana, Nigeria and Senegal have urged Burkina Faso to appoint a transitional government'.

[49] The 2000 Arusha Agreement mentions the 'institution of a new political, economic, social and judicial order in Burundi' (Arusha Agreement, art. 5.1) following the 'speedy establishment of the transitional institutions' (art. 5.3) under the chapter 'solutions' (Chapter 2) immediately following the chapter 'nature and historical causes of the conflict' (Chapter 1), leaving no doubt as to the *conflict resolution function* of TG.

[50] With respect to the transition in Côte d'Ivoire, the 2003 Linas-Marcoussis Accord provides: 'a Government of National Reconciliation will be set up immediately after the conclusion of the Paris Conference *to ensure a return to peace and stability*' (Linas-Marcoussis Accord of 13 January 2003, art. 3.a). Own emphasis.

[51] The 2002 Pretoria agreement mentions among its 'transition objectives', 'the setting up of structures that will lead to a new political order' (Pretoria Agreement, II.5) in the DRC.

[52] In Nepal, the 'progressive restructuring of the state' is a principal component of the 2011 Comprehensive Peace Agreement between the Government of Nepal and the Communist Party of Nepal of 22 November 2011, Preamble.

[53] Berghof Foundation and UNDPPA, *Constitutions and Peace Processes – A Primer*, 2020.

[54] P. Chitalkar, D. M. Malone, 'The UN Security Council and Iraq', UNU Working Paper Series, Nr. 1, November 2013, p. 4. Own emphasis.

character'[55] (limitations *ratione temporis*), but also, beyond these self-evident temporal limits, confine public powers during the interregnum (limitations *ratione materiae*).[56] A set of institutions and rules govern the transition itself.[57] These rules, sometimes called transitional provisions,[58] are mostly secondary, power-conferring norms in the Hartean sense. The transition itself is subject to rules and procedures to avoid a legal hiatus between the demise of the old regime and the establishment of a new order.

States in transition thus have, to some degree, their 'hands tied'. The story of how Ulysses avoided the fatal temptation of the Sirens has become part of the established imaginary in constitutional literature but is also relevant beyond that field. Let us take a listen to Ulysses himself:

> We must keep clear of the Sirens, who sit and sing most beautifully . . . Therefore, take me and bind me to the crosspiece half way up the mast; bind me as I stand upright, with a bond so fast that I cannot possibly break away . . . If I beg . . . to set me free, then bind me more tightly still.
>
> I had hardly finished telling everything to the men before we reached the island of the two Sirens. . . . Meanwhile I look a large wheel of wax . . . Then I stopped the ears of all my men, and they bound me hands and feet to the mast . . . but they went on rowing themselves.
>
> When we had got within earshot of the land . . . the Sirens . . . began with their singing . . . and as I longed to hear them further I made by frowning to my men that they should set me free; but they quickened their stroke, and . . . bound me with still stronger bonds till we had got out of hearing of the Sirens' voices.[59]

Ulysses' self-constraint allowed him and his crew to transit safely through the Strait of Messina without giving in to the beautiful but deadly Sirens. This parable is often used to symbolise the utility of 'permanent' constitutions. But, perhaps even more, it shows that of *interim* constitutionalism and *transitional* governance as well: the need for self-regulation or 'structured caution'[60] in tempestuous times. Interim constitutionalism is

[55] C. Jackson, 'What's in a Name? Reflections on Timing, Naming, and Constitution-Making', *Wm. & Mary L. Rev.*, 49, 2007–8, p. 1260.

[56] Chapter 6.

[57] Chapter 3, Section B.2 about the purpose of TI, under 'self-limitation'.

[58] Democracy Reporting International (DRI), 'Ensuring a Smooth Transition to the new Constitutional Order: Transitional Provisions in the Libyan Draft Constitution and Political Agreement', January 2016.

[59] Homer, *The Odyssey*, translated by Samuel Butler, CreateSpace Independent Publishing Platform, 2018. First phrase lightly adapted.

[60] A. Sachs, 'South Africa's Unconstitutional Constitution', op. cit., p. 1252.

CONTEMPORARY TRANSITIONAL GOVERNANCE 11

a 'new paradigm of constitution-making'. It successfully combines the need of a provisional government with the requirement of subjecting this form to constitutional limitations'.[61] The same is true of TG generally, which may be regulated by legal instruments *other* than constitutions proper.[62]

3 Non-Constitutionality

The third feature of TG, its non-constitutional origin, refers to texts or actions, which are, if not *contra constitutionem*, at least *praeter constitutionem*. Non-constitutionality, broadly understood, concerns constitutional modifications outside the existing constitutional (amendment) procedures, or the establishment of (transitional) institutions not foreseen by the constitution. In the first case, the goal is to radically transform the existing constitutional order; acts are then unequivocally unconstitutional, for example the Libyan 2011 Constitutional Declaration. In the second case, the aim can be to restore an older order with the assistance of TA; acts are then *praeter constitutionem* without being unconstitutional, for example the *Accord Cadre de mise en oeuvre de l'engagement solennel* of 1 April 2012 regarding Mali, or the *Pacto de Transição Política* of 16 May 2012 regarding Guinea-Bissau, which both also confirmed the relevance of the previous constitution.

This book is not a study on constitutional changes ('*Verfassungsänderungsprozessen*').[63] A non-constitutional *rupture* must have taken place, for example against the background of a revolution, an agreement between warring factions, an external intervention or a restoration of an older (constitutional) regime. Broadly defined, such a rupture is already consumed when TI, at the time of their entry into force, partly aspire to a legal force superior to the existing and forthcoming constitutions ('supra-constitutionality'). This wide definition of 'rupture' is used throughout the book.

---

[61] A. Arato, *Constitution Making under Occupation*, op. cit. Own emphasis.

[62] Chapter 3, Section B.2 where the concept of 'transformative constitutionalism' is introduced. It refers to the triple aspiration of (interim) constitutions and other documents fulfiling a constitutional role in times of transition: pacification, self-limitation and reconstitutionalisation.

[63] M. Böckenförde, 'Die Einbindung der Bevölkerung in Verfassungsänderungsprozessen – Ein Überblick' in H. P. Hestermeyer, Nijhoff (et al.) (eds.), *Coexistence, Cooperation and Solidarity*, Brill Nijhoff, 2011, pp. 1107–23.

4 *Formal Domestic Nature*

Recent transitions are characterised by secondary legal frameworks which depart from the previous constitutional order with the view of introducing a new one. After 1989, TG increasingly became a process whereby TA introduce a state renaissance as regulated by a supraconstitutional framework. In addition, TG is *at least formally* carried out by domestic actors, in two senses: the (main) stakeholders and beneficiaries are domestic actors (4.1), and the transition does not give rise to a new state (4.2).

4.1 Domestic Stakeholders

TG is to be qualified as domestic in light of the non-international identity and portfolio of the (main) stakeholders and beneficiaries appointed in the transition. Domestic actors are tasked with carrying out TG, also when they receive international assistance. This can result in 'channel[ing] international intervention through a range of filters and conduits that sought to anchor them in the local such that there was local ownership of global governance'.[64]

The domestic nature of TG is not incompatible with the factual and legal internationalisation of the interregnum. The *factual internationalisation* refers to (1) the international context in which the transition is triggered, for example internationally brokered negotiations, and to (2) the international assistance during the transition (the 'assistance model'),[65] for example through contact groups and UN missions.[66] The *legal internationalisation* refers the increased reliance on international law to regulate transitions.

By default, sovereigns are tasked with leading the transition in spite of the clear imprint left by this two-sided internationalisation of the interregnum. Note also that external assistance does not amount to direct international territorial administration ('ITA') if the transition is – at least on paper – in the hands of domestic actors: the signatories and/or ratifying parties of the TI, and their main stakeholders, are national actors.[67] The TI for Afghanistan and Burundi, for example, were negotiated in international

---

[64] V. Nesiah, 'The Ambitions and Traumas of Transitional Governance: Expelling Colonialism, Replicating Colonialism', p. 141, in E. De Groof, M. Wiebusch (eds.), International Law and Transitional Governance: Critical Perspectives, Routledge, 2020.

[65] M. Saul, 'From Haiti to Somalia: The Assistance Model and the Paradox of State Reconstruction in International Law', *International Community Law Review* 11, no. 1, 2009.

[66] Table 1.1.

[67] Chapter 4, Section A.1.

CONTEMPORARY TRANSITIONAL GOVERNANCE 13

conferences (the Bonn Conference and the Arusha peace process, respectively). Yet, these countries were never considered to be under ITA. Although internationalised, the interregnum was formally domestic.

4.2 No State Creation

If current trends continue, state-internal TG is likely to become more prominent. This study therefore does not focus on transitions giving rise to new states. Transitions that do *not* (directly) give rise to new states will retain our attention. Processes of decolonisation, but also of state dissolution related to the fall of communism, are indeed largely part of history since the end of the Cold War. This is why the number of states is now more or less stagnating, as shown in Figure 1 which runs until 2019.[68] Since 2010, one country, South Sudan, has joined the UN organisation.

Against this background, I disregard transitions giving rise to state creation, for example in the context of state secession[69] or decolonisation.[70] Transitions in the context of the disintegration of Yugoslavia (1990s), the dissolution of the Soviet Union (1991) furthermore raise questions, for example in relation to state succession, which are not handled here.

This choice is based on what I believe to be the current course of history but is also informed by limitations of time and space. In this book TA are thus understood to aspire to state transformation while respecting the state's territorial integrity, contrary for example to secessionist entities or *de facto* states aspiring to perpetuity, that is 'territories which have

---

[68] S. Rosière, 'La fragmentation de l'espace étatique mondial', L'Espace Politique [Online], 11, 2010–2. Last consulted on 24 March 2020. Available on http://journals .openedition.org/espacepolitique/1608.

[69] 'Interim settlements resolv[ing] the self-determination conflict by establishing the secessionist unit as a constitutional self-determination entity' are increasingly deployed, notes M. Weller, 'Self-Governance in Interim Settlements – The Case of Sudan' in M. Weller, S. Wolff (eds.), *Autonomy, Self Governance and Conflict Resolution: Innovative Approaches to Institutional Design in Divided Societies*, Routledge, 2005, p. 138. The creation of South Sudan in 2011 on the basis of the 2005 Naivasha Agreement is largely disregarded. The same is true of the interim settlement preceding the declaration of independence of Kosovo in 2008, and of the transition in Ethiopia/Eritrea leading to Eritrea's independence in May 1993. The (potential) secession of Scotland, Catalonia or other regions are not examined either.

[70] For example, the rights and obligations of the *Gouvernement provisoire de la république algérienne*, the government-in-exile of the Algerian National Liberation Front during the latter part of the Algerian War of Independence (1954–62), are not examined, even if this government was to manage a transition *sensu lato*.

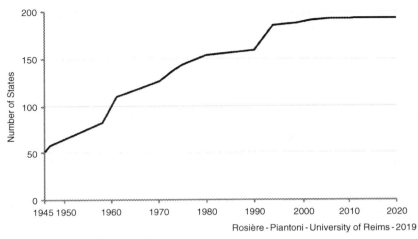

Figure 1 Surge of UN member states

gained *de facto* independence – often following warfare and/or state collapse – but have failed to gain international recognition or are, at best, recognised by only a few states',[71] such as Northern Cyprus, Somaliland, South Ossetia or Abkhazia.

Also, in this study transitions are understood to profoundly alter the state without challenging its legal continuity. The transformation is so profound though that some do see a certain kinship between TG and state creation.[72] This analogy, in light also of the principles of territorial integrity and legal continuity, allows us to speak of a state *renaissance*.

5 A Contemporary Phenomenon

The features discussed above characterise post-1989, or what we may call contemporary TG. In short, the features of TG are (1) its international relevance in light of the peace-through-transition-paradigm, (2)

---

[71] N. Caspersen, 'Playing the Recognition Game: External Actors and *De Facto* States', *The International Spectator*, Vol. 44, no. 4, December 2009, p. 47. See p. 48 about the goal of permanence.

[72] K. Stathopoulou, 'Self-Determination, Peacemaking and Peace-Building: Recent Trends in African Intrastate Peace Agreements' in D. French (ed.), *Statehood and Self-Determination: Reconciling Tradition and Modernity in International Law*, Cambridge University Press, 2013, p. 283: 'transformations occurring within the confines of pre-defined states ... often appear to be akin to the creation of states, as the power structures within the state are hugely altered'.

CONTEMPORARY TRANSITIONAL GOVERNANCE

its self-regulation and temporality, (3) its non-constitutionality and (4) its formal domestic nature. Cumulatively combined, the distinctive features of contemporary TG were generally absent in prior forms of interim governance:

- In post-War Germany and Japan, transitions occurred through 'quick clean breaks and new permanent constitutions under occupying forces'[73]. The transition was not subject to extensive formal *self-regulation*.
- The 'pacted constitutional transitions' of the 1989 Autumn of Nations in Eastern and Central Europe were constitutional as they 'proceeded in a more piecemeal fashion, guided by round table discussions whose conclusions were acted upon by legislative bodies in *formal compliance* with the amendment process of prior constitutions'.[74] Also, these transitions were generally left ungoverned by secondary rules.[75]
- In the context of other pre-Cold War transitions, for example in Latin America, transitions were generally not regulated by specific rules, or governed by institutions set up for that specific purpose.[76]

Categorisations of transitions between 1945 and 1989 abound.[77] Pre-Cold War transitions, or transitions without transitional institutions and

---

[73] V. C. Jackson, 'What's in a Name?', op. cit., p. 1261.

[74] Id., p. 1267.

[75] There was a coalition government with elements both from the communist party and the opposition in Czechoslovakia ruling the country in the months following the Velvet Revolution. But to my knowledge the functioning of this government was not subject to a particular set of rules governing the interim period, even if the whole constitutional system came to be altered.

[76] IDEA, 'Interim Constitutions in Post-Conflict Settings', Discussion Report, 4–5 December 2014', p. 16: '[w]ith two exceptions (Nicaragua and Guatemala, both of which are deemed unrepresentative cases), Latin American countries have not used interim constitutions' (observation by J. Couso).

[77] See, for example the distinction between '*classical transitions*': 'the extension of democracy in advanced capitalist countries between 1860 and 1920'; '*neoclassical transitions*': 'democratisations in basically capitalist countries after the Second World War (West Germany, Italy, and Japan in the 1940s; Spain and Portugal in the 1970s; some Latin American countries in the 1970s and 1980s; South Korea and Taiwan in the 1980s)'; '*market-oriented reform* in non-communist countries': 'West Germany and other Western countries after the Second World War; South Korea and Taiwan in the early 1960s; Chile in the 1970s; Turkey and Mexico in the 1980s; Argentina in the 1990s'; and '*Asian post-communist transition*': 'China since the late 1970s and Vietnam since the late 1980s'. L. Balcerowicz, 'Understanding Post-Communist Transitions' in W. Kostecki, K. Zukriwska, B. J. Goralczyck, *Transformations of Post-Communist States*, Macmillian Press, 2000, pp. 225.

16   TRANSITIONAL GOVERNANCE TODAY

elaborate self-regulatory frameworks will only occasionally be referred to as transitions *sensu lato*.

B Scope of the Book

This book zooms in on the non-forcible aspects of conflict-related TG (1) while focusing on the transition itself (2).

1 Non-Forcible Aspects of Conflict-Related TG

In spite of the often violent context of or antecedents to TG (1.1), this study prioritises the analysis of non-forcible aspects of TG (1.2).

1.1 Conflict-Related TG

We are concerned with contemporary TG which furthermore unfolds against the background of armed conflicts or threats to peace and security. Two yardsticks shall be adopted to distinguish between (more or less) peaceful and conflict-related TG: the existence of armed conflict and/or the threat to international peace and security. Non-constitutional transitions often occur in such contexts because, cynically enough, the association between non-constitutionality and violence is almost natural.[78]

Transitions in the context of internal disturbances[79] not posing a threat to international peace and security will mostly be disregarded. Admittedly, the distinction between internal disturbances and armed conflicts is not always clear-cut and this study may also generate insights for the former category.[80] The relatively peaceful revolutions of the 1989 Autumn of Nations,[81] several regime changes in Europe and Latin

---

[78] Fundamentally, this is because 'current constitutional legitimacy is ultimately based in violence'. A. A. i Ninet, *Constitutional Violence: Legitimacy, Democracy and Human Rights*, Edinburgh University Press, 2012, p. 3. As the state in principle has the legitimate monopoly on exercising power (violence/use of force to suppress revolt or enforce law), non-constitutional change is often associated with violent revolution.

[79] Protocol Additional to the Geneva Conventions of 12 August 1949, and relating to the Protection of Victims of Non-International Armed Conflicts (Protocol II), 8 June 1977, art. 1.2.

[80] Y. Dinstein, *Non-International Armed Conflict in International Law*, Cambridge University Press, 2014, p. 21. Internal disturbances: 'may be large-scale and rife with violence, perhaps inflicting incalculable human fatalities and/or colossal damage to property, but they do not become a non-international armed conflict as long as . . . they are not coordinated and sustained over a stretch of time'.

[81] L. Balcerowicz, 'Understanding Post-Communist Transitions' in W. Kostecki, K. Zukriwska, B. J. Goralczyck, *Transformations of Post-Communist States*, op. cit., pp.

SCOPE OF THE BOOK

America in the 1970s and 1980s,[82] the relatively stable multiparty transitions in a number of African countries during the 1990s,[83] took place in the context of 'mere' internal disturbances and tensions. The same is true of the installation of the interim cabinet of the Egyptian Supreme Council installed in February 2011,[84] the creation of the *Gouvernement d'union nationale de la transition* in Madagascar in August 2009,[85] the formation of the coalition government in Greece in November 2011[86] and projected transitions in Algeria, Sudan and Venezuela (2019). References to 'mere' (political) crisis-related TG will be kept to a minimum.

Peaceful large-scale institutional modifications in line with the existing constitutional order also fall outside the scope of this book. Such modifications are neither violent nor non-constitutional. The book disregards cases in which the politico-legal constitutional regime remains largely unquestioned, even when there are significant constitutional modifications (for example Belgium's step-by-step evolution from a unitary State in 1831 to a federal State in 1993) or when political powers are temporarily exercised by a caretaker or technical government (for example Belgium's administration *en affaires courantes* from June 2010 until December 2011, and again in 2019–20).

Occasionally, non-violent crises are addressed by a *non-constitutional* transition led by an interim government or a technocrat government – for example the interim leadership of Emmerson Mnangagwa after the

---

227–8: '[a] [fourth] exceptional feature of East-Central European economic and political transitions is their lack of violence ... ECE has undergone a peaceful revolution, with massive changes in political and economic institutions resulting from negotiations between the surviving communist elite and the leaders of the opposition'. Cf. also J. Elster, C. Offe, U. K. Preuss, *Institutional Design in Post-communist Societies – Rebuilding the Ship at Sea*, Cambridge University Press, 1998, p. 3: 'non-military and non-violent nature of the collapse and transition'. The exception of the (violent) Romanian transition should be mentioned.

[82] Argentina (1973), Greece (1974), Portugal (1974), Spain (1975), Brazil (1985), and Uruguay (1985). These situations did not reach the level of armed conflict and, given the inactivity of the UNSC during the Cold War, were not considered to pose a threat to international peace and security.

[83] E.g. in Benin (which led the way in the wave of democracy movements in West Africa in the early 1990s), Burkina Faso (military coups and military regimes alternating with other forms of government, but no armed conflict), Cameroon (although during the Cameroon Insurgency of 1955–60 more than 100 people were killed in riots), Cabo Verde and Ghana.

[84] After the resignation of President Mubarak.

[85] Based on the Maputo Agreement of 8 August 2009 following the 2009 Malagasy political crisis marked by an unconstitutional change of government.

[86] Following calls from the EU in light of the sovereign debt crisis.

army quietly seized power from Robert Mugabe in Zimbabwe in 2017. The peace-through-transition paradigm is less relevant for non-violent crises, for example the case of a bloodless coup.[87] These cases are rather rare, and interactions between domestic and international actors, thus usually international legal relevance, decrease when TG is pursued in a non-violent context.

1.2 Non-Forcible Aspects

The background of armed conflicts or threats to peace and security notwithstanding, we will focus on the *non-forcible* aspects of conflict-related TG. The recourse to violence has been a measure of last resort under international law since war was outlawed as a means for resolving international disputes. This is true since the 1928 Briand-Kellogg Pact, and remains largely applicable under the more recent 'responsibility to protect' framework ('R2P').[88] We are therefore better advised to investigate what international law allows for *within* the range of non-forcible (yet sometimes coercive) measures to maintain or restore international peace and security; and hereby to concentrate on TG as an instrument of choice to this end.

Today, contrary to the decolonisation era,[89] it hardly makes sense to examine whether *forcible* support to movements pursuing internal self-determination is permissible. Such support is simply forbidden.[90] In our age, the analysis should rather focus on *non-forcible* support in similar or comparable situations also leading to regime change. Can transitions be vitiated by coercion short of force?[91] Are there procedural safeguards

---

[87] The case of Guinea Bissau and the 2012 *Pacto de Transição Política* is occasionally referred to.

[88] Also under the 'responsibility to react', military intervention is seen as a last resort remedy, and 'can only be justified when every non-military option for the prevention or peaceful resolution of the crisis has been explored'. ICISS Report of the International Commission on Intervention and State Sovereignty, p. XII.

[89] Forcible support to national liberation movements was then allowed. A/RES/29/3314 of 14 December 1974, art. 7. N. Ronzitti, *Le guerre di liberazione nazionale e il diritto internazionale*, Pacini, 1974. N. Ronzitti, Resort to Force in Wars of National Liberation in A. Cassese (ed.), *Current Problems of International Law, Essays on U.N. Law and on the Law of Armed Conflict*, Giuffrè editore, 1975.

[90] UN Charter, art. 2, § 4. A/RES/2625 of 24 October 1970 ('1970 Friendly Relations Declaration'). Cf. also Accordance with International Law of the Unilateral Declaration of Independence in Respect of Kosovo, Advisory Opinion, ICJ Reports 2010, p. 403, §§ 80–81.

[91] Cf. Part IV. This question becomes relevant when decision-makers do not shy away from defending the idea of 'imposed democracy' even if, as history has amply shown, 'the survival of imposed democracy is by no means assured'. A. J. Enterline, J. M. Greig,

SCOPE OF THE BOOK 19

against this risk? What does international law say about indirectly imposed regime change? Such questions suggest that non-forcible aspects of TG should be analysed on their own merits. Topics such as humanitarian intervention, violent 'remedial secession' or forcible countermeasures will thus be carefully avoided.

This study on conflict-related TG will therefore not privilege the analysis of the use of force in transition contexts. How to evaluate the invitation by a Malian TA to France to use force (resulting in *Opération Serval*, 2013–14)? How was the Libyan TA to behave as a belligerent party when the Arab Spring erupted in 2011? Was the 'transformative occupation' in Iraq after the 2003 US invasion lawful? Delicate questions relating to *ius ad bellum* and *ius in bello* in the context of transitions still merit attention, yet we shall focus on the legal-regulatory aspects surrounding TG,[92] also when we discuss indirectly imposed regime change.[93]

2 *The Voyage Is the Destination*

This study analyses the transitions themselves, rather than to fetishise, so to speak, their – legitimate, illegitimate, democratic or undemocratic – precedents or outcomes. We will focus on specific types (2.1) and actors of TG (2.2).

2.1 Focus on Replacement and Transplacement

Among transitions from authoritarian regimes to democracy, distinctions were made between:

- 'transformations', by which 'those in power in the authoritarian regime take the lead and play the decisive role in ending that regime and changing it into a democratic system';[94]
- 'replacements', by which 'democratisation . . . results from the opposition gaining strength and the government losing strength until the government collapses or is overthrown'; and

---

'Against All Odds? The History of Imposed Democracy and the Future of Iraq and Afghanistan', *Foreign Policy Analysis*, 2008, 4, 321–47.

[92] Chapter 4, Section B.1.3 about the severability between civilian/political and forcible/military aspects of TG. Cf. also the notion of *civilian* TA under Chapter 4, Section B.1.

[93] Chapters 9 and 10.

[94] S. P. Huntington, *The Third Wave: Democratisation in the Late Twentieth Century*, Julian J. Rothbaum Distinguished Lecture Series v. 4, University of Oklahoma Press, 1991, p. 124.

- 'transplacements', by which 'democratisation is produced by the combined actions of government and opposition'.[95]

These distinctions were developed when the idea of a 'worldwide democratic revolution' still had wide traction. Although this is much less the case at the time of writing, characterised by what some consider to be a global democratic recession,[96] the distinctions between transformation, replacement and transplacement remain useful.

The first form of transition results from a self-initiative. In such case, the transition is in fact a reform undertaken by the incumbent in line with the existing constitution. These are chiefly domestic, government-led matters, and therefore least relevant from an international legal perspective.[97] As such self-reform initiatives are carried out in line with the constitution, transitions by transformation are no further considered.

This book focuses on the two latter transition models, that is replacements and transplacements. Replacements are unilateral or confrontational, and follow uprisings, revolutions, coups or armed conflict. TA installed by replacement will be referred to as 'oppositional TA', which can be defined as 'political/civilian entities that have the publicly proclaimed aim of introducing a new political regime by non-constitutionally reconfiguring the constitutional order, without (initially) collaborating with the incumbent power'.[98] As we live in the age of constitutional geopolitics, defined as external actors' political interest and involvement in shaping the constitutional identity of other states, this scenario raises important questions under international law, notably under the principles of self-determination and non-intervention.

The third form of transition, transplacement, is agreement-based, yet often non-constitutional. Domestic TA with a consensual origin are mostly set up as part of a peace process and based on power-sharing or peace agreements. Such TA will be referred to as 'consensual TA'.

---

[95] Id.

[96] T. Gerald Daly, 'Democratic Decay: Conceptualising an Emerging Research Field', *Hague Journal on the Rule of Law*, Vol. 11, no. 1, 2019, pp. 9–36. L. Diamond, 'Facing Up to the Democratic Recession', *Journal of Democracy*, no. 1, 2015, pp. 41–55.

[97] Such as the Moroccan transition, initiated by King Mohammed VI who organised the 2011 referendum and subsequent constitutional reforms. Indonesia's interim government after President Suharto's resignation in 1998 also represents the 'incumbent caretaker model of [a] transition'. M. S. Malley, 'Inchoate Opposition, Divided Incumbents – Muddling toward Democracy in Indonesia, 1998–99' in K. Guttieri, J. Piombo (eds.), *Interim Governments – Institutional Bridges to Peace and Democracy?*, op. cit., pp. 147–69.

[98] Id.

SCOPE OF THE BOOK

2.2 Focus on States in Transition, Official Reactions and the UNSC

This study, and the accompanying Report published on the website of the Political Settlements Research Programme,[99] refers to extensive international practice. Which practice? A variety of actors may intend to influence TG, and the ensuing political/constitutional reconfiguration of a state's order. We will focus on states in transition; reactions by other states; occasionally regional international organisations ('IO') and the UN, especially the UNSC; and practitioners' guidelines to complement our insights.

This study concentrates primarily on the practice of *states in transition*; or the practice of TA attributable to states. It draws on the observation of practice and transition instruments of more than twenty interested states, which are, or were said to be in transition.[100]

Second, views expressed by *other states*, including during contact group reunions, complement this observation. The conclusions of such meetings are taken on behalf of dozens of states and IO. With the necessary nuances, views from third states allow to take the temperature of potentially emerging state practice and/or *opinio iuris*. Their practice with regard to TG is at least insightful. Consider, for instance, the role of Turkey and Egypt as temporary hosts of the Syrian oppositional TA; or national programmes monitoring transitions (such as the Office of Transition Initiatives from the United States Agency for International Development). Consider also chancelleries which often view or promote TG as a conflict resolution mechanism. The influence on transitions exercised by governmental or government-funded agencies is underestimated, too.[101]

Third, *regional IO and the UN* often influence TG. Regional organisations include the African Union ('AU'), whose 'mandate, especially in transition contexts, appears to have gradually expanded over time',[102] and Economic Community of Central African States ('ECCAS') and

---

[99] E. De Groof, 'The Features of Transitional Governance Today', *Political Settlements Research Programme*, University of Edinburgh, 2019, first edition. This report is available on www.politicalsettlements.org/publications-database/features-of-transitional-govern ance-today, op. cit.

[100] See Tables 1.1 and 3.1 and E. De Groof, 'The Features of Transitional Governance Today', op. cit.

[101] S. Bisarya, 'No Strings Attached? Constraints on External Advice in Internationalised Constitution-Making', op. cit., in E. De Groof, M. Wiebusch (eds.), International Law and Transitional Governance, Routledge, 2020.

[102] IDEA, *Rule of Law and Constitution Building, The Role of Regional Organisations*, 2014, p. 3.

Economic Community of West African States ('ECOWAS'). Regional organisations may also be involved in state renaissance through agencies such as the European Endowment for Democracy (a private foundation funded by the EU) and the EU Civil Society Facility (an EU strategy created under the European Neighbourhood Policy).[103] At the UN, the Constitutional Focal Point was 'established in 2013 in response to increased demand for UN assistance in constitution-making processes'.[104] The Peacebuilding Commission; the UN Department of Political and Peacebuilding Affairs ('UNDPPA') Mediation Support Unit ('MSU') with its Standby Team of Mediation Experts; the 'Rule of Law Coordination and Resource Group'; and UN field missions with mandates relating to the rule of law are also engaged with TG. The practice of the UNSC will be given particular attention as it plays an important role in divulging the peace-through-transition paradigm, notably by adopting resolutions through which it catalyses or spreads relevant *opinio iuris*.

Reference is also made to practitioners' and deontological guidelines. Such guidelines partly account for the socialised origin of TG practices.[105] They are often prepared by non-governmental or academic organisations working on TG.[106] Their reading assists us in unveiling the socialised origin of TG, thus in understanding why TG is replicated, and why specific norms in relation to it are germinating.

The variety of actors concerned with TG touches upon the invisible yet unexplored *fil rouge* of this study: the implicit tension between domestic and international engagement during transitions which often end up in disasters. Who is responsible for the ineffectiveness or malfunctioning of TG, or sometimes malpractices and illegalities affecting it? By the end of this book, it should become clearer under which circumstances TA and external actors potentially engage their responsibility. But I shall not enquire whether or how responsibility must be shared. More modestly, this study uncovers norms and policies which, if current trends are

---

[103] R. Balfour, 'Changes and Continuities in EU-Mediterranean Relations after the Arab Spring' in S. Biscop, R. Balfour, M. Emerson (eds.), *An Arab Spring for EU Foreign Policy?*, Egmont Paper 54, January 2012.

[104] See the factsheet on CFP, available on https://peacemaker.un.org/sites/peacemaker.un .org/files/ConstitutionMaking_Factsheet_May2016.pdf, last accessed 23 February 2019.

[105] Introduction, Section A.1, and the peace-through-transition paradigm.

[106] For example the NGOs DRI and International IDEA to name but a few. Religious organisations have also played a role in state transformation processes. For example the mediation by the Catholic Church leading to the 1989 power-sharing agreement in Poland. Cf. Observations by L. Garlicki in IDEA, 'Interim Constitutions in Post-Conflict Settings', op. cit., p. 17.

consolidated, should by and large be respected by *both* sets of actors. The question of attribution, then, comes second, as it depends on a minutious case-by-case assessment.

C The Argument: No Absolute Freedom in Times of Transition

The last section presents the research hypothesis (1) and exposes the reasons why international law was chosen to analyse TG, thus why this book was written (2).

1 *Partial Invalidation of Initial Hypothesis*

Do transitions entirely depend on domestic political contingencies? Does TG constitute a playfield on which both domestic and international actors may intervene without any legal constraints ('*legibus soluti*'), even as they influence a state renaissance? My initial research hypothesis was that, legally speaking, such freedom would reign – and that the law of the jungle would predominate. This book dismantles the initial hypothesis for its lack of nuance. In light of the practice and policy in relation to more than twenty 'interested states', that is countries that have undergone a - transition,[107] described in a separate report[108] and analysed in this book, the hypothesis is indeed proven to be partly wrong, and partly justified.

Undeniably, both domestic actors and international actors enjoy much freedom in times of transition. TG is first and foremost influenced by politics, domestic and international. At the same time, a number of red lines place TG under marginal yet meaningful legal scrutiny. Some of these red lines already exist under international law while others are currently being traced.

As a distinct politico-legal phenomenon, TG was to some extent already regulated under international law; it is now increasingly so. While international law does not prescribe the precise identity of the 'newborn child' (that is the post-transition state), the rules governing the birth process[109] or rather *re*generation of the state are now gaining detail. Existing and evolving legal norms with regard to TG will be examined in

---

[107] Table 3.1 and Introduction, Section A.

[108] E. De Groof, 'The Features of Transitional Governance Today', op. cit.

[109] Imagery of J. d'Aspremont, 'Les administrations internationales de territoire et la création internationale d'Etats démocratiques', 2018, available on https://esil-sedi.eu /wp-content/uploads/2018/04/DAspremont.pdf, p. 1, where it is used in a different

24 TRANSITIONAL GOVERNANCE TODAY

light of TI, state practice, UNSC resolutions and deontological guidelines. As they develop under the umbrella of the pre-existing principle of self-determination, norms currently in flux include the temporal and material limits to the powers of TA, as follows.

TA should exercise their duties on a temporary basis, that is without suspending or delaying the interregnum, and with the aim of being replaced. They should commit to a predefined timeframe. Such temporal limitations reinforce the following substantive limitations. TA should not preshadow the future entirely. While preparing for major institutional changes, the leeway for defining the post-transition constitutional order is limited. At a maximum, they may define beforehand the 'big principles' for the post-transition. Furthermore, the legal position of other states and the rights of private persons acquired before the transition should be respected. Lastly, TA are themselves entrusted with completing TG and ensuring the daily running of the state even when receiving extensive international assistance.

In several respects, the law applicable to TG is currently evolving or only germinating, and can therefore only robustly be defined. If current trends continue, though, *ius in interregno*, feeding itself from existing international legal principles, can gain coherence also without becoming a so-called self-contained regime.[110] The greater such coherence, the more (political) arbitrariness is reduced, subjecting TG in that sense to the rule of law.[111] International law may then have an 'essential role to play in informing and regulating ... transitional political arrangements'.[112]

---

sense (with ITA, the international community 'cannot entirely control the birth of states [but] strives to choose the gender of the "newborn child"').

[110] In its narrow sense, i.e. defined as a 'special set of secondary rules [claiming] priority over the secondary rules in the general law of State responsibility'. Report of the study group on the fragmentation of international law, finalised by M. Koskenniemi, A/CN.4/L.682, 13 April 2006, p. 66. See p. 68 for the distinction between self-contained regime in a narrow and broader sense.

[111] I adopt the following large definition of the international rule of law: 'the power of the State may not be exercised arbitrarily. This incorporates the rejection of "rule of man", but does not require that state power be exercised for any particular purpose. It does, however, require that laws be prospective, accessible, and clear'. S. Chesterman, 'An International Rule of Law?', *The American Journal of Comparative Law*, Vol. 56, no. 2, 2008, p. 342. TG is progressively removed from the *exclusive* sphere of politics. For an article advocating a reductionist view of the rule of law in conjunction with constitutionalism, see F. Venter, 'The Rule of Law as a Global Norm for Constitutionalism' in J. R. Silkenat, J. E. Hickey Jr, P. D. Barenboim (eds.), *The Legal Doctrines of the Rule of Law and the Legal State*, Springer, 2014, pp. 91–104.

[112] J. I. Levitt, *Illegal Peace in Africa*, op. cit., p. 43.

NO ABSOLUTE FREEDOM IN TIMES OF TRANSITION 25

Ius in interregno thus refers to existing international legal principles, and to emerging custom inferred from currently shared practices and associated beliefs, which will be compared so as to find their lowest common denominator. This comparison is based on a *skeletonisation*, one could say, of TG practices – the reversed action of what some in the field of comparative constitutional law have called the 'IKEA theory':[113] by de-assembling we discover commonalities.

The law must be stable, and yet it cannot stand still. International law applicable to TG, too, is stable, yet does not stand still. The core or frame of *ius in interregno* is stable. It is based on firmly established principles of international law such as the principles of self-determination and non-intervention, and on secondary norms such as those on state responsibility or the sources of law. To this stable beacon, the law as it currently evolves in relation to TG is arguably adding some nuance and body.

Language, similarly characterised by changing trends evolving around a self-referential set of rules, can also gain nuance and body. Alternatively, and depending on the zeal of its aficionados and detractors, language can lose precision. In some cases, a declining collective memory and loss of structure may even lead to its implosion, a fate possibly reserved to endangered languages such as Guaraní (Paraguay, Argentina, Brazil), Breton (France) or Kobiana (Senegal, Guinea-Bissau).

Similarly, the frame of *ius in interregno* can be refined. In law, the task of specifying the frame, characterised by its generality and abstraction, may be fulfiled by individual customary rules based on practice and *opinio iuris*.[114] But if customary rules supposedly adding precision, nuance and body to international law are discontinued, progressively or abruptly, then such 'added value' will either fade out or vanish. A more radical scenario is the case of an aggressive reversal of the practice and *opinio iuris* which initially informed customary norm germination around established principles and secondary norms. Such a U-turn could in the long run even erode the core of international law itself. This scenario is not really envisaged in this book – but it cannot be excluded by it either.

The argument developed in this book will be centred around this self-referential, cyclic and multilayered vision of international law. Even those

---

[113] G. Frankenberg, 'Constitutional Transfer: The Ikea Theory Revisited', *International Journal of Constitutional Law*, Vol. 8, no. 3, 1 July 2010.

[114] Here I paraphrase A. Cassese, *Self-determination of Peoples: a Legal Reappraisal*, Hersch Lauterpacht Memorial Lecture Series, Cambridge University Press, 1995, p. 129.

who argue and predict that an ongoing evolution will probably be confirmed in the near future must accept, as I do, that germinating individual customary rules currently sculpting the frame of international law might, in the long run, either be confirmed, fade out or even radically change to the point of eroding established international law. We are now at a tilting point as we cannot predict whether current widespread practice surrounding TG, potentially co-constituting substantive and temporal legal limits to TG, will be confirmed or discontinued in the future.

After reading this book, we will thus find ourselves, one may dare say, in the position of the attentive observer who, sometime between the beginning and end of Spring, notes that red leather skirts are indeed becoming en vogue, yet awaits the Summer to see if the trend will be confirmed and perhaps become *incontournable*. Some readers may frown at this image. The point I am trying to make, here with Weber, is that: 'experience reveals a continuous scale of transitions from norms of conduct guaranteed by mere convention to those which are regarded as binding and guaranteed by law ... It should be clear that ... the transitions from mere usage to convention and from it to law are fluid.'[115]

Without disposing of a crystal ball, there is no 'burden of proof' to substantiate that the law will further develop in the direction it seems to have just taken, as will be described in the following chapters. Instead, I argue that yesterday we were at a crossroads, that today we are just beyond that point but still only around the corner, and that, except if we backtrack now, a step has been taken *towards* crystallising current practices, which, then, tomorrow may add nuance and body to existing international law.

2 Why Analyse Transitions under International Law?

Political science has addressed transitions for some time.[116] The rise of TG has not yet been subjected to comprehensive international legal study, though, in spite of the active external entanglement with TG, and in spite

---

[115] M. Weber, *On Law in Economy and Society*, Harvard University Press, 1954, pp. 30–53.

[116] Y. Shain, J. Linz, *Between States – Interim Governments and Democratic Transitions*, Cambridge University Press, 1995; K. Guttieri, J. Piombo (eds.), *Interim Governments – Institutional Bridges to Peace and Democracy?*, op. cit.; J. Strasheim, H. Fjelde, 'Pre-Designing Democracy: Institutional Design of Interim Governments and Democratisation in 15 Post-Conflict Societies', *Democratization*, Vol. 21, no. 2, 2014; Y.-P. Mandjem, 'Les Gouvernements de transition comme sites d'institutionnalisation de la politique dans les ordres politiques en voie de sortie de crise en Afrique', *African Journal of International Affairs*, Vol. 12, no. 1 and 2, 2009, pp. 81–182.

NO ABSOLUTE FREEDOM IN TIMES OF TRANSITION 27

of international law remaining the language of diplomacy. This gap may be explained by the subtlety marking the topic, 'less striking than belligerent occupation or international territorial administration'.[117] Few have thus scrutinised how the South African two-stage transition was repeated in other contexts; how this model became increasingly influenced by international actors; and how the recurrence and internationalisation of TG may modestly contribute to the development of international law.[118] This book represents the first such attempt. It does so using the existing international legal language.

The originality of this approach does not lie so much in the terms *ius in interregno*, which is not a legal concept or a self-contained regime but simply a term, used for ease of reference, covering international legal norms, both stable and evolving, applicable to TG. This book is not supposed to be *original* as much as it intends to be *creative* by pouring new wine (TG as a contemporary and distinct politico-legal phenomenon) into old bottles (existing references of international law) – hopefully solid bottles, containers of quality resilient enough to accommodate the change. In a sense, we engage in a 'theorisation-within-the-law enterprise'.

Using international law is not to deny the contingency of individual transitions. Also, international law represents just one approach among many others. Then, why dedicate an entire treatise to TG under international law? A common reference frame – however robust – is indispensable for a pluralist international society.[119] International law constitutes 'a social discourse and argumentation practice in constant evolution',[120] thus providing a formally self-referential and ever evolving framework for a principled debate on TG. This is essential because in the absence of

[117] M. Saul, 'From Haiti to Somalia', op. cit., p. 133.

[118] B. Bowden, H. Charlesworth, J. Farrall (eds.), *The Role of International Law in Rebuilding Societies after Conflict: Great Expectations*, Cambridge University Press, 2009; N. Youssef, *La transition démocratique et la garantie des droits fondamentaux*, Publibook, 2011.

[119] In 1980, R.-J. Dupuy highlighted the role of scholarship in observing international norm creation in a heterogeneous world. R.-J. Dupuy, Leçon inaugurale faite le Vendredi 22 Février 1980, Collège de France, Chaire de Droit International, 1980, pp. 16–17.

[120] O. Corten, *Méthodologie du droit international public*, Éd. de l'Université de Bruxelles, 2009. Own translation. This is not to deny the validity of other conceptions of international law. Cf. J. d'Aspremont, *Epistemic Forces in International Law*, Elgar International Law, 2015, p. vii: 'there is not necessarily any inconsistency in simultaneously thinking of international law as a set of rules and institutions, a set of authoritative processes, a combination of rules and processes, a set of legal relations, a discourse, a tool to create authoritative claims, a political project, etc.'.

28 TRANSITIONAL GOVERNANCE TODAY

a true homogeneous international community, global governance remains polycentric and heterarchical, also in relation to TG.

The international impact on TG and its susceptibility to external influences explain the legal and factual internationalisation of the interregnum. The proliferation of TG is expedited by the partial shift from a politico-military to a legal-regulatory approach to international peace and security, although the pendulum may swing back. The peace-through-transition paradigm is also propagated by the UNSC and several components of the international community. This mainstreaming however hardly conceals underlying disparities, which are unavoidable given the diversity of goals pursued by an array of actors. While some actors may be genuinely interested in a domestically driven and inclusive transition (say, arguably the parties to the Pretoria Agreement leading to the transition in the DRC), others aim at extending their geopolitical grip (say, external actors involved in transitions in Libya, Sudan and Ukraine).

International law, as one among other epistemological registers, is then promoted as a tool for analysing TG so as to change the *mode* of debating this polemical topic, also to the advantage of states undergoing a transition. The aim is thus to provide an analytical grid and argumentative toolbox also *for actors or states, often in the Global South, suffering from unlawful TG practices or in search of legal arguments to defend themselves from being, directly or indirectly, 'lured into' a transition.* A culture of formalism can help in depoliticising the theme.[121] This is neither a politically innocent choice[122] nor an attempt at maximising the regulatory grip of international law.[123] Analysing TG under international law is not to be confused with blind norm entrepreneurship. International law is not, and should not be, ubiquitous. The law applicable to TG will never deal even with most aspects of TG, and its evolution may be halted if current common practices were disrupted. Those who

---

[121] M. Koskenniemi, *The Gentle Civilizer of Nations: The Rise and Fall of International Law 1870–1960*, Cambridge University Press, 2004.

[122] M. Koskenniemi, *From Apology to Utopia*, Cambridge University Press, 2005, p. 616: 'its ideals include those of accountability, equality, reciprocity and transparency, and it comes to us with an embedded vocabulary of (formal) rights'.

[123] There is no 'wishful thinking' in this regard, as described by Pellet: 'une certaine tendance à prendre leurs désirs pour des réalités et à tenir pour vérités juridiques des tendances encore balbutiantes ou, pire, qui n'existent que dans leurs espoirs'. A. Pellet, 'Droits-de-l'hommisme et droit international', Conférence commémorative Gilberto Amado, 18 juillet 2000. I thus avoid a 'committed argument'. Cf. G. I Hernández, 'The Activist Academic in International Legal Scholarship', *ESIL Reflections*, Vol. 2, no. 11, 16 December 2013.

consider, rightly or wrongly, these practices to be disingenuous or ineffective may even welcome such a reversal. It is not the purpose of this book to enter this controversy.

This book limits itself to unveiling the partly evolving legal framework in relation to TG, regardless of the moral or political desirability of how specific norms evolve. Potential norm crystallisation carries both opportunities and risks. This book does not go at length in explaining what these are. This question is left to fields outside or about the law which may wish to engage in a critical assessment about what the consequences, positive or adverse, may be of *ius in interregno* further gaining terrain.

PART I

The Unchartered Territory of Transitional Governance

This part explains why the legal analysis of TG is overdue in light of its proliferation and internationalisation since the end of the Cold War (Chapter 1). As current literature does not offer sufficient guidance (Chapter 2), we will turn to existing legal yardsticks and a perusal of relevant practice in subsequent chapters.

1

The Rise and Internationalisation of Transitional Governance

TG has 'become more complicated and, so, require[s] greater and more protracted effort, and support, to accomplish and consolidate. Transition periods, and the anocratic regimes associated with such transitions, then, tend to last longer than they had in the past'.[1] Transitions are also becoming more numerous, making it a challenge to follow the rhythm by which they pop up. In addition, TG has become a matter of international concern. This chapter analyses the discourse underpinning its proliferation (Section A) and internationalisation (Section B).

A The Rise of Transitional Governance

What are the reasons explaining the widespread reliance on TG? This section situates the proliferation of TG in its historic-economic context (1), and problematises the legal grounds that might be invoked to justify and consolidate this trend (2).

1 The Turn to the 'Light Footprint'

The relative diminution of state creation and unsustainability of direct ITA are the historic-economic factors explaining the rise of contemporary TG. First, the creation of new states has become relatively rare compared to the second half of the twentieth century, especially after the epoch of decolonisation and the dissolution of the USSR and ex-Yugoslavia. In the twenty-first century, more recent and sometimes forcible attempts to redraw the borders of Ukraine (annexation of Crimea by Russia) or Syria and Iraq (the so-called Islamic State of Iraq and the Levant), for example, do not amount to state creation.

---

[1] M. G. Marshall, B. R. Cole, Center for Systemic Peace, 'Global Report 2014, Conflict, Governance, and State Fragility', p. 25.

34   THE RISE AND INTERNATIONALISATION OF TG

Attempts to create states like Kosovo, Abkhazia, South Ossetia or Catalonia remain legally unsettled to this date. This can in no way be compared to the general consensus (sometimes *ex post*) concerning the dissolution processes of the USSR[2] and Yugoslavia[3] or decolonisation in the 1960s and 1970s (notwithstanding individual[4] or longtime objectors[5]). Compared to the second half of the twentieth century, the creation of states in the twenty-first century has become rare. From a geopolitical viewpoint, influencing TG rather than supporting state creation seems to create less resistance.

Furthermore, since the turn of the millennium, instances of direct international/foreign territorial administration, whether or not in conjunction with belligerent occupation, are decreasing, notwithstanding the scholarly attention they continue to receive.[6] All trusteeship operations were suspended in 1994. Since then, most instances of ITA, especially those in East Timor (UNTAET) and Kosovo (UNMIK), have been criticised both on normative[7] and material (costs and ponderousness[8]) grounds. ITA in these countries required the UN almost to substitute for a sovereign state.[9]

---

[2] For the consensual basis of the dissolution, cf. The Belavezha Accords of 8 December 1991, and the Alma-Ata Protocols of 21 December 1991.

[3] Cf. conclusions of Arbitration Commission of the Peace Conference on Yugoslavia ('Badinter Commission').

[4] For example, Serbia in the case of Yugoslavia's dissolution.

[5] Portugal in the decolonisation process. Colonising states absented their vote on the 'Declaration on the Granting of Independence to Colonial Countries and Peoples'.

[6] See e.g. E. De Brabandere, *Post-Conflict Administrations in International Law: International Territorial Administration, Transitional Authority and Foreign Occupation in Theory and Practice*, Martinus Nijhoff Publishers, 2009; B. Knoll, *The Legal Status of Territories Subject to Administration by International Organisations*, Cambridge University Press, 2008.

[7] R. Wilde, *International Territorial Administration – How Trusteeship and the Civilizing Mission Never Went Away*, Oxford University Press, 2008. Cf. also C. Bull, *No Entry Without Strategy – Building the Rule of Law under UN Transitional Administration*, United Nations University Press, Tokyo, New York, Paris, 2008.

[8] C. Bull, *No Entry Without Strategy – Building the Rule of Law under UN Transitional Administration*, op. cit.

[9] Y. Daudet, 'L'exercice des compétences territoriales par les Nations Unies' in: Organización de los estados Americanos, Comité jurídico interamericano. Curso de Derecho Internacional XXXIV 2007, Secretariá General OEA, Washington DC, 2007, pp. 54, 58 : 'Dès lors que les Nations Unies *se substituent* à des Etats défaillants ou remplissent sur des territoires non autonomes des missions comparables à celles dont étaient investies des puissances mandataires ou chargées d'une tutelle, *les compétences dont elles disposent sont celles d'Etats souverains*'. Own emphasis. Own translation : 'Since the United Nations replaces States that are in default or performs duties on non-self-

THE RISE OF TRANSITIONAL GOVERNANCE

The UN changed its method first in Afghanistan by opting for a 'light footprint' approach:[10] 'the UN could be the *midwife* for the birth of an interim Afghan government as the first step in an agreed process of transition ... but we would have no pretensions to run Afghanistan'.[11] Close observers confirmed that the 'emphasis has been placed on ensuring Afghan ownership of the reconstruction process'.[12] Under the light footprint approach, the UN is expected (only) to *assist* states in transition, rather than to (directly) administer them. The reason for adopting this approach was to correct the 'heavy international footprint'[13] of the past.

The new approach was 'hailed as a major conceptual revolution ..., developed out of the perceived failures in Kosovo, East Timor and elsewhere'.[14] Its novelty consisted in combining a two-staged domestic transition – in its very basic structure akin to the South African model – with international assistance.

governing territories comparable to those for which proxy powers or trusteeship were vested, the powers available to the United Nations are akin to those of sovereign States'.

[10] Report of the Secretary-General, 'The situation in Afghanistan and its implications for international peace and security', A/56/875–S/2002/278 of 18 March 2002, p. 16: 'UNAMA should aim to bolster Afghan capacity (both official and non-governmental), relying on as limited an international presence and on as many Afghan staff as possible, and using common support services where possible, thereby leaving a light expatriate "footprint."'

[11] K. Annan, N. Mousavizadeh, *Interventions – A Life in War and Peace*, Penguin Books, London, 2012, p. 338. Own emphasis.

[12] E. Afsah, A. Guhr, 'Afghanistan: Building a State to Keep the Peace', *Max Planck Yearbook of United Nations Law*, 9, 2005, p. 382. In the same sense: E. De Brabandere, *Post-Conflict Administrations in International Law*, op. cit. p. 42: 'that Afghanistan would not be a "full" UN-led international administration like UNMIK or UNTAET. ... [T]he focus was on the greatest possible participation of local actors and less international involvement. ... [T]he Bonn Agreement did not give the UN a mandate to exercise administrative authority over the territory, nor a direct responsibility for the administration of the territory'.

[13] E. Newman opposes the 'light footprint' to the 'heavy international footprint'. E. Newman, 'Liberal Peacebuilding Debates' in E. Newman, R. Paris, O. P. Richmond, *New Perspectives on Liberal Peacebuilding*, United Nations University Press, Tokyo, New York, Paris, 2009, p. 32. Assisting TG rather than bearing direct responsibility for conducting ITA must be seen as a 'possible correction to the trend towards ever-expanding [UN transitional] mandates' (S. Chesterman, *You, The People, The United Nations, Transitional Administration, and State-Building*, Oxford University Press, 2004, p. 49). It was a reaction to the 'well-known set-backs and over-extension of UN peace operations in the early 1990s' (M. Griffin, B. Jones, 'Building peace through transitional authority: New Directions, major Challenges', *International Peacekeeping*, 7:4, 2007, 75–90).

[14] E. Afsah, A. Guhr, 'Afghanistan: Building a State to Keep the Peace', op. cit., p. 382.

Despite the so-called light footprint approach, however, international actors went beyond acts of assistance, and exercised significant leverage on the Afghan transition and state-building process.[15] For some, 'the United Nations, continued to operate, far too often, through parallel structures that did provide some services to the population but undermined rather than helped the state establish and sustain its credibility'.[16] Because states and IO provided 'direct service delivery',[17] their involvement triggered dependency schemes resulting in Afghanistan becoming a rentier state.[18] The 'light footprint' approach becomes a fiction when 'formal authority remains with domestic actors but governance is dependent on international actors'.[19] This deep contradiction has affected several countries since the approach was introduced.

2 Prima Facie Legal Reasons behind the Rise of Transitional Governance

Might legal considerations also explain the increased recourse to TG? At first sight, the legal adventurer might think of three such considerations. First, TG may constitute an alternative option when ITA seems difficult to justify in light of the principle of equal sovereignty (2.1). Second, TG

---

[15] M. Schoiswohl, 'Linking the International Legal Framework to Building the Formal Foundations of a State at Risk: Constitution-Making and International Law in Post-Conflict Afghanistan', *Vanderbilt Journal of Transnational Law* 39, 2006, p. 861: 'This assistance is not imposed, *at least technically*, but provided on the basis of the normative framework enshrined in the 2001 Bonn Agreement', which 'reflects a compromise between a domestic program for the consolidation of power and specific benchmarks to ensure that the state-building agenda evolves in a manner acceptable to the international community. In the latter regard, the international community acts as a watchdog of democracy, *whose financial means in the form of bilateral and multilateral 'benevolence' entail significant leverage to inform the way by which Afghanistan is to rise to the circle of democratic states'*. Own emphasis.

[16] L. Brahimi, 'State-Building in Crisis and Post-Conflict Countries', paper presented at the 7th Global Forum on Reinventing Government, Vienna, Austria, 26-29 June 2007, p. 6.

[17] 'Conference Conclusions of the International Afghanistan Conference entitled 'Afghanistan and the international community: from transition to the transformation decade', A/66/597–S/2011/762 of 9 December 2011, p. 3.

[18] A. Suhrke, *When More Is Less: The International Project in Afghanistan*, Columbia University Press, 2011.

[19] M. Saul, 'The Search for an International Legal Concept of Democracy: Lessons from the Post-Conflict Reconstruction of Sierra Leone', *Melbourne Journal of International Law*, Vol. 13, no. 1, 2012, p. 7. Cf. also N. Roehner, *UN Peacebuilding – Light Footprint or Friendly Takeover?*, CreateSpace Independent Publishing Platform, Berlin, 2012.

may allow international actors to influence a country's future with lesser legal constraints (2.2). Third, TG may be represented as a means for avoiding shared international responsibility between domestic and other actors involved in the transition (2.3).

Deliberately formulated in a superficial way, these prima facie legal justifications will be briefly presented, and immediately rebuked. The piercing of this superficiality serves to underscore the subtlety of analysing TG under international law.

2.1 International Territorial Administration As a Last Resort: TG As the Alternative?

When resorting to TG, international actors may invoke principles of proportionality, subsidiarity and state sovereignty to justify their choice. As a response to serious crises and conflicts, the UN, regional IO and states increasingly support, empower or even create domestic TA.[20] This cost-efficient approach may seem preferable over their own direct intervention or over ITA. It has been argued indeed that direct ITA, when international actors and notably the UN exercise direct responsibility for governance (in German known as *VN-Übergangsverwaltung*), should be limited by the principles of proportionality and subsidiarity: it must be inversely proportional to possible restrictions on state sovereignty, and can only be used if peace and security cannot be achieved by other means.[21]

As ITA is considered a *'solution de dernier recours'*,[22] assisting TA could be presented as the law-abiding alternative in all other cases. By favouring nationally owned transitions, the risk of violating the principle of self-determination while influencing transitions seems less high. In reality, however, the choice for TG does not annihilate this risk. It also matters how TG is pursued, who offers international assistance to TG and at what point in time. Part III thus argues that TA are increasingly expected to comply with the principle of self-determination, and Part IV explains that international actors must not hinder a self-determination-compliant transition.

---

[20] Part IV.

[21] T. Marauhn, 'Konfliktbewältigung in Afghanistan zwischen Utopie und Pragmatismus', op. cit., pp. 480–511.

[22] K. Ardault, C.-M. Arion, D. Gnamou-Petauton, M. Yetongnon, 'L'administration internationale de territoire à l'épreuve du Kosovo et du Timor oriental: la pratique à la recherche d'une théorie', *Revue belge de droit international*, 2005/1–2, p. 301.

2.2 Less Constraints under International (Humanitarian) Law?

When external influence is channelled via TA in the absence of, or independently from, belligerent occupation, the leverage to influence a state's laws and institutions becomes enormous. By contrast, in the case of belligerent occupation, the Hague and Geneva Conventions require that domestic laws be further applied. The latter convention explicitly provides that the occupant shall, 'unless absolutely prevented', respect the laws in force in the country.[23] As a result, 'the authority of the occupant is *limited* by specific constraints emanating from . . . the limited regulatory powers of the occupant'.[24] Belligerent occupation must be 'order-preserving'.[25]

In the absence of belligerent occupation, or when legislative changes are carried out directly by domestic TA, neither of said conventions is applicable, and their legal requirements cannot be violated. The international involvement with TG can trigger constitutional changes that are constitutive of a new politico-legal order. The aim of constituting a new order could, then, be achieved to a lesser cost[26] and with a seemingly lower risk of legal non-compliance, given the non-applicability of said conventions.[27]

---

[23] 1907 The Hague Convention, art. 43: 'the authority of the legitimate power having in fact passed into the hands of the occupant, the latter shall take all the measures in his power to restore, and ensure, as far as possible, public order and safety, while respecting, unless absolutely prevented, the laws in force in the country'. Cf. also the Fourth 1949 Geneva Convention, art. 64.

[24] C. Stahn, *The Law and Practice of International Territorial Administration*, Cambridge Studies in International and Comparative Law, 2010, p. 115. Own emphasis. Stahn adds: 'the laws of occupation are not intended to provide a general framework for reconstruction and law reform' (p. 119).

[25] N. Bhuta, 'Antinomies of Transformative Occupation', *EJIL*, Vol. 16, no. 4, 2005, p. 727.

[26] Financial, material and human capital costs flowing from military occupation would be avoided.

[27] With a grain of irony, Saul observes that, where domestic TA consent to international assistance, the 'order-preserving' legal instruments central to the law of occupation do not apply: 'The law of occupation applies, when a state comes into *uninvited* effective control of the territory of a third state, to regulate the administration of the occupied territory. Its rationale, which includes the preservation of the occupied states' sovereignty and the humanitarian well-being of the people, explains a strict emphasis on conservation of the state and civil infrastructure. That this law does not apply in the assistance model can *help project the international involvement as benevolent and of little threat to political independence because, one might reason, if there were a threat to political independence, surely the law of occupation would apply?'*. M. Saul, 'From Haiti to Somalia', op. cit., p. 140. Own emphasis.

THE RISE OF TRANSITIONAL GOVERNANCE 39

This reasoning, too, must be strongly nuanced. Even when order-preserving legal instruments do not apply, TA or external actors do not enjoy absolute freedom when redefining the social contract of a country in transition. I will argue that there are limits to this, notably under the principle of self-determination: neither domestic TA nor external actors enjoy absolute freedom in reconfiguring the state order.

2.3 Primary Responsibility of Domestic Transitional Authorities?

A third factor potentially accounting for the reduction of ITA and the correlative rise of TG may be linked to discourses around international responsibility. TG is often misleadingly portrayed as falling under the primary or even exclusive responsibility of TA. Domestic TA are deemed responsible for 'their' peace-building and state-building enterprises (2.3.1). This monolithic vision will lead us to question whether, under such an assumption, the responsibility regime of TG would constitute an improvement as compared to the much-criticised ITA responsibility regime (2.3.2).

2.3.1 Insistence by UNSC, UNGA and PBC on Domestic Responsibility for TG The peace-through-transition paradigm heavily relies on the (formal) domestic nature of TG, even to the extent that 'local ownership becomes a dimension of global governance'.[28] Domestic actors are deemed primarily responsible for observing TG. This, at least, is what the so-called international community tirelessly repeats. At the UN level, especially, the primary responsibility of domestic TA has been consistently emphasised.

In the resolution by which the Peacebuilding Commission ('PBC') was established late 2005, the UNGA: 'affirm[ed] the primary responsibility of . . . transitional Governments and authorities of countries emerging from conflict or at risk of relapsing into conflict . . . in identifying their priorities and strategies for post-conflict peacebuilding'.[29] The principle of domestic *ownership* (e.g. under the 2005 Paris Declaration on Aid Effectiveness)[30] has been conflated with domestic *responsibility*. The

---

[28] V. Nesiah, 'The Ambitions and Traumas of Transitional Governance: Expelling Colonialism, Replicating Colonialism', op. cit., p. 141.

[29] A/RES/60/180 of 30 December 2005, Preamble and § 10.

[30] L. Brahimi, 'State-Building in Crisis and Post-Conflict Countries', op. cit., p. 6: 'foreign assistance is just that: assistance; it can in no way be a substitute for a national agenda aiming at rebuilding the national state'.

2009 'Report of the Secretary-General on peacebuilding in the immediate aftermath of conflict', for instance, emphasised the imperative of local ownership and responsibility.[31] During the middle of 2014, the PBC again referred to the 'principle of national responsibility'.[32] Domestic responsibility is consistently recalled by the UNSC, too,[33] e.g. with regard to transitions in CAR[34] and Iraq.[35]

Contact groups and diplomatic coalitions – their new weight on the international scene will be explained later[36] – also emphasise that TA are responsible for TG. The CAR international contact group, representing more than thirty-five states and IO[37] 'recalled the primary responsibility of the CAR stakeholders ..., stressing that the role of the international community is to support national efforts and not replace them'.[38]

Domestic responsibility is emphasised even when external actors such as contact groups are deeply involved in the transition. With regard to the DRC, for instance, the *Comité international d'accompagnement de la*

---

[31] Report of the Secretary-General on peacebuilding in the immediate aftermath of conflict' of 11 June 2009, A/63/881-S/2009/304, § 7.

[32] S/PV.7217, Report of the Peacebuilding Commission on its seventh session (S/2014/67) of 15 July 2014, p. 14.

[33] S/PRST/2015/2 of 14 January 2015 in which the UNSC 'underline[d] that the primary responsibility for successful peacebuilding lies with national governments and relevant local actors, including civil society, in countries emerging from conflict'.

[34] S/RES/2149 of 10 April 2014 in which the UNSC welcomes the designation of the TA in CAR and 'urges' the TA 'to accelerate the preparations in order to hold free, fair, transparent and inclusive presidential and legislative elections' and to launch 'an inclusive political dialogue'. Even if the transition in CAR is influenced by international monitoring activities and other external factors, the UNSC 'underscores the primary responsibility of the Central African authorities' (S/RES/2121 of 10 October 2013, § 6. Cf. also S/RES/2149 of 10 April 2014), e.g. to provide security and protect the law. The UNSC furthermore called on CAR TA to complete their transition in line with the 'Transitional Framework' (S/RES/2127 of 5 December 2013, S/RES/2134 of 28 January 2014, S/RES/2149 of 10 April 2014).

[35] In Iraq, too, the UNSC repeatedly affirmed the domestic responsibility for TG. See for example S/RES/1723 of 28 November 2006 which repeatedly affirms the responsibility of Iraq (in various fields); or S/RES/1509 of 19 September 2003 which '[r]eaffirm[s] that the primary responsibility for implementing the Comprehensive Peace Agreement and the ceasefire agreement rests with the parties, and urging the parties to move forward with implementation of these agreements immediately in order to ensure the peaceful formation of a transitional government by 14 October 2003'.

[36] Chapter 1, Section B.1.3.

[37] Consult the list on www.peaceau.org/uploads/com-icg-car-08-07-2013eng.pdf, last accessed on 23 February 2019.

[38] Conclusions of the fourth meeting of the International Contact Group on the Central African Republic of 21 March 2014, § 9. Available on www.peaceau.org/uploads/auc.conclusions.4th-mtg.icg.car.pdf. Last accessed on 25 March 2020.

THE RISE OF TRANSITIONAL GOVERNANCE   41

transition ('CIAT'), representing several states and IO,[39] was particularly active during the interregnum. It saw itself as a representative of the so-called international community, and was massively involved in the transition.[40] Yet, 'the primary responsibility ... rests with the Transitional Government', the Secretary General noted.[41]

These examples – among others[42] – suggest that TA often operate under the guidance and impulsion of the UNSC or regional/international organisations or diplomatic coalitions. At the same time, TA are held responsible for the transition. Across the globe, this responsibility usually relates *inter alia* to the execution of the transition roadmap as well as the safeguarding of safety and order.[43]

Some questions seem to be avoided by holding TA systematically responsible for 'their transition'. By relying on TG as a discrete and cost-efficient form of (proxy) governance, states and IO exercise a considerable influence on the ground even/also without exercising territorial control. Notwithstanding such 'massive international involvement',[44] their support to domestic TG may be instrumental to side-stepping responsibility for wrongful acts potentially committed under their own impulse during the interregnum.

2.3.2 Correction of ITA Accountability Gap? Is the monolithic vision of the UNSC, UNGA and PBC – that is the systematic absence of division of responsibility for internationally assisted TG – sustainable? To put things in perspective, let us question whether this vision, if it were accurate, would be an improvement as compared to the ITA responsibility

---

[39] UNSC members as well as representatives from Angola, Belgium, Canada, Gabon, South Africa, Zambia, the AU, the EU and the UN.

[40] Chapter 1, Section A.2.3.1.

[41] 'Third special report of the Secretary-General on the United Nations Organisation Mission in the Democratic Republic of the Congo' of 16 August 2004, S/2004/650, § 54 ('Third UNSG special report on DRC Mission').

[42] Chapter 5, Section B.2.3. Cf., for instance, regarding Iraq: S/RES/1723 of 28 November 2006 which repeatedly affirms the responsibility of Iraq (in various fields); or S/RES/1509 of 19 September 2003.

[43] Chapter 6.

[44] M. Brandt, J. Cottrell, Y. Ghai, and A. Regan, 'Constitution-making and Reform – Options for the Process', *Interpeace*, 2011, pp. 73–74: '[a] key factor is whether the process is driven by local or external factors. If external, there are two possibilities: (a) the country is taken into international care and the United Nations or a regional organisation takes over management of state affairs (as in Cambodia, Kosovo, and Timor-Leste), or (b) there is massive international involvement (as in Afghanistan, Bosnia-Herzegovina, Iraq, and Namibia)'.

regime. Some might argue that the delegation of responsibility from the international to the domestic level addresses some of the shortcomings of ITA. ITA is directly created by the UNSC. The question of which responsibility regime, if any, applies to ITA as an 'outgrowth' of the UNSC remains unanswered. This lack of clarity has been severely criticised.[45]

The increased recourse to TG and the continuous insistence on the primary responsibility of the state in transition appears to bring with it a welcome simplification of the responsibility regime as compared to ITA. The issue of attribution of responsibility would now be unambiguous. This apparent straightforwardness may, in part, explain the traction of contemporary TG. In addition, when presented as a challenge to the culture of dependency,[46] the emphasis on TA's domestic responsibility appears laudable from a policy perspective.

Such a representation however barely conceals the tensions underlying the – proverbial – light footprint approach. Tensions inherent to *externally* assisted *domestic* TG are unavoidable when 'the responsibilities of leadership or ownership lie with the domestic state but their partners (or joint stakeholder) decode the policies';[47] in short, when there is a 'disaggregation of power ... through internationalisation of domestic governance ... often presented as "transitional" to a future agreed alternative'.[48]

B   The Internationalisation of Transitional Governance

Although this study concerns the role of *domestic* institutions in domestic transitions that are unrelated to decolonisation, secession or dissolution processes, this is not only an internal matter. TG is viewed, often

---

[45] Cf. e.g. Y. Daudet, 'L'exercice de compétences territoriales par les Nations Unies', op. cit., p. 58. Wilde argues that ITA represented a regression even from the older mandate (1919–45) and trusteeship (1945–94) systems. R. Wilde, 'From Trusteeship to Self-Determination and Back Again: The Role of the Hague Regulations in the Evolution of International Trusteeship, and the Framework of Rights and Duties of Occupying Powers', *Loyola of Los Angeles International and Comparative Law Review*, Vol. 31, 2009, pp. 134–5.

[46] Interview with Carlos Westendorp cited in Y. Daudet, 'L'exercice de compétences territoriales par les Nations Unies', op. cit., p. 30.

[47] D. Chandler, *Empire in Denial – The Politics of State-Building*, Pluto Press, 2006, p. 39.

[48] C. Bell, *On the Law of Peace – Peace Agreements and the Lex Pacificatoria*, Oxford University Press, 2008, p. 117.

THE INTERNATIONALISATION OF TG   43

erroneously, as a panacea for solving all kinds of problems.[49] Obstruction by so-called spoilers to TG is therefore not accepted. Thus, a top UN official declared with regard to Burkina Faso in February 2015 that 'the international community will not tolerate any obstacle to the transition. Those who threaten the transition should be aware that the international community is watching and will hold them accountable'.[50]

Since the end of the Cold War, the 'international community' has placed a heavy burden on TG. It has, in a sense, *aggrandised, lionised* even, its core function. The painting on the cover of this book by Jacob Jordaens stands symbol for this. In line with the peace-through-transition paradigm, TG and constitution-making have been assigned the challenging task of bringing peace to conflict-affected countries, leading authors to question 'whether constitutions can bear the conflict resolution and democratisation burdens being ascribed to them in political transitions'.[51] The 2015 Review of the UN Peacebuilding notes how TG, beyond the central exercise of constitution-making, has become a conflict resolution tool of choice:

> Over the last couple of decades, a rough template seems to have emerged for international response to post-conflict challenges. First, mediators achieve a peace agreement, usually fragile and not always sufficiently reflective of the local dimensions of the conflict. *This is followed by a limited "Transition" period, often accompanied by temporary power-sharing arrangements and/or some form of "National Dialogue" process.* Within a year or so, a new constitution is drafted and adopted. The culmination is the holding of new and democratic elections – usually a massive logistical exercise.[52]

There are manifold ways in which states and IO influence the interregnum, in virtually all its aspects, ranging from justice and security reform and economic and fiscal policies to the very origins of TG: 'despite the domestic character and significance of governance transitions, the assembly and maintenance of interim structures has increasingly become an international project'.[53] The transition roadmaps themselves are often

---

[49] For a critique in this sense, see Y.-P. Mandjem, 'Les Gouvernements de transition comme sites d'institutionnalisation de la politique dans les ordres politiques en voie de sortie de crise en Afrique', op. cit., pp. 81–82.

[50] UN News Centre, 'International community "will not tolerate" obstacles to Burkina Faso transition, says UN political chief', 4 February 2015.

[51] C. Bell, 'Introduction: Bargaining on Constitutions – Political Settlements and Constitutional State-Building', *Global Constitutionalism*, 6:1, 2017, p.14. See also H. Ludsin, 'Peacemaking and Constitution-Drafting: A Dysfunctional Marriage', op. cit., p. 241, and 310.

[52] 2015 Review of the UN Peacebuilding architecture, op. cit., § 31. Own emphasis.

[53] K. Guttieri, J. Piombo (eds.), *Interim Governments – Institutional Bridges to Peace and Democracy?*, op. cit., p. 3. Own emphasis.

44 THE RISE AND INTERNATIONALISATION OF TG

generated in international contexts and produced by small epistemic communities.

The external impact on various components of TG, the considerable budgets allocated to it[54] and the international assistance well-nigh systematically offered to states in transition allow us to speak of the *factual internationalisation of TG*, as mentioned in the Introduction (Section A.4.1). The *legal internationalisation of TG* refers to manifold references to international law in texts regulating the interregnum. The remainder of this section examines the actors behind the factual internationalisation of TG (1), and challenges the assumption that external actors fulfil an assisting role only (2).

1 The Multitude of Actors Influencing Transitional Governance

The conviction that TG is conducive to peace transpires in the discourse and practice of actors operating at the global, regional and state level. The peace-through-transition paradigm suggests that TG – including a country's reconstitutionalisation – is widely seen as a way to cope with armed conflict and/or threats to peace and security.

This explains why several actors offer their *assistance* in installing, monitoring or completing transitions: 'by the late 1990s and early 2000s . . . the role of the international community increased. Great powers and international institutions – no longer stymied by Cold War rivalry – took on expanded and more direct roles in the creation and maintenance of interim governments'.[55] Both the UN (1.1), regional organisations (1.2), diplomatic coalitions or contact groups (1.3) and individual states (1.4) contribute to the internationalisation of TG.

1.1 The UN

The UN often relies on TG to accompany states going through a stage of convalescence. Since the end of the Cold War, the UN has been closely involved in at least thirty reconstitutionalisation processes.[56] It regularly

---

[54] J. Strasheim and H. Fjelde, 'Pre-Designing Democracy: Institutional Design of Interim Governments and Democratisation in 15 Post-Conflict Societies', *Democratisation* 21, no. 2, 24 December 2012, p. 336: 'the international community continues to allocate vast resources to support interim regimes'.

[55] K. Guttieri, J. Piombo (eds.), *Interim Governments – Institutional Bridges to Peace and Democracy?*, op. cit., p. 7.

[56] Afghanistan, Bhutan, Burundi, Cambodia, DRC, East Timor, Ecuador, Egypt, Eritrea, Gambia, Guyana, Haiti, Iraq, Kosovo, Liberia, Libya, Malawi, Maldives, Namibia, Nauru, Nepal, Rwanda, Sierra Leone, Solomon Islands, Somalia, South Sudan, Sudan, Tokelau,

helps installing transitional governments,[57] or assists countries in triggering transitions: 'following the Cold War, [the UN] assisted conflict-prone sovereign and independent states in sculpting new constitutions and in shaping political institutions. It now engages in internal governance not to decolonize, but to prevent conflicts and build peace'.[58] To this end, the PBC and the UN Peacebuilding Trust Fund (and the UN Secretariat)[59] increasingly turn their attention to countries in transition.[60]

The UNSC bears the primary responsibility for the maintenance of international peace and security.[61] More and more, it tries to discharge this obligation by having recourse to TG. TG is assigned the task not (only) of dealing with regime succession but also, and more ambitiously, of coping with armed conflicts or threats against international peace and security. As already noted (Introduction, Section A), the pacificatory function of TG thus comes to overarch and overshadow the functions historically attributed to TG.

The UNSC establishes UN missions to monitor transitions, sometimes in collaboration with the UN Development Programme. In various cultural and political settings, such missions keep a close eye on TG. In CAR, Somalia and Libya for example, UN missions were explicitly

---

Tunisia, Zambia, Zimbabwe. This list is an aggregation of the countries under international constitutional assistance mentioned in two articles: V. C. Franke, A. Warnecke, 'Building Peace: An Inventory of UN Peace Missions Since the End of the Cold War', *International Peacekeeping*, 16:3, 2009, pp.407–36. V. Y. Sripati, 'UN Constitutional Assistance Projects in Comprehensive Peace Missions: An Inventory 1989–2011', op. cit., pp. 93–113.

[57] M. Ottaway, B. Lacina, 'International Intervention and Imperialism: Lessons from the 1990s', *SAIS Review*, Vol. 23, no. 2, Summer–Fall 2003, p. 82: 'UN post-conflict interventions have followed one of three basic approaches, which vary greatly in the way in which they interfere with existing power structures. In most cases, missions have simply relied on the existing administrative and even political structures; *in others, the missions have helped to install a local transitional government instead*'. Own emphasis.

[58] V. Y. Sripati, 'UN Constitutional Assistance Projects in Comprehensive Peace Missions', op. cit., p. 94.

[59] The UNSG was for example closely involved in the constitutional transformation of Kenya where it mediated 'a transitional arrangement that was to lead to a full process of root-and-branch constitutional reform'. K. Annan, N. Mousavizadeh, *Interventions – A Life in War and Peace*, op. cit., p. 202.

[60] Although they had been created to ensure a comprehensive approach towards international rather than domestic transitional administrations. 'A more secure world: our shared responsibility', Report of the High-level Panel on Threats, Challenges and Change, A/59/565 of 2 December 2004.

[61] UN Charter, art. 24.

mandated to support the implementation of the transition.[62] 'Although each UN peacekeeping operation is different, there is a *considerable degree of consistency* in the types of mandated tasks assigned by the Council.'[63] A mandate typically includes assisting reconstitutionalisation processes. This is often directly foreseen in UNSC resolutions. The task can also result from the UN mission's requirement to monitor a (peace) process which, itself, would require constitutional adjustments. It may also be known under other denominators such as peace-building,[64] rule of law assistance[65] or electoral reform.[66] To be sure, assistance to reconstitutionalisation has become central to the portfolio of several UN missions.

Rather than deploying ITA or (exclusively) relying on blue helmets or military intervention to address armed conflicts or threats to peace, the UNSC increasingly places its confidence in TG. In light of the historic-economic context of the peace-through-transition paradigm, the renaissance of a state is nowadays seen as an instrument for advancing collective security. It comes as no surprise, then, that in recent years constitutional assistance has become an 'established field'[67] within the UN. Further testament to this evolution is the creation of the UN Mediation Support Unit in 2006 and a UNSG High-Level Advisory

---

[62] In the Central African Republic, MINUSCA was mandated with the 'support for the implementation of the transition' (UNSC/RES/2149 of 10 April 2014, § 30.b). In Somalia, the UNSC has underscored 'the importance of UNSOM's support to the Somali-Government-led inclusive political process ... and constitutional review processes' (S/RES/2408 of 27 March 2018, § 3). In Libya, UNSMIL was mandated to support 'subsequent phases of the Libyan transition process, including the constitutional process' (S/RES/2434 of 13 September 2018, § 1.4, § 8).

[63] See the page on 'Mandates and the legal basis for peacekeeping', last consulted 28 June 2019. Own emphasis.

[64] The UN 2006 Peacebuilding Capacity Inventory includes constitution-making under the heading of governance and participation.

[65] The 2000 Brahimi report advocated for a doctrinal shift in the use of rule of law elements in peace operations. Constitutional reform can be regarded as a reform area of UN rule of law assistance. See R. Sannerholm, 'The United Nations Security Council, Peacekeeping and the Rule of Law', Working Paper No. 3.2, 2012.

[66] Sripati rightly notes that 'the UN has long used the generic term "electoral assistance" to cover for constitutional assistance, thereby indicating that it has merely a facilitating rather than a directing or overseeing role'. V. Sripati, 'United Nations Constitutional Assistance in Statebuilding' in D. Chandler, T. D. Sisk (eds.), *Routledge Handbook of International Statebuilding*, op. cit., p. 144.

[67] V. Y. Sripati, 'UN Constitutional Assistance Projects in Comprehensive Peace Missions', op. cit., p. 93.

THE INTERNATIONALISATION OF TG 47

Board on Mediation in 2017 (these teams include constitutional experts), and of a meanwhile understaffed UN Constitutional Focal Point in 2013.

1.2 Regional Organisations

The peace-through-transition paradigm was also appropriated by a number of regional or subregional organisations. The most elaborate provisions with regard to domestic non-constitutionality are part of the post-colonial African regional legal framework[68] (previously, the OAU supported non-constitutional transitions as a way of realising self-determination).[69] Since its 2000 Constitutive Act, the AU has adopted a policy of condemning unconstitutional changes of government.[70] This policy indirectly promotes TG as it obliges any unconstitutional government or political organisation to relinquish power. This can take months or years, and will often be accompanied by a transition.

Furthermore, a number of subregional organisations have been encouraging and monitoring TG. The Economic Community of Central African States (ECCAS) deeply impacted the transition in CAR.[71] On the same continent, no one doubts that the Economic Community of West African States (ECOWAS) strongly influenced the transitions in Burkina Faso, Guinea, Guinea-Bissau, Liberia and Mali. The Gulf Cooperation Council (GCC), lastly, had a heavy hand in the (unsuccessful) transition in Yemen. The 2011 Agreement was designed

---

[68] M. Olivier, 'The Emergence of a Right to Democracy – An African Perspective' in C. Panara, G. Wilson, eds., *The Arab Spring, New Patterns for Democracy and International Law*, Martinus Nijhoff Publishers, 2013.

[69] A historical example whereby a regional organisation supported the triggering of a non-constitutional transition in the specific context of a liberation struggle is provided by the 'Declaration of the OAU Ad-hoc Committee on Southern Africa on the question of South Africa' or the so-called Harare Declaration: 'permanent peace and stability in Southern Africa can only be achieved when the system of apartheid in South Africa has been liquidated and South Africa transformed into a united, democratic and non-racial country'; 'the outcome [of such a process] should be a new constitutional order' (Preamble, § 4; nr. 16).

[70] The 2000 African Union Constitutive Act. Cf. also the 2000 Lomé Declaration on the Framework for an OAU Response to Unconstitutional Changes in Government and the 2007 African Charter on Democracy, Elections and Governance.

[71] ECCAS 'quickly took responsibility for the political management of the crisis and masterminded the 11 January 2013 Libreville Agreement, almost appearing to place the CAR "under its supervision"' (ICG Report nr. 203, 11 June 2013, 'Central African Republic: priorities of the transition', p. 11). It was also involved in setting up the 'National Transitional Council' responsible for managing the transition in the CAR (Id.).

48 THE RISE AND INTERNATIONALISATION OF TG

under its auspices and provided in detail how this transition was supposed to unfold.

1.3 Contact Groups: A New International Coordination Mechanism?

In order to compensate for ineffective global leadership, states and IO gather in ad hoc diplomatic coalitions ('contact groups' or 'friends of groups') with a view to steering or monitoring transitions. Contact groups are generally composed of several representatives of states and IO, sometimes including the UN as an observer or active participant.[72] Regional organisations like the AU, ECCAS, ECOWAS and the EU regularly take part in these groups or create them. In February 2019, the EU thus created a contact group to monitor the situation (and the projected transition in) Venezuela.[73]

Contact groups are not without antecedents in history,[74] yet are relative newcomers.[75] The CIAT, for instance, was described as 'a new form of an international coordination mechanism'.[76] Their number has sharply risen since the end of the Cold War, which broadly corresponds with the period during which TG, too, has increased almost exponentially. Table 1.1 provides a non-exhaustive overview of contact groups/implementation committees, and includes another indicator – the presence of UN/regional missions – of interregnums being increasingly internationalised.

---

[72] How should the participation of the UN in policy-oriented contact groups be legally assessed. This question is not addressed in this book. Of course, the UN must itself respect the principle of non-intervention in domestic affairs (UN Charter, art. 2 § 7). For some, this principle is then more stringent. See B. Conforti, 'The Principle of Non-Intervention' in M. Bedjaoui, *International Law: Achievements and Prospects*, UNESCO and Martinus Nijhoff, 1991.

[73] Cf. e.g. the crucial role of the Western Contact Group for the transition to independence of Namibia. The constitutional principles of Namibia's 1990 constitution 'had emerged from negotiations between the Western Contact Group, "front line" states, the then Soviet Union and Namibian "discussants"'. IDEA, 'Constitutionbuilding after Conflict: External Support to a Sovereign process', op. cit., p. 13.

[74] M. Saul, 'From Haiti to Somalia', op. cit., p. 131: 'particularly noticeable are the conferences of friends at which the reconstruction targets of the state are mapped out and international assistance promised on this basis'.

[75] M. de Goede and C. van der Borgh, 'A Role for Diplomats in Postwar Transitions? The Case of the International Committee in Support of the Transition in the Democratic Republic of the Congo', *African Security* 1, no. 2, 2008.

[76] 'International Contact Group on Venezuela', EEAS press statement, 4 February 2019. Available on https://eeas.europa.eu/headquarters/headquarters-homepage/57639/international-contact-group-venezuela_en. Last accessed on 25 March 2020.

THE INTERNATIONALISATION OF TG 49

Table 1.1 *The internationalised interregnum*

	International contact groups/international follow-up/implementation committees	UN missions/ Regional missions
Afghanistan	Contact Group on Afghanistan and Pakistan. UN Special Representative to '*monitor and assist in the implementation*' of Bonn Agreement.[77]	UNAMA
Burkina Faso	International Contact Group for Burkina Faso[78] or 'International follow-up and support group for the transition in Burkina Faso'.[79] ECOWAS also to monitor implementation.[80]	Joint UN-AU-ECOWAS mission
Burundi	International Contact Group on Great Lakes. (No country-specific contact group at the time of the 2000 Arusha Agreement. In 2014, the creation of a contact group had been proposed by the US government, but was not materialised).[81] Implementation Monitoring Committee.[82]	ONUB
Cambodia	Request for assistance in the implementation.[83]	UNTAC
Central African Republic	International Contact Group on the Central African Republic or 'ICG-CAR'. *Comité de Suivi.*[84]	MINUSCA
Comoros	*Comité de suivi présidé par l'OUA et composé des Parties comoriennes signataires du présent Accord et des observateurs officiels.*[85]	–
Côte d'Ivoire	Conference of Heads of State on Côte d'Ivoire.[86] *Comité d'évaluation et*	UNOCI

[77] Bonn Agreement, Annex II, art. 2.

[78] Set up by UN, AU and ECOWAS. Composition: Senegal, Ghana, Togo.

[79] Conclusions of 30 March 2015 of the international follow-up and support group for the transition in Burkina Faso.

[80] 'ECOWAS to monitor implementation of one-year transition in Burkina Faso', News Agency of Nigeria, 6 November 2014.

[81] See the declassified document of 18 March 2014 on the 'Elements of a regional solution to the crisis in Burundi'.

[82] Arusha Agreement, Protocol V. The Implementation Monitoring Committee is also composed of representatives of the UN and the (then) OAU.

[83] Paris Agreement, art. 26: '[t]he Signatories request other States, international organisations and other bodies to cooperate and assist in the implementation of this Agreement and in the fulfilment by UNTAC of its mandate'.

[84] l'Accord de Libreville, art. 11.

[85] Accords d'Antananarivo, art. 4.

[86] S/2003/99 of 27 January 2003, Annex II, § 6.

50 THE RISE AND INTERNATIONALISATION OF TG

Table 1.1 (*cont.*)

	International contact groups/international follow-up/implementation committees	UN missions/ Regional missions
	d'accompagnement (CEA).[87] Monitoring Committee.[88]	
DRC	CIAT (*Comité international d'accompagnement de la transition*) to 'guarantee the Proper implementation of this Agreement and to support the program for transition in the DRC'[89]/Committee for Follow-up of the Agreement.[90]	MONUC
Guinea	International Contact Group on Guinea.[91] The signatories of the 2010 Ouagadougou declaration 'insistently invited the international community to provide political, financial and technical assistance for [its] enforcement'.[92]	/
Guinea-Bissau	No specific provision regarding the implementation of the 2012 *Pacto de Transição Política* but reactivation of the International Contact Group on Guinea Bissau.	UNIOGBIS
Iraq	The creation of a contact group may have been proposed but never materialised.[93] The 2004 Law of Administration for the State of Iraq for the Transitional Period provides for the possibility of consultation with the UN for implementing the first phase of the transition.	UNAMI
Liberia	International Contact Group on the Mano River Basin (ICG-MRB).[94] Implementation	UNMIL

---

[87] Accord Politique de Ouagadougou, art. 7.2.

[88] Linas-Marcoussis Accord of 13 January 2003, art. 4.

[89] Pretoria Agreement, Annex IV.

[90] Pretoria Agreement, Annex III.

[91] E.g. S/2009/140 of 12 March 2009.

[92] 2010 Ouagadougou Declaration, art. 11.

[93] K. Katzman, 'Iraq: Post-Saddam Governance and Security' in S. J. Costel (ed.), *Surging out of Iraq?*, Nova Science Publishers, 2007, p. 101.

[94] E.g. the conclusions of the International Contact Group on the Mano River Basin of 21 March 2005.

THE INTERNATIONALISATION OF TG

Table 1.1 (*cont.*)

	International contact groups/international follow-up/implementation committees	UN missions/ Regional missions
	Monitoring Committee/Joint Monitoring Committee (JMC) established under the terms of the Ceasefire Agreement, and composed of representatives of ECOWAS, the UN, AU, ICGL and Parties to the Ceasefire Agreement.[95]	
Libya	International Contact Group for Libya.	UNSMIL
Mali	OIC Contact Group on Mali. Support and Follow-Up Group in Mali. Art. 54 of the 2015 Agreement for peace and reconciliation in Mali provides: 'the international community is the guarantor of the scrupulous implementation'.	MINUSMA
Nepal	No country-specific contact group. Yet, monitoring of human rights-related provisions by United Nations Office of the High Commissioner Human Rights, Nepal.[96]	UNMIN
Sierra Leone	International Contact Group on the Mano River Basin (ICG-MRB).[97] Joint Implementation Committee[98] and call for international support: 'call on the International Community to assist them in implementing the present Agreement'.[99]	UNAMSIL
Somalia	International Contact Group on Somalia.	UNOSOM
Syria	Follow-up by ICG-S, and by High Level Meeting on Somalia.[100]	UNSMIS (abandoned)

[95] 2003 CPA, art. III.3. Cf. also art. IV.1.

[96] 2007 Interim Constitution, art. 9.1.

[97] E.g. the Secretary-General's message to the 12th session of the International Contact Group on the Mano River Basin, op. cit.

[98] 1999 Lomé Agreement, Part VI.

[99] 1999 Lomé Agreement, art. XXXV. Composition: Benin, Burkina Faso, Côte d'Ivoire, Ghana, Guinea, Liberia, Libyan Arab Jamahiriya, Mali, Nigeria, Togo, the United Kingdom and the United States of America, the UN, the OAU, ECOWAS and the Commonwealth of Nations.

[100] Chairman's Summary of High Level Meeting on Somalia of 23 September 2011.

52 THE RISE AND INTERNATIONALISATION OF TG

Table 1.1 (*cont.*)

	International contact groups/international follow-up/implementation committees	UN missions/ Regional missions
Sudan	See Implementation Agreements to the CPA[101] and annexure II to CPA which *inter alia* sets up a Constitutional Task Team. Follow-up by IGAD.	UNMIS
Tajikistan	Contact Group.[102] See also Protocol on the guarantees of implementation of the General Agreement on the Establishment of Peace and National Accord in Tajikistan, signed at Tehran on 28 May 1997.[103]	UNMOT
Ukraine	Weimar Triangle/Trilateral Contact Group (Ukraine, Russia, OSCE). Supervision and monitoring of Minsk Agreements by OSCE.[104]	/
Yemen	Friends of Yemen Group. UNSG, Secretary-General of GCC, members of GCC, permanent members of the UNSC, the EU and the League of Arab States are called on to support implementation of the GCC Agreement.[105]	UNMHA

Contact groups fulfil various functions. These include, beyond the classical mediation between warring parties, preventing non-constitutional changes of government;[106] preparing and monitoring transitions and

---

[101] For instance the Agreement between the Government of the Sudan and the Sudan People's Liberation Movement/Sudan People's Liberation Army (SPLM/SPLA) on Implementation Modalities of the Protocols and Agreements of 31 December 2004.

[102] Composition: OSCE, Europe, Russia, Kyrgyzstan, Kazakhstan, Iran, Afghanistan and Uzbekistan. Cf. 'Contact group calls for support for Tajikistan peace process', Agence France-Presse, 1 May 1999.

[103] Protocol on the guarantees of implementation of the General Agreement on the Establishment of Peace and National Accord in Tajikistan, Tehran, 28 May 1997.

[104] Minsk Agreement, arts. 3 and 10.

[105] 2011 GCC Agreement, arts. 28–30.

[106] Vandeginste suggests that 'contact groups' are used as a diplomatic tool by the AU to prevent unconstitutional changes of government. Cf. S. Vandeginste, 'The African Union, Constitutionalism, and Power-Sharing', Working Paper 2011.05, p. 12. In the same sense, the 2010 'Report of the chairperson of the Commission on the prevention of unconstitutional changes of government and strengthening the capacities of the AU to manage such situations', § 28.iii.

THE INTERNATIONALISATION OF TG 53

negotiating constitutions;[107] and implementing peace processes.[108] Contact groups may have regulatory powers and exercise financial leverage[109] or apply accountability/monitoring mechanisms.[110] They may be deployed to support initiatives by the UNSG.[111] The most notable development, however, is that although in the past they often dispensed independent mediation services,[112] now contact groups are usually established to 'coordinate the policy of a coalition'.[113]

Collaboration with contact groups is generally seen in a positive light. For de Goede and van den Borgh, 'coordination, in the form of friends groups or a lead role by specific actors, has in past cases proved to have a positive effect on the implementation of peace agreements'.[114] The UN Guidance for Effective Mediation similarly commends this practice.[115] In countries like CAR,[116]

[107] P. Dann, Z. Al-Ali, 'The Internationalised Pouvoir Constituant', *Max Planck UNYB* 10, 2006, p. 43.

[108] T. Whitfield, 'Working with Groups of Friends', United States Institute of Peace, Washington D.C.

[109] With regard to financial oversight on Afghanistan, cf. e.g. the following excerpt: '[r]egarding oversight of Afghanistan's transitional funds and procedures, Mr. Dobbins said the Contact Group was satisfied that the proper procedural steps were being followed', Press Conference on Meeting of International Contact Group, 20 September 2013.

[110] In the case of Afghanistan, the members of the International Contact Group on Afghanistan, together with the Afghan government decided to 'establish a follow-up mechanism to review their mutual long-term commitments laid out in this Declaration and the Tokyo Framework, and to verify the fulfillment of these commitments based on the notion of mutual accountability'. Cf. Conclusions of the Tokyo conference on Afghanistan of 8 July 2012, § 25. Cf. also, Annex on the Tokyo Mutual Accountability Framework, which 'continue[s] to serve as a reference for relations between donors and a new Afghan Government' (Chairman Statement's International Contact Group Meeting, New Delhi, 16 January 2014, § 4).

[111] M. W. Doyle, N. Sambanis, *Making War and Building Peace: United Nations Peace Operations*, Princeton University Press, 2011, p. 305: '[c]omposed of *ad hoc*, informal, multilateral diplomatic mechanisms that join together states in support of initiatives of the Secretary-General, it legitimates with the stamp of UN approval the pressures interested states can bring to bear the to further the purposes of peace and the UN'.

[112] G. R. Berridge, A. James, L. Lloyd, *The Palgrave Macmillan Dictionary of Diplomacy*, Palgrave Macmillan, 2012. Own emphasis.

[113] Id. Own emphasis.

[114] M. de Goede and C. van der Borgh, 'A Role for Diplomats in Postwar Transitions?', op. cit.

[115] 2012 UN Guidance for Effective Mediation, 2012, p. 18.

[116] About one year following a recommendation by the PBC in April 2013 ('Meeting of the CAR configuration of the Peacebuilding Commission', 17 April 2013, § 5), the UNSC recommended to set up a contact group in the CAR in order to accompany the transition. S/RES/2149 of 10 April 2014, § 10: '[e]ncourages the TA with the support

Yemen,[117] the DRC[118] and Afghanistan[119] (reverse chronological order), the role of contact groups for TG was generally lauded.

This praise needs to be critically assessed. The variety of functions ascribed to contact groups do not guarantee their independence. Contact groups increasingly function as 'groups of the major powers interested in the outcome of a conflict', and have been 'vehicles for these powers' direct diplomacy'.[120] As noted, especially in recent times contact groups assume the role of *policy coordinators* rather than conflict mediators. It is

> of key members of the International Contact Group to take immediate measures to revitalize the political process by agreeing on certain key parameters, which could include the possible creation of an international mechanism which would include key stakeholders, including the AU, ECCAS, the United Nations and the EU, as well as the International Financial Institutions (IFIs) as appropriate, to accompany the transition while respecting the sovereignty of the CAR, and requests the Secretary-General to report to the Council on progress taken in this regard'. The International Contact Group convened several times to monitor the (extended) transition.

[117] With regard to the transition in Yemen, the UNSC affirmed the crucial role of the 'Friends of Yemen' by 'affirm[ing] their view that the Friends of Yemen have a particularly important role to play by bringing together the main international actors in a common endeavour to support Yemen's overall transitional plans during the next two years'. S/PRST/2012/8 of 29 March 2012.

[118] The UNSG called for 'sustained dialogue between the CIAT and the Transitional Institutions' ('Statement on the launch of the Joint Verification Mechanism to address DRC-Rwanda border security issues' of 22 September 2004) and the CIAT has been described as playing an essential role in 'the extremely complex transition process' and in 'reducing the opportunities for the unruly transitional government to manipulate the peace process' (M. de Goede and C. van der Borgh, 'A Role for Diplomats in Postwar Transitions?', op. cit., p. 115). The contact group may even have prevented the peace agreement and the whole transition from collapsing (Id., p. 126). The CIAT was 'widely credited as a beneficial and needed force to maintain progress' (Cable signed by Amb. Roger Meece of 5 November 2004, available on Wikileaks). Yet, other commentators are much more critical: 'représentativité tronquée, légitimité contestée, multilatéralisme biaisé, violations et atteintes à la souveraineté de l'Etat; des dysfonctionnements qui provoquent une 'crise de confiance', toujours menaçante par excès de politisation ou de bureaucratisation; insuffisance de moyens ...; soumission aux intérêts des plus puissants'. Y.-P. Mandjem, 'Les Gouvernements de transition comme sites d'institutionnalisation de la politique dans les ordres politiques en voie de sortie de crise en Afrique', op. cit., p. 130. Own translation : 'truncated representativeness, contested legitimacy, biased multilateralism, violations and infringements of state sovereignty; dysfunctions provoking a "crisis of confidence", constant threats by excessive politicisation or bureaucratisation; insufficient means ...; submission to the interests of the most powerful'.

[119] With regard to the transition in Afghanistan, the participants of the Bonn Conference took 'note with appreciation of the close collaboration of the International Contact Group with the Afghan Government and their work, and encourage them to continue their joint efforts'. Conference Conclusions 'Afghanistan and the international community: from transition to the transformation decade', op. cit., p. 4.

[120] T. Whitfield, 'Working with Groups of Friends', op. cit., p. 33.

THE INTERNATIONALISATION OF TG 55

misleading to portray them as agents of the international community,[121] a controverted term which 'has an important political function in generating legitimacy for those who act in its name'.[122] Contact groups are mostly 'self-selecting'[123] or 'self-serving'[124] as they include 'states with an overriding strategic interest in the outcome of a particular conflict, or [with] a proxy relationship with one of the parties'.[125] It is in this sense that contact groups, with the strong presence or remarked absence of some powers, have supported *their* version of TG in Libya and Syria.[126]

Designated committees, linked to contact groups, are often mandated to monitor compliance with specific preset goals. CIAT was for instance assigned a mediation role and 'given a formal role in the interim constitution of 2005'.[127] Further, the International Contact Group on Guinea reportedly 'adopted a very firm position setting out the list of measures to be taken to allow Guinea to resume her transition process'.[128] Even at an earlier stage, before the interregnum formally starts, contact groups may intervene. As powerful policy coordinators, they can catalyse constitutional and/or regime change in conflict-striven countries,[129] sometimes without having the mandate to do so. When conflict or crisis is followed by a contact group's involvement with (sometimes self-proclaimed) TA, this may result in fundamental polity modifications of the target country.[130]

---

[121] For de Goede and van der Borgh, for example, CIAT, the contact group monitoring the transition in the DRC, 'enabled the *international community* to speak with one voice . . . [as] it was very well understood that a firm and united position from the international community would be key to the implementation of the transitional agenda'. Cf. M. de Goede and C. van der Borgh, 'A Role for Diplomats in Postwar Transitions?, op. cit. Own emphasis.

[122] B. Buzan and A. Gonzalez-Pelaez, '"International Community" after Iraq', *International Affairs* 81, no.1, January 1, 2005, p. 31.

[123] T. Whitfield, 'Working with Groups of Friends', op. cit., p. 6, p. 26.

[124] Id.

[125] Id., p. 37.

[126] G. R. Berridge, A. James, L. Lloyd, *The Palgrave Macmillan Dictionary of Diplomacy*, op. cit.

[127] Id., p. 119.

[128] Press statement of 13 October 2009, available on file.

[129] For a critique, see M. D. Nazemroaya, 'With "Friends" like these . . . : America's "Contact Group Industry" is Overthrowing Governments', *Russia Today*, 27 August 2012.

[130] In some cases, the involvement by contact groups is paired with forcible intervention though, e.g. the NATO interventions in Libya (2011) and Yugoslavia (1999). Regarding the latter, see I. Brownlie, C. J. Apperley, 'Kosovo Crisis Inquiry: Memorandum on the International Law Aspects', *The International and Comparative Law Quarterly*, Vol. 49, no. 4, 2000, pp. 878–905, §§ 82 a.f., cf. also § 7: 'a major justification for the . . . aerial

By triggering or endorsing constitutional and/or regime change, contact groups thus 'risk replicating the conflict dynamics'[131] in the realm of TG. Their early involvement can permeate the whole transition – and beyond that. As shall be discussed in Part IV, such acts can leave a permanent imprint on the state order of a country, during and beyond the interregnum, and must therefore be critically assessed.

1.4 Individual States

Among the actors professing the peace-through-transition paradigm, individual states cannot be left unmentioned. Examples are legion.

Like other countries, the US has developed a bilateral assistance-to-transition policy,[132] and has tried to leave its marks on the reconstitutionalisation of South Sudan, Sri Lanka and Ukraine, among other countries. Thus, not long after civil war erupted in South Sudan, its overall constitutional structure was reconsidered. During a meeting of the UNSC in August 2014, the US ambassador 'reiterated the need for both leaders [of the civil war] to put together a transitional authority'.[133] In Sri Lanka, the US closely followed the transition because it was 'keen to bolster ties with countries throughout Asia as part of its effort to *counterbalance* an increasingly powerful and assertive China'.[134] In Ukraine, the transition was purportedly influenced not only by the US[135] but also by the Weimar Triangle (composed of Poland, Germany and France), which brokered an agreement unsuccessfully calling for a national unity government.[136] After President Yanukovych's non-constitutional ouster,[137] the Yatsenyuk interim government received financial support

---

bombardment ... was to induce Yugoslavia to accept the "demands" of the Contact Group' (peace talks at Rambouillet).

[131] 2012 UN Guidance for Effective Mediation, op. cit., p. 19.

[132] US National Security Strategy, February 2015. Cf. the section about 'Supporting Emerging Democracies' (pp. 20–21). Cf. also policies and programmes of the European Endowment for Democracy.

[133] 'Security Council concludes South Sudan visit', UNMISS Press Release, 13 August 2014.

[134] 'US security adviser Rice pledges help for Sri Lanka "transition"', *Reuters*, 7 February 2015. Own emphasis.

[135] 'Obama told that Washington "had brokered a deal to transition power in Ukraine"', CNN interview, 1 February 2015.

[136] Agreement on the Settlement of Crisis in Ukraine of 21 February 2014.

[137] Even those who defend the Ukrainian revolution write that 'there were no constitutional grounds for shortening the presidential term'. Cf. 'The Ousting of Yanukovych was Legal', 15 March 2014. It seems that the impeachment votes did not reach the required three quarters of the 449-seated parliament. See 'Russia in Ukraine: A Reader Responds',

from the EU,[138] Canada[139] and the US.[140] After Crimea's annexation, Russia, too, raised her voice about how Ukraine's constitutional structure should be reconfigured.[141]

Examples on the African continent or in the Middle East also abound. In 2012, the UNSG called on individual UNSC members, and all countries with influence in Syria, to exert joint pressure for a transition to a legitimate government;[142] this exercise was being continued eight years into the war and beyond.[143] In 2014, 'the presidents of Ghana, Nigeria and Senegal urged Burkina Faso to appoint a transitional government'.[144] In 2015, Iran pushed for a unity government to initiate a transition in Yemen.[145]

Finally, we should not be oblivious to the fact that agencies or non-governmental organisations, when providing assistance in times of transition, are often funded by individual states. Bisarya mentions DRI, IDLO, International IDEA, Interpeace, NDI, PILPG and USIP in this regard.[146] Furthermore, trust funds such as the Middle East and North Africa Multi-Donor Trust Fund (created to 'support countries in the region that are [currently] undergoing historic transition')[147] also rely on contributions from individual states.

The foregoing testifies to the fact that, in our day and age, individual states increasingly 'meddle', for the better or for the worse, with TG in other countries. The constitutional structure of states has become

---

Lawfareblog, 5 March 2014, a post in which A. Deeks argues that 'Yanukovych is still the incumbent and legitimate President of the Ukraine'.

[138] 'EU offers Ukraine $15 billion, but help hinges on IMF deal', Reuters, 5 March 2014.

[139] 'Ukraine to get $220M in financial support from Canada', CBC News, 13 March 2014.

[140] White House fact sheet: 'International Support for Ukraine' of 4 March 2014.

[141] See, for example, 'Russia says it wants east Ukraine to stay with Kiev under reformed constitution', Constitutionnet, 16 December 2014. Also, reportedly Obama told CNN's Zakaria that Washington 'had brokered a deal to transition power in Ukraine' following on the heels of the deadly 'protests on Maidan and Yanukovich then fleeing'. See 'Obama openly admits "brokering power transition" in Ukraine', 1 February 2015.

[142] K. Annan, N. Mousavizadeh, *Interventions – A Life in War and Peace*, op. cit., p. 369.

[143] Cf. the role of EU countries in the Brussels II Conference, 24–25 April 2018, under the title 'Supporting the future of Syria and the region'.

[144] 'Thousands gather in Burkina Faso to denounce "military coup"', *The Guardian*, 2 November 2014.

[145] 'Iran says working to help Yemen form unity government to fix crisis', *Reuters*, 8 April 2015.

[146] S. Bisarya, 'No Strings Attached? Constraints on External Advice in Internationalised Constitution-Making', op. cit., p. 58.

[147] See https://www.worldbank.org/en/programs/middle-east-and-north-africa-multi-donor-trust-fund last consulted on 25 March 2020.

a matter of international interest and sometimes avidity. In one breath, external actors' political interest and involvement in shaping the constitutional identity of other states can be called 'constitutional geopolitics'.

2 Unravelling the Assistance Model

The support by external actors on the occasion of regime changes has been referred to as the *assistance model*.[148] The higher the external impact on TG, the less this model can be wedded to the light footprint approach. This subsection observes that the various actors influencing TG can act concurrently (2.1) and can go beyond offering mere assistance (2.2), with the result that such assistance actually vacillates between multilateral state transformation and unilateral constitutional geopolitics (2.3).

2.1 Concurring Assistance

Multilateral, collective and state-to-state assistance to TG are often exercised in tandem. How transitions are influenced is a factor to be taken into account in the legal analysis of TG.[149] The multitude of actors concurrently influencing TG was palpable in Afghanistan and Nepal, for instance. In Afghanistan, there were at least 'six communicative circles of empire' during the interregnum (2001–4), including the interim government and three 'international community actors' (the 'six-plus-two group', the UN mission and the UNSC).[150] In Nepal,

> while the peace process is largely domestically driven, it has been accompanied by wide-ranging international involvement, including initiatives in peacemaking by NGOs, the United Nations, and India, which, throughout the process, wielded considerable political influence; significant investments by international donors; and the deployment of a Security Council-mandated UN field mission.[151]

This is not to deny that regime trajectories self-evidently undergo domestic influences. In the context of the Arab Spring, for example, regime

---

[148] M. Saul, 'From Haiti to Somalia', op. cit.

[149] Chapter 8, Section A.

[150] M. Bothe, A. Fischer-Lescano, 'Protego et obligo, Afghanistan and the Paradox of Sovereignty' in R. A. Miller, P. C. Zumbansen, eds., *Comparative Law as Transnational Law, A Decade of the German Law Journal*, Oxford University Press, 2012, pp. 291–9.

[151] S. von Einsiedel, D. M. Malone, S. Pradhan, eds., *Nepal in Transition: From People's War to Fragile Peace*, Cambridge University Press, 2012.

THE INTERNATIONALISATION OF TG

trajectories were much influenced by domestic military elites or defectors from the military.[152] Yet, such domestic influences mostly form just one (far from negligible) part of the picture. To describe or even encourage the concurring influence of external actors in other states, some authors have developed notions like 'co-sovereignty' and 'shared sovereignty',[153] or even 'suspension of sovereignty'. These notions have been dismissed as awkward.[154] From a legal perspective, distinctions between 'empirical' and 'juridical' sovereignty are largely irrelevant.[155] But the mere fact that such notions have been developed to describe certain realities, has a self-explanatory significance.

2.2 Beyond Assistance

Assistance to TG is often represented as a service.[156] UN assistance or, more generally, external assistance to TG easily evolves into something more or else than that. It often fills a governance gap – frequently ascribed to the failure of a state[157] – of such proportions that, notwith-standing the *nominal* ownership by TA, international actors perform 'quasi-governmental functions in war-shattered states, or ... "proxy governance"'.[158] The external impact on TG in Burundi and the DRC, for example, was particularly strong:

---

[152] K. Köhler, 'Political Militaries in Popular Uprisings: A Comparative Perspective on the Arab Spring', *International Political Science Review*, Vol. 38, no. 3, 2017, pp. 363–77.

[153] For the development of the concept of 'shared sovereignty', see S. D. Krasner, 'Sharing Sovereignty – New Institutions for Collapsed and Failing States', *International Security*, Vol. 29, no. 2, 2004, pp. 85–120: 'the engagement of external actors in some of the domestic authority structures of the target state for an indefinite period of time' (p. 108).

[154] K. Guttieri, J. Piombo (eds.), Interim Governments – Institutional Bridges to Peace and Democracy?, op. cit., p. 4: '[o]ne of the contradictions in this process rests in the awkward attempt to create a sovereign state by suspending sovereignty. Most recent state-building attempts entail removing a state's ability to govern itself in order to reconstruct a new, sovereign state from without'.

[155] J. Moses, *Sovereignty and Responsibility – Power, Norms and Intervention in International Relations*, Palgrave Macmillan, 2014, pp. 22-23, with reference to R. Jackson, *Quasi-States: Sovereignty, International Relations and the Third World*, Cambridge University Press, 2011.

[156] S/2009/189 of 8 April 2009, 'Report of the Secretary-General on enhancing mediation and its support activities', § 20.

[157] For a short but trenchant critique of the notion of 'failed states', see R. Wilde, 'The Skewed Responsibility Narrative of the Failed States Concept', *ILSA Journal of International & Comparative Law*, Vol. 9, 2002–3, pp. 425–9.

[158] R. Paris, 'International Peacebuilding and the Mission Civilisatrice', *Review of International Studies*, Vol. 28, no. 4, 2002, p. 645.

> While domestic actors managed these interim governments, *external actors had significant input* as to who could participate in the peace talks leading to the *creation* of the temporary regimes and who could lead those transitional governments once they were created. In this way, external facilitation in creating peace agreements left a *strong imprint* on the character and functioning of the *subsequent* domestic regime in each country.[159]

In the DRC, the CIAT exercised enormous leverage during the transition.[160] Indicative of the CIAT's influence is that J.-P. Bemba (then vice-president in the transitional government) had written to the CIAT 'asking for [its] intervention to resolve the political impasse over allocation of the state companies' senior positions'.[161] This is just one example of how the CIAT was involved in virtually all aspects of the DRC transition.[162] Also in the case of CAR, the external impact on TG was enormous, as mentioned above (Section B.1.2).

The same trend was observed on the occasion of the Arab Spring. Since 2011, a number of 'transitional institutions' were created under different forms and denominations in countries like Libya, Syria and Yemen. Public reports and press articles portrayed these institutions throughout 2011 under a naively positive light. What is more, domestic and international actors sometimes *anticipatively* entrusted TA with a constitution-building and interim governance role.

In South Sudan, too, external influence on TG materialised before independence, and before the Transitional Constitution entered into force. A panoply of international actors gathered at a Thai Restaurant in Juba in December 2010, rivalling with each other as to who would assist the authorities in preparing for a transition.[163] Following its independence in 2011 (and especially since civil war erupted following a split within the ruling Sudan People's Liberation Movement towards the end of 2013), another debate took place regarding South Sudan's constitutional structure. During the Summer of 2014, this structure was discussed

---

[159] D. Curtis, 'Transitional Governance in Burundi and the Democratic Republic of the Congo' in K. Guttieri, J. Piombo (eds.), *Interim Governments – Institutional Bridges to Peace and Democracy?*, op. cit., p. 171. Own emphasis.

[160] Chapter 1, Section A.2.3.1.

[161] Cable signed by Amb. Roger Meece of 30 November 2004, available on Wikileaks.

[162] Cable signed by Amb. Roger Meece of 5 November 2004, available on Wikileaks.

[163] S. Bisarya, 'No Strings Attached? Constraints on External Advice in Internationalised Constitution-Making', op. cit., p. 58.

on the basis of a position paper proposing the creation of a (new) transitional government,[164] an initiative the US insisted on.[165]

2.3 Between Multilateral State Transformation and Unilateral Constitutional Geopolitics

Several strata of the 'international community' have an interest in promoting TG. The peace-through-transition paradigm both reflects and reinforces this tendency. It pretends to entrust TG with a pacificatory function. Although unrelated to decolonisation, secession or dissolution processes, TG has become a matter of international concern, and therefore is extremely susceptible to external influences. The 'international community' continues to portray the installation and monitoring of TA as a panacea, although the failures in Libya, Syria and Yemen have sensibly tempered the enthusiasm at least in expert circles. Several actors but also global citizens, often well-intentioned, nevertheless continue to rely on the paradigm to justify their involvement with TG.

In spite of the appearances, peace through transition is not an identical goal pursued by a homogeneous international community, which, except perhaps as a categorical imperative, does not exist. In 1980 already, R.-J. Dupuy warned against the misleading words 'communauté internationale'.[166] For lack of homogeneity and shared vision, today's pluralist international society can hardly be called a community[167] although perhaps 'an international community of liberal states has formed *within* the wider, politically pluralist international society'.[168] These reservations should be borne in mind whenever the concept is used.

In sum, international actors are not animated by similar motivations when they rely on the peace-through-transition paradigm. Seen from a favourable eye, IO such as the UN and the AU offer their assistance to TG for rational reasons, that is to efficiently delegate their responsibilities over international peace and security; and contact groups and individual

---

[164] The 'Position Paper' of 17 July 2014 is available on 'Commentary: The First Six Months of Transition in Post-Independent South Sudan', *The New Sudan Vision*, 15 February 2012.

[165] 'Security Council concludes South Sudan visit', UNMISS Press Release, 13 August 2014.

[166] R.-J. Dupuy, Leçon inaugurale faite le Vendredi 22 Février 1980, op. cit., p. 9.

[167] B. Urquhart, 'The International Community – Fact or Fiction?', *Macalester International*, 1995, Vol. 1, Article 7. Except, of course, if one advances a very thin definition of international community. H. Mosler, *The International Society as a Legal Community*, Sijthoff, 1980, p. 2.

[168] R. Buchan, *International Law and the Construction of the Liberal Peace*, Hart Publishing, 2013, p. 5. Own emphasis.

states would do so for selfless reasons, that is in the best interest of the states concerned.

The devil's advocate may well argue, however, that the UN and regional organisations promote TG to 'get rid' of their responsibilities by placing this burden on TG; and that contact groups and individual states would favour TG for strategic interests, that is to bolster ties with countries or to counterbalance the geopolitical ambitions of peers, as some states have explicitly recognised.[169] The circumstances of each case combined with a careful analysis of the facts will dictate a different judgement. What is already clear, however, is that the internationalisation of TG can vacillate between bona fide multilateral state transformation and interest-based unilateral constitutional (proxy) politics. Against this tension, this book analyses how international law relates to TG. Such analysis is only relevant though if current literature does not provide sufficient guidance. This is what we shall enquire in the following chapter.

[169] 'US security adviser Rice pledges help for Sri Lanka "transition"', *Reuters*, 7 February 2015.

2

Limitations of Existing Literature

The examination of existing literature (and of its limitations) will lead to the following conclusion: in light of its proliferation and internationalisation, TG under international law deserves to be an object of study in its own right. However relevant a number of concepts or fields may seem to be, they are of little avail for our enquiry.

At first sight, two fields of scholarship seem particularly relevant for the study of TG: *ius post bellum* and TJ, as these fields address the question of how law and justice are applied in post-conflict – and often transitional – settings (Section A). Further, the concepts of 'legitimacy' and 'democracy' are often invoked in relation to TG, too, and therefore merit some attention (Section B).

A   Limitations Inherent to Transitional Justice and *Ius Post Bellum* Literature

Neither the field of TJ (1) nor the doctrine of *ius post bellum* (2) offer sufficient guidance for uncovering how international law applies to TG.

1   Limitations to Transitional Justice

The field of TJ studies how a post-conflict society can come to terms with its own past, through retributive and/or restorative justice mechanisms, and how it can achieve national reconciliation. It is almost systematically applied or at least considered in transition states. In this sense, there is undoubtedly a correlation between TJ and state renaissance.

If only a TJ perspective were chosen to analyse TG, a number of its weaknesses would however contaminate, so to speak, the study of TG. These weaknesses relate to the scope as well as to the normative under-pinnings of TJ, and can be summarised by formulating a dilemma, in the following way. At least initially (1970–90), the general emphasis in TJ literature was on questions relating to TJ *sensu stricto*: the role of amnesty and truth and reconciliation commissions in post-conflict societies to 'digest the past', that is, to cope with situations of past large-scale human rights violations, in short to ensure a form of *Vergangenheitsbewältigung*, to use an accurate German term. Considering this particular emphasis and the traditional focus of TJ on human rights violations, the tendency towards *droits-de-l'hommisme*, that is, activist, militant scholarship to promote human rights,[1] would come at the expense of analysing the overarching institutional context of TJ – a concern which Levitt and Chesterman seem to share.[2]

This tendency or bias, some may say, has not disappeared in TJ literature even if the field has been steadily growing and now includes the analysis of procedural and institutional questions going well beyond the initial focus on (individual and societal) accountability for large-scale human rights violations: 'transitional justice is ... *spilling over* into what have traditionally been "peacebuilding" activities'.[3] There is a 'risk of overstretch'.[4] If, at its beginnings, the TJ literature underemphasised the fundamental role of procedures and institutions in transforming the state, it now risks outgrowing itself by dealing with such questions (TJ *sensu latissimo*),[5] yet without being cleansed, so to speak, of its predisposed focus on seeking justice after human rights violations.

Where to 'box', then, from a legal perspective, TG? Either TG could be analysed under the framework of TJ *sensu latissimo*, at the risk of tainting the analysis with the normative underpinnings of this field. Or

---

[1] A. Pellet, 'Droits-de-l'hommisme et droit international', op. cit.

[2] J. I. Levitt, *Illegal Peace in Africa*, op. cit. Chesterman already observed that '"[t]ransitional justice" is frequently used to refer to both prosecution of war criminals and the establishment of a legal system, but it is typically the former that receives the most attention and resources', S. Chesterman, 'An International Rule of Law?', op. cit., p. 343.

[3] C. L. Sriram, 'Transitional Justice and the Liberal Peace' in E. Newman, R. Paris, O. P. Richmond, *New Perspectives on Liberal Peacebuilding*, op. cit., pp. 116–17. Own emphasis.

[4] J. Iverson, 'Transitional Justice, *Jus Post Bellum* and International Criminal Law: Differentiating the Usages, History and Dynamics', *The International Journal of Transitional Justice*, Vol. 7, 2013, p. 413. See also D. N. Sharp, 'Beyond the Post-Conflict Checklist: Linking Peacebuilding and Transitional Justice Through the Lens of Critique', op. cit., p. 177. TJ 'has begun to move *beyond* its roots and association with the political transitions of the late 1980s and 1990s to Western liberal democracy, and it has become associated with postconflict peacebuilding situations *more generally*, even including those that do not involve a liberal transition'. Own emphasis.

[5] The superlative is used not only to emphasise the considerable expansion of TJ's field of enquiry but also because further below, under Chapter 7, Section C, a distinction will be drawn between transitional justice *sensu stricto* (truth and reconciliation) and *sensu lato* (including criminal justice and international commissions of enquiry).

a traditional international legal perspective could be privileged. By opting for the latter choice, this book reclaims a role for general international law and hopes to lay the groundwork for a less value-driven analysis of practices and procedures that often encompass, albeit are distinct from, TJ.[6]

2   *Limitations to* Ius Post Bellum

As a toolbox for analysing TG, the *ius post bellum* literature suffers from shortcomings, which will lead us to dismiss this concept in further analysis. First, transitions may span periods with or without armed conflict. The *ius post bellum* project, with its emphasis on the role of law *after* armed conflicts, is therefore of little avail.[7] Moreover, it is not always easy to make a distinction between *before* and *after* the war, given that 'many societies emerging from [civil] war can be described as experiencing "no war, no peace" situations'.[8] Jessup wrote in 1954 already that 'legal thinking . . . finds it difficult if not impossible to escape from the confining walls of the firmly established distinction between war and peace'.[9] This study tries to build more immunity to this challenge.

Another weakness of *ius post bellum* is its 'entrenchment' in the law of occupation and focus on the role of international or foreign actors: 'Jus post bellum should apply to the exercise of governmental and public powers by external entities such as IO and foreign states.'[10] But transitional situations do not necessarily follow or coincide with situations during which international humanitarian law applies, and are often (formally) 'managed' by domestic actors.

Third, *ius post bellum* would artificially exclude the analysis of transitions presenting a threat to international peace and security without constituting an armed conflict. As we just observed, transitions can

---

[6] About the conceptual expansion of TJ, see C. L. Sriram, 'Transitional Justice and the Liberal Peace', op. cit., p. 117.

[7] Cf. also Chapter 4, Section A.2.

[8] R. M. Ginty, 'No War, No Peace: Why so Many Peace Processes Fail to Deliver Peace', *International Politics* 47, no. 2, March 2010, p. 145. Cf. also P. C. Jessup, 'Should International Law Recognise an Intermediate Status between Peace and War?', *The American Journal of International Law* 48, no. 1, 1954, 98–103. In the same sense, M. Saul, *Popular Governance of Post-Conflict Reconstruction*, op. cit., p. 5.

[9] P. C. Jessup, 'Should International Law Recognise an Intermediate Status between Peace and War?', op. cit., pp. 98–103.

[10] K. E. Boon, 'Obligations of the New Occupier: The Contours of Jus Post Bellum', op. cit., p. 76.

66   LIMITATIONS OF EXISTING LITERATURE

span periods of armed conflict and peace, but can also be realised in the context of a threat to international peace and security without the level and intensity of armed conflict. For instance, in Yemen, the UNSC determined that the situation constituted such a threat in February 2014;[11] only later, in March 2015, did the situation evolve into an armed conflict. The unsuccessful transition based on the 2011 Gulf Cooperation Agreement thus spanned both moments.

Lex pacificatoria (the law of peacemakers) developed by Bell[12] is sometimes regarded as a part of *ius post bellum*,[13] and this is why I briefly treat it here. *Lex pacificatoria* concentrates on the use of peace agreements from a legal perspective.[14] Bell emphasises the hybrid nature of peace agreements, which 'address both the external position of the state on the international realm, and the internal constitutional structure of the state'. By developing the notion of 'peace agreement constitutions',[15] Bell recognises that peace agreements may fulfil both pacificatory and constitutional functions. She offers a rich account of how the legal form of peace agreements influences issues of compliance considering that such agreements do not easily fit conventional legal categories.[16]

Yet, *lex pacificatoria* does not account for other sorts of texts fulfiling similar (pacificatory and constitutional) functions. It does not consider TG as a conceptually distinct phenomenon, which can also be regulated by constitutional texts or unilateral declarations.[17] In light of the different object and perspective of *lex pacificatoria*, TG cannot be comprehensively examined under this doctrine either.

*

Before turning to the legal analysis and practice-based observation of TG, under the following parts of the book, we will briefly discuss two other notions often heard *en lien* with TG: the concepts of democracy and legitimacy, both inherent to the so-called transition paradigm.

---

[11] S/RES/2140 of 26 February 2014.
[12] C. Bell, *On the Law of Peace: Peace Agreements and the Lex Pacificatoria*, Oxford University Press, 2008.
[13] J. Iverson, 'Transitional Justice, *Jus Post Bellum* and International Criminal Law: Differentiating the Usages, History and Dynamics', *The International Journal of Transitional Justice*, Vol. 7, 2013, p. 427.
[14] C. Bell, *On the Law of Peace: Peace Agreements and the Lex Pacificatoria*, op. cit., abstract.
[15] Id., p. 151.
[16] Id., p. 160.
[17] Chapter 3.

B Irrelevance of the Transition Paradigm

This book deals with transitions in spite of the 'uneasiness about the term and the idea of "transitions" [which] presupposes the "end of history" (transition to what?)'.[18] The term is charged with many connotations. Five assumptions solidly underpin the 'transition paradigm', which Carothers summarises as follows: (a) any country said to be in transition moves toward democracy; (b) democratic teleology ensures that states in transition almost naturally go through a number of stages until an end point is reached; (c) elections generate democracy; (d) structural conditions – e.g. cultural and socioeconomic features – do not much influence the transition and (e) existing state structures can be employed for the transition. One by one, these presuppositions were dismantled in the literature. Today, the transition paradigm, as based on the above assumptions, has crashed altogether.[19]

The end of the transition paradigm led us to propose a more neutral understanding of 'transition'. In this book, this concept refers to the procedures carried out during interregnums, while state and constitutional structures are held in abeyance. And, as already explained, TG is based on a number of features: its association with the peace-through-transition paradigm, and its self-regulatory, temporal, non-constitutional and domestic nature. By concentrating solely on the interregnum, this study furthermore makes abstraction from the – democratic or undemocratic; legitimate or illegitimate – origin and outcome of TG.

Yet, more often than not, the concepts of legitimacy or democracy are evoked in press articles and political discourses about TG. Although regularly heard in such contexts, these concepts remain controversial, especially from a legal perspective. I therefore adopt an *agnostic* viewpoint on them. For the purposes of this book, I do *not* consider that regimes are 'described as transitional on the assumption that they were an intermediate point on a trajectory from authoritarianism to liberal democracy'.[20]

Avoiding the 'democratising bias' allows us to disassociate legal analysis from disputed legitimacy or democracy considerations. This study

---

[18] R. Iveković, 'Partition as a Form of Transition' in S. Bianchini, S. Chaturvedi, R. Iveković and R. Samaddar, *Partitions: Reshaping States and Minds*, Routledge, 2005, p. 13.

[19] T. Carothers, 'The End of the Transition Paradigm', op. cit., pp. 5–21.

[20] M. Tuschnet, 'Authoritarian Constitutionalism – Some Conceptual Issues' in T. Ginsburg, A. Simpser, *Constitutions in Authoritarian Regimes*, Cambridge University Press, 2014, p. 37. With reference to S. Levitsky and L. Way, *Competitive Authoritarianism: Hybrid Regimes after the Cold War*, Cambridge University Press, 2010, pp. 3–4.

therefore makes largely abstraction from both concepts, which are often related to the intended outcome of a transition. Instead, we focus on the transition itself. To say it with Confucius, the journey becomes the destination. Only by way of exception shall we pause on the concepts of legitimacy (1) and democracy (2) in the two following subsections.

1   The Legitimacy Controversy

The concept of legitimacy cannot be used to legally frame, let alone analyse, TG. In the following lines, legitimacy refers to the legitimacy of an established government or of a political body aspiring to such status. Even when one narrows the enquiry down to legitimacy of governmental authority (among other objects of 'legitimacy'), the semantic ambiguity remains.

Departing from the traditional effective control test, states and IOs increasingly assess the 'legitimacy' of an oppositional or consensual political body considered to be a potential alternative and valid successor to a (governmental) regime deemed to be illegitimate or ineffective: 'within the international legal discourse, it is [indeed] a relatively recent phenomenon that the attribute "legitimate" has been added to "government" with frequency'.[21]

The controversy surrounding the legitimacy *vel non* of governments in time of transition becomes sharper as the tests of legitimacy and effective control interact variably. Different readings in scholarship reflect a variety of nuances about how both tests interrelate: (1) the legitimacy of a government can be denied in spite of its effective control; (2) the legitimacy of a government can only be questioned if it loses effective control; (3) legitimacy can be accorded beforehand to a political body even if it lacks effective control.

According to the first reading, a government's effective control over a state territory does not automatically endow it with legitimacy. In other words, legitimacy does not follow effective control.[22] The lack of correlation between effective control and legitimacy would result in a 'broad-

---

[21] Y. Rim, 'Two Governments and One Legitimacy: International Responses to the Post-Election Crisis in Côte d'Ivoire', *Leiden Journal of International Law*, Vol. 25, no. 3, September 2012, p. 693.

[22] J. Vidmar, 'Human Rights, Democracy and the Legitimacy of Governments in International Law: Practice of States and UN Organs' in C. Panara, G. Wilson (eds.), *The Arab Spring, New Patterns for Democracy and International Law*, Martinus Nijhoff Publishers, 2013, p. 53.

IRRELEVANCE OF THE TRANSITION PARADIGM   69

based movement towards reconsideration of the legal legitimacy that traditional doctrine has automatically conferred on governments in effective control'.[23] As regards the conditions for denying legitimacy, it has been argued, in relation to two countries which triggered my thinking on TG, that 'while international law does not yet provide any clear rules for the assessment of governmental legitimacy, the Libyan and Syrian situations show an emerging consensus that governments which use excessive force against their own population to secure their position *lose their legitimacy* and must or should go'.[24]

According to the second reading, the legitimacy criterion only becomes relevant where the government's effective control is being challenged. In other words, legitimacy could only be invoked as a subsidiary criterion, not to be considered as long as effective control is secured.[25] The third reading, finally, considers that legitimacy can compensate for the lack of effective control. Legitimacy could, then, be invoked from an external perspective to endorse an opposition-generated government, and to (purportedly) confer a status upon it.[26] Legitimacy then becomes a criterion for (anticipatively) recognising a government.[27]

The different readings reveal a conceptual indeterminacy. As a *concept*, legitimacy encompasses several *conceptions*. One can furthermore

---

[23] See B. R. Roth, *Governmental Illegitimacy in International Law*, Oxford University Press, 1999, p. 303; pp. 196–7.

[24] S. Talmon, 'Recognition of Opposition Groups as the Legitimate Representative of a People', *Chinese JIL*, 2013, no. 2, p. 238. Own emphasis.

[25] See B. R. Roth, *Governmental Illegitimacy in International Law*, op. cit., p. 303; pp. 196–7.

[26] For Tomuschat, legitimacy 'compensates' for the lack of effective control: '[i]n July 2011, the NTC was at the most a government *in statu nascendi*. But its lack of factual power was *compensated* by its legitimacy which it possessed as the voice of the Libyan people, although not confirmed by formal elections'. C. Tomuschat, 'The Arabellion – Legal Features', *Zeitschrift für ausländisches öffentliches Recht und Völkerrecht*, Vol. 3, 2012, p. 464. Own emphasis.

[27] In this sense, Nesi observes that 'practice also shows that States' decisions have been based not only on traditional elements such as the effective control of parts of the State territory; but that other elements, such as the *legitimacy* of the parties, have also been considered as parameters to be taken into account in relation to recognition or the absence thereof'. G. Nesi, 'Recognition of the Libyan National Transitional Council: When, How and Why', Symposium: The Libyan Crisis and International Law, *The Italian Yearbook of International Law*, Vol. XXI, 2011, p. 59. Own emphasis. Wippman notes that the legitimacy of a political body lacking effective authority is invoked even to accept its invitation to forcibly intervene. D. Wippman, 'Military Intervention, Regional Organisations, and Host-State Consent', *Duke Journal of Comparative & International Law* 7, 1996–7, p. 238: '[i]ncreasingly . . . states are prepared to consider the democratic *legitimacy* of an inviting authority as a counterbalance to considerations of power and effective control'. Own emphasis.

distinguish between legal, moral and social legitimacy.[28] Can 'legitimacy' be gauged in isolation, or is it to be articulated against the opposite criteria of 'illegitimacy' or 'loss of legitimacy'? Is it on this ground that the criterion of legitimacy has compensatory power? Regardless of whether these concepts refer to an illegitimate but effective government or to a legitimate but ineffective political body, the indeterminacy persists. The question thus remains whether 'legitimacy', with its strong value connotation, can be assessed in legal terms.

Should legitimacy assessments concentrate on the legal and constitutional foundation of the exercise of political power – 'legitimacy of origin' – or on the manner in which this power is actually exercised – 'legitimacy of exercise' – or on both?[29] Does it matter, to mention another distinction developed by d'Aspremont and De Brabandere, whether the origin or exercise of power is perceived to be legitimate by domestic actors ('internal legitimacy') or third actors ('external legitimacy')? These are only a few among many interrogations provoked by letting legitimacy adventure into the realm of law.

To be clear, grave and persistent violations of international law can be illegitimate under any acceptable definition doing justice to the ordinary meaning of 'illegitimacy'. Law and morals belong to separate registers. But they both belong to the larger field of normativity and, as such, can intersect. Violating the principle of self-determination, running a racist government or illegally occupying a country can be illegitimate, and sometimes conspicuously so. Thus, the artificial creation of Bantustans, the apartheid regime or the occupation of South West Africa were generally deemed to be illegitimate.

In these cases, all relating to pre-transition South Africa, as well as in other cases (e.g. the territorial illegitimacy of North Cyprus and Crimea), the word illegitimacy was used to label instances in which gross or systematic internationally wrongful acts occurred, that is, to illegality. In other words, illegitimacy was associated with gross and systematic

---

[28] C. A. Thomas, 'The Concept of Legitimacy and International Law', LSE Law, Society and Economy Working Papers 12/2013.

[29] d'Aspremont and De Brabandere write: 'while the legitimacy of origin has constituted the classical measure to evaluate the legitimacy of governments, recent practice has shifted the paradigm toward the legitimacy of exercise'. J. d'Aspremont, E. De Brabandere, 'The Complementary Faces of Legitimacy in International Law: The Legitimacy of Origin and the Legitimacy of Exercise', *Fordham International Law Journal*, Vol. 34, no. 2, 2011, p. 192. Other variants of legitimacy have been proposed in literature: 'input legitimacy'; 'output legitimacy'; 'procedural legitimacy'. See V. Röben, 'Legitimacy of UN Member States', op. cit., p. 1508.

IRRELEVANCE OF THE TRANSITION PARADIGM

illegality. If illegitimacy is to mean something else than this, the rhetorical question remains: what, precisely, does this concept cover *in law*?

Identifying the 'right' post-transition government, or the 'right' political body for governing the interregnum on the basis of legitimacy criteria is a doubtful enterprise. More generally, even if it were verified that the international community has been undergoing a structural and value-driven change by departing from traditional effectiveness criteria,[30] the concept of 'legitimacy' cannot replace them. Its usage is too fresh, its contents unstable and its legal nature contested. Because legitimacy is an elusive notion, *other concepts and criteria* should be identified as benchmarks for legally framing and assessing TG. This is what this book intends to do: it frames TG using the law beyond concepts such as legitimacy – or democracy.

2   The Democracy Controversy

The concept of 'democracy' does not enlighten us more on how TG can be analysed from a general international legal perspective. Democracy cannot be used as a benchmark for legally framing TG. It cannot serve to identify the post-transition government or, even less so, to appoint the 'right' political body for governing the interregnum – note that transitions are seldom triggered by elections.[31] Nevertheless, the concept of democracy invariably marches in when discussing TG. This is not surprising since the transition paradigm is traditionally linked to the idea of democracy.[32]

---

[30] E. Šarčević, 'Völkerrechtlicher Vertrag Als "Gestaltungsinstrument" Der Verfassungsgebung: Das Daytoner Verfassungsexperiment Mit Präzedenzwirkung?', *Archiv Des Völkerrechts*, 39, no. 3, 1 September 2001, p. 324: '[a]n der Schwelle zum 21. Jahrhundert erlebt die Staatengemeinschaft den fundamentalen Strukturwandel des Völkerrechts: Die bisher eher auf dem Grundsatz der Effektivität und des status quo fußende völkerrechtliche Ordnung wandelte sich nach und nach zu einem stärker wertorientierten Völkerrecht'. Own translation: 'On the eve of the twenty-first century, the international community is experiencing how international law has structurally and fundamentally changed. Hitherto rather based on the principles of effectiveness and the status quo, it has gradually transformed itself into a more value-oriented international law.'

[31] This point will be revisited in Chapter 7, Section A.

[32] N. Bhuta, 'Democratisation, State-Building and Politics as Technology' in B. Bowden, H. Charlesworth, J. Farrall (eds.), *The Role of International Law in Rebuilding Societies After Conflict – Great Expectations*, Cambridge University Press, 2009, p. 58: 'After the cold war, the academic research programme of democratic transition held out the promise of a rationalised method of managing "transitions to democracy." Not unlike modernisation theory before it, the newly consecrated discipline of "transitology" filled

72 LIMITATIONS OF EXISTING LITERATURE

The transition paradigm and its various assumptions have been criticised from a political science perspective.[33] Often democracy does not yield the desired results. According to the democratic peace theory, 'consolidated democracies do not go to war with each other because democracies have institutional constraints upon leaders that make initiating conflict with other countries more difficult'.[34] Even if this theory were waterproof, it would need to be distinguished from the question whether, *on the domestic plane*, democratisation is conducive to peace. At least in this sense, there seems to be no direct or exclusive causality between formal democracy and peace.[35] Especially in transitional contexts, ironically democratisation efforts might even form an incentive for violence.[36]

From a legal perspective, there are three interrelated reasons why the international law analysis of non-constitutional transitions does better without the concept of democracy. The question 'what is democracy?' can be addressed in two parts, which relate to the fluctuating conceptions (2.1) and inconsistent practice and uncertain legal status of democracy (2.2).

2.1 The Variety of Definitions of Democracy

A panoply of definitions and conceptions exist, and, in descending order, they may be subdivided into three categories. First, there is the expansive/ substantive approach to democracy, based on a positive definition which associates the exercise of democracy with the respect for human rights. This vision can be found in the Human Rights Committee General Comment on article 25 of the ICCPR, which considers that the freedom of expression, assembly and association are essential preconditions of the right to participate in public affairs.

a cognitive gap among policy intellectuals and donors facing a new period of uncertainty in the politics of the Third World. It became, in the words of one democracy-promoting insider, "a universal paradigm for understanding democratisation"'.

[33] E. Newman, 'Liberal Peacebuilding Debates', op. cit., p. 39: '[t]he Political Instability Task Force, after conducting a large-scale analysis of conflict from 1955 to 2003, came to the conclusion that, in terms of statistical correlation, the risk of conflict is highest not among democracies or authoritarian states but in partial democracies or transitional states'.

[34] E. Newman, R. Paris, O. P. Richmond, *New Perspectives on Liberal Peacebuilding*, op. cit., p. 11.

[35] S. Bastian and R. Luckham, *Can Democracy Be Designed?: The Politics of Institutional Choice in Conflict-Torn Societies*, Zed Books, 2003.

[36] E. Newman, 'Liberal Peacebuilding Debates', op. cit, p. 11: 'significant amount of research suggests that transitional societies ... may be more likely to experience civil conflict, especially in poor and divided societies'.

IRRELEVANCE OF THE TRANSITION PARADIGM

A deeper concept of democracy is also promoted in the UNCHR's 1999 resolution 'Promotion of the Right to Democracy', and in the 1990 Charter of Paris.[37] Generally, the expansive/substantive approach to democracy is based on the following elements: the actual exercise of governmental power by the freely chosen representatives; the participation of citizens in public affairs; the institutionalised constraints on the exercise of power; the guarantee of civil liberties; and the (equal application of the) rule of law.[38]

The formalist/procedural approach to democracy is primarily based on the right to free elections.[39] This approach is not incompatible with 'illiberal democracy', that is, the rule by autocratic regimes entrenched through regular elections. Yet, as most of the state practice centres on elections,[40] the formalist/procedural approach to democracy may well be the predominant one.[41]

The minimalistic approach to democracy, finally, embraces a negative definition of democracy: 'states where the effective holder of the power is not chosen through free and fair elections and where basic civil rights are seriously and blatantly infringed are usually considered non-democratic in contemporary practice'.[42] According to this approach, consensus

[37] 1990 'Charter of Paris for a new Europe': 'democratic government is based on the will of the people, expressed regularly through free and fair elections. Democracy has as its foundation respect for the human person and the rule of law. Democracy is the best safeguard of freedom of expression, tolerance of all groups of society, and equality of opportunity for each person. Democracy, with its representative and pluralist character, entails accountability to the electorate, the obligation of public authorities to comply with the law and justice administered impartially'.

[38] M. Saul, 'The Impact of the Legal Right to Self-Determination on the Law of Occupation as a Framework for Post-Conflict State Reconstruction' in N. Quinivet, S. Shah-Davis (eds.), *International Law and Armed Conflict*, T.M.C. Asser Press, 2010, p. 407.

[39] J. Salmon, 'Le droit international à l'épreuve au tournant du XXI siècle', *Cours Euro-Méditerranéens Bancaja*, Vol. VI, 2002, p. 298–301: 'dans les rapports de force actuels au sein des relations internationales, c'est la conception purement formaliste de la démocratie axée sur le droit à des élections libres et honnêtes qui domine. Cette conception occulte le fait que ce type de démocratie est souvent fictif'. Own translation: 'in the current balance of power of international relations, the purely formalist conception of democracy based on the right to free and fair elections dominates. This conception obscures the fact that this type of democracy is often fictitious'.

[40] G. Fox, 'Democracy, Right to, International Protection', MPEPIL.

[41] G. Fox, 'The Right to Political Participation in International Law' in G. Fox and B. Roth, *Democratic Governance and International Law*, Cambridge University Press, 2000, p. 49: 'International law has [however] come to understand "democracy" in narrower, more *process-oriented* terms'. Own emphasis.

[42] J. d'Aspremont, *L'Etat non démocratique en droit international*, A. Pedone, 2008.

74   LIMITATIONS OF EXISTING LITERATURE

would only exist about a number of parameters which, if they are met, would define the *absence* of democracy.

2.2   Inconsistent Practice and Uncertain Legal Status

In light of these conceptual controversies, it is not surprising that the practice of states and IO in relation to democracy is inconsistent.[43] With specific reference to the practice of UN Charter organs, who seem to privilege a thin concept of democracy,[44] democracy lacks both determinate legal content and consistent practice.[45] As a result of these indeterminacies, democracy practices strongly vary according to the regional context.[46]

Besides the uncertainty about how democracy should be defined – substantially, procedurally or negatively – and the persistent doubts about whether it can be consistently applied under any approach, the legal status of the concept – '*lex lata, de lege ferenda* or mere political aspirations'?[47] – also causes controversy. A plausible argument for denying that, *de lege lata*, all states are obliged to be or to become democratic is that democratisation efforts mostly *follow* state consent. Because democratisation practices mostly occur on a voluntary basis, international practice does not support the conviction that democracy is compulsory[48] – unless (for example in the framework of regional organisations) there was a prior commitment to this end.

---

[43] G. H. Fox, B. R. Roth, 'Democracy and International Law', *Review of International Studies*, 27, 2001, p. 346.

[44] C. Steinorth, 'The United Nations, Post-Conflict Institution-Building and Thin Concepts of Democracy', *Journal of Intervention and Statebuilding*, Special Issue, 2011, pp. 305–21.

[45] N. Bhuta, 'Democratisation, State-building and Politics as Technology', *op. cit*, p. 46: 'even if the shifting geopolitical context opened a space for a renewed effervescence of liberal internationalism, it has *not necessarily resulted in a conforming legal practice among international institutions*. ... In the practice of UN Charter organs, resolutions increasingly refer to "democracy" or "periodic and genuine elections" as desiderata in the context of specific regional conflicts, but there is little evidence that "democracy" has developed a determinate legal content in international law'. Own emphasis.

[46] For an overview of the formal importance accorded to democracy on regional levels, see T. Christakis, *Le droit à l'autodétermination en dehors des situations de décolonisation*, CERIC, 1999, p. 503. Cf. also V. Saranti, 'Pro-Democratic Intervention, Invitation, or "Responsibility to Protect"? Challenges to International Law from the "Arab Spring"' in C. Panara, G. Wilson, eds., *The Arab Spring, New Patterns for Democracy and International Law*, op. cit., pp. 171–2.

[47] G. H. Fox, 'Democracy, Right to, International Protection', Wayne State University Law School Research Paper No. 07–22, 2007, p. 4.

[48] G. H. Fox, B. R. Roth, 'Democracy and International Law', op. cit., p. 344.

The interconnected interrogations about the definition, implementation and legal status of democracy leave us empty-handed. Even if a consensus about the contents of democracy existed, the uncertainty about its implementation and legal status would persist. As a result, '"democracy" becomes identified with whichever choice engages our sympathies', Roth writes.[49] For other authors, accepting a 'right to democracy' could even have adverse effects, and serve as a justification for imposing polities abroad, in violation of the principles of state sovereignty and self-determination;[50] or democratic legitimacy would not even have the *potential* of governing state transformation processes which, in order to be effective, would need to be predicated on bold non-democratic power.[51]

There is no need to engage with these more or less provocative statements. Suffice it, here, to note that 'democracy' suffers from legal indeterminacy. It is thus better dispensed with to analyse TG. This choice will be confirmed further in Part III when we shall conclude that TG is neither the fruit of formal/procedural democracy nor an exercise of substantive democracy.[52] At best, TG can be seen as an *undemocratic means of realising democracy*,[53] whereby the absence of democracy during the interregnum should, less and less, be confused with a lack of normativity.

Unavoidably, then, the agnostic position taken with regard to 'legitimacy' or 'democracy' extends to the (positive or negative) *outcome* of transitions – this may be called 'irrelevance of outcome'. I therefore avoid the terms 'legitimate transition' or 'democratic transition'.[54] Even though the declared purpose of many transitions is to install a (more) legitimate and democratic

---

[49] B. R. Roth, 'Democratic Intolerance: Observations on Fox and Nolte' in G. H. Fox and B. R. Roth, *Democratic Governance and International Law*, op. cit., p. 442.

[50] S. Mclaughlin Mitchell, P. F. Diehl, 'Caution in What You Wish For – The Consequences of a Right to Democracy', *Stanford Journal of International Law*, Vol. 48, no. 2, 2012, p. 289.

[51] See the reference to and explanation of R. Hardin's account of state transformation/formation in N. Bhuta, 'New Modes and Orders: The Difficulties of a Jus Post Bellum of Constitutional Transformation', *University of Toronto Law Journal*, Vol. 60, no. 3, Summer 2010, pp. 20–1.

[52] Chapter 7, Section A.

[53] R. Ponzio, *Democratic Peacebuilding, Aiding Afghanistan and Other Fragile States*, Oxford University Press, 2011, p. 220: '[r]ather than decelerating or impeding democratisation, [such] case specific and transformative governance innovation are necessary to build a viable and durable democratic state over the medium to long term'.

[54] Contrary to N. Youssef, *La Transition démocratique et la garantie des droits fondamentaux*, op. cit.

regime based on the respect of fundamental rights,[55] this goal – whether achieved or not – does not inform us about the norms and practices *of the transition*. The challenge is to analyse the transition *itself* – that is, the period during which the state is held in abeyance – from an international legal perspective *without* relying on controverted concepts.

Conclusion of Part I

The recourse to TG is flourishing, especially as state creation has passed its zenith, and ITA is considered too costly while also being normatively contested. Through TG, international involvement can furthermore be cost-efficient and discrete while leaving its marks on virtually all state components.

Besides this historic-economic context, another, less self-evident, factor may explain the rise of TG: some might try to argue that TG is preferable on pseudo-legal grounds related to the persistent idea that domestic actors should not only 'own' their transition but also systematically be legally responsible for it – in spite of its increased internationalisation. The first chapter suggested that this idea of systematic domestic responsibility for TG (often associated to the principles of state sovereignty and self-determination) is superficial, especially if it constitutes an extra incentive for external actors to actively intervene in transitions while their slate remains clean no matter what happens. The piercing of this superficiality clears the path for a more nuanced analysis.

State transformations are subject to internal and external influences in many fields. This book concentrates on a field going to the core of a state's business: regime transformation and reconstitutionalisation. TG is placed centre stage in international diplomacy, and already plays an important role for the international security system.[56] The UN and regional IOs as well as diplomatic coalitions and individual states are

---

[55] Id., p. 45. True, the circumstance that, over the last decades, no newly created state has *not* committed itself to democracy might be indicative of a putative international democratic principle. But such a principle in relation to state creation, if its existence is verified, is not transposable to the realm of TG. Further, a pre-commitment to democracy should not be confused with the actual and immediate exercise of or abidance by democracy – even formally defined – during the interregnum, which seems rather utopian. If compliance with democracy is to be realised *gradually*, the question remains what international law expects – if anything at all – from the state during this interim period.

[56] E. De Groof, 'The Peace-Through-Transition Paradigm: Domestic Interim Governance As the New Center Piece of the International Security System', op. cit., pp. 79–94.

CONCLUSION OF PART I

increasingly concerned with TG. In public discourse, this involvement is often associated with the peace-through-transition paradigm and the assistance model. As this model is often overstretched, such discourse barely conceals that goals other than international peace and security – namely constitutional geopolitics – can be pursued through assistance to TG. As a multifaceted phenomenon, the internationalisation of TG can thus vacillate between multilateral state transformation and unilateral constitutional geopolitics.

The proliferation and internationalisation of TG invite us to treat it as an object of study in its own right under international law. From this specific angle, TG is largely unchartered territory. Given the limitations in literature, this study has to be carried out afresh. The fields of TJ and *ius post bellum* and the concepts of legitimacy and democracy are only of limited utility in this regard. In light of the 'irrelevance of outcome',[57] this study is not so much concerned with the question of to what extent the decision of a political system is purely a domestic matter. It rather focuses on the state renaissance preceding and accompanying that decision: the very operation of choosing or replacing a political system, to which the *Nicaragua* judgment refers,[58] in many cases *takes time*. It often results from a protracted process which includes, but is not limited to, reconstitutionalisation. How this process unfolds is very much influenced by the secondary norms regulating TG, so-called TI, which transitional authorities are called upon to implement. It is to the analysis of TA, and the instruments which regulate the transition, that we now turn.

---

[57] Chapter 2, Section B.2.2.

[58] This principle was pronounced by the ICJ in *Military and Paramilitary Activities in and against Nicaragua (Nicaragua v. United States of America)*, Merits, Judgment, *ICJ Reports*, 1986, p. 14., § 258 ('Nicaragua Case'). This position was already announced in the Western Sahara case: 'no rule of international law ... requires the structure of the State to follow any particular pattern, as is evident from the diversity of the forms of State found in the world today', *Western Sahara*, Advisory Opinion, ICJ Reports 1975, p. 12, § 94. Cf. also J. Vidmar, 'Democracy and Regime Change in the Post-Cold War International Law', *NZJPIL*, 11, 2013, p. 358: 'even the post-Cold War international law adheres to the Nicaragua case principle: the choice of the political system and electoral method is a domestic matter of states'.

PART II

Foundation and Actors of Transitional Governance * Sources of *Ius in Interregno*

The aim of this part is to unveil which instruments, actors and sources are relevant for the law applicable to TG, a multifaceted but distinguishable politico-legal phenomenon. It analyses the foundation of TG (Chapter 3), and further conceptualises TA as political bodies (purportedly) introducing a state transformation in their respective states (Chapter 4). It ends with an assessment of the sources of *ius in interregno* (Chapter 5).

3

The Foundation of Transitional Governance

The written instruments that are constitutive of non-constitutional TG, that is the '*actes fondateurs de la transition*,'[1] are referred as constituent transition instruments or simply transition instruments ('TI'). Of varying legal nature and created in various contexts, the TI discussed in this chapter and listed in Table 3.1 also form the material for the report accompanying this book.[2]

This chapter analyses such legal documents triggering and regulating TG. TA are installed through non-constitutional processes such as peace deals, power-sharing agreements but also unilateral declarations or interim constitutions. Section A is dedicated to the non-constitutional origin or context of TG. Section B deals with the supraconstitutional function of transition instruments and their constitutional transformation purpose.

A Origin or Context: Non-Constitutionality

This section defines the origin or context of TG, non-constitutionality (1), and observes that international law is in principle neutral vis-à-vis non-constitutionality (2).

1 Definition of Non-Constitutionality

Non-constitutionality defines the origin or context of TG. The return to 'permanent' constitutionality usually announces its end.[3] The words 'non-constitutionality' or 'non-constitutional' refer to the violation of a constitution or its modification without following the available amendment or revision procedures; or to the creation of oppositional or consensual TA not foreseen by the constitution. An oppositional TA comes into being on the

---

[1] N. Youssef, *La transition démocratique et la garantie des droits fondamentaux*, op. cit., p. 110.
[2] E. De Groof, 'The Features of Transitional Governance Today', op. cit.
[3] Chapter 4, Section A.2.4 for other yardsticks defining a transition's end.

82 THE FOUNDATION OF TRANSITIONAL GOVERNANCE

Table 3.1 *Transition instruments and their non-constitutional origin*

Country	Transition instruments	Legal nature	Non-constitutional Context/Origin
Afghanistan	2001 Bonn Agreement	Intrastate agreement	Ousting of Taliban (1996–2001)
Burkina Faso	2014 Charte de la Transition	Domestic law	Ousting of Pres. Blaise Compaoré (31 October 2014).
Burundi	2000 Arusha Agreement	Intrastate agreement	Peace process in context of Burundi civil war (1993–2005).
Cambodia	1991 Paris Peace Accords	Int'l treaty	Peace process in context of Cambodian-Vietnamese war (1977–91).
Central African Republic	2013 Déclaration de N'Djamena 2013 Charte Constitutionelle	Domestic law	Ousting Pres. Bozizé & Suspension constitution (March 2013) by Séléka coalition.
Comoros	1999 Accords d'Antananarivo	Intrastate agreement	Coup in April 1999 deposing Pres. Massounde.
Côte d'Ivoire	2003 Linas-Marcoussis Accord 2007 Ouagadougou Political Agreement	Intrastate agreement	Peace process in context of Fist Ivorian Civil War (2002–7).
DRC	2002 Pretoria Agreement 2002 Draft Constitution of the Transition	Int'l treaty/ domestic law	Peace process in context of Second Congo War (1998–2003).

ORIGIN OR CONTEXT: NON-CONSTITUTIONALITY

Table 3.1 (*cont.*)

Country	Transition instruments	Legal nature	Non-constitutional Context/Origin
Guinea	2010 Ouagadougou Declaration	Domestic law	Coup by CNDD on 23 December 2008 following death Pres. Conté.
Guinea-Bissau	2012 ECOWAS Communiqué *Pacto de Transição Política*	Int'l resolution Domestic law	Coup on 12 April 2012 deposing Pres. Pereira.
Iraq	2004 Transitional Administration Law	Domestic law	Ousting of Pres. Hussein in 2003 and dissolution of Ba'ath party.
Kyrgyzstan	2010 Provisional Government Decree No 19 and 20	Domestic law	Ousting of Pres. Bakiev and his government in April 2010.
Liberia	2003 Accra Comprehensive Peace agreement	Intrastate agreement	Peace process in context of Second Liberian Civil war (1999–2003).
Libya	2011 Constitutional Declaration 2015 Libyan Political Agreement	Domestic law	Unilateral transition procedure and ousting of Colonel. Gaddafi in context of Libyan Civil War (2011).
Mali	2012 Framework Agreement See also 2015 Agreement on Peace and Reconciliation in Mali emanating from the Algiers process of 15 May 2015.	Intrastate agreements	Coup on 22 March 2012 deposing Pres. Touré. Unrest in Northern Mali.

84 THE FOUNDATION OF TRANSITIONAL GOVERNANCE

Table 3.1 (*cont.*)

Country	Transition instruments	Legal nature	Non-constitutional Context/Origin
Nepal	2006 Comprehensive Peace Agreement 2007 Interim Constitution	Intrastate agreement	Ousting of King Gyanendra (May 2006) in aftermath of Nepalese Civil War (1996–2006).
Rwanda	1993 Arusha Agreement	Intrastate agreement/ domestic law	Peace process in the aftermath of Rwandan Civil War (1990–3).
Sierra Leone	1999 Lomé agreement	Intrastate agreement	Peace process in the aftermath of Sierra Leone Civil War (1991–2002).
Somalia	2004 Somali Transitional Charter	Domestic law	Peace process in the context of Somali Civil War (1986– present).
South Africa	1994 Interim Constitution	Domestic law	Abolition of apartheid (1948–94).
Syria	Coalition Principles (undated)/2015 Basic Principles	Soft law or domestic political declaration	Attempt of unilateral transition procedure and ousting of Pres. Al-Assad in the context of Syrian Civil War (2011– present).
Sudan	2005 Sudan Comprehensive Peace Agreement	Int'l treaty/ intrastate agreement	Peace process in the context of Second Sudanese Civil War (1983–2005).

ORIGIN OR CONTEXT: NON-CONSTITUTIONALITY 85

Table 3.1 (cont.)

Country	Transition instruments	Legal nature	Non-constitutional Context/Origin
Ukraine	2015 Minsk Agreement 2014 Agreement on the Settlement of Crisis in Ukraine	Int'l treaty/ intrastate agreement	Peace process in the context of War in Donbass (2014–present).
Yemen	2011 Gulf Cooperation Council Agreement 2015 Constitutional Declaration	Intrastate agreement / domestic political declaration	Departure of Pres. Saleh; Yemeni Civil War (2015).

basis of a supraconstitutional unilateral declaration overtly defying the constitutional order (the case of intended *replacement*, for example the Libyan Transitional National Council self-proclaimed in March 2011)[4] while a consensual TA is created by a supraconstitutional agreement departing from and redefining the existing constitutional order (the case of *transplacement*, for example the 2000 Burundi Arusha Agreement).[5] In both cases, a rupture has taken place.

Non-constitutionality should not be conflated with large-scale constitutional/institutional modifications carried out with due regard to the existing institutions and applicable constitutional provisions. This study does not engage in a comparison of constitutional reforms ('*Verfassungsänderungsprozessen*');[6] or of illegitimate transitions through formally lawfully adopted amendments, that is the issue of so-called unconstitutional constitutional amendments.[7]

---

[4] Chapter 9, Section A.1.2.

[5] See E. De Groof, 'The Features of Transitional Governance Today', op. cit. for details.

[6] M. Böckenförde, 'Die Einbindung der Bevölkerung in Verfassungsänderungsprozessen – Ein Überblick', op. cit.

[7] A. Barak, 'Unconstitutional Constitutional Amendments', *Israel Law Review*, Vol. 44, 2011, p. 321: an unconstitutional constitutional amendment is 'an amendment to the constitution that has been made pursuant to the formal requirements of the constitution but [that] deviates from its basic structure' (p. 321). Roznai observes that a 'global trend is moving towards accepting the idea of limitations – explicit or implicit – on constitutional amendment power'. Y. Roznai, 'Unconstitutional Constitutional Amendments—The Migration and Success of

86   THE FOUNDATION OF TRANSITIONAL GOVERNANCE

Furthermore, non-constitutionality is not incompatible with transition texts referring to previous constitutional systems (as in Afghanistan,[8] Somalia),[9] or even confirming the continued application of the previous constitutional system if, at the same time, such texts claim to be partly supraconstitutional,[10] that is supersede the previous regime (as in Afghanistan,[11] Burkina Faso,[12] Burundi,[13] Côte d'Ivoire,[14] South Africa,[15] South Sudan[16] and Yemen[17]) at least in part. Sometimes one can find, within the same TI, the affirmation that it has supraconstitutional value side by side with a reference to the previous constitutional and legal order, for example to ensure the continued application of existing laws inasmuch as these are not overridden by the TI. The non-

a Constitutional Idea', *The American Journal of Comparative Law*, Vol. 61, 2013, p. 658. See also Section A.2.2.

[8] The Bonn Agreement, art. II.1.1, giving rise to the Afghan TA, explicitly refers to the continued application, in principle, of the Afghan Constitution of 1964.

[9] The Somali Transitional Charter refers to the 1960 Somali Constitution. Cf. the Transitional Federal Charter for the Somali Republic, February 2004, art. 71.2.

[10] Table 3.2 for an overview.

[11] Bonn Agreement, Section V.5: '[a]ll actions taken by the Interim Authority shall be consistent with Security Council resolution 1378 (14 November 2001) and other relevant Security Council resolutions relating to Afghanistan'.

[12] The Burkinabé Charte de la Transition of 16 November 2014 provides: '[e]n cas de contrariété entre la Charte de la transition et la Constitution, les dispositions de la présente charte prévalent'. Own translation: 'in the event of a conflict between the Transitional Charter and the Constitution, the provisions of this Charter prevail'.

[13] In the case of Burundi, the Arusha Agreement, Protocol II, Ch. II, art. 15 provides that '[w]hen there is any conflict between [the Constitution of the Republic of Burundi of 13 March 1992] and the Agreement, the provisions of the Agreement shall prevail'. Also, the Chair of the Specific Configuration on Burundi of the Peacebuilding Commission 'appeal[ed] for an inclusive process and a revision that didn't undermine the basic principles of the Arusha Agreements' (Chair's Summary of the Informal meeting of the Burundi Specific Configuration of the PBC, New York, 12 March 2014).

[14] Linas-Marcoussis Agreement, 3.a, IX. See also S/RES/1721 of 1 November 2006, Preamble and § 4.

[15] The South African interim constitution (art. 71) provides that the new constitutional text shall comply with 34 constitutional principles.

[16] For South Sudan, the 2005 CPA, which ended the civil war in that country, could be seen as an '*Überconstitution*': 'the negotiation and conclusion of the CPA was considerably influenced by external factors. *And it was the CPA that determined the procedural and substantial framework for the constitution-making process*' (P. Dann, Z. Al-Ali, 'The Internationalised Pouvoir Constituant', op. cit., pp. 443–8). Own emphasis.

[17] The 'Agreement on the Implementation Mechanism for the Transition Process in Yemen' provides that '[t]he GCC Initiative and the Mechanism shall supersede any current constitutional or legal arrangements. They may not be challenged before the institutions of the State'. (Agreement on the Implementation Mechanism for the Transition Process in Yemen in Accordance with the Initiative of the Gulf Cooperation Council (GCC) of 5 December 2011, § 4).

ORIGIN OR CONTEXT: NON-CONSTITUTIONALITY 87

constitutional basis of all the transitions just mentioned in passing is actually a moot point: no one doubts that the constitutional orders of these countries were fundamentally altered as a result of TG generated by a non-constitutional rupture. This is so irrespective of whether the TI contain references to the previous constitutional order.

In most cases under scrutiny, the non-constitutional origins of the transition eventually evolve into the adoption of a new constitution ('reconstitutionalisation') and the creation of a new regime. Between these two moments, that is during the interregnum, typically one or more TA administer the state, and ensure the return to (permanent) constitutionality on the basis of the election/appointment of a constituent body and the organisation of a constitutional referendum or general elections.

Non-constitutionality does not exclude interim constitutionalism. Domestic transitions are composite procedures. They go through a number of stages, and mostly build on a sequence of interim acts or documents. The non-constitutionality that initially characterises them can subsequently be remedied, in one or more steps (through staged constitution-making). Non-constitutionality in such contexts is not a linear or continuing state of affairs. Interim constitutional acts or documents can depart from the previous constitutional order, and at the same time provide a provisional legal foundation for the regime to come. For example, the 1993 South African Constitution repealed South Africa's first constitution, adopted in 1909, and at the same time laid the basis for the 1996 constitution and post-apartheid South Africa. TA established on the basis of such acts or documents are non-constitutional but interim-constitution based, like South Africa's Government of National Unity (April 1994–February 1997). They are, thus, constitutional in a sense, even if they were set up in the larger context of a non-constitutional transition.

Finally, in the context of TG, the non-constitutional nature of TA is qualitatively different from the non-constitutionality characterising *de facto* governments, that is non-constitutional governments (or puta-tive governments of *de facto* states)[18] as opposed to *de iure* govern-ments. The non-constitutionality of TA is paired with (pretensions of) supraconstitutionality, allowing the pursuit of TG.[19] The non-constitutionality of *de facto* governments, on the other hand, is reduced

[18] Introduction, Section A.4.2.
[19] Chapter 3, Section B.

88   THE FOUNDATION OF TRANSITIONAL GOVERNANCE

to its unlawful nature.[20] The concept of *de facto* governments is premised on this idea of illegality, and, in this sense, is rather one-dimensional. It is also premised on the idea that the replacement of a *de iure* by a *de facto* government, or vice versa, is done almost instantaneously. Further, even though the precise moment of replacement is not always easy to pinpoint,[21] *under the scenario of de facto governments, institutions set up to regulate the substitution itself are usually not envisaged*. In the context of TG, these become indispensable as substitution is not an instantaneous or quasi-instantaneous act.

This subtlety, together with the more obvious distinction between temporary and permanent governance,[22] allows us to differentiate TG from governance by *de facto* governments. TG can be, or become incrementally, constitutional (in spite of their non-constitutional origins), while *de facto* governments are commonly seen as unequivocally non-constitutional.

---

[20] This feature of *de facto* governments was accepted since the 1920s. N. Henry, *Les gouvernements de fait devant le juge*, Guillon, Paris, 1927, § 2: 'le gouvernement de fait est celui dont le pouvoir est entaché d'irrégularité'. Own translation : 'the *de facto* government is one whose power is tainted with irregularity'. J. Spiropoulos, *Die de facto-Regierung im Völkerrecht*, Verlag des Instituts für internationales Recht an der Universität Kiel, 1926, p. 1: '[u]nter einer *de facto*-Regierung versteht man die im Widerspruch zu einer bestehenden Verfassung, oder bei Nicht-Existenz einer Staatsordnung ipso facto ins Leben getretenem *ohne verfassungsmäßige Grundlage* die Regierungsgewalt ausübende Behörde'. Own emphasis and translation: 'by a *de facto* government is understood the authority exercising governmental authority contrary to an existing constitution or, in the absence of a state order, the government created ipso facto, that is without a constitutional basis'. See also S. Gemma, 'Les gouvernements de fait', *Collected Courses of the Hague Academy of International Law*, Vol. 4, 1924, p. 307: 'un gouvernement qui n'est pas conforme, qui est même contraire à l'ordre juridique existant'. Own translation: 'a government that is not in compliance with, even contrary to the existing legal order'. *De iure* governments, on the other hand, are governments that took office in accordance with the existing constitutional order.

[21] S. Gemma, 'Les gouvernements de fait', op. cit., p. 318 : 'il n'est pas toujours facile d'établir le moment juridique où l'ancien gouvernement a cessé d'exister, où le nouveau l'a remplacé. L'ancien ordre juridique, en effet, ne peut pas prévoir son anéantissement, ni même sa transformation radicale, et le nouveau ne peut pas trouver dans un droit préexistant (parce qu'alors il ne serait plus nouveau) le titre de sa suprématie. Les deux moments: l'initial, celui de la sortie de la légalité et le terminal, celui de la rentrée, ne peuvent souvent se déterminer qu'approximativement'. Own translation: 'it is not always easy to establish the legal moment when the old government ceased to exist, where the new one replaced it. The old legal order, indeed, cannot foresee its annihilation, nor even its radical transformation, and the new one cannot find in a pre-existing right (because then it would not be new) the title of its supremacy. The two moments: the initial (that of the exit of the legality) and the terminal (that of the re-entry) can often be determined only approximately'.

[22] Chapter 4, Section A.2.

Unidimensional and immediate non-constitutionality characterises *de facto* governments while incremental and interim constitutionality characterises TA.

2 Non-Constitutionality under International Law and Regional Frameworks

Non-constitutionality is chiefly a domestic legal matter. If a durable constitution concerns the 'rules of the game' defining how public power is limited, then (on yet another level) TI purport to determine 'the rules of the game defining the rules of the game'. They are, then, secondary norms in the Hartean sense – or even 'tertiary' norms, one could say, and for the remainder of the book this neologism will be used. In spite of this, their domestic validity is not guaranteed from the start – precisely because of their non-constitutional origin or context. Non-constitutionality refers to a possible conflict of norms within the domestic order, and in principle does not concern the relationship between national and international law. Why? On the global level, international legal frameworks addressing non-constitutionality are lacking (2.1) while on the regional level, non-constitutionality is sometimes sanctioned, but incoherently so (2.2).

2.1 Non-Constitutionality on the Global Level: International Law's Neutrality

There are no global (multilateral) international legal instruments directly applying to domestic non-constitutionality. Propositions *de lege ferenda* in this regard, for example the idea to create an International Constitutional Court, are unrealistic.[23] Apart from regional organisation instruments mentioned below, there is just one well-known international-treaty-based reference to domestic non-constitutionality. The 1969 VCLT provides that (under strict conditions) the violation of internal law of fundamental importance – read: constitutional law – relating to treaty-concluding powers may lead to the invalidation of the consent to be bound by a treaty.[24]

---

[23] The Tunisian President suggested that an International Constitutional Court be created (speech to the UNGA in September 2012). See also www.constitutionaltransitions.org /tunis-international-constitutional-court, last accessed on 25 March 2020, and L. Nasrawin, 'Towards the Establishment of an International Constitutional Court', *ICL Journal*, Vol. 10, 4/2016.

[24] VCLT, art. 46. The manifest violation of internal laws 'of fundamental importance' regarding a state's competence to conclude a treaty potentially invalidates that state's consent to be bound by that treaty under the VCLT.

90 THE FOUNDATION OF TRANSITIONAL GOVERNANCE

The drafting history of article 27 of the VCLT confirms that the autonomy of international law must however be upheld, also vis-à-vis constitutional law.[25] The ILC, too, has underlined the autonomy of international law (albeit in another field, the law of international responsibility) vis-à-vis domestic law.[26] For the same reason, the Tobar doctrine, according to which international recognition of unconstitutional (insurgent) governments should be refused, has gained little acceptance.

Apart from the issues of recognition and of accreditation of delegates in the UNGA on the basis of a constitutionality criterion,[27] domestic non-constitutionality or illegality is thus of little concern for international law, notwithstanding nuanced discussions in literature.[28] Since there is no legal framework regulating the formally absent dynamics between domestic non-constitutionality and international illegality, contexts of non-constitutionality are generally regarded as *neutral* – neither forbidden nor allowed.[29] In a sense, the neutrality of international law vis-à-vis non-constitutional TI can be compared to international law's neutrality vis-à-vis declarations of independence (potentially) leading to the birth of a new state.[30]

[25] A. de Hoogh, 'The Relationship between National Law and International Law in the Report of the Georgia Fact-Finding Mission', *EJIL:Talk!*, 4 January 2010.

[26] See, for example, DASR, art. 3: '[t]he characterization of an act of a State as internationally wrongful is governed by international law. Such characterization is not affected by the characterization of the same act as lawful by internal law'.

[27] Cf. the accreditation of delegates of Kuwait (1990), Afghanistan (1996–2001), Haiti (1992) and Sierra Leone (1997). For a discussion, cf. J. d'Aspremont, 'Duality of Government in Côte d'Ivoire', *EJIL:Talk!*, 4 January 2011. Cf. also J. d'Aspremont, 'Legitimacy of Governments in the Age of Democracy', op. cit., p. 905, and M. Griffin, 'Accrediting Democracies: Does the Credentials Committee of the United Nations Promote Democracy through its Accreditation Process, and Should it?', *NYU J. Int'l & Pol.*, 32, 1999–2000, pp. 725–85, arguing that, while the UNGA Credentials Committee starts to take democracy into account, there is no general rule in this regard (which, in any event, would be inadvisable for Griffin).

[28] For Vidmar, 'it appears that an extra-constitutional regime change in international law is generally – at least – tolerated; except where the overthrown government enjoys democratic legitimacy' (J. Vidmar, 'Democracy and Regime Change in the Post-Cold War International Law', op. cit., p. 380. See also the concept of 'democratic coup d'état': O. O. Varol, 'The Democratic Coup d'Etat', *Harvard International Law Journal*, Vol. 53, no. 2, 2012. For others, 'contemporary practice weathers an incremental de-emphasising of the democratic origin of governments'. J. d'Aspremont, '1989-2010: The Rise and Fall of Democratic Governance in International Law', in J. Crawford (ed.), *Select Proceedings of the European Society of International Law*, Hart Publishing, 2011, p. 8.

[29] J. Salmon, 'Le droit international à l'épreuve au tournant du XXI siècle', op. cit., p. 93.

[30] Declarations of independence, too, are legally neutral under international law. Accordance with International Law of the Unilateral Declaration of Independence in Respect of Kosovo, Advisory Opinion, ICJ Reports 2010, p. 403. See, however, J. Vidmar,

ORIGIN OR CONTEXT: NON-CONSTITUTIONALITY 91

In the absence of a clear, let alone consistently implemented, international legal framework, it is little surprising that international reactions to domestic non-constitutionality are often incoherent, save exceptions (for example with regard to Burkina Faso in 2014).[31] Occasionally, the UNSC condemns non-constitutionality.[32] It sometimes rejects non-constitutional transitions,[33] and may observe that they present a threat to international peace and security.[34] On other occasions, though, it (indirectly) approves of a non-constitutional transition by endorsing a TA. It thus turned a blind eye on unconstitutional transitions (for example the Libyan transition triggered in 2011), especially where a government allegedly breaching international law was incapacitated.

2.2 Non-Constitutionality under Regional Frameworks: Incoherent Implementation

On the regional level, a number of provisions directly apply to domestic non-constitutionality. The most elaborate such provisions are part of the African regional legal framework as developed after the decolonisation process.[35] During decolonisation, the OAU often supported non-constitutional transitions as a means of realising self-determination.[36] After decolonisation, support to non-constitutional transitions became increasingly banned. In 1999, the AU Assembly of Heads of State decided

'Conceptualizing Declarations of Independence in International Law', *Oxford Journal of Legal Studies*, Vol. 32, no. 1, 2012.

[31] In the case of Burkina Faso, the AU, ECOWAS and the UN seemed to agree about how to react vis-à-vis a non-constitutional transition, as their joint declaration of 2 November 2014 indicates. AU, ECOWAS, UN joint declaration of 2 November 2014.

[32] The UNSC has only seldom labelled the unseating of the constitutionally elected government as a threat to international peace and subsequently approved the use of military force to restore constitutionally elected leaders. UNSC/RES/940 of 31 July 1994. UNSC Statement by the Pres. of the UNSC of 26 February 1998. On the other hand, the UNSC 'regularly invokes Chapter VII to condemn coups against democratically elected regimes'. Cf. G. H. Fox, 'Regime Change', MPEPIL. But the UNSC 'has not responded to the vast majority of cases of regime change in the post-war era' (Id.), and in any event non-constitutional foundational moments do not directly impact the legality of TG practices.

[33] In 2002 the USNC 'expresse[d] its strong support to the decisions of the OAU Heads of State and Government at the Algiers Summit held in 1999 denying recognition to Governments that come to power through unconstitutional means'. S/PRST/2002/2 of 31 January 2002, p. 2.

[34] Cf. for instance UNSC resolutions with regard to Haiti and Rhodesia.

[35] Cf. also M. Olivier, 'The Emergence of a Right to Democracy – An African Perspective', in C. Panara, G. Wilson (eds.), *The Arab Spring, New Patterns for Democracy and International Law*, op. cit.

[36] UNGA/RES/1514 (XV), known as the 'Charter of decolonisation'. Cf. also UNGA/RES/ 3280 (XXIX).

92 THE FOUNDATION OF TRANSITIONAL GOVERNANCE

that 'member States whose Governments came to power through unconstitutional means . . . should restore constitutional legality'.[37]

Since its 2000 Constitutive Act, the AU has confirmed the principle that unconstitutional changes of governments shall be condemned, and that unconstitutional governments shall be rejected from the Union's activities.[38] In the same period, the so-called Lomé Declaration[39] elaborated a definition of unconstitutional change of government, as follows:

1) military coup d'état against a democratically elected Government;
2) intervention by mercenaries to replace a democratically elected Government;
3) replacement of democratically elected Governments by armed dissident groups and rebel movements;
4) the refusal by an incumbent government to relinquish power to the winning party after free, fair and regular elections.

The 2007 Governance Charter declared that the adherence to the rule of law is 'premised upon the respect for, and the supremacy of, the Constitution and constitutional order in the political arrangements of the State Parties'.[40] It promoted the 'total rejection of unconstitutional changes of government' into a fundamental principle.[41]

In other regions, the 2001 Inter-American Democratic Charter and the 2011 South Asian Association for Regional Cooperation Charter of Democracy contain provisions on unconstitutional changes of government. These instruments provide that unconstitutional changes of government should be followed by a condemnation and suspension of membership.[42]

In contrast, EU treaties do not contain provisions specifically relating to unconstitutional changes of government. Yet, under the Treaty on the European Union ('TEU'), the EU Council can, under certain conditions,

---

[37] Decision 142 (XXXV) of 12–14 July 1999.

[38] AU Constitutive Act of 11 July 2000, artt. 4 and 30.

[39] Lomé Declaration of 12 July 2000 on the Framework for an OAU Response to Unconstitutional Changes in Government.

[40] African Charter of 30 January 2007 on Democracy, Elections and Governance ('Governance Charter'), Chapter 2, art. 2.2.

[41] Id., Chapter 3, art. 3.10.

[42] AU Constitutive Act, artt. 4 and 30; Inter-American Democratic Charter, art. 20; South Asian Association for Regional Cooperation Charter of Democracy, seventh commitment. With regard to the AU, cf. also 2007 Governance Charter and the Lomé Framework for an OAU Response to Unconstitutional Changes in Government ('Lomé Declaration').

'determine that there is a clear risk of a serious breach'[43] of the values of democracy and the rule of law.[44] The Commission has proposed that the Council proceed as such vis-à-vis Poland in December 2017, after new Polish law had lowered the retirement age of Supreme Court judges.[45] This proposal followed a fierce debate about which legal arsenal could be activated to combat (the formally constitutional) 'unconstitutional constitutional amendments' and 'authoritarian backsliding' in this country as well as in Hungary. These situations do not concern *formal domestic* non-constitutionality; the European Commission, and later the EU Court of Justice, based its reasoning on violations of EU law instead.[46] One can imagine though that the relevant TEU provisions may also be invoked when EU law and constitutional law are simultaneously being violated.

In theory, thus, the policy of non-interference with regard to non-constitutionality is making place for a policy of non-indifference, in various regions of the world.[47] This evolution however encounters two hurdles. First, where regional provisions rejecting and condemning unconstitutional changes of government are available, they do not foresee *how* the constitutional order must be restored, and how the period between the unconstitutional change of government and return to constitutionality (including, as the case may be, the interim constitution-making process) must be bridged.[48] They also remain silent about non-constitutional changes of government that are *praeter constitutionem* without being unconstitutional.

Second, the policy of non-indifference with regard to non-constitutionality has been inconsistently applied, including under the

---

[43] TEU, art. 7.

[44] Id., art. 2.

[45] 'Rule of Law: European Commission acts to defend judicial independence in Poland', European Commission Press Release, 20 December 2017.

[46] 'Rule of Law: European Commission refers Poland to the European Court of Justice to protect the independence of the Polish Supreme Court', European Commission Press Release, 24 December 2018. EU Court of Justice (Grand Chamber), Judgment of 21 June 2019 (C-619/18). (See also M. Wiebusch, 'The Role of Regional Organizations in the Protection of Constitutionalism', IDEA Discussion Paper 17/2016, p. 30.

[47] J. d'Aspremont, 'Coups d'Etat in International Law', Tulane J. of Int'l & Comp. Law, Vol. 18, 2009–10, p. 463: 'there are quite a number of international organisations that sanction the overthrow of a government, particularly when the latter benefits from some democratic legitimacy'.

[48] For policy guidelines on how to return to constitutional order, see M. Wiebusch, 'The Role of Regional Organizations in the Protection of Constitutionalism', op. cit.

AU framework.[49] The Arab Spring, for instance, exposed 'the limitations of the union's current conceptualisation of unconstitutional changes in government'.[50] Regional organisations have also been inconsistent in relation to transitions in Guinea-Bissau[51] and Burundi.[52] This observation can be extended to regional frameworks in other continents as well, in light of the equivocal reactions to the 2017 Venezuelan constitutional crisis[53] or the large absence of reactions following the 2013–14 political crisis and coup d'état in Thailand, for instance.[54]

*

Literature has much focused on the evolution from non-interference to non-indifference vis-à-vis non-constitutional acts or instruments. Yet, if non-indifference there is, it is sporadic because based on a couple of poorly implemented regional frameworks. In any event, rather than pausing on non-constitutional moments, this study deals with TG *resulting from or following* such moments. This 'irrelevance of origin' complements the 'irrelevance of outcome' already discussed.[55] As neither

---

[49] Z. Yihdego, 'The African Union: Founding Principles, Frameworks and Prospects', *European Law Journal*, Vol. 17, no. 5, September 2011, pp. 568–94. U. Engel, 'Unconstitutional Changes of Government – New AU Policies in Defence of Democracy', Working Paper Series, 2010, No. 9.

[50] G. M. Wachira, 'The Role of the African Union in Strengthening the Rule of Law and Constitutional Order in Africa' in IDEA, *Rule of Law and Constitution Building, The Role of Regional Organisations*, 2014, p. 22.

[51] The reactions to the creation of the transitional government in Guinea-Bissau evidence this inconclusiveness. This government was recognised by ECOWAS, which deployed a mission (ECOMIB) in the country. But it was not recognised by the Community of Portuguese-Language countries (CPLP), or by the EU. The AU and the *Organisation internationale de la Francophonie* suspended Guinea-Bissau. In its resolution of 18 May 2012, the UNSC had condemned the coup and had called for a restoration of the constitutional order. It had specifically requested the UNSG 'to *harmonize* the respective positions of international bilateral and multilateral partners, particularly the AU, ECOWAS, the CPLP and the EU, and ensure maximum coordination and complementarity of international efforts' (S/RES/2048 of 18 May 2012, § 3), but to no avail. Own emphasis.

[52] In Burundi, the hinge on power by President Nkurunziza was generally regarded as non-constitutional. Here, too, reactions have been mixed. The *Organisation internationale de la Francophonie* has suspended Burundi while the AU has refused to do so or to condemn Nkurunziza's third term in power.

[53] 'OAS nations wind up empty handed on Venezuela condemnation', *Reuters*, 21 June 2017 – whereas MERCOSUR condemned the country. In January 2019, the OAS Permanent Council agreed 'to not recognize the legitimacy of Nicolas Maduro's new term' (Resolution on the situation in Venezuela, 10 January 2019).

[54] 'Why ASEAN has not condemned Thailand', *Japan Times*, 7 August 2014.

[55] Chapter 2, Section B.2.2.

international law nor regional frameworks are informative about the non-constitutional context forming the breeding ground for TG, such contexts are not examined in detail. Instead, the following section analyses how TI purport to remedy the (initial) non-constitutionality by (partly) supplanting the previous constitutional order and laying the foundations for the order to come.

B   Supraconstitutionality and Transformative Constitutionalism

This section concerns the common function and purpose of instruments laying the foundation of, and regulating, TG. It observes that constituent TI have a supraconstitutional function (1) and pursue the larger purpose of transformative constitutionalism (2).

1   The Function of Transition Instruments: Supraconstitutionality

Non-constitutionality hinges on supraconstitutionality, that is the claim that, at the time of its entry into force and until a new constitution is adopted, the TI is at least partly superior both to the previous and future constitution.[56] Through such two-dimensional provisional supraconstitutionality, TI alter the existing constitution, and then aim either at (progressively) replacing the old constitutional order by another, or, more rarely, at partly restoring an older constitutional order in a non-constitutional way (the TI is then *praeter constitutionem*).

TI can be subdivided into three categories. They are either international agreements, intrastate agreements or interim constitutions/unilateral proclamations. This sequence seems to indicate that the international legal *nature* of TI decreases in this list from one category to the other. This is not entirely false, yet we shall see that the function and even international legal *relevance* (rather than legal force) of TI for the progressive development of *ius in interregno* does not entirely depend on their nature.

Table 3.2 of TI reveals their variety. It also shows that, independently of their legal nature, they fulfil a supraconstitutional function by (partly) overriding the existing constitutional order.

---

[56] This definition of supraconstitutionality is broader than what Bell and Forster describe as the 'supra-constitutional arrangements involv[ing] peace agreements that sweep away and displace the existing constitutional order without formally amending it'. See their contribution in E. De Groof, M. Wiebusch (eds.), *International Law and Transitional Governance: Critical Perspectives*, op. cit., p. 33.

96 THE FOUNDATION OF TRANSITIONAL GOVERNANCE

Table 3.2 *Legal nature of supraconstitutional transition instruments*

Transitions	Supraconstitutional provisions/decisions	Legal nature
Afghanistan	Bonn Agreement, Section V.5[57]	Intrastate agreement
Burkina Faso	Charte de la transition, artt. 2, 25[58]	Domestic legislation or act

[57] The Bonn Agreement provides that 'until the adoption of the new Constitution' the Constitution of 1964 shall be applicable (Section V.5) but only 'to the extent that its provisions are not inconsistent with those contained in this agreement' (Bonn Agreement, II.1.i). At the same time, this agreement provides how and according to which timetable the next constitution is to be adopted (Bonn Agreement, I.6). Its supraconstitutionality thus concerns both the past and the future. In spite of the Bonn Agreement being an intrastate agreement, the UNSC has 'reiterat[ed] its endorsement . . ., in particular its annex 2 regarding the role of the United Nations during the interim period' (S/RES/1401 (2002). Annex 2 is about the UN advising the Interim Authority during the interim period, confirming that this intrastate agreement was internationally endorsed and monitored, notably by the UNSC. For a discussion of the legal nature of the Bonn Agreement, cf. T. Marauhn, 'Konfliktbewältigung in Afghanistan zwischen Utopie und Pragmatismus', op. cit., pp. 480–511. See also M. Schoiswohl, for whom this agreement 'escapes traditional distinctions between domestic agreements and international treaties', and notes that, in any event, it was endorsed in a UNSC resolution (S/RES/1383 of 6 December 2011). Cf. M. Schoiswohl, 'Linking the International Legal Framework to Building the Formal Foundations of a State at Risk: Constitution-Making and International Law in Post-Conflict Afghanistan', op. cit., pp. 828 a.f.

[58] The *Charte de la Transition* of 13 November 2014 refers to the 1991 constitution in its preamble, on which it is based, but also provides that it 'completes' this constitution (Charte de la Transition of 13 November 2014, Preamble), and is superior to it. Also, art. 2 of the Charte de la Transition provides that the President can exercise its powers according to the provisions of the 1991 constitution except for those that are incompatible with this charter: '[l]e Président de la transition occupe les fonctions de Président du Faso et de Chef de l'Etat. Il veille au respect de la Constitution et de la Charte de la transition. Ses pouvoirs et prérogatives sont ceux définis par la présente Charte et au Titre III de la Constitution du 2 juin 1991 *à l'exception de ceux incompatibles avec la conduite de la transition*". Own emphasis and translation: 'the President of the transition holds the office of President of Burkina Faso and Head of State. He ensures the respect of the Constitution and of the Charter of the transition. His powers and prerogatives are those defined by this Charter and by Title III of the Constitution of June 2, 1991 *with the exception of those incompatible with the conduct of the transition*'. Cf. also art. 14. The claim of supraconstitutionality, here too, is clear.

Table 3.2 (*cont.*)

Transitions	Supraconstitutional provisions/decisions	Legal nature
Burundi	Arusha Agreement, art. 5.5; art. 15.2[59]	Intrastate agreement
Cambodia	Paris Accords, art. 23[60]	Int'l agreement[61]

[59] The Arusha Agreement provides that constitutional provisions were to be adopted 'pursuant to the provisions of Protocol II to the Agreement' (Protocol I, Ch. II, art. 5.5). This agreement, too, has supraconstitutional value. It furthermore provides: 'the constitutional provisions governing the powers, duties and functioning of the transitional Executive, the transitional Legislature and the Judiciary, as well as the rights and duties of citizens and of political parties and associations, shall be as set forth hereunder and, *where this text is silent*, in the Constitution of the Republic of Burundi of 13 March 1992. When there is any conflict between that Constitution and the Agreement, the *provisions of the Agreement shall prevail*' (Protocol II, Ch. II, art. 15.2). Own emphasis. On a third occasion, the Arusha Agreement affirms its supraconstitutional nature by providing that '[t]he transitional National Assembly shall as a priority review all legislation in force with a view to amending or repealing legislation incompatible with the objectives of the transitional arrangements and the provisions of the present Protocol' (art. 16.2). Given its supraconstitutional nature 'the Arusha Agreement clearly shaped the framework for the continued mediation of the conflict and in the end decisively shaped Burundi's current Constitution of 18 March 2005', Vandeginste remarks (S. Vandeginste, 'Power-Sharing, Conflict and Transition in Burundi: Twenty Years of Trial and Error', *Africa Spectrum*, 44, no. 3, January 1, 2009, p. 72). Even after completion of the transition this agreement continued to bear upon domestic politics. Cf. for example Chair's Summary of the Informal meeting of the Burundi Specific Configuration of the PBC, New York, 12 March 2014. After the political crisis which started in 2015, especially the opposition continued to invoke 'the spirit' of the Arusha Agreement.

[60] The Paris Accords are explicitly supraconstitutional. Article 23 provides that Cambodia 'will incorporate [...] [b]asic principles, including those regarding human rights and fundamental freedoms as well as regarding Cambodia's status of neutrality'. The rights and freedoms to be incorporated into the Cambodian legal order are further detailed in the fifth annex to this treaty. The provisions concerning the constitution to be adopted require that the basic principles must be incorporated into the new Cambodian Constitution. The supraconstitutionality of the Paris Agreement not only concerns the future but also relates to the past constitutional order, as this agreement (at least implicitly) departs from the 1976 Khmer Rouge Constitution of Democratic Kampuchea.

[61] The 1991 Paris Accords, signed by various sovereigns, is an international treaty in the sense of the VCLT.

98   THE FOUNDATION OF TRANSITIONAL GOVERNANCE

Table 3.2 (*cont.*)

Transitions	Supraconstitutional provisions/decisions	Legal nature
Central African Republic	Déclaration de N'Djamena, art. 4, art. 8[62]	Domestic legislation or act
Comoros	Accord-Cadre de Réconciliation Nationale, artt. 4, 9.i, 11.ii, 17, 18, 29[63]	Intrastate agreement
Côte d'Ivoire	Linas-Marcoussis Agreement, art. 3.a, IX[64]	Intrastate agreement

[62] The *Déclaration de N'Djamena* provides that a constitutional referendum is to take place (art. 4), and that a 'Conseil national de Transition' is to prepare a draft constitution: 'l'urgente mission du Conseil National de Transition est d'élaborer et *d'adopter une Charte constitutionnelle* de la transition organisant l'ensemble des pouvoirs publics de la transition *conformément à l'Accord de Libreville, à la Déclaration de N'Djamena . . .*' (art. 8). Own emphasis and translation: 'the urgent mission of the National Transitional Council is to elaborate and adopt a Constitutional Charter of the Transition organising all the public authorities of the transition in accordance with the Libreville Agreement, the Declaration of N'Djamena'. The Preamble of the *Charte constitutionnelle* of 18 juillet 2013 explicitly refers to the Déclaration de N'Djamena.

[63] The *Accord-Cadre de Réconciliation Nationale* of 17 February 2001 regulates the procedure for organising a constitutional referendum and for adopting the coming constitution in Comoros (Accord-Cadre de Réconciliation Nationale, artt. 4, 9.i, 11.ii, 17, 18). Its article 29 states: 'toutes dispositions contraires aux dispositions du présent Accord sont nulles et non avenues'. Own translation : 'any provisions contrary to the provisions of this Agreement are null and void'.

[64] The 2003 Linas-Marcoussis Agreement provides that a 'Government of National Reconciliation [will] be set up immediately after the conclusion of the Paris Conference to ensure a return to peace and stability [which] will implement the appended Round Table program which includes, in particular, provisions in the *constitutional*, legislative and regulatory sphere' (art. 3.a. Own emphasis). The same agreement also provides that 'the Government of National Reconciliation will ensure that the *constitutional,* legislative and regulatory reforms arising from the decisions it is required to make are introduced without delay' (Id., IX), leaving no doubt as to the obligatory nature of this supraconstitutional provision. Own emphasis. The UNSC confirms this when deciding that 'no Ivorian party should invoke *any* legal provision to impede the peace process' (S/RES/1721 of 1 November 2006, Preamble and § 4. Own emphasis). This indicates that the UNSC deemed the Linas-Marcoussis agreement to be superior to all Ivorian laws, even of constitutional nature. In spite of the UNSC's exhortations, the Linas-Marcoussis peace process failed, which resulted in a second (leg of the) transition. Concluded on

Table 3.2 (cont.)

Transitions	Supraconstitutional provisions/decisions	Legal nature
DRC	Pretoria Agreement, VII.a[65]	International agreement
	The 2002 Draft Constitution of the Transition[66]	Domestic legislation or act
Guinea	Déclaration conjointe de Ouagadougou of 15 January 2010, artt. 1–12[67]	Domestic legislation or act

4 March 2007, the Preamble of the 'Ouagadougou Political Agreement' referred back to the Linas-Marcoussis Agreement. This agreement is arguably an internationalised intrastate agreement. The 'Round Table of the Ivorian political forces' consisted of domestic actors (Linas-Marcoussis Agreement, art. 1). But the Conference of Heads of State on Côte d'Ivoire of 25 and 26 January 2003, consisting of the EU member states, about eighteen other states, and representatives of the Organisation de la Francophonie, UNDP, WB, IMF, ADB, UNHCR and ICRC, among other actors, explicitly 'endorsed' this agreement. Annex II to S/2003/99 of 27 January 2003, § 6.

[65] The Pretoria Agreement provides that 'the transitional *constitution* shall be drafted *on the basis of this inclusive Agreement* on transition in the DRC and shall form an integral part thereof' (Pretoria Agreement, VII.a. Own emphasis). Mangu observes that 'both instruments were the only source of Power during the transition'. A. M. B. Mangu, 'The Conflict in the Democratic Republic of Congo and the Protection of Rights under the African Charter', *AHRLJ*, Vol. 3, no. 2, 2003, pp. 253. Own emphasis. It is not clear to which instrument Mangu is referring here (the interim constitution, the Pretoria agreement, or another legal instrument). Both the 2006 Constitution (Constitution de la République du Congo, February 2006) and the 2002 'Draft Constitution of the Transition' refer in their respective preambles to the Pretoria Agreement. The latter instrument recognises, in its first article, that the Constitution of the transition of the DRC was drawn up based on the Pretoria Agreement.

[66] The 2002 'Draft Constitution of the Transition' provides that 'all previous *constitutional provisions*, in particular Statutory Order No. 03 of May 27th 1997 pertaining to the exercise of power as modified to date, are *repealed and replaced* by this Transitional Constitution of the Democratic Republic of Congo' (2002 Draft Constitution of the Transition, art. 202. Own emphasis).

[67] The *Déclaration conjointe de Ouagadougou* of 15 January 2010 enumerates a number of measures to be taken in order to ensure a return to constitutional order. Eventually, this declaration would pave the way for the promulgation of the constitution on 7 May 2010, which in its Preamble explicitly refers to it (Constitution of 7 May 2010).

100 THE FOUNDATION OF TRANSITIONAL GOVERNANCE

Table 3.2 (cont.)

Transitions	Supraconstitutional provisions/decisions	Legal nature
Guinea-Bissau	Pacto de Transição Política of 16 May 2012, art. 5.1. See also Final communiqué of the Extraordinary summit of ECOWAS heads of state and government, Dakar, 3 May 2012, § 21[68]	Domestic legislation or act
Iraq	Law of Administration for the State of Iraq for the Transitional Period, artt. 2B, 3, 26, 58B, 59, 60, 61[69]	Domestic legislation or act
Kyrgyzstan	Provisional Government Decree No 19, 20 (April 2010)[70]	Domestic legislation or act

[68] The 'Final communiqué' of 3 May 2012 of the 'Extraordinary summit of ECOWAS heads of state and government' held in Dakar, ECOWAS 'confirm[ed] its previous decision to establish a twelve-month transition, during which *the following measures shall be taken* with the assistance of ECOWAS: a review of legal texts (*constitution*, electoral code, etc.) to achieve greater efficiency' ('Final communiqué' of the Extraordinary summit of ECOWAS heads of state and government, Dakar, 3 May 2012, § 21). Own emphasis.

[69] The 'Law of Administration for the State of Iraq for the Transitional Period' includes several supraconstitutional provisions. It states that it is 'the Supreme Law of the land' (art. 3.A), and that 'any legal provision that conflicts with this Law is null and void' (art. 3.B). It regulates when and how (artt. 2.B, 59, 60, 61), and in light of which standards (art. 58b), the permanent constitution should be drafted.

[70] After the April 2010 popular uprisings, a draft constitution was adopted on 26 April 2010 (Club de Madrid, Political Leadership for Democratic Transition in the Kyrgyz Republic; 'New Kyrgyz Constitution Strong on Promises, Vague on Checks and Balances', Eurasianet, 4 May 2010). After the referendum of 27 June 2010, this draft (for 90 per cent based on the Venice Commission's proposals – cf. 'How Strong Is Kyrgyzstan's New Constitution?', Radio Free Europe, 2 July 2010) was adopted. About the distinctions between the 2010 and the 2007 constitutions, see the Venice Commission's Opinion on the draft constitution of the Kyrgyz Republic, adopted on 4 June 2010. The transitional period was extremely short, and the texts regulating the transition are not easily accessible. According to the OSCE, 'the legal framework for the referendum derives from various decrees adopted by the provisional government, which, according to a decree, *supersede other constitutional laws*'; 'Decrees No 19 and 20 stipulate that constitutional laws should guide the administration of the referendum unless they contradict the decrees; in such cases the *decrees supersede constitutional laws*'. OSCE Office for Democratic Institutions and Human Rights Referendum Observation Mission, Constitutional Referendum Kyrgyz Republic 2010, Interim report, 21 May–13 June 2010, 17 June 2010. Own emphasis.

TRANSFORMATIVE SUPRACONSTITUTIONALITY 101

Table 3.2 (*cont.*)

Transitions	Supraconstitutional provisions/decisions	Legal nature
Liberia	2003 Accra Comprehensive Peace Agreement, art. 35[71]	Intrastate agreement
Libya	Draft Constitutional Charter For the Transitional Stage, artt. 34, 35[72]	Domestic legislation or act
Mali	2012 Accord Cadre de mise en œuvre de l'engagement solennel, art. 5; 2015 Agreement for peace and reconciliation in Mali, Annex 1.[73]	Intrastate agreement

[71] The 2003 Accra Agreement 'prescribed extralegal rules and processes for sharing power that *abrogated constitutionally based superior rules*'. J. I. Levitt, *Illegal Peace in Africa*, op. cit., p. 86. This agreement indeed provides that there is a 'need for an *extra-Constitutional arrangement* that will facilitate its formation and take into account the establishment and proper functioning of the entire transitional arrangement' (Accra Agreement, Part 10 'Implementation of the Peace Agreement', art. XXXV.1a). Again, the supraconstitutional function of this agreement also relates to the past: 'the provisions of the present Constitution of the Republic of Liberia, the Statutes and all other Liberian laws, which relate to the establishment, composition and powers of the Executive, the Legislative and Judicial branches of the Government, are hereby *suspended*. [c] For the avoidance of doubt, relevant provisions of the Constitution, statutes and other laws of Liberia which are inconsistent with the provisions of this Agreement are also hereby *suspended*. [d] All other provisions of the 1986 Constitution of the Republic of Liberia shall remain in force' (art. XXXV, b–d). Own emphasis.

[72] The 'Draft Constitutional Charter for the Transitional Stage' provides that 'the constitutional documents and laws which were applicable before applying this Declaration shall be repealed' (Draft Constitutional Charter for the Transitional Stage, art. 34; see also art. 35: '[a]ll the provisions prescribed in the existing legislations shall continue to be effective in so far as they are not inconsistent with the provisions hereof until they are amended or repealed'). This TI also defines when and how, and in light of which standards, the permanent constitution should be drafted (Draft Constitutional Charter For the Transitional Stage, artt. 1–16; 31–3).

[73] The restoration of the (existing) constitutional order was the aim of the 'Accord Cadre de mise en oeuvre de l'engagement solennel' of 1 April 2012. At the same time, this agreement indicates that, given the exceptional circumstances, it is impossible to follow the constitution (i.e. to organise elections within forty days), and necessary to establish transitional institutions (*Accord Cadre de mise en oeuvre de l'engagement solennel*, artt. 5 and 6). It is in this sense that the Malian TI, even if it intends to restore the constitutional order, has supraconstitutional value (without being unconstitutional).

102 THE FOUNDATION OF TRANSITIONAL GOVERNANCE

Table 3.2 (*cont.*)

Transitions	Supraconstitutional provisions/decisions	Legal nature
Nepal	Interim Constitution of Nepal, 2063 (2007), artt.1, 167, schedules 2, 3 (with reference to Comprehensive Peace Agreement of 22 November 2006)[74]	Domestic legislation or act Intrastate agreement[75]
Rwanda	Peace Agreement between the Government of the Republic of Rwanda and the Rwandese Patriotic Front of 4 August 1993, artt. 3.1 and 3.2[76]	Intrastate agreement

[74] The Interim Constitution 2063 provides in its first article that 'all laws inconsistent with this constitution shall, to the extent of such inconsistency, be void'. Art. 167 provides that 'the Constitution of the Kingdom of Nepal, 2047 (1990) has hereby been terminated'. Part VII provides how the constituent assembly is to be formed, when it is to meet, and how it must pass bills relating to the constitution (art. 63 a.f.).

[75] The 'Decisions of the Summit Meeting of the Seven-Party Alliance and the Communist Party of Nepal (Maoist)' of 8 November 2006 briefly provides the procedure by which the interim constitution and new constitutional council are to be promulgated. 'Decisions of the Summit Meeting of the Seven-Party Alliance and the Communist Party of Nepal (Maoist)', artt. III.1 and VI resp. III.6 and III.9. It also contains provisions about the future 'structure of the state' (art. III.10) and its 'socio-economic transformation' (art. III.11). The 'Comprehensive Peace Agreement between the Government of Nepal and the Communist Party of Nepal', an intrastate agreement concluded on 22 November 2006, contains several provisions on the interim constitution and transition institutions. It was integrated into the Interim Constitution of Nepal, 2063 (2007) (see Schedule 3). This interim constitution provides that the final constitution – which came into force on 20 September 2015 – shall be promulgated in accordance with the peace agreement just mentioned (see Schedule 2).

[76] The 'Protocol of Agreement on Power-Sharing within the Framework of a Broad-based Transitional Government between the Government of the Republic of Rwanda and the Rwandese Patriotic Front' of 9 January 1993 establishes a 'Legal and Constitutional Commission' that is to 'prepare a preliminary draft of the Constitution which shall govern the country after the Transitional Period' (art. 24.B.2). The 'Peace Agreement between the Government of the Republic of Rwanda and the Rwandese Patriotic Front' of 4 August 1993 provides that 'the Constitution of 10th June, 1991 and the Arusha Peace Agreement shall constitute indissolubly the Fundamental Law that shall govern the Country during the Transition period'. At the same time, this peace agreement replaces forty-seven articles of this constitution (art. 3.1), and provides that 'in case of conflict between the other provisions of the Constitution and those of the Peace Agreement, the provisions of the Peace Agreement shall prevail' (art. 3.2).

Table 3.2 (cont.)

Transitions	Supraconstitutional provisions/decisions	Legal nature
Sierra Leone	Lomé Agreement, art. X[77]	Intrastate agreement
Somalia	Somali Transitional Charter, artt. 3.2, 3.3, 71.9[78]	Domestic legislation or act/Intrastate agreement
South Africa	Art. 71 of the Interim Constitution[79]	Domestic legislation or act
Syria	Coalition's Principles nr. 4; basic principles for a political settlement to the Syrian conflict,	Domestic legislation or act

[77] The Lomé Agreement (which served as a template for the Accra Agreement) did not suspend the constitution, but provided that 'in order to *ensure* that the Constitution of Sierra Leone represents the needs and aspirations of the people of Sierra Leone and that *no constitutional or any other legal provision prevents the implementation of the present Agreement*, the Government of Sierra Leone shall take the necessary steps to establish a Constitutional Review Committee to review the provisions of the present Constitution' (art. X). Own emphasis. There is thus no doubt as to the supraconstitutional of the Lomé Agreement.

[78] The 'Transitional Federal Charter for the Somali Republic' of February 2004 also shows the features of double supra-constitutionality. Vis-à-vis the past, it provides that it 'shall be the supreme law binding all authorities and persons and shall have the force of law throughout the Somali Republic. If any law is inconsistent with this Charter the Charter shall prevail' (Somali Transitional Charter, art. 3.2), and that 'the validity, legality or procedure of enactment or promulgation of this Charter shall not be subject to challenge by or before any court or other State organ' (art. 3.3). Art. 71.2 of the same instrument provides: 'the 1960 Somalia Constitution and other national laws shall apply in respect of all matters not covered and not inconsistent with this Charter'. Towards the future, it provides that 'it shall be the basis for the federal constitution whose draft shall be completed within two and half years and be adopted by popular referendum during the final year of the transitional period' (art. 71.9).

[79] As a notable precursor of contemporary domestic TG, the South African interim constitution (art. 71) provided that the new constitutional text shall comply with a set of no less than thirty-four constitutional principles.

104 THE FOUNDATION OF TRANSITIONAL GOVERNANCE

Table 3.2 (cont.)

Transitions	Supraconstitutional provisions/decisions	Legal nature
	February 2015.[80] See call by the UNGA for a 'review of the constitution on the basis of an inclusive national dialogue'[81] and similar calls by the UNSC.[82]	
Sudan	2005 Sudan Comprehensive Peace Agreement[83] 2019 Political Agreement on establishing the structures	Intrastate agreements[84]

[80] 'Overthrowing the Assad regime' is part of the Mission Statement of this coalition (http://en .etilaf.org/about-us/goals.html last consulted on 25 March 2020). See also the 'Declaration by the National Coalition for Syrian and Opposition forces' outlining how a transition should be carried out (http://en.etilaf.org/coalition-documents/declaration-by-the-national-coalition-for-syrian-revolutionary-and-opposition-forces.html last consulted on 25 March 2020). This suggests that the principles claimed supra-constitutional value. If the transition were to unfold according to the Coalition's plan – *quod non* – one can imagine that said principles would be adopted in a new (interim) constitution; the same is true of the '13-item draft document of basic principles for a political settlement to the Syrian conflict' adopted by the Coalition's General Assembly on the occasion of its Istanbul meetings from 13 to 15 February 2015 (Communiqué of the 19th General Assembly meeting', 17 February 2015). This document provides that the purpose of resuming the political process is 'to institute a radical comprehensive change within the current political system from the top down'. Draft Document of Basic Principles for a Political Settlement in Syria, Principle 3, on file.

[81] A/RES/67/262 of 4 June 2013 § 25.

[82] S/RES/2254 of 18 December 2015 § 4.

[83] The 2005 Comprehensive Peace Agreement is, in the words of Dann and Al-Ali, an '*Überconstitution*'. P. Dann, Z. Al-Ali, 'The Internationalised Pouvoir Constituant', op. cit., p. 448: 'the negotiation and conclusion of the CPA was considerably influenced by external factors. And it was the CPA that determined the procedural and substantial framework for the constitution-making process' (p. 443). The authors re-emphasise that 'the process and substance of the constitution was almost entirely predetermined by the CPA. In fact, the domestic constitutional process only executed what had been agreed upon in the CPA . . .' (p. 447).

[84] Its (domestic) intrastate nature is contested. The 2005 'Comprehensive Peace Agreement Between the Government of the Sudan and the Sudan People's Liberation Movement/Sudan People's Liberation Army' arguably constitutes an international treaty: 'it is difficult to see the CPA solely as an agreement to be implemented at the national level. It is clearly an agreement with both a constitutional and international legal character'. S. P. Sheeran; 'International Law, Peace Agreements and Self-Determination: The Case of The Sudan', *International and Comparative Law Quarterly*, Vol. 60, no. 2, 2011, p. 439.

TRANSFORMATIVE SUPRACONSTITUTIONALITY

Table 3.2 (cont.)

Transitions	Supraconstitutional provisions/decisions	Legal nature
	and institutions of the transitional period, Chapter 2, § 8. Constitutional Charter for the 2019 Transitional Period, Chapter 1, § 1.	
Ukraine	Minsk Agreement of 12 February 2015, art. 11[85]	International agreement[86] Intrastate agreement[87]
Yemen	2011 GCC agreement, § 4[88]	Intrastate agreement

[85] At the time of writing, the implementation of the Second Minsk Agreement is still on hold (T. B. Peters, A. Shapkina, 'The Grand Stalemate of the Minsk Agreements', country report, Konrad Adenauer Stiftung, February 2019) while in December 2019 new mediation efforts are deployed. This agreement provided for the 'passing of a constitutional reform in Ukraine with the entry into force by the end of 2015 of a new constitution, which shall incorporate decentralization as a key element' (Minsk Agreement of 12 February 2015, art. 11), thus affirming the claim of supraconstitutionality. It was followed by a presidential decree whereby a constitutional commission was established (Presidential Decree number 119/2015 of 3 March 2015).

[86] The Second Minsk Agreement was brokered by France and Germany and concluded between Ukraine and Russia on 12 February 2015.

[87] The draft intrastate compromise agreement brokered by the Weimar Triangle (composed of Poland, Germany and France), and calling for the establishment of a national unity government and 'constitutional reform' (Agreement on the Settlement of Crisis in Ukraine, art. 2) failed. In February 2015, the Second Minsk Agreement was concluded to re-initiate the constitutional reform.

[88] The 'Agreement on the Implementation Mechanism for the Transition Process in Yemen' provides that 'the GCC Initiative and the Mechanism shall supersede any current constitutional or legal arrangements. They may not be challenged before the institutions of the State' (GCC Agreement, § 4). This agreement is also an 'internationalised intrastate agreement' since it clearly relies on the international community for its implementation. See artt. 28 and 29: '[i]n order to ensure the effective implementation of this Mechanism, the two parties call on the States members of the GCC and the United Nations Security Council to support its implementation. They further call on the States members of the GCC, the permanent members of the Security Council, the European Union and its States members to support the implementation of the GCC Initiative and the Mechanism'; '[t]he Secretary-General of the United Nations is called upon to provide continuous assistance, in cooperation with other agencies, for the implementation of this Agreement. He is also requested to coordinate assistance from the international community for the implementation of the GCC Initiative and the Mechanism'.

106 THE FOUNDATION OF TRANSITIONAL GOVERNANCE

Table 3.2 (*cont.*)

Transitions	Supraconstitutional provisions/decisions	Legal nature
	2015 Constitutional Declaration, art. 1[89]	Domestic legislation or act

This overview shows how TG can be based on (1) intrastate agreements, (2) domestic legislation or acts and (3) treaties. These three categories of supraconstitutional TI will be briefly introduced here whereas their relevance for unveiling nascent custom will be discussed later.[90]

a   Domestic Intrastate Agreements

In most cases, TG is regulated by supraconstitutional *domestic intrastate agreements*. Often such agreements contain various references to international law, and are endorsed by international mediators, other states and/or regional or global organisations. In addition, their implementation is frequently internationally monitored.[91] These three elements indicate that such agreements are particularly permeable to international (legal) influence,[92] and therefore are sometimes called 'internationalised intrastate agreements'. These are often peace agreements which include provisions on constitutional reform,[93] implying that 'provisions included as a result of international involvement at the negotiation stage will themselves achieve constitutional status, at least until such times as a longer, more participatory, constitutional process is complete'.[94]

---

[89] The 'Constitutional Declaration to organise the foundations of governance during the transitional period in Yemen' (Houthi Constitutional Declaration of 6 February 2015) adopted by the Houthi Revolutionary Committee provides, in its first article, that 'the provisions of the constitution in force shall continue to apply, *provided that they do not conflict with the provisions of the present Declaration*'. Own emphasis. Its fourteenth article provides: 'ordinary legislation shall remain in force unless it explicitly or implicitly contradicts texts of the present Declaration'.

[90] Chapter 5, Section B.

[91] Chapter 1, Section B. Table 1.1.

[92] Chapter 5, Section A.1.

[93] J. S. Easterday, 'Peace Agreements as a Framework for Ius Post Bellum' in C. Stahn et al. (eds.), *Jus Post Bellum: Mapping the Normative Foundations*, Oxford University Press, 2014, p. 379.

[94] C. Turner, R. Houghton, 'Constitution Making and Post-Conflict Reconstruction' in M. Saul, J. A. Sweeney (eds.), *International Law and Post-Conflict Reconstruction*, Routledge, 2015, p. 126.

Intrastate agreements regulating TG contain explicit supraconstitutional provisions. This is for example the case in Afghanistan, Burundi, Comoros, Côte d'Ivoire, Liberia, Mali, Nepal, Rwanda, Sierra Leone, Sudan, Ukraine and Yemen. The supraconstitutionality characterising intrastate agreements in these countries enable them to function as TI, that is to introduce TG and transform the existing constitutional order.

b   Domestic Transitional Instruments

In several cases, TG was regulated by supraconstitutional domestic TI such as interim constitutions, transitional declarations, communiqués, charters or laws.[95] Interim arrangements are then generally part of domestic law, even if they are part of, or annexed to, an international treaty (for example the 1991 Paris Agreement) or an internationalised intrastate agreement (for example the 2005 Sudan CPA and the 2019 Political Agreement on establishing the structures and institutions of the transitional period). Domestic laws applicable to TG have also be coined 'droits de transition'.[96]

An interim, transitional or temporary constitution can be defined as a constitution that 'limits its own term and lapses at its expiration date unless re-enacted through regular constitutional amendment procedures'.[97] This allows us to differentiate them from other, permanent, constitutions, which, in a different respect, have a transitional component too: 'any constitution that "lasts" must have a capacity to be "transitional" in allowing for contest over changing understandings and new circumstances'.[98] The distinguishing criterion is that so-called

---

[95] Burkina Faso, Central African Republic, DRC, Guinea, Guinea-Bissau, Iraq, Kyrgyzstan, Libya, Nepal, Somalia, South Africa, Syria and Yemen.

[96] *Ius in interregno* is not used in the sense of a 'droit de transition' as defined by X. Philippe, which refers to *domestic* legal rules applicable to transitions: '[l]e droit de transition peut se définir comme l'ensemble des règles juridiques qui sont adoptées ou confirmées dans un ordre politique et juridique en mutation et qui sont destinées à permettre au nouveau régime de s'instaurer dans la durée et la stabilité'. Own translation : 'the law on transitions can be defined as the set of legal rules that are adopted or confirmed in a changing political and legal order and that are intended to bring long-term stability to the new regime'. X. Philippe, 'La spécificité du droit de transition dans la construction des Etats démocratiques. L'exemple de l'Afrique du Sud', *Droit et Démocratie en Afrique du Sud*, l'Harmattan, 2001, p. 36. *Ius in interregno* rather refers to the set of international legal rules applicable to TG whereby these rules stem both from principles of international law and from emerging custom based on a broad comparison of recent 'droits de transition'.

[97] O. O. Varol, 'Temporary Constitutions', op. cit., p. 409.

[98] V. C. Jackson, 'What's in a Name?', op. cit., p. 1281.

108   THE FOUNDATION OF TRANSITIONAL GOVERNANCE

permanent constitutions do not announce their own termination or otherwise compromise their own existence.

In addition to interim constitutions, instruments like charters, (joint) declarations, communiqués or decrees may regulate transitions. In Burkina Faso, CAR, DRC, Guinea, Guinea-Bissau, Iraq, Kyrgyzstan, Libya, Nepal, Somalia, South Africa, Syria and Yemen, for example, domestic TI have regulated TG. A variety of documents serve as interim or transitional constitutions. Their supraconstitutionality is central to the function of TI: the initiation of an interregnum to transform the constitutional order. By virtue of their supraconstitutional provisions, the declarations, pre- or constitutional texts mentioned in the table above directly relate to TG.

c International Agreements

Occasionally, TG is regulated by supraconstitutional international agreements. A number of TI are enshrined in international agreements, for example the Paris Agreement (Cambodia), the Pretoria Agreement (DRC) and arguably the Minsk Agreement (Ukraine).

*

Since the end of the Cold War, the number of TI has increased exponentially if one considers all documents fulfiling a constitutional or state-power-modifying function in the context of TG.[99] Whether materialised in intrastate agreements, transitional constitutions or declarations, or treaties, the TI mentioned above fulfil a supraconstitutional function in a double sense. They (claim to) *supersede*, in whole or in part, the previous constitution and (claim to) *pre-define*, at least to some degree, the coming constitution.

As they claim to be superior not only to the previous constitution but also, at the time of their enactment, to the constitution ensuing from the transition, they can be considered, and have been called, '*Überconstitutions*';[100] in Section 2, I suggested a generic term less loaded: 'tertiary norms'. Just like every constitution has extra-legal origins,

---

[99] Interpeace, 'Constitution-Making for Peace', Interim constitutional Arrangements: 'It has been estimated that one third of all constitutional design processes from 1975 to 2003 involved interim documents. If the meaning of the word "document" extends beyond constitutions, then the number of interim arrangements would be even larger, as some of them are based on understandings, treaties, or peace arrangements that affect the way state power is to be exercised, but are not constitutions. Several terms can be used to refer to what we call here "interim arrangements": provisional, temporary, interim, and transitional constitutions.'

[100] P. Dann, Z. Al-Ali, 'The Internationalised Pouvoir Constituant', op. cit.

Überconstitutions claim to be supraconstitutional. Self-evidently, it would be more difficult to imagine the reconstitutionalisation of a state without supraconstitutionality. Such claim to supraconstitutionality must be borne in mind in the following chapter, when the sources and indicators of nascent custom are discussed, and in Part IV, when the legality of external support to TG will be discussed.

2 The Purpose of Transition Instruments: Transformative Constitutionalism

Whichever form they take, TI purport to serve three purposes, relating to the past, present and future, respectively: (1) resolving conflicts and creating the conditions for peace (peace through transition); (2) regulating the exercise of public powers *ad interim* (defining the interim rule) and (3) projecting and preparing the coming constitutional order (constitutional reconfiguration). These three functions are interrelated: the constitutional reconfiguration of the state is only one – albeit crucial – aspect of the interim rule,[101] which itself is observed to cope with a situation of crisis or armed conflict.

The first purpose – pacification – echoes the peace-through-transition paradigm. The conflict-resolution and peace-conducive function of TI led several states to consider that 'constitutional reform' is a *principle* underpinning post-conflict national reconciliation.[102] Becoming 'part of the process of conflict transformation',[103] interim constitutions, as one category of TI, are increasingly being used as 'instruments of peace-keeping and as efforts to reconstitute or transform their societies'[104] or, more broadly, as 'crisis management tools'.[105]

---

[101] Other aspects of the interim rule include economic reconstruction, demilitarisation and TJ.

[102] EU member states, Norway, Iceland and Turkey. S/PV.4903 (Resumption 1) of 26 January 2004 p. 4: '[t]he fifth principle is constitutional reform. In many cases, a new beginning will require the fundamental rewriting of an existing constitution or the elaboration of a new constitution'.

[103] V. Hart, 'Constitution-Making and the Transformation of Conflict', *Peace & Change*, Vol. 26, no. 2, 2001, p. 153. This is not entirely a new phenomenon. It seems that in Colombia, for example, constitutions from the nineteenth century served as peace pacts. Cf. also A. Tadjdini, 'The Constitutional Dimension of Peace' in C. M. Bailliet and K. M. Larsen (eds.), *Promoting Peace through International Law*, Oxford University Press, 2015, p. 395 a.f.

[104] V. C. Jackson, 'What's in a Name?', op. cit., p. 1255.

[105] IDEA, 'Constitutionbuilding after Conflict: External Support to a Sovereign process', op. cit.

110   THE FOUNDATION OF TRANSITIONAL GOVERNANCE

The second purpose – self-limitation – directly relates to the idea of self-constraint and self-regulation central to TG, symbolised by Ulysses' foresight in having his hands tied to avoid temptation by mellifluous Sirens:[106] 'abandoning the old constitutional framework raises the question of how to define the rules and institutions that guide the process of making the new constitution'.[107] This question must be extended to TG generally. In the realm of TG, self-regulation depends on clear limitations *ratione temporis* and *ratione materiae* to the interim rule, which will be detailed in Part III.

The third purpose of TI – reconstitutionalisation – is to reconfigure the constitution of states in transition. The depth of reconstitutionalisation depends on the supraconstitutional aspirations of TI. Inversely, depending on the degree to which reconstitutionalisation effectively materialises, will TI (retroactively) have had *constituent* or *constitutional* value.

Through reconstitutionalisation, the original non-constitutionality may thus be (progressively) cured by the transition a TI generates and regulates. The incremental return to, or restoration of, constitutional legality precisely hinges on TG. As tertiary supraconstitutional norms, TI may become domestically valid early on in the transition. This is often the case when they emanate from consensual and inclusive processes, and have not been externally imposed (for example the 2002 Pretoria Agreement for the DRC). A TI may also (in whole or in part) acquire domestic legal validity *ex post* when, in spite of its oppositional origin, it comes to effectively regulate the transition or part of it (e.g., but for some time only the 2011 Constitutional Declaration for Libya).[108] In such case, the supraconstitutional nature of a TI will be confirmed with certainty only once the subsequent regime has been installed following the successful completion of a transition. The *ex post* validation of an initially unconstitutional TI may then be seen as a form of acquiescence.[109]

---

[106] Introduction, Section A.2.

[107] G. Anderson and S. Choudhry, *Constitutional Transitions and Territorial Cleavages*, IDEA, 2015, p. 12.

[108] Since the adoption of the Political Agreement of 17 December 2015, the domestic validity of the 2011 Constitutional Declaration is under discussion. DRI, 'Ensuring a Smooth Transition to the New Constitutional Order: Transitional Provisions in the Libyan Draft Constitution and Political Agreement', op. cit. See also, DRI, 'Libya's Transition – The Constitutional Declaration: A Basis for Democracy?', Briefing Paper, December 2011.

[109] N. Sérgio Marques Antunes, 'Acquiescence', MPEPIL: the 'consent tacitly conveyed . . . unilaterally through silence or inaction, in circumstances such that a response expressing disagreement or objection . . . would be called for'. If a situation calls for some reaction

Together, the three functions of TI serve the larger purpose of transformative constitutionalism: 'while in ordinary times constitutions are conceived as fully forward-looking, in periods of radical change such constitutions are simultaneously backward- and forward-looking'.[110] In this study, *transformative constitutionalism* relates not only to constitutional documents *sensu stricto* but to all sorts of TI – such as peace agreements, unilateral declarations and laws – aiming at reconstitutionalising a country.

As both backward- and forward-looking instruments, TI form a 'historic bridge', to echo the 1993 South African Interim Constitution's postscript. In post-conflict settings, they fulfil a palliative (peace-building) and preventive (conflict prevention) function. In contrast to 'preservative constitutions', TI often emphasise '*disassociation* with rather than continuation of norms'.[111] In the context of a wholesale state transformation, however, disassociation can only occur incrementally. For such a transformation to be successful, there must be some *attachment* with former laws and institutions:

> Reconstructions often involve a two-step process: disentrenchment or rupture from the former regime followed by reconstitutionalism. The probability of successfully accomplishing both in one fell swoop is

within a reasonable period on the part of state authorities, and they do not do so, they are held to have acquiesced the situation. Cf. Case concerning the Temple of Preah Vihear (Cambodia v. Thailand), Merits, Judgment of 15 June 1962, ICJ Reports, 1962, p. 23. See also cf. S. Wheatly, 'The Security Council, Democratic Legitimacy and Regime Change in Iraq', *EJIL*, 17, 2006, p. 550. For the link between acquiescence and estoppel, cf. I. Sinclair, 'Estoppel and Acquiescence' in V. Lowe, M. Fitzmaurice (eds.), *Fifty Years of the International Court of Justice, Essays in Honor of Sir Robert Jennings*, Cambridge University Press, 1996, pp. 104–20. Acquiescence is only dealt with in passing in this book.

[110] R. Teitel, 'Transitional Jurisprudence: The Role of Law in Political Transformation', *Yale L.J.*, 106, 2009, p. 2015. Transitional constitutionalism is a feature of transitions *sensu lato* such as the Southern European (post-Franco Constitution of 1978; Portuguese constitutions 1976) and Southern American transitions (1988 Brazilian Constitution, Chile's 1991 Constitution, 1990 Colombian referendum). In these cases, transitional constitutionalism was used to 'broker out' of authoritarian rule. Teitel also refers to West Germany's Basic Law of 1949 and Japan's post-war constitution of 1946 as instances of victor's (transitional) constitution-making; as well as to constitutions in post-Communist countries resulting from the 1989 revolutions.

[111] J. Mendez, 'Constitutionalism and Transitional Justice' in M. Rosenfeld and A. Sajó (eds.), *The Oxford Handbook of Comparative Constitutional Law*, Oxford University Press, 2012. p. 1282: '[t]ransformative constitutions are founded upon a need to break with the past, and form a thick line between what was, and what will be. This stands in contrast to constitutions that, as Sunstein emphasises, are more preservative of tradition ["preservative constitutions"]; for transformative constitutions, the point is disassociation with rather than continuation of norms'.

low. ... it may often be necessary to temporarily *preserve* governance structures from the former regime as new institutions are formed during reconstitutionalism constitution-making process.[112]

Constitutional association and disassociation characterise both oppositional and consensual forms of TG. The emphasis on disassociation is naturally stronger though in the context of oppositional TG, which usually results from unilateral constitution-making. Unilateral (transitional) constitution-making 'reflects the somewhat paradoxical nature of the revolutionary concept of constitution-making. It is an act of politics, ultimately *unrestricted* by the old legal order, but it creates a new normative order, binding new actors'.[113] Yet, as shall be argued below,[114] oppositional transitions also respect some degree of continuity, especially in relation to international legal obligations. Inversely, disassociation is also featured, if to a lesser degree, in consensual TG, partly detached itself from the previous order through supraconstitutional instruments.

TI of all sorts and shapes echo the demands of constitutional association and disassociation. Thus, peace processes and agreements may also honour the purposes of transformative constitutionalism, or be closely associated to it.[115] Depending on their object and purpose, declarations or bills, too, may fulfil constitutional functions. The Libyan Constitutional Declaration of August 2011, for instance, contributed to transforming the Libyan legal order. The Law of Administration for the State of Iraq for the Transitional Period' of 8 March 2004 ('TAL') also 'functioned as something of an interim constitution'.[116] This is not to *nominally* extend the notion of constitution to documents which, traditionally, would not be denominated as such.[117] But one cannot escape the

---

[112] O. O. Varol, 'Temporary Constitutions', op. cit., p. 426. Own emphasis.

[113] P. Dann, Z. Al-Ali, 'The Internationalised Pouvoir Constituant', op. cit., p. 427. Own emphasis.

[114] The assertion that oppositional transitional constitution-making is 'unrestricted' by the old legal order will be strongly nuanced below, under Chapter 6, Section B.2, which is about how TA must respect the past.

[115] L. Brahimi, 'State-Building in Crisis and Post-Conflict Countries', op. cit., p. 7: 'the constitutional process is intimately linked to the peace process. A new constitution ultimately is needed to serve as the framework of principles and rules upon which the new state will be based. The other elements of the peace process, if properly sequenced and implemented, will help facilitate a successful constitutional process. Reciprocally, a well-conceived and implemented constitutional process will be a decisive contributor to the overall success of the peace process'.

[116] V. C. Jackson, 'What's in a Name?', op. cit., p. 1273.

[117] Mambo writes that constitutions suffer from an 'extensibilité sémantique, surtout en temps de crise' or, in English, a 'semantic extensibility, especially in times of crisis'

TRANSFORMATIVE SUPRACONSTITUTIONALITY 113

observation that more and more documents, regardless of their legal nature, and despite the doubts expressed as to the capability of such polyvalence,[118] acquire *transformative constitutional functionality*. The penholders of TI thus potentially dispose of enormous powers. The limits to the powers of institutions created by such instruments will be discussed under Part III. Sometimes external actors, too, dispose of significant power in defining TI. The legal limits to external assistance in relation to TI will be discussed under Part IV. Before turning to these matters, we will examine the reality and legal nature of TA, and then the sources of *ius in interregno*.

(P. Mambo, 'Les Rapports entre la Constitution et les Accords Politiques dans les Etats africains: Réflexion sur la Légalité Constitutionnelle en Période de Crise', op. cit., p. 925). He refers in particular to internationalised agreements taking precedence over constitutional arrangements (p. 931). For Mambo, constitutions would become 'semantically extensible' and transformative constitutionalism would extend the notion of constitution itself.

[118] H. Ludsin, 'Peacemaking and Constitution-Drafting: A Dysfunctional Marriage', op. cit.

4

The Actors of the Interregnum

Political bodies like 'interim governments', 'transitional governments', 'transitional councils' created and/or regulated by TI and operating in the context of TG are referred to in this book as TA, regardless of their consensual or oppositional origin. This term is also used in practice.[1]

Several domestic TA have a consensual origin. Consensus-created domestic TA include those in Afghanistan (2001–4); Burundi (1998–2005); Côte d'Ivoire (2007); the DRC (2002–6); Liberia (2003–6); Mali (2012–present); Rwanda (1993–2003); Somalia (2004–12); Sudan (2005–11); Tajikistan (1997) and Uganda (1979–80). Some domestic TA have an oppositional origin – a unilateral proclamation or declaration – like those in Kyrgyzstan (2010) and Libya (2011). In spite of their oppositional origin and without always exercising effective control,[2] such TA nearly systematically take a vow to 'inclusivity',[3] and thus promise to progressively abandon their oppositional origin during the transition, as shall be observed in Chapter 7.

Towards the end of this book, the two final chapters will primarily deal with oppositional TA. Such authorities can be further defined as follows: political/civilian (non-military) entities that have the publicly proclaimed aim of non-constitutionally reconfiguring the constitutional order and introducing a new regime, without (initially) collaborating with the incumbent regime. External involvement with oppositional TA represents a thorny issue. It cannot simply be glossed over considering what is at stake: indirect regime change through external involvement with

---

[1] Cf. e.g. the 'Report of the Working Group on the issue of discrimination against women in law and in practice', A/HRC/23/50 of 19 April 2013, § 97.

[2] M. Saul, *Popular Governance of Post-Conflict Reconstruction*, op. cit., p. 78: 'a post-conflict situation in which there is an absence of independent effective control of the territory is not incompatible with the existence *or creation* of an entity with governmental status'. Own emphasis.

[3] E. De Groof, 'The Features of Transitional Governance Today', op. cit. See 'Practice 4'.

THE ACTORS OF THE INTERREGNUM 115

oppositional TG. This issue is therefore reserved for the end of the book. The present and following chapters, on the other hand, deal with TA, generally, referring both to revolutionary quasi-governmental,[4] pre-governmental[5] and power-sharing or consensual interim governmental bodies.[6]

TA clearly mirror a diverse politico-legal reality. Sometimes they represent the state *ab initio*, sometimes only *ex post*, and sometimes, when they remain embryonic, never at all. TA may, or may not, be internationally recognised governments of the state during the interregnum. This may be the case if they exercise effective control during the transition, are representative and possess the capacity to enter into relations with other states.[7] This is generally not contested for consensual TA whose power to represent the state is not seriously, or only marginally, contested. If, on the other hand, TA originate from an oppositional movement, they may come to represent the state only after the (successful) completion of the transition, or at a certain point of the interregnum after acquiring effective control.[8] In such case, TG acts can be retroactively attributed to the state.

TI and the set of tertiary norms they contain inform us on the consensual or oppositional origins and (more or less inclusive, and sometimes evolving) composition of TA. Together with the stage of maturity of TA and larger factual context, these factors are not without consequence. They form the criteria co-defining not only whether TA are representative, and whether their actions are attributable – instantly or only in hindsight – to the state but also, we shall see, whether or how other states and organisations can legitimately engage with them.

In spite of their diversity, TA are amenable to a common conceptualisation. The distinction between oppositional or consensual TA is an important yet not all-defining dividing line. Their common conceptualisation is based not only on the rather obviously shared feature of their domestic and provisional nature. Two further elements can be retained. First, oppositional and consensual TA share a purpose. In both cases TA

---

[4] The adjective *quasi-governmental* emphasises that TA may be endowed with government-like features, e.g. representation powers in international fora.

[5] The adjective *pre-governmental* emphasises that TA often have the intention of governing the state *ad interim*, and anticipatively engage in constitution-making.

[6] Y. Shain, J. Linz, *Between States – Interim Governments and Democratic Transitions*, op. cit., p. 5.

[7] Montevideo Convention, 26 December 1933, art. 1.

[8] Exceptionally they would do so already at an earlier stage. See the acceptance of credentials at the UNGA of the Libyan TNC during September 2011.

116 THE ACTORS OF THE INTERREGNUM

aim at bridging a transition from one regime to another, often under international assistance, and sometimes pressure. Their shared raison d'être justifies that they be analysed together. They both rely, genuinely or only in appearance, as the case may be, on the peace-through-transition paradigm, and pursue a common finality: a rupture with the past and the creation of a new constitutional order, without disrupting the state's territorial integrity.

Furthermore, in both cases TG is characterised by self-regulation: TI foresee a set of tertiary norms regulating the interregnum. In Part III we shall unveil that oppositional and consensual TA generally adopt basic analogous practices and commit to similar obligations, as introduced in the Introduction (Section A.2 and Section C.1). Although limited in number, some duties become increasingly incumbent on TA enjoying functional, relative international legal personality, regardless of their governmental status *vel non*.[9] The level of intensity of these duties also depends on the question whether actual practice by TA and interested states is contributing to the development of international law in relation to TG. This in turn depends on whether such practice is indicative of relevant emerging state behaviour, thus potentially co-constitutive of international custom adding 'body' to existing international principles.

A number of distinctive features of TA will now be discussed. In Section A, the domestic and provisional nature of TA will be elaborated on. In Section B, the concept of TA will be further refined by reference to their raison d'être.

A Nature of Transitional Authorities: Domestic, Provisional and Relative Legal Personality

TA are domestic (1) and provisional (2), and, depending on a number of variables, may enjoy international legal personality (3).

1 Domestic Nature

Domestic forms of TG can be conceptually contrasted against foreign and international forms of interim governance. The domestic nature of TA hinges on the non-international identity of the (main) stakeholders and beneficiaries appointed in the transition. Domestic institutions formally hold the reigns over TG. In the absence of direct ITA, TA are

---

[9] Chapter 4, Section A.3.

NATURE OF TRANSITIONAL AUTHORITIES

entrusted with managing the transition, even if the interregnum is substantially internationalised.[10] The following lines briefly elaborate on the non-foreign (1.1) and non-international (1.2) character of domestic TA, while recognising that the distinction between domestic and foreign or international governance can be a matter of degree (1.3).

1.1 No Foreign Administration

The TA examined in this book are domestic in nature. This distinguishes them from ITA or foreign/occupying powers.[11] The implication of a foreign power is however not incompatible with domestic TG. Foreign rule and domestic governance can alternate. For instance, while the US-led Coalition Provisional Authority and its Iraqi Governing Council (13 July 2003–1 June 2004) lacked domestic ownership, the Iraqi Interim Government (28 June 2004–3 May 2005) and the Iraqi Transitional Government (3 May 2005–20 May 2006), set up after the formal transfer of sovereignty, were formally domestic TA.

Furthermore, military occupation does not exclude the presence of a domestic TA, and vice versa. The Afghan TA (Afghan Interim Administration, 22 December 2001–13 July 2002; the Afghan Transitional Administration, 13 July 2002–3 January 2004) were at least formally in domestic hands although the country was under occupation. In Mali, the TA requested military assistance from ECOWAS,[12] and later from France, which resulted in *Opération Serval* and consent-based partial occupation of the country. In such cases, the interregnum is simultaneously characterised by domestic TG and foreign occupation, with the two modes of governance being formally dissociated one from another.

1.2 No International Administration

While TA may receive assistance from the UN or other external actors, they are *formally* domestic, unlike ITA. Within the assistance model, degrees of assistance vary. Even if external actors, notably the UN, are to 'guide, not direct',[13] at times assistance to TG amounts to a form of

---

[10] As discussed in Chapter 1, Section A.2.3, the UNSC and UNGA affirmed the responsibility of TA. This is confirmed by relevant practice discussed under Chapter 6, Section B.1.

[11] M. Saul, 'From Haiti to Somalia', op. cit.: a 'key distinction from belligerent occupation and international territorial administration is that a domestic government administers the reconstruction process'.

[12] Letter of the TA of Mali of 1 September 2012 to ECOWAS requesting military assistance.

[13] S/PV.4903 of 26 January 2004, p. 16.

(implicit) indirect rule.[14] The distinction between international administration and the assistance model should nevertheless be made: 'in the assistance model, the external actors do not exercise direct political authority. Political authority is reserved for the favoured domestic actors. These domestic actors are subject to the influence of the external actors, but not to the extent that there is a complete absence of autonomy'.[15] The assistance model distinguishes TG from ITA. According to Caplan's definition, ITA is 'a formally constituted international body that has been entrusted temporarily with responsibility for the principal governance functions of a state or territory'.[16] Wilde observes that ITA 'has been used as a device to replace local actors in the activity of administration',[17] and uses the criterion of supervision, control and direct operation to conceptually isolate it.[18] The *formal* absence of international supervision, control and direct operation characterises TG.

Distinguishing between ITA (supervision and control) and the assistance model is not always straightforward.[19] On the basis of the

---

[14] See the examples in Chapter 1, Section B.

[15] M. Saul, *Popular Governance of Post-Conflict Reconstruction*, op. cit., pp. 6–7.

[16] R. Caplan, 'Transitional Administration' in V. Chetail (ed.), *Post-Conflict Peacebuilding*, op. cit., p. 359. Own emphasis.

[17] Id., p. 587.

[18] Wilde adds that 'ITA should be contrasted with merely monitoring and/or assisting local actors in operating such a structure, although the *distinction is sometimes difficult to make* in practice, particularly in the case of conduct and assistance.' R. Wilde, 'From Danzig to East Timor and Beyond: The Role of International Territorial Administration', *The American Journal of International Law* 95, no. 3, July 1, 2001, p. 585. Own emphasis. Cf. also the definition by I. Prezas, *L'administration de collectivités territoriales par les Nations Unies – Etude de la substitution de l'organisation internationale à l'état dans l'exercice des pouvoirs de gouvernement*, L.G.D.J., 2012, p. 26: '*substitution* d'une autorité étrangère d'origine internationale à un Etat [...] dans l'exercice direct de pouvoirs gouvernementaux formellement identiques à ceux résultant habituellement pour un Etat de son titre territorial'. Own emphasis and translation: '*substitution* of a state by a foreign authority of international origin [...] in the direct exercise of governmental powers which are formally identical to those usually resulting from a State's territorial title'.

[19] R. Wilde, *International Territorial Administration: How Trusteeship and the Civilizing Mission Never Went Away*', op. cit., p. 33: '[a]lthough *the distinction between assistance, on the one hand, and supervision or control*, on the other, is contested and can be difficult to make in practice, as an idea it *is key to understanding how the activity of territorial administration is compared with other activities performed by international organisations*, and treated as distinctive as a result. Because of these considerations relating to distinctiveness and originality, the difference between supervision/control/conduct, on the one hand, and mere assistance/advice, on the other, is adopted as a key component in defining the nature of the involvement in territorial administration by international actors'. Own emphasis.

NATURE OF TRANSITIONAL AUTHORITIES

supervision and control criterion, Wilde ranges the following scenario under ITA: 'situations where particular administrative activities are performed by local actors, but under the *overall authority* of the international organisation'.[20] The international transitional administration in Kosovo (UNMIK) and East Timor (UNTAET),[21] and their historical precedents,[22] thus constitute instances of ITA. In contrast, in light of the absence of formal overall authority, supervision and control by international actors, the main responsibility for TG formally lies with domestic TA.[23]

1.3 Gradations of International Involvement

Some cases are not clear-cut and defy the distinction between international/foreign administration and assisted TG. To reflect this nuance, scholars have developed various, more or less complex, classifications and models of international involvement in transitional situations. An overview, as shown in Table 4.1, should suffice.

The table below reflects the diversity of external involvement in transitional situations, allowing us to better situate TG. Clearly, the distinction between international/foreign administration and internationally assisted TG is not a clear-cut dichotomy. While Caplan only differentiates between direct UN governance and UN supervision,[24] Chopra makes a distinction between (1) governorship, that is the UN assuming full responsibility for the transition; (2) control, that is the UN exercising direct control over the transition; (3) partnership, that is the UN exercising a veto and final say over the transition and (4) assistance, that is the UN just supporting the transition without any binding powers. Doyle differentiates between four models of international administration, depending on the legal authority and effective capacity exercised by the UN. In descending order, models of international administration range

---

[20] Id., fn. 95. Own emphasis.
[21] L. Aucoin and M. Brandt, 'East Timor's Constitutional Passage to Independence' in L. E. Miller (ed.), *Framing the State in Times of Transition: Case Studies in Constitution Making*, United States Institute of Peace Press, 2010.
[22] R. Wilde, 'From Danzig to East Timor and Beyond: The Role of International Territorial Administration', op. cit., pp. 583–606.
[23] There may be grounds for piercing the veil separating actions by international and domestic actors during transitions. This depends on factual questions of attribution and direction and control, not analysed in this book.
[24] R. Caplan, *International Governance of War-Torn Territories*, Oxford University Press, 2005, pp. 17–21.

120 THE ACTORS OF THE INTERREGNUM

Table 4.1 *Categories and degrees of external involvement*

[1]	Ottaway and Lacina	[a] International transitional administrations [int'l admin. by High Representative in Bosnia; UNMIK; UNTAET] [b] Installation of local transitional government [Afghanistan, DRC, Liberia, Rwanda, Somalia] [c] Reliance on existing structures
[2]	Caplan	[a] Direct UN governance [UNTAES; UNMIK; UNTAET] [b] 'Between direct governance and supervision' [int'l admin. by High Representative in Bosnia] [c] Supervision [no direct role for UN, relatively little authority, e.g. UNTAC]
[3]	Chopra	[a] Governorship [UNMIK] [b] Control [int'l admin. by High Representative in Bosnia] [c] Partnership [d] Assistance
[4]	Doyle	[a] Supervisory authority [UNTAET; UNMIK] [b] Executive authority [UNTAES; UNOMIL; int'l admin. by High Representative in Bosnia] [c] Administrative authority [ONUMOZ; UNTAC; MINURSO; int'l admin. by High Representative in Bosnia] [d] Monitoring [UNTAG; UNMOT; UNMIH; MINUGUA; UNAVEM; UNOMIG; UNFICYP; UNAMIR; UNOSOM I; MONUC; UNPROFOR; UNOMSIL]
[5]	Wilde	[a] Supervision/control/conduct [incl. UNMIK; UNTAET] [b] Assistance/advice
[6]	Chesterman	Depending on the purpose and trajectory of the transition: [a] Decolonisation and independence [Namibia, East Timor] [b] Temporary admin. of territory pending peaceful transfer of control to existing government [West New Guinea, Western Sahara, Eastern Slavonia] [c] Temporary admin. of territory pending holding of elections [Cambodia] [d] Interim admin. as part of peace process without an end state [Bosnia and Herzegovina, Kosovo]

NATURE OF TRANSITIONAL AUTHORITIES

Table 4.1 *(cont.)*

		[e] *De facto* administration or responsibility for basic law and order in the absence of governing authority [Congo 1960–1964, Somalia 1993–1995, Sierra Leone 1999]
[7]	Shain and Linz[25]	[a] Revolutionary provisional governments [b] Power-sharing interim governments [c] Incumbent caretaker governments [d] International interim governments
[8]	Not the focus of this book	1.a; 2.a; 2.b; 3.a; 3.b; 4.a, 4.b, 4.c; 5.a; 7.c; 7.d.

from supervisory authority to executive authority, administrative authority and mere monitoring.[26] For Croissant, only the latter model (similar to Saul's assistance model) is compatible with TG being truly domestic.

There are grey zones. The experiences in Bosnia and Herzegovina and Cambodia, for instance, may be difficult to classify either under ITA or TG. In Bosnia and Herzegovina, the division of labour and prerogatives was explicitly foreseen in the Dayton Agreement.[27] As this case lies somewhere 'between direct governance and supervision',[28] we will consider it a transition *sensu lato*.

In the case of Cambodia, sovereignty during the transitional period was vested in the country's representatives, but all powers necessary to ensure the implementation of the transitional arrangements of the 1991 Paris Accords were delegated to the UN.[29] Interim governance in Cambodia was formally domestic, although some powers were thus delegated to

---

[25] Y. Shain, J. Linz, *Between States – Interim Governments and Democratic Transitions*, op. cit., p. 5.

[26] M. W. Doyle, 'War Making and Peace Making – The United Nations' Post-Cold War Record' in C. A. Crocker, F. O. Hampson, P. Aall (eds.), *Turbulent Peace, the Challenges of Managing International Conflict*, United States Institute of Peace Press, 2001, p. 551, table 2.

[27] See J. C. O'Brien, 'The Dayton Constitution of Bosnia and Herzegovina' in L. E. Miller (ed.), *Framing the State in Times of Transition*, op. cit., p. 332.

[28] R. Caplan, *International Governance of War-Torn Territories*, Oxford University Press, 2005.

[29] S. P. Marks, 'The Process of Creating a New Constitution in Cambodia' in L. E. Miller (ed.), *Framing the State in Times of Transition*, op. cit. Cf. also G. Curtis, 'Transition to what? Cambodia, UNTAC and the peace process', UN Research Institute for Social Development, 1993.

122 THE ACTORS OF THE INTERREGNUM

UNTAC.[30] UNTAC did not exercise all its powers though, and regularly met and consulted with the Supreme National Council ('SNC'), using it as a sounding board.[31] For some authors, 'the UN's control over Cambodia's civil administration was largely nominal'.[32] In any event, exclusive international governance was avoided. The situation can best be qualified as 'formal co-governance',[33] with the SNC as a 'semisovereign mechanism'.[34]

2 Provisional Nature

TA are by definition provisional. They observe the interim rule, regulated by a set of tertiary transition norms, and in doing so (purport to) 'rule for

---

[30] On the one hand, the domestic 'supreme National Council [was] the unique legitimate body and source of authority in which, throughout the transitional period, the sovereignty, independence and unity of Cambodia are enshrined' (Paris Agreement, art. 3). On the other hand, this domestic body agreed to delegate to the UNTAC 'all powers necessary to ensure the implementation of this Agreement' (art. 6). Cf. also C. Bull, *No Entry Without Strategy – Building the Rule of Law under UN Transitional Administration*, op. cit., p. 29: UNTAC 'was delegated only those powers necessary for it to fulfil its mandate. Although the SNC continued to conduct many government functions, UNTAC had direct authority over the organisation and conduct of free elections, including the establishment of laws and administrative procedures; over all administrative agencies that could influence the outcome of the elections (foreign affairs, defense, finance, public security and information); over the police force, over relevant law enforcement and judicial processes in consultation with the SNC; and over military operations'.

[31] S. P. Marks, 'The Process of Creating a New Constitution in Cambodia' in L. E. Miller (ed.), *Framing the State in Times of Transition*, op. cit., p. 212.

[32] J. Dobbins, 'A History of UN Peacekeeping' in I. Shapiro, J. Lambert, *Charter of the United Nations*, Yale University Press, 2014, p. 199. In the same sense, Croissant notes that the SNC exercised full legislative power, and UNTAC could only act when this council was deadlocked. A. Croissant, 'International Interim Governments, Democratisation, and Post-Conflict Peace Building: Lessons from Cambodia and East Timor' in K. Guttieri, J. Piombo (eds.), *Interim Governments – Institutional Bridges to Peace and Democracy?*, op. cit., p. 227: 'UNTAC and its special representative, Yasushi Akashi, were given the authority to decide matters only when the factions within the council were deadlocked and Prince Sihanouk did not act. ... UNTAC thus exercised executive power only indirectly'.

[33] C. Stahn, *The Law and Practice of International Territorial Administration*, op. cit., p. 269: 'It presented a midway point between the accidental UN governance experiences of the Cold War period and the comprehensive UN statebuilding missions of the mid- to late 1990s.'

[34] M. W. Doyle, 'War Making and Peace making – The United Nations' Post-Cold War Record' in C. A. Crocker, F. O. Hampson, P. Aall, *Turbulent Peace, the Challenges of Managing International Conflict*, United States Institute of Peace Press, 2001, p. 543. Doyle and Sambanis also consider the Commission on the Peace in El Salvador and the National Consultative Council in East Timor as 'semisovereign mechanisms'. See M. W. Doyle, N. Sambanis, *Making War and Building Peace: United Nations Peace Operations*, Princeton University Press, 2011.

NATURE OF TRANSITIONAL AUTHORITIES

a limited amount of time until a permanent government can come to power'.[35] Interim public powers encompass various matters such as the running of daily affairs, the provision of security, monitoring the logistics of the transition (for example by organising a national dialogue or preparing for elections) and constitution-making.

The constitution-making process is pivotal to interim rule. During the interregnum, TA (endeavour to) pre-define the coming constitutional order, through staged constitution-making processes: 'transitional constitutionmaking is frequently impermanent, and involves *gradual change*'.[36] Such a process is by nature provisional if carried out in accordance with the TI's relevant provisions. Staged constitution-making has been qualified as 'post-sovereign constitutionmaking'[37] because the constitution-making process *itself* is predefined or at least constrained beforehand.

In this book we give a very specific meaning to 'transitional constitution-making' as the designing and drafting of supraconstitutional (constituent) TI, whereas 'constitution-making' *tout court* (without further qualification) refers to the designing and drafting of the permanent post-transition constitution. Note, from the outset, that 'transitional constitution-making' can have an effect on constitution-making *tout court*. Because of the third function of TI, constitutional reconfiguration, the TI is, partly and indirectly, also a *regulator of the post-transition order*. This is precisely the reason why I suggested characterising TI as 'tertiary norms'.

Staged constitution-making takes place against the background of longer transitions, which, if broadly defined, can be subdivided into four stages. Youssef's subdivision centres on the level of protection of human rights before, during and after the transition.[38] As Table 4.2 shows, the subdivision proposed here revolves around material events and/or juridical texts: the pre-transition, the foundation of TG, the interregnum itself and the post-transition stage.

The subdivision of transitions follows, apart from the pre-transition, an internal, self-referential, structure. It is not formally dependent on external circumstances such as the presence, absence or degree of intensity of the crisis or conflict surrounding the transition.

---

[35] Definition provided by the African Elections Database.
[36] R. Teitel, 'Transitional Jurisprudence: The Role of Law in Political Transformation', op. cit., p. 2057. Own emphasis.
[37] A. Arato, *Constitution Making Under Occupation*, op. cit.
[38] N. Youssef, *La Transition démocratique et la garantie des droits fondamentaux*, op. cit., p. 43.

124 THE ACTORS OF THE INTERREGNUM

Table 4.2 *Four stages of a transition: concepts*

1. Pre-transition stage	2. Foundation of the transition: IT/TA	3. The interregnum	4. Post-transition
Starts with a political event (e.g. ceasefire, formal opening negotiations) until foundation of transition.	The adoption of the constituent TI (usually in combination with the creation of the TA).	The interim rule or transition as such, starting with the explicitly foreseen commencement date or, in the absence thereof, the actual functioning of the TA.	From the approval of the new constitution/ holding general elections/ creation new government onwards.

In some cases, TA are created during armed conflict. Both the establishment of the Libyan National Transitional Council by self-proclamation and the subsequent promulgation of its core tasks occurred during a (non-international, then both non-international and international)[39] armed conflict. In other cases, transitions start in the aftermath of an armed conflict, for example the DRC transition following the Second Congo War. These examples illustrate how the analysis of sometimes lengthy transitions can be decoupled from the distinction between 'before' and 'after' the war.[40] Table 4.3 applies the subdivision into four stages to some of the cases referred to.

Let us now discuss in turn the pre-transition (2.1); the foundation of TG (2.2); the interregnum (2.3) and the post-transition (2.4).

---

[39] P. Thielbörger, 'The Status and Future of International Law after the Libya Intervention', *Göttingen Journal of International Law* 4, 2012, 1, 11–48.

[40] This distinction is central to *ius post bellum*, which is why this doctrine is not fit for the purpose of studying conflict-related transitions. See Chapter 2, Section A.2. See, for example, the critique by Bell who 'reject[s] a project of developing and clarifying a holistic jus post bellum as a regulatory legal framework for transitions from conflict to peace'. C. Bell, 'Of *Jus Post Bellum* and Lex Pacificatoria – What's in a Name?' in C. Stahn, J. S. Easterday, J. Iverson (eds.), *Jus Post Bellum – Mapping the Normative Foundations*, Oxford University Press, 2014, p. 182.

Table 4.3 *Four stages of a transition: examples*

	Pre-transition	Foundation of the transition	The interregnum	After the transition
Afghanistan (2001–4)	11 September 2001–5 December 2001	5 December 2001 (Bonn Agreement)	5 December 2001–3 January 2004	Since 3 January 2004
Burundi (1998–2005)	23 October 1993–6 June 1998	6 June 1998 (Constitutional Act of Transition)	6 June 1998–18 March 2005	Since 18 March 2005
DRC (2002–5)	15 October 2001 (opening Inter-Congolese Dialogue)–16 December 2002	16 December 2002 (Pretoria Agreement)	16 December 2002–19 December 2005 (Const. referendum)	Since 19 December 2005
Iraq (2003–6)	19 March 2003 (US invasion)–28 June 2004 (transfer of sovereignty)	8 March 2004 (Law of admin. signed)	28 June 2004–May 2006 (formation government National Unity)	Since May 2006
Liberia (2003–6)	May 2003 (Taylor consents to peace talks)–18 August 2003	18 August 2003 (Accra Comprehensive Peace Agreement)	18 August 2003–8 November 2005 (presidential elections)	Since 8 November 2005
Libya (2011–?)	15 February 2011 (protests Benghazi)–5 March 2011	5 March 2011 (Establishment Libyan Transitional National Council)	5 March 2011–? (*tentative completion*)	/

2.1 Pre-Transition

The period before the transition usually starts with a political event – for example a ceasefire, the formal start of negotiations, civil unrest – eventually leading to the creation of a TA. The choice in picking the event triggering the pre-transition stage is entirely context-based.[41] The pre-transition ends when a transition formally starts or a TA is founded.

During the pre-transition, candidate TA are either non-existent or just embryonic. When TA, lacking (sufficient) international support, or for other reasons, remain blocked in the pre-transition, without ever activating TG, they can be either *aspirational* or *embryonic*. The Chinese TA (2008) and the Ugandan National Transition Council (2011) respond to this qualification.

The little-known 'Charter of the TA of China', published late February 2008, provides in some detail how this authority would be composed. It also details its missions, including its own dissolution 'once the task of rejecting the totalitarian rule of the CCP's [Chinese Communist Party] bureaucratic group is completed and following the establishment of democracy based on a national referendum'.[42] This initiative had poor outreach, little media attention and no success. The same is true of the Uganda National Transition Council. Late August 2011, perhaps inspired by the international recognition of the Libyan Transitional National Council then gaining momentum, Ugandan citizens decided to set up a Uganda National Transition Council.[43]

The gravitas and level of organisation of both these aspirational TA was never sufficiently high so as to plausibly trigger a transition. This need not always be the case though. As aspirational TA can evolve either way, grow or fade out, they are relevant for our enquiry. External support to aspirational TA potentially results in regime change. Their political purpose – the reconfiguration of a state order – must be taken into account when examining the

---

[41] Where the interregnum is based on a peace agreement, the pre-transition may correspond to what Bell, under a 'stage-function classification', described as the 'stage producing pre-negotiation agreements'. C. Bell, *On the Law of Peace*, op. cit., p. 53.

[42] Cf. the *Charter of the TA of China*, available on www.dossiertibet.it/news/charter-transitional-authority-china (last retrieved on 16 October 2015, not available anymore), A.2.c. The title of the URL indicates that the initiative is linked to Tibet's quest for sovereignty. E-mail sent on 17 February 2015 to ask for information remains unanswered.

[43] www.musevenimustgo.com last consulted on 17 February 2015 (not available anymore). E-mail sent on the same date to ask for information about the Uganda National Transition Council remains unanswered.

NATURE OF TRANSITIONAL AUTHORITIES

leeway third states have in supporting them. This issue will be discussed under Part IV.

2.2 Foundation of the Transition

The foundation of the transition refers to the public adoption of the constituent TI in combination with the creation of the TA. The TI can explicitly provide when a TA is to be established. In Rwanda, for example, a peace agreement foresaw that 'the Transitional Institutions shall be set up within thirty-seven days following the signing of the Peace Agreement'.[44] By the time of its foundation, the TA's organisational structure and portfolio have generally been defined in the relevant TI. In some cases, several texts, entering into effect on different moments, are to be read together, for example a constitutional act (such as the Constitutional Act of Transition of 6 June 1998 for Burundi) and an intrastate agreement (such as the 2000 Arusha Agreement for Burundi) in order to understand the specific design of a transition.

The foundation of a TA need not always trigger an interregnum. This is the scenario of the non-inaugurated transition. A TA can be founded, receive recognition and become (relatively) influential without the transition roadmap eventually being executed. Such a TA is more than aspirational or embryonic without ever becoming effective. We can call this an *inchoate* TA.

In Syria, for instance, an agreement reached on 11 September 2012 during a meeting in Doha of Syrian opposition groups formalised the founding of the National Coalition for Syrian Revolutionary and Opposition Forces (the 'Coalition'). Towards the end of 2012, the first countries to 'recognise'[45] this Coalition were France, Turkey, Qatar and then Britain.[46] This Coalition also enjoyed the support of the Council of the EU[47] and of the Gulf Cooperation Council.[48] Even prior to the foundation of this Coalition, the involvement by states and organisations

---

[44] Peace Agreement between the Government of the Republic of Rwanda and the Rwandese Patriotic Front of 4 August 1993, art. 7.

[45] A discussion on the 'recognition' of oppositional TA will follow under Chapter 9, Section A.1 and Section B.1.

[46] 'Syria criticises 3 countries for recognising opposition', *IHT*, 19 November 2012.

[47] Conclusions on Syria at the 3199th Foreign Affairs Council meeting of 19 November 2012.

[48] 'Opposition in Syria war is urged to pick leaders; U.S. and others want to see a political structure that could replace regime', *IHT*, 7 December 2012.

in the process leading to its creation conferred it considerable political weight. Their aim was clear from the start: creating governance structures and triggering a regime change through TG.[49] Although TG was still envisaged as a solution for the Syrian crisis during 2019,[50] this attempt has not materialised at the time of writing. The foundation of this TA therefore did not result in the initiation of TG. Albeit in a different context, something similar happened in Venezuela where an interim government, led by opposition leader Juan Guaidó but without effective territorial control yet recognised by dozens of like-minded countries, unsuccessfully tried to trigger a transition.

This division into various stages reflects the changing dynamics of transitions, also in relation to effective control. The notion of TA is thus not premised on effective control or on TA exhibiting governmental features, contrary to the concept of the *de facto* state[51] or *de facto* government[52] which presupposes the factual, that is effective, control over state territory. Table 4.4 emphasises the gradual nature of transitions, with concrete examples of (1) embryonic, (2) inchoate, (3) halfway or (4) completed transitions at the time of writing.

2.3 Interregnum

The interregnum lasts from the explicitly foreseen commencement date (or, in the absence thereof, the actual functioning of the TA) until the end of the transition. The end of the interregnum, we shall discuss in the following subsection, can be marked by various events such as general elections, the dissolution of the TA, resumption of powers by a post-transition government and/or the adoption of a new constitution.

---

[49] 'Obama threatens Syria over chemical weapons; Warning to Assad suggests use could be met with military force', *IHT*, 5 December 2012.

[50] 'Brussels to host third Conference on Supporting the Future of Syria and the Region', EEAS Press Release, 1 February 2019: 'The overarching objective of the Brussels Syria Conferences is to support the Syrian people and further mobilise the international community behind the work to achieve a lasting political solution to the Syria crisis, in line with UN Security Council Resolution 2254.' Cf. also the Statement of the International Syria Support Group of 17 May 2016, especially the last part on 'advancing a political transition'.

[51] Introduction, Section A.4.2.

[52] Chapter 3, Section A.1, *in fine*.

Table 4.4 *Embryonic, inchoate, midway or completed transitions*

	1. Pre-transition	2. Foundation	3. Interregnum	4. End of transition
A. Tentative foundation of TG *(aspirational or embryonic TA)*	- China - Uganda	/	/	/
B. Tentative interregnum *(inchoate TA)*	- South Sudan - Syria	- South Sudan (agreement formation unity government) - Syria (National Council; National Coalition)	/	/
C. Tentative completion of interregnum	- Burkina Faso - CAR - Libya - Mali - Ukraine	- Burkina Faso - CAR - Libyan TNC/GNC - Mali - Ukraine	- Burkina Faso - CAR - Libyan TNC/GNC - Mali[53] - Ukraine	/

[53] At the time of writing, the reconstitutionalisation was not yet completed. See S/2018/58 of 31 January 2018, p. 4. See also A. Diallo, 'Mali: 2019, année de la révision de la Constitution?', *Jeune Afrique*, 21 February 2019.

Table 4.4 (*cont.*)

	1. Pre-transition	2. Foundation	3. Interregnum	4. End of transition
D. Completed transition	- Afghanistan - Burundi - Côte d'Ivoire - DRC - Guinea - Guinea-Bissau - Iraq - Kyrgyzstan - Liberia - Nepal	- Afghanistan - Burundi - Côte d'Ivoire - DRC - Guinea - Guinea-Bissau - Iraq - Kyrgyzstan - Liberia - Nepal	- Afghanistan - Burundi - Côte d'Ivoire - DRC - Guinea - Guinea-Bissau - Iraq - Kyrgyzstan - Liberia - Nepal	- Afghanistan - Burundi - Côte d'Ivoire - DRC - Guinea - Guinea-Bissau - Iraq - Kyrgyzstan - Liberia - Nepal

NATURE OF TRANSITIONAL AUTHORITIES

Timing is thus mostly planned beforehand. To pave the way for long-term institutional development, some practitioners and scholars argue we would be served by relatively long transitions:[54] 'a fair amount of time for deliberation, compromise, education, participation, and renewed discussion *prior to* efforts to solidify agreements in a comprehensive and final constitution is conducive to successful constitution-making in situations of serious post-conflict regime change'.[55] TI regularly provide the length of the interregnum, for example in Cambodia,[56] Côte d'Ivoire[57] and the DRC.[58] The interregnum can last from a couple of months (Kyrgyzstan, April–October 2010) to almost a decade (Nepal, 2007–17) and even longer, as in Somalia[59] or in Palestine, where the five-year transition foreseen by the 1993 Oslo Accords evolved into 'Palestine's permanent transition'.[60]

---

[54] J. Benomar, 'Constitution-Making After Conflict: Lessons for Iraq', op. cit., p. 87. In the same vein, Samuels argues that 'supporting longer time-frames between the negotiation of peace agreements and constitutions' would 'minimize the inherent tensions in a postwar constitution building'. K. Samuels, 'Postwar Constitution Building' in R. Paris and T. D. Sisk (eds.), *The Dilemmas of Statebuilding – Confronting the Contradictions of Postwar Peace Operations*, op. cit., p. 175. Ould-Abdallah even goes as far as suggesting that 'in many African countries the introduction of democracy should be allied with a ten- to twenty-year transitional period of constitutional power sharing'. A. Ould-Abdallah, *Burundi on the Brink 1993–1995. A UN Special Envoy Reflects on Preventive Diplomacy*, United States of Peace Press, 2000, p. 71. Papagianni, too, emphasises the link between inclusivity and sustainability. K. Papagianni, 'Political Transitions after Peace Agreements: The Importance of Consultative and Inclusive Political Processes', op. cit., p. 47. See also p. 50: 'the peacebuilding agenda is served by extended transitional periods, which provide avenues for political representation beyond the signatories of peace agreements before elections are held'.

[55] V. C. Jackson, 'What's in a Name?', op. cit., pp. 1270–1. Own emphasis.

[56] Paris Agreement, art. 1: 'the transitional period shall commence with the entry into force of this Agreement and terminate when the constituent assembly elected through free and fair elections, organised and certified by the United Nations, has approved the constitution and transformed itself into a legislative assembly, and thereafter a new government has been created'.

[57] Accord de Ouagadougou, Annexe 'Chronogramme de mise en oeuvre de l'Accord de Ouagadougou', nr. 4: 'formation du gouvernement [s]e fait cinq semaines après la signature de l'Accord'. Translation: 'the government will be formed five weeks after the signing of the Agreement'.

[58] Pretoria Agreement, IV.

[59] IDEA, 'Interim Constitutions in Post-Conflict Settings', Discussion report, 4–5 December 2014, p. 22, observation by A.-S. Jama: 'in 2012, the international community declared that the 12-year transition had ended and recognised the Somali government, despite the absence of legitimate institutions, and indeed ongoing conflict'.

[60] Z. Miller, 'Perils of Parity: Palestine's Permanent Transition', *Cornell International Law Journal*, Vol. 47, 2014, p. 331–412.

132   THE ACTORS OF THE INTERREGNUM

Transitions can also be consecutive, as was the case in Côte d'Ivoire (2003–6; 2006–10), and is still the case in Somalia at the time of writing (2004–12; 2012–present) where the 2012 Provisional Constitution was described as essentially 'handing over from one interim authority to another, from one transition to another'.[61] A second consecutive transition, led by a temporary Government of National Accord, was also supposed to be implemented, for better or worse, in Libya, still largely in anarchy at the time of writing.[62]

During the interregnum, TA (purport to) administer the country and execute the transition roadmap. Although there is much debate about what sequencing guarantees the best results and although activities can overlap, the following roadmap is generally followed:

- Setting up of TA;
- Election or appointment of a constituent assembly;
- National dialogue/Roundtables;
- Reconstitutionalisation, validated either by referendum or general elections;
- Organisation of TJ.

2.4   End of the Transition

TI sometimes explicitly indicate when the transition is to end. This is the case with TI relating to Burkina Faso (installation of new institutions),[63] Burundi (presidential election),[64] Cambodia (approval of the constitution and creation of a new government),[65] DRC (election of a new

---

[61] A. Ainte, 'Somalia – Legitimacy of the Provisional Constitution', *Accords*, Issue 25, 2014, p. 60 (quoting A. Hashi of ICG). In May 2018, Somalia launched a constitutional review process with a view to replacing the 2012 Provisional Constitution.

[62] Libyan Political Agreement of 17 December 2015, art. 1.4. 'A Crisis Deepens in Libya but Where Are the Cameras?', IPS, 16 February 2018. The UNSC still referred to the Libyan Political Agreement of 17 December 2015: SC/13120 of 14 December 2017; S/RES/2441 dd. 5 November 2018. About its difficult implementation, cf. M. Toaldo, 'Libya's Political Stalemate', *The Cairo Review of Global Affairs*, 6 February 2016.

[63] *Charte de la Transition* of 13 November 2014, art. 21: '[l]es institutions de la période de la transition fonctionnent jusqu'à l'installation effective des nouvelles institutions'. Own translation: 'the institutions of the transition period will function until the actual establishment of the new institutions'.

[64] Arusha Agreement, Protocol II, chapter II, art. 13: '[t]he transition period shall culminate upon the election of the new President'.

[65] Paris Agreement, art. 1: 'the transitional period shall commence with the entry into force of this Agreement and terminate when the constituent assembly elected through free and fair elections, organised and certified by the United Nations, has approved the constitution and

NATURE OF TRANSITIONAL AUTHORITIES

President),[66] Guinea Bissau (the new President assuming office),[67] Iraq (formation of an elected government),[68] Libya (ratification of a permanent constitution),[69] Nepal (new constitution 'framed' by a constituent assembly)[70] and Rwanda (general elections[71]/fixed period of 22 months).[72]

But which yardstick should be used to mark a transition's end in the absence of explicit provisions? As the word transition is used in a technical sense, this question should not depend on whether the stage of a well-functioning human rights-based democracy has been reached – this is an ever-to-be-renewed process anyhow.[73] Also, larger questions as to the link between the *end* and the *ends* (in the sense of purpose) of

---

transformed itself into a legislative assembly, and thereafter a new government has been created'.

[66] Pretoria Agreement, IV.

[67] *Pacto de Transição Política* of 16 May 2012, art. 2.1.

[68] TAL, art. 2: '[t]he term "transitional period" shall refer to the period beginning on 30 June 2004 and lasting until the formation of an elected Iraqi government pursuant to a permanent constitution as set forth in this Law . . .'.

[69] The 'Draft Constitutional Charter For the Transitional Stage', Preamble: '[t]he interim Transitional National Council has decided to promulgate this Constitutional Declaration in order to be the basis of rule in the transitional stage until a permanent Constitution is ratified in a plebiscite'.

[70] Interim Constitution of Nepal, 2063 (2007), Preamble: 'hereby promulgate this Interim Constitution of Nepal, 2063 (2007), prepared through a political consensus *enforceable until a new Constitution is framed by the Constituent Assembly*'. Own emphasis.

[71] Protocol of Agreement on Power-Sharing within the Framework of a Broad-Based Transitional Government between the Government of the Republic of Rwanda and the Rwandese Patriotic Front of 9 January 1993, art. 23.a.2: '[t]he Broad-based Transitional Government shall implement the programme comprising the following: . . . [p]repare and organise general elections to be held at the end of the Transition Period'.

[72] 'Protocol of Agreement between the Government of the Republic of Rwanda and the Rwandese Patriotic Front on Miscellaneous Issues and Final Provisions' of 3 August 1993, art. 22 on the 'transitional period': '[t]he duration of the Transition period shall be *twenty two (22) months*, effective from the date of establishment of the Broad-Based Transitional Government, with the possibility of one (1) extension if warranted by exceptional circumstances impeding the normal implementation of the programme of the Broad-Based Transitional Government'. Own emphasis.

[73] N. Youssef, *La Transition démocratique et la garantie des droits fondamentaux*, op. cit., p. 28: 'la transition démocratique *se détache de la période transitoire* pour s'étendre bien *au-delà* la fin de cette période et jusqu'au temps nécessaire pour renforcer et consolider le régime de l'Etat de droit fondé sur la démocratie et la protection des droits fondamentaux'. Own emphasis and translation: 'the democratic transition *should be detached from the transitional period*. It extends well *beyond* the end of this period until the time needed to strengthen and consolidate the rule of law based on democracy and the protection of fundamental rights'. See also, about democracy being an ever-to-be-renewed process, W. Van den Eynde, *Fortisgate: een stresstest voor justitie*, op. cit.

134 THE ACTORS OF THE INTERREGNUM

a transition are not addressed here.[74] How, then, should the end of a transition be marked? The textual references just referred to put forward three main options:

- Resumption of power by a permanent domestic government;[75]
- National elections;[76]
- Adoption of the new constitution ('reconstitutionalisation').

Mostly, however, TI explicitly define the transition's end. This constitutes another criterion to distinguish TA from *de facto* governments,[77] which do not aspire at guiding an interregnum. *De facto* governments rather intend to transform their control into a permanent or at least non-transitory state of affairs. While TA, by definition *and increasingly also by law*, set temporary limits on their own existence.[78]

3 Functional International Legal Personality

The subdivision in four stages *assists* us in defining when TA acquire functional international legal personality.[79] Legal personality must be strictly separated not only from international responsibility[80] but also

---

[74] Z. Miller, 'The End(s) of Transition' in E. De Groof, M. Wiebusch (eds.), *International Law and Transitional Governance: Critical Perspectives*, op. cit., p. 115.

[75] K. Guttieri, J. Piombo (eds.), *Interim Governments – Institutional Bridges to Peace and Democracy?*, op. cit., p. 24: 'a transitional period has ended when a *new or reconstituted, permanent, domestic government* is able to wield effective internal sovereignty. By effective internal sovereignty we mean the *dissolution of the interim structures* and the resumption of law and order functions by the domestic regime'. Own emphasis.

[76] J. Strasheim, H. Fjelde, 'Pre-Designing Democracy: Institutional Design of Interim Governments and Democratisation in 15 Post-Conflict Societies', op. cit., p. 342.

[77] Chapter 3, Section A.1, *in fine*.

[78] This restriction is frequently recalled by the UNSC. TA must not intend to perpetuate themselves in light of the limits *ratione temporis* to the interim rule. Chapter 6, Section A. See also E. De Groof, 'The Features of Transitional Governance Today', op. cit. See 'Practice 2'.

[79] Distinctions between *Völkerrechtspersönlichkeit*, *Völkerrechtssubjektivität*, *Völkerrechtsfähigkeit* are not further analysed here. Adopting a functional approach, this book largely equates international legal personality to international legal capacity. For a similar approach, see C. Walter, 'Subjects of International Law', MPEPIL.

[80] International responsibility and international legal personality are separate issues. The ECtHR affirmed that 'each State Party to the Convention nonetheless remains *responsible* for events occurring anywhere within its national territory' including for events occurring on the territory of what the Court calls 'self-proclaimed authorities' (ECtHR, *Assanidze v. Georgia*, Judgment of 8 April 2004, 39 EHRR 32, § 146). This finding is not incompatible with the reasoning that such authorities – and, *mutatis mutandis*, TA– may enjoy international legal personality. Considering the principle of state unity (*LaGrand*,

NATURE OF TRANSITIONAL AUTHORITIES 135

from the question whether TA with international legal personality are 'lawmakers' under the doctrine of sources.[81] At this stage, the issue of international legal personality matters only for having a better indication and understanding of the scope *ratione personae* of *ius in interregno*, which precisely depends on when TA acquire international legal personality. Three interrelated variables are indicative of international legal personality.

First, when TA are considered to be addressees of certain obligations, their international legal personality is acknowledged in practice. States and IO – not in the least the UNSC – regularly 'urge' or 'require' TA to execute specific legal obligations, thus consider them to be addressees of international law. The UNSC has for example 'call[ed] on the Transitional institutions'[82] or has 'urge[d]'[83] TA to adopt specific behaviour, in the context of the DRC and CAR transitions, respectively. It has determined responsibilities of the Transitional National Assembly[84] and of the Interim Government of Iraq.[85] It has also addressed itself to the Mali TA[86] and even to aspirational TA.[87]

Part III and the Report accompanying this book[88] contain several other references showing that states and IO regard TA as addressees of certain obligations. International legal personality arguably stems from the circumstance that certain entities have international obligations (and rights) under international law.[89] In short, sometimes

---

Germany v. United States of America, judgment, ICJ, Reports 2001, p. 466), it cannot be said that the international responsibility of a state for one of its sub-entities would exclude such entities from enjoying (partial) international legal personality. This is evidenced, for example, by the treaty-concluding powers Belgian federated entities have in their respective field of competences.

[81] I thank J. d'Aspremont for insisting on the latter distinction.

[82] S/RES/1635 of 28 October 2005.

[83] S/RES/2149 of 10 April 2014.

[84] S/RES/1546 of 8 June 2004 § 4.c.

[85] Id., § 26.

[86] UNSC/RES/2056 of 5 July 2012; UNSC/RES/2071 of 12 October 2012.

[87] UNSC/RES/2201 of 15 February 2015; UNC/RES/2216 of 14 April 2015, both addressing Houthi's (Yemen).

[88] E. De Groof, 'The Features of Transitional Governance Today', op. cit.

[89] O. Krönert, *Die Stellung nationaler Befreiungsbewegungen im Völkerrecht*, Europäische Hochschulschriften, Reihe 2, Rechtswissenschaft. Bd. 404, Frankfurt/M., Bern, Nancy, New York, 1984, p. 83: 'in diesem Zusammenhang bedeutet der Ausdruck 'funktionelle' Völkerrechtssubjektivität nicht anderes, als dass die Wirkungseinheit nicht –wie die Staaten– die volle Rechtsfähigkeit hat, sondern nur Adressat der Rechte und Pflichten ist, die für ihre spezielle Rechtsstellung und Funktion im Völkerrecht notwendig sind'. Own translation: 'in this context, the term 'functional' subject of international law means

136 THE ACTORS OF THE INTERREGNUM

international legal personality inevitably *follows* the existence of such obligations and rights.

Second, to the extent that TA, as publicly instituted bodies, exercise public functions, they possess (a degree of) international legal personality. A functional and dynamic approach to international legal personality, based on the criterion of effectiveness, is to be favoured. This approach has been applied to *de facto* regimes and is defended by several authors.[90] Arguably, 'if international law grants even insurgents the status of partial subjects of international law, this must *a fortiori* apply to quasi-State entities that have consolidated their positions . . .. The principle of effectiveness means that they can *gradually* be granted international legal personality'.[91] The same is true of TA effectively implementing a state renaissance.

Third, when, after their public foundation, TA act on behalf of the state or nation, they enjoy international legal personality. The question of attribution will be addressed in the following chapter.[92]

---

no more than that the subject does not enjoy full legal capacity, as the States, but is only the addressee of the rights and obligations necessary for their special status and function in international law'. See also C. Walter, 'Subjects of International Law', op. cit.: 'subjects of international law may be defined as entities which are capable of possessing international rights and duties'.

[90] This includes the Taliban, a group that has regularly been directly addressed by the UNSC. The UNSC stated that the Taliban was obliged to comply with international law. See SC/RES/1267 of 15 October 1999, S/RES/1333 of 19 December 2000, S/RES/ 1363 of 30 July 2001, S/RES/1378 of 14 November 2001. R. Wolfrum, C. Philipp, 'The Status of the Taliban: Their Obligations and Rights under International Law' in J. Frowein, R. Wolfrum (eds.), *Max Planck Yearbook of United Nations Law*, Vol. 6, 2002, p. 601.

[91] H.-J. Heintze, 'Are *De Facto* Regimes Bound by Human Rights?' in Institute for Peace Research and Security Policy at the University of Hamburg / IFSH (ed.), *OSCE Yearbook 2009*, Nomos Verlagsgesellschaf, Baden-Baden 2010, pp. 267–75. Own emphasis. In the same vein, J. Frowein writes: '[a]uch ein Regime, das nicht als Staat oder Regierung anerkannt ist, kann aber möglicherweise als Völkerrechtssubjekt in gewissem Umfang anerkannt sein'. Own translation: 'even a regime that is not recognised as a state or government, may be recognised as an international law subject to some extent'. J. Frowein, *Das de facto-Regime im Völkerrecht, Eine Untersuchung zur Rechtsstellung 'nichtanerkannter Staaten' und ähnlicher Gebilde*, Carl Heymanns Verlag Kg, 1968, p. 14. Cf. Also M. Schoiswohl, '*De Facto* Regimes and Human Rights Obligations – The Twilight Zone of Public International Law?', *Austrian Rev. Int'l & Eur. L.* 45, 6, 2001. See also Report of the International Commission of Inquiry on Darfur to the United Nations Secretary-General Pursuant to Security Council Resolution 1564 of 18 September 2004, 25 January 2005, § 172.

[92] Chapter 5, Section B.2.1.

NATURE OF TRANSITIONAL AUTHORITIES 137

The international legal personality of TA is *relative* because *correlative* to the legal position ('*Rechtsstellung*') assigned to them by other subjects of international law, and to the public functions they exercise. Just like with national liberation movements ('NLM'), the issue of legal personality of TA is relevant only during a limited period, that is the time it effectively functions or until the transition elapses, as Table 4.5 shows.[93]

Table 4.5 shows how international legal personality is relative as it depends on the three variables – norm addressees, effectiveness or state representation – identified above, which in turn also hinge on timing:

- In the pre-transition and when TA are merely embryonic, usually none of the three criteria are satisfied.
- After their public foundation, inchoate TA gaining wider support without effectively starting the interregnum (or being almost immediately aborted) and oppositional TA[94] will enjoy international legal personality only to the extent that they exercised effective public powers or became addressees of international law, and only during that period. Consensual TA will also enjoy legal personality if, *ab initio*, they acted on behalf of the state.
- TA observing the interregnum enjoy international legal personality to the extent they effectively exercised public powers and/or were sufficiently representative, which also depends on their consensual origin or, for oppositional TA, on whether they gradually became more inclusive.
- Finally, there is no doubt that TA enjoy international legal personality when the interregnum succeeds and comes to completion. In such cases, TA act as organs of the state, and their acts become attributable to the state, which, per definition, enjoys international legal personality.[95]

As mentioned above, the subdivision in four stages allows us to better define the scope *ratione personae* of *ius in interregno*, that is depending on when in the transition TA acquire international legal personality.

---

[93] J. Verhoeven, *Droit international public*, Larcier, 2000, p. 291.

[94] E.g. the opposition-based Libyan Transitional National Council when it exercised public powers *ad interim*. According to the Constitutional Declaration, the TNC was 'the supreme power in the State of Libya' that had to 'undertake the works of the supreme sovereignty' (Constitutional Declaration of 3 August 2011, art. 17). When it actually undertook this task, the international community generally treated it as the sovereign ruler.

[95] DASR, art. 4. See also Chapter 5, Section B.2.1.

Table 4.5 *Functional international legal personality*

	1. Pre-transition	2. Public foundation of TA	3. Interregnum	4. End transition
A. Tentative foundation of TG *(aspirational or embryonic TA)*	No int'l legal personality	/	/	/
B. Tentative interregnum *(inchoate TA)*	No int'l legal personality	Int'l legal personality to the extent: - TA is addressee of international obligations - Consensual TA is created to act on behalf of state - Oppositional TA ambitions to act on behalf of state, and has initiated exercising public powers e.g. during a power vacuum	/	/

C. Tentative completion of interregnum	No int'l legal personality	Int'l legal personality to the extent: - TA is addressee of international obligations - Consensual TA is created to act on behalf of state - Oppositional TA ambitions to act on behalf of state, and has initiated exercising public powers e.g. during a power vacuum	Int'l legal personality to the extent TA exercises public powers during interregnum	/
D. Completed transition	No int'l legal personality	Int'l legal personality to the extent: - TA is addressee of international obligations - Consensual TA is created to act on behalf of state - Oppositional TA ambitions to act on behalf of state, and has initiated exercising public powers e.g. during a power vacuum	Int'l legal personality to the extent TA exercises public powers during interregnum	TA has acted on behalf of state, and *ipso facto* enjoys int'l legal personality

140 THE ACTORS OF THE INTERREGNUM

Related to that, the subdivision also assists us in understanding *when* the law is applicable, and how its scope is differentiated depending on the stage. Thus, in the pre-transition stage and towards the foundation of the interregnum, external involvement with TG should be subject to higher scrutiny under the principles of self-determination and non-intervention, Part IV will argue. The constitution and institutions are then in abeyance, rendering the state fragile, and making the threshold for external actors to violate these principles easier to reach. Furthermore, during the interregnum, a shared core of emerging customary rules in relation to TG – the 'lowest common denominator' as detailed in Part III – is gaining terrain.[96]

B Raison d'être of Transitional Authorities: State Renaissance in the Post-Colonisation Era

Besides their domestic and provisional character, TA can be further conceptually isolated by the state renaissance they pursue, a purpose which stands out as being civilian or political in nature (1). Given their historic context, they must also be distinguished from national liberation movements (2).

1 State Transformation Aim: A Civilian/Political Purpose

Although TA may, and often do, have ties with the military or armed groups, they can mostly be separated from each other (1.1). Where there is a significant entanglement, the acts concerning civilian and political aspects of TG can be conceptually isolated (1.2). It is thus generally possible, and indeed necessary, to sever the civilian from the military/forcible aspects of TG (1.3).

1.1 Separate Structure, Hierarchy or Recognised Status

The distinction between a TA and affiliated (parallel or parent) organised armed groups is often straightforward. In order to verify their civilian nature, the definition of civilians developed by the ICRC can be of further assistance. In the absence of any treaty definition, the ICRC has provided (negative) definitions of 'civilians' in international and non-international armed

---

[96] N. Youssef, *La Transition démocratique et la garantie des droits fondamentaux*, op. cit., p. 73. TA then increasingly respect specific norms in relation to TG, resulting in what Youssef calls the minimum of the *Etat légal intérimaire*.

RAISON D'ÊTRE OF TRANSITIONAL AUTHORITIES 141

conflict.[97] It follows from these definitions, accepted as authoritative,[98] that a person who (1) is not member of the state armed forces[99] or of an organised armed group,[100] (2) nor participant in a *levée en masse*,[101] (3) nor directly takes part in hostilities,[102] is undoubtedly a civilian, regardless of whether the armed conflict is international or non-international. A group mainly composed of such persons is a civilian group as opposed to an armed group.[103]

[97] N. Melzer, ICRC, 'Interpretative Guidance on the Notion of Direct Participation in Hostilities under International Humanitarian Law', May 2009, p. 20.

[98] For a discussion, see C. Garraway, 'Direct Participation and the Principle of Distinction: Squaring the Circle' in C. Harvey, J. Summers, N. D. White (eds.), *Contemporary Challenges to the Laws of War: Essays in Honour of Professor Peter Rowe*, Cambridge University Press, 2014. Cf. also G. Aivo, *Le statut de combattant dans les conflits armés non internationaux*, Primento, 2013; especially second chapter, part 2, title 1.

[99] The notion of state armed forces is relatively broad, and includes 'both the regular armed forces and other armed groups or units organised under a command responsible to the state' (N. Melzer, ICRC, 'Interpretative Guidance on the Notion of Direct Participation in Hostilities under International Humanitarian Law', op. cit., p. 31). Yet, even in a country at war, persons exercising political powers within a group that has the intent of constitutionally and institutionally reconfiguring the state are not necessarily members of that state's armed forces, or of its national guard, customs or police forces. The execution of TG is mostly not a state's army's business, even though this is not excluded, as the role by the military (the interim cabinet of the Supreme Council of the Armed Forces installed in February 2011) in the transition *sensu lato* in Egypt illustrates.

[100] The category of 'organised armed group' does not directly relate to TG either. This category includes both dissident armed forces and other organised armed groups. Concerning the membership in organised armed groups other than dissident armed forces, one should follow a functional criterion. If an individual does not exercise continuous combat function in an organised armed group, s/he (again) acquires civilian status. N. Melzer, 'Interpretative Guidance on the Notion of Direct Participation in Hostilities under International Humanitarian Law', op. cit., pp. 32–3.

[101] Art. 2 H IV R; Art. 4 [6] GC III; Art. 50 [1] AP I.; N. Melzer, ICRC, 'Interpretative Guidance on the Notion of Direct Participation in Hostilities under International Humanitarian Law', op. cit., p. 25. TG is not an improvised exercise. TI pre-define the transition roadmap sometimes in quite some detail. This is why TG cannot easily rely on 'inhabitants of a non-occupied territory who, on the approach of the enemy, spontaneously take up arms to resist the invading forces without having had time to form themselves into regular armed units', which is the definition of a *levée en masse* (p. 32).

[102] For lack of 'belligerent nexus' – which is defined in relation to the (purported) causation of military harm (N. Melzer, 'Interpretative Guidance on the Notion of Direct Participation in Hostilities under International Humanitarian Law', op. cit., pp. 47 and 58) –, 'the concept of direct participation in hostilities [*excludes*] the lawful exercise of *administrative, judicial or disciplinary authority* on behalf of a party to the conflict'. Own emphasis. This is why the exercise of political authority on behalf of a political – even warring – party to a conflict cannot be compounded with direct participation in hostilities.

[103] Z. Dabone, *Le Droit International Public Relatif Aux Groupes Armés Non Étatiques*, L.G. D.J., Schulthess Éditions Romandes, Université de Genève, Faculté de Droit, 2012, p. 85.

142   THE ACTORS OF THE INTERREGNUM

A civilian group functioning as a TA is a civilian TA. In this book, the adjective 'civilian' is however generally omitted. Civilian TA can either be parallel to (for example the Libyan council and Syrian coalition) or originate from (for example the Eritrean provisional government) an armed group. The criteria of separate structure and hierarchy imply that civilian TA are organised following their own organogram and chain of command, in plain, are directed by someone else than the superior of the military wing, if there is one. It is furthermore possible that the military status of a group, over time, gives way to a political status, as was observed with national liberation movements. Thus, the military status of the ANC 'had been suspended with the beginning of negotiations for transition'.[104]

On the basis of the separate structure and hierarchy criterion, there was a clear distinction, for instance, between the 'National Coalition for Syrian Revolutionary and Opposition Forces' (the 'Coalition'), on one hand, and the 'Free Syrian Army' and 'Supreme Military Council Command', on the other. These organisations were based in different cities – Istanbul and Reyhanli respectively – and the Coalition only had '*tenuous* links with fighters on the ground'.[105] The distinction also stemmed from official statements, including the conclusions of the November 2012 Doha meeting where the Coalition was created.[106] When on 15 December 2012 the Military Council issued a statement clarifying its legal status, the Coalition was not mentioned.[107] The Coalition and Supreme Military Council were

> Dabone focuses on the use of arms for belligerent purposes in order to define an armed group. This definition can be used *a contrario* to describe a 'civilian group'.

[104] K. Ginther, 'Liberation Movements' in R. Bernhardt, P. Macalister-Smith, and Max-Planck -Institut für Ausländisches Öffentliches Recht und Völkerrecht (eds.), *Encyclopedia of Public International Law*, North-Holland, 1992, pp. 213–15.

[105] 'Western-backed Syrian opposition body elects new leadership', *Reuters*, 5 January 2015: '[d]espite having *tenuous links* with fighters on the ground . . ., the National Coalition remains one of the main parties in international discussions to find solutions to the almost four-year civil war'. Own emphasis.

[106] Draft of the 'Syrian Coalition Doha Agreement', fourth conclusion, first consulted on the pages of www.etilaf.org where it is not available anymore. Last consulted on 26 March 2020 on https://m.dailykos.com/stories/1237058. The fourth conclusion provided that the Coalition would 'creat[e] a Supreme Military Council that oversees all military councils and entities. The Coalition will also aid in the composition of the Supreme Military Council, including all organisational and structural specifications'. During early October 2013 the Syrian Coalition, through the 'Government on forming Ministry of defense', and the Free Syrian Army took steps to institutionalise their reciprocal ties. See media statement of 8 October 2013, and the statement by the Supreme Military Council of 5 October 2013.

[107] 'Statement on the Formation of the Supreme Military Council Command of Syria' of 15 December 2012.

clearly separate entities, functioning under a distinct organisation and hierarchy.

1.2 Focus on the Civilian/Political Portfolio

Sometimes the armed/military groups and political factions are rather entangled. Even then, the acts (and sometimes persons) concerned with the civilian/political aspects of TG can mostly be conceptually isolated. When the criteria of separate structure and hierarchy cannot be applied, the criterion of functionality takes precedence. When TA purport to reconstitutionalise their respective countries, this is a civilian/political activity, and eminently so, even if it is carried out against the background of violent crisis, an armed conflict or threat to international peace and security.

The label of civilian TG could then also be used when a group exercises political and administrative authority on behalf of a party to the conflict,[108] and even for segments within the army itself. The Guinean TA, for example, was 'composed of civilians *and* the military',[109] yet its portfolio was political as it held 'legislative powers, with a view to achieving the objectives of the transition'.[110] In relation to the transition in Egypt (a transition *sensu lato*), the Egyptian Supreme Council of the Armed Forces conferred political powers upon itself after adopting a constitutional declaration in March 2011, and a number of 'basic principles for the new constitution'. Although it had jeopardised civilian oversight *during* the interregnum, it clearly pledged to a civilian outcome of the transition – privileging the ballot over bullets.[111] The Supreme Council thus came to deal with a political portfolio as if it were a civilian transitional authority. The latter observation also applies to another transition *sensu lato*, in Sudan where the military, on the basis of an agreement concluded with the opposition early July 2019, in an initial stage observed the interim rule.

When armed (opposition) groups or the military play a dominant role in TG, it is often required that TG be handed over to civilians, or at least

---

[108] It can also occur that civilian parties involved in TG lose control over their military/armed counterparts, as in the DRC during the 2002-2005 transition. Thus, for ICG, '[n]one of the signatories of the Sun City Agreement, which ushered in the transition in 2003, has strong control of either its military or political wing'. 'The Congo's transition is failing: crisis in the Kivus', ICG, Africa Report n. 91, 30 March 2005, p. i.

[109] Final communiqué of the Extraordinary Summit ECOWAS heads of state and government of 10/11 January 2009, § 13.1. Own emphasis.

[110] Id.

[111] 'Egypt military pledges transition to civilian rule', *BBC*, 13 February 2011.

144 THE ACTORS OF THE INTERREGNUM

that a transition to civilian rule be facilitated. Sanctions can be applied to political but also military stakeholders trying to derail a transition. The UNSC threatened to do so, for instance, in Guinea-Bissau, urging *both* political and military leaders 'to refrain from any action that could hamper' the transition.[112] Under the African Charter on Democracy, Elections and Governance, 'State Parties shall strengthen and institutionalise constitutional *civilian* control over the armed and security forces to ensure the consolidation of democracy and constitutional order'.[113] It is thus not surprising that, in Burkina Faso, ECOWAS and a contact group called for the 'urgent designation of a suitable eminent *civilian* person to lead the transition'[114] during November 2014, a request doubled with threats of sanctions[115] and also echoed by the AU which 'reaffirm[ed] the imperative of a civilian-led and consensual transition'.[116] Alternatively, there is much insistence on the military interregnum at least paving the way to civilian rule.[117]

1.3 Severability Civilian/Political Versus Forcible/Military Aspects of TG

Civilian TG is thus conceptually distinguishable on two sets of grounds. Either the TA has a separate structure, obeys its own hierarchy or has its civilian status recognised. Absent these criteria, one can look at the nature of the tasks the TA is concerned with: the civilian/political portfolio and the proclaimed aim of primarily pursuing a state renaissance – a political activity, and eminently so.

---

[112] S/PRST/2013/19, p. 2.

[113] Art. 14. Own emphasis.

[114] See, for example, 'ECOWAS names contact group on Burkina Faso', 7 November 2014, calling for the 'urgent designation of a suitable eminent *civilian* person to lead the transition'. Own Emphasis. See, in the same vein, 'The African Union appoints a special envoy for Burkina Faso', AU Press Release of 3 November 2014.

[115] 'Burkina Faso crisis: African leaders in army handover talks', BBC News Africa, 5 November 2014. On 5 November 2014, it was reported that ECOWAS will 'hold a series of meetings to press for the quick handover, following a threat by the AU to *impose sanctions if the military did not act within two weeks*'. Cf. also 'Thousands gather in Burkina Faso to denounce "military coup"', *The Guardian*, 2 November 2014, reporting how UN officials called for the return to civilian rule, 'adding that *sanctions were a possibility* if there was no progress'. Own emphasis.

[116] Communiqué of the AU Peace and Security Council, 3 November 2014, p. 2.

[117] Thus, when the Supreme Council of the Armed Forces seemed to avert the possibility of civilian oversight contrary to an earlier pledge, other states continued to demand a return to civilian rule. See 'Egypt military pledges transition to civilian rule', *BBC*, 13 February 2011; and 'US urges Egypt's army commander on peaceful civilian transition', *Reuters*, 6 July 2013.

RAISON D'ÊTRE OF TRANSITIONAL AUTHORITIES 145

Why is it relevant to sever the civilian from the military/forcible aspects of transitions? This is so for three interrelated reasons. First, and on a general note, the distinction allows us to deprioritise questions related to the use of force – a commitment made for specific reasons and from the outset.[118] Second, it helps unveiling the practices that are relevant for *ius in interregno*, and for clarifying its scope. Third, civilian TG and military or armed activities should be evaluated differently under international law. For example, the thresholds for evaluating assistance to civilian TG as opposed to assistance to armed activities under the principle of non-intervention are different (for instance in relation to the definition of 'coercion')[119] although the principle itself remains relevant for both sets of circumstances.

2 Historic and Conceptual Distinction from National Liberation Movements

Today, the quest for self-determination increasingly takes place *within* the frontiers of transition states, and *through* TG. This is likely to be continued. The principle of self-determination will become pivotal to TG, and, conversely, TG will add specificity to this principle. The argument of a new life for the principle itself will be developed under Part III,[120] where only occasionally parallels will be drawn between TA and NLM all the while keeping a clear distinction. After a brief discussion of the historic criteria for recognising NLM (2.1), we shall observe that these are only of indirect relevance for TG (2.2).

2.1 Historic Criteria for Recognising NLM

Within the OAU, a Liberation Committee was established to 'provide for collective recognition and support of liberation movements on the African continent'.[121] Yet, the criteria used for recognising NLM were unclear. The pursuance of self-determination – the raison d'être of NLM – is an evident identification criterion;[122] relevant UNGA resolutions always mention the struggle for self-determination. The UNGA made several calls to discontinue any support to self-determination-

---

[118] Introduction, Section B.1.2.
[119] Chapter 5, Section A.2.2.
[120] Chapter 7, Section B.5 'A Revival of the Principle of Self-Determination'.
[121] K. Ginther, 'Liberation Movements', op. cit., § 17.
[122] In the same sense, O. Krönert, *Die Stellung nationaler Befreiungsbewegungen im Völkerrecht*, op. cit., p. 24.

146 THE ACTORS OF THE INTERREGNUM

violating states, and to lend support to NLM instead.[123] It thus invited 'all States to provide material and moral assistance to the national liberation movements in colonial Territories'.[124] But it never defined NLM nor identified their recognition criteria. Subsequent resolutions did not clarify this point.[125] The so-called Goodwill Mission Report is sometimes cited as an authoritative text in this regard.[126] Talmon, for instance, refers to this text, and draws a parallel with TA: 'in the 1960s, the Organisation of African Unity's Coordinating Committee for the Liberation of Africa developed *certain standards, albeit vague*, for the recognition of national liberation movements fighting the incumbent government as the sole legitimate representative of a people which, it is suggested, *may equally be applied to the recognition of the [Libyan] NTC*'.[127]

Scholarship generally agrees that effective territorial control was not a criterion to recognise NLM.[128] Neither regional organisations nor the UN used effective control over state territory as a criterion for recognising NLM. In contrast, political control over, and organised allegiance of, the people represented by NLM were considered as the relevant criteria conferring the effectiveness to NLM.[129]

---

[123] Note that, to my knowledge, the UNGA did not make any calls to recognise or engage with the Libyan and Syrian TA; it did not consider that it is a legal obligation to discontinue support to the incumbents, and to assist the TA. In September 2011, however, the Credentials Committee accepted that the TNC represent Libya at the UNGA.

[124] UNGA/RES/2105 of 20 December 1965 § 10. Call repeated in UNGA/RES/2787 of 6 December 1971 § 3.

[125] UNGA/RES/2787 of 6 December 1971; UNGA/RES/2625 of 24 October 1970; UNGA/RES/2787 of 6 December 1971. UNGA/RES/2878 of 20 December 1971. In resolution UNGA/RES/2908 of 2 November 1972 the UNGA refers to the 'arrangements relating to the participation in the work of the Special Committee of representatives of the national liberation movements' without further detail. UNGA/RES/3280 of 10 December 1974.

[126] General Report of the Goodwill Mission of the Coordinating Committee for the Liberation of Africa to the Angolan Nationalists, Léopoldville, July 13–18, 1963, quoted in J. Marcum, *The Angolan Revolution*, Vol. II, Exile Politics and Guerrilla Warfare (1962-1976), Appendix 2, pp. 304 a.f.

[127] S. Talmon, 'Recognition of the Libyan National Transitional Council', op. cit. Own emphasis.

[128] K. Ginther, 'Liberation Movements', op. cit., pp. 211–12: 'unlike insurgency in a civil war or a *de facto* regime, the recognition of liberation movements does *not require proof of any effective territorial control*'. Own emphasis.

[129] Id.: 'according to OAU and LAS practice, and according to the overwhelming majority of UN member States, liberation movements may gain recognition if evidence exists of *political control* over, and *organised allegiance* of, the people they claim to represent'. Own emphasis. See also O. Krönert, *Die Stellung nationaler Befreiungsbewegungen im Völkerrecht*, op. cit., p. 250, p. 253.

RAISON D'ÊTRE OF TRANSITIONAL AUTHORITIES 147

The requirement of effectiveness was however relative.[130] All that was required was national liberation to be pursued by a 'movement' reaching a certain degree of organisational capacity and representativity;[131] 'until self-determination can be freely and openly exercised, one has to be content with certain indices of the representative character of liberation movements'.[132] Scholars sometimes regarded international support as a complementary criterion for recognising NLM.[133]

In practice, the criteria of domestic allegiance and international support were not consistently applied. A wide variety of NLM existed in South-East Asia, Africa and the Americas. Their power and popular support was not constant. In some cases, NLM acquired popular support only progressively. Also, NLM were not always fully prepared to govern once they transformed into ruling political parties.[134] The UNGA actually declared that 'inadequacy of political, economic, social or educational preparedness should never serve as a pretext for delaying independence'.[135]

As the UNGA was not clear about the NLM recognition criteria, the debate was never settled.[136] This lacuna conferred enormous powers on

---

[130] O. Krönert, *Die Stellung nationaler Befreiungsbewegungen im Völkerrecht*, op. cit., p. 246, 248: 'an die Effektivität der Bewegung [sind] geringere Anforderungen zu stellen als an die Effektivität von Regierungen eines Staates'. Own translation: 'the effectiveness of national liberation movements is less demanding than the effectiveness of state governments'.

[131] Id., p. 23: '[i]m Sprachgebrauch der internationalen Politik werden grundsätzlich nur organisierte Bewegungen unter den Befreiungsbegriff gefasst. Das lässt sich damit erklären, dass spontan sich bildende und agierende Gruppen nicht das Maß an Stabilität und Dauerhaftigkeit aufweisen, das nun einmal erforderlich ist, um zu einem relevanten Faktor zu werden'. Own translation: 'In the usage of international politics, only organised movements are included in the concept of liberation movements. This can be explained by the fact that groups both formed spontaneously and acting spontaneously do not have the required degree of stability and permanence for becoming relevant actors.'

[132] G. Abi-Saab, 'Wars of National Liberation in the Geneva Conventions and Protocols', *Collected Courses of the Hague Academy of International Law*, Vol. 165, 1979-IV, p. 413.

[133] B. A. Boczek, *International Law: A Dictionary*, Scarecrow Press, 2005: 'the status of the movements rested not on the control of the territory but on the international support of the anti-colonial forces for the principle of self-determination of peoples'.

[134] M. N. Younis, *Liberation and Democratisation: The South African and Palestinian National Movements*, 1st edition, University of Minnesota Press, 2000: in South Africa, for instance, 'The shortage of personnel made the ANC's ability to assume control over the various apparatuses of the state, which were retained rather than dismantled, let alone the economic enterprises of the country, virtually impossible.'

[135] UNGA/RES/1514 of 14 December 1960, § 3.

[136] J. Faundez, 'International Law and Wars of National Liberation: Use of Force and Intervention', *African Journal of International and Comparative Law*, Vol. 1, no. 1, 1989, p. 97.

148   THE ACTORS OF THE INTERREGNUM

regional organisations like the OAU and the League of Arab States. The UN granted observer status only to NLM previously recognised by these regional organisations,[137] which thus 'began to play a role as powerful intermediaries between liberation movements and the international community'.[138] This became established practice.[139] The UNGA's recognition of NLM often resulted from the cooperation between the Special Committee on Decolonisation and the Economic Commission for Africa and the OAU.[140] Yet, it remains contested whether the recognition by regional organisations was *constitutive* of NLM.[141]

2.2 Indirect Relevance for Transitional Governance

Analogies between TA and NLM have been made in literature.[142] But full comparisons fall short because, contrary to TA, NLM pursued external self-determination. TA pursue the explicit aim of reconfiguring the constitutional order *within* their respective countries. This clearly differentiates them from NLM which – save for exceptions, notably the position of the Palestinian Liberation Organisation – in the specific context of

---

[137] UNGA/RES/3280 of 10 December 1974, §6, in which the UNGA 'decides to invite as observers ... representatives of the national liberation movements recognised by the Organisation of African Unity to participate in the relevant work of the Main Committees of the General Assembly and its subsidiary organs concerned, as well as in conferences, seminars, and other meetings held under the auspices of the United Nations which relate to their countries'. See also Preamble mentioning 'the positive results achieved in the work of the United Nations bodies concerned as a direct consequence of the participation of representatives of the national liberation movements recognised by the Organisation of African Unity'. Cf. also UNGA/RES/3247 of 29 November 1974, and A/RES/43/160 of 9 December 1988 § 2 in which the UNGA '[c]alls once more upon the States concerned to accord to the delegations of the national liberation movements *recognised by the Organisation of African Unity and/or by the League of Arab States* and accorded observer status by international organisations, the facilities, privileges and immunities necessary for the performance of their functions'. Own emphasis.

[138] Id., p. 863. Own emphasis.

[139] O. Krönert, *Die Stellung nationaler Befreiungsbewegungen im Völkerrecht*, op. cit., p. 208.

[140] This modus operandi was notably observed in the Fourth Committee, i.e. the Special Committee on Decolonisation and the Economic Commission for Africa. R. Wolfrum and C. Philipp, *United Nations: Law, Policies, and Practice*, Martinus Nijhoff, 1995, p. 859.

[141] E. U. Olalia, *The Status in International Law of National Liberation Movements and Their Use of Armed Force*, International Association of People's Lawyers, 2002, p. 17.

[142] P. Thielbörger, 'Die Anerkennung oppositioneller Gruppen in den Fällen Libyen (2011) und Syrien (2012)', *Journal of International Law of Peace and Armed Conflict*, 26. Jahrgang, 1/2013.

RAISON D'ÊTRE OF TRANSITIONAL AUTHORITIES 149

decolonisation[143] struggled to gain independence from the distant 'metropolitan' states (*'Fremdherrschaft'*). In short, the aim of NLM was to realise, reassess or reconfirm external self-determination while the aim of domestic TA is naturally to realise internal self-determination. To pursue this goal, TA seek to reverse or transform the institutional and constitutional framework of their respective countries.

Furthermore, TA do not correspond to a specific legal category but simply reflect a specific, recurring, politico-legal phenomenon. In contrast, 'from being a political concept, the national liberation movement became a specific legal category with its own conditions for recognition and a legal system of rights and duties'.[144] Also, whereas the 'legality of the peoples' struggle for self-determination and liberation from colonial and foreign domination and alien subjugation'[145] cannot be doubted, international law remains mostly neutral vis-à-vis – neither permitted nor prohibited – domestic calls to transform the political and constitutional order of a country,[146] and generally prohibits external intervention to encourage such transformations.[147] The absence of a legal status or special legal regime for TA, and the corresponding lack of explicitly formulated rules, are precisely the reason why this book analyses which obligations TA must increasingly honour under international law generally (Part III), and under which circumstances TA may be endorsed or supported by third states (Part IV).

---

[143] UNGA/RES/1514 (XV), known as the 'Charter of decolonisation'. Cf. also UNGA/RES/3280 (XXIX).

[144] R. Ranjeva, 'Peoples and National Liberation Movements' in M. Bedjaoui, *International Law: Achievements and Prospects*, UNESCO and Martinus Nijhoff, 1991, p. 107. See also C. Lazarus, 'Le statut des mouvements de libération nationale à l'Organisation des Nations Unies', *Annuaire français de droit international*, Vol. 20, 1974. pp. 173–200.

[145] UNGA/RES/2787 of 6 December 1971. Cf. also UNGA/RES/3103 of 12 December 1973.

[146] Chapter 3, Section A.2.

[147] Chapter 9.

5

The Sources of *Ius in Interregno*

Ius in interregno has no other meaning than *international law applicable to TG*, and does not pretend to evolve towards a self-containing regime. International law applicable to TG is stable, yet does not stand still. It includes both pre-existing and evolving norms applicable to TG.

Two contrasting examples illustrate this. First, if a state using coercion imposes laws on another state, in transition, in order to (indirectly) entrench the post-transition era, this would be unlawful under the principle of non-intervention, which is part and parcel of existing international law. *Ius in interregno* therefore prohibits such an intervention.[1] Second, when a TA tries to involve several segments of society in a state renaissance, this is generally commended and appreciated – but is such behaviour compulsory under international law? Is there an *obligation* for TA to attempt being inclusive? Widespread, and widely accepted, practice points to an emerging customary rule in this sense.[2] But even those who predict that this evolution will probably be confirmed must accept that, as it is presently merely germinating, this rule may radically change or fade out in the future.

At this stage, these introductory propositions simply aim at familiarising the reader with the following idea: individual customary rules are germinating in relation to TG but of course not in complete isolation from existing law, and notably the principle of self-determination. Also in the context of TG, the task of specifying the issues that this principle does not address is fulfilled by individual customary rules.[3]

This final chapter of Part II is a springboard to Part III, which is based on a close observation of transition practice and policies (available in a

---

[1] Part IV.

[2] Part III.

[3] Paraphrasing A. Cassese, *Self-Determination of Peoples: A Legal Reappraisal*, op. cit., p. 129. Own emphasis.

EXISTING LAW AS THE BASIS OF *IUS IN INTERREGNO*   151

separate report),[4] and which will argue that customary rules are emerging under the auspices of existing international legal principles. Before delving into this, this chapter exposes the theory behind the idea that both existing international law (Section A) and evolving law in the form of nascent custom (Section B) are relevant for TG.

A   Existing Law as the Basis of *Ius in Interregno*

A perusal of TI shows how international law plays a predominant role for transitions (1). This, in turn, suggests that fundamental international law principles are pivotal to *ius in interregno* (2).

1   International Law As Residual Law of the Interregnum

TG is increasingly becoming an international project. International assistance to TG has a broad impact on various – legal and non-legal – components of state-building and constitution-making. The factual internationalisation of the interregnum was already discussed.[5] In the legal sphere, the internationalisation of the interregnum is apparent from the increased reliance on international law, which acquires a 'heightened legitimacy as a domestic political reference point during transition'.[6] The reliance of TI on international law is thus a method to foster legitimacy.[7] The widespread legal internationalisation of the interregnum suggests that the exercise of public authority during the interregnum *must* be guided by the respect of international legal norms. TA pledge to let the transition and its outcome be guided by international law, which often comes to be directly applicable in the interim legal order. In this section, we shall put the legal internationalisation of TG in context and turn to some examples.

Post-Cold War TI generally contain multiple references to international law, including humanitarian law[8] and especially human rights

---

[4] E. De Groof, 'The Features of Transitional Governance Today', op. cit.

[5] Introduction, Section A.4. Chapter 1, Section B, Table 1.1.

[6] C. Bell, *Navigating Inclusion in Peace Settlements, Human Rights and the Creation of the Common Good*, British Academy, 2017, p. 57.

[7] C. Goss cited in C. Rodrigues, 'Letting Off Steam: Interim Constitutions as a Safety Valve to the Pressure-Cooker of Transitions in Conflict-Affected States?', *Global Constitutionalism*, 2017, 6:1, p. 39.

[8] This is also true for transitions that are not the primary focus of this study, e.g. the one in Cambodia. On the role of international law in the constitution-making process in Cambodia, see S. P. Marks, 'The Process of Creating a New Constitution in Cambodia'

152   THE SOURCES OF *IUS IN INTERREGNO*

law.[9] The growing tendency to integrate international law references into TI also results from the multitude of actors influencing TG.[10] During an interregnum, the reliance on international law ensures that, when the constitutional structure of the state is held in abeyance, there is no descent into state of nature. International law becomes the *residual* law of TG. With the domestic legal sphere in limbo, it steps in to fill the normative vacuum.

Compliance with international law *during* or *after* the interregnum are distinct issues. The legal internationalisation of the interregnum should be distinguished from the commitment, often made beforehand, that the post-transition legal order will be based on international law or will conform to a set of general principles. Often, TA pledge to let the transition *and* its outcome be guided by international law. In Part III, we shall see that TA do not have the power to predetermine their future constitutional order at least in full detail.[11] Yet, they can define the general principles (often with reference to international law) to which the coming constitutional order must conform. The commitment by TA to respect international law during the interregnum is a distinct matter. The Libyan TA, for instance, affirmed its 'strict compliance'[12] with international humanitarian law during the interregnum, and, on a

---

in L. E. Miller, *Framing the State in Times of Transition: Case Studies in Constitution Making*, op. cit., p. 208 and p. 228.

[9] Youssef observes that the 'protection théorique et juridictionnelle des droits fondamentaux a été prise en considération par les Etats menant la transition démocratique. La plupart d'entre eux ont adopté des Constitutions consacrant les droits fondamentaux'. Own translation: 'the protection of fundamental rights, in its theoretical and jurisdictional aspects, has been taken into consideration by the states steering democratic transitions. Most of them have adopted Constitutions recognising fundamental rights'. More generally, 'if there is one substantive area where most states have shown great willingness to be open to principles of international law, it has been in the area of human rights'. T. M. Franck, A. K. Thiruvengadam, 'International Law and Constitution-making', *Chinese JIL*, 2, 2003, p. 518. The prospective abidance by human rights law is not unrelated to the 'growing acceptance of the idea that conformity to human-rights norms is a necessary condition of the legitimacy of governments and even of states'. Cf. A. Buchanan, 'Human Rights and the Legitimacy of the International Legal Order', *Legal Theory*, 14, 2008, pp. 39–70. See also W. Wahiu, *A Practical Guide to Constitution Building: Building a Culture of Human Rights*, IDEA, 2011.

[10] Chapter 1, Section B.1.

[11] Chapter 6, Section B.3. See also E. De Groof, 'The Features of Transitional Governance Today', op. cit. Refer to 'Practice 3'.

[12] Declaration regarding 'The Treatment of Detainees and Prisoners' of 25 March 2011, available on www.ntclibya.org/english/prisoners (last retrieved on 5 May 2012, available *en cache*).

EXISTING LAW AS THE BASIS OF *IUS IN INTERREGNO*   153

different note, pledged that 'Libya *will* be a State that fully respects the international law and international declarations on human rights'.[13] The Constitutional Declaration confirms this.[14]

International legal obligations are increasingly directly transplanted into the realm of TG. This is true both of oppositional and consensual instruments founding TA. As to oppositional TI, the legal internationalisation of the interregnum is often clearly stipulated in opposition-based interim or transitional constitutions. Sometimes as part of their communication strategy,[15] oppositional TA thus pledge to respect international law.[16] Besides the example I just gave of the Libyan Constitutional Declaration, the constitutional declaration adopted by the Houthi revolutionary Committee in Yemen, for instance, was also explicit in this sense.[17]

Consensual TI are often peace agreements. In-depth comparative research explains why human rights references are increasingly integrated into such agreements: 'because . . . peacemaking is often, to some extent, constitution making, and peace agreements are often distinctively "transitional" constitutions, human rights are essential in such processes'.[18] As a result, 'a typical feature of contemporary peace accords and power-sharing agreements are references to human rights'.[19] Human rights references abound both in the preambles and substantive parts of peace agreements. This is especially the case when peace agreements fulfil functions beyond ending armed conflict or installing a ceasefire, that is when, as TI, they constitute tertiary normative frameworks regulating TG.[20]

---

[13] The Interim Transitional National Council Statement of 22 March 2011, available on www.ntclibya.org/english/the-Statement (last retrieved on 5 May 2012, available *en cache*). Own emphasis.

[14] Constitutional Declaration of 3 August 2011, op. cit., art. 7: 'human rights and his basic freedoms shall be respected by the State. The State shall commit itself to join the international and regional declarations and charters which protect such rights and freedoms'.

[15] M. Saul, 'Legitimising Transitional Authorities through the International Law of Self-Determination' in E. De Groof and M. Wiebusch (eds.), *International Law and Transitional Governance: Critical Perspectives*, op. cit., p. 95.

[16] See above-cited declarations by Libyan, Syrian, Yemeni (Houthi) and Ukrainian TA.

[17] Constitutional Declaration to organise the foundations of governance during the transitional period in Yemen of 6 February 2015, art. 4: 'the foreign policy of the State shall be based on adherence to the good neighbor principle, non-interference in the internal affairs of other countries, adoption of sound and peaceful means to resolve disputes'. Note that this initiative was rejected by the 'international community'.

[18] S. Aroussi, S. Vandeginste, 'When Interests Meet Norms: The Relevance of Human Rights for Peace and Power-Sharing', op. cit., pp. 183–203.

[19] Id.

[20] Id., p. 190. See also Chapter 3, Section B.2.

The reception of international law into domestic transitional constitution-making is not an isolated phenomenon.[21] It is part of the increased internationalisation of constitutional law: 'contemporary constitution-making processes are increasingly open to international law'.[22] The internationalisation of constitutional law is now extended to interim constitutions,[23] especially since both the contents and form of such constitutions are influenced by a relatively small transnational epistemic community (in spite of the plurality of actors engaged with TG) which regards TI as conflict resolution tools.

The systematic incorporation of international law, and especially human rights principles, into post-conflict (interim or transitional) constitutions is recommended expert practice.[24] The UN, too, actively promotes compliance with international law during the constitution-making stage; it even 'encourages constitutional approaches that *directly* incorporate and make supreme international human rights standards'.[25] As a result, the internationalisation of constitutional law applies not only to traditional constitutions but also to TI enshrined for instance in peace agreements or interim constitutions.

[21] P. Dann, Z. Al-Ali, 'The Internationalised Pouvoir Constituant', op. cit., p. 428. H. Tourard, *L'Internationalisation des constitutions nationales*, L.G.D.J, 2000.

[22] G. Bartolini, 'A Universal Approach to International Law in Contemporary Constitutions: Does it Exist?', op. cit., pp. 1–34, esp. p. 9 noting a 'significant trend of contemporary constitution-making processes to facilitate the openness of domestic legal systems towards international law'. Cf. also A. Cassese, 'Modern Constitutions and International Law', *Receuil des cours* 192, 1985, 331–476, and T. M. Franck, A. K. Thiruvengadam, 'International Law and Constitution-Making', *Chinese JIL*, 2003. Tourard came to a similar conclusion. H. Tourard, *L'Internationalisation des constitutions nationales*, L.G.D.J, 2000, p. 8. Id., p. 12: 'd'une part, il existe un développement de la prise en considération par les constitutions nationales du rapport de l'Etat avec le droit international ; d'autre part, on constate une pénétration croissante des normes internationales en droit constitutionnel et donc une soumission au droit international de l'ensemble des dispositions constitutionnelles'. Own translation: 'on the one hand, national constitutions increasingly take into account the relation of the state vis-à-vis international law; on the other hand, there is a growing penetration of international standards in constitutional law and thus a submission to international law of all constitutional provisions'. Cf. also T. M. Franck, A. K. Thiruvengadam, 'International Law and Constitution-Making', op. cit., pp. 516–18.

[23] IDEA, 'Interim Constitutions in Post-Conflict Settings', op. cit., p. 6. See also Bell's remarks on 'internationalised constitutionalism', C. Bell, 'Introduction: Bargaining on Constitutions – Political Settlements and Constitutional State-Building', op. cit., p. 18.

[24] J. Benomar, 'Constitution-Making After Conflict: Lessons for Iraq', op. cit., p. 90.

[25] UN Rule of Law Unit, www.unrol.org/article.aspx?n=Constitution-making, last accessed 9 May 2013 (not available anymore), available en cache. Own emphasis. See also J. Harper, 'International Constitutional Law', https://lawin.org/international-constitutional-law, last accessed on 28 March 2020.

EXISTING LAW AS THE BASIS OF *IUS IN INTERREGNO*   155

Finally, ensuring conformity with international law is seen as a deontological obligation. International mediators are supposed to ensure that peace agreements respect international law.[26] With regard to constitution-making, the UNSG Guidance Note on assistance to constitution-making provides that 'the UN should consistently promote compliance of constitutions with international human rights and other norms and standards. Thus, it should *speak out* when a draft constitution does not comply with these standards'.[27] The prevalence of international law for TG implies that, in post-conflict situations, 'public officials *have to* interpret national law through the lens of international law and standards'.[28]

The fact that experts should speak out when international norms and standards are not sufficiently integrated in constitutional texts suggests that socialisation directly contributes to the internationalisation of transitional legal orders. This 'rapid internationalisation'[29] is seen in several countries. States in transition generally express or reaffirm their commitment to international law. Notable precursors in this regard are Cambodia, Rwanda and South Africa. After the turn of the century, TA in Burundi, Afghanistan, DRC, Liberia, Somalia, Haiti, Iraq and Côte d'Ivoire, for instance, also expressed their deference to international law during the interregnum, as I have shown in a separate report.[30]

The internationalisation of TG shows and explains that TG is permeable to external influences. The manifold references to international law in TI are a clear expression of this. Such is particularly evident from the reconstitutionalisation of a country, a central aspect of TG. International actors often directly impact supraconstitutional interim frameworks. When there is a power vacuum, they tend to rely on international legal references. For domestic TA, too, international law is seen as the residual legal system whenever a domestic legal system is being transformed. The perusal of post-Cold War TI (in the separate report) confirms that international law

---

[26] 2012 UN Guidance for Effective Mediation, op. cit., p. 20. See also M. Saliternik, 'Reducing the Price of Peace: The Human Rights Responsibilities of Third-Party Facilitators', *Vanderbilt Journal of Transnational Law*, Vol. 48:179, 2015.

[27] 'Guidance note of the Secretary-General on UN assistance to constitution-making processes', op. cit., p. 4. Own emphasis. See also R. Sannerholm, *Rule of Law after War and Crisis*, op. cit., p. 237.

[28] R. Sannerholm, *Rule of Law after War and Crisis*, op. cit. Own emphasis.

[29] Id., p. 237.

[30] E. De Groof, 'The Features of Transitional Governance Today', op. cit., See under 'Practice 1'.

156   THE SOURCES OF *IUS IN INTERREGNO*

directly influences both their general *ratio legis* and individual provisions.[31]

In the long run, the legal internationalisation of TG potentially carries more weight than the internationalisation of traditional constitutional law. It implies that international law serves as an authoritative interpretive framework for national legal systems that are in limbo, spreading its influence to the domestic sphere 'through the backdoor', so to speak. Increasingly, TA must abide by international law during the interregnum. Even when the constitutional structure of a state is in flux, the international legal obligations incumbent on a state cannot be dispensed with. TG and its legal internationalisation thus consolidate the role of international law in the domestic sphere both during and after the interregnum.

2   International Law Principles

As international law is increasingly seen as the residual law of the interregnum, it becomes self-explanatory that, also in times of transition, its fundamental principles continue to play a pivotal role for governing relations between states. Principles widely accepted by the community of states are not on hold during a state renaissance. Part III will revolve around the principle of self-determination (2.1), and Part IV around the principle of non-intervention in domestic affairs (2.2), but here is the right place to introduce each principle.

2.1   Principle of Self-Determination

In the post-Second World War era, the 1960 UNGA resolution on the 'Granting of Independence to Colonial Countries and Peoples',[32] also known as the Charter of decolonisation, formed the basis for the implementation of self-determination in the context of decolonisation. Its second paragraph provides that 'all peoples have the right to self-determination; by virtue of that right they freely determine their political status and freely pursue their economic, social and cultural development'. The first article of the 1966 ICCPR and ICESCR sanctions this principle in exactly the same wordings without limiting their scope to the

---

[31] E. De Groof, 'The Features of Transitional Governance Today', op. cit. See under 'Practice 1'.
[32] UNGA/RES/1514 (XV) of 14 December 1960, *Declaration on the Granting of Independence to Colonial Countries and Peoples.*

EXISTING LAW AS THE BASIS OF *IUS IN INTERREGNO*   157

context of decolonisation.[33] By virtue of this common article, peoples have the right to *freely* determine their political status, thus also 'free from any manipulation or undue influence from the *domestic* authorities themselves'.[34]

Seen from the right-holder perspective, three layers of internal self-determination can be distinguished:[35]

- The people's right to determine the *pouvoir constituant* and 'constitute its own political system'[36] (defining the rules of the game);
- The people's right to change the constitution, that is 'to have a say in amending the constitution'[37] (modifying the rules of the game);
- The people's right to participate in public affairs, elections, referenda, etc. (taking part in the game).

In 2004 the ICJ confirmed the continuing validity of the principle of self-determination, stating that 'it is one of the essential principles of *contemporary* international law'.[38] Although not uncontested,[39] self-determination is often seen as an *erga omnes* norm under international law.[40] Writing in 1995, the ICJ found that the 'assertion that the right of peoples to self-determination, as it evolved from the Charter and from United Nations practice, has an *erga omnes* character, is irreproachable'.[41]

---

[33] J. Crawford, 'The Right of Self-Determination in International Law: Its Development and Future' in P. Alston (ed.), *Peoples' Rights*, Oxford University Press, 2001, p. 27.

[34] A. Cassese, *Self-Determination of Peoples: A Legal Reappraisal*, op. cit., p. 53.

[35] Id., p. 249.

[36] Id.

[37] Id.

[38] Legal consequences of the construction of a wall in the occupied Palestinian territory, Advisory opinion, ICJ Reports 2004, p. 136, § 154. Own emphasis.

[39] Summers writes that self-determination is not a *ius cogens* norm, and that its *erga omnes* character is also questionable (self-determination could simply be explained as a customary norm). J. Summers, *Peoples and International Law*, op. cit., pp. 387–92. See also J. Summers, 'The Internal and External Aspects of Self-Determination Reconsidered' in D. French (ed.), *Statehood and Self-Determination*, Cambridge University Press, 2013, p. 397.

[40] Cassese went a step further by confirming that 'self-determination constitutes a peremptory norm of international law'. A. Cassese, *Self-Determination of Peoples: A Legal Reappraisal*, op. cit., p. 140.

[41] Case concerning East Timor, judgment of 30 June 1995, ICJ Reports 1995, 90, § 29 ('*Case concerning East Timor*'). With references to the UN Charter and to ICJ jurisprudence (Legal Consequences for States of the Continued Presence of South Africa in Namibia (South West Africa) notwithstanding Security Council Resolution 276 (1970), Advisory Opinion, ICJ Reports 1971, p. 16; Western Sahara, Advisory Opinion, ICJ Reports 1975, pp. 31–3, §§ 54–9. Confirmation in: Legal consequences of the construction of a wall in the occupied Palestinian territory, Advisory opinion, ICJ Reports 2004, p. 136, § 88.

158 THE SOURCES OF *IUS IN INTERREGNO*

Today, a narrow interpretation of the right of self-determination cannot be defended anymore. Self-determination is not reduced to the decolonisation process.[42] The 1970 Friendly Relations Declaration precisely states that, in addition to the establishment of an independent state or the free association or integration with another state, 'the emergence into any other political status freely determined by a people' constitutes a mode of implementing the right of self-determination.[43] In a study based on treaty law, resolutions and declarations of IO, as well as state practice, jurisprudence and literature, Raič convincingly concludes that self-determination has a *'continuing* character ... beyond the traditional colonial context'.[44] International jurisprudence amply confirms that, at least in its internal dimension, self-determination is less controversial today than it used to be.[45]

Perhaps we are even going towards the monopoly of self-determination in its internal dimension. If self-determination is here to stay,[46] then the 'resort to external self-determination, in the sense of separation from an existing state, will gradually disappear in the future, except in its consensual form, giving way to the increasing prevalence of internal

[42] J. Crawford, 'The Right of Self-Determination in International Law: Its Development and Future' in P. Alston (ed.), *Peoples' Rights*, op. cit., pp. 37–8. In the same sense: C. Tomuschat, 'Self-Determination in a Post-Colonial World' in C. Tomuschat, *Modern Law of Self-Determination*, op. cit., pp. 2–4; M. Saul, *Popular Governance of Post-Conflict Reconstruction*, op. cit., p. 67. See also G. Arangio-Ruiz, *The normative role of the General Assembly of the United Nations and the Declaration of Principles of Friendly Relations*, Collected Courses of the Hague Academy of International Law, Vol. 137, Brill Nijhoff, 1972, p. 566: 'self-determination is not just another word for decolonisation in a narrow sense'.

[43] 1970 Friendly Relations Declaration, principle e. See also G. Arangio-Ruiz, *The Normative Role of the General Assembly of the United Nations and the Declaration of the Principles of Friendly Relations*, op. cit., p. 567.

[44] D. Raič, *Statehood and the Law of Self-Determination*, Kluwer Law International, 2002, p. 228. Own emphasis.

[45] The *Gambian coup* case (Joined Communications 147/95 and 149/96, *Jawara v. The Gambia*, (2000) A.H.R.L.R. 107 (ACHPR 2000) (Thirteenth Annual Activity Report), § 73); African Commission on Human and Peoples' Rights, Communication 75/92, *Katangese Peoples' Congress v. Zaire* (2000) A.H.R.L.R. 72 (ACHPR 1995) (Eighth Annual Activity Report); Supreme Court of Canada, reference re Secession of Quebec [1998] 2 SCR 217; Committee on the Elimination of Racial Discrimination, General Recommendation No. 21, Right to Self-Determination (adopted at the forty-eighth session, on 23 August 1996), § 4.

[46] G. Arangio-Ruiz, *The Normative Role of the General Assembly of the United Nations and the Declaration of the Principles of Friendly Relations*, op. cit., p. 566.

EXISTING LAW AS THE BASIS OF *IUS IN INTERREGNO*   159

self-determination'.[47] The continuing character of self-determination thus 'refers to an *internal* dimension or aspect of the right of self-determination, that is to say, to an implementation of self-determination *within* States'.[48]

Internal self-determination is least controversial when disassociated from the right to secession. Controversies especially arise when self-determination is invoked for justifying the secession from a state[49] as 'international law is not a suicide club for States'.[50] The scepticism about self-determination conceived as a right to secede was already palpable during the *travaux préparatoires* of the UN Charter,[51] and was later confirmed in jurisprudence, notably by the African Commission on Human and Peoples' Rights and the Supreme Court of Canada.[52]

Generally, TA challenge the existence or continuity of a regime, not of the state itself.[53] In relation to TG, internal self-determination is not to be understood as a right to secede. By generating a state renaissance, TA thus pursue the *least controversial form of internal self-determination*. This observation must be borne in mind when (inclusive) state renaissance will be further discussed, under Part III.

2.2   Principle of Non-Intervention

Under the principle of non-intervention, no state has the right to intervene, directly or indirectly, in the internal or external affairs of any other state. Based on the principle of equal sovereignty, and codified by the 1945 UN Charter,[54] the non-intervention principle was further enshrined in the 1965

---

[47] A. Yusuf, 'The Role That Equal Rights and Self-Determination of Peoples Can Play in the Current World Community' in A. Cassese (ed.), *Realising Utopia*, op. cit., p. 383.

[48] D. Raič, *Statehood and the Law of Self-Determination*, op. cit., p. 234.

[49] J. Crawford, 'The Right of Self-Determination in International Law: Its Development and Future', op. cit., p. 39; p. 64.

[50] P. Thornberry, 'The Democratic or Internal Aspect of Self-Determination' in C. Tomuschat, *Modern Law of Self-Determination*, op. cit., p. 118. In the same sense, G. Arangio-Ruiz, *The Normative Role of the General Assembly of the United Nations and the Declaration of the Principles of Friendly Relations*, op. cit., p. 567.

[51] As described in C. O. Quaye, *Liberation Struggles in International Law*, Temple University Press, 1991, p. 217.

[52] African Commission on Human and Peoples' Rights, Communication 75/92, *Katangese Peoples' Congress v. Zaire* (2000) A.H.R.L.R. 72 (ACHPR 1995) (Eighth Annual Activity Report); Supreme Court of Canada, reference re Secession of Quebec [1998] 2 SCR 217: '[t]he recognised sources of international law establish that the right to self-determination of a people is normally fulfilled through internal self-determination' (§ 126).

[53] The 2005 CPA for Sudan is a special case as it submitted the decision for South Sudan to separate from Sudan to a referendum.

[54] UN Charter, art. 2 § 1, § 7.

160   THE SOURCES OF *IUS IN INTERREGNO*

UNGA resolution, and in the 1970 Friendly Relations Declaration. This declaration's third principle is key to our further discussion:

> No state has the right to intervene, directly or indirectly, for any reason whatever, in the internal or external affairs of any other state. Consequently, armed intervention and all other forms of interference or attempted threats against the personality of the state or against its political, economic and cultural elements, are condemned.
>
> No state may use or encourage the use of economic, political or any other type of measures to coerce another state in order to obtain from it the subordination of the exercise of its sovereign rights or to secure from it advantages of any kind. Also, no state shall organise, assist, foment, finance, incite or tolerate subversive, terrorist or armed activities directed towards the violent overthrow of the regime of another state, or interfere in civil strife in another state.

The scope of the prohibition is quite large. The preamble to this declaration states that '*any* attempt aimed at the *partial or total disruption* of the national unity and territorial integrity of a state or country or at its political independence is incompatible with the purposes and principles of the Charter'. The declaration forbids 'all . . . forms of interference or attempted threats against the personality of the state *or* against its political, economic and cultural elements'.

The non-intervention principle also applies to areas other than the use of force.[55] This book is not concerned with the use of force even in combination with TG.[56] Scholarship often concentrates on *forcible* regime change, much less on *coercive but non-forcible* regime change. There is sometimes even confusion between coercive and forcible intervention.[57] In law, a range of coercive actions, whilst proscribed under

---

[55] UN Charter, art. 2, § 4. P. Kunig, 'Prohibition of Intervention', MPEPIL: '[t]he new and broader definition of intervention forbids not only direct military force but also indirect interference through economic, political, and diplomatic means'. See also *Nicaragua Case*, op. cit.: there is no general right to intervene in support of an opposition group; and a distinction must be made between arming and training a rebel group (threat or use of force) vs. supplying funds (not a threat or use of force, but rather a violation of principle of non-intervention).

[56] Suffice to remind that 'attempts to elevate pro-democratic intervention into one of the few limitations to the prohibition to use force have failed to bring about a new entitlement to use (or threat to use) force under international law'. J. d'Aspremont, 'Duality of Government in Côte d'Ivoire', op. cit. See also J. Vidmar, 'Human Rights, Democracy and the Legitimacy of Governments in International Law: Practice of States and UN Organs', op. cit., pp. 71–3.

[57] G. Arangio-Ruiz, *The Normative Role of the General Assembly of the United Nations and the Declaration of the Principles of Friendly Relations*, op. cit., p. 553, who refers to the 'embellishment of downright aggression into intervention'.

EXISTING LAW AS THE BASIS OF *IUS IN INTERREGNO*   161

the principle of non-intervention, could be undertaken without further objections under the prohibition of the use of force.

In spite of the broad wordings, the scope of the non-intervention principle is limited in two ways. Only when (1) coercion is exercised (2) in the '*domaine réservé*', is the principle violated.[58] Coercion forms 'the very essence of prohibited intervention', according to the ICJ.[59] But what is coercion? Not all unfriendly acts are coercive. A simple critique or condemnation is not coercive. Also, pressure and influence are part of normal foreign policies between states.[60] States have the right to react, also in critical terms, to events in other states. Intervention in a state's political choice is coercive when the measure used to intervene is 'objectively capable of modifying [this] choice[s]'.[61] According to its ordinary

---

[58] O. Corten, P. Klein, 'Droit d'ingérence ou obligation de réaction ? Les possibilités d'action visant à assurer le respect des droits de la personne face au principe de non-intervention', *Revue belge de droit international*, 1990/2; Collection de Droit International 26, Editions Bruylant, Bruxelles, 1992, p. 10: '[d]eux éléments doivent donc être démontrés pour conclure à l'existence d'une intervention illicite. Premièrement, il faut une utilisation de 'moyens de contrainte'; à défaut, il ne saurait être question d'intervention interdite. ... Deuxièmement, ces moyens de contrainte doivent porter sur des matières où l'Etat a préservé des droits souverains'. (Own and free translation: 'two conditions must be fulfilled to conclude that there was unlawful interference. Firstly, it is necessary to show that there was coercion; otherwise, there can be no question of prohibited intervention. ... Second, coercion must relate to matters in which the State has preserved sovereign rights'). See also pp. 13 a.f.

[59] *Nicaragua Case*, op. cit, §§ 202–4: 'in view of the generally accepted formulations, the principle forbids all states or groups of states to intervene directly or indirectly in internal or external affairs of other states. A prohibited intervention must accordingly be one bearing on matters in which each state is permitted, by the principle of state sovereignty, to decide freely. One of these is the choice of a political, economic, social and cultural system, and the formulation of foreign policy. Intervention is wrongful when it uses methods of coercion in regard to such choices, which must remain free ones. The element of coercion, which defines, and indeed forms the very essence of, prohibited intervention, is particularly obvious in the case of an intervention which uses force, either in the direct form of military action, or in the indirect form of support for subversive or terrorist armed activities within another state'.

[60] O. Corten, P. Klein, 'Droit d'ingérence ou obligation de réaction? Les possibilités d'action visant à assurer le respect des droits de la personne face au principe de non-intervention', op. cit., p. 16: 'il est évident que ... toute politique étrangère vise à influencer le comportement des autres Etats, et ce y-compris dans des domaines où il exerce sa souveraineté'. (Own translation: 'it is obvious that ... any foreign policy aims to influence the behaviour of other states, including in areas where it exercises sovereignty.')

[61] B. Conforti, 'The Principle of Non-Intervention', op. cit., pp. 471–2.

162   THE SOURCES OF *IUS IN INTERREGNO*

meaning,[62] coercion signifies 'the action of making somebody do something that they do not want to do'.[63]

In interstate relations, 'coercion ... involves the government of one State compelling the government of another State to think or act in a certain way by applying various kinds of pressure, threats, intimidation or the use of force'.[64] The ILC defines coercion as 'conduct which forces the will of the coerced state'.[65] In UNGA resolution 2131 and in the Friendly Relations Declaration, coercion is associated to the *subordination* of sovereign rights.

The non-intervention principle is violated when coercion is used in relation to the *domaine réservé*.[66] The *domaine réservé* concerns the areas of state activity that are internal affairs of a state.[67] As far back as 1858, von Martens wrote that the constitutional system of a country is a domestic matter.[68] Also more recently it 'appears to be the prevailing opinion among public international lawyers who regard the domestic affairs of a state, including its constitutions, as remaining outside the jurisdiction and evaluation of other states'.[69] Constitution-making is 'traditionally the *hallmark* of sovereignty and the *ultimate expression* of national self-determination'.[70] Clearly, the non-constitutional reconfiguration of a state goes directly to the heart of the *domaine réservé*. Please bear this in mind when the external triggering of oppositional TG will be discussed.[71]

---

[62] VCLT, art. 31.1.

[63] Oxford Advanced Learner's Dictionary.

[64] C.C. Joyner, 'Coercion', MPEPIL.

[65] DASR, commentaries to art. 18, adopting a relatively broad definition of coercion: 'coercion could possibly take other forms, e.g. serious economic pressure, provided that it is such as to deprive the coerced State of any possibility of conforming with the obligation breached'.

[66] '[a] prohibited intervention must ... be one bearing on matters in which each state is permitted, by the principle of state sovereignty, to decide freely', *Nicaragua Case*, op. cit., § 205.

[67] K. S. Ziegler, 'Domaine réservé', MPEPIL.

[68] G. F. von Martens, *Précis du droit des gens moderne de l'Europe*, op. cit.: 'une affaire intérieure de la société, qu'elle peut régler à l'exclusion de tous les étrangers'. (Own translation: 'an internal affair of society, which it can regulate to the exclusion of all foreigners').

[69] U. K. Preuss, 'Perspectives on Post-Conflict Constitutionalism: Reflections on Regime Change through External Constitutionalisation', op. cit., p. 473.

[70] P. Dann, Z. Al-Ali, 'The Internationalised Pouvoir Constituant', op. cit., p. 424. Own emphasis.

[71] Part IV.

B Nascent Custom

International law applicable to TG includes emerging customary rules. After a non-constitutional rupture, TA generally follow a similar set of *policies and practices* during the interregnum, regardless of their oppositional or consensual origin. They generally accept to fulfil a fiduciary role on the basis of a mandate that is limited both in time and substantively; and they commit to an inclusive state renaissance through gradual self-*re*determination. We shall detail in Part III what the substance is of these policies and practices, and argue that TA and other actors are becoming convinced that such policies and practices are more than just that – that is that a series of customary rules with regard to TG are *emerging around* existing international law.

Custom is based on general practice, both extensive and virtually uniform (*usus*), and the conviction that such practice reflects or amounts to law (*opinio iuris*) and is required by political, social or economic exigencies (*opinio necessitatis*).[72] Before proceeding with the argument of Part III, this last section first explains that the peace-through-transition paradigm forms the 'ecosystem' for *opinio necessitatis* to emerge, in turn a fertile breeding ground for custom creation (1), second, details which elements can be taken into account for evidencing *usus* and *opinio iuris* (2), and, finally, draws our attention to a number of pitfalls to be avoided in any reasoning about custom creation (3).

1 The Peace-through-Transition Paradigm As the 'Ecosystem' for Opinio Necessitatis

The peace-through-transition paradigm replaced the ITA model and adjusted the until then prevailing 'New York Consensus' on state-building.[73] Historic and socioeconomic reasons explaining the rise of TG were already advanced.[74] It is in this context that the conviction arises that TG practices are required by political, social or economic exigencies of our times. *Opinio necessitatis* is especially important during the custom's infancy, and this is why we treat it first: 'at least in the early formative stages of the custom, the conduct may be perceived as more of a social necessity than a legal obligation'.[75] In

---

[72] A. Cassese, *International Law*, Oxford University Press, 2001, p. 119.
[73] M. Kahler, 'Statebuilding after Afghanistan and Iraq', op. cit.
[74] Chapter 1, Section A.
[75] B. Conforti, A. Labella, *An Introduction to International Law*, op. cit., p. 33.

164 THE SOURCES OF *IUS IN INTERREGNO*

our case, we shall see that respecting common practices further substantiated under Part III is perceived as a political (1), social (2) and economic (3) exigency.

To begin with, the installation and monitoring of TG by the international community is viewed – often wrongly – as a political heal-all for all kinds of problems. The peace-through-transition paradigm is strongly anchored in practice. The creation of TA in Burkina Faso during Autumn 2014, and (formal or informal) proposals made in this sense for South Sudan during Summer 2014,[76] for Burundi during 2019[77] and for Syria during 2015,[78] 2016[79] and 2019[80] confirm this trend. Since 2019, transitions *sensu lato* were considered in at least two more countries (Algeria and Sudan). The result often is that domestic constituencies will more easily yield to political pressure presenting TG as the adequate means of promoting peace and stability, a template finding large resonance in the Global South.[81]

[76] During Summer 2014, the constitutional structure of South Sudan was being discussed on the basis of a 'position paper' proposing the creation of a (new) transitional government (The 'Position Paper' of 17 July 2014 is available on 'Commentary: The First Six Months of Transition in Post-Independent South Sudan', *The New Sudan Vision*, 15 February 2012. During a UNSC meeting, the US ambassador insisted on establishing a TA ('Security Council concludes South Sudan visit', UNMISS Press Release, 13 August 2014).

[77] 'Rejet d'un "Gouvernement de transition" pour débloquer la crise au Burundi', Arib Info, 4 February 2019: 'Le vice-président burundais, Gaston Sindimwo, a indiqué dimanche sur les antennes de la radio publique avoir rejeté une proposition d'un "Gouvernement de transition" qui a été émise par le médiateur dans la crise burundaise, Benjamin William M'Kapa, au 20ème Sommet des chefs d'Etat de la Communauté est-africaine.' (Own translation: 'Burundian Vice President Gaston Sindimwo said on Sunday that public radio stations had rejected a proposal to create a "transitional government" issued by the mediator in the Burundi crisis, Benjamin William M'Kapa, at the 20th Summit of Heads of State of the East African Community.'

[78] During September and October 2015, Germany, Iran, Russia and Saudi Arabia, the UK, have at least pondered the creation of a transitional government. 'Germany calls for Syria transitional government', *Yahoo News*, 27 September 2015. 'Forming Transitional Government: Iran Solution for Syria Crisis', *Alalam*, 25 October 2015. 'U.S., Russia, Saudi Arabia, Turkey meet on possible transitional government for Syria', *Triblive*, 23 October 2015. Position of UK, cf. 'Deal to end civil war in Syria could allow president Bashar al-Assad to stay', *The Observer*, 26 September 2015.

[79] Statement of the International Syria Support Group of 17 May 2016.

[80] 'Brussels to host third Conference on Supporting the Future of Syria and the Region', EEAS Press Release, 1 February 2019.

[81] R. M. Ginty, 'No War, No Peace: Why So Many Peace Processes Fail to Deliver Peace', *International Politics* 47, no. 2, March 2010, pp. 154. Thus, the 'African solutions to African problems' approach 'resemble[s], in many respects, western approaches'.

NASCENT CUSTOM

Second, as TG practices give effect to the peace-through-transition paradigm, they reflect a 'social sedimentation',[82] that is an 'accumulation of the patterns of behaviour and convictions of the members of a given society, the international society'.[83] There is a 'broad social consensus, that is to say a widespread awareness in the society concerned of the necessity of respecting certain rules of conduct'.[84] In spite of some scepticism in specialised circles on the effectiveness of such consensus, the growing community of practitioners remains immersed in the peace-through-transition paradigm and remains convinced that transitions, *grosso modo*, should follow similar patterns. What are the underlying reasons for this conviction and discourse?

This dominant discourse is the result of acculturation and repeated interaction catalysed by a small epistemic community. Although the community of *practitioners* including diplomats and civil servants engaged in post-war countries and especially constitution-building is constantly growing, the *epistemic* community dealing with these issues has a rather modest size, creating a habitat favourable to the reproduction of professional practices by emulation. The reoccurrence of TG, and the reiteration of specific features associated with it, can thus be attributed to particular social phenomena such as the 'interaction of transnational actors and norm entrepreneurs',[85] acculturation in contact groups,[86] the (recommended *vel non*)[87] presence of international mediators and

---

[82] L. Condorelli, 'Custom' in M. Bedjaoui, *International Law: Achievements and Prospects*, op. cit., p. 180.

[83] Id.

[84] Id., p. 181.

[85] 'An international rule is interpreted through the interaction of transnational actors in a variety of law-declaring fora, then internationalised into a nation's domestic legal system.' H. J. Koh, '1998 Frankel Lecture: Bringing International Law Home', Faculty Scholarship Series, Paper 2102, 1998, p. 626.

[86] For example, participants of the contact group 'encouraged countries that have undergone similar processes to share their experiences with the CAR'. See Conclusions of the fourth meeting of the International Contact Group on the Central African Republic of 21 March 2014, § 9.

[87] J. Benomar, 'Constitution-Making After Conflict: Lessons for Iraq', *Journal of Democracy*, Vol. 15, no. 2, April 2004, p. 90: '[i]t is particularly important to try to mobilize as much national expertise as possible during the constitution-making process. Foreign advisors may be helpful as well, but should not effectively replace the local participants in the process. Such advisors can usefully offer counsel or lay out options, but under no circumstances should they act on behalf of any local political party or group'. See also V. C. Jackson, 'What's in a Name?', op. cit., pp. 1270–1.

166   THE SOURCES OF *IUS IN INTERREGNO*

experts, the use of templates for peace-building,[88] but also the 'migration of constitutional ideas'[89] and 'constitutional borrowing'.[90]

This mimesis explains why specific TG practices gain currency. This is even more so since professionals, such as the former members of the UN Mediation Support Unit, rely on 'a conception of mediation emphasising generic and depoliticised expertise',[91] thus 'emphasis[ing] knowledge that can be transferred from one conflict to another and from one mediator to the next',[92] and perhaps de-emphasise the role of context-related conflict analysis. The tendency to characterise external mediation and assistance to TG as a technocratic and depoliticised action reinforces its supposed transposability. Custom creation and the germination of norms are partly predicated on these socialised practices and convictions. It is for this reason that policy guidelines and deontological obligations are no innocent texts.

Third, and crucially, TA adopt analogous practices with the hopes of increasing their (perceived) legitimacy, and of gaining also financial support from international community actors (often acting through contact groups). Such strategic calculations increase the odds of receiving budgetary support. The Comoros TI, for instance, literally emphasised the need to organise TG in order *to obtain funds* from the international community.[93] With regard to Guinea-Bissau, it was similarly observed that respecting the temporal limits to the interregnum would 'enabl[e] the full re-engagement of international partners'.[94]

---

[88] One proposal voiced at a UNSC meeting was thus to 'prepare a compendium of model practices for use by the United Nations in each post-conflict situation'. UNSC discussion on the role of the UN in post-conflict national reconciliation. S/PV.4903 of 26 January 2004, p. 16. See also D. N. Sharp, 'Beyond the Post-Conflict Checklist: Linking Peacebuilding and Transitional Justice through the Lens of Critique', *Chicago Journal of International Law*, Vol. 14, no. 1, 2013–14, p. 169, fn. 16.

[89] S. Choudry, *The Migration of Constitutional Ideas*, Cambridge University Press, 2011.

[90] D. M. Dennis, 'Constitutional Borrowing: The South Africa Experience', *International Journal of Constitutional Law*, 1 (2), pp. 181–95.

[91] E. Convergne, 'Learning to Mediate? The Mediation Support Unit and the Production of Expertise by the UN', *Journal of Intervention and Statebuilding*, 2015, p. 3.

[92] Id., p. 8.

[93] Accord sur les dispositions transitoires aux Comores of 20 December 2003, Part I (Principles): 'la nécessité de parachever rapidement la mise en place des institutions de l'Union des Comores, afin ... d'encourager la communauté internationale à débloquer l'assistance technique et financière'. (Own translation: 'the need to complete rapidly the establishment of the Union of Comoros institutions, in order ... to encourage the international community to release technical and financial assistance'.) Own emphasis.

[94] S/PV/6963 of 9 May 2013, 'The situation in Guinea-Bissau'.

NASCENT CUSTOM

While the assistance model may be less expensive than ITA, it does not come without costs and 'the international community continues to allocate vast resources to support interim regimes'.[95] As one delegation put it at a UNSC debate, 'the international community has an important role to play in providing financial and technical support to transitional Governments'.[96] The international involvement with TG requires financial commitments often on the basis of aid agreements, conditionality programmes or donations. The UNSC underscores that peace-building in transition states requires sustained financial support.[97]

This translates in considerable sums, also committed bilaterally, for example the $875 million provided by the US to Yemen since the transition began in November 2011 until September 2014,[98] soon after which the transition collapsed. The financial commitments to the Afghan transition have been widely reported.[99] The same applies to the Central-African,[100] Congolese,[101] Guinean[102] and other transitions. The UNGA

---

[95] J. Strasheim, H. Fjelde, 'Pre-Designing Democracy: Institutional Design of Interim Governments and Democratisation in 15 Post-Conflict Societies', op. cit., p. 336.

[96] The Egyptian delegation added that such support must continue for elected governments after the transition, and that the aim of the support was to establish 'the necessary frameworks to provide for all of these elements, including special tribunals, truth commissions, information strategies to enable individuals and groups to recover from the conflict and move to a phase of peaceful coexistence, and effective disarmament, demobilization and reintegration programmes'. S/PV.4903 (Resumption 1) of 26 January 2004 p. 9.

[97] S/PRST/2015/2 of 14 January 2015.

[98] Remarks at the Friends of Yemen Ministerial, 24 September 2014.

[99] A. Suhrke, *When More Is Less: The International Project in Afghanistan*, op. cit. The constitutional process alone cost US $12 million. Cf. C. McCool, 'The Role of Constitution-Building Processes in Democratisation', IDEA, 2004, p. 13.

[100] Cf. Declaration of the third meeting of the ICG-CAR of 8 November 2013: 'Participants pledged to facilitate and speed up, at the bilateral and multilateral levels, the procedures for financial assistance, taking into account the urgency and the magnitude of needs of the CAR. They agreed to reactivate the ongoing assistance programmes which had been interrupted as a result of the crisis. They urged the authorities of the Transition to work closely with the World Bank, the IMF, the African Development Bank (AfDB) and the EU, in order to establish quickly a transparent management system of the financial resources.'

[101] Third UNSG Special Report on DRC Mission, op. cit., § 17: '[a]s soon as the Sun City Agreement was signed, the DRC government and the World Bank signed a loan agreement of US $120 million to rebuild the economy, followed by US $120 million to rebuild the economy, followed by US $214 million in emergency support a few months later'; 'The donors reiterated their commitment to support a well-designed plan endorsed by all the components of the Transitional Government.'

[102] Déclaration conjointe de Ouagadougou, janvier 2010, § 11: 'les signataires de la présente déclaration appellent instamment la communauté internationale à apporter son

went as far as considering that 'in an era when dozens of States are under stress or recovering from conflict, there is a clear *international obligation to assist States* in developing their capacity to perform their sovereign functions effectively and responsibly',[103] and the UNSC often calls on states to financially support transitional institutions.[104]

But support to TG is seldom unconditional. Through 'implicit coercion', 'there can be a strong, implicit signal that the level of international support will be attached to the government's commitment to consistency with international human rights law',[105] to give one example. For the better or for the worse (a discussion for another occasion), social, political but also financial incentives and exigencies explain why TA (pledge to) follow common behavioural patterns. The same reasons explain why they often effectively comply with these practices, or at least spare no effort to do so. They perceive abidance to be a *necessity* also in light of economic incentives.

In short, against the backdrop of the peace-through-transition paradigm, TA and other actors are more and more convinced that, in times of transition, a specific set of TG practices are required by the political, social and economic exigencies of our times. Such *opinio necessitatis* then clears the way for spreading state practice (*usus*) and reinforcing the conviction that such practice amounts to law (*opinio iuris*).

concours politique, financier et technique pour la mise en œuvre des mesures ci-dessus arrêtées'. (Own translation: 'the signatories of this declaration urge the international community to immediately provide political, financial and technical assistance for the implementation of the above measures'.)

[103] 'A more secure world: our shared responsibility', Report of the High-Level Panel on Threats, Challenges and Change, A/59/565 of 2 December 2004, § 261. Own emphasis.

[104] For example, the UNSC has 'call[ed] on Member States, international and regional organisations to provide rapid and tangible support to the TA of the CAR including contributions for the payment of salaries and other needs of the TA of the CAR'. S/RES/2149 of 10 April 2014. Cf. also M. Saul, *Popular Governance of Post-Conflict Reconstruction*, op. cit, p. 28: 'international actors can [also] be expected to provide substantial funding for post-conflict reconstruction'. Cf. also sections on aid agreements (pp. 208–23).

[105] M. Saul, *Popular Governance of Post-Conflict Reconstruction*, op. cit, p. 106. With regard to Afghanistan, Saul writes: '[t]he clarity of the message that international actors expected a concern for human rights also had implications for the domestic actors that assumed governing responsibilities on the basis of the Bonn Agreement. It strengthened the signal that continued and extended international support was likely to have some connection to the approach taken to compliance with international law' (pp. 164–5). With sharper criticism, D. Chandler, *Empire in Denial – The Politics of State-Building*, op. cit., p. 39.

NASCENT CUSTOM 169

2 Usus *and* Opinio Iuris

State practice (*usus*) can be evidenced by a wide range of actions and documents: 'treaties, participation in the resolutions of international organisations, diplomatic correspondence, statutes, the decisions of domestic courts, and administrative acts' may evidence state practice.[106] In 2016, the Special Rapporteur on the identification of custom also adopted a relatively broad definition of state practice.[107] The following documents can thus be considered:

> diplomatic correspondence, policy statements, press releases, the opinions of government legal advisers, official manuals on legal questions (e.g. manuals of military law), executive decisions and practices, orders to military forces (e.g. rules of engagement), comments by governments on ILC drafts and corresponding commentaries, legislation, international and national judicial decisions, recitals in treaties and other international instruments (especially when in 'all States' form), an extensive pattern of treaties in the same terms, the practice of international organs, and resolutions relating to legal questions in UN organs, notably the General Assembly.[108]

The conviction that practice reflects or amounts to law (*opinio iuris*), as a natural extension of *opinio necessitatis*, is instrumental to custom creation. Legal conviction must not always be inferred from separate acts: *opinio iuris* and state practice can both be derived from the TI, other relevant documents, and reactions to these documents, amply cited in this book and the accompanying report.[109] Besides the already present

---

[106] B. Conforti, A. Labella, *An Introduction to International Law*, op. cit., p. 32, with reference to domestic jurisprudence.

[107] Fourth report on identification of customary international law, op. cit., p. 21, draft conclusion 6, § 3: 'Forms of State practice include, but are not limited to: diplomatic acts and correspondence; conduct in connection with treaties; executive conduct, including operational conduct "on the ground"; legislative and administrative acts; and decisions of national courts.'

[108] J. Crawford, *Brownlie's Principles of Public International Law*, Oxford University Press, 2008, p. 24. In the same sense, cf. V. Đ. Degan, *Sources of International Law*, Martinus Nijhoff Publishers, 1997, p. 174 a.f.

[109] For someone who infers *opinio iuris* partly from state practice, see C. Tams, *Enforcing Obligations Erga Omnes in International Law*, Cambridge University Press, 2005, p. 238. For the other way around, J. Wouters and C. Ryngaert, 'Impact on the Process of the Formation of Customary International Law' in M. T. Kamminga and M. Scheinin (eds.), *The Impact of Human Rights Law on General International Law*, Oxford University Press, 2009. See furthermore A. Bleckmann, 'Die Praxis des Völkergewohnheitsrecht als konsekutive Rechtsetzung' in R. Bernhardt, W. K. Geck, G. Jaenicke, H. Steinberger (eds.), *Völkerrecht als Rechtsordnung, Internationale Gerichtsbarkeit, Menschenrechte*, Springer-Verlag, 1983, p. 91: '[es] [w]ird ersichtlich, dass dann Übung und Äußerung

170   THE SOURCES OF *IUS IN INTERREGNO*

opinio necessitatis, arguably *opinio iuris* seems to be increasingly accompanying the practices described under Part III.

Both *usus* and *opinio iuris* are only relevant to the extent they are attributable to states in transition. Let us first consider this question (2.1) before our enquiry concentrates on how *usus* and *opinio iuris* in relation to TG can be revealed in TI (2.2) and receive broad confirmation from international actors (2.3).

2.1   The Question of Attribution

Most of the transitions under examination are or were led by *consensual* TA. When TA are consensual – for example unity governments – their conduct is naturally attributable to the state. Under specific conditions, conduct by *oppositional* TA may also be regarded as relevant practice. During the interregnum, publicly instituted oppositional TA acquire international legal personality to the extent that they effectively exercise important public functions, and bear international obligations. This was observed in Chapter 4. The functional international legal personality of TA however does not confer international lawmaking power on them. In other words, it is not because TA may enjoy international legal personality that they generate relevant practice under international law.[110] To qualify for this, the conduct of oppositional TA must (either immediately or in hindsight) be attributable to a state in transition.

Two scenarios can be envisaged, as follows. First, conduct by oppositional TA may be regarded as relevant practice when, eventually, it can be attributed to a state in transition.[111] If oppositional TA, as addressees of international obligations and having exercised public powers during the interregnum, evolve into the government of the state, their policy statements, opinions, manuals or other relevant texts thus become relevant for the assessment of custom germination. If oppositional TA are successful in reconstitutionalising the state, their conduct can be (retroactively) attributed to the state.

---

der Rechtsüberzeugung nicht, wie die Lehre vorauszusetzen scheint, in zwei unterschiedlichen Akten zu suchen sind, sondern in einem einzigen Akt zusammenfallen' (Own translation: 'it becomes apparent that then the practice and expression of the conviction do not manifest themselves, as the doctrine seems to presuppose, in two separate acts, but coincide in a single act'). Bleckmann insists on the seriousness of practice (which can be evidenced by institutional guarantees). Id., p. 98.

[110] Fourth report on identification of customary international law, op. cit., p. 21 (draft conclusion 4, § 3).

[111] DASR, art. 10.

The ILC considered that the conduct of an insurrectional movement subsequently becoming the new government of the state 'shall be considered an act of that state under international law'.[112] This conclusion can be applied *mutatis mutandis* to oppositional TA. The conduct of oppositional TA may be attributed *ex post* to the state if TG has proven to be successful. Through this avenue, the conduct of such authorities can also be informative for assessing in which direction *ius in interregno* is evolving.

Second, conduct by oppositional TA may be regarded as relevant practice when, eventually, it can be attributed to, *or is acknowledged by*, a state in transition. Conduct can be acknowledged and adopted by a transition state as its own sometimes through acquiescence.[113] For instance, in the period immediately following the 2011 Constitutional Declaration, the Libyan TNC exercised important functions, yet there was certainly no consensus about it then representing the Libyan state. This declaration was however accepted and acknowledged as foundational by subsequent TA, and therefore remains informative for an international law analysis of TG.

2.2 Transition Instruments as Evidence of Nascent Custom

The plurality and variety of TI as 'tertiary norms' reflect a rich and creative practice based on a common paradigm. TI are enshrined in intrastate agreements, domestic legislation and international treaties. The three categories of TI were introduced in Chapter 3 (Section B.1). This variety, already observed in literature,[114] reflects the creative power and casuistic approach of lawyers, policymakers, mediators, diplomats and advisors who, within their respective constituencies or on behalf of their own organisations, happen to be involved in a similar enterprise becoming common currency nowadays: TG. Casuistry concerns the form or sequence of instruments used for realising the peace-through-transition paradigm, not the paradigm itself. Nor does this casuistry alter the fact that TG is a distinct phenomenon,[115] and that TI, too, with their

---

[112] DASR, art. 19. Cf. also the commentaries. *Yearbook of the International Law Commission, 2001*, Vol. II (Part Two).

[113] DASR, art. 11: 'Conduct which is not attributable to a State under the preceding articles shall nevertheless be considered an act of that State under international law if and to the extent that the State acknowledges and adopts the conduct in question as its own.'

[114] N. Youssef, *La Transition démocratique et la garantie des droits fondamentaux*, op. cit., pp. 112 a.f.

[115] Introduction, Section A.

172 THE SOURCES OF *IUS IN INTERREGNO*

shared function (supraconstitutionality) and purpose (transformative constitutionalism), are discernible.[116]

TG practices are often self-imposed in domestic interim constitutional texts or intrastate agreements, or are obligatory as the result of an international treaty. As noted, TI pursue a triple purpose, that is peace through transition, self-regulation and constitutional reconfiguration based on their supraconstitutional nature. The idea that constitutional practice may cement into custom is not new. The idea that supraconstitutional practice may contribute to it, perhaps is.[117] Some may be surprised by this idea. But denying supraconstitutional TI even the *potential* to inform custom creation would fly in the face of their triple purpose, intimately related to the heart of a state's affairs. Saying that supraconstitutional practice and what I call 'tertiary norms' could never be indicative of emerging state practice seems somewhat similar, to end with a lighter note, to excluding that hominoids were the predecessors of the *homo sapiens*. In sum, there is little reason, other than pervasive silo-thinking, to systematically deny *any* relevance to comparative (supra) constitutional norms under general international law.[118]

In the following lines we shall thus suggest that supraconstitutional TI, enshrined in intrastate agreements (2.2.1), domestic legal acts (2.2.2) and international treaties (2.2.3) can be – if attributable to state practice – be indicative of emerging custom, especially when international reactions confirm the trend.

2.2.1 Domestic Intrastate Agreements as Evidence of Nascent Custom

Supraconstitutional intrastate agreements (also without being treaties in the sense of the VCLT) regulate transitions,[119] and can be indicative of emerging custom. Intrastate agreements are frequently 'internationalised', especially when they exhibit the following features: (1) the signatories are subjects of international law; (2) the agreement has been endorsed by other subjects of international law;[120] (3) the agreement contains various references to international law; (4) the agreement has

---

[116] Chapter 3.

[117] This paragraph is inspired by a discussion with S. Choudry at the ICON-S conference in Berlin in June 2016 for which I am very grateful.

[118] The mission statement of the International Society of Public Law also suggests this. See www.icon-society.org/mission, last accessed on 26 March 2020.

[119] Twelve such cases were discussed above. Afghanistan, Burundi, Comoros, Côte d'Ivoire, Liberia, Mali, Nepal, Ukraine, Rwanda, Sierra Leone, Sudan and Yemen.

[120] See e.g. the *Comores Accord sur les dispositions transitoires aux Comores* of 20 December 2003.

consistently been invoked or referred to in binding UNSC resolutions and (5) its implementation is internationally monitored. On the basis of these five features, the Arusha Agreement (Burundi), the Pretoria Agreement (DRC), the Bonn Agreement (Afghanistan), the Global Comprehensive Agreement (Sudan) and the GCC Agreement (Yemen) can be regarded as internationalised intrastate agreements.

Whether or under which circumstances intrastate agreements acquire international (or internationalised) legal status remains a contested point.[121] What is their residual legal system: domestic or international law? This question may affect the international legal status of 'internationalised' intrastate agreements. But the question of status of such agreements triggering and regulating TG is not central to our argument. Regardless of their status, such agreements can (indirectly) acquire international legal *relevance* to the extent that they manifest state practice and *opinio iuris*. State practice can be evidenced by 'all branches of the (central) government of the State, be they executive, legislative, or judicial'.[122] As supraconstitutional intrastate agreements have considerable legislative effects and sometimes form a basis for executive acts, they, too, may, sometimes retroactively or through acquiescence, be indicative of state practice, thus co-constitutive of custom.

Furthermore, and from a whole different angle, if attributable to the state in transition, intrastate agreements may constitute 'unilateral declarations', that is 'formal declarations formulated by a State with the intent to produce obligations under international laws',[123] consolidating custom creation. As to their form, unilateral declarations are not dictated

---

[121] L. Vierucci, *Gli accordi fra governo e gruppi armati di opposizione nel diritto internazionale*, Editoriale Scientifica, 2013, p. 100: 'nonostante gli indubbi elementi di suggestioni presenti nel filone dottrinale che qualifica gli accordi come "ibridi" o "internazionalizzati", preme osservare che *da questa dottrina non emerge con chiarezza quale sia l'ordinamento di riferimento di questo tipo di atti*. Non è chiaro, infatti se l'ordinamento di inquadramento degli accordi "ibridi" o "internazionalizzati" sia quello interno, e in tal caso il diritto internazionale avrebbe una funzione limitata, ad esempio, al diritto applicabile, oppure se l'ordinamento di base sia quello internazionale, e al diritto interno sia fatto un mero "rinvio"'. Own emphasis. Own free translation: 'some scholarship qualifies certain agreements as "hybrid" or "internationalised". But this doctrine does not clearly show under which legal order such agreements fall. It is not clear, in fact, whether the classification of "hybrid" or "internationalised" is internal or international. In the former case, international law would have a limited function, for example to define which domestic law is applicable. In the latter case, international law would be the law by default containing a mere reference to domestic law'.

[122] M. Wood, O. Sender, 'State Practice', MPEPIL, § 9.

[123] 'Guiding Principles Applicable to Unilateral Declarations of States Capable of Creating Legal Obligations', *Yearbook of the International Law Commission, 2006*, Vol. II, Part Two.

174 THE SOURCES OF *IUS IN INTERREGNO*

by special or strict requirements.[124] If given publicly, and with intent to be bound, unilateral declarations are binding.[125] For evidencing these elements, the second (international endorsement by co-signature), third (international law referencing) and fifth (international monitoring) of the internationalisation features mentioned above will be particularly relevant.

2.2.2 Domestic Transitional Instruments as Evidence of Nascent Custom

Both national courts, the ICJ and the ILC have considered domestic legislation as primary evidence of state practice,[126] a position confirmed in 2016 by the Special Rapporteur on custom identification.[127]

Domestic legal texts often come into existence as a direct consequence of, or in connection with, a parent TI. For example, the 2004 Constitution of Afghanistan would not have seen the light of day without the 2001 Bonn Agreement. In Burundi, the 1998 Constitutional Act of Transition initiated the Arusha peace negotiations, affirmed the necessity of a transitional period, and eventually led to the 2000 Arusha Agreement. This agreement was followed by another agreement determining the structure of the transitional government,[128] a ceasefire agreement[129] and a post-transition constitution.[130] In the DRC, the 'Mémorandum sur le mécanisme pour la formation d'une armée nationale, restructurée et intégrée' of 6 March 2003 was adopted in line with the Pretoria Agreement, and should be seen as part of its context. Similarly, the domestic decrees of 29 March 2007 and 7 April 2007 regarding the creation and composition of the transitional

---

[124] Id., art. 5. Cf. *The Mavrommatis Palestine Concessions*, Judgment of 30 August 1924, PCIJ, Series A, No. 2, p. 34; *Application of the Convention on the Prevention and Punishment of the Crime of Genocide (Bosnia-Herzegovina v. Yugoslavia)*, Judgment of 11 July 1996, *ICJ Reports 1996*, p. 612, § 24 and p. 613, § 26; *Case Concerning the Temple of Preah Vihear (Cambodia v. Thailand), Preliminary Objections*, Judgment of 26 May 1961, *ICJ Reports 1961*, p. 31; *Nuclear Tests (New Zealand v. France), ICJ Reports 1974*, pp. 267–8, § 45, and p. 473, § 48.

[125] *Nuclear Tests (New Zealand v. France), Judgment, ICJ Reports 1974*, p. 457, § 46.

[126] M. Akehurst, 'Custom As a Source of International Law' in M. Koskenniemi, *Sources of International Law*, Ashgate, 2000, p. 259. Akehurst notably refers to the ICJ Nottebohm and North Sea Continental Shelf cases to substantiate this claim.

[127] Fourth report on identification of customary international law, A/CN.4/695, 8 March 2016, p. 21 (draft conclusion 6).

[128] Agreement on the legal framework and the structure of the transitional government, and the composition of the cabinet, the senate and the transitional national assembly of 11 October 2001.

[129] Global Ceasefire Agreement of 16 November 2003.

[130] Post-Transition Interim Constitution of the Republic of Burundi of 18 March 2005.

NASCENT CUSTOM

government in Côte d'Ivoire are part of the context of the 2007 Ouagadougou Political Agreement.

The practices of TA often stem from self-imposed obligations. Even at early stages of the interregnum, TA commit themselves to following a transition roadmap, often emulating other transition contexts. In the early twentieth century already, Gemma accepted the importance and legal relevance of obligations imposed by provisional governments upon themselves.[131] More recently, Samuels considered that TA should conform to their self-imposed constitutional framework.[132] Here too, when TA express their intention to be bound under international law through domestic TI, and such intention becomes attributable to the state in transition, it confers a legal character on the position taken,[133] thus reinforcing custom creation.

2.2.3 International Agreements as Evidence of Nascent Custom

Treaties can also evidence nascent custom. A number of TI are enshrined in international agreements, for example the Paris Agreement (Cambodia), the Pretoria Agreement (DRC) and arguably the Minsk Agreement (Ukraine). Such agreements are treaties in the sense of the VCLT, that is 'an international agreement concluded between states in written form and governed by international law ... *whatever its particular designation*'.[134] This definition does not require treaties to be registered with the UN Secretariat,[135] and accepts a variety of nomenclatures. It is flexible enough so as to include even joint communiqués between states.[136]

There is no doubt as to the international legal relevance of TI taking the form of treaties for custom creation considering the 'unending interplay between custom and treaty'.[137] The UNSC can give an extra impetus in this regard, for instance when it 'underlin[ed] the necessity for the full

---

[131] S. Gemma, 'Les gouvernements de fait', op. cit., pp. 383–4.

[132] K. Samuels, 'Postwar Constitution Building' in R. Paris and T. D. Sisk, *The Dilemmas of Statebuilding – Confronting the Contradictions of Postwar Peace Operations*, op. cit., p. 175: 'one of the benchmarks in the international community's relationship with a postwar transitional government could be the expectation that the government will abide by the constitution negotiated as part of the transition'.

[133] J. Salmon, *Dictionnaire de droit international public*, Bruylant, 2001, p. 305.

[134] VCLT, art. 2.1.a. Own emphasis.

[135] This is in principle required by UN Charter, art. 102, and by the VLCT, art. 80. This obligation has never been consistently respected though and, in any event, the definition of a treaty does not depend on it.

[136] Aegean Sea continental shelf, Judgment, ICJ Reports 1978, p. 3, § 96.

[137] B. B. Jia, 'The Relations between Treaties and Custom', *Chinese Journal of International Law*, Vol. 9, no. 1, 1 March 2010, pp. 81–109, § 67.

176   THE SOURCES OF *IUS IN INTERREGNO*

cooperation of the Supreme National Council of Cambodia ... in the implementation of the agreements'.[138] It also referred to the Pretoria Agreement for the DRC,[139] and to other agreements.[140] In such instances, the UNSC simply confirms pre-existing international obligations. As traditional sources of international law, TI enshrined in international treaties also help us understand how TG is considered from an international legal perspective, and inform us on the obligations increasingly becoming incumbent on TA.[141]

A suggested in the previous subsection, treaties and domestic laws are sometimes to be read in conjunction with each other, and then jointly deliver insights about emerging custom. In the absence of a direct incorporation into a treaty, interim or pre-constitutional texts may still *refer* to an international agreement. Where domestic acts or declarations complement existing treaties, such instruments are part of the 'context' of the treaty,[142] or can be seen as 'instrument[s] related to the treaty'[143] or 'subsequent practice in the application of the treaty'.[144] In the reverse sense, too, treaties can shed light on prior or subsequent domestic practice, also when there is a clear contextual association but no explicit textual link between the relevant treaty and domestic law.

2.3 International Reactions Confirming Nascent Custom

The emerging customary nature of specific practices and policies incumbent on TA may also find confirmation in reactions from other actors. Such reactions are not necessarily by themselves constitutive of custom but can confirm or evidence the normative progression. UNSC practice in relation to TG, for example, is not, in itself, formative of custom. But the cumulative actions of the UNSC can impact on the shaping of international law, or at least elevate the momentum in this regard, Gowlland-Debbas argued.[145] TI

---

[138] UNSC/RES 718 of 31 October 1991, Preamble. In another resolution, it 'call[ed] upon the Supreme National Council of Cambodia to fulfil its special responsibilities set out in the agreements'. UNSC/RES 745 of 28 February 1992, § 5.

[139] See e.g. S/RES/1565 of 1 October 2004.

[140] See also E. De Groof, 'The Features of Transitional Governance Today', op. cit.

[141] B. B. Jia, 'The Relations between Treaties and Custom', op. cit.

[142] VCLT, art. 31.1.

[143] VCLT, art. 31.2.b. Own emphasis.

[144] VCLT, art. 31.3.b.

[145] V. Gowlland-Debbas, 'The Limits of Unilateral Enforcement of Community Objectives in the Framework of UN Peace Maintenance', op. cit., p. 377: '[g]enerally speaking, the Council's resolutions are not legislative in the sense of applying outside the framework of particular cases of restoration of international

may thus acquire additional international legal *relevance* when UNSC resolutions refer to them explicitly, especially if these resolutions call for their implementation.

The UNSC has thus confirmed the binding nature of domestic intrastate agreements by endorsing them in its resolutions. It explicitly referred to the Bonn Agreement for Afghanistan,[146] the Arusha Agreement for Burundi,[147] the Accra Comprehensive Peace Agreement for Liberia,[148] Yemen's Transition Agreement,[149] the Libreville Agreements regarding CAR[150] and the Ouagadougou Preliminary Agreement relating to Mali.[151] The UNSC has also referred to other sorts of domestic interim arrangements, such as the N'Djamena Declaration of 18 April 2013 and the Constitutional Charter for the Transition of 18 July 2013. The UNSC resolutions in which such TI come to be cited contribute to norm diffusion.[152] In the same vein, for self-imposed unilateral declarations to produce legal effects, there is no need for international reactions in the form of acknowledgements.[153] Yet, such reactions can serve for evidentiary purposes, and may add impetus to custom creation.[154]

> peace and security. Moreover, they cannot – by analogy with General Assembly resolutions – be said to reflect either *opinio juris*, nor the generality of the requisite state practice. It is undeniable on the one hand that the cumulative actions of the Security Council under Chapter VII, in instituting collective responses to situations involving breaches of community norms, have had an impact on the shaping of an international public policy and that core norms of human rights, humanitarian law and international criminal law have been affected and strengthened through the impetus thus provided'.

[146] For several references, E. De Groof, 'The Features of Transitional Governance Today', op. cit.

[147] Cf. for example UNSC/RES/1375 of 29 October 2001.

[148] UNSC/RES/1509 of 19 September 2003.

[149] UNSC/RES/2051 of 12 June 2012, Preamble. See also § 1.

[150] UNSC/RES/2149 of 10 April 2014 in which the UNSC '[r]eiterates its support for the Libreville Agreements of 11 January 2013'.

[151] S/2014/403 of 9 June 2014 with reference to the Agreement of 23 May 2014.

[152] See e.g. S/RES/2149 of 10 April 2014, which, after referring to the Libreville Agreements of 11 January 2013, N'Djamena Declaration of 18 April 2013, and Constitutional Charter for the Transition of 18 July 2013, 'urges' the TA to continue with the transition.

[153] *Nuclear Tests (New Zealand v. France), Judgment, ICJ Reports 1974*, p. 457, § 46.

[154] The monitoring by the so-called international community of transition situations, and declarations made by various contact groups, can account for the *reactions* to unilateral declarations by TA. Such reactions may be taken into account when determining the legal consequences of these declarations. Id., art. 3. *Nuclear Tests (New Zealand v. France), ICJ Reports 1974*, pp. 269–70, § 51, and pp. 474–5, § 53; *Case concerning the Frontier Dispute (Burkina Faso v. Republic of Mali), ICJ Reports*

In addition, UNSC practice is often echoed and endorsed in larger collective settings. Contact groups are one example. Contact groups gather a panoply of states and IO monitoring TG. Their members often reiterate which TG practices should be followed. The documents they issue (and to which the perusal under Part III and the corresponding report regularly refer) allow us to take stock of broadly shared practices and opinions. During UN meetings, too, states express their opinion about transitions in other countries.[155] Such meetings serve as complementary evidence that, in relation to specific themes, legal convictions increasingly converge. A similar logic can be applied when IO react to breaches of their resolutions on TG. Such collective initiatives and reactions reinforce the conviction of states in transition that specific behaviour in relation to TG is not only desirable but also compulsory.

Besides the exhortatory collective reactions and reminders, TG practices may also be *imposed*. The UNSC, for instance, or regional organisations such as the AU or ECOWAS may exercise their competence to supervise transition states, beyond formulating mere recommendations. Binding resolutions can thus foresee when and how transitions are to be followed. Dozens of UNSC resolutions directly relate to TG. Crucially, these resolutions are regularly adopted under Chapter VII of the UN Charter, and sometimes establish a sanctions regime. On this legal basis, the UNSC can:

- Endorse existing TI;
- Monitor TG;
- Call on TA to:
  - Respect their limited mandate,
  - Engage in an inclusive transition,
  - Organise TJ,
  - Respect international law generally;
- Adopt or threaten to adopt sanctions against individuals trying to derail the transition.

1986, pp. 573-4, §§ 39-40; Case concerning Armed Activities on the Territory of the Congo (New Application: 2002) (Democratic Republic of the Congo v. Rwanda), Jurisdiction and Admissibility ICJ Reports 2006, p. 6, § 49; Nicaragua Case, op. cit., § 261.

[155] This study for example refers to the 'Review of the United Nations peacebuilding architecture' (A/64/868 – S/2010/393 of 21 July 2010).

NASCENT CUSTOM

In line with the increased reliance on a legal-regulatory approach to peace and security,[156] the UNSC has adopted binding resolutions under Chapter VII with regard to (projected) transitions in South Sudan,[157] Somalia,[158] Libya,[159] Mali,[160] Côte d'Ivoire,[161] CAR,[162] Yemen,[163] Guinea-Bissau,[164] Libya,[165] Haiti[166] and Afghanistan[167] (reverse chronological order). The UNSC increasingly addresses threats to international peace and security by monitoring TG, in the spirit of the peace-through-transition paradigm.[168] Comforted by its broad discretionary powers in determining whether there is a threat to peace, and by the gradual expansion of this 'very vague and elastic' concept over the years,[169] the UNSC is developing a detailed jurisprudence, one could say, on TG.

The above enumeration of binding UNSC resolutions is not exhaustive. The list of 'sanction resolutions' should also be complemented with UNSC resolutions serving as decisions (that is deriving their binding nature from their operational parts).[170] Also when an explicit reference

[156] See Introduction, Section A.1.

[157] S/RES/2187 of 25 November 2014.

[158] S/RES/2182 of 24 October 2014 relating to Somalia, in which the UNSC is '[h]ighlighting in particular the FGS's commitment to establish interim regional administrations by the end of 2014 which is an essential step under the "Vision 2016" programme, and emphasising the importance of this being an inclusive and consultative process'.

[159] S/RES/2174 of 27 August 2014.

[160] S/RES/2164 of 25 June 2014.

[161] S/RES/2153 of 29 April 2014 in which the UNSC refers to the Ouagadougou Agreement and '[d]ecides that the Ivoirian authorities shall submit biannual reports to [a] Committee . . . on progress achieved in relation to DDR and SSR'.

[162] S/RES/2149 of 10 April 2014.

[163] S/RES/2140 of 26 February 2014.

[164] S/RES/2048 of 18 May 2012.

[165] S/RES/2009 of 16 September 2011 in which the UNSC directly addressed itself to the National Transitional Council on the topic of the transition.

[166] S/RES/1529 of 29 February 2004, § 1.

[167] S/RES/1386 of 20 December 2001 in which the UNSC refers to the Bonn Agreement, which regulates the transition in Afghanistan. The Bonn Agreement, furthermore, explicitly refers to S/RES/1378 of 14 November 2001. Cf. also T. Marauhn, 'Konfliktbewältigung in Afghanistan zwischen Utopie und Pragmatismus', op. cit., p. 496.

[168] Introduction, Section A.1.

[169] B. Conforti, *The Law and Practice of the United Nations*, Kluwer Law International, 2000, p. 173. See also 2005 World Summit Outcome, UNGA Res. 60/1 of 24 October 2005, §§ 6 and 69. See also 'In Larger Freedom: Towards Development, Security and Human Rights for All', UN Doc/59/2005, op. cit.

[170] UNSC resolutions do not always indicate on which basis they were adopted. In such case, their classification depends on the analysis of the operative part of the resolution. Art. 25 of the UN Charter indeed states that all *decisions* of the Security Council in accordance

180 THE SOURCES OF *IUS IN INTERREGNO*

to Chapter VII is lacking, UNSC resolutions relating to TG can be binding if the language used is not merely exhortatory,[171] that is when the resolutions are 'of an operational nature'[172] and/or constitute decisions rather than recommendations.

UNSC resolutions are often paired with the threat or application of sanctions against so-called spoilers. The UNSC reserves itself the power to take sanctions against anyone trying to impede the transition. It used this power or threatened to do so against potential 'transition spoilers'[173] in Yemen, CAR, Guinea Bissau, Somalia, and Côte d'Ivoire (reverse chronological order):

- In February 2014, after determining that the situation in Yemen presented a threat to international peace and security, the UNSC established a committee to monitor the activities of individuals or entities that could aggravate this threat by 'obstructing or undermining the successful completion of the political transition'.[174]

with the Charter must be executed. Cf. also *Legal Consequences for States of the Continued Presence of South Africa in Namibia (South West Africa) notwithstanding Security Council Resolution 276 (1970), Advisory Opinion, ICJ Reports 1971*, p. 16, § 114: '[t]he language of a resolution of the Security Council should be carefully analysed before a conclusion can be made as to its binding effect. In view of the nature of the powers under Article 25, the question whether they have been in fact exercised is to be determined in each case, having regard to the terms of the resolution to be interpreted, the discussions leading to it, the Charter provisions invoked and, in general, all circumstances that might assist in determining the legal consequences of the resolution of the Security Council'. The UN occasionally 'underscor[es] that Member States are obligated under Article 25 of the Charter of the United Nations to accept and carry out the Council's decisions'. S/RES/2165 of 14 July 2014, Preamble. Cf. also *Legal Consequences for States, ICJ Reports (1971)*, §§ 114–16. *Contra*: B. Simma (ed.), *The Charter of the United Nations – A Commentary*, op. cit., p. 613.

[171] For example, in its resolution S/RES/1383 of 6 December 2001, the UNSC '[c]alls on all Afghan groups to implement this Agreement in full, in particular through full cooperation with the Interim Authority which is due to take office on 22 December 2001'. For another binding UNSC resolution (without reference to UN Charter Ch. VII), also impacting the transition, cf. S/RES/2186 of 25 November 2014 (Guinea-Bissau).

[172] B. Conforti, *The Law and Practice of the United Nations*, op. cit., p. 152.

[173] S. J. Stedman, 'Spoiler Problems in Peace Processes', *International Security*, Vol. 22, no. 2, 1997. Spoilers can be described as groups that 'readily position themselves against the efforts of the international "custodians of the peace" (usually UN missions) and transitional governmental arrangements, in a bid to spoil any peace that does not accord with their interests'. P. Nadin, P. Cammaert, V. Popovski, *Spoiler Groups and UN Peacekeeping*, International Institute for Strategic Studies, 2015, p. 12.

[174] See S/RES/2140 of 26 February 2014, in which the UNSC 'determin[ed] that the situation in Yemen constitutes a threat to international peace and security in the region', '[w]elcomes the recent progress made in the political transition of Yemen and expresses strong support for completing the next steps of the transition', and

NASCENT CUSTOM

On 14 April 2015, the UNSC adopted sanctions against Ahmed Saleh because he 'hinder[ed] Yemen's peaceful transition'.[175]

- In December 2013, the UNSC closely monitored the transition in CAR, and 'decide[d] that any attempt to delay, impede or violate the transitional arrangements . . . shall be considered as an impediment to the peace process and could lead to the imposition of appropriate measures'.[176] After the possibility of a sanctions regime was (implicitly) mentioned, dozens of states and organisations gathering in a contact group 'stressed the need for the imposition of sanctions against all CAR individuals and entities attempting to hinder the transition'.[177] Less than a month after this statement, a UNSC sanctions regime was established, targeting 'individuals and entities . . . engaging in or providing support for acts that undermine the peace, stability or security of the CAR [or] *that impede the political transition process*'.[178]
- The UNSC urged both political and military stakeholders in Guinea-Bissau to refrain from any action that could hamper the transition. It considered applying targeted sanctions against potential spoilers.[179]
- In Somalia, the UNSC decided that individuals or entities can be sanctioned if they engage in or provide 'support for acts that threaten the peace, security or stability of Somalia, including acts that threaten

---

establishes a sanction committee monitoring the activities of individuals or entities that may threat the peace, security or stability of Yemen by '[o]bstructing or undermining the successful completion of the political transition'. Cf. also S/PRST/2014/18, Statement by the President of the Security Council of 29 August 2014, and S/2013/173 of 19 March 2013 § 9, mentioning 'actions aimed at undermining . . . the transition process despite . . . the [UNSC's] readiness to consider further measures, including under Article 41 of the Charter of the Unites Nations'. Already in June 2012, the UNSC was 'expressing concern at the recent deterioration of cooperation among some political actors and actions that could adversely affect or delay the political transition process' (S/RES/2051 of 12 June 2012).

[175] S/RES/2216 of 14 April 2015, Annex, § 2. Cf. also S/RES/2204 of 24 February 2015 in which the UNSC emphasised the critical importance of the sanctions regime.

[176] S/RES/2127 of 5 December 2013, § 10.

[177] Conclusions of the fourth meeting of the International Contact Group on the Central African Republic of 21 March 2014, § 19. Cf. also § 9.

[178] S/RES/2149 of 10 April 2014. Own emphasis.

[179] It 'urge[d] stakeholders in Guinea-Bissau, including political and military leaders to refrain from any action that could hamper the electoral process and the implementation of reforms, which are key to the long-term stability of Guinea Bissau. The Security Council recall[ed] its resolution 2048 (2012) and, in this regard, reiterate[d] its readiness to consider further measures, as it deems necessary, including targeted sanctions against individuals who undermine efforts to restore the constitutional order', S/PRST/2013/19, p. 2. Cf. also S/RES/2048 of 18 May 2012, § 6.a.

182   THE SOURCES OF *IUS IN INTERREGNO*

the Djibouti Agreement of 18 August 2008 or the political process'.[180] This agreement forms the backbone of the Djibouti peace process in the context of which a Transitional Federal Government was formed.[181]

- With regard to Côte d'Ivoire, too, the UNSC decided on 15 November 2004 (during the first transitional period from 13 January 2003 to 4 March 2007)[182] that sanctions could be applied against 'spoilers' of the reconciliation process.[183]

- In 2004, the UNSC considered assisting the DRC in 'mobilising the resources necessary to deter spoilers from derailing the transition'.[184]

Since the turn of the millennium, the UN, sometimes backed up by regional organisations, thus regularly considers adopting sanctions against 'spoilers' allegedly derailing the transition.[185] When TA or persons acting on their behalf disobey binding UNSC resolutions, they risk breaching the UN Charter,[186] and potentially engage the responsibility of

---

[180] S/RES/1844 of 20 November 2008, § 8.a.

[181] For an overview, cf. 'Somali Peace Process' on AMISOM webpage, http://amisom-au .org/about-somalia/somali-peace-process, last accessed on 26 March 2020.

[182] The transition period based on the Linas-Marcoussis agreement of 13 January 2003.

[183] S/RES/1572 of 15 November 2004, § 9: '[d]ecides that all States shall take the necessary measures, for a period of twelve months, to prevent the entry into or transit through their territories of all persons designated by the Committee established by paragraph 14 below, who constitute a threat to the peace and national reconciliation process in Côte d'Ivoire, in particular those who block the implementation of the Linas-Marcoussis and Accra III Agreements'. Implemented on the EU level by Council Decision 2004/852/ CFSP of 13 December 2004. An overview of sanctions can be found online. The measures imposed were reviewed on a regular basis 'in the light of progress accomplished in the peace and national reconciliation process in Côte d'Ivoire as defined by the Linas-Marcoussis and Accra III Agreements', S/RES/1572 of 15 November 2004, § 13.

[184] Id., § 119. Own emphasis. See also S/2004/650 of 16 August 2004 §§ 57, 65 and 119.

[185] The EU, for example, threatened with suspending its support on the occasion of the transition in the Central African Republic. The EU thus 'stressed in Brazzaville that the democratic credentials of the transitional institutions would be critical for the resumption of any type of support'. Informal meeting of the Central African Republic configuration of the Peacebuilding Commission, Chairman's Summary, 16 May 2013, § 6. See also R. Caplan, *International Governance of War-torn Territories*, op. cit., p. 21. The High Representative had the 'power to dismiss local officials deemed to be obstructing implementation of the accord and to issue interim laws if the local parties are "unable" (that is, unwilling) to do so'.

[186] Three articles of the UN Charter are relevant in this regard. First, art. 25 by virtue of which UN members 'agree to accept and carry out' decisions of the UNSC. Second, art. 41 by virtue of which the UNSC may call upon UN Members to apply 'measures not involving the use of armed force'. Third, art. 103 by which UN members give precedence to obligations under the UN Charter.

NASCENT CUSTOM

their state. Concomitantly to the rise of TG, the UNSC exercises such a tighter control, suggesting that we are beyond the stage of a free electron syndrome.

3 Coutume Sauvage, *Contested Utility and Non-Compliance*

As a final consideration of this part, I will turn to a number of pitfalls to be avoided in any reasoning about custom creation. Let us first discuss the risk of norm entrepreneurship (3.1) and then suggest that the contested utility of TG and even issues if non-compliance only have a limited impact on custom creation (3.2).

3.1 Avoiding *Coutume Sauvage*

The effects of dominant discourse and mimesis I described earlier entice a common (legal) culture accounting for both the (socialised) origin of, and (legal) compliance with, specific behavioural patterns. This fertile breeding ground also explains why such patterns are formalised through the adoption of TI. But does Weber's recognition that 'transitions from mere usage to convention and from it to law are fluid',[187] exposing this continuum between *opinio necessatis* and *opinio iuris*, not generate the risk of perhaps well-intentioned yet wild norm creation?

Many scholars criticise norm entrepreneurs who, by loosely invoking custom creation, make their will their way – especially when norm entrepreneurs happen to be *droit-de-l'homme-istes* or campaigners who have decided, for good or bad reasons, to dedicate their academic life to a cause.[188] Although from a legal viewpoint I would be tempted to agree with the critics, there is no reason here to engage with this point, for the following simple reason. While the initiative to analyse TG from an international legal perspective in itself of course constitutes a normative

---

[187] M. Weber, *On Law in Economy and Society*, Harvard University Press, 1954, pp. 30–53.

[188] B. Simma, P. Alston, 'The Sources of Human Rights Law: Custom, *Jus Cogens*, and General Principles', *Australian Year Book of International Law*, Vol. 12, 1988, p. 83: 'the temptation to adapt or re-interpret the concept of customary law in such a way as to ensure that it provides the "right" answers is strong, and at least to some, irresistible'. For a text arguing that in the field of human rights and humanitarian law 'the traditional requirement of consistency of state practice may be played down a bit, provided that a strong opinio juris, democratically informed by global state consent, has crystallised in international fora', see J. Wouters and C. Ryngaert, 'Impact on the Process of the Formation of Customary International Law' in M. T. Kamminga and M. Scheinin, *The Impact of Human Rights Law on General International Law*, op. cit., p. 131.

choice,[189] merely witnessing that customary rules in relation to TG are *nascent* at the dawn of the third millennium (as I will do in Part III on the basis of rather abundant practice evidencing, *inter alia*, the substantive and temporal normative limits to inclusive TG) carries little risk of creating a '*coutume sauvage*'.[190]

In Part III, I will sketch how yesterday we were still at a crossroads whereas today we are just around the corner, going *towards* crystallising current practices, potentially adding nuance, precision and body to international law in the near future. In the remainder of this book, the aim is not to substantiate that the law is *bound* to further develop in the direction it has now taken. It is rather to show that, except if there is clear backtracking, a step towards crystallising current practices into norms has been taken, for the better or for the worse. Of this ongoing evolution there is, I would submit, ample evidence. Actually, the elements currently confirming this evolution are manifesting themselves rather indiscreetly.

The perusal of practice and policy in this book and the separate report is based on a relatively short period of thirty years, that is from 1989 to 2019.[191] In the North Sea Continental Shelf Case, the ICJ observed that 'the passage of only a short period of time [is] not necessarily a bar to the formation of a new rule of customary international law'.[192] The future will indicate whether custom in relation to TG results from 'a transformative development in which new rules and doctrines of customary international law emerge with unusual rapidity and acceptance'.[193]

For the time being, early-stage, currently germinating international customary rules can be derived from consistent and recurrent TG practices. The conviction that these practices, as observed in Part III, must not be dispensed with, meanwhile is well alive, especially with states whose interests are affected – that is, states in transition. While 'the Rubicon which divides custom (in our sense of "usage") from law is crossed

---

[189] Introduction, Section C.2.

[190] R.-J. Dupuy, 'Coutume sage et coutume sauvage' in C. E. Rousseau, *La communauté internationale, Mélanges offerts à Charles Rousseau*, A. Pedone, 1974, p. 75.

[191] For a discussion on time in relation to custom formation, cf. M. Akehurst, *British Yearbook of International Law*, Vol. 47, no. 1, 1975, pp. 1–53.

[192] North Sea Continental Shelf, Judgment, ICJ Reports 1969, p. 3, § 74. An example in this regard concerns the freedom of movement into outer space, discussed by Judge Lachs in his dissenting opinion in the same case.

[193] M. P. Scharf, *Customary International Law in Times of Fundamental Change – Recognising Grotian Moments*, Cambridge University Press, 2013, p. 5.

silently, unconsciously and without proclamation',[194] that passage was not crossed at the time of writing. Perhaps it has at the time of reading.

By recognising that customary rules in relation to TG are only nascent at the time of writing, there is little risk of creating a *'coutume sauvage'*.[195] In the future, *ius in interregno* might or might not be further refined; germinating customary rules might extinguish or consolidate. Whatever happens, international law is not ubiquitous and will never regulate all aspects of regime change. Whenever the law is silent, ambiguous or non-existent, political and diplomatic actors simply enjoy more legal leeway.

3.2   Limited Impact of Contested Utility and Non-Compliance

The contested utility of TG, and even issues of non-compliance, have a relative impact on custom creation. True, since it became en vogue since the end of the Cold War, TG has sometimes generated doubtful results. In Rwanda, the non-implementation of the August 1993 Arusha Agreements, which was to establish a Broad-Based Transitional Government ('BBTG'), was followed by a genocide. The close to disastrous situations in Afghanistan, DRC, Iraq, Libya, South Sudan and Yemen at the time of writing show that TG has not yielded desirable results, to say the least. In other states, like Burundi (failed coup during May 2015, continuing unrest after contested elections) and CAR (Séléka versus anti-Balaka conflict during the 2014–15 transition; fragile peace deal of 5 February 2019), the political situation remains delicate.

Verbal commitments do not always make a positive difference or are simply not implemented. This is sometimes the case with the promise of inclusivity.[196] Actual compliance leaves much to be desired.[197] Even when a transition is inclusive, 'there is not even a scintilla of evidence that it improves the durability or the democratic content of constitutions', according to one author.[198] With regard to another common feature of TG, the commitment to provide security, in some cases 'the

---

[194] Sir J. Fisher Williams, *Aspects of Modern International Law*, Oxford University Press, 1939, p. 44.

[195] R.-J. Dupuy, 'Coutume sage et coutume sauvage', op. cit., p. 75.

[196] J. Arnault, 'Legitimacy and Peace Processes – International Norms and Local Realities' in A. Ramsbotham and A. Wennmann (eds.), *Legitimacy and Peace Processes, From Coercion to Consent*, op. cit.

[197] E. Newman, R. Paris, O. P. Richmond, *New Perspectives on Liberal Peacebuilding*, op. cit., p. 4; p. 13.

[198] L. Diamond, F. Fukuyama, D. L. Horowitz, M. F. Plattner, 'Reconsidering the Transition Paradigm', *Journal of Democracy*, Vol. 25, no. 1, January 2014, p. 100.

186 THE SOURCES OF *IUS IN INTERREGNO*

transitional period *contributed little to the demilitarisation of politics.* Weak interim regimes failed to institutionalise consultation and joint decision making, thereby leaving in place the powerful and unreconstructed institutions of war'.[199] Such failures are attributable to unrealistic expectations or to the gap between commitments and implementation – between words and deeds.

From an international legal perspective, the contested utility of TG, and even issues of non-compliance or weak implementation, are however of relative relevance, for two reasons. First, states in transition have not been led to abandon their commitment to socialised TG practices.[200] For want of alternatives or sufficient imagination, perhaps, the overall project continues.[201] In the meantime, even mere commitments to TG practices can account for – incipient, yet relevant – practice, also when the expected results are not achieved. If TA purport to comply with prevailing international practice because they are convinced that – beyond a political, social and economic exigency – this is also a legal requirement, then *opinio iuris* is also ascertained. Another reason why clearly formulated commitments carry some weight is that several obligations under *ius in interregno* are obligations of means (requiring a duty of best efforts) rather than obligations of result.[202]

Second, non-compliance does not, in itself, disconfirm the validity of a legal rule. A breach of fundamental principles of international law should of course be considered as such: a violation of international law. The same is true of individual customary obligations which are being developed under the umbrella of these principles. When such obligations are violated (for example lack of inclusivity in transitions in Afghanistan and Iraq),[203] this does not make them 'less compulsory'. In the same vein, for a rule to be established as customary, the corresponding practice must not be in absolute rigorous conformity with the rule. Breaches of customary rules, even early stage, do not automatically invalidate them.[204]

---

[199] T. Lyons, 'Post-Conflict Elections and the Process of Demilitarizing Politics: The Role of Electoral Administration', *Democratisation*, Vol. 11, no. 3, 2004, p. 57. Own emphasis.

[200] Part III. E. De Groof, 'The Features of Transitional Governance Today', op. cit.

[201] Id., p. 13.

[202] Chapter 7.

[203] E. De Groof, 'The Features of Transitional Governance Today', op. cit.

[204] Furthermore, in international law a broad conception of legal compliance can be favoured. G. H. Fox, 'International Law and the Entitlement to Democracy After War', *Global Governance* 9, 2003, pp. 190–1: legal compliance 'occurs through indirect processes of acculturation and legitimation . . ., [and] is not a discernible end point but an ongoing process of articulating and inculcating law-compliance as a cherished value'.

CONCLUSION OF PART II

Although admittedly this issue is more delicate when norms are in the process of being created, the ICJ considered that:

> in order to deduce the existence of customary rules, the Court deems it sufficient that the conduct of States should, in general, be consistent with such rules, and that instances of State conduct inconsistent with a given rule should generally have been treated as breaches of that rule, not as indications of the recognition of a new rule.[205]

When norms are in the process of germination, a temporal dimension should finally be considered. The actual practice of states in transition can be 'expressive, *or creative*, of customary rules', to paraphrase the ICJ[206] as well as the Special Rapporteur on the identification of customary law.[207] Only time will confirm or disconfirm whether socialised TG practices – discussed in detail in the following part – will further ascend into the realm of law.

Conclusion of Part II

As a multifaceted but distinct politico-legal phenomenon, TG touches upon transversal issues seldom treated together. From the outset, a distinction was made between consensual ('transplacement') and oppositional ('replacement') TA, leaving the analysis of transitions triggered and executed solely by the incumbent ('transformations') for another day. Transitions by transplacement and by replacement are analysed together because consensual and oppositional TA are both children of the peace-through-transition paradigm. The goal of pursuing a state renaissance is common to both modes of transition.

This part analysed the foundation (1) and actors of TG (2), and examined the sources of *ius in interregno* (3). First, as to the foundation of TG, TI come in all shapes and sizes. They are enshrined in international treaties, intrastate agreements or domestic legal acts and laws. The TI we examined however share a number of features. To begin with, their origin or common breeding ground: non-constitutionality. As a central feature of contemporary TG, non-constitutionality calls for a nuanced analysis as TG progressing in stages can be 'interim-constitution-based'.

---

[205] ICJ Nicaragua Case, op. cit., § 186. Own emphasis. There is no perfectly consistent practice, there can be an 'individual deviation [which] may not lead to the conclusion that no rule has crystallised' (A. Cassese, *International Law*, op. cit., p. 120).

[206] Tunisia/Libya Continental Shelf Case, 1982 ICJ Reports, p. 46, § 43. Own emphasis.

[207] Fourth report on identification of customary international law, op. cit., p. 21 (draft conclusion 4).

Another feature concerns the method of supraconstitutionality, allowing TI to (partly) supersede, if only temporarily, both the previous and coming constitutional order. Supraconstitutionality furthermore serves as a catalyser for yet another common feature of TI: the shared triple purpose of pacification, self-limitation and reconstitutionalisation.

Second, as to the actors of TG, whether consensual or oppositional, TA have a civilian nature or portfolio and are to be contrasted with realities or concepts like armed opposition groups and NLM. TG is not exactly a military activity. Even if TA entertain links with armed groups, the finality of TG is not armed struggle but the exercise of political power during the interregnum in view of a state renaissance. The forcible/military and non-forcible/non-military aspects of transitions are severable. When military and political rule are confounded during transitions, the UNSC, regional organisations and third states usually urge a return to civilian rule.

TA furthermore act in a specific historic context: the rise of the peace-through-transition paradigm since the end of the Cold War. TG can be contrasted with other forms of interim governance, notably foreign and international administration, and with historic forms of interim governance, which predominantly focused on regime succession. In our day and age, the role of contemporary TG has been aggrandised, lionised even, as it takes up a formidable challenge: peace through transition.

TG is by definition pursued on a provisional basis. Often TI explicitly foresee when TA must cease to exist – this also distinguishes TA from *de facto* governments or states. Transitions can be divided into four stages, with the two middle stages (foundation and interregnum) being most relevant for our analysis. This subdivision is helpful in analysing when, and to what extent, TA enjoy (functional) international legal personality. During the interregnum, the redefinition of the state order is an exercise of public power, and eminently so. Even without being allotted governmental status (as of yet), TA may enjoy international legal personality to the extent that they effectively exercise such power, are seen as addressees of international obligations, or (subsequently) come to represent the state.

Third, as to the sources of *ius in interregno* I suggested that both stable and evolving norms applicable to TG should be considered. Individual customary rules are germinating in relation to TG but not in isolation from the existing principles of self-determination and non-intervention, which were introduced in this part. As to the evolving part of *ius in interregno*, I argued that TI may testify to the emergence of custom. To that extent, they

CONCLUSION OF PART II

have international legal *relevance* independently of their domestic or international legal nature. Both domestic laws, unilateral declarations, intrastate agreements or international treaties can indeed be taken into account. Socialisation explains why these instruments incorporate TG-relevant patterns, and also accounts for UNSC and IO resolutions directly or indirectly (by reference to TI) echoing these patterns, providing an extra impetus for custom creation.

*

Whether TI are valid on the domestic plane *ab initio* or may become so only in hindsight is not directly relevant for our enquiry. International law adopts a position of neutrality vis-à-vis the domestic legality of TI. Compliance with international law is furthermore expected regardless of how the transition was triggered, that is regardless of the transition's '(il) legitimacy of origin'.[208] The question whether or not TG was initiated in a domestically lawful fashion should therefore not directly affect the following, different question: when does the exercise of public powers during the interregnum comply with international law? This question concerns the 'legitimacy of exercise' of interim rule, the main focus of the following part.

That TG is a distinguishable politico-legal phenomenon should be amply clear by now. What we learned in this part about the foundation and actors of TG, and the sources of *ius in interrego*, allow us to tackle the next step. How does international law evolve in relation to the 'legitimacy of exercise' during the transition? Are customary rules emerging in relation to the interregnum itself – and what are these in substance? Could their rudimentary nature do justice to a rich and rapidly expanding practice? On the basis of a perusal of policies and practices becoming commonplace in times of transition (as evidenced in a separate report),[209] the following part addresses these questions.

---

[208] For a brief discussion of this concept, see Chapter 2, Section B.1.

[209] E. De Groof, 'The Features of Transitional Governance Today', op. cit.

PART III

Self-Determination through Transitional Governance

This part focuses on the conduct of TA *during* the interregnum. It builds on a perusal of features and procedures common to TG. The argument developed on this part builds on two conceptual levels: (a) customary rules are nascent in relation to TG, and increasingly limit the powers of TA; (b) these rules are to be read through the lens of the principle of self-determination. For both conceptual levels, the distinction between 'obligations of means' and 'obligations of result' will be relevant. Obligations of means or best efforts imply that TA should do what can be reasonably expected from them, that is that they should at least do their best to achieve certain standards. Obligations of result require that TA actually realise specific standards.

Nascent Customary Rules

During the interregnum, some (externally or self-imposed) policies become more than just that, as they are *evolving* into obligations, mostly of conduct, incumbent on TA. Given the 'irrelevance of outcome' adopted in this book (and, some may add, in line with the Nicaragua principle),[1] this part neither promotes any political order to be pursued after the interregnum nor pays much attention to post-transition general elections.[2] It rather argues that international law is less and less indifferent to the *mode* of observing public authority during the transition.

---

[1] Part I, Conclusion.

[2] Post-conflict elections will not be given much attention. Traditionally, a high burden rests on elections. As a prime expression of politics, they are often expected to continue war by other means (inversing Clausewitz's famous line that war is a continuation of politics by other means) and to stop armed conflict. The perusal of practices on which this part is based concentrates on practices preceding elections, i.e. those *of the interregnum* rather than on elections closing transitions. For some the latter focus is 'overblown' anyhow. R. M. Ginty, 'No War, No Peace: Why So Many Peace Processes Fail to Deliver Peace', op. cit., pp. 156–7. Also here, TG is in a sense the continuation of conflict through other means. Cf. Bell and Pospisil's concept of 'formalised political unsettlement', 'wherein the

192   PART III

TG commitments analysed in this part form the lowest common denominator of emerging customary rules in relation to TG, and it is certainly possible for TA to go beyond that.[3] Nascent customary rules are relevant both for oppositional and consensual TA when they effectively exercise power during the interregnum or (come to) represent the state.[4] In a nutshell, these rules entrust TA with the fiduciary role of organising a time-constrained but inclusive state renaissance.

This part draws on an observation of practice and *opinio iuris* of more than twenty states, which are, or were said to be in transition, complemented with reactions from other states. This perusal shows the richness and geographical breadth of specific practices repeated in the context of TG. As space is limited here, the perusal has been published in a separate report[5] allowing the reader to verify the evidence of two strands of practices which, I shall argue, contribute to the emergence of two sets of obligations:

- To begin with, the limits *ratione temporis* and *ratione materiae* to TG require a double course of action. TA must manage the country during the interregnum, and then relinquish power. This time limitation imposes mainly an obligation (still in the make) of result. Furthermore, the fiduciary powers of TA do not go much beyond managing the transition itself and administering the country *ad interim*, which includes providing security. These are obligations of best efforts (also in the make). Both sets of obligations will be discussed under Chapter 6.
- Second, requirements of 'inclusion' and 'domestic ownership' must be respected during the interregnum. In some regards, specific results are required, whereas in others obligations of best efforts suffice. This argument will be elaborated under Chapter 7.

---

conflict is translated into political and legal institutions rather than being resolved'. C. Bell, *Navigating Inclusion in Peace Settlements, Human Rights and the Creation of the Common Good*, British Academy, 2017, p. 55. See also C. Bell, J. Pospisil, 'Negotiating Inclusion in Transitions from Conflict: The Formalised Political Unsettlement', *Journal of International Development*, Vol. 29, no. 5, 2017.

[3] In the words of Youssef, TA must at least respect the requirements of an *Etat légal intérimaire* but can do more, and sometimes effectively do so when, as of the beginning of the transition, they build an *Etat de droit intérimaire* announcing the transformation into a substantive democracy respectful of fundamental rights. N. Youssef, *La Transition démocratique et la garantie des droits fondamentaux*, op. cit., pp. 72 a. f.

[4] Chapter 4, Section A.3.

[5] E. De Groof, 'The Features of Transitional Governance Today', op. cit.

PART III   193

The first category concerns mainly but not exclusively *limitations* directly derived from the temporary nature of the interim rule. The second category concerns mainly *positive obligations* informing TA as to how they must pursue TG. Usually, both oppositional and consensual TA commit to the aforementioned practices so as to comply with transition instruments, self-imposed commitments or legitimate demands by external actors. A perusal of practice and *opinio iuris* thus suggests that today TA more readily accept to follow especially duties of conduct in the exercise of public authority, which, I submit, should be read in light of the principle of self-determination – or, one could say, of progressive self-*re*determination.

Self-Redetermination

Since the end of the Cold War, the quest for self-determination or rather self-redetermination increasingly takes place within the frontiers of transition states, and through TG. The principle of self-determination is central to TG, and, conversely, the practices and beliefs of the interregnum will *add specificity* to the principle of self-determination, through nascent custom. This part does not examine how the right to self-determination may or may not be invoked by its right-holder, the peoples, to trigger a transition (*ius ad interregnum*).[6] It rather analyses the structuring role and absorbing capacity of self-determination seen as a principle once the transition is set in motion. Some authors recognise that self-determination has become an umbrella principle for (specific) state alterations other than transitions or for peace-building.[7] Literature has not been explicit about this principle potentially gaining specificity through the effective self-*re*determination of a country. Yet, 'self-determination is one of the typical legal principles of the present

---

[6] This choice is partly inspired by the observation that the principle of self-determination is not individually 'justiciable' as far as art. 1 of the ICCPR and ICESCR are concerned. Cf. also Human Rights Committee, *Ivan Kitok v. Sweden*, Communication No. 197/1985 (CCPR/C/33/D/197/1985), final views of 27 July 1988; Human Rights Committee, *Diergaardt et al. v. Namibia*, Communication No. 760/1997 (CCPR/C/69/D/760/1997), final views of 25 July 2000.

[7] Saxer considers that the principle of self-determination has become an umbrella principle for *Staatenwandel* understood as alterations to the state with territorial implications. Cf. U. Saxer, *Die internationale Steuerung der Selbstbestimmung und der Staatsentstehung*, Springer-Verlag, 2010. K. Stathopoulou, 'Self-Determination, Peacemaking and Peace-Building: Recent Trends in African Intrastate Peace Agreements' in D. French (ed.), *Statehood and Self-Determination: Reconciling Tradition and Modernity in International Law*, op. cit. See also M. Saul, 'Legitimising Transitional Authorities through the International Law of Self-Determination' in E. De Groof, M. Wiebusch (eds.), *International Law and Transitional Governance: Critical Perspectives*, op. cit., p. 95.

194 PART III

world community. With the other fundamental principles it shares a high degree of generality and abstraction. . . . The task of specifying the issues that the principle does not address is fulfilled by individual customary rules.'[8] This part argues that the principle of self-determination informs how TG must be pursued, and, vice versa, that TG is instructive about the slightly expanding contents and scope of this principle. The limits *ratione temporis* and *ratione materiae* to the interregnum as well as another recurrent TG practice – inclusivity and domestic ownership – can be read through the lens of this principle. The argument is premised on the following ongoing interactions:

- TG is one of the *means of implementation* of the principle of self-determination. Self-determination can indeed be implemented by the 'emergence into any other political status freely determined by a - people'.[9] In our day and age, the dynamics behind such emergence are more and more regulated through TG rather than through state creation, alteration or the free association or integration with another state.

- TG *specifies* the principle of self-determination. The contents of this principle gain in precision, and its contemporary relevance and validity thus come to be confirmed through TG. The principle is partly losing its indeterminacy in the context of TG, as its scope of application is being extended in three regards:
  - Even in cases where TG is initiated in an exclusionary fashion, it must gradually open up to the participation and representation of various, though not all, factions of society which, in the past, were not always considered an essential part of the definition of the people. As a result, the *personal scope of application* of the principle of self-determination is being expanded.
  - Self-determination is to be exercised also during the transition through a set of relatively novel procedures which ensure that the voice of various factions of society are taken seriously, either through direct participation or through representation. As a result, the *material scope of application* of the principle of self-determination is being diversified.
  - From the start and during the interregnum as a whole, not only on the occasion of the constitutional referendum and/or general election towards the end of it, TA should aim at progressively involving the

---

[8] A. Cassese, op. cit., 1995, p. 129. Own emphasis.
[9] 1970 Friendly Relations Declaration, principle e. Own emphasis.

PART III

195

people in the interim rule. As a result, the *temporal scope of application* of the principle of self-determination is being extended.

- The principle of self-determination remains a *directive guideline*, also in relation to TG. It informs how TG must be observed, and what the minimum requirements are for inclusivity, as a TG practice, to be self-determination compliant.

Thus, the principle of internal self-determination as applicable to TG will require *more* than just the (thin, procedural) holding of a constitutional referendum or elections towards the end of the interregnum – but *less* than what (substantive) democracy would require. Before proceeding with this argument, I should formulate some caveats.

Introductory Caveats: Transitional Governance Practices Are Rudimentary and Contested

The lowest common denominator of emerging customary rules in relation to TG is based on an observation of practices and policies which are rudimentary (a) and contested (b) in spite of being widespread through socialisation. As a result, *ius in interregno* is itself rudimentary and, like other normative frameworks, generated by socialised practices which are not always uncontested.

Rudimentary Nature of Transitional Governance Practices

The recurrent TG practices (summarised above and substantiated below and in the report)[10] which give rise to relevant customary rules are of a rudimentary, that is undetailed, nature. This should not be a concern. If practices commonly adopted during transitions do not operate on a high level of detail, and *ex hypothesi* give rise to custom, this may shield a practice as casuistic as TG from overstandardisation. There is no need to artificially engage in norm entrepreneurship. Overregulation would hinder contextual sensitivity, denying that 'any effort to generate a *rigid* template for reconstructing the institutions of law and order in a post-conflict environment is . . . likely to fail',[11] a situation Chesterman rightly cautions against.

---

[10] E. De Groof, Contemporary Transitional Governance: Key Political and Legal Features, op. cit.

[11] S. Chesterman, 'Ownership in Theory and in Practice: Transfer of Authority in UN Statebuilding Operations', *Journal of Intervention and Statebuilding*, Vol. 1, no. 1, 2007, p. 3. Own emphasis.

196   PART III

This caveat is essential. This chapter, and indeed the book as a whole, is not intended to be an artificial contribution to 'legal globalisation'[12] or to create blueprints out of the blue. Rather, it witnesses the expansion of specific practices and designs relating to TG pursued by TA (purportedly or progressively) acting on behalf of the state.[13] To the extent that these practices and designs enter the realm of law, the interregnum will become subject to regulation. The law applicable to TG thus allows for path-dependency. At the same time, *ius in interregno* will be indicative of a number of basic red lines that must not be crossed.

Transitional Governance Practices Are Contested on Extra-Legal Grounds

The normative underpinnings of TG are often questioned.[14] The assistance-to-TG model is frequently considered to be biased inasmuch it relies on the liberal/democratic peace(-building) paradigm,[15] that is 'the idea that certain kinds of (liberally constituted) societies will tend to be more peaceful, both in their domestic affairs and in their international relations than illiberal states are'.[16] The idea of liberal peace, itself criticised, would be spreading its tentacles, so to speak, to the realm of TG – especially as intervention through constitution-making, a central part of TG, historically would be more in the remit of (western) liberal states.[17] The systematic integration of TJ mechanisms into state-building allegedly also contributes to a biased narrative in this sense.[18]

---

[12] J. H. Peterson, '"Rule of Law" Initiatives and the Liberal Peace: The Impact of Politicised Reform in Post-Conflict States', *Disasters*, 34, 2010, S20.

[13] TA either are already governmental bodies enjoying international legal personality, or may, akin to insurrectional movements (DASR, art. 10), retroactively gain this status when, after completion of the transition, they are succeeded by the (effective) representatives of the states. See also Chapter 5, Section B.2.1.

[14] See the critical approach to state-building which calls into question the very assumptions of liberalism and state-building. D. Chandler, *Empire in Denial – The Politics of State-Building*, op. cit., p. 32. See also the criticism on 'inclusion' under Chapter 7, Section B.4.1.

[15] Chapter 2, Section B, 'Irrelevance of the Transition Paradigm'.

[16] E. Newman, R. Paris, O. P. Richmond, *New Perspectives on Liberal Peacebuilding*, op. cit., p. 11. Cf. also R. M. Ginty, 'No War, No Peace: Why So Many Peace Processes Fail to Deliver Peace', op. cit., pp. 145–62.

[17] V. Mayer-Schönberger, 'Into the Heart of the State: Intervention through Constitution-Making', *Temp. Int'l & Comp. L.J.*, 8, 315, 1994.

[18] C. L. Sriram, 'Transitional Justice and the Liberal Peace' in E. Newman, R. Paris, O. P. Richmond, *New Perspectives on Liberal Peacebuilding*, op. cit., p. 112.

PART III 197

Another criticism in relation to contemporary TG concerns its defective compliance and/or undesired results.[19] As noted before, such criticism does not amount to a *legal* contestation. However politically contested, the TG practices and beliefs this part refers to are so widespread since the Cold War that, at least in their lowest common denominator, they seem to be indicative of emerging, rudimentary customary rules. The first set of widespread practices concerns the temporal (*ratione temporis*) and substantive (*ratione materiae*) limits to TG.

[19] Chapter 5, Section B.3.2.

6

Limits *Ratione Temporis* and *Materiae* to Transitional Governance

A perusal of practice suggests that TA are restrained by limits *ratione temporis* (Section A) and *ratione materiae* (Section B). Combined, these limits help calibrating the power of modification and duty of conservation in times of transition (Section C).

A   Limits *Ratione Temporis*

The interregnum is limited *ratione temporis*. TG, even if programmed to last for a long period, cannot be prolonged artificially, although flexible arrangements for extensions may be built *in* the TI itself.[1] Whatever the case may be, 'that a government has declared itself provisional, interim, transitional (or uses other similar appellations) bespeaks a choice'.[2] That transitions are time-limited may seem to be a tautology, and in a certain way it is, but it is not one devoid of significance either on the policy or the legal level.

From a policy perspective, realistic temporal limitations would contribute to an incremental and solid transition.[3] A prolonged interregnum, like in Eritrea, Libya and Côte d'Ivoire, 'could arguably itself be a sign of continued instability, if elections are pushed back repeatedly because the situation is not deemed "ripe"'.[4] Defining feasible and clear limits *ratione temporis* to the interregnum is thus instrumental to prevent TG from failing.[5] This is not to say that transitions must be short. For

---

[1] This was done in the Central African Republic. For a discussion, see C. Rodrigues, 'Letting off Steam: Interim Constitutions as a Safety Valve to the Pressure-Cooker of Transitions in Conflict-Affected States?', op. cit., p. 49.

[2] Y. Shain, J. Linz, *Between States – Interim Governments and Democratic Transitions*, op. cit., p. 8.

[3] Id., p. 31.

[4] J. Strasheim, H. Fjelde, 'Pre-Designing Democracy: Institutional Design of Interim Governments and Democratisation in 15 Post-Conflict Societies', op. cit., p. 350.

[5] N. Youssef, *La Transition démocratique et la garantie des droits fondamentaux*, op. cit., p. 28: 'sinon, la transition va se prolonger ce qui peut la rendre obsolète et peut contribuer à

200   LIMITS *RATIONE TEMPORIS* AND *MATERIAE* TO TG

instance, the assertion that a country's security and long-term institutional development would be 'served by extended transitional periods'[6] is perfectly compatible with the proposition that clear time limits must be set.

There is also a legal issue at stake. From the various cases under analysis, it stems that TA *must* manage TG without frequent or long interruptions, and subsequently transfer power. Temporal limitations are explicitly foreseen in TI.[7] They usually have a general and specific component. Generally, the powers of TA are limited in time, and, more specifically, transition leaders or even all transition office-holders are in most cases ineligible to hold office after the transition. Such limitations are often self-imposed in TI.[8] In addition, external

---

son échec'; '[é]tablir un calendrier de la transition déterminant les étapes et les démarches à suivre durant un délai déterminé favorise les chances d'atteindre les buts souhaités, et de mener à bien le processus transitoire' (p. 61). Own translation: 'otherwise, the transition will be prolonged which may make it obsolete and may contribute to its failure'; 'establishing a transition timeline that identifies the steps and initiatives to take during a specific time period will increase the chances of achieving the desired goals, and will help completing the transitional process'. Youssef mentions Lebanon (and the Taif Agreement) as a counter-example (p. 101).

[6] K. Papagianni, 'Political Transitions after Peace Agreements: The Importance of Consultative and Inclusive Political Processes', *Journal of Intervention and Statebuilding*, Vol. 3, no. 1, March 2009, p. 50. In the same sense, see J. Benomar, 'Constitution-Making After Conflict: Lessons for Iraq', op. cit., p. 87. While Jackson writes that 'a fair amount of time for deliberation, compromise, education, participation, and renewed discussion prior to efforts to solidify agreements in a comprehensive and final constitution is conducive to successful constitution-making in situations of serious post-conflict regime change', she also warns that 'comparison and generalization here are remarkably difficult. There are many confounding factors that may affect analysis and predictions in particular cases'. V. C. Jackson, 'What's in a Name?', op. cit., pp. 1270–1. In the same vein, Samuels argues that 'supporting longer time-frames between the negotiation of peace agreements and constitutions' would 'minimize the inherent tensions in a postwar constitution building'. K. Samuels, 'Postwar Constitution Building' in R. Paris and T. D. Sisk, *The Dilemmas of Statebuilding – Confronting the Contradictions of Postwar Peace Operations*, op. cit., p. 175.

[7] This observation suffers few exceptions. If it were a TI, the 1989 Taif Agreement could be seen as an exception. Youssef considers that limits *ratione temporis* of the reforms in Lebanese society should have been provided in this agreement, and that this omission has contributed to the failure of the transition in Lebanon. N. Youssef, *La Transition démocratique et la garantie des droits fondamentaux*, op. cit., p. 28. Cf. also pp. 99 a.f.

[8] For example, 'the Transitional Government held during this volatile period [July 2003] and Buyoya – true to form – agreed to step down at the appointed hour of his relinquishing the presidency of the transitional government in April 2003', T. Sisk, *International Mediation in Civil Wars*, Routledge, 2009, p. 142.

actors may echo them. When TA do not hand over power or perpetuate their reign, also external actors view this as unlawful. When the Eritrean provisional government, for example, was reluctant to end its provisional reign, this 'demonstrate[d] a typical case of *illegal perpetuation of transitional government* beyond the reasonable transitional period'.[9] The UNSC or regional organisations thus often underline that powers of TA are temporal, and that the transition must be implemented in a timely fashion, after which the interim rule must be relinquished.

Several cases evidence that the TI themselves as well as external actors have taken a clear stance on the temporal limitation to TG. This can also impact transition leaders' eligibility, which is often retracted after the transition ('ineligibility-after-transition practice'). Table 6.1 shows how TI, and, as the case may be, the UNSC or regional organisations, have imposed temporal limits on TG in Afghanistan, Burkina Faso, Burundi, Cambodia, CAR, Comoros, Côte d'Ivoire, DRC, Guinea, Guinea Bissau, Iraq, Kyrgyzstan, Liberia, Libya, Mali, Nepal, Somalia, Syria, Ukraine and Yemen. More details on a case-by-case basis are provided in the separate report.[10]

As mentioned, limitations *ratione temporis* to TG have a general and specific component. First, as a general rule, TA must exercise their duties on a temporary basis, that is without suspending or delaying the interregnum, and with the aim of being replaced. As a perusal of practice shows consistency in demanding that a replacement actually take place, this limitation *ratione temporis* can safely be qualified as a customary obligation of result albeit in the make. This obligation should be seen in connection with the limited substantive powers of TA (following section). Limitations *ratione temporis* indeed diminish the substantive powers of TA. This can be illustrated, *a contrario*, by the following events that occurred in Ghana in the 1990s: 'the PNDC [Provisional National Defence Council] refused to declare its political neutrality. Instead, it openly sought to control the entire transition period *and to give itself maximum advantage*. While it accepted the report of the National Commission on Democracy ('NCD') to return the country to constitutional rule,

---

[9] S. M. Weldehaimanot, 'The Status and Fate of the Eritrean Constitution', op. cit., p. 133. Own emphasis.

[10] E. De Groof, 'The Features of Transitional Governance Today', op. cit. See 'Practice 2'.

Table 6.1 *Overview limitations* ratione temporis *to interregnum*[11]

Transitions	Limitations transitional period on the basis of TI and UNSC resolutions	Ineligibility
Afghanistan	Bonn Agreement, Preamble, § 7; art. I.4; art. I.5 S/2002/278 (2002)	/
Burkina Faso	Charte de la Transition of 16 November 2014, artt. 20, 21	Charte de la Transition of 16 November 2014, artt. 4, 13, 16
Burundi	Arusha Agreement, protocol II, Chapter II, 'Transitional Arrangements' (artt. 1–11) S/RES/1545 (2004) S/RES/1577 (2004) S/RES/1602 (2005)	Arusha Agreement, Ch. 1, Art. 20, § 11
Cambodia	Paris Accords, art. 23 S/RES/745 (1992), § 3 S/RES/783 (1992), § 2 S/RES/792 (1992), Preamble §3; §2	Dissolution SNC
Central African Republic	Déclaration de N'Djamena, § 4 S/RES/2127 (2013), §§ 5 and 6 S/RES/2149 (2014), § 8	Charte Constitutionnelle du 18 juillet 2013, art. 106 S/RES/2127, § 3
Comoros	Accords d'Antananarivo, art. 3.b Accord-cadre de réconciliation nationale of 17 February 2001, titre II Accord sur les dispositions transitoires aux Comores, I. Principes.	Accords d'Antananarivo, art. 3.a Accord-cadre de réconciliation nationale of 17 February 2001, III, art. 18

---

[11] This table first appeared in E. De Groof, 'The Features of Transitional Governance Today', op. cit. Courtesy of Political Settlements Research Programme (University of Edinburgh).

Table 6.1 (*cont.*)

Transitions	Limitations transitional period on the basis of TI and UNSC resolutions	Ineligibility
Côte d'Ivoire	Linas-Marcoussis Agreement, art. 3.a, IX S/RES/1933 (2010)	Linas-Marcoussis Accord, art. 3.c Premier accord complémentaire à l'accord politique de Ouagadougou (unnumbered)
DRC	Pretoria Agreement, IV S/RES/1457 (2003) S/RES/1468 (2003) S/RES/1565 (2004) S/RES/1592 (2005) S/RES/1635 (2005)	Draft Constitution of the Transition, art. 200 (exception for President of the transition)
Guinea	Déclaration conjointe de Ouagadougou, artt. 1–12 ECOWAS Final communiqué 10/11 January 2009, artt. 13.1, 13.3	Déclaration conjointe de Ouagadougou, art. 8 ECOWAS Final communiqué 10/11 January 2009, § 13 S/2009/422, § 7 S/PRST/2009/27
Guinea-Bissau	ECOWAS Final communiqué 3 May 2012, § 21 S/PRST/2013/19	Pacto de Transição Política, art. 5.3 ECOWAS Final communiqué 3 May 2012, § 25
Iraq	Transitional Administration Law, artt. 2B, 58B, 59, 60, 61 Agreement on Political Process	Dissolution GC
Kyrgyzstan	Provisional Government Decree No. 19, 20 (April 2010)	
Liberia	Accra Comprehensive Peace Agreement, art. 35	Article cited below (p. 206) by Roehner (primary source not available)

Table 6.1 (*cont.*)

Transitions	Limitations transitional period on the basis of TI and UNSC resolutions	Ineligibility
Libya	Constitutional Declaration art. 30 Libyan Supreme Court ruling of 6 November 2014	Art. 21 of the 2011 Constitutional Declaration
Mali	Accord Cadre de mise en oeuvre de l'engagement solennel, art. 5 S/RES/2423 (2018), § 2 S/RES/2480 (2019), § 1	Implicitly in Accord Cadre de mise en oeuvre de l'engagement solennel, art. 6.a
Nepal	Interim Constitution of Nepal, 2063 (2007), artt. 1, 167, schedules 2, 3 (with reference to Comprehensive Peace Agreement of 22 November 2006)	N/A although art. 45.4 of the Interim Constitution limits the term of the 'legislature-parliament'
Somalia	Somali Transitional Charter, artt. 3.2, 3.3, 71.9	Somali Transitional Charter, art. 32.4 (for members of parliament)
Sudan	2019 Political Agreement on establishing the structures and institutions of the transitional period, Chapter 2, § 6 and 7; Chapter 5, § 2 Constitutional Charter for the 2019 Transitional Period, Chapter 2, § 6	2019 Political Agreement on establishing the structures and institutions of the transitional period, Chapter 2, § 12
Syria	Coalition's Principles nr. 4 Basic principles for a political settlement to the Syrian conflict, February 2015. See also Final communiqué of the Action Group for Syria and its § 9 about 'irreversible steps in the transition according to a fixed time frame'.	Transition was not initiated

Table 6.1 (cont.)

Transitions	Limitations transitional period on the basis of TI and UNSC resolutions	Ineligibility
Ukraine	Second Minsk Agreement, art. 11 S/RES/2202 (2015) with reference to 'Package of Measures for the Implementation of the Minsk Agreements', § 11	Transition aborted/ collapsed
Yemen	GCC agreement, artt. 6, 7, 10 S/RES/2216 (2015) S/RES/2402 (2018), § 1 S/RES/2456 (2019), § 1	Transition aborted/ collapsed

it did not commit itself to any timetable.[12] Similarly, in the DRC, elites 'tried to prolong the transition for as long as possible, and to postpone the elections' only to continue war exploitations during the transition.[13] Such examples – and, generally, any attempt to cling on to power – show how temporal and substantive limitations to the interregnum are connected. TA tempted to act *ultra vires* will do so with more ease by disregarding the temporal limits to TG. Sometimes, non-compliance with a predefined timetable is the only way for TA to overstep their limited mandate: stealing time to abuse power.

Second, the ineligibility-after-transition practice is relatively consistent although it has suffered (nuanced) exceptions in the past.[14] If current trends

[12] E. Gyimah-Boadi, 'Ghana – The Political Economy of 'Successful' Ethno-Regional Conflict Management' in S. Bastian and R. Luckham, *Can Democracy Be Designed?: The Politics of Institutional Choice in Conflict-Torn Societies*, Zed Books, 2003, p. 130. Own emphasis.

[13] M. de Goede and C. van der Borgh, 'A Role for Diplomats in Postwar Transitions?', op. cit, p. 120.

[14] In Afghanistan, Karzai was appointed during the transition. In the DRC, the ineligibility rule was generally applicable, with the exception of the President. In Iraq, the GC was dissolved before the reigns were taken over by the interim council and transitional government. An exception seems to concern Yemen where the ineligibility-after-transition was not explicitly enshrined in the 2011 GCC Agreement. Yet, Saleh *de facto* quit office (although he continued to exert significant powers behind the scenes until his assassination in December 2017).

206 LIMITS *RATIONE TEMPORIS* AND *MATERIAE* TO TG

continue and generalise, this limitation *ratione temporis* may be qualified as an obligation of best efforts, also currently in the make. Note that the ineligibility-after-transition practice is not a TJ measure, for example in the context of vetting procedures, and should not be invoked to justify long-term exclusions in the post-transition era.[15] It does not target members from the pre-transition regime (contrary to, for instance, the de-Baathification process in Iraq or the vetting procedures in post-1989 Central and Eastern Europe). Instead, it bars transition office holders from taking office after completion of the transition.

The rationale behind the ineligibility-after-transition practice is double. First, it ensures that transition office holders do not have incentives to trigger TG merely to monopolise power after the interregnum. Second, the transition purportedly becomes depoliticised. The (appearance of) technocratic function of the transition finds confirmation in the ineligibility-after-transition practice. For the same reason, in some cases the constituent assembly must not, during the interregnum, include sitting members of parliament.[16]

In the same context, TI may provide that transition office holders are not allowed to buy or rent state property, or to conclude contracts with the state as suppliers or contractors.[17] Such limitations on their legal capacity corroborate the disincentive that transition office holders should not expect to gain personal advantages from holding power during the interregnum.[18] This

---

[15] In Egypt, the Supreme Constitutional Court declared a political exclusion law unconstitutional in 2012.

[16] For Egypt, cf. Ruling Higher Administrative Court, April 2012 cited in R. Grote, T. Röder, *Constitutionalism, Human Rights, and Islam after the Arab Spring*, Oxford University Press, 2016, p. 14.

[17] See, for example, the Constitutional Declaration of 3 August 2011 regarding Libya, art. 21: 'during the term of his membership, the member [of the Interim Transitional National Council], his wife or his sons may not buy or rent any State property or lease or sell to or barter with the State any of his own property, or conclude a contract with the Sate in his capacity as obligator, supplier or contractor'. These examples could be complemented with texts relating to the transition in Burundi.

[18] Admittedly, in at least one case, i.e. Liberia, this has had the contrary effect. Roehner writes, with regard to the transition in Liberia, that '[a]s terms in office of the NTGL members were limited until the national elections in November 2005, they did not have a great interest in sustainable reforms but rather aimed at securing economic benefits for themselves'. N. Roehner, *UN Peacebuilding – Light Footprint or Friendly Takeover?*, op. cit., p. 184. Mehler and Strasheim write: '[d]agegen gibt es Hinweise, dass wichtige Reformen gezielt verhindert wurden: Ehemalige Bürgerkriegsparteien in der Übergangsregierung Liberias . . . nutzten die Machtbeteiligten, um sich persönlich zu bereichern und eine grundlegende Justizreform zu blockieren'. Own translation: 'on the other hand, there are indications that important reforms have been deliberately prevented: former civil war parties in the interim

LIMITS *RATIONE MATERIAE* 207

logic is connected to, but distinct from, the prohibition contained in the African Charter on Democracy, Elections and Governance according to which 'the perpetrators of unconstitutional change of government shall not be allowed to participate in elections held to restore the democratic order or hold any position of responsibility'.[19] By analogy, and more subtly, the ineligibility-after-transition and the concomitant reduction of legal capacity discourage political actors from initiating TG for personal or political advantages.

B   Limits *Ratione Materiae*

TG is also limited substantively. Practice indicates that TA generally do not take the liberty to dominate the present, review the past or entrench the future. The limitations *ratione materiae* thus influence their powers in three ways: TA cannot adopt decisions for the present which go beyond their managerial mandate, nor erase the past and affect acquired rights nor take a full grip on the post-transition stage. Rather, they must execute the transition and administer the country on a provisional basis, including by restoring security (1), respecting past laws and treaties (2) and preparing for the future without foreshadowing it (3).

1   Administer the Country during the Transition, and Ensure Security

TI mostly centre around two tasks. First, to stick to the main assignment, that is bringing the transition – including the constitution-making process – to completion. Second, to ensure the day-to-day conduct of state affairs, that

government of Liberia ... used the power to enrich themselves and to block fundamental judicial reform'. N. Ansorg, F. Haass, A. Mehler, J. Strasheim, 'Institutionelle Reformen zur Friedenskonsolidierung', *GIGA Focus*, Nr. 6, 2012, p. 5. Some suggest that this could have been remedied by a wider participation in the NTGL: 'Third parties need to advocate for wider participation because the members of power-sharing governments often have no interest in such efforts. The National Transitional Government of Liberia (NTGL) inaugurated in October 2003 demonstrates the attitudes of power-sharing elites. . . . Due to the lack of accountability mechanisms during the transitional period, the members of the NTGL devoted more attention to the division of the spoils of the state than to making and implementing public policies,' K. Papagianni, 'Power Sharing, Transitional Governments and the Role of Mediation', op. cit., p. 50.

[19] African Charter on Democracy, Elections and Governance of 30 January 2007, art. 25.4. The distinction is emphasised because the transitions under scrutiny are not necessarily unconstitutional, but can also be 'just' non-constitutional, as we have seen in Chapter 3, Section A.

is essential government services, which includes the core business of the Weberian state: demilitarising politics, monopolising legitimate force, providing security and restoring effective control over the state territory. The portfolio of TA is thus limited: do not lose sight of daily business and priorities, and in the interval pursue state transformation. In South Africa, thus, the 'Record of Understanding between ANC and Government' of 26 September 1992 precisely addressed these two issues. It committed the participants of the ANC and the South African government to a transition[20] as well as to a more secure environment following the 1991 National Peace Accord.[21] Limiting TG on the basis of this double assignment has another notable historic precedent: the powers of the 1814 French provisional government.[22]

Monitoring transitions and seeing to daily business while ensuring security are two tasks increasingly 'delegated' to domestic constituencies, also when international peace and security are concerned and in spite of the factual internationalisation of the interregnum. Even a rough sketch of state practice illustrates how TA are entrusted with (1) completing a transition and (2) ensuring the daily business of state affairs in a secured environment.[23] TA worldwide have been concerned with, and deemed responsible for the execution of the transition roadmap and the provision of security. Besides in South Africa, this trend was evident in Burundi, Afghanistan, DRC, Haiti, Iraq, Côte d'Ivoire and Nepal. Since 2010, it was confirmed in Yemen, Guinea Bissau, CAR, Burkina Faso, Ukraine and Libya. The details can be found in a separate report.[24] Let us briefly consider both tasks in turn.

First and foremost, TA have the ultimate responsibility for completing the transition. This is not limited to constitution-making – usually delegated to a constituent assembly – but also involves organising sur-

---

[20] Record of Understanding between ANC and Government of 26 September 1992, § 2.e, § 2.a and especially § 2.b.

[21] National Peace Accord of 14 September 1991. See especially Chapter 4 (regarding the mission and Code of Conduct of the South African Police) and Chapter 6 (regarding the establishment of a Commission of Inquiry on the prevention of public violence and intimidation).

[22] In the context of the 'Restauration', 'Acte du Sénat qui nomme un gouvernement provisoire chargé de pourvoir aux besoins de l'administration, et de présenter au sénat un projet de constitution', of 1–2 April 1814. This provisional government had a double function as indicated in the title of the Act.

[23] E. De Groof, 'The Features of Transitional Governance Today', op. cit. See 'Practice 3'.

[24] Id.

LIMITS *RATIONE MATERIAE*

rounding activities, such as national dialogues, referenda and elections. Such activities should be 'inclusive' and aim at *progressively* realising the principle of internal self-determination, we shall see below.[25] TA in principle are entrusted with, and generally considered responsible for, these activities even if TG is subject to international influence.[26]

The second task – daily business and provision of security – is reminiscent of the function of caretaker governments[27] in running day-to-day affairs and, as part of their daily concerns, maintaining public order and safety. As they cope with considerable security issues, TA purport to restore (full) effective control over state territory, also by providing 'critical arenas in which ex-combatants and civilians make assessments' regarding their future.[28] A successful state renaissance and reconstitutionalisation also depends on an incremental restoration of peace during the transition by demilitarising political dialogue. This is how TA are expected to break the conundrum that 'peace cannot occur without a constitution and a successful constitution cannot be achieved without peace'.[29]

Considering the volatile environments they work in, TA do not always succeed in demilitarising politics. The quasi-symbolic securitisation of the capital city in some states, or the need to rely on an international presence to dissipate physical threats to the transition, are cases in point.[30] TA nevertheless see to it that politics are demilitarised during the interregnum. They frequently execute disarmament, demobilisation and reintegration programs ('DDR'), which are commonplace in transition settings,[31]

---

[25] Chapter 7.

[26] Chapter 1, Section A.2.3.

[27] In French: *gouvernements de gestion* or *gouvernements en affaires courantes*. The Australian 2013 Guidance on Caretaker Conventions, for example, ensures that during the caretaker period major policy decisions, significant appointments and the entering into major contracts or undertakings are avoided.

[28] T. Lyons, 'Post-Conflict Elections and the Process of Demilitarizing Politics: The Role of Electoral Administration', op. cit., pp. 36–62.

[29] H. Ludsin, 'Peacemaking and Constitution-Drafting: A Dysfunctional Marriage', op. cit., p. 254.

[30] K. Guttieri, J. Piombo (eds.), *Interim Governments – Institutional Bridges to Peace and Democracy?*, op. cit., p. 13: 'states like Somalia seem to be stuck with a series of virtually permanent "transitional governments" that cannot even govern the capital city. Other countries like Afghanistan have gone beyond the "transitional government" phase, yet the resultant central government can barely project force beyond the capital city'. E. Newman, 'Liberal Peacebuilding Debates', op. cit., pp. 33–4.

[31] N. Ansorg, F. Haass, A. Mehler, J. Strasheim, 'Institutionelle Reformen zur Friedenskonsolidierung', op. cit.: 'Weder führt die militärische Integration von Rebellen in die nationalen Streitkräfte noch die einfache Demobilisierung solcher Rebellengruppen – zwei sehr unterschiedliche Reformlogiken – zwangsläufig zu einer

a technique promoted by dozens of non-transitioning states as well.[32] In spite of the diversity of DDR contexts,[33] the treatment itself has been quite consistently applied.

The two core tasks of TA, administering the transition and seeing to daily business, are related to each other, and all the more so in light of the 'inextricable – perhaps even mutually constitutive – connection between effective power and successful legitimation during . . . founding periods and processes'.[34] A secure environment is conducive to a successful transition, as evidenced by the contrast between the relatively successful South African transition and the difficult Afghan transition.[35] Security is central to the process of self-*redetermination* during TG[36] as a lack thereof inhibits meaningful debate, consensus-

---

Reduzierung der Gewalt. . . . Die häufigsten Maßnahmen in diesem Bereich waren Programme zur Entwaffnung, Demobilisierung und Reintegration ehemaliger Rebellengruppen (nach der englischen Bezeichnung "Disarmament, Demobilization, and Reintegration", abgekürzt DDR)'. Own emphasis and translation: 'neither the military integration of rebels into the national armed forces nor the simple demobilisation of such rebel groups – two very different reform logics – inevitably leads to a reduction in violence. . . . The most common measures in this area were programs for the disarmament, demobilisation and reintegration of former rebel groups'.

[32] EU states, China, Iceland, Morocco, Nigeria, Norway, Pakistan, Turkey, US. The EU states, Iceland, Norway and Turkey accentuate that DDR must go hand in hand with social and economic integration (S/PV.4903 of 26 January 2004, p. 27). China considers DDR to be '[t]he first priority, at the outset of the post-conflict national reconciliation period' (Id., p. 28). Morocco considers that the reintegration of former combatants is a 'pivotal element[s] in the lasting settlement if conflicts' (S/PV.4903 of 26 January 2004 (resumption 1) p. 22). Nigeria (Id., p. 35). Pakistan insists on full-fledged peacekeeping operations including DDR programmes. The US sees DDR as an instrument for post-conflict national reconciliation (Id., p. 20).

[33] M. Berdal, D. H. Ucko (eds.), *Reintegrating Armed Groups after Conflict*, Routledge Studies in Intervention and Statebuilding, 2009, p. 3: 'diversity in the character of armed groups that have, with very uneven levels of success, been subject to DDR'.

[34] See Bhuta's review of Weber's, Schmitt's and Arendt's theories of state formation/ transformation. N. Bhuta, 'New Modes and Orders', op. cit., p. 19.

[35] K. Annan, N. Mousavizadeh, *Interventions – A Life in War and Peace*, op. cit., p. 342. Annan noted about the Afghan transition how 'the security reality began lagging behind the formal political transition. The inability to close this gap became the greatest threat to the transition itself'.

[36] This observation was made in relation to TJ, and can be expanded to TG. E. Stover, H. Megally, H. Mufti, 'Bremer's Gordian Knot: Transitional Justice and the US Occupation of Iraq', *Human Rights Quarterly*, 27.3, 2005, p. 834: 'in a post-conflict situation like Iraq in which the state has collapsed, security trumps everything: it is the central pedestal that supports all else. Without some level of security, transitional justice processes are doomed to fail'.

building and transparency.[37] This is why the UNSC noted, in relation to Sudan, that 'without a ceasefire and a fully inclusive peace process the implementation of certain other provisions of the Agreement, including constitution-making and post-transition elections, should not take place'.[38] If successful, the restoration of security and control – *inter alia* through DDR initiatives – will positively influence other components of the transition. These components include public participation in the state order reconfiguration[39] as well as the realisation of TJ,[40] topics which will be addressed in the following chapter.

In short, TA usually assume a double core mission. They execute the transition and see to day-to-day state affairs, including by doing everything within their power to restore public security and effective control over the state territory. If current trends continue and become more generalised, this limitation *ratione materiae* may be qualified as an international obligation (now in the make) of best efforts.

2 Respect the Past vis-à-vis Third States and Private Persons

State continuity and the respect of acquired (private) rights demand that TA, even if they introduce a break with history, respect the past in certain

---

[37] J. Benomar, 'Constitution-Making after Conflict: Lessons for Iraq', op. cit., p. 83.

[38] S/RES/2406 of 15 March 2018, § 4.

[39] K. Papagianni, 'Political Transitions after Peace Agreements: The Importance of Consultative and Inclusive Political Processes', op. cit., p. 47: '[p]rogress in the demilitarization and demobilization efforts and improvements in public security are essential before political participation is expanded significantly. Improved public security allows debate to take place and opinions to be expressed without the danger of destabilization'. See also p. 55. Conversely, inclusivity can also enhance security. M. Saul, *Popular Governance of Post-Conflict Reconstruction*, op. cit., p. 177. In some cases, the gender aspects of inclusive security are emphasised. With regard to the CAR transition, for example, dozens of states and organisations 'stressed the importance of . . . ensuring their [women's] involvement in the processes relating to disarmament, demobilization and reintegration (DDR), as well as to security sector reform (SSR)'. Cf. Declaration of the third meeting of the International Contact Group on the Central African Republic', Bangui, 8 November 2013.

[40] This is why a UNDP official stated that 'unless citizens feel that their personal security is being met by effective policing of their streets and communities, a lot of the rest of reconciliation and peace-building is hard to achieve'. Cf. S/PV.4903 of 26 January 2004, p. 7. In the same sense, the Russian delegation (id., p. 21). The link between security through DDR and reconciliation was also made with respect to Sierra Leone, as the UN regarded 'the process of reintegration as an essential component of national reconciliation, with special focus on ex-combatants' (S/PV.4903(Resumption 1) of 26 January 2004, p. 8). In the same sense, France (S/PV.4903 of 26 January 2004, p. 17).

regards.[41] TA generally strike this balance. It would therefore be inaccurate to say that (even oppositional) transitional constitution-making is 'unrestricted by the old legal order',[42] and it is no coincidence that TI often contain references to preceding constitutional systems.[43] TG and post-sovereign constitution-making purport to avoid a 'legal and institutional state of nature',[44] and a reference to existing law can be instrumental to that effect. State continuity is not necessarily at odds with the non-constitutional origin and supraconstitutional function of TG. The supraconstitutional function of TI leaves ordinary legislation and previously concluded treaties generally untouched. TA are not in the position to repeal them *en bloc*. There is no *tabula rasa*. TA see to state transformation, not state creation.

A level of continuity concerns both the domestic and international legal plane, and is upheld in deference both to private interests and third states. The principle of state continuity remains applicable in times of transition, regardless of whether it was explicitly enshrined in relevant instruments. Although this is not strictly necessary, various TI do however reiterate that international treaties must be upheld. In the DRC, the 2002 Draft Constitution of the transition specified that the delegates of the Inter-Congolese Dialogue would respect previously ratified international and regional legal instruments.[45] Similarly, the 2004 Somali Transitional Charter provides that 'the Transitional Federal Government of the Somali Republic shall uphold all bilateral

---

[41] About state continuity, see, generally, A. Zimmermann, 'Continuity of States', MPEPIL: '[s]tate practice has over time always confirmed that any such internal changes are irrelevant for purposes of international law'. State continuity does not pose a particular problem when profound regime changes are not accompanied by territorial changes. Further, referring to transitions from Tsarist to communist Russia (1917), from the Ottoman Empire to the Turkish Republic (1921), from republican Spain to Francoist Spain (1937), from federal to unitary Indonesia (1950), and from the Japanese empire to post-War Japan, Verzijl notes that in spite of important constitutional changes these states remained the same persons, and their 'international rights and obligations subsist in principle unaltered'. J. H. W. Verzijl, *International Law in Historical Perspective*, op. cit., pp. 118–19. Cf. also, about state continuity and interim governments, S. Gemma, 'Les gouvernements de fait', op. cit., p. 342. About state continuity and *de facto* governments, see N. Henry, *Les gouvernements de fait devant le juge*, op. cit., § 185.

[42] P. Dann, Z. Al-Ali, 'The Internationalised Pouvoir Constituant', op. cit., p. 427.

[43] Chapter 3, Section A.1.

[44] A. Arato, 'Post-Sovereign Constitution-Making and Its Pathology in Iraq', op. cit., p. 541.

[45] These delegates reaffirm their 'attachment to ... all international and regional legal instruments adopted within the framework of the United Nations Organisation and of the African Union duly ratified by the Democratic Republic of Congo'. Cf. 2002 Draft Constitution of the Transition, Preamble.

LIMITS *RATIONE MATERIAE* 213

agreements'.[46] State continuity also explains why, in September 2011, the UNSC, in the context of the Libyan transition, 'call[ed] upon the Libyan authorities to honour extant contracts and obligations'.[47] The *Pacto de Transição Política* regarding the transition in Guinea-Bissau in 2012 also provided that the TA were to respect international treaties previously concluded.[48]

Further, post-transition constitutional texts generated by TG often refer to the continuing validity of treaties and, more generally, confirm the pre-eminence of international law. When the Venice Commission, which has now extended its activities well beyond Europe, issues opinions on draft constitutions, it consistently advises that respect for existing treaties be mentioned in final constitutions.[49] Treaties concluded prior to the interregnum thus remain in force unless the initiation of TG constitutes a 'supervening impossibility of performance'[50] or a 'fundamental change of circumstances'[51] under the strict conditions imposed by the VCLT.

TI furthermore frequently confirm that the major part of previously enacted domestic law remains in place. Briefly, six examples. In 1992, before the South African transition (1994–1997) had started, 'the Government and the ANC agreed that during the interim/transitional period there shall be *constitutional continuity*'.[52] In Burundi, the 2000 Arusha Agreement provided that 'all laws in force prior to the commencement of the transition shall *remain in force* until amended or repealed' whilst accepting the possibility of reviewing legislation contrary to the transitional arrangements.[53] In the DRC, the 2002 Draft Constitution of the Transition similarly provided that 'legislation currently in force, where it is not contrary to the Transitional Constitution, remains applicable for as long as it is not amended or repealed'.[54] In

---

[46] 2004 Somali Transitional Charter, art. 69.

[47] S/RES/2009 of 16 September 2011.

[48] *Pacto de Transição Política* of 16 May 2012, art. 1.2.

[49] See e.g. Opinion 733/2013 on the final draft constitution of the Republic of Tunisia (2013), §§ 38–40.

[50] VCLT, art. 61.

[51] VCLT, art. 62.

[52] Record of Understanding between ANC and Government of 26 September 1992. Own emphasis.

[53] Arusha Agreement, Protocol II, Ch. II, art. 16.1. Own emphasis. Art 16.2 provides: '[t]he transitional National Assembly shall as a priority review all legislation in force with a view to amending or repealing legislation incompatible with the objectives of the transitional arrangements and the provisions of the present Protocol'.

[54] Draft Constitution of the Transition, art. 203.

214   LIMITS *RATIONE TEMPORIS AND MATERIAE* TO TG

Liberia, the 2003 Accra Agreement provided that 'all suspended provisions of the Constitution, Statutes and other laws of Liberia, affected as a result of this Agreement, shall be deemed to be *restored* with the inauguration of the elected Government by January 2006'.[55] In Côte d'Ivoire, previous laws, including the controversial 'Law 98–750 of 23 December 1998 on Rural Land Tenure',[56] were in principle upheld.[57] In Iraq, the 2004 TAL provided that 'except as otherwise provided in this Law, the laws in force in Iraq on 30 June 2004 *shall remain in effect* unless and until rescinded or amended by the Iraqi Transitional Government in accordance with this Law'.[58] Inasmuch as it is compatible with supraconstitutional TI, continuity is the rule while rescission or amendment is the exception.

State continuity protects the legal position of third states as well as the private interests of citizens and acquired rights of foreign investors. This need not be explicitly recognised, even if at times TI do so. In the context of the Rwandan transition, for example, the right of refugees to repossess their properties was confirmed explicitly.[59] The protection of private property, generally, was also confirmed on the occasion of transitions in Burkina Faso[60] and CAR.[61] In the same vein, citizens' rights and legitimate expectations require that acts such as the registration of births, deaths and marriages

---

[55] Accra Agreement, Part 10 'Implementation of the Peace Agreement', art. XXXV, e. Own emphasis. For a discussion, cf. E. P. Morgan, 'Interim Government in Liberia – Peace Building toward the Status Quo' in K. Guttieri, J. Piombo (eds.), *Interim Governments – Institutional Bridges to Peace and Democracy?*, op. cit., p. 195.

[56] Linas-Marcoussis Accord of 13 January 2003, art. IV.1.

[57] The continuity of domestic legislation of course does not amount to an interdiction of any reform. It was for instance decided that: '[t]he Government of National Reconciliation will within one year *overhaul* the general regime governing the press so as to strengthen the role of the regulatory authorities, guarantee neutrality and impartiality of the State broadcasters and foster the financial independence of the media'. Linas-Marcoussis Accord of 13 January 2003, art. V.2. Own emphasis.

[58] TAL, art. 26. Own emphasis.

[59] Protocol of Agreement between the Government of Rwanda and the Rwandese Patriotic Front on the Repatriation of Rwandese Refugees and the Resettlement of Displaced Persons of 9 June 1993, art. 4: 'All refugees shall therefore have the right to repossess their property on return. . . . refugees who left the country more than 10 years ago should not reclaim their properties, which might have been occupied by other people. The Government shall compensate them by putting land at their disposal and shall help them to resettle.' The fact that this issue is related to the transition as such is evidenced in artt. 34–35 of this protocol, which links the repatriation program to the establishment of the Broad-Based Transitional Government.

[60] 'ECOWAS names contact group on Burkina Faso', ECOWAS Press Release, 7 November 2014.

[61] *Déclaration de N'Djamena*, art. 7.

LIMITS *RATIONE MATERIAE*

concluded under the previous order not be invalidated by the TA. The perspective of the citizen as point of reference during temporary administration is not unknown to international law. It was central to the ICJ's ruling that South Africa's administration of the Namibian territory could not affect the validity of acts 'the effects of which can be ignored only to the detriment of the inhabitants of the Territory'.[62]

Even against the background of a state renaissance, TA generally do not question the validity of private acts like those just mentioned. The 'Namibia principle' can be applied *mutatis mutandis* to TG. Upon a liberal interpretation, this principle may explain why contracts or concessions granted by TA may be rescinded if they manifestly conflict with the citizens' interests. Thus, when government officials of the Liberian National Transitional Government (allegedly) committed fraud and misappropriated $1.3 million – manifestly overstepping their fiduciary mandate – a good number of contracts and concessions were reviewed and sometimes cancelled by other states or organisations.[63]

Furthermore, foreign investors enjoy protection against governmental changes of revolutions, including in a transition setting.[64] This is in line

---

[62] Legal consequences for states of the continued presence of South Africa in Namibia (South West Africa) notwithstanding Security Council Resolution 276 (1970), Advisory opinion, ICJ Reports 1971, p. 16, § 125.

[63] C. Bruch et al., 'International Law, Natural Resources and Post-Conflict Peacebuilding: From Rio to Rio+20 and Beyond', *Review of European Community & International Environmental Law*, Vol. 21, no. 1, April 1, 2012, p. 50: 'the World Bank and other donors insisted on –and the transitional Liberian government ultimately accepted– putting in place the Governance and Economic Management Assistance Program (GEMAP) to *review all contracts and concessions granted by the transitional government* as well as the first few years of the new government. GEMAP applied international accounting, financial management and transparency standards to all concessions and contracts, not just those relating to timber or other natural resources. *The reviews led to the cancellation or renegotiation of fifty contracts* and the approval of fifty-two contracts, yielding a substantial improvement in the proportion of concessions and contracts meeting minimum legal standards. While this may have yielded improved outcomes, it also was intrusive – all contracts required two signatures: one from the relevant Liberian official and one from the World Bank'. Own emphasis. Saul writes: 'the fact that Charles Gyude Bryant, former Chairman of the National Transitional Government of Liberia, stands charged with economic sabotage for misappropriating $1.3 million during his tenure is a further illustration of the inherent risk that the international involvement will put a self-interested government in control of the state in question'. M. Saul, 'From Haiti to Somalia', op. cit., p. 139. Bryant was acquitted in April 2009, and further charges were dropped during September 2010.

[64] M. Fink, 'Grenzen des arabischen Wandels aufgrund von Investitionsschutzrecht?', *Zeitschrift für ausländisches öffentliches Recht und Völkerrecht, HJIL*, Vol. 72, no. 3, 2012, pp. 483–519.

with the 1923 Tinoco Claims Arbitration.[65] If investors' rights are not respected during the interregnum, the international responsibility of the TA or the successor government may be engaged on the basis of general international law and/or of specific investment-protection regimes. The Libyan TA, for instance, was to exercise due diligence in protecting the rights of investors. Dozens of states and organisations represented in the 'International Contact Group for Libya'[66] thus 'welcomed the commitment of the NTC to ... honour any existing legal contracts signed under the Qaddafi regime'.[67] On the basis of the due diligence principle, and of a joint Italian-Libyan declaration dated 21 January 2012,[68] foreign investors could in principle vindicate their rights.[69]

Financial institutions, too, can invoke the protection of investment. This would apply even to so-called odious debts contracted by previous regimes. For Howse, the theory of the odious debt confirms that, outside the context of state succession, 'relationships with financial institutions that had odious dealings with the previous regime [should be continued] when the economic and financial stability of the transition suggests such a course of action'.[70] Applying this rule however also depends on the

---

[65] *Great Britain v. Costa Rica*, 1 U.N. Rep. Int'l Arb. Awards 369, 1923.

[66] Including the Arab League, the EU, the GCC, the NATO, and the UN.

[67] US Department of State Press Release, Fourth Meeting of the Libya Contact Group – Chair's Statement of 15 July 2011, § 12.

[68] F. Francioni, 'Lo status del transitional national council della Libia e gli effetti del cambiamento di regime sui diritti degli investitori esteri', *Giornate di Studio sulla Libia*, Recenti sviluppi dello scenario libico dopo la crisi – Implicazioni giuridiche ed economiche, Atti delle Giornate di Studio organizzate dalla SIOI, Editoriale Scientifica, 2012, p. 32.

[69] Id., p. 36: 'nonostante le incertezze sul piano politico e la fluidità sul campo in Libia, l'Italia ha buoni argomenti per tutelare i diritti degli investitori in Libia sulla base dei trattati in vigore e avrebbe sia l'interesse, sia buoni argomenti giuridici per sostenere la perdurante operatività dei trattati in vigore'. Own translation: 'despite the uncertainties on the political level and the changing dynamics on the battlefield in Libya, Italy has good arguments to protect the rights of investors in Libya on the basis of the treaties in force. It would have both an interest and strong legal arguments to support the continuing applicability of the treaties in force'.

[70] R. Howse, 'The Concept of Odious Debt in Public International Law', UN Conference on Trade and Development, Discussion Papers, July 2007, No. 185. J. Crawford, on the other hand, has briefly proposed to 'develop a system under which third parties dealing with a grossly unrepresentative regime would be required to take the risk of doing so. This would apply both to States and to private parties, including corporations. It would put them on a notice that if they wish to deal with a regime lacking any legitimacy or popular support, they would take the risk of the review of the transaction by a subsequent representative government', J. Crawford, 'Democracy and the Body of International

LIMITS *RATIONE MATERIAE* 217

question whether the contracting of the debt was beneficial for the population concerned. For Howse, a 'special transitional tribunal' should be created to consider such claims.[71]

In any case, the principle of state continuity is not fundamentally challenged by TG, even in the context of a state renaissance. *Ius in interregno* here simply echoes existing international law. The principle of state continuity imposes restraint when managing state affairs. It protects the legal position not only of any state entertaining a legal relation with countries in transition, but also of their citizens legitimately expecting their rights not to be fundamentally altered during or after the interregnum; and of third investors, for similar reasons.

Not unlike belligerent occupiers[72] or ITAs,[73] TA act as *trustees* also of third-state and private interests. This confirms the fiduciary nature of

---

Law' in G. H. Fox, B. R. Roth, *Democratic Governance and International Law*, op. cit., p. 109.

[71] R. Howse, 'The Concept of Odious Debt in Public International Law', op. cit., p. 4, p. 25.

[72] The principle of 'conservationism' in international humanitarian law and 'stewardship' during transitional periods, which Boon deems central to *ius post bellum*: Conservationism: 'Occupiers are [therefore] obliged to protect the civilian population, by acting as trustees and reserving fundamental political and legal changes to future governments representing the occupied population.' K. E. Boon, 'Obligations of the New Occupier: The Contours of Jus Post Bellum', op. cit., p. 60; Stewardship 'require[s] that administrators respect the rights and safeguard the interests of inhabitants under their purview. This obligation entails acting in the best interests of the populations concerned, because local populations are vulnerable to the risk of misconduct' (id., p. 81). While introducing major constitutional changes, interim rule is thus based on a fiduciary or commissarial type of administration. This is reminiscent of situations of belligerent occupation (cf. Hague Convention (IV) respecting the Laws and Customs of War on Land of 18 October 1907, artt. 43 and 55; Fourth Geneva Convention relative to the Protection of Civilian Persons in Time of War, Geneva, 12 August 1949, art. 64, enshrining a 'prohibition of fundamental legislative and institutional change'). For Saul, '[t]here is a clear emphasis on the indication of areas where administration must be conducted rather than on change and development. ... *Any attempts to make permanent changes would therefore be of doubtful legality'.* M. Saul, 'The Impact of the Legal Right to Self-Determination on the Law of Occupation as a Framework for Post-Conflict State Reconstruction', in N. Quinivet, S. Shah-Davis, *International Law and Armed Conflict*, op. cit., p. 298 a.f. Own emphasis.

[73] For Diamond, '[a]ll international post-conflict interventions to reconstruct a failed state on democratic foundations confront a fundamental contradiction. Their goal is, in large measure, democracy – popular, representative, and accountable government in which "the people" are sovereign. Yet their means are undemocratic – in essence, some form of imperial domination, however temporary and transitional. How can the circle be squared? ... This requires a balancing of international *trusteeship* or imperial functions with a distinctly non-imperial attitude and a clear and early specification of an acceptable timetable for the restoration of full sovereignty', L. Diamond, 'Building Democracy After Conflict. Lessons from Iraq', *Journal of Democracy*, 16(1), 2005, pp. 9–23. Own emphasis.

218   LIMITS *RATIONE TEMPORIS* AND *MATERIAE* TO TG

TG. It echoes the idea of stewardship deemed central to *ius post bellum* which 'require[s] that administrators respect the rights and safeguard the interests of inhabitants under their purview. This obligation entails acting in the best interests of the populations concerned'.[74] The context of TG cannot be invoked as an excuse to deny third-state or private interests. Notwithstanding the transformative nature of TG, their legal position remains in principle unaltered. Although TA rupture with history, they must respect the past without entirely foreshadowing the future.

3   Prepare for the Future without Entrenching it

TA prepare for the future, generally by following a comparable roadmap: arranging an inclusive interregnum, setting up a constituent assembly for drafting a new constitution, organising a constitutional referendum to have the draft constitution adopted or rejected and/or preparing general elections. These are among the core *procedural duties* of TA. In addition, just as pre-transition governments are sometimes barred from taking actions that would hinder the transition (for example in Rwanda[75] and Burundi),[76] TA must not negatively affect their country's future nor have it cast in stone. It is for this reason that one must 'separate discussions on [transitional] frameworks from debates on new constitutional arrangements'.[77]

The limited power in predefining the future has an impact on TG in general, and constitution-making in particular. With regard to constitutional arrangements contained in peace agreements, for instance, Papagianni argues 'against the inclusion of fixed, long-term institutional arrangements in peace agreements. . . . [P]eace agreements should define the *processes through which* political leaders will reach decisions on

---

[74] Id.

[75] Peace Agreement between the Government of the Republic of Rwanda and the Rwandese Patriotic Front of 4 August 1993, art. 8: '[t]he current Government shall, in no case, take decisions which may be detrimental to the implementation of the Broad-Based Transition programme'.

[76] 2000 Arusha Agreement regarding the transition procedure in Burundi, Protocol II, Ch. II, art. 22.8: '[t]he Government shall be responsible for the day-to-day government of Burundi during the interim period. If during that period the Government should, without the approval of the Implementation Monitoring Committee, take any of the actions indicated in subparagraphs (a)–(d) below, *such action may subsequently be reviewed by the transitional Government and, if found not to have been in the interests of good governance, summarily cancelled or reversed*'. Own emphasis.

[77] K. Papagianni, 'Transitional Politics in Afghanistan and Iraq: Inclusion, Consultation, and Public Participation', *Development in Practice*, Vol. 15, no. 6, 2005, p. 747.

LIMITS *RATIONE MATERIAE*

constitutional arrangements, *but should not define the long-term consti-tutions themselves*.[78] One way of avoiding the entrenchment of long-term institutional arrangements is by limiting detail. If too detailed, TI risk becoming 'ossified',[79] which can result in a protracted interregnum, as the Nepalese transition of almost a decade on the basis of the very detailed 2007 interim constitution illustrates.

The idea that unelected TA should not pre-empt the future is not new. In the early 1950s, in the context of the planned decolonisation of Libya under UN assistance, UN Commissioner Adriaan Pelt feared 'the extent to which the Provisional Libyan Government, as yet unable to account for its actions to an Elected Parliament, could bind the future duly constituted Government'. Pelt thus proposed to circumscribe the man-date of the provisional government.[80] Subsequent practice confirms that TA have limited powers in predefining – other than procedurally – the future of their country. The analysis of TG in practice, in a separate report,[81] reveals that the predefinition of broad supraconstitutional principles is the maximum allowed, although obligations taken up during the transition which fit the TA's fiduciary role are usually inherited by the post-transition government (as the transition in Liberia illustrates).[82]

A TG practice, relatively consistent so far, can thus be unveiled: TA 'midwife' the process of state transformation without predefining substantively the coming constitutional order. At a maximum, TI predetermine a set of general supraconstitutional principles.[83] These principles often refer to international law or to fundamental goals of

---

[78] K. Papagianni, 'Political Transitions after Peace Agreements: The Importance of Consultative and Inclusive Political Processes', op. cit., p. 52. Own emphasis.

[79] IDEA, 'Interim Constitutions in Post-Conflict Settings', op. cit., p. 6, p. 10 (under 'stickiness and scope').

[80] A. Pelt, *Libyan Independence and the United Nations: a Case of Planned Decolonisation*, Carnegie Endowment for International Peace, 1970, p. 827: 'the Provisional Government, while assuming full responsibilities for all measures necessary during its period in office to build up federal governmental machinery, should *limit its other obligations to the strictest minimum*, so as to leave as much liberty of action as possible to the Government that would take office on the declaration of independence'. Own emphasis.

[81] E. De Groof, 'The Features of Transitional Governance Today', op. cit. See 'Practice 3'.

[82] The Accra Agreement, regarding the transition in Liberia, provides that '[a]ll legal obligations of the transitional government shall be inherited by the elected government'. Accra Agreement, art. 35.e.

[83] V. C. Jackson, 'What's in a Name?', op. cit., p. 1282: 'some transitional constitutions seek not only to entrench themselves as law for a short period of time, but also to advance entrenched principles or rules from which future constitution makers cannot depart'.

the transition.[84] As tertiary norms, TI thus define the *method* and perhaps *broad objectives* for reconstitutionalising a state without predetermining the *contents* of the future constitutional order. The idea that TI should determine the modalities of TG without fixing the contents of the ensuing long-term constitution is largely verified in practice.[85] Fundamental legal changes are reserved for elected bodies and/or for the post-transition stage. If current trends continue and become more generalised, this limitation *ratione materiae* may be qualified as an obligation of best efforts (now in the make), also to be understood in light of the principle of self-determination: while the 'broad principles' are considered permanent, they do not pre-empt the people's power to reconstitutionalise their country.

It almost sounds like a contradiction. Although they prepare for major institutional changes, TA have little leeway for defining the post-transition constitutional order. TG is therefore best qualified as *fiduciary*. This also triggers the question whether, during an interregnum, TA may grant long-term concessions to foreign investors for the exploitation of natural resources. This question deserves separate analysis, also specifically in relation to relevant TI.[86] The fiduciary nature of TG is reminiscent of – but not identical to – the conservation principle, that is the prohibition of fundamental legislative and institutional change in situations of belligerent occupation,[87] a parallel drawn by other

---

[84] N. Youssef, *La Transition démocratique et la garantie des droits fondamentaux*, op. cit., p. 125.

[85] See also, in about the same wordings, K. Papagianni, 'Power Sharing, Transitional Governments and the Role of Mediation', op. cit., p. 51: 'need to define the processes through which political leaders will reach decisions on constitutional arrangements without actually defining the long-term constitutions themselves'.

[86] In transition settings, the question often arises whether TJ should also pursue a redistributive aim, i.e. the reordering of material resources to correct past injustices resulting from socio-economic disparities. Haysom and Kane recommend that the division of natural resources be explicitly addressed in TI (as was done, for instance, in the context of the Sudanese, and in much less detail the South African transition): 'particularly in situations where natural resources are or may have been a driver of conflict, the handling of natural resources should be a central component of subsequent peace or constitutional negotiations'. N. Haysom, S. Kane, 'Negotiating Natural Resources for Peace: Ownership, Control and Wealth-Sharing', Center for Humanitarian Dialogue, 2009. Cf. also IDEA, *Oil and Natural Gas: Constitutional Frameworks for the Middle East and North Africa*, 2015. See also A. Wennmann, 'Sharing Natural Resource Wealth during War-to-Peace Transitions' in P. Lujala, S. A. Rustad (eds.), *High-Value Natural Resources and Peacebuilding*, Routledge, 2011.

[87] Fourth Geneva Convention relative to the Protection of Civilian Persons in Time of War, Geneva, 12 August 1949, art. 64, which enshrines a 'prohibition of fundamental legislative

LIMITS *RATIONE MATERIAE*

authors too.[88] Under the conservation principle, the 'expectation is that change will be deferred until the end of occupation. Any attempts to make permanent changes would therefore be of doubtful legality';[89] the occupying power 'act[s] as trustees and reserve[es] fundamental political and legal changes to future governments representing the occupied population'.[90] At its core, the principle of self-determination underpins the conservation principle.[91]

To a lesser degree, and under a nuanced form, the conservation principle applies to TG. TA have to exercise self-constraint. They may prepare for the future but cannot hold it hostage. Besides being commended by scholarship and sometimes confirmed by the UNSC, the prohibition on leaving a detailed imprimatur on the successor order has been quite consistently verified since the end of the Cold War.[92] The conservation principle combined with the fiduciary nature of TG entails two other consequences, both of which were already discussed: TA must focus on their primary task – completing the transition – while remaining attentive to running the state on a daily basis, and TG should not, in principle, negatively affect the legal position of third states or of private persons.

---

and institutional change'. See also Hague Convention (IV) respecting the Laws and Customs of War on Land, 18 October 1907, artt. 43 and 55. The fiduciary nature of TG could also be compared to ITA being limited by its conservation function. See I. Prezas, *L'administration de collectivités territoriales par les Nations Unies – Etude de la substitution de l'organisation internationale à l'état dans l'exercice des pouvoirs de gouvernement*, op. cit.

[88] In relation to the Iraqi TA, see R. Wolfrum, 'Iraq – from Belligerent Occupation to Iraqi Exercise of Sovereignty: Foreign Power versus International Community Interference', op. cit., p. 40.

[89] M. Saul, 'The Impact of the Legal Right to Self-Determination on the Law of Occupation as a Framework for Post-Conflict State Reconstruction' in N. Quinivet, S. Shah-Davis, *International Law and Armed Conflict*, op. cit., p. 298 a.f. Own emphasis.

[90] K. E. Boon, 'Obligations of the New Occupier: The Contours of Jus Post Bellum', op. cit., p. 60.

[91] J. L. Cohen, 'Sovereignty and Human Rights in "Post-Conflict" Constitution-Making: Toward a *Jus Post Bellum* for "Interim Cccupation"', op. cit., p. 223: 'if post-conflict constitution-making is to be an exercise in self-determination instead of foreign imposition, if the sovereignty of the occupied state and people is to remain intact while that state and the constitution is being reconstructed, then occupying forces *must not themselves engage in expansive legislative and institutional changes that pre-empt autonomous political decision-making by the occupied regarding the nature of their political, social, and economic regime*'.

[92] E. De Groof, 'The Features of Transitional Governance Today', op. cit. See 'Practice 3'.

C Calibrating the Power of Modification and the Duty of Conservation

The scope of TG is confined both *ratione temporis* and *ratione materiae*. In the limited time allotted to them, TA prepare for the future without predefining it, initiate reforms while respecting the continuity of the state, prepare a state renaissance while attending to daily business. Such practices are not considered merely a matter of politeness or morality but are increasingly framed as legal obligations, sometimes of result, and sometimes of best efforts.

TA come into being in a non-constitutional fashion with the aim of reconfiguring the state's constitutional order. At the same time, they commit to stability, and accept that their role is constrained. They thus strike a balance between the *power of modification* (within the limits imposed by their mandate) and the *duty of conservation* (regarding the matters not covered by their mandate). They commit both to change (managing the transition) and stability (state continuity; respect of private rights). Enormous procedural powers – a state renaissance no less – are combined with limited substantive powers. This tension, inherent to transformative constitutionalism, manifests itself during the entire interregnum. It is normatively addressed in the following way: because mostly unelected, TG is a fiduciary type of administration facilitating the realisation of internal self-*re*determination.

Because TA are generally unelected indeed,[93] their mandate is circumscribed. Back in 1951, Pelt recognised the necessity of this limitation. Temporal and substantive limitations to TG are not trivial because TA, being unelected, are undemocratic, under the formal understanding of democracy and sometimes beyond.[94] Undemocratic TA carry out a reconstitutionalisation process, often in the name of democracy. This kind of paradox also tainted ITA.[95] The only way for ITA to avoid being embroiled in the contradiction was for a temporary unelected

---

[93] Report of the Secretary-General on peacebuilding in the immediate aftermath of conflict' of 11 June 2009, A/63/881-S/2009/304, §§ 11 and 12: 'many post-conflict countries are governed by transitional political arrangements until the first post-conflict elections are held. National authorities are often *appointed rather than elected*, put in place through a brokered agreement between parties to the conflict who may not be fully representative or recognised by the population'. Own emphasis.

[94] For definitions of democracy, cf. Chapter 2, Section B.2.1.

[95] L. Diamond, 'Building Democracy After Conflict. Lessons from Iraq', op. cit., pp. 9–23.

THE POWER OF MODIFICATION & DUTY OF CONSERVATION 223

administration to function under a limited mandate.[96] This required 'balancing of international trusteeship or imperial functions with a distinctly non-imperial attitude and a clear and early specification of an acceptable timetable for the restoration of full sovereignty'[97] – in a sense, limits *ratione materiae* and *ratione temporis*. The same reasoning now applies to TG which, as was noted, has largely supplanted ITA as a technique for (indirectly) administering conflict- or crisis-riven societies. The non-imperial, fiduciary nature of TG also explains the increased emphasis on inclusion, a topic we shall tackle in the next chapter.

---

[96] S. Chesterman, *You, The People, The United Nations, Transitional Administration, and State-Building*, op. cit., p. 257: 'to exercise state-like functions, [the UN and other international actors] must not lose sight of their *limited mandate* to hold that sovereign power in trust for the population that will ultimately claim it'. Own emphasis. See also I. Prezas, *L'administration de collectivités territoriales par les Nations Unies – Etude de la substitution de l'organisation internationale à l'état dans l'exercice des pouvoirs de gouvernement*, op. cit., p. 213. Prezas explains the limits *ratione materiae* ('principe de conservation') and *ratione temporis* of ITA.

[97] L. Diamond, 'Building Democracy after Conflict. Lessons from Iraq', op. cit., pp. 9–23.

7

The Practice and Discourse of Inclusion

In this chapter we dissect the notion of 'inclusion' or 'inclusivity' and explore the interaction between inclusive TG and the principle of self-determination. Since the end of the Cold War, 'inclusivity' and 'domestic ownership' have been jointly promoted in relation to TG. As the more general term, 'inclusion' or 'inclusivity' refers to the involvement of various groups with a direct interest in the social contract and its redefinition. The aim of inclusion is to ensure national ownership over the transition and especially constitution-making so as to increase their legitimacy. For some commentators, without inclusion, 'the constitution is unlikely to achieve either peacemaking or constitution-drafting goals'.[1] More generally and beyond the constitution, progressive inclusion during the interregnum as a whole is deemed instrumental on all three levels of transformative constitutionalism: resolving conflicts and creating the conditions for peace (peace through transition); regulating the exercise of public powers *ad interim* (defining the interim rule); and projecting and preparing the coming constitutional order (constitutional reconfiguration).

Inclusion can be realised through representation or participation. For the purposes of this book, 'representation' refers to the inclusion of *delegates* or *representatives* of the various groups that wish to be included and their interests to be defended in the interregnum.[2] It depends on including peoples' delegates or key political players during the transition ('elite involvement'). 'Participation' refers to the direct inclusion of the *population* during the interregnum by means of general consultation, national dialogues,[3] public referenda or other modes of popular governance. It aims at involving the population at large ('popular involvement').

---

[1] H. Ludsin, 'Peacemaking and Constitution-Drafting: A Dysfunctional Marriage', op. cit., p. 276.
[2] N. Töpperwien, 'Participation and Representativeness in Constitution-Making Processes' in IDEA, *Constitution Building: A Global Review (2013)*, 2014, p. 8.
[3] See Berghof Foundation, National Dialogue Handbook, April 2017, for an introduction to the topic.

THE PRACTICE AND DISCOURSE OF INCLUSION 225

While some authors emphasise the importance of representation,[4] others stress the importance of participation and popular governance,[5] and still others both.[6]

To be included, attendance at the party usually does not suffice – the various groups should also be invited to dance. It has become a mantra that 'a system of institutional transition cannot be unilaterally defined by the new *de facto* authorities in power; rather, a genuine broad dialogue within the political parties and civil society must be initiated'.[7] Inclusive national ownership has been described as a shared national responsibility requiring the participation by segments of society such as minority groups, women's platforms, youth, labour organisations, political parties, civil society – and rarely also the private sector and diaspora. In essence, the people, in its diversity although not all segments of it, must be taken seriously during a state renaissance.[8]

Since the early 1990s, inclusivity was emphasised as a guiding principle or in more specific, operational terms in countries like South Africa, Comoros, Burundi, Afghanistan, DRC, Liberia, Côte d'Ivoire and Iraq. Since 2010, inclusivity was again promoted for (purported) transitions in countries like Kyrgyzstan, Guinea, Libya, Somalia, Yemen, Syria, Guinea-Bissau, CAR, Burkina Faso and Ukraine. The separate report provides more detail on these cases. It evidences how the commitment to inclusive transitions has become commonplace.[9] Beyond these examples, it appears that, especially since the early 1990s, over a period spanning three decades and in more than hundred jurisdictions, 'ensuring that political

---

[4] J. Benomar, 'Constitution-Making After Conflict: Lessons for Iraq', op. cit., p. 84.

[5] M. Saul, *Popular Governance of Post-Conflict Reconstruction*, op. cit., p. 30.

[6] Papagianni commends that both forms of inclusion be respected in transition contexts. K. Papagianni, 'Political Transitions after Peace Agreements: The Importance of Consultative and Inclusive Political Processes', op. cit., p. 58: '[e]xperiences in a number of countries demonstrate that consultative and inclusive mechanisms, which facilitate *bargaining and negotiation among elites and participation by the public*, contribute to the acceptance of the transitional political process and its outcomes'. Own emphasis.

[7] 'Situation of human rights in Burundi' (A/51/459), report of 7 October 1996, § 37.

[8] This formulation is inspired by J. Klabbers, 'The Right to be Taken Seriously: Self-Determination in International Law', *Human Rights Quarterly*, Vol. 28, no. 1, 2006.

[9] E. De Groof, 'The Features of Transitional Governance Today', op. cit. See 'Practice 4'.

settlements are inclusive is key to the attempts of negotiating transitions from conflict'.[10]

This 'inclusion cascade' is also attributable to socialisation. Practitioners' and organisations' guidelines, manuals and policy briefs echo and perpetuate the mantra that transitions must be inclusive.[11] Such documents systematically refer to inclusivity as a pivotal concern for TG generally, and constitution-making processes specifically. This is also well established in UN language. As a general rule, the UN's approach is 'centred on national ownership and support for inclusive, participatory and transparent processes'.[12] Creating the conditions for 'participatory governance' and assisting parties 'to develop legitimate and broad-based institutions' are seen as effective peacekeeping operations exit strategies.[13] A 2018 UN-led dialogue with governments and other stakeholders[14] reiterates what the Review of the UN Peacebuilding architecture already noted in this sense.[15] Since the

---

[10] C. Bell and J. Pospisil, 'Navigating Inclusion in Transitions from Conflict: The Formalised Political Unsettlement', *Journal of International Development*, 29:5, 2017.

[11] For example the Briefing Note 'Preventing Violence through Inclusion', Inclusive Peace & Transition Initiative, January 2018. D. N. Sharp, 'Beyond the Post-Conflict Checklist: Linking Peacebuilding and Transitional Justice Through the Lens of Critique', op. cit., p. 183: 'the importance of local or national ownership has now become a virtual *UN mantra* in official policy documents'. See also, in relation to peace processes, Conciliation Resources, PSRP, Accord, 'Navigating Inclusion in Peace Processes', Issue 28, March 2019: 'There is a *broad global consensus* that inclusion matters in peace processes'. Cf. also the nuanced study 'Pathways for Peace: Inclusive Approaches to Preventing Violent Conflict', World Bank, United Nations, Washington D.C., 2018: 'the importance of nationally led, inclusive processes came up *continually, across many different contexts*. When states take ownership of their peace processes, and those processes include women, youth, other marginalised groups, and local organisations, significant progress tends to be made toward peace and stability'. Own emphasis in the three quotes.

[12] UN Rule of Law Unit, www.unrol.org/article.aspx?n=Constitution-making, last accessed 9 May 2013 (not available), available en cache. See also J. Harper, 'International Constitutional Law', https://lawin.org/international-constitutional-law accessed on 28 March 2020.

[13] 'No exit without strategy: Security Council decision-making and the closure or transition of United Nations peacekeeping operations', S/2001/394, Report of the Secretary-General of 20 April 2001.

[14] Letter of 14 February 2018 of the President of the UNGA to all permanent representatives and observers at the UN, on file with author. See also A/72/707–S/2018/43 dd. 18 January 2018, § 60; and the High-Level Meeting on Peacebuilding and Sustaining Peace in New York on 24–25 April 2018.

[15] A/64/868 – S/2010/393 of 21 July 2010 ('review of the United Nations peacebuilding architecture'), § 18: 'the principle of national ownership is *widely invoked and accepted*'.

TG THROUGH THE LENS OF SELF-DETERMINATION   227

turn of the millennium, the UNGA,[16] UNSC[17] and UNSG reports[18] have increasingly emphasised the centrality of inclusivity.

The socialised 'inclusion cascade' is not devoid of legal significance. This point will be developed in this chapter, which is divided in three sections. First, we shall make the association between inclusivity and self-determination more explicit (A). Then, we shall dissect the concept of inclusivity, and see how through its many facets it may contribute to the principle of self-determination gaining specificity (B). In the last section, we shall briefly explain how inclusivity and self-determination relate to post-conflict justice (C).

A   Inclusive Transitional Governance through the Lens of Self-Determination

The need to ensure inclusive TG may rest on sound policy considerations, and, within practitioners' circles, is required as a socialised practice. But more is at stake. This section further elaborates on the idea that inclusive TG should be read through the lens of the principle of self-determination *as a general yet qualified rule.*

If peoples have the right to 'freely determine their political status', it is difficult to see how this right could not be relevant for state renaissance and reconstitutionalisation, especially as democratic requirements are too ambitious in times of transition. The thresholds associated with inclusive TG are lower than those associated with substantive democracy. Inclusivity is less high a standard than democracy, certainly if inclusivity mainly revolves around obligations of means and democracy is seen as a substantive right or obligation. TG is neither the fruit of procedural democracy nor can be equated to the actual exercise of governmental

---

Own emphasis. See also A/67/312–S/2012/645 of 15 August 2012 ('civil capacity in the aftermath of conflict').

[16] A/RES/60/180 of 30 December 2005, Preamble and § 10. In the resolution establishing the PBC, the UNGA thus mandated the PBC to 'work in cooperation with national or TA . . . with a view to *ensuring national ownership of the peacebuilding process*'. Own emphasis.

[17] S/PRST/2015/2 of 14 January 2015 in which the UNSC 'emphasise[d] the importance of inclusivity'.

[18] 'The rule of law and transitional justice in conflict and post-conflict societies', S/2004/616 of 23 August 2004. The 2004 UNSG report considers that participation in decision-making is required under the rule of law. Cf. also the 'Report of the Secretary-General on peacebuilding in the immediate aftermath of conflict' of 11 June 2009, A/63/881-S/2009/304, § 9. The 2009 UNSG report notes the importance of 'effective communication and an inclusive dialogue between national authorities and the population'.

power by freely chosen representatives. TA are installed through non-constitutional, often undemocratic means, sometimes in clear defiance of, and always rupturing with, the established legal order.[19] They are indeed mostly appointed or self-selected. Seldom, if ever, do transitions as defined in this study result from democratic processes.[20]

Further, inclusive TG is not (necessarily) testament to a genuine deference to democratic ideals. 'Only the thinnest forms of democracy, justice, or stability tend to co-exist in transition.'[21] Like other TG practices, inclusivity is rudimentarily defined and can be honoured in various ways. No matter the avenue chosen, the systematic insistence on 'representation', 'participation' and 'ownership' does not miraculously transform TG into a textbook example of democracy. A government's representativity and its democratic character, for instance, are two different things, d'Aspremont rightly emphasises.[22] The same is true of national dialogues. With regard to the 2004 national conference in Iraq, for instance, it was observed that 'while such a national dialogue would not be fully democratic, it could be made relatively inclusive, transparent, and participatory'.[23]

While democracy is seen as the greater good, inclusivity is seen as a temporary Ersatz and lesser evil. We shall indeed conclude that, in the context of TG, the principle of internal self-determination goes *further* than the thin procedural right to a constitutional referendum and general elections towards the end of the interregnum (as the people should be progressively involved on a larger scale also during the interregnum), yet requires *less* than substantive democracy.

The undemocratic origin, exercise and sometimes result of TG strongly suggest that TG should be disassociated from democracy.[24]

---

[19] See also C. Rodrigues, 'Letting Off Steam: Interim Constitutions as a Safety Valve to the Pressure-Cooker of Transitions in Conflict-Affected States?', op. cit., p. 51.

[20] Note the exception of double transitions, i.e. when one elected TA follows up on a selected/appointed one. Also, the transitional constituent assembly can be voted, and function both as a parliament/house of representatives and constitutional body, e.g. in Nepal.

[21] Z. Miller, 'The End(s) of Transition' in E. De Groof, M. Wiebusch (eds.), *International Law and Transitional Governance*: Critical Perspectives, Routledge, 2020, p. 128.

[22] J. d'Aspremont, 'Les administrations internationales de territoire et la création internationale d'Etats démocratiques', op. cit., pp. 7–8: on se gardera de confondre la représentativité d'un gouvernement et son caractère démocratique'. Own translation: 'one should not confuse a government's representativeness with its democratic nature'.

[23] J. Benomar, 'Constitution-Making After Conflict: Lessons for Iraq', op. cit., p. 94.

[24] The formalist/procedural vs. substantive understandings of democracy were discussed under Chapter 2, Section B.2.1.

TG THROUGH THE LENS OF SELF-DETERMINATION 229

Instead, inclusive TG has been regarded as an avenue for realising self-determination. In the absence of democracy during the interregnum, inclusivity fulfils a double function. First, a compensatory function. The provisional absence of democratic legitimacy is, in a way, remedied 'by substituting principles like pluralistic inclusion ... *for the missing principle of democratic legitimacy*'.[25] To cope with the (provisional) lack of democracy, inclusivity is put forward. Second, inclusivity is seen as a precursor to democracy. This view does not garner full consensus as the correlation between inclusive transitions and democratisation is contested.[26] In spite of what they often publicly aspire to or announce, inclusive transitions do not necessarily result in democratic outcomes.[27] Dominant discourse nevertheless accepts the premise that inclusivity – through representation and participation – paves the way for democracy. Awaiting democracy, inclusivity is seen as the alternative requirement for the interregnum, *as if* this requirement *anticipated* the democratic character of the state.[28]

The suggestion that inclusive transitions should be read through the principle of self-determination rather than democracy has a notable precedent. The principle of self-determination provided the legal basis for NLM's struggle in the context of decolonisation. While no proof of

[25] A. Arato, 'Post-Sovereign Constitution-Making and Its Pathology in Iraq', op. cit., p. 540. Own emphasis. Cf. also M. Schoiswohl, 'Linking the International Legal Framework to Building the Formal Foundations of a State at Risk: Constitution-Making and International Law in Post-Conflict Afghanistan', op. cit., p. 825: 'the democratic deficit inherent in the self-appointment of a transitional authority mandated to re-institute permanent state structures after civil war can only be overcome by designing a process that sufficiently allows for the emergence of a democratic dialogue and participation'.

[26] J. Strasheim, H. Fjelde, 'Pre-Designing Democracy: Institutional Design of Interim Governments and Democratisation in 15 Post-Conflict Societies', op. cit., p. 347.

[27] N. Youssef, *La Transition démocratique et la garantie des droits fondamentaux*, op. cit., p. 81. J. Strasheim and H. Fjelde, 'Pre-Designing Democracy: Institutional Design of Interim Governments and Democratisation in 15 Post-Conflict Societies', op. cit., p. 347. This is perhaps especially true when inclusive transitions lead to premature elections.

[28] J. d'Aspremont, 'Les administrations internationales de territoire et la création internationale d'Etats démocratiques', op. cit., pp. 7–8: 'cela n'est finalement guère surprenant. Il est en effet difficile de concevoir qu'un gouvernement intérimaire – c'est-à-dire une autorité qui a vocation à mettre en place les principes de l'exercice futur du pouvoir – puisse prétendre à quelque autre légitimité que celle procédant de sa représentativité'. Own translation: 'this is hardly surprising. It is difficult to imagine that an interim government – that is to say, an authority whose vocation is to materialise the principles of the future exercise of power – can claim some other legitimacy than that stemming from its representativeness'.

230   THE PRACTICE AND DISCOURSE OF INCLUSION

territorial control or stringent effectiveness criteria had to be verified, the allegiance of the people (claimed to be represented) was necessary for a NLM to be recognised as such.[29] In the context of TG, the progressive implementation of inclusivity during the interregnum also aims at garnering the people's allegiance through a participatory and/or representative reformulation of the social contract, even when TA do not exercise effective control. Popular allegiance and 'inclusion' constitutes the tool both for NLM and TA to pursue self-determination. Such thematic (rather than historic) continuity suggests that drawing a connection between inclusivity and self-determination is nothing revolutionary.

After the era of decolonisation, inclusive TG has indeed been analysed in light of the principle of self-determination, at least in concrete instances. Authors have observed an *incidental* or *ad hoc* relation between inclusion and self-determination,[30] for example by connecting this principle to local ownership in the specific context of peacebuilding and post-conflict reconstruction.[31] Before and after the turn of the millennium, a good number of transitions designed around inclusivity have been interpreted against the principle of self-determination rather than democracy. This has for example been the case with regard to transitions in Cambodia,[32] South

---

[29] Chapter 4, Section B.2.1.

[30] S. Chesterman, 'Ownership in Theory and in Practice: Transfer of Authority in UN Statebuilding Operations', op. cit., p. 20, observing that the 'broadest use of the term [ownership] is sometimes akin to self-determination'. M. Saul, 'Local Ownership of Post-Conflict Reconstruction in International Law: The Initiation of International Involvement', *Journal of Conflict & Security Law*, Vol. 16, No. 1, 2011, pp. 190–1. M. Saul, *Popular Governance of Post-Conflict Reconstruction*, op. cit., pp. 33–4.

[31] E. Demir, 'The Right to Internal Self-Determination in Peacebuilding Processes: A Reinterpretation of the Concept of Local Ownership from a Legal Perspective', *The Age of Human Rights Journal*, 8, 2017, p. 18: 'the right to internal self-determination offers a legal "checklist" for the UN to provide both legitimacy and sustainability to peacebuilding processes'. Based on a perusal of the language generally used in peace agreements, Stathopoulou points at the intrinsic link between peacemaking and self-determination, without making the link to TG. K. Stathopoulou, 'Self-Determination, Peacemaking and Peace-Building: Recent Trends in African Intrastate Peace Agreements', op. cit. Saul observes that 'In some instances, the commitment of the lead actors to the right to self-determination has been expressed in key documents and resolutions setting out the basis for international involvement and plans for how to enhance the transitional period'. M. Saul, 'Local Ownership of Post-Conflict Reconstruction in International Law: The Initiation of International Involvement', op. cit., pp. 190–1.

[32] It was thus noted that 'it is most accurate to describe the *essence* of the Cambodian process as an exercise in political *self-determination*'. S. P. Marks, 'The Process of Creating a New Constitution in Cambodia' in L. E. Miller, *Framing the State in Times of Transition: Case Studies in Constitution Making*, op. cit., p. 208. Own emphasis. After reaffirming its

TG THROUGH THE LENS OF SELF-DETERMINATION 231

Africa,[33] Afghanistan,[34] Iraq,[35] South Sudan[36] and (intended) transitions of the Arab Spring.[37]

In my view, inclusive TG should be read through the lens of the principle of self-determination *as a general yet qualified rule*. As observed earlier, this principle is a continuing one,[38] and cannot but be relevant

---

support for the 1991 Paris Accords, the UNSC indeed affirmed its intention to contribute to 'the assurance of the right to self-determination'. S/RES/745 of 28 February 1992, Preamble.

[33] The South African transition was also considered 'a problem of self-determination'. A. Sachs, 'South Africa's Unconstitutional Constitution: the Transition from Power to Lawful Power', op. cit., p. 1255.

[34] In Afghanistan, the insistence on a broad based and fully representative administration 'should [rather] be understood as a requirement for representativeness of various ethnic groups and peoples in the context of the right to self-determination'. J. Vidmar, 'Human Rights, Democracy and the Legitimacy of Governments in International Law: Practice of States and UN Organs' in C. Panara, G. Wilson (eds.), *the Arab Spring, New Patterns for Democracy and International Law*, op. cit., p. 64. Marauhn also finds that both the Bonn Agreement and the ensuing transition must be understood in light of the principle of self-determination. T. Marauhn, 'Konfliktbewältigung in Afghanistan zwischen Utopie und Pragmatismus', op. cit., p. 492: '[d]er somit vorhandene faktische Zusammenhang zwischen den Unterzeichnern des Abkommens und dem afghanischen Volk lässt sich nur auf der Grundlage des Selbstbestimmungsrechts in einen rechtlichen Zusammenhang transformieren'. Own free translation: 'From a legal point of view, the existing link between the signatories of the agreement and the Afghan people can only be understood in light of the principle of self-determination'. The signatories of the Bonn Agreement were thus (temporarily) entrusted with honouring the right to self-determination. The UNSC supported a 'broad based' and 'fully representative' transitional administration. S/RES/1378 of 14 November 2001. But it did not call for any particular political system: 'one cannot argue that Security Council Resolution 1378 expressed support for a particular political system – that of Western style liberal-democracy. The use of the term "democracy" itself was avoided. The resolutions also failed to call for an enactment of a particular political system or electoral method'. J. Vidmar, op. cit., p. 64.

[35] Regarding the Iraqi transition, 'the principle governing the transition of Iraq from the former governmental regime via the power exercised by the occupying states to a government under a new national regime is the principle of self-determination'. R. Wolfrum, 'Iraq – from Belligerent Occupation to Iraqi Exercise of Sovereignty: Foreign Power versus International Community Interference', op. cit., p. 43.

[36] S. P. Sheeran, 'International Law, Peace Agreements and Self-Determination: The Case of the Sudan', op. cit., p. 444.

[37] J. Vidmar, 'Human Rights, Democracy and the Legitimacy of Governments in International Law: Practice of States and UN Organs' in C. Panara, G. Wilson (eds.), *The Arab Spring, New Patterns for Democracy and International Law*, op. cit., p. 64. Vidmar writes that the inclusion requirement is to be associated to an exercise of internal self-determination.

[38] Chapter 5, Section A.2.1.

232   THE PRACTICE AND DISCOURSE OF INCLUSION

during a state renaissance, lest one ignore the ordinary meaning of the words 'freely determine a political status'.

I will thus argue that the principle of self-determination is an umbrella principle for TG, and, moreover, that it potentially gains specificity through TG practices, that is through the effective self-*re*determination of a country. More accurately, the principle serves as a directive guideline for TG imposing some *obligations of result* while it also gains in precision through practices increasingly seen as *obligations mainly of conduct* applicable to TG. As shown in Table 7.1 below, this development has already been inaugurated, and its further course will depend on whether practices of inclusion will be maintained and preserve their many facets.

B   Facets of Inclusivity

Although the multifaceted requirement of inclusivity is somewhat under-determined, it does contribute to reducing the relative indeterminacy of the principle of self-determination. We already mentioned that, to be included, attendance at the party usually does not suffice – one should also be invited to dance. The question then is whom to invite, to which dance and at what stage of the party.

As more answers to this threefold question are being provided, the principle of self-determination is gaining precision. As a result, its contemporary relevance and validity come to be confirmed through the emergence of individual customary rules entrenching specific obligations especially of conduct as to (1) 'who' should be included in TG, (2) 'how' and (3) 'when'. We will then ask 'whither' current trends will evolve (4) before concluding that said obligations are adding flesh to the bones of the principle of self-determination (5).

1   Who? Plurality of Groups to Be Involved in Transitional Governance (Expansion Ratione Personae)

Who is the people? Inclusivity aims at fostering the cohesion of 'the people' in a conflict-related situation.[39] Through a broad 'constitutional conversation',[40] involving a plurality of groups during TG contributes

---

[39] W. F. Murphy, 'Constitutions, Constitutionalism, and Democracy' in D. Greenberg et al. (ed.), *Constitutionalism and Democracy*, Oxford University Press, 1993.

[40] S. Chambers, 'Contract or Conversation? Theoretical Lessons from the Canadian Constitutional Crisis', *Politics and Society*, 26, 1998, pp. 143–72.

FACETS OF INCLUSIVITY

to the creation of this 'meaningful corporate identity'.[41] The challenge seems to consist in dealing with various claims for recognition coming from the people, and to 'build trust and consent through its process' in order to arrive at a 'mediated peace'.[42] This seems a mammoth task. Especially as 'there is no such thing as "the people"; there are religious groups, ethnic groups, the disabled, women, youth, forest people, pastoralists, sometimes "indigenous peoples", farmers, peasants, capitalists and workers, lawyers, doctors, auctioneers, and practising, failed or aspiring politicians, all pursuing their own agenda'.[43] Should they *all* be included in state renaissance? Who are the rightholders of the principle of self-determination *of peoples* in times of transition?

From the perusal published separately,[44] a couple of considerations can be drawn which are instructive for the notion of 'peoples' in TG settings. First, peoples are not necessarily 'natural', 'pre-political' or even territory-dependent but can be constituted through the exercise of self-*re*determination. The role of the *process* of group formation is essential here.[45] Second, inclusivity relates to the *entitlement to be taken seriously* and to be involved in the transition.[46] This entitlement is usually associated to the following groups: (1) the political factions or armed groups/military previously in conflict with each other;[47] (2) ethnic groups and indigenous peoples;[48] (3) regional or local entities, provinces;[49] (4) civil

[41] V. Hart, 'Constitution-Making and the Transformation of Conflict', *Peace & Change*, Vol. 26, no. 2, 2001, p. 156.

[42] Id., p. 167. Own emphasis.

[43] Y. Ghai, G. Galli, *Constitution Building Processes and Democratisation*, op. cit., p. 15.

[44] E. De Groof, 'The Features of Transitional Governance Today', op. cit. See 'Practice 4'.

[45] B. Mello, 'Recasting the Right to Self-Determination: Group Rights and Political Participation', *Social Theory and Practice*, 30, 2004, pp. 193–213, criticising statist and cultural understandings of self-determination.

[46] This formulation is inspired by J. Klabbers, 'The Right to be Taken Seriously: Self-Determination in International Law', *Human Rights Quarterly*, Vol. 28, no. 1, 2006.

[47] This was the case for instance in South Africa, Burundi, DRC, Kyrgyzstan, Yemen, Burkina Faso, Liberia. See E. De Groof, 'The Features of Transitional Governance Today', op. cit.

[48] See for example, S/RES/2250 of 9 December 2015, § 2.b, mentioning "indigenous processes for conflict resolution".

[49] For instance in DRC, Somalia, Libya, Yemen. See E. De Groof, 'The Features of Transitional Governance Today', op. cit.

society;[50] (5) traditional and religious leaders;[51] (6) youth;[52] and (7) women.[53] The voice of these categories and factions of society carry increasing weight throughout the interregnum. This list confirms that the concept of 'population' is not strictly associated with territoriality or national culture,[54] and goes well beyond former belligerents or opponent political parties – so-called horizontal inclusion – demanding a seat at the table.

The involvement of women as a cross-cutting category and at various intervals of the interregnum is almost systematically commended.[55] The UNSC has 'urg[ed] the full, equal and effective participation of women in *all activities* relating to the democratic transition'.[56] The UNSG deems the full participation of women in transitions to be essential.[57] In the same vein, the UNSC President noted that women play an important role for the 'design and implementation of reconciliation strategies',[58] an opinion shared by the EU.[59] The UN Guidance Note for Effective Mediation further finds that women may play an effective role in high-level mediation processes, and converts this finding into a deontological

---

[50] See the same report in relation for instance to South Africa, Somalia, Kyrgyzstan, Yemen.

[51] Id. in relation for instance to Burkina Faso.

[52] Id. in relation for instance to Yemen. See also S/RES/2419 of 6 June 2018, § 2, linking inclusion to youth; and S/RES/2250 of 9 December 2015, § 1, which encourages "meaningful participation of youth in peace processes".

[53] See the same report in relation for instance to Afghanistan, DRC, Iraq, Libya, Yemen, Guinea-Bissau, CAR, Burkina Faso.

[54] In the same sense, B. Mello, 'Recasting the Right to Self-Determination: Group Rights and Political Participation', op. cit.

[55] The 2015 Review of the UN Peacebuilding architecture, op. cit., § 44. Specifically about the inclusion of women during transitions, cf. the Report of the Working Group on the issue of discrimination against women in law and in practice, A/HRC/23/50 of 19 April 2013. This working group recommends that states '[s]upport and ensure women's equal participation in and benefit from all areas of political decision-making during times of political transition'. This includes women's participation in 'all transitional authorities and mechanisms', including transitional justice initiatives (id., § 97. d) and arguably constitution-making. See S. Suteu, C. Bell, 'Women, Constitution-Making and Peace Processes', PSRP, UN Women, 2018.

[56] S/RES/2434 of 13 September 2018, Preamble, § 19; § 4. Own emphasis.

[57] 'Report of the Secretary-General on peacebuilding in the immediate aftermath of conflict' of 11 June 2009, A/63/881-S/2009/304, §§ 11 and 12.

[58] S/PV.4903 (resumption 1) of 26 January 2004, p. 2.

[59] Id., p. 4: '[n]ational reconciliation will not take root if some groups or sections of the population are excluded from the process of nation-building. In this regard, greater attention should continue to be paid to the role of women'. The EU considers 'inclusiveness' to be a principle underpinning national reconciliation.

guideline.[60] It has also been suggested that 'women's participation in peace negotiations contributes to the quality and durability of peace'.[61] The same is said of female involvement in power-sharing agreements.[62] Their inclusion would also have beneficial socioeconomic effects lasting beyond the transition.[63]

The inclusion of women is thus nigh-systematically required in transitional settings.[64] Beyond a socialised practice, this has arguably become a normative requirement even in places where traditionally there is no rosy picture when it comes to involving women in society (think of Yemen). 'Women are almost always among the groups considered relevant today'.[65] A landmark UNSC resolution encourages the development of a strategic plan 'calling for an increase in the participation of women at decision-making levels in conflict resolution and peace processes'.[66] This is analogous to, yet broader than, gender-mainstreaming in response to the historic under-involvement of women in transitional justice.[67]

A question usually left unaddressed in the literature is whether exiles or members of the diaspora are to be included, and have an entitlement to influence TG. There is no shared practice in this regard in spite of the

---

[60] 2012 UN Guidance for Effective Mediation, op. cit., p. 11: '[w]omen leaders and women's groups are often effective in peacemaking at community levels and should therefore be more strongly linked to the high-level mediation process'; see also pp. 9 and 13. This guidance note also mentions that the gender dimension of the mediation process should be explicitly addressed in peace agreements (p. 21).

[61] J. Krause, W. Krause, P. Bränfors, 'Women's Participation in Peace Negotiations and the Durability of Peace', *International Interactions*, 44:6, 2018, p. 985. See also T. Paffenholz, N. Ross, S. Dixon, A.-L. Schluchter, J. True, 'Making Women Count – Not Just Counting Women: Assessing Women's Inclusion and Influence on Peace Negotiations', Geneva: Inclusive Peace and Transition Initiative, The Graduate Institute of International and Development Studies, UN Women, April 2016.

[62] Since the UNSC resolution 1325 on women, peace and security a 'remarkable trend in power-sharing agreements is the presence of references to gender and women's rights'. S. Aroussi, S. Vandeginste, 'When Interests Meet Norms: The Relevance of Human Rights for Peace and Power-Sharing', *The International Journal of Human Rights*, Vol. 17, no. 2, 2013, p. 188.

[63] M. Saul, *Popular Governance of Post-Conflict Reconstruction*, op. cit., pp. 41–2.

[64] E. De Groof, 'The Features of Transitional Governance Today', op. cit. See 'Practice 4'. For examples through quotas for women in transitional legislatures, see C. Bell, R. Forster, 'Women and the Renegotiation of Transitional Governance Arrangements', PA-X Spotlight: Gender, 2019.

[65] IDEA, *Constitution Building: A Global Review (2013)*, 2014, p. 6

[66] S/RES/1325 of 31 October 2000, § 2.

[67] S. Buckley-Zister, R. Stanley, *Gender in Transitional Justice*, Palgrave Macmillan, 2012, p. 6.

'immense potential of diaspora communities for conflict transformation'.[68] That the diaspora or foreigners are not expected to contribute to domestic transitions may seem obvious, but in the context of the factual and legal internationalisation of the interregnum, pressure can mount high to pay attention to external input, and not only from 'expat experts'. Business representatives are usually not (directly) considered either, in spite of the transformational power they, too, may have.[69]

2 How? Diversified but Limited Choice for Implementing Inclusive TG (Expansion Ratione Materiae)

Inclusivity is associated to the following methods: transitional constitution-making (2.1); constitution-making *tout court* (2.2); the exercise of public authority during the interregnum (2.3); constitutional referenda and general elections (2.4).

2.1 Transitional Constitution-Making

Transitional constitution-making, that is the drafting or adoption of a TI, can be *triggered* by a popular vindication of self-determination in the context of large-scale popular protests, as was the case of the Arab Spring.[70] Even in such contexts, TI are however generally drafted by political elites, not by the people. The people seldom play a role in

---

[68] W. Zunzer, 'Diaspora Communities and Civil Conflict Transformation', Berghof Occasional Paper Nr. 26, 2004, p. 2. See also how the diaspora tried to influence TG in Iraq and Libya. IDEA, 'Interim Constitutions in Post-Conflict Settings', op. cit. on p. 19 and p. 22 respectively.

[69] J. L. Kaye, 'The Business of Peace and the Politics of Inclusion: What Role for Local Business Elites in Peace Mediation? The Case of Yemen (2011–2016)' in C. Turner, M. Wählisch (eds.), *Rethinking Peace Mediation: Critical Approaches to International Peace Making*, Bristol University Press, 2021, forthcoming. Similarly, economic questions are often excluded from the field of transitional justice, argues Miller who speaks of the 'invisibility of economics'. Z. Miller, 'Effects of Invisibility: In Search of the 'Economic' in Transitional justice', *The International Journal of Transitional Justice*, Vol. 2, 2008, pp. 266–91.

[70] V. Saranti, 'Pro-Democratic Intervention, Invitation, or "Responsibility to Protect"? Challenges to International Law from the "Arab Spring"' in C. Panara, G. Wilson (eds.), *The Arab Spring, New Patterns for Democracy and International Law*, Martinus Nijhoff Publishers, 2013, pp. 169–201: 'the claims of the heterogeneous group of demonstrators and insurgents, even though diversified, could be summed up as follows: freedom, democracy, human rights protection, establishment of functioning institutions and the rule of law, free and fair election and regime change; namely, *especially regarding the latter, the people vindicated the right to self-determination, in its internal dimension*'. Own emphasis.

defining or drafting TI in this beginning stage, be it *grosso modo* or in the specifics. Yet, the very parameters for the transition (including the constitution-making process itself, and the ensuing constitutional order) are already being predefined in these tertiary norms.

As TI anticipate how the social contract will be redefined, the question of inclusivity from the outset is of course no minor issue. For example, 'the understanding of interim constitutions as political agreements aimed at achieving peace has shaped a view that public participation might not be required in the transitional period, only in the drafting of the final constitution. *Yet an interim constitution's legitimacy is likely to depend on a certain degree of inclusivity*, even if this falls short of full public participation.'[71] Along these lines, some practitioners suggest that, at that initial stage already, there be at least some level of *representation* of, rather than full-scale participation by, the people. But such views supporting the early involvement of the people are rather uncommon, and there is all but extensive and uniform practice in this sense.

2.2 Constitution-Making *Tout Court*

Inclusivity especially resonates with 'constitution-making *tout court*', that is constitution-making – through roundtable negotiations, nationwide consultations, national dialogues or conferences[72] – seen as an occasion to redefine the post-transition social contract: 'if the constitution is to be a social contract between different communities, understood as ethnic, linguistic, cultural and/or religious communities ... then these communities must also be included in the constitution-making process'.[73] Constitution-making with popular input on the basis of direct (calls to the public) or indirect (via civil society representatives) consultations or dialogues is becoming more frequent than in the past.[74] Here, the epistemic community catalysing knowledge on TG as well as the broader community of practitioners seem to be on the same page.

---

[71] IDEA, 'Interim Constitutions in Post-Conflict Settings', op. cit., p. 6. Own emphasis.

[72] See for example the cases of SA, Burundi, Afghanistan, Kyrgyzstan and Libya. E. De Groof, 'The Features of Transitional Governance Today', op. cit. See 'Practice 4'.

[73] IDEA, *Constitution Building: A Global Review (2013)*, op. cit., p. 4.

[74] The national conferences in Francophone Africa since 1989, on the other hand, 'allowed a broad and inclusive participation involving representatives from key political and civic groups'. K. Samuels, 'Postwar Constitution Building' in R. Paris and T. D. Sisk, *The Dilemmas of Statebuilding – Confronting the Contradictions of Postwar Peace Operations*, op. cit., p. 177. In contrast, the Autumn of Nations transitions, for instance, were guided by roundtable discussions.

'Inclusivity, participation and transparency' are listed as core principles guiding UN assistance to constitution-making processes.[75] A UNDP report also underscores that 'the UN's constitutional assistance should seek to support a nationally owned and led process that is inclusive, transparent and participatory'.[76] Transition leaders worldwide have similarly recognised that, whatever the process chosen for designing a new constitution, a wide range of participants must be involved 'upstream', and the core demands of key contending groups should be accommodated.[77] In the same vein, influential constitution-makers have enumerated public participation, inclusiveness and national ownership as emerging guiding principles.[78] The introduction of inclusive constitution-making into the legal realm is clearly being propagated by socialisation. Earlier observations about dominant discourse and emulation as fertile grounds for custom creation need not be reminded here.[79]

The obligation to involve the people in *constitution-making* is arguably on the verge of becoming one of result. 'Broad-based popular participation is *fast becoming a norm* in constitution building, but questions remain regarding how to structure effective participation and how to balance mass participation with pact making by the political elite.'[80] How can the people be involved? A rich menu: representation at roundtable negotiations, national dialogues or conferences or participation in nationwide consultations[81] (so-called vertical inclusion). The people's voice is then usually non-binding, but may provide input to a constituent assembly or impact the

---

[75] 'Guidance note of the Secretary-General on UN assistance to constitution-making processes', op. cit., p. 4: '[t]he UN should make every effort to support and promote *inclusive, participatory and transparent constitution-making processes* given the comparative experiences and the impact of inclusivity and meaningful participation on the legitimacy of new constitutions. A genuinely inclusive and participatory constitution-making process can be a transformational exercise'. Own emphasis.

[76] M. Brandt, 'Constitutional Assistance in Post-Conflict Countries, The UN Experience: Cambodia, East Timor & Afghanistan', op. cit., p. 27.

[77] A. F. Lowenthal, S. Bitar, *From Authoritarian Rule Towards Democratic Governance: Learning from Political Leaders*, IDEA 2015, p. 30. Own emphasis.

[78] M. Brandt, J. Cottrell, Y. Ghai, A. Regan, 'Constitution-making and Reform – Options for the Process', op. cit., pp. 9–10. Cf. also K. Samuels, 'Post-Conflict Peace-Building and Constitution-Making', *Chicago Journal of International Law*, Vol. 6, nr. 2, pp. 663 a.f.

[79] Chapter 5, Section B.1.

[80] IDEA, *Constitution Building: A Global Review (2013)*, 2014, p. 2. Own emphasis.

[81] South Africa, Yemen. 'A degree of inclusiveness seems necessary before any process can be dubbed a "national dialogue". The term "dialogue" is usually also intended to signal a desire to move from oppositional politics that reinforce differences and division to a process in which thought is given to understanding different positions and considering the possibility of agreement'. C. Murray in IDEA, *Constitution Building: A Global Review*, op. cit., p. 11.

method by which the assembly must discharge its duties. In some cases, the constituent assembly, sometimes also functioning as a general assembly, is voted into power by the people. This range of options shows that, although engaging the people in designing the constitution is increasingly seen as an obligation of result, there is much leeway as to how to realise this goal.

With the 'postimperial paradigm shift in constitutionalism',[82] constitution-making has become subjected to popular scrutiny. This shift is also apparent in relation to the interim rule, understood as the exercise of public powers during the interregnum, generally (see following subsection), but remains most palpable in relation to constitution-making, specifically.[83] Inclusive constitution-making is considered as the *minimum minimorum* in the wider context of inclusive interim rule. This is not only a policy issue or question of 'best practices'. From the right-holder perspective, self-determination, seen as a right to participate in the conduct of public affairs, applies to constitution-making.[84] This was recognised by the UNCHR,[85] and confirmed by authors like Raič,[86] Preuss,[87] Dann and Al-Ali,[88] Franck and

[82] J. Tully, 'Strange Multiplicity: Constitutionalism in an Age of Diversity', op. cit.

[83] Id., p. 175. Own emphasis. Y. Ghai, G. Galli, *Constitution Building Processes and Democratisation*, op. cit., p. 13. This text mentions the aim of 'developing a collective agenda for social and political change – negotiated rather than imposed. . . . If these are the contemporary functions of constitutions, then the process for making them is crucial to developing a national consensus'. J. Benomar, 'Constitution-Making after Conflict: Lessons for Iraq', op. cit., p. 84; K. Samuels, 'Constitution-Building Processes and Democracy: A Discussion of Twelve Case Studies', IDEA. For Samuels, 'in all cases where the constitutional process was inclusive, representative or participatory, the constitution-building process has led to incremental democratisation of the state'. K. Samuels, 'Postwar Constitution Building' in R. Paris and T. D. Sisk, *The Dilemmas of Statebuilding – Confronting the Contradictions of Postwar Peace Operations*, op. cit., p. 174.

[84] ICCPR, art. 1 *cum* art. 25

[85] UNCHR, *Marschall v. Canada* § 5.2 & 5.3: 'at issue in the present case is whether the constitutional conferences constituted a 'conduct of public affairs' . . . [and] the Committee cannot but conclude that they do indeed constitute a conduct of public affairs'.

[86] After observing that the right to self-determination serves as a basis for a people to 'participate (a right to have a say) in the decision-making processes of the State', Raič writes that 'the right of participation *would, in any case, relate to the determination or constitution* of the political system of the State (*pouvoir constituant*)'. D. Raič, *Statehood and the Law of Self-Determination*, op. cit., p.237. Own emphasis.

[87] Preuss, too, observes that 'constitution-making demands the constituent power of a collective that defines itself as a political entity and disposes of the institutional means to develop and express its own political will. In other words, constitution-making is an act of political self-determination'. U. K. Preuss, 'Perspectives on Post-Conflict Constitutionalism: Reflections on Regime Change through External Constitutionalisation', op. cit., p. 478.

[88] For Dann, this concerns the most fundamental act of self-determination. P. Dann, Z. Al-Ali, 'The Internationalised Pouvoir Constituant', op. cit., p. 426.

240 THE PRACTICE AND DISCOURSE OF INCLUSION

Thiruvengadam,[89] Hart[90] and Jackson.[91] There is no reason for this conclusion not to apply to constitution-making in times of transition. We can call this the prohibition of *internally* imposed constitution-making.

2.3 The Exercise of Public Authority during the Interregnum (Inclusivity of the Interim Rule)

Apart from inclusive constitution-making *tout court*, inclusivity can also relate to the interim rule, understood as the exercise of public powers during the interregnum. It can for example be observed through power-sharing TA or governments of national unity. The people can then be (progressively) involved in the administration of the country, usually less by taking directly part in the conduct of public affairs than by sending their representatives. Cases in which TG is directly *exercised* (rather than triggered) by the people, or exercised in conformity with their will as expressed through elections or referenda, are rare if not inexistent at the time of writing. That is because TG, as defined in this study, is exercised on a non-constitutional basis, and is accompanied by a pledge to recon-stitutionalise after the holding of a referendum and elections.

In the absence of a power-sharing or unity government, the accepted alternative, so recent history shows, is to have a TA committing itself to progressively involving other political factions in constitution-making and decision-making. Opposition-based interim governments, for example, are then supposed to gradually open up to other political factions.

---

[89] While arguing that there is 'no persuasive evidence that customary law requires any particular modalities to be followed in the process of writing a state's constitution', Franck and Thiruvengadam write that the methods for drafting constitutions are not unlimited. On the basis of observations regarding UN-supervised practice of decolonisation and of textual requirements of the ICCPR, the authors find that there is a 'general requirement of public participation in governance' and a 'growing convergence around universal principles of legitimate governance [which] are tending to be applicable also to the process of constitution drafting'. T. Franck, A. Thiruvengadam, 'Norms of International Law Relating to the Constitution-Making Process' in L. E. Miller, *Framing the State in Times of Transition*, op. cit., pp. 14–15.

[90] V. Hart, 'Constitution Making and the Right to Take Part in a Public Affair' in id. Hart confirms that participation is a 'requirement of a constitution-making process'; 'The public has a right to take part in the *foundational affair of constitution making*, and the powerful interests that will always be involved in the process must recognise and respect that right'. Own emphasis.

[91] V. C. Jackson, 'What's in a Name?', op. cit., p. 1293: there is an 'emerging international consensus that "legitimate" constitution-making requires public participation or ratification'.

Formulated as a public commitment, such an approach can also be a tactical move to attract international recognition or support.[92]

The inclusivity of the transition – its foundation, the interregnum, constitution-making – also hinges on the state respecting, protecting and fulfiling the rights to freedom of expression, assembly and association (as guaranteed by articles 19, 21 and 22 of the ICCPR, respectively).[93] Self-determination is generally associated with the protection of such rights.[94] (The link between self-determination and human rights, especially the protection of minorities, goes further back in history than the association between self-determination and decolonisation.[95])

In the context of TG, TA generally confirm the continued relevance during the interregnum of instruments protecting human rights, as we saw in Chapter 5 ('the internationalisation of the interim legal order'). The *prospect* of compliance with these rights is also used as a benchmark for evaluating the 'legitimacy' of interim governments.[96] Arguably, TA must at the very minimum *respect* universal human rights which under-gird the principle of self-determination throughout the transition. This is

[92] With d'Aspremont, we can observe this 'trait nouveau de la pratique contemporaine: pour voir son existence ou, à tous le moins, ses pouvoirs internationalement reconnus, *le gouvernement intérimaire doit être "représentatif"* de la population qu'il assujettit'. See his article 'Les administrations internationales de territoire et la création internationale d'Etats démocratiques', op. cit., p. 8. Own emphasis and translation: there is a 'new feature of contemporary practice: to have its existence or, at the very least, its powers internationally recognised, *the interim government must be "representative"* of the population it exercises power over'.

[93] Cf. A. Cassese, *Self-determination of Peoples: a Legal Reappraisal*, op. cit., p. 53 where he links self-determination to freedom of expression and association. Cf. also J. Crawford, 'The Right of Self-Determination in International Law: Its Development and Future', op. cit., p. 40: 'if self-determination is a continuing right . . . then its normal manifestation will be through the exercise of civil, political and social rights . . . within the framework of the relevant state'.

[94] CCPR General Comment No. 12: Article 1 (Right to Self-determination). In this comment, the Human Rights Committee recognises that 'this right and the corresponding obligations concerning its implementation are interrelated with other provisions of the Covenant and rules of international law' (§ 2).

[95] B. Simma (ed.), *The Charter of the United Nations, A Commentary*, Oxford University Press, 1995, p. 64. Cf. also UN Charter, art. 55 § c. For the link between human rights and self-determination, see also G. Arangio-Ruiz, *The Normative Role of the General Assembly of the United Nations and the Declaration of the Principles of Friendly Relations*, Recueil Des Cours, Collected Courses, 1972, Vol. 137, p. 565. See also the declaration by Italy submitted in this regard (id., p. 571).

[96] M. Saul, *Popular Governance of Post-Conflict Reconstruction*, op. cit., p. 178. M. Saul, 'Legitimising Transitional Authorities through the International Law of Self-Determination' in E. De Groof, M. Wiebusch (eds.), *International Law and Transitional Governance: Critical Perspectives*, op. cit., p. 95.

242 THE PRACTICE AND DISCOURSE OF INCLUSION

an obligation of result in the sense that they should refrain from interfering with or curtailing the enjoyment of human rights.

2.4 Constitutional Referenda and General Elections

Towards the end of the transition, the constitution for the post-transition era is usually adopted by referendum. Alternatively, the transition's closure is directly or indirectly validated through general elections. Commitments in this sense undertaken by TA then confirm existing obligations (enshrined notably in ICCPR, article 25) with regard to the citizenry's participation in public affairs and elections.

The essential nucleus of the principle of self-determination already requires that TA, when coming to represent the state, ascertain the wishes of the population while 'there may be various procedures acceptable for the expression of popular will (referenda, popular consultations, etc.), provided that they enable the population to manifest its choice in a "free and genuine" way'.[97] The popular approval of the constitution or organisations of elections, referenda or at least consultations in closing the transition are in this sense obligations of result already incumbent on TA. Self-determination at present already informs 'downstream constraints' (that is procedures for approving the constitution), and imposes limits on how a new constitution is adopted. Abundantly analysed already, the right to political participation under the procedural conception of democracy, that is mostly seen as an entitlement to fair, open and transparent elections, needs no further comment here.[98]

When it relates to the manifestation of a free and genuine choice in relation to the closure of the transition and pending reconstitutionalisation – mostly through the popular approval of the constitution or general elections – inclusivity can already be considered an obligation of result (*de lege lata*), also in light of the prohibition of internally imposed constitution-making. Such an obligation of result imposes itself towards the end of the interregnum. Public participation then constitutes a red line that cannot be crossed.

---

[97] A. Cassese, 'The International Court of Justice and the Right of Peoples to Self-Determination' in V. Lowe, M. Fitzmaurice (eds.), *Fifty years of the International Court of Justice, Essays in honor of Sir Robert Jennings*, op. cit., p. 359–60. With reference to Western Sahara, Advisory Opinion, ICJ Reports, 1975, pp. 28–9, §§ 71–2.

[98] Cf. for example G. H. Fox, 'International Law and the Entitlement to Democracy after War', op. cit., esp. p. 183.

FACETS OF INCLUSIVITY

3   When? Involving the People throughout the Interregnum (*Expansion* Ratione Temporis)

As one understands from the variety of methods of inclusion just discussed, representation of or participation by the people is relevant at various stages of the transition. The three layers of internal self-determination, already discussed above, can be replicated within the realm of TG, as follows.

- The people's involvement in transitional constitution-making: influencing the *pouvoir pré-constituant* and the tertiary transition instruments that will eventually impact the 'rules of the game' (constitutional law);
- The people's involvement in constitution-making *tout court* for the post-transition order: influencing the *pouvoir constituant* and thus the 'rules of the game' themselves;
- The people's involvement in the interim rule: participating in public affairs.

The commitment to inclusivity can be expressed at various intervals of the interregnum.[99] At the foundation of the interregnum, transitional constitution-making, that is the drafting of the supraconstitutional constituent TI, from a pure factual perspective can be more or less inclusive. The same is true of constitution-making *tout court* and of the interim rule during the interregnum. We could add that, towards the end of the interregnum, the procedure chosen for approving the post-transition constitution or closing the transition can also be more or less inclusive. In all cases, inclusivity can be attained through participation or representation.

Inclusive decision-making in relation to constitutional and institutional arrangements *of the transition* itself is thus to be distinguished from inclusive decision-making in relation to durable such arrangements *for the post-transition* stage. Inclusivity focuses on both aspects in a different way: it is (and should be) gradually applied in relation to participatory or representative governance and constitution-making during the transition[100] while it is nigh-systematically (and should be)

---

[99]   E. De Groof, 'The Features of Transitional Governance Today', op. cit. See 'Practice 4'.

[100]   See, in this sense, K. Papagianni, 'Political Transitions after Peace Agreements: The Importance of Consultative and Inclusive Political Processes', op. cit., p. 52. Specifically with regard to power-sharing, cf. A. K. Jarstad, 'Sharing Power to Build States' in D. Chandler and T. D. Sisk (eds.), *Routledge Handbook of International Statebuilding*, op. cit., p. 254.

244 THE PRACTICE AND DISCOURSE OF INCLUSION

applied towards the end of the transition on the occasion of a referendum or general elections.

4 Whither? Inclusivity Adding Detail to Self-Determination

In spite of its contested utility and criticism on other grounds (4.1), inclusivity is gaining ground and arguably adds detail to the principle of self-determination (4.2).

4.1 Criticism: Inclusivity in the Dock

The multifaceted practice of inclusivity receives positive (4.1.1) and negative (4.1.2) criticism, yet any criticism only has relative legal impact (4.1.3).

4.1.1 Positive Criticism For a significant part of the community of practitioners and experts engaged with TG, inclusive TG leads to a (more) stable post-transition period. It can break the cycle of prior domination by specific groups,[101] and pave the way for stability as 'bargaining and negotiation among elites and participation by the public, contribute to the acceptance of the transitional political process and its outcomes'.[102] Transitions 'that are broadly inclusive ... have the best chance of creating the legitimacy needed for effective post-war governance'.[103] According to some authors, inclusion would furthermore be 'least threatening to traditional elites' as their seat around the table is guaranteed.[104] During transitions, representative and shared decision-making thus yield positive results, so the inclusion aficionados say.

---

[101] S/PV.4903 of 26 January 2004, p. 14.

[102] Id., p. 58. Papagianni summarises the policy reasons behind the requirements of inclusion or expansion of participation during the transition as follows: 'improving perceived legitimacy of a power-sharing government, representing newly formed opposition groups, enabling the emergence of new leaders, and laying foundations for long-term institutional development', K. Papagianni, 'Power Sharing, Transitional Governments and the Role of Mediation', op. cit., p. 47.

[103] T. D. Sisk, 'Elections and Statebuilding after Civil War, Lurching toward Legitimacy' in D. Chandler, T. D. Sisk (eds.), *Routledge Handbook of International Statebuilding,* op. cit., p. 259.

[104] R. Ponzio, *Democratic Peacebuilding, Aiding Afghanistan and other Fragile States,* op. cit., p. 220: 'while discouraging the international community from rushing into electoral contests that inevitably result in winners and losers, transitional governance arrangements send the signal that political change is under way in a manner that is both inclusive of the general population and least threatening to traditional elites'.

FACETS OF INCLUSIVITY

245

Exclusive processes, on the other hand, would produce adverse consequences. It seems transitions in Colombia, Ethiopia and Venezuela were negatively affected by a lack of inclusivity.[105] Transitions in Cambodia (no inclusive constitution-making process)[106] and Thailand (restriction of communication rights)[107] have also been mentioned as counter-examples, whereas for some commentators the outbreak of violence in Ukraine during 2014 could have been avoided, had there been inclusive TG.[108]

4.1.2 Negative Criticism The concrete implementation of inclusion often leaves to be desired (as the Afghan and Iraqi cases illustrate). Apart from this basic observation, commentators consider inclusivity to be vulnerable to criticism from various angles, both of a practical and more principled nature.

From a practical point of view, the noticeable expansion of the notion of 'people' during the interregnum may slow down the transition or otherwise hinder its effectiveness, as 'more actors will, *ceteris paribus*, increase the difficulty of reaching agreement'.[109] Marginalised segments of society – such as youth, women and minorities – are increasingly expected to contribute to peace transitions, whereas actors who already wield considerable, albeit often hidden power – such as business elites, and sometimes, to use a shorthand-term, illicit nobility – remain on the margins of such

---

[105] See J. Benomar, 'Constitution-Making after Conflict: Lessons for Iraq', op. cit., p. 85. The lack of representation during the Ethiopian transition would have led to secessionist claims. The lack of representation in the constitutional process in Venezuela in 1999 has led to a deadlock between pro- and contra-Chavez forces. The exclusion of two large rebel groups has impeded peace during long in Colombia.

[106] S. P. Marks, 'The Process of Creating a New Constitution in Cambodia' in L. E. Miller, *Framing the State in Times of Transition: Case Studies in Constitution Making*, op. cit., p. 213: '[h]ad the Paris Agreements provided for the appointment of an inclusive and independent constitutional commission to direct a constitution-making process that included a comprehensive program of public participation, the process itself may have been more transparent and democratic'.

[107] J. Strasheim, 'Interim Governments: Short-Lived Institutions for Long-Lasting Peace', op. cit., p. 7: 'allegations include arbitrary arrests and the restriction of freedom of expression and assembly. Amnesty International claims that *such restrictions are unfavourable to an inclusive institutional reform process* as well as national reconciliation. The situation in Thailand is that without consulting civil society in the institutional reform process, Thailand's interim leaders are risking a hard landing: not only will reforms not supported by civil society be unsustainable, but an *exclusive interim period might promote further unrest in the country*'. Own emphasis.

[108] Id., p. 6.

[109] J. Blount, Z. Elkins, T. Ginsburg, *Does the Process of Constitution-Making Matter?*, Cambridge University Press, 2012, p. 51. S. J. Steadman, 'Spoiler Problems in Peace Processes', *International Security*, Vol. 22, no. 2, 1997, pp. 5–53.

246 THE PRACTICE AND DISCOURSE OF INCLUSION

processes.[110] Inclusion, as it is nowadays interpreted, for some commentators may then partly defeat the purpose of an effective and efficient state renaissance. The picture can become even more complex when inclusion leads to overrepresentation in a country marked by territorial cleavages.[111]

Among the modes for implementing inclusivity, especially the power-sharing model has been criticised both on legal and extra-legal grounds.[112] Power-sharing as a temporary governance device should however be discerned from power-sharing as a permanent, post-transition, mode of governance.[113] It is more easily accepted as a time-finite measure. It is then not a prefiguration of the post-transition stage but fulfils a different function, that is to familiarise both voters and authorities with new procedures, conflicts to subside[114] and to advance reconciliation.[115] Yet, even as an *ad interim* institutional design, power-sharing is sometimes criticised as 'Eurocentric and derived from academic laboratories and states in the West',[116] ineffective[117] or even counterproductive when it forms an incentive for

---

[110] J. L. Kaye, 'The Business of Peace and the Politics of Inclusion: What Role for Local Business Elites in Peace Mediation? The Case of Yemen (2011–2016)', op. cit.

[111] S. Bisarya, IDEA, 'Constitutional Transitions and Territorial Cleavages', 2015.

[112] For critique on power-sharing generally, cf. I. S. Spears, 'Africa: The Limits of Power-Sharing', *Journal of Democracy*, Vol. 13, no. 3, July 2002, pp. 123–36; S. Vandeginste, C. L. Sriram, 'Power Sharing and Transitional Justice: A Clash of Paradigms?', *Global Governance*, Vol. 17, no. 4, 2011, pp. 489–505; C. L. Sriram, M.-J. Zahar, 'The Perils of Power-Sharing: Africa and Beyond', op. cit. D. Rothchild, 'Executive Power-sharing Systems – Conflict Management or Conflict Escalation?' in K. Guttieri, J. Piombo (eds.), *Interim Governments – Institutional Bridges to Peace and Democracy?*, op. cit., pp. 73–93; J. Strasheim, H. Fjelde, 'Pre-Designing Democracy: Institutional Design of Interim Governments and Democratisation in 15 Post-Conflict Societies', op. cit., p. 347. Levitt argues that this model, as applied in Liberia and Sierra Leone, was – at least domestically – illegal. J. I. Levitt, *Illegal Peace in Africa*, op. cit.

[113] A. K. Jarstad, 'Sharing Power to Build States' in D. Chandler and T. D. Sisk (eds.), *Routledge Handbook of International Statebuilding*, op. cit., p. 254 who argues that 'power-sharing should be a temporary provision'.

[114] I. S. Spears, 'Africa: The Limits of Power-Sharing', op. cit., p. 114: 'incompatibilities between political leaders are more easily overcome if *power sharing is seen as a transitional and time-finite step* towards more competitive elections. On the other hand, such transitional agreements still allow voters and constituents to familiarise themselves with democratic procedures, or for tensions between groups and individuals to subside and, ideally, for the integration of former disputants into common institutions before a non-power-sharing system is adopted'. Own emphasis.

[115] Id., p. 114.

[116] J. I. Levitt, *Illegal Peace in Africa*, op. cit., p. 244.

[117] I. S. Spears, 'Understanding Inclusive Peace Agreements in Africa: The Problems of Sharing Power', *Third World Quarterly*, Vol. 21, no. 1, pp. 105–18, 2000. Note that this article does not focus on power-sharing as a TG method.

FACETS OF INCLUSIVITY

armed groups to step up violence in the hope to accede to power. The model is nevertheless regularly used in transitional settings where, through representation, it constitutes a method which, by its very nature, tends to honour the inclusion requirement, at least in its horizontal variant.

As to inclusive constitution-making, some commentators have observed that 'the claim that participatory design processes generate constitutions with higher levels of legitimacy and popular support has been subject to only limited study'.[118] Linked to this epistemological challenge is the claim that participatory constitution-making processes often breed paper tigers, especially in the case of a 'dissonance between those who influence the outcome of the drafting process and those who will be called upon to operate the constitution'.[119] Such processes may raise expectations that cannot be implemented, and 'the pressures to accept the views of the people lead to complex and ambitious constitutions which the government may not (or often does not) have any intention of fulfilling'.[120]

Then there is the sober, realpolitik-based assessment that, without involving elites, direct participatory processes are no sufficient condition for *institutionalising* a country.[121] In development studies, the engagement of formal and informal elites and power structures based on a 'political settlement mapping' is considered to be the only guarantee for real change. Without taking into account the 'primary actors that hold power', the interests of the elites and existing institutions,[122] change is simply not grounded in reality. There must be a connection between effective power and legitimation in a foundational period, especially in so-called anocracies.

Inclusivity is finally seen as an approach off-the-shelf, non-reflexive and uniform: 'standardised peace manifests itself in everything from women's empowerment schemes to human rights training for local government officials'.[123] Waving the flag of inclusivity would, moreover,

---

[118] J. Blount, Z. Elkins, T. Ginsburg, *Does the Process of Constitution-Making Matter?*, Cambridge University Press, 2012, p. 22.

[119] Y. Ghai, G. Galli, *Constitution Building Processes and Democratisation*, IDEA, 2006, p. 10.

[120] Id., p. 15.

[121] Id., p. 16.

[122] T. Parks, W. Cole, 'Political Settlements: Implications for International Development Policy and Practice', Occasional Paper no. 2, July 2010, p. 28.

[123] R. M. Ginty, 'No War, No Peace: Why So Many Peace Processes Fail to Deliver Peace', op. cit., p. 159.

often amount to little else than window dressing. Financial incentives for conforming to the discourse would be appealing enough for inclusivity to be only nominally upheld, that is as a ticking-the-box exercise and with the sole aim of attracting international support and financing.[124] It would thus be naive to say that the concept is never manipulated or subjected to justificatory rhetoric. The sharpest criticism, finally, is that inclusive TG could constitute yet another object for Western laboratories experimenting with state and society formation, relying on, while largely overestimating, the malleability of socio-politics.[125]

4.1.3 Relative Legal Impact of Extra-Legal Criticism No matter how valid or unjustified, the above criticism does not thwart the *emerging* mandatory nature (for the major part through obligations of conduct) of some components of the widely observed practice and discourse of inclusivity. This study tackles a politicised phenomenon from a legal perspective, and therefore maintains the separation between the legal and political registers, even when discussing as delicate an issue as norm germination in relation to TG. The requirements of 'inclusion', 'representation' and 'participation' are now solidly embedded in international discourse and practice.[126] This observation should be separated from the discussion of their political opportunity *vel non*. The peace-through-transition paradigm can thus safely be requalified, without negative or positive connotations intended, as the peace-through-*inclusive*-transition paradigm.

Aside from being a socialised norm, commended or criticised, inclusivity increasingly penetrates the legal sphere. There is now a strong conviction and commitment that it cannot be dispensed with in times of transition: 'it should no longer be acceptable to exclude the conflict-affected public from efforts to define the new order'.[127] The fact that the UNSC applies sanctions when so-called spoilers obstruct an inclusive transition points in the same direction. This is so regardless of the socialised origins of this evolution or the criticism it generates. Reservations, whether founded or not, do not fundamentally alter the perusal of practice. I thus suggest that inclusivity, broadly understood, is

---

[124] Id., pp. 89–90.

[125] N. Bhuta, 'Against State-Building', *Constellations*, Vol. 15, no. 4, 2008, p. 524. His criticism concerned state-building but could be applied, *mutatis mutandis*, to TG.

[126] E. De Groof, 'The Features of Transitional Governance Today', op. cit. See 'Practice 4'.

[127] Conciliation Resources, PSRP, Accord, 'Navigating Inclusion in Peace Processes', Issue 28, March 2019, p. 97.

FACETS OF INCLUSIVITY

widespread in transition settings (*usus*) and, at certain points of the transition, increasingly seen as a political, social and economic exigency (*opinio necessatis*), paving the way for a legal conviction in this sense (*opinio iuris*) and, eventually, for custom.

4.2 How Inclusivity Details and Extends Self-Determination

As the requirement of 'inclusion' is now solidly embedded in international discourse and practice, it has the potential of expanding the scope of the principle of self-determination, at least in the context of TG, in three regards, as pictured in the following Table 7.1 (see also Table 7.3).

TG *further extends and specifies* the contours of the principle of self-determination, qualified as an entitlement to be taken seriously. We have already seen that this entitlement is held by several segments of society, can be satisfied through various means among which some are indispensable, and must be respected *crescendo* throughout the interregnum. In this subsection, we shall conclude that, slowly but surely, these socialised practices are expanding the personal (4.2.1), material (4.2.2) and temporal (4.2.3) scope of application of the principle of self-determination.

4.2.1 Expansion *Ratione Personae*

Inclusivity practices arguably allow for a re-evaluation and redefinition of the concept of 'peoples', which is gaining precision and also operational clout as several segments of society are increasingly expected to be involved in state renaissance. Various segments of society are to be taken seriously and should (progressively) be involved in TG. As a result, and unless current trends drastically change, the application *ratione personae* of the principle of self-determination is being specified in this sense, and the principle's indeterminacy somewhat reduced in two ways: (1) several though not all categories of persons can claim to be part of the 'people' and be progressively included in the transition; (2) this claim is most clearly and systematically formulated in relation to women's involvement.

First, transitions are often initially steered by elite negotiations, and subsequently become more inclusive. We saw that inclusivity *can* play a role at various stages of the interregnum. The principle of internal self-determination protects the right of the people to be closely and gradually involved in the interregnum and self-*re*determination of the country, through representation and participation. Even in cases where TG is initiated

Table 7.1 *The relation between self-determination and inclusivity*

Principle of self-determination *gaining detail* through common practices	TG practices in relation to inclusion. Increasingly, seen as customary obligations, mostly of best efforts.
A. Expanding scope *ratione personae*	A. Wide interpretation of 'the people': progressive involvement of wider society even when transition initiated in an exclusionary fashion (obligation of best efforts). Women's inclusion almost systematically required (on the verge of an obligation of result).
B. Expanding scope *ratione materiae*	B. A set of procedures to ensure that the voice of various factions of society be taken seriously and that public input be provided to the state renaissance. Only an obligation of best efforts in relation to transitional constitution-making but almost systematically required for constitution-making *tout court* (on the verge of an obligation of result).
C. Expanding scope *ratione temporis*	C. During the interregnum as a whole (including transitional constitution-making), and not only on the occasion of the constitutional referendum and/or general election towards the end of it, TA should aim at progressively involving the people. Only an obligation of best efforts in relation to progressive involvement (for the final validation of the constitution or final elections, obligation of result already).
How self-determination currently gaining detail may eventually impact it as a directive principle	
Principle of self-determination as a *directive principle* for TG	- Some TG inclusive practices are already compulsory under self-determination, mostly as obligations of result (popular approval of constitution or general elections to close the transition; respect of basic human rights during interregnum as enablers of the state renaissance).
	- Over time, threefold expansion of principle of self-determination will further corroborate it as a *directive principle* for inclusive TG.

FACETS OF INCLUSIVITY

in an exclusionary fashion, it must *open up* to the participation and representation of several groups of society.[128] The progressive inclusion of the people during the interregnum can remediate poor popular involvement at the beginning of the interregnum and decreases the chance that decisions taken in the early stages are irrevocable.

Towards the end of the interregnum, the people must always be involved in the constitution-making process. In short, even when TG was initially generated by a replacement, the interregnum must evolve into a transplacement.[129] In light of the prohibition of internally imposed constitution-making, TA are prevented from arbitrarily excluding groups from constitution-making on the basis of race, creed, political allegiance and increasingly of gender.[130]

Second, the expectation of progressively involving various segments of society in the state renaissance is most clearly and systematically formulated in relation to women's involvement. The encouragement to include women's representatives in TG is however seldom formulated *en lien* with the principle of self-determination. Whether the principle of self-determination makes the inclusion of women's representatives compulsory as an obligation of result during TG is controverted. Some authors are sceptical about this,[131] while others advocate for a *lex specialis* on this matter, thus implicitly recognising that the law as it stands now does not (sufficiently) deal with it.[132]

Yet, the (discursive) practice about women inclusion arguably *adds specificity* to the principle of self-determination also from a right-holder perspective. The obligation, albeit still in the make, within this evolution is on the verge of becoming one of result. The pond dividing

---

[128] Power-sharing agreements in Liberia and Sierra Leone were concluded in violation of the principle of self-determination, Levitt contends. J. I. Levitt, *Illegal Peace in Africa*, op. cit., p. 46. This argument hinges on an analysis of the *foundation* of TG in both countries. It does not consider whether or not the gradual involvement of the people might have served as a corrective for this initial violation.

[129] This terminology was introduced in the Introduction, Section B.2.1.

[130] Gana expresses reservations about self-determination being currently applicable to and protective of women's participation. R. L. Gana, 'Which "Self"? Race and Gender in the Right to Self-Determination as a Prerequisite to the Right to Development', *Wisconsin International Law Journal*, 14, 1995, pp. 133–53. See also C. Chinkin, H. Charlesworth, *Building Women into Peace: The International Legal Framework*, Routledge, 2008, pp. 233–53. See also S/RES/1325 of 31 October 2000 on Women, Peace and Security.

[131] R. L. Gana, 'Which "Self"? Race and Gender in the Right to Self-Determination as a Prerequisite to the Right to Development', op. cit. See also C. Chinkin, H. Charlesworth, 'Building Women into Peace: the international legal framework', op. cit., pp. 233–53.

[132] M. Saul, *Popular Governance of Post-Conflict Reconstruction*, op. cit., p. 170.

obligations of conduct from obligations of result may sooner or later be crossed in this respect. (By contrast, inclusion is least clearly articulated in relation to the involvement of business elites and diaspora, where it does not even attain the level of a nascent obligation of best efforts.)

4.2.2 Expansion *Ratione Materiae* If it is correct that TG should be considered as one of the means of implementation of the principle of self-determination, as suggested from the outset in this part, this in itself considerably extends its material scope of application and confirms its relevance today. This introductory point is the most fundamental one. Further, four considerations as to the extended scope *ratione materiae* can be retained here: (1) the *diversification* of methods deemed acceptable for implementing inclusivity; (2) the emphasis on *procedural* inclusion over substantive requirements; (3) the requirement of *progressive* inclusion; and (4) the increased *rejection of internally imposed constitutionalism* during the transition.

First, a whole range of procedures is available to ensure that the voice of various factions of society are taken seriously. Unless current trends drastically change, the scope *ratione materiae* of the principle of self-determination is being expanded (and, concomitantly, the principle's indeterminacy somewhat reduced) through the *diversification* of methods deemed acceptable for implementing inclusivity throughout the interregnum. In several ways, the groups and segments of society mentioned further above can be included, through obligations of conduct requiring the involvement of the people on the basis of political representation or popular participation. Through representative and/or participatory processes, and with varying degrees of intensity, peoples are involved in the redefinition of their social contract. There is not one method for a people to freely determine its political status. Popular involvement can be expressed in various ways and degrees, and as a general rule gradually increases during the interregnum. While in theory popular participation can be applied to all methods, representation is relevant for all of them except for elections and referenda when the people itself, as a matter of *lex lata*, is called to the ballot.

Second, inclusivity will generally be required in relation to 're-foundational' procedures, that is by public consultations during constitution-making, electing the constituent assembly, approving the draft constitution or through general elections closing the transition. The design of the interregnum especially relates to so-called upstream procedural constraints, that is the application of participatory/representative procedures *preceding* the adoption of the constitution.[133] Rather than posing substantive requirements as to the *outcome* of TG, TI specify the modalities for inclusively implementing self-determination *during* the interregnum.

Third, inclusivity is generally seen as an obligation to be implemented *progressively* over the course of the transition. It does not guarantee (a) that representation or participation of all segments of society is ensured from the start, or (b) that these segments must be included in the post-transition phase. It usually requires though that secondary norms coming to existence during the transition are based on inclusive consultations. The interregnum as a whole, beyond the constitution-making process, must be considered an avenue and occasion for state renaissance. It must (progressively) open up to the people, and not evolve from inclusive on paper to exclusive on the ground, as was arguably the case in South Sudan,[134] let alone remain exclusive from end to end, as was arguably the case in Iraq.

The progressive involvement during the interregnum is supposed to balance out initial elite powers by popular involvement. If the transition first depends on negotiations between elite players, it subsequently becomes more inclusive. The question is thus not whether to 'focus "horizontally" on the conflict parties, or "vertically" on broader societal groups', but rather how both forms of inclusion can be nested in each other.[135] From a diplomatic perspective, this implies that multi-track diplomacy should be privileged by official so-called Track I diplomacy actively involving Track II diplomacy, defined as 'unofficial dialogue and problem-solving

---

[133] This definition is a free adaptation of J. Elster's definition. For the distinction between upstream and downstream constraints, cf. J. Elster 'Forces and Mechanisms in the Constitution-Making Process', *Duke Law Journal*, Vol. 45, 1995, p. 373: 'upstream constraints are imposed on the assembly before it starts to deliberate. Downstream constraints are created by the need for ratification of the document the assembly produces'. Cf. also J. Elster, *Ulysses Unbound*, Cambridge University Press, 2000.

[134] G. Storaas, 'Participation on Paper but not in Practice? – The South Sudan Constitutional Review Process', Berghof Foundation, 2015: 'The permanent constitution process was designed by the Presidency to look inclusive. It had mechanisms for participation from the grassroots and marginalized communities, but was not genuinely inclusive. Even if the first phases had been genuinely participatory, the adoption of the constitution would still be by an elite appointed body. The constitution-making process was therefore not genuinely inclusive'.

[135] J. Pospisil, 'Peacebuilding and Principled Pragmatism' in Conciliation Resources, PSRP, Accord, 'Navigating Inclusion in Peace Processes', Issue 28, March 2019, p. 19.

activities aimed at building relationships between civil society leaders and influential individuals who have the ability to impact Track I dynamics';[136] and even Track III diplomacy, defined as 'people-to-people interactions at the grassroots level'.[137] Self-determination-compliant TG and constitution-making based on public participation finally also depends on the whole process being transparent.[138]

Fourth, while popular involvement at the time of defining a TI (transitional constitution-making) is not expected although appreciated, TA must try to make the exercise of public powers during the interregnum, and especially the constitution-making process for the post-transition stage, inclusive. Here, too, the line dividing obligations of conduct from obligations of result may be crossed over time. In spite of the 'considerable scope for a discretionary approach to matters of popular governance',[139] internally imposed constitutionalism, even at the drafting stage, will be increasingly out of the question. Obligations of inclusion incumbent on TA are most clearly being strengthened in relation to popular involvement in constitution-making, and were already applicable *de lege lata* to the final approval of the constitution.

4.2.3 Expansion *Ratione Temporis* A static view of self-determination, to be invoked at one specific moment or to exhaust its effects within a limited time frame[140] is not relevant for TG. Self-determination is a continuing principle,[141] in a double sense: it continues to apply, also outside the context of decolonisation, and is continuously applicable, that is cannot be instantly applied, in the context of TG. It is in the latter sense

---

[136] K. Göldner-Ebenthal, V. Dudouet, 'From Power Mediation to Dialogue Support? Assessing the European Union's Capabilities for Multi-Track Diplomacy', Research Report, Berghof Foundation, Berlin, 2017, p. 8.

[137] Id.

[138] In Cambodia, for example, the constitution-making process suffered from a lack of transparency: 'although the elections were free and fair and enjoyed massive participation, the continued flaring of political violence became an excuse for a *brief and secretive constitution-making process*'. J. Benomar, 'Constitution-Making after Conflict: Lessons for Iraq', op. cit., p. 83. Own emphasis. Inclusive transitional constitution-making was hindered because of an 'opaque and non-transparent' constitution-drafting process. IDEA, 'Interim Constitutions in Post-Conflict Settings', op. cit., p. 14.

[139] M. Saul, *Popular Governance of Post-Conflict Reconstruction*, op. cit., p. 107.

[140] E.g. the question whether the unilateral declaration of independence by Kosovo complies with this principle.

[141] J. Crawford, 'The Right of Self-Determination in International Law: Its Development and Future', op. cit., p. 40.

that the principle of self-determination is being sensibly extended *ratione temporis*, as the following Table 7.2 shows.

Various combinations between the scenarios depicted in Table 7.2 below are possible, and popular or elite involvement can vary in degree or over time. For instance, the foundation of TG by certain elites can be combined with a constitution-making process for the post-transition stage on the basis of a national dialogue and/or public consultations.

As obligations, especially of conduct, are taking shape, the lack of participation or representation under some of the scenarios below or their combinations, also depending on timing, is (increasingly) problematic under international law. For example, if an opposition-based body refuses to progressively include other political factions in the interim rule, this is increasingly seen as unlawful. Already considered unlawful is the case of a post-transition constitutional framework which was not approved by the people; or (as we shall see under Part IV) of an externally imposed TA or TI. Further, during the transition unrepresentative or secret negotiations on the constitution are increasingly seen as unlawful while, at the start of the transition, elite transitional constitution-making is not (yet?) considered unlawful if subsequently constitution-making *tout court* is gradually opened up to popular participation or at least representation.

The temporary nature of TG cannot be invoked as an excuse to hinder the progressively inclusive nature of TG. Two-stage transitions are precisely designed to allow for a progressive opening. The powers of elites designing the TI are intentionally curbed when this is followed by a more inclusive interregnum[142] 'enabl[ing] a shifting of emphasis from an elite bargain among combatants to a broader, more participatory process and constitutional bargain'.[143] The people expects to be involved throughout the interregnum and not only towards the end of it. As it currently evolves, inclusivity is for the larger part to be qualified as an obligation of conduct. TA must honour this requirement throughout the interregnum, must choose the approaches for realising it, and, if it originated from an elite movement, must gradually open up interim governance to various

---

[142] C. Bell, 'Introduction: Bargaining on Constitutions – Political Settlements and Constitutional State-Building', op. cit., p. 23.

[143] C. Rodrigues, 'Letting off Steam: Interim Constitutions as a Safety Valve to the Pressure-Cooker of Transitions in Conflict-Affected States?', op. cit., pp. 49–50.

Table 7.2 *Inclusivity deconstructed (based on timing)*

INCLUSIVITY	[a] Pre-transition and foundation of the transition (upstream constraints)	[b] Interregnum / Interim governance (upstream constraints)	[c] Towards the end or after the transition (downstream constraints)
[1] Popular involvement (participation)	Constituent supraconstitutional TI prepared with direct popular input (*Rare if not inexistent*) Foundation non-constitutional transition/adoption TI after popular consultation by referendum or election (*Rare if not inexistent*)	Interim rule observed in conformity with popular will on the basis of α elections and referendum (*Rare*) or β national dialogue (*Occasional*) Election of constituent assembly (*Occasional*) Constitution-making process carried out on basis of national dialogue and/or public consultations (*Common*)	Post-transition constitutional framework approved and adopted by popular referendum or general election (*Frequent*)

| [2] Elite involvement (representation) | Constituent supraconstitutional TI prepared by representative body (*Frequent with consensual transitions, rare with oppositional transitions*) Foundation non-constitutional transition/adoption TI by fairly representative body (*Frequent with consensual transitions, rare with oppositional transitions*) | Interim rule observed by: α interim power-sharing/unity government (*Frequent with consensual transitions*) or β by opposition-based body progressively including other political factions in interim decision-making processes (*Common with oppositional transitions*) Constituent assembly appointed by representative body (*Common*) Constitution-making by representative body but carried out in confidential negotiations / closed roundtables (*Common*) | Post-transition constitutional framework approved and adopted by representative body but without popular approval (*Rare: the scenario of elite players both devising and adopting the permanent constitution behind closed doors to end the transition is rather exceptional today*) |

258 THE PRACTICE AND DISCOURSE OF INCLUSION

segments of society. This is not always a minor feat as TG can last from a couple of months to several years.[144]

The redetermination of the social contract hinges on *deliberation* during the entire interregnum providing a 'political space in which a population can begin a conversation about what kind of country they want to be theirs'.[145] The allegiance of the people requires such a process of deliberation among various segments of society: factions previously at war, political parties, civil society representatives, armed movements, regional entities, women's groups, etc. Their right to be taken seriously during the interregnum then translates into a *continuous* obligation of conduct incumbent on TA. This obligation of conduct is on the verge of becoming one of result when constitution-making is concerned.[146] As to the final approval of the reconstitutionalisation, inclusion already constitutes an obligation of result.

5   A Revival of the Principle of Self-Determination

Through variations of the inclusivity requirement, obligations of conduct sensibly *extend* the principle of self-determination in its internal variant, which is likely to predominate in the future.[147] This principle remains contested as a basis for secession. In relation to TG it has sensibly gained ground since the end of the Cold War. In the past it was often considered indeterminate 'with the exception of the stricture that a government must *represent* the population of the territory without systematic exclusion or discrimination against groups on the basis of race, creed, or colour'.[148] Until today, the principle, without doubt, also serves as a basis for a people to '*participate* (a right to have a say) in the decision-making processes of the State'.[149] We already saw that *representation* and *participation* constitute two cross-cutting modes for realising inclusive TG. Through specific expressions of representation

---

[144] Table 4.3.
[145] For a comparison with constitutionalism, cf. S. Chesterman, 'An International Rule of Law?', op. cit., p. 954.
[146] V. Hart, 'Constitution-Making and the Transformation of Conflict', *Peace & Change*, Vol. 26, no. 2, 2001, pp. 169–70.
[147] Chapter 5, Section A.2.1.
[148] See J. L. Cohen, *Globalization and Sovereignty: Rethinking Legality, Legitimacy, and Constitutionalism*, op. cit., p. 253. Own emphasis.
[149] D. Raič, *Statehood and the Law of Self-determination*, op. cit., p.237. Own emphasis.

FACETS OF INCLUSIVITY

and participation specifying the personal, substantive and temporal scope of application of self-determination, said principle is further losing some of its indeterminacy.

As an instrument of internal self-determination, inclusivity offers a rudimentary legal benchmark for assessing transitions. Except towards the end of the interregnum, TA enjoy considerable discretionary powers as inclusivity can be applied in various ways, and at various stages of the transition. It will consequently often become debatable whether or when the principle of self-determination, especially under the form of an obligation of conduct, was respected during the interregnum. A culture of debate on the basis of legal yardsticks and some red lines is precisely to be encouraged. The standard to be lived up to, self-determination, is rudimentary, but some limits become increasingly clear. The bottom-line is that TG is time-limited and power-constrained, must be progressively inclusive, and leaves no room for internally imposed constitution-making, under any form whatsoever.

The general and systematic focus on 'inclusion', 'representation', 'participation' and 'ownership' puts considerable weight on the application of a *proceduralised* self-determination:[150] the people's approval of the constitution (usually through a referendum or final elections) is required as an obligation of result. But also substantively the requirement of inclusivity is to be implemented progressively throughout the interregnum, at least as an obligation of conduct, by involving the people if not in the formulation of the TI then at least in the interim rule and in constitution-making *tout court*. The multifaceted practice of inclusion adds specificity to the principle of self-determination through such obligations of best efforts which are in the make. Some of them, notably the obligation to involve the population at large in constitution-making *tout court* and to involve women in TG more generally, are already bending towards obligations of result, albeit also in the make.

In conclusion, inclusivity is increasingly considered mandatory for TG. As TG is about reconstitutionalisation and is intended to facilitate an orderly reconsideration of the social contract, inclusivity bears a clear connection with the principle of self-determination which precisely protects the right to 'freely determine a political

---

[150] J. L. Cohen, 'The Role of International Law in Post-Conflict Constitution-Making: Toward a Jus Post Bellum for "Interim Occupations"', op. cit., p. 527.

status'. The role of self-determination for TG should be neither over- nor underestimated, as shown in the following Table 7.3. In the future, TG practices alongside 'practical and flexible management tools or guidelines to operationalise the various forms of "ownership"'[151] may further expose the flesh on the bone of internal self-determination unless current trends are discontinued and TG practices become less detailed and consistent.

C Ownership of Transitional Justice

This section briefly analyses how TJ contributes to the development of international law applicable to TG. TJ can be defined as 'the *full range* of processes and mechanisms associated with a society's attempts to come to terms with a legacy of large-scale past abuses'.[152] These processes and mechanisms 'may include both judicial and non-judicial mechanisms, with differing levels of international involvement (or none at all)'.[153] For the purposes of this book, TJ should be understood as a chapeau concept, comprising three categories:

- TJ *sensu stricto* (truth and reconciliation commissions);
- Post-conflict domestic or international criminal justice ('transitional criminal justice');[154]
- International fact-finding missions or inquiries.

In a broad sense, TJ thus includes not only so-called alternative tools for dealing with the past but also 'transitional criminal justice'[155] and fact-finding missions. Under any definition, the *aim* of TJ goes well beyond redressing large-scale human rights violations of the past: it contributes to the convalescence of a country after widespread human rights abuses. TJ must be 'understood as a moment in the creation of a new political and

---

[151] S. Chesterman, 'Ownership in Theory and in Practice: Transfer of Authority in UN Statebuilding Operations', op. cit., p. 21. Cf. for example 2012 UN Guidance for Effective Mediation, op. cit., p. 15, giving practical indications on how mediators can promote national ownership.

[152] 'The rule of law and transitional justice in conflict and post-conflict societies', S/2004/616 of 23 August 2004. Own emphasis.

[153] Id.

[154] A. Fijalkowski and R. Grosescu, *Transitional Criminal Justice in Post-Dictatorial and Post-Conflict Societies*, Intersentia, 2015, p. 1: 'mechanisms of judicial accountability carried out in post-dictatorial or post-conflict states'.

[155] Id.

Table 7.3 *Mutual relevance of self-determination and transitional governance*

	Pre-transition	Foundation of the transition	Interregnum	End of the transition (or towards it)
Inclusivity through participation (popular involvement) or representation (elite involvement)	*- Inclusive exercise of ius ad interregnum (not addressed in this book);* *- Popular or representative input to transitional constitutionmaking*	*- Elite foundation to be followed by progressive inclusivity during interregnum* - Prohibition under existing legal standards on externally instigating transitions (Chapters 8 & 9)	*- Inclusivity of constitutionmaking tout court (on the verge of an obligation of result)* *- Progressive inclusivity of interim rule (in relation to women's inclusion, on the verge of an obligation of result)* - Respect of existing human rights standards related to self-determination	Popular validation of closure of transition and of reconstitutionalisation (existing obligation of result under the principle of self-determination)

- *In italics: TG & inclusivity potentially add specificity to self-determination*
- Other text: Self-determination as (existing) directive principle

legal order'.[156] Being instrumental to state order transformation, TJ is almost systematically part of TG. When transitions come to an end, foreseeing TJ, under one of its many available forms, has become generalised practice.

I am not concerned here with the question of whether or how retributive and restorative justice should (best) be combined to achieve reconciliation and thus contribute to effective state transformation. For some states, such a combination should be predefined[157] while for others restorative justice should take precedence in certain circumstances.[158] I shall rather simply observe that, as a socialised phenomenon and as confirmed by state practice, TJ has become a standard component of TG (1) although there are limits to the discretionary powers of TA in designing and implementing TJ (2).

1   The Transitional Justice Cascade

> [T]he growth of transitional justice practices may be creating a 'justice cascade', a new *global norm of accountability* that helps give rise to new trials and truth commissions year after year.[159]

The conviction that TJ is part and parcel of TG is confirmed by state practice.[160] In most cases, TA commit themselves to organising TJ. If not, the UNSC underscores the relevance, and even compulsory nature, of TJ and the fight against impunity. Before the turn of the millennium, TA in

---

[156] D. Dyzenhaus, 'Justifying the Truth and Reconciliation Commission', *The Journal of Political Philosophy*, Vol. 8, Nr. 4, 2000, p. 494, defending the idea of *transformative justice*.

[157] Id., pp. 12–13. See, for instance, the intervention of German delegation: 'both mechanisms, taken together, cover the whole spectrum of injustices committed during a conflict, without leaving an impunity gap'.

[158] When 'the attainment of retributive justice is not feasible at the onset of the reconciliation process because of the inability of transitional institutions to provide justice through conventional means'. S/PV.4903 of 26 January 2004 p. 4, p. 25. Intervention of Philippine delegation.

[159] D. N. Sharp, 'Beyond the Post-Conflict Checklist: Linking Peacebuilding and Transitional Justice Through the Lens of Critique', op. cit., p. 166. Own emphasis. Citing K. Sikkink, *The Justice Cascade: How Human Rights Prosecutions Are Changing World Politics*, Norton, 2011 (arguing that a global increase of human rights prosecutions demonstrates the emergence of a new international norm of accountability); and P. B. Hayner, *Unspeakable Truths: Transitional Justice and the Challenge of Truth Commissions*, Routledge 2d. ed., 2011 (discussing the phenomenon of truth commissions and their spread throughout the world).

[160] S/PV.4903 of 26 January 2004.

OWNERSHIP OF TRANSITIONAL JUSTICE

Cambodia, Rwanda and South Africa for example committed to TJ. After the turn of the millennium, TA in Burundi, Afghanistan, DRC, Liberia, Somalia, Haiti, Iraq, Côte d'Ivoire, Guinea, Libya, Yemen, Guinea Bissau, CAR, Burkina Faso, Ukraine, Gambia and Sudan also pledged to organise TJ.[161]

In the vast majority of cases, TA are thus required, or they imposed on themselves, to address the past in their respective countries in one way or another. 'Increasingly, *the question is not whether* some kind of justice will be delivered during periods of transition but what the sequencing and modalities might be'.[162] Teitel speaks of the 'expansion and normalisation of transitional justice'.[163] Considering the worldwide expansion of TJ, most TA implement mechanisms to this effect, or are asked to do so by the UNSC. The perusal published elsewhere,[164] for example concerning DRC and Liberia, shows how the UNSC insists that commitments to organise TJ and to combat impunity be effectively carried out. The UNSC sometimes expects that TJ measures also concern the members themselves of TA.[165]

As a result, TJ is systematically considered even if there is 'no evidence that [TJ] [makes] a difference in terms of the durability or sustainability of [those] peace processes'.[166] Adopting TJ in post-conflict societies is becoming mainstream. Although making TJ context-sensitive remains a challenge, it is generally agreed that, towards the end of the interregnum, TJ must be planned or at least conceptualised. Sierra Leone for instance considered that 'post-conflict national reconciliation should be compulsory'[167] and immediately addressed after the cessation of conflict, adding that 'a mechanism for post-conflict reconciliation should be included in all peace agreements'.[168] Not only transition states share this view. At a

---

[161] E. De Groof, 'The Features of Transitional Governance Today', op. cit. See 'Practice 5'.

[162] D. N. Sharp, 'Beyond the Post-Conflict Checklist: Linking Peacebuilding and Transitional Justice Through the Lens of Critique', op. cit., p. 176. Own emphasis.

[163] R. Teitel, 'Transitional Justice Generalogy', *Harvard Human Rights Journal*, 16, 2003, p. 89. In the same sense, K. McEvoy, 'Beyond Legalism: Towards a Thicker Understanding of Transitional Justice', *Journal of Law and Society*, 34 (4), 2007, p. 412.

[164] E. De Groof, 'The Features of Transitional Governance Today', op. cit. See 'Practice 5'.

[165] Cf. for instance Third UNSG Special Report on DRC Mission, op. cit., § 111, and S/RES/1592 of 30 March 2005.

[166] J. Arnault, 'Legitimacy and Peace Processes – International Norms and Local Realities' in A. Ramsbotham, A. Wennmann, *Legitimacy and Peace Processes, From Coercion to Consent*, Accord Issue 25, April 2014, p. 25. Own emphasis.

[167] Id., p. 8.

[168] Id.

UNSC meeting,[169] the EU member states, Norway, Iceland and Turkey found that TJ constitutes a 'principle' underlying national reconciliation.[170]

TJ becoming part of the dominant legal discourse is the result of acculturation.[171] Experts recommend that TJ mechanisms be integrated in TI.[172] As a result, tools of TJ are 'increasingly embedded in peace-building and democratisation or rule of law strategies'.[173] This main-streaming also results from the proactive work by the Office of the UN High Commissioner for Human Rights, and of Special Rapporteurs this office relies on.[174] Worldwide, transition leaders have felt the combined pressure to organise a form of TJ.[175] As a consequence, TJ 'has in many ways been *institutionalised, regularised, and mainstreamed*'.[176] This development is further expedited by the fact that TJ is detaching itself from the liberal-peace-based transition paradigm it was first anchored in, a normative disassociation which is favourable to the generalisation of TJ.[177]

2 Scope of Transitional Justice: No Blanket Amnesty and Domestic Ownership

TA have wide discretionary powers for organising TJ but no unbridled freedom. Institutional capacity and political choices may impact TJ. More specifically, the unilateral or consensual origin of TG, and the balance of power during the initial stages of the transition can influence the mode and implementation of TJ. As a matter of law, there are two

[169] S/PV.4903 of 26 January 2004.
[170] S/PV.4903 (Resumption 1) of 26 January 2004 p. 4.
[171] Id., p. 192: '[i]t has been argued that as transitional justice practices have spread around the world, they have done so not necessarily by adapting themselves *de novo* to each new context, but through a process of "acculturation" whereby a dominant script or practice is replicated again and again as a result of repeated information exchanges and consultations'.
[172] D. Bloomfield, T. Barnes, L. Huyse (eds.), *Reconciliation after Violent Conflict, A Handbook*, IDEA, 2003, pp. 43–44.
[173] C. L. Sriram, 'Transitional Justice and the Liberal Peace' in E. Newman, R. Paris, O. P. Richmond, *New Perspectives on Liberal Peacebuilding*, op. cit., p. 113.
[174] Their work 'has led to the establishment of truth commissions and other transitional justice and accountability mechanisms around the world'. 'Implementing the responsi-bility to protect – Report of the Secretary-General', A/63/677 of 12 January 2009, § 33.
[175] A. F. Lowenthal, S. Bitar, *From Authoritarian Rule Towards Democratic Governance: Learning from Political Leaders*, op. cit., p. 36.
[176] Id., p. 176. Own emphasis.
[177] Chapter 2, Section A.1.

OWNERSHIP OF TRANSITIONAL JUSTICE

clear limitations to the domestic competence of organising TJ. Although there is wide discretion as to how TJ can be implemented, it is generally agreed that amnesty cannot be accorded for serious crimes (2.1), and that TJ must be nationally owned (2.2).

2.1   No Blanket Amnesty

Amnesty cannot be granted for serious crimes, that is war crimes, genocide and crimes against humanity. Such serious crimes must be submitted to transitional *criminal* justice. There is 'a strong trend in international law contending that the duty of states to prosecute is binding only in respect of those most responsible for international crimes'.[178] Although contested in literature,[179] this position is widely held by states and is confirmed in international conventions and jurisprudence. It is also reflected in deontological guidelines.

To begin with, most states do not accept that amnesty be applied to serious crimes. This position was defended for example by Brazil,[180]   Burundi,[181]   Costa   Rica,[182]   Iceland,[183]   Japan,[184] Liechtenstein,[185]   Norway,[186]   Pakistan,[187]   Rwanda,[188]   Sierra Leone,[189] Turkey[190] and all EU states (including the UK).[191] At

---

[178] P. P. Soares, 'Positive Complementarity: Fine-Tuning the Transitional Justice Discourse', in A. Fijalkowski and R. Grosescu, *Transitional Criminal Justice in Post-Dictatorial and Post-Conflict Societies*, op. cit., p. 191. This author further nuances that 'prosecution needs to be at least an available avenue at the end of a non-criminal investigation' (id.).

[179] L. Mallinder, *Amnesty, Human Rights and Political Transitions, Bridging the Peace and Justice Divide*, op. cit., p. 135: 'state practice . . . shows that although states are increasingly willing to exclude crimes under international law from amnesty laws, they tend to do so when the exclusion complements their domestic or international policy objectives. . . . Therefore, it is not yet possible to assert that state practice established an absolute prohibition on amnesties for crimes under international law'.

[180] S/PV.4903 of 26 January 2004 p. 19.

[181] S/PV.4903 (Resumption 1) of 26 January 2004 p. 27.

[182] Id., p. 21.

[183] Id., p. 5.

[184] Id., p. 23.

[185] Id., p. 35.

[186] Id., p. 5.

[187] S/PV.4903 of 26 January 2004, p. 20.

[188] S/PV.4903 (Resumption 1) of 26 January 2004, p. 31.

[189] Id., p. 8.

[190] Id., p. 5.

[191] Id., p. 5: '[w]hile a balance must be struck, the European Union also agrees with the Secretary-General that there should be no granting of amnesties for war crimes, genocide, crimes against humanity or other serious violations of international human rights

266 THE PRACTICE AND DISCOURSE OF INCLUSION

the 2005 World Summit, *all* states confirmed this position by adopting the R2P framework.[192] It is thus generally accepted that 'justice must always be rendered for the most serious crimes under international law, as defined in the Rome Statute of the International Criminal Court',[193] a position confirmed by the UN, too.[194]

The prohibition of a blanket amnesty for serious crimes is furthermore predicated on a dense international legal framework, based on instruments such as the Rome Statute, the ICCPR, the International Convention Against Torture, the Genocide Convention, the ECHR, the Inter-American Convention on Human Rights and the African Charter of Human Rights. Jurisprudence has evolved from a rather permissive stance to a stringent approach on this matter. International Courts, including the Inter-American Court on Human Rights[195] and the European Court of Human Rights,[196] agree that there should be zero tolerance for amnesty of serious crimes. International law has become more protective of the victims of such crimes, even though the issue of individual rights to effective remedy remains on the table.[197]

The limitation to states' discretion in choosing how to implement TJ has finally given rise to concrete deontological guidelines.[198] Mediators

and humanitarian law'''. See also the separate statements by Germany (S/PV.4903 of 26 January 2004 p. 4, p. 13) and France (id., p. 17).

[192] 'Implementing the responsibility to protect – Report of the Secretary-General', A/63/677 of 12 January 2009, § 54.

[193] S/PV.4903 (Resumption 1) of 26 January 2004, p. 34. Position of Liechtenstein.

[194] S/PV.4903 of 26 January 2004, p. 3. See also S/2000/915 of 4 October 2000, 'Report of the Secretary-General on the establishment of a Special Court for Sierra Leone', §§ 22–24: 'Amnesty clauses in peace agreements must exclude amnesties for war crimes, genocide, crimes against humanity and other serious violations of international human rights and humanitarian law'.

[195] *Barrios Altos v. Peru,* Judgment of 14 March 2001, Inter-Am.Ct.H.R. Cf. §§ 41 – 43. See also finding 51; *Gelman v. Uruguay,* Judgment of 24 February 2011, Inter-Am.Ct.H.R. See §§ 225, 229, observing the 'incompatibility of the amnesty laws with the American Convention in cases of serious violations of human rights'.

[196] *Bazorkina v. Russia,* 69481/01, Council of Europe: European Court of Human Rights, 27 July 2006. *Sahin v. Turkey,* Application no. 44774/98, Council of Europe: European Court of Human Rights, 10 November 2005, §§ 69–70.

[197] In *Velasquez Rodriguez Case,* Judgment of 29 July 1988, Inter-Am.Ct.H.R. (Ser. C) No. 4 (1988), the Inter-American Court of Human Rights found that states must at least '*attempt to restore* the right violated and provide compensation as warranted for damages resulting from the violation' (§ 166). Own emphasis.

[198] Guidance Note of the Secretary-general, United Nations Approach to Transitional Justice, March 2010, p. 4, p. 10.

have to draw the same distinction between serious and other crimes.[199] As they contribute to normative acculturation, such guidelines indirectly reinforce pre-existing limits to states' discretionary powers in dealing with the past.

In short, the development of international criminal law since the eve of the twenty-first century precludes the pardon of serious crimes.[200] The Rome Statute explicitly foresees 'that it is the duty of every State to exercise its criminal jurisdiction over those responsible for international crimes'.[201] There is thus little room for challenging the conclusion that serious crimes cannot be amnestied, especially since this treaty (which under certain circumstances also applies to non-signatories)[202] has the specific ambition of putting an end to impunity for the perpetrators of the most serious crimes of concern to the international community as a whole.[203] Importantly, the limitation to states' discretion with regard to TJ also affects the position of third states, we shall see under Part IV.[204]

2.2 Domestic Ownership

TJ must be nationally owned. This argument is based on the following reasoning:

- TJ also contributes to the political transformation, that is the *re*-determination, of a country.
- By virtue of the principle of self-determination, all peoples have the right to freely determine their political status.
- TJ must be carried out in accordance with the peoples' right to freely determine their political status. It must be domestically owned, and its design must be the result of inclusive consultations.

Exclusive TJ is criticised, and 'to the extent possible, all sectors of a war-ravaged society – the individual, community, society and state – should become engaged participants in – and not merely auxiliaries to – the

---

[199] 2012 UN Guidance for Effective Mediation, op. cit., p. 11; see also p. 17. Mediators 'cannot endorse peace agreements that provide for amnesties for genocide, crimes against humanity, war crimes or gross violations of human rights, including sexual and gender-based violence'.
[200] S/PV.4903 of 26 January 2004 p. 4, p. 15. Position of Algeria.
[201] Id., § 7.
[202] Rome Statute, art. 13.b (referral by UNSC); art. 15 (investigation *proprio motu*).
[203] Rome Statute, Preamble, § 6.
[204] Chapter 8, Section A.6.

268 THE PRACTICE AND DISCOURSE OF INCLUSION

processes of transitional justice and social reconstruction'.[205] A safe environment will encourage such wide engagement, which also depends on the respect of basic rights such as the freedom of expression and assembly.[206]

No matter which TJ approach is chosen, there is consensus that it must be 'owned' by the population of the state in transition, and that it cannot be externally imposed. This position is shared not only by the transition states discussed in a separately published report[207] but also by Angola,[208] China,[209] Costa Rica,[210] Japan,[211] Korea,[212] Liechtenstein,[213] Serbia and Montenegro,[214] the Philippines[215] and

---

[205] E. Stover, H. Megally, H. Mufti, 'Bremer's Gordian Knot: Transitional Justice and the US Occupation of Iraq', op. cit., p. 835. See the criticism about exclusive TJ in Iraq or the criticism about the Rwandan *Gacaca* courts limited jurisdiction (exclusion crimes committed by soldiers of the ruling party RPF).

[206] Insecurity and the lack of respect for basic rights may hamper inclusive TJ, as was arguably the case in Thailand (J. Strasheim, 'Interim Governments: Short-Lived Institutions for Long-Lasting Peace', op. cit., p. 7) and Kosovo (S/PV.4903 of 26 January 2004 (resumption 1) p. 29–30).

[207] E. De Groof, 'The Features of Transitional Governance Today', op. cit. See 'Practice 5'.

[208] S/PV.4903 of 26 January 2004 p. 26: '[e]very process of national reconciliation must, however, be participative, must enjoy popular adherence'.

[209] Id., p. 29: 'national reconciliation within a country will depend, in the final analysis, on the efforts of all the parties concerned in the country. The support and assistance of the international community must therefore be based on an understanding of and respect for local conditions, traditions, history and culture, and its focus must be on their local interests and needs. Nothing should be imposed upon them'.

[210] S/PV.4903 of 26 January 2004 (resumption 1) p. 20: '[t]he international community must actively support local efforts at reconciliation, but it should not try to act as a substitute. In this context, the United Nations has an important part to play as a facilitator, assisting in crafting the mechanisms and agreements that are required to initiate the process of reconciliation'.

[211] Id., p. 23: '[i]t is vital for a post-conflict society to choose the policy measures which it considers best suited to its unstable transitional situation'.

[212] Id., p. 28: 'reconciliation cannot be imposed upon a society from the outside'.

[213] Id., p. 34: '[o]wnership is also a key concept when it comes to striking a balance between the ideals of justice on the one hand and reconciliation on the other'.

[214] Id., pp. 29–30: '[r]eady-made solutions cannot merely be imposed from the outside. A *genuine internal process* is necessary and local actors must take responsibility for pushing it forward'. Own emphasis.

[215] S/PV.4903 of 26 January 2004 p. 24: 'national reconciliation is essentially an internal process and cannot be imposed externally on communities in conflict. . . . *No external body or organ can decree reconciliation from the outside*. . . . Stakeholders in postconflict societies must have the sense of having ownership of the process if it is to bring about the emergence of institutions and practices capable of creatively resolving the kind of social and political tensions that led to past violent conflict. This is not to say, however, that the expertise and the guidance that could be provided by outside groups such as the United Nations have no place in national reconciliation processes'. Own emphasis.

CONCLUSION OF PART III

all EU states (with individual but concurring positions by Germany[216] and the UK).[217] The EU considers that inclusivity is a *principle* underpinning national reconciliation.[218]

Conclusion of Part III

The crisis conditions surrounding the birth and life of TA might convey an impression of lawlessness. At first sight, such context seems incompatible with the proposition that TG may be governed by a set of rules and obligations – and, by extension, with the idea that compliance with these rules and obligations will determine the 'legitimacy of exercise' of TG. This impression of lawlessness explains why the initial research hypothesis was based on the assumption that domestic (and international) actors could act freely and without any legal constraints during a state renaissance.[219]

This assumption is proving to be partly inaccurate. An international rule of law regulating TA is currently germinating.[220] Instead of being subjected to the state of nature, TG in conflict-riven states is increasingly regulated by international norms, sometimes sanctioned in practice. Contrary to the view that 'the rule of law vacuum [is] evident in so many post-conflict societies',[221] TG is less and less

---

[216] Id., p. 13. Germany 'recall[s] that judicial and non-judicial mechanisms need local acceptance and legitimacy', and mentions that transitional justice mechanisms must 'meet with broad popular support', i.e. that 'judicial and non-judicial mechanisms need local acceptance and legitimacy'.

[217] Id., p. 23: 'a reconciliation process has the best chance of success if it is built from the ground level. Durability is best guaranteed by local ownership'.

[218] S/PV.4903 (Resumption 1) of 26 January 2004 p. 5. It furthermore considered that '[n]ational reconciliation will not take root if some groups or sections of the population are excluded from the process of nation-building. In this regard, greater attention should continue to be paid to the role of women' (Id., p. 23).

[219] Introduction, Section C.1.

[220] For the conception of 'rule of law' used in this book, refer to Introduction, Section C.1.

[221] 'The rule of law and transitional justice in conflict and post-conflict societies', S/2004/616 of 23 August 2004. Rule of law support to post-conflict countries should be preceded by and based upon a thorough analysis of what the state of the law is during transitional periods. This is an important observation, as the UNSC has had 'mandated support for the rule of law in many peacekeeping and political missions, including in Afghanistan, Burundi, the Central African Republic, Chad, Côte d'Ivoire, the Democratic Republic of the Congo, Guinea-Bissau, Haiti, Iraq, Liberia, Sierra Leone, South Sudan, the Sudan and Timor-Leste. There are currently 18 Security Council mission mandates that include strengthening the rule of law', E. Selous, G. Bassu, 'The Rule of Law and the United Nations' in J. R. Silkenat, J. E. Hickey Jr and P. D. Barenboim (eds.), *The Legal Doctrines of the Rule of Law and the Legal State*, Springer, 2014, p. 357.

270   THE PRACTICE AND DISCOURSE OF INCLUSION

observed in a legal void. Perhaps ironically, this is the case even when the state in transition, and its very constitutional backbone, are held in abeyance.

The reader is now surely familiar with two ideas which suffuse this book as a whole, the one by Antonio Cassese that the task of *specifying* the principle of self-determination is fulfiled by *individual customary rules*, and the other by Roscoe Pound that *the law must be stable, yet cannot stand still*. These ideas were intimately interrelated in this part. An international rule of law regulating the conduct of states in transition is currently germinating around a core of existing law. If it is confirmed in the future, it can *grosso modo* be defined from two complementary angles: (1) temporal and substantive limitations to the interregnum; (2) the inclusivity of the transition.

First, TG is limited *ratione temporis* and *ratione materiae* (Chapter 6). Limitations *ratione temporis* imply that TA should accept that their powers and mandate are limited. They should direct the transition towards permanent institutions, and then relinquish power. They should thus exercise these duties on a temporary basis, that is with the aim of being replaced on the basis of new elections or laws. This usually means that TA are barred from suspending or perpetuating the interim rule, and often from having their leaders and/or members running for office after the transition.

The powers of TA are also limited *ratione materiae*. The fiduciary nature of TG precludes TA from carrying out activities that would go beyond their mandate, which usually contains three components: TA prepare for the future without fully predefining it; they respect state continuity both internally (vis-à-vis their own citizens) and externally (vis-à-vis other international legal persons, and foreign investors). They concentrate on managing the present, including the transition, and are themselves tasked with administering the country *ad interim* in spite of the extensive external assistance they may receive.

Considering TG's fiduciary function (and undemocratic origin), substantive decision-making should be deferred to elected bodies; or validated by elections. Also in light of the principle of self-determination, fundamental state transformation choices are left open for decision by the national constituencies after or towards the end of the transition. In addition, the power to conclude political or alliance treaties is arguably limited during the interregnum.[222] The same rationale of TA as trustees

---

[222] As with *de facto* governments, it can be argued that TA 'would have the legal capacity to bind the state to treaties of a technical, apolitical nature (e.g. postal and aeronautical

CONCLUSION OF PART III   271

explains why the previous legal order cannot be completely overhauled, and why their main responsibility is limited to completing the transition.

Second, TG must be carried out inclusively, and with due respect for the continuously applicable principle of self-determination (Chapter 7). In the context of TG, the 'inclusion cascade' read in conjunction with this principle goes *further* than the thin procedural right to a constitutional referendum or general elections towards the end of the interregnum, yet requires *less* than substantive democracy. TA are expected to favour broad and progressively inclusive political participation during the interregnum whereby answers to questions as to *whom* to include, *how* and *when* are gaining precision. Thus, the concept of population is being redefined beyond mere national territoriality and although inclusivity can be associated to a myriad of actions, it becomes a must for some techniques (notably constitution-making) and at some moments (notably towards the end) of the transition. In the same context, TA usually commit to some form of inclusive TJ – now a standard in conflict-riven states given the 'TJ cascade' – and, subject to a few limitations, may choose how to do so.

Should it appear that there is a systematic gap between the commitment to inclusivity and the actual practice – with self-determination becoming only a utopian legal benchmark for TG – then this should result in an invitation to readjust the practice and reconsider the normative concepts underpinning them. Day and Malone thus suggest that the 'scant record of clear success may well prompt a reconsideration of the current approaches to transitional governance'.[223] Pending this reassessment, inclusivity *cum* self-determination increasingly constitutes a compelling benchmark against which TG must be legally assessed. As inclusion practices meanwhile arguably are turning into customary rules, they furthermore help specifying the principle of self-determination, showing the principle's continuing vitality and potential for expansion.[224]

This part argued that these two broad strands of practices, discussed in Chapter 6 and Chapter 7 respectively, contribute to custom formation in relation to TG, and increasingly limit the powers of TA. It furthermore

---

conventions), though not to *partisan* alliances . . .'. B. R. Roth, *Governmental Illegitimacy in International Law*, op. cit., p. 158.

[223] A. Day, D. Malone, 'Contextualising Conflict-Related Transitional Governance since 1989' in E. De Groof, M. Wiebusch (eds.), *International Law and Transitional Governance: Critical Perspectives*, op. cit., p. 25.

[224] J. Crawford, 'The Right of Self-Determination in International Law: Its Development and Future', op. cit., p. 65.

advanced that such custom is to be read through the lens of the principle of self-determination. If peoples have the right to 'freely determine their political status', this right cannot but be relevant in times of state renaissance and reconstitutionalisation. Moreover, TG can function as a stepping stone for realising self-determination only if the limits *ratione temporis* and *ratione materiae* are respected, and additionally, the obligation of inclusivity, based on participation and representation, is complied with. This is the core business of TA, which are created precisely to facilitate an inclusive state renaissance.

At the same time, I argued that the principle of self-determination also gains in precision through practices mostly seen as obligations of conduct during TG. The limits *ratione temporis* and *ratione materiae* to TG thus also specify this principle, in ways already explained above: unelected TA are prevented from exceeding their fiduciary mandate. TA and their members should not artificially or forcefully suspend or prolong the interregnum, and must not entrench the future, a task to be left to the electorate and representative institutions. Inclusivity also 'adds a layer' to the principle of self-determination, notably in relation to *whom* to include (for example the widespread consensus on the obligatory inclusion of women), *how* (for example in relation to constitution-making for the post-transition stage), and *when* (progressively during the interregnum and in any event towards the end). In short, while the principle of internal self-determination is central to *ius in interregno*, TG practices also contribute to the development of the principle itself.

Internal self-determination thus forms a composite standard for broadly assessing the process of state renaissance, which can last a couple of months or carry on for several years. Both consensual and oppositional TA increasingly commit to the (progressive) inclusivity of a transition. As an obligation of conduct, this requirement remains pertinent when, initially, TG was elitist or imposed, that is resulted from a '*transition de fait*'.[225] Both consensual and oppositional transitions call for (progressive) inclusivity. This culminates in the exercise of constitution-making needing popular approval, whereby such approval already qualifies as an obligation of result while the inclusivity of constitution-making during the interregnum is on the verge of becoming one.

In conclusion, in the context of TG, the principle of self-determination requires less than substantive democracy but more than the organisation

---

[225] N. Youssef, *La Transition démocratique et la garantie des droits fondamentaux*, op. cit., p. 90. Youssef gives the examples of Mauritania, Romania and Iraq.

CONCLUSION OF PART III

of elections. TG practices 'adding a layer' to the principle of self-determination are neither underspecified – going well beyond a yes-or-no-plebiscitary choice – nor extremely detailed – leaving ample room for path-dependency. The principle therefore provides a basis for exercising so-called marginal scrutiny: on its fringes, TG can be legally assessed while several of its aspects remain ungoverned by international law. Still, the set of practices and corresponding emerging duties identified in this part form benchmarks against which acts and omissions of TA effectively in power can be legally assessed, and – perhaps more importantly – debated. An *argumentarium* in relation to self-determination through TG can provide powerful ammunition in lawfare about transitions.

Crucially, the actual compliance with said duties, and sometimes the commitment to abide by them in the early stages of the transition, reveal their importance much beyond the domestic plane: they are factors which external actors dealing with TA should also take into account. The argument that domestic duties incumbent on TA are mirrored to the international level will be developed in the following and final Part.

PART IV

Moderating External Influence on Transitional Governance

In the age of constitutional geopolitics, external actors play a significant role in TG. They have become 'supervisors of all aspects of postwar transitions'.[1] Today, this observation suffers less and less exceptions. As a result, 'the concern for the constitutional character of a country has become an important element of international politics'.[2] International assistance to TG can yield considerable effects when there actually is a (tertiary) interim legal framework on which influence can be exerted. State transformation that is not based on such a framework is less prone to international influence. From the outset, we underscored the international influence on contemporary TG and on the peace-through-transition paradigm, and the increasing predominance of the assistance model.

External influences on TG and constitution-making processes have always existed. But assistance to TG, and especially to transitional constitution-making, has significantly intensified.[3] Rightly or wrongly, some consider this to be a neocolonial enterprise in disguise. Since the end of the Cold War, the UN – through UNSC, UN missions and/or UNDP – has been closely involved in at least thirty reconstitutionalisation processes.[4] But also regional IO and contact groups are involved. As a result, 'international involvement in intra-state constitution-making is regarded as an emerging pattern of connecting domestic governance of states with the international and transnational space characteristic of a globalizing world'.[5]

---

[1] G. H. Fox, 'International Law and the Entitlement to Democracy after War', op. cit., p. 179.
[2] U. K. Preuss, 'Perspectives on Post-Conflict Constitutionalism: Reflections on Regime Change through External Constitutionalisation', op. cit., p. 493.
[3] P. Dann, Z. Al-Ali, 'The Internationalised Pouvoir Constituant', op. cit., p. 427.
[4] Chapter 1, Section B.1.1.
[5] U. K. Preuss, 'Perspectives on Post-Conflict Constitutionalism: Reflections on Regime Change through External Constitutionalisation', op. cit., p. 494. Own emphasis.

The argument of this final part can be summarised as follows. External actors assisting TG, and constitution-making specifically, must respect, and refrain from obstructing, the obligations increasingly incumbent on TA which were identified in the previous part. To the extent that recurrent TG practices are indicative of emerging customs, external actors must pay heed to their lowest common denominator. This calls for a *duty of restraint* and a number of concrete prohibitions. But on which ground? There are two potential legal bases dependent on whether or not TA represent a state:

- External actors engage their responsibility *indirectly* when they aid or assist a *consensual* TA (progressively) representing the state in violating emerging customary norms under *ius in interregno*, which in turn would impact the legality of the transition state's self-redetermination. This argument is based on the ILC's DASR, widely regarded as reflecting international custom:[6]

  > A State which *aids* or *assists* another State in the commission of an internationally wrongful act by the latter is internationally responsible for doing so if: (a) That State does so with knowledge of the circumstances of the internationally wrongful act; and (b) The act would be internationally wrongful if committed by that State.[7]

- External actors may engage their responsibility *directly* under the twin principles of self-determination and non-intervention as further specified under *ius in interregno* when they have dealings with *oppositional* transitional authorities.

This part challenges the assumption that international law, including relevant emerging custom and the principle of self-determination, could not be informative about how external assistance to TG must be pursued. It will start with an analysis of the limits to external involvement with TG, generally; and will then zero in on such limits specifically in relation to oppositional TG.

The question of how the right to self-determination is affected or curtailed by belligerent occupation has received much attention in literature. The issue as to whether this right can be affected by external actors

---

[6] A. Pellet, 'The ILC's Articles on State Responsibility for Internationally Wrongful Acts and Related Texts' in J. Crawford, A. Pellet, S. Olleson, *The Law of International Responsibility*, Oxford University Press, 2010. For a brief discussion about the DASR as a codification of customary international law, cf. A. Aust, *Handbook of International Law*, Cambridge University Press, 2010, pp. 376–7.

[7] DASR, art. 16. Own emphasis.

PART IV

independently of any occupation or armed force has attracted less attention. This issue is crucial, however, especially in the case where a state
renaissance takes place, and a reconstitutionalisation unfolds, either
independently from or parallel to foreign occupation. The law of occupation has limited relevance for *domestic* TG formally led by national
actors,[8] even in cases where TG is accompanied by belligerent occupation. Before going to the heart of the matter, I will clarify two concepts
that will be used throughout this part, assistance and consent.

Defining Assistance

Assistance to TG is defined broadly; ranging from political and financial
support to TA, to (so-called) technical support in drafting processes, to
constitutional assistance and rule-of-law and state-building assistance.
This chapter adopts the perspective of individual states providing assistance. In order to reduce the arbitrariness of constitutional geopolitics,
'external influence should ... be channelled through multilateral institutions', Dann argues.[9] Ghai and Galli also find that intervention by external
parties in constitution-building processes 'should be on a multilateral
basis'.[10] But the main assumption here is that assistance is provided by
individual states. This approach allows us to define the minimum legal
constraints on external assistance in TG – which can then be extrapolated
to groups of states for instance gathering in contact groups. In principle,
the legal restraints to TG are indeed, *mutatis mutandis*, applicable to
groups of states. In addition, reference will occasionally be made to
deontological rules for example of mediators acting on behalf of (groups
of) states. I will therefore use the neutral terminology of 'external actors'.

Assistance to TG can take various forms, which are often dependent
on the *actor* offering the assistance. Further, a distinction can be made
on the basis of the *form* of assistance being offered: through normative
activity, through advisory activity, through mediation, through education and through promotion of standards.[11] In relation to that, one can

---

[8] P. Dann, Z. Al-Ali, 'The Internationalised Pouvoir Constituant', op. cit., p. 451: 'in the few
instances where occupation law actually does apply, it often has a minimal impact'. Cf.
also K. E. Boon, 'Obligations of the New Occupier: The Contours of Jus Post Bellum', op.
cit., p. 64.

[9] P. Dann, Z. Al-Ali, 'The Internationalised Pouvoir Constituant', op. cit., p. 461.

[10] Y. Ghai, G. Galli, *Constitution Building Processes and Democratisation*, IDEA, 2006, p. 10.

[11] G. Malinverni, 'The Venice Commission of the Council of Europe', The International
Influences of National Constitutional Law in States in Transition, *Proceedings of the
Annual Meeting (American Society of International Law)*, Vol. 96, 2002, p. 390.

examine the *specific type* of assistance offered. External actors can offer technical assistance: providing a venue for dialogue, sharing expertise, facilitating the exchange of various experiences, providing training or finance, promoting peer group communication, etc.[12] They can also try to influence the substantive aspects of TG, for example by facilitating the participation of a political group holding strong opinions about the post-transition stage or by influencing the constitution-making process. In addition, a distinction can be made on the basis of the *degree* of external assistance: is the influence total, partial or only marginal?[13] Lastly, forms of assistance should also be distinguished depending on *when* it is offered. Thus, external support can impact the constituent TI (assistance to transitional constitution-making), the exercise of public powers during the interregnum (the interim rule) or constitution-making for the post-transition era.

Assistance to constitution-making at the outset of and during the interregnum can be quite impactful. Our enquiry concentrates on the legality of external assistance in relation to both transitional constitution-making and constitution-making *tout court* for the post-transition era.

First, transitional constitution-making concerns the *foundation* of the transition, that is the drafting and entry into force of the supraconstitutional (constituent) TI. TG is either based on non-constitutional domestic instruments, which are neutral under international law, or on non-constitutional international legal instruments, regarded either as lawful or unlawful under international law.[14] Whichever form they take, TI (for example the Iraqi Transitional Administration Law) regulate the course of the interregnum. Assistance to transitional constitution-making does not always concern constitutional documents *sensu stricto*. As already explained, TI take various forms and still fulfil the triple purpose of transformative constitutionalism, that is peace through transition, self-

---

[12] IDEA, *From Authoritarian Rule to Democratic Governance: Learning from Political Leaders*, op. cit., pp. 37–9. For example, 'the UN, United States, EU, and some EU member states also offered technical expertise to support the NDC and the constitutional process'. P. B. Holzapfel, 'Yemen's Transition Process: Between Fragmentation and Transformation', op. cit., p. 16.

[13] P. Dann, Z. Al-Ali, 'The Internationalised Pouvoir Constituant', op. cit., p. 428.

[14] International law adopts a position of neutrality vis-à-vis domestic non-constitutionality (Chapter 3, Section A.2). TG can also be triggered by international legal instruments, which can be either internationally lawful (e.g. a validly concluded treaty) or internationally unlawful (e.g. a treaty vitiated by fraud, corruption, coercion or a violation of *ius cogens*).

PART IV

regulation and constitutional reconfiguration.[15] The exact denomination of the TI is irrelevant as long as they fulfil these functions. Transitional constitution-making can thus generate various documents including peace agreements or declarations that rupture, lightly or forcefully, with the previous regime.

Second, constitution-making *tout court* relates to the *constitution-making process* triggered by the transition in view of establishing the post-transition constitutional framework. This form of constitution-making typically takes place during the interregnum, and pertains to the constitutional texts which regulate the post-transition stage (for example the Iraqi constitution-making process).

Defining Consent

Consent is relevant in any area in which the principle of non-intervention in domestic affairs might be relevant: 'valid consent by a State to the commission of a given act by another State precludes the wrongfulness of that act in relation to the former State to the extent that the act remains within the limits of that consent'.[16] The reconstitutionalisation process of a state pertains to the heart of its *domaine réservé*. The issue of consent to external assistance to TG is therefore crucial. When TA agree that the very catalyser of TG (that is the constituent TI) be shaped under external assistance, there is no doubt that such consent must be valid and representative. Consent to the internationalisation of interim constituent power should not be lightly presumed, precisely because this matter touches upon the heart of a state's *domaine réservé*.

A parenthesis: any consent to the use of force must emanate from a *representative* government. In case of duality of government or of a government of national unity, consent to the use of force must be given by both governmental bodies or by all governmental factions, respectively. If doubts as to the legitimate representative of the state persist, 'international law ... imposes a duty of abstention'.[17] With regard to TA embracing former warring parties, 'transition governments which, following a peace agreement, are composed of all important parties to an internal conflict, cannot, as a general rule, invite

[15] Chapter 3, Section B.2.
[16] DASR, art. 20.
[17] O. Corten, *The Law Against War – The Prohibition on the Use of Force in Contemporary International Law*, Hart Publishing, 2012, p. 280.

280   PART IV

foreign troops without the *consent of its main component political forces*.[18] This is justified by the principle of self-determination.[19] The same reasoning applies by analogy in the field of TG. The validity of consent thus plays a role beyond the use of force, in relation with which it has already been examined.[20]

Since TG must be pursued in conformity with the principle of self-determination, any request for assistance may only be accepted if it emanates from TA that are truly inclusive and representative,[21] or at least seriously commit to the obligations of conduct and of result identified in the previous part. In this chapter, valid consent plays a role at various stages of the transition:

- Consent to be bound by an externally designed constituent TI;
- Consent to receiving assistance for observing public powers during the interregnum;
- Consent to the internationalisation of the constitution-making process for the post-transition stage.

***

Chapter 8 analyses how external assistance to TG is legally circumscribed. It deals with both consensual and oppositional transitions. Both the limits of third party assistance to TG generally, and to

---

[18] G. Nolte, 'Intervention by Invitation', MPEPIL. Own emphasis. In the same sense, K. Bannelier, T. Christakis, 'Under the UN Security Council's Watchful Eyes: Military Intervention by Invitation in the Malian Conflict', *Leiden Journal of International Law*, Issue 4, Vol. 26, 2013, pp. 855–74. This article analyses the legality of a military intervention *at the request of the TA of Mali* under interim president Dioncounda Traoré. The actual request came after the formation of the (internationally recognised) Transitional Government of National Unity on 21 August 2012.

[19] O. Corten, *The Law Against War – The Prohibition on the Use of Force in Contemporary International Law*, op. cit., p. 289: the 'people and not the government of a State here enjoy a right which can be considered infringed when a foreign State intervenes to favour one or other party in an internal political conflict'.

[20] Cf. for example K. Bannelier, T. Christakis, 'Under the UN Security Council's Watchful Eyes: Military Intervention by Invitation in the Malian Conflict', op. cit.

[21] In the same sense: '[t]he law of self-determination is argued to be useful because it affords international actors a high level of discretion to determine when a request for their involvement is a sufficient reflection of the will of the people. However, it is also contended that the sustainability of this legal framework rests on international actors exercising their discretion responsibly. This entails refusing to initiate involvement on the basis of a request from a government with little claim to be an embodiment of the will of the people, unless there is strong contextual justification for such a course of action', M. Saul, 'Local Ownership of Post-Conflict Reconstruction in International Law: The Initiation of International Involvement', op. cit., p. 168.

(transitional) constitution-making specifically are examined. As external involvement with oppositional TA raises additional questions, Chapter 9 is entirely dedicated to that topic. Chapter 10 goes a step further and examines whether or not external actors may exceptionally empower oppositional TA, thus indirectly trigger regime change.

8

Limits to External Involvement with Transitional Governance

What are the limits to external assistance to consensual or oppositional TG? In addressing this question, this chapter concentrates on the foundation of the transition (stage 2) and the transition itself (stage 3). The internationalisation of TG is now a fact. From a policy perspective, commentators regularly advocate for an even greater involvement by the international community.[1] This issue has almost become a moot point as external involvement with TG, whether commendable or not, is now commonplace. The question as to whether the international community should expand its role in TG has thus become largely irrelevant, or at least should receive a different emphasis.

The more relevant enquiry is what external actors, when providing assistance to TG, are legally *prevented* from doing.[2] The answer to this question can be summarised as follows: external actors assisting TG must respect, and refrain from obstructing, the obligations incumbent on TA. They must avoid any misalignment with the lowest common denominator of emerging customary rules in relation to TG. We saw that TA must pursue TG in accordance with specific obligations of conduct and of result. These rules unveiled under the previous part, partly in flux, become *opposable* to external states, either indirectly when external actors aid or assist TA (progressively) representing the state or directly in light of the principle of self-determination when they engage with oppositional TA.[3]

---

[1] K. Papagianni, 'Power Sharing, Transitional Governments and the Role of Mediation', op. cit., pp. 42–54: 'the international community has an important role to play in assisting powersharing governments to manage their countries' political transition'.

[2] About the link between the right to self-determination and the right to non-intervention, cf. B. Conforti, 'The Principle of Non-Intervention', op. cit. Cf. also J. Crawford, 'The Right of Self-Determination in International Law: Its Development and Future', op. cit., pp. 40–1.

[3] This reasoning is based on the DASR, art. 16, already cited in full.

283

The neutrality of international law vis-à-vis domestic non-constitutionality is not quite replicated vis-à-vis TG. Even if TG originates from non-constitutionality, not all forms of external assistance to TG are permitted. This remains true even if external assistance *initiates* on a consent-base. At the very start of a transition, TA may indeed consent to external actors assisting them in reconstructing a country during the interregnum. For Saul, such consent 'allows states on both sides of the debate to support international involvement in post-conflict reconstruction, because it provides a platform to claim consistency with sovereignty *and thereby to avoid discussion of the permissible level of interference*'.[4] While the first proposition is perfectly sound, the second proposition (presented in italics, and admittedly taken in isolation) can surely be contested on its face value.

Initial consent to external assistance does not absolve the assisting state from its international legal obligations.[5] To the extent that transition practices progressively amount to rudimentary albeit distinct customary obligations of the interregnum, these also apply beyond the moment of initial consent (if consent there is). Not all forms of external assistance are permissible after initial consent was given. In the same vein, even if TG starts on the basis of a TI deemed lawful under domestic or international law, this does not render all forms of assistance to TG *ipso facto* lawful.

Compliance with *ius in interregno* including the principle of self-determination remains relevant beyond the moment of consent, both for TA and for external actors. Such compliance then calls for heightened scrutiny: during the interregnum, the state is in limbo and its constitution and institutions are held in abeyance, thus rendering the state fragile, which makes the threshold for violating this principle easier to reach. External involvement during the interregnum occurs, therefore, if not *in tempore suspecto* then at least *in tempore fragili*.

TA usually commit to the legal internationalisation of the transitional legal order. In light of the residual role of international law during transitions, TG cannot be pursued in a legal vacuum. For external actors, international law is relevant in at least three respects:

- External actors cannot act at variance with the international obligations incumbent on TA (Section A in this chapter on prohibitions applicable to external actors);

---

[4] M. Saul, *Popular Governance of Post-Conflict Reconstruction*, op. cit., p. 64. Own emphasis.
[5] See also DASR, art. 20, which makes clear that consent is circumscribed and not a blank check.

- External actors can demand that TA abide by their self-imposed obligations or by international law generally[6] (Section B.2 in this chapter and remarks throughout on permissible pressure);
- Compliance by TA with international law is a factor to be taken into account when evaluating the legality of international support to oppositional TA (cf. Chapter 10, Section B.2.2.4).

To a lesser degree, TG suffers from the same contradictions that used to affect ITA. The paradox inherent to ITA was already mentioned.[7] ITA 'envisages the respect of the state sovereignty and self-determination, on the other hand, it requires a prolonged and forcible interference in its domestic affairs'.[8] There thus seems to be, in essence, a conceptual discrepancy between the goal pursued – self-determination – and the means to reach this goal – unelected rule, encroachment on sovereignty.

Under subtler forms, this tension materialises in the realm of international assistance to TG, especially when such assistance exceeds the initially agreed boundaries. For example, states and IO can exercise significant influence on TG, which, in some cases, may amount to interference in a state's domestic affairs: 'actors with authority in the aftermath of war that are concerned about the *perceived* consistency of a reconstruction process with the notion of self-determination at stake should seek to maximise the quantity and quality of popular involvement across all dimensions of governance'.[9] This issue is not a matter of political perception alone. Consistency with self-determination during TG is a legal matter, too. Accordingly, a number of *prohibitions* apply to external actors (Section A) which in no way prevent them from demanding that TA abide by their self-imposed obligations and international law more generally (Section B).

---

[6] Thus, the Venice Commission encouraged the Tunisian National Constituent Assembly to recognise the superior status of international treaties, and to refer in the new constitution's preamble to international general principles and international custom. Opinion 733/2013 on the final draft constitution of the Republic of Tunisia (2013), §§ 38–40.

[7] Chapter 6, Section C.

[8] A. Carati, 'Intervention and Promotion of Democracy. The Paradoxes of External Democratisation and the Power-Sharing Between International Officials and Local Political Leaders', op. cit., p. 136.

[9] M. Saul, *Popular Governance of Post-Conflict Reconstruction*, op. cit., p. 38. Own emphasis.

A Prohibitions Applicable to External Actors

Under the UN Charter, states must refrain from all activities that would be inconsistent with the development of friendly relations based *inter alia* on the respect of the principle of self-determination.[10] Part III demonstrated the current relevance of this principle in its internal variant, through TG: states in transition are increasingly expected to facilitate its progressive realisation during the interregnum, which in turn depends on their abidance by a set of emerging customary rules. External actors, too, should pay heed at least to their lowest common denominator as the implementation of these rules precisely influences if and how the principle of self-determination is being honoured during the interregnum. If they refuse to do so, they risk violating this principle in its various and newly detailed components, at distinct stages of the transition, either directly (by dealing straight with an oppositional TA) or indirectly (by aiding or assisting TA progressively representing the state). To avoid this, external actors must respect six prohibitions:

1. Prohibition on imposing the constituent TI at the foundation of TG;
2. Prohibition on violating the limits *ratione temporis* of the transition;
3. Prohibition on violating the limits *ratione materiae* of the transition;
4. Prohibition on undermining inclusivity during the interregnum;
5. Prohibition on externally imposing constitutionmaking for the post-transition stage;
6. Prohibition on externally imposing modes of TJ.

These prohibitions will be addressed in the relevant order (see also Table 8.1). Distinctions should thus be made between: the prohibition on imposing a constituent TI (subsection 1); the prohibition on pre-defining the post-transition era, through TI or otherwise (subsection 3); and the prohibition on pre-defining the post-transition era through constitution-making *tout court* (subsection 5).

1 Prohibition on Externally Imposing (Consensual) TG

In light of the principle of self-determination, states or IO must not impose any form of TG, be it oppositional or consensual, on other states. Any involvement with the interregnum must in principle be consent-based. Two consequences flow from this.

---

[10] UN Charter, art. 1§2.

PROHIBITIONS APPLICABLE TO EXTERNAL ACTORS   287

Table 8.1 *Prohibitions applicable to external actors (per stage)*

Stage 1. Pre-transition	Stage 2. Foundation of transition	Stage 3. Transition	Stage 4. Post-transition
Prohibition on empowerment of oppositional TA (Chapters 9 & 10).	1. Prohibition on externally imposing consensual TG either by triggering a constituent TI or by artificially creating a consensual TA.	2. Prohibition on violating limits *ratione temporis* to TG. 3. Prohibition on violating limits *ratione materiae* to TG: - prohibition on leaving definitive imprint on post-transition order; - respect for state continuity. 4. Prohibition on favouring groups during interregnum or on otherwise undermining inclusivity. 5. Prohibition on externally imposed constitution-making *tout court*.	6. Prohibition on externally imposing modes of TJ.

- During the pre-transition, external actors must not empower oppositional (embryonic or inchoate) TA by financing them or lending them political support with the aim to pre-define the course of TG. The external empowerment of such oppositional TA raises specific issues and merits separate analysis. It will thus be examined later, under the two final chapters.
- When approaching the moment of founding TG, external actors must not impose, in whole or in part, constituent TI, even of consensual TA; or artificially create consensual (non-oppositional) TA in view of truncating consent. The prohibition to impose TI or create TA resulting in the external instigation and framework-setting of consensual

288   LIMITS TO EXTERNAL INVOLVEMENT WITH TG

TG, in short, the 'prohibition on externally imposing consensual TG', is dealt with now, in the present subsection.

Let us start with a reminder of the triple function of constituent TI: resolving conflicts and creating the conditions for peace (peace through transition); regulating the exercise of public powers *ad interim* (defining the interim rule); and projecting and preparing the coming constitutional order (constitutional reconfiguration). This subsection focuses on the external imposition of TI and TA *as regulators of public powers during the interregnum*, and therefore primarily concerns the second function of constituent TI. TI as regulators of the post-transition order will be dealt with later.[11]

TI are often shaped in international contexts. This is true of international treaties, but can also apply to (especially internationalised)[12] intrastate agreements and even domestic laws, acts or constitutions. In the latter case, one speaks of 'transnational constitutions'.[13] The very existence of TA can also be tributary to international efforts. Some commentators remark that in Cambodia, for example, 'international efforts *facilitated* the bringing together of the two main factions to form a single entity, the Supreme National Council, *which was created solely for the purpose of consenting to the international involvement*'.[14]

If constituent TI are negotiated and elaborated in international settings, the transition state must consent to the (possible) internationalisation of interim constituent power. This mitigates the risk that TG is considered to be a product of coercion, and that TI will be invalidated *ex post*. Consent to the internationalisation of interim constituent power must be *valid*. This begs the question of who is authorised to bind the state at the eve of the interregnum. In order to gauge the validity of consent, one must consider 'whether the agent or person who gave the consent was authorised to do so on behalf of the State (and if not, whether the lack of that authority was known or ought to have been known to the acting State), or whether the consent was vitiated by coercion or some other factor'.[15]

---

[11] Subsection 3.1 'Prohibition on leaving post-transition imprint through transition instruments'.

[12] See Chapter 5, Section B.2.2.1 for the criteria.

[13] V. C. Jackson, 'What's in a Name?', op. cit., p. 1256: they 'are often clearly shaped by external participants, and may require further external participants as guarantors to effectuate the transition'.

[14] M. Saul, 'Local Ownership of Post-Conflict Reconstruction in International Law: The Initiation of International Involvement', op. cit., p. 198. Own emphasis.

[15] DASR, Commentaries to art. 20. See also, in the domain of the law of treaties, VCLT, art. 7.

Any form of externally imposed TG is prohibited, and would be incompatible with the principle of self-determination.[16] This has deontological consequences for external mediators who may dominate the process by predetermining the rules even of consensual TG.[17] When offering their assistance to TG, mediators should thus be sensible to said prohibition.[18] Several commentators have seriously questioned whether, in a number of countries, TG resulted from genuinely domestic political choices or, on the contrary, derived from externally imposed TI or TA. Such a critical assessment has been made in relation to Afghanistan, Burundi, Iraq and Somalia, as follows.

In Afghanistan, TG was the result of an elite arrangement, allegedly compounded by threats. The Bonn Conference produced the 2001 Bonn Agreement regulating TG in Afghanistan. During this conference, Rabbani's government consented to the transfer of power.[19] McCool and Papagianni observe that 'the Bonn Conference was, in effect, a gathering of some interested groups which set out to allocate positions of power and determine a sequence of events and timeline for this to take place'.[20] The withdrawal of former Afghan King Mohammed Zahir Shah was reportedly obtained under pressure,[21] and the US ambassador 'threatened that the US would hold accountable anyone who opposed the peace process'.[22]

In Burundi, TG was regulated by the Arusha Agreement, which was also concluded under pressure. For Vandeginste, 'international pressure . . . has

---

[16] M. Saul, *Popular Governance of Post-Conflict Reconstruction*, op. cit., p. 70: 'an imposed governance arrangement would be in breach [of the right to self-determination], as this would hinder enjoyment of all of the elements that are covered in the standard definition of the right'.

[17] C. Daase, 'The Law of the Peacemaker: The Role of Mediators in Peace Negotiations and Lawmaking', *Cambridge Journal of International and Comparative Law* (1)3, 2012, p. 109.

[18] M. Saliternik, 'Reducing the Price of Peace: The Human Rights Responsibilities of Third-Party Facilitators', op. cit., p. 232–3.

[19] M. Saul, *Popular Governance of Post-Conflict Reconstruction*, op. cit., p. 160: 'Rabbani's government was represented at Bonn and consented to the outcome (the official transfer of power was implemented on 22 December through Rabbani signing a document at the inauguration of Karzai)'.

[20] C. McCool, 'The Role of Constitution-Building Processes in Democratisation', op. cit., pp. 7–8. In the same sense: K. Papagianni, 'Transitional Politics in Afghanistan and Iraq: Inclusion, Consultation, and Public Participation', op. cit., pp. 749–50: 'the Afghan participants at the Bonn Conference were initially chosen by the West and at a difficult moment the *international community exerted pressure* to push the process forward'. Own emphasis.

[21] E. Afsah, A. Guhr, 'Afghanistan: Building a State to Keep the Peace', op. cit., p. 422.

[22] Id., pp. 411–12.

290 LIMITS TO EXTERNAL INVOLVEMENT WITH TG

decisively contributed to the *design* and initial implementation of the power-sharing arrangement'.[23] This is not insignificant considering that the Arusha Agreement 'clearly shaped the framework for the continued mediation of the conflict and in the end *decisively shaped Burundi's current Constitution'.*[24]

In Iraq, the constituent TI, the 2004 TAL, was produced both under internal and external pressure. The internal imposition is discussed elsewhere.[25] The external imposition results from the fact that the TAL was promulgated during US occupation, and 'emanated from negotiations between the CPA and the IGC: an occupying power and its appointed body'.[26] As this law was 'partly drafted and officially approved and signed into law by their occupiers',[27] it is widely considered to be a product of the US administration. In addition, the drafting discussions were carried out in secrecy.[28] As a consequence, the TAL was 'resisted by the Iraqi people because it reflected the will of the occupying power'.[29] It was not explicitly endorsed by the UN either.[30] 'C'est une transition imposée, hasardeuse et mal menée', Youssef summarises.[31]

In Somalia, TG resulted from the premature recognition of the Somali Transitional Federal Government, created in 2004 by the Somali Transitional Charter. In the literature, concerns were voiced about international intervention being excessive and bypassing Somalia's sovereignty

---

[23] S. Vandeginste, 'Power-Sharing, Conflict and Transition in Burundi: Twenty Years of Trial and Error', op. cit., p. 83. Own emphasis. See also, in the same sense, H. Wolpe, 'Making Peace after Genocide – Anatomy of the Burundi Process', United States Institute of Peace, Peaceworks No. 70, 2011.

[24] S. Vandeginste, 'Power-Sharing, Conflict and Transition in Burundi: Twenty Years of Trial and Error', op. cit., p. 72. Own emphasis.

[25] E. De Groof, 'The Features of Transitional Governance Today', op. cit. See 'Practice 4'.

[26] J. Benomar, 'Constitution-Making after Conflict: Lessons for Iraq', op. cit., pp. 92–3.

[27] Id.

[28] K. Papagianni, 'Transitional Politics in Afghanistan and Iraq: Inclusion, Consultation, and Public Participation', op. cit., p. 751.

[29] L. Brahimi, 'State-Building in Crisis and Post-Conflict Countries', op. cit., p. 8.

[30] D. Romano, 'Reflections on an Iraqi Sojourn: Alice through the Looking Glass?', Policy Options, November 2004: 'the TAL was dealt a severe blow by the United Nations, however, when Security Council Resolution 1546 failed to refer to it and hence provide it with international recognition'. The UNSC endorsed the transition roadmap as established by the TAL but never acknowledged TAL's existence, which 'is an indication that it recognised that the document was lacking internal and international legality'. P. Dann, Z. Al-Ali, 'The Internationalised Pouvoir Constituant', op. cit., p. 453.

[31] N. Youssef, *La Transition démocratique et la garantie des droits fondamentaux*, op. cit., p. 98. Own translation: 'the transition is an imposed one, carries risks and is misgoverned'.

as well as the will of its people.[32] If these concerns are justified, the international creation and recognition of the Somali Transitional Federal Government arguably runs counter to the principle of self-determination.

These four examples show that, according to commentators, the very initiation even of consensual (non-oppositional) TG can result from external pressure. Regularly, concerns are raised about TG being initiated through external political pressure. In other cases, however, there is consensus that the constituent TI was not externally imposed. Few would contend that the 2002 Pretoria Agreement and the ensuing 2003 transitional constitution in the DRC were externally imposed,[33] and no one would argue this in relation to the 1993 South African interim constitution.

Seen as a merely theoretical possibility at present, attempts to invalidate TI under international law should not be excluded in the future. If a constituent TI were externally imposed without being subsequently acquiesced to,[34] its validity could be questioned, in two ways. When it is enshrined in an international treaty, a TI can be invalidated under the law of treaties if a country was *coerced* into TG,[35] at least when there was a 'direct causal relationship between coercion and the conclusion of the treaty'.[36] When it is embodied in a domestic legal act, its validity can be

[32] See, for example, A. Ainte, 'Somalia – Legitimacy of the Provisional Constitution', op. cit. Ainte describes how 'the level of external oversight of the Roadmap has undermined Somalia's sovereignty' (p. 60).

[33] D. Curtis, 'Transitional Governance in Burundi and the Democratic Republic of the Congo', op. cit., p. 180.

[34] When, despite the constituent TI being imposed, TA willingly install post-transition institutions, this may evidence their *acquiescence* of that instrument.

[35] A treaty can be invalidated if it was concluded under coercion (art. 52 VCLT) or in violation of *ius cogens* (art. 53 VCLT). Cf. also J. A. Frowein, 'Die Verpflichtungen erga omnes im Völkerrecht und ihre Durchsetzung' in R. Bernhardt, W. K. Geck, G. Jaenicke, H. Steinberger (eds.), *Völkerrecht als Rechtsordnung, Internationale Gerichtsbarkeit, Menschenrechte*, op. cit., pp. 260–1: '[z]wang gegen den Staat durch Drohung oder Anwendung von Gewalt muss nach Ansicht der Kommission zur absoluten Nichtigkeit führen, weil es sich hierbei um Verletzungen von Völkerrechtsnormen handelt, deren Einhaltung alle Staaten angeht'. With reference to Yearbook ILC 1966 II, p. 246 a.f. Own translation: 'Coercion against the state through threat or use of force must, in the Commission's view, lead to absolute nullity, because it is a violation of international law of concern to all states'. Cf. also *Fisheries Jurisdiction (United Kingdom v. Iceland)*, Jurisdiction of the Court, Judgment, ICJ Reports 1973, p. 3. Cf. § 24. See also E. Šarčević, 'Völkerrechtlicher Vertrag Als "Gestaltungsinstrument" Der Verfassunggebung: Das Daytoner Verfassungsexperiment Mit Präzedenzwirkung?', op. cit., pp. 327–8; and J. Benomar, 'Constitution-Making after Conflict: Lessons for Iraq', op. cit., p. 88.

[36] M. E. Villiger, *Commentary on the 1969 Vienna Convention of the Law of Treaties*, Martinus Nijhoff Publishers, 2009, pp. 644–5.

challenged under general international law if it is the product of a violation of the principle of self-determination.

Would an externally imposed and invalid TI influence the legality of the entire ensuing transition (and external assistance thereto) on the basis of the adage *ex iniuria ius non oritur*, meaning literally that 'injustice or illegal acts cannot create law'?[37] The relation between the invalidity of a TI and the validity of TG itself merits to be carefully examined as a topic in its own right, and will not be tackled in this book.

2 Prohibition on Violating Limits Ratione Temporis

During the interregnum, external actors must respect the limits *ratione temporis* to TG. As noted earlier, the prohibition on impeding the progressive realisation of internal self-determination through TG applies beyond the moment of consent and continues to apply after the TA are created. The contention that a 'contravention of the right to self-determination in international law could be avoided through a consensual basis'[38] is therefore, on these specific terms, incomplete. As a continuing principle, self-determination applies throughout the interregnum. Emerging customary rules revolving around this principle now require that TA must pursue TG on a temporary basis before relinquishing power.[39] External time pressure can negatively affect the progressive realisation of internal self-determination. External actors must thus respect the limitations *ratione temporis* of the

---

[37] Does this adage affect the (legal, constitutional and institutional) consequences flowing from unlawful TI? For example, could the external imposition (and, arguably, invalidity) of the Iraqi TAL – which outlined a transition roadmap, including the constitution-making process – result in this process being null and void? The relation between an *ex hypothesi* unlawful, externally imposed TI and the legality *vel non* of external assistance to the interregnum is not addressed in this book. In political science, it has been suggested that 'good' TG could serve as a corrective to an earlier externally imposed constituent TI. Arato thus asked whether 'the democratisation process initiated by externally imposed liberation could succeed *if the constitution-making process escaped the framework of imposition*'. A. Arato, 'Post-Sovereign Constitution-Making and Its Pathology in Iraq', op. cit., p. 537. Own emphasis. Transposed to the realm of law, the question is whether the illegal (because externally coerced) initiation of TG automatically affects the legality of any subsequent external assistance to TG including assistance to transitional constitution-making. This issue deserves an in-depth analysis, which should take into consideration whether or not (1) the external actor unlawfully initiating TG is the same actor that offers assistance to TG, and (2) the externally imposed constitutional framework was subsequently acquiesced to.

[38] M. Saul, *Popular Governance of Post-Conflict Reconstruction*, op. cit., p. 193.

[39] Chapter 6, Section A. E. De Groof, 'The Features of Transitional Governance Today', op. cit., 'Practice 2'.

interregnum, not only as a matter of deontology but also increasingly of law, to the extent such limitations have entered the international legal realm indeed.

The obligation for external actors to respect the limitations *ratione temporis* of the interregnum is not insignificant. A recurring problem is that external actors impose tight deadlines: 'instead of encouraging national leaders to initiate inclusive political processes, external actors often prevent adequate consultation by imposing deadlines related to their own timetables and interests'.[40] Whenever external actors attempt to exert influence on the transition agenda, the nationally defined or approved transition agenda should be taken as the point of reference. As a matter of deontology, practitioners are thus required to 'protect the mediation process from the undue influence of other external actors, especially with regard to unrealistic external deadlines or incompatible agenda'.[41] The 2015 Review of the UN Peacebuilding architecture, too, advised against haste and impracticable timelines, especially when transitions are influenced or driven by mediation groups with 'varying levels of international legitimacy'.[42]

The interregnum must not be artificially prolonged, shortened or otherwise influenced, by the domestic TA themselves or by external actors. This is not only a matter of policy or deontology but also, to a greater extent as time passes, of law. International law applicable to TG increasingly prohibits external actors from artificially influencing the agenda and duration of the interregnum. Since external actors must respect how TA, more and more, tend to abide by these precepts, they must not aid, assist or direct them in violating them; or directly deal with an oppositional TA acting in urgency. Otherwise they could influence the transition agenda and negatively affect the inclusive redefinition of the social contract. They must be all the more sensible to this prohibition as the threshold of coercive pressure is more easily reached when, during its renaissance, the state is held in abeyance.

---

[40] K. Papagianni, 'Power Sharing, Transitional Governments and the Role of Mediation', op. cit., p. 43. In the same sense, D. L. Horowitz, 'Conciliatory Institutions and Constitutional Processes in Post-Conflict States', op. cit., p. 1229: 'especially if the conflict might turn back to violence, many third parties will put reaching a *quick constitutional settlement above all other goals*'. See also O. O. Varol, 'Temporary Constitutions', op. cit.: external actors 'anxious to terminate their involvement in a constitutional reconstruction, may . . . *impose external time restraints* on the design process'. Own emphasis.

[41] 2012 UN Guidance for Effective Mediation, op. cit., p. 15. Cf. also M. Saliternik, 'Perpetuating Democratic Peace: Procedural Justice in Peace Negotiations', *European Journal of International Law*, Vol. 27, no. 3, August 2016, pp. 617–42.

[42] 2015 Review of the UN Peacebuilding architecture, op. cit., § 33.

In a number of countries, external time constraints imposed on TG have been severely criticised. The transitions in Afghanistan, Iraq, Somalia and Yemen, show how external actors can influence the duration of TG, including the constitution-making process. In Afghanistan, the Bonn Agreement had been agreed 'under extreme time pressure'.[43] Following this agreement, 'international actors ... required the constitution-design process in Afghanistan to be completed within two years – a formidable challenge in a society emerging from twenty-five years of civil war'.[44] Following a hastily concluded TI, the ensuing transition itself, too, followed a tight time schedule.

In Iraq, the US occupation 'forced a *rushed* constitutional-design process, which was completed in less than six months through a process that excluded Sunni factions'; 'these *temporal restraints* on the constitutional-design process often *do not permit sufficient deliberation* ... and invite short-term cognitive biases to infect a durable document'.[45] It seems thus that the occupying powers exerted pressure on the duration of the Iraqi transition, which prevented any consensus from ripening;[46] 'the views and opinions of the Iraqi people were at best secondary',[47] also due to time pressure. Similar concerns were raised with regard to Somalia[48] and Yemen.[49]

---

[43] Id., p. 384.

[44] O. O. Varol, 'Temporary Constitutions', op. cit.

[45] Id. Own emphasis.

[46] See comments by Jackson and Welikala in IDEA, 'Interim Constitutions in Post-Conflict Settings', op. cit. V. C. Jackson, 'What's in a Name?', op. cit., p. 1273. 'In contrast to the two years of the Multi-party Negotiation Process in South Africa followed by two years of constitution-drafting, the 2005 constituent assembly in Iraq had only a few months and did not take advantage of an extension period contemplated by the TAL under pressure from the occupying authorities'. IDEA, 'Interim Constitutions in Post-Conflict Settings', op. cit.: '[t]he urgency of the timeframe was essentially dictated by President Bush's campaign promise that Iraq would have a constitution by the 2006 mid-term elections. The drafting committee was given six months to draft the permanent constitution, and due to internal sectarian divisions (along with continuing insecurity), this ended up being just two weeks. Due to the *unrealistic timeline*, the final days of the Iraqi process were messy and *highly pressured'*. Own emphasis.

[47] P. Dann, Z. Al-Ali, 'The Internationalised Pouvoir Constituant', op. cit., p. 458.

[48] A. Ainte, 'Somalia – Legitimacy of the Provisional Constitution' in A. Ramsbotham, A. Wennmann, *Legitimacy and Peace Processes, from Coercion to Consent*, op. cit.: 'a key challenge to the domestic legitimacy of the constitutional process relates to ... the extent to which the process has been engineered and *accelerated to hit external benchmarks*. The public consultation phase of the constitutional process was *truncated under pressure* (widely perceived as coming *from international partners*) to deliver a draft constitution before the end of transition on 1 August'. Own emphasis.

[49] O. Hammady, 'International support to legal and constitutional reforms in the MENA transitional processes', presentation during International Expert Seminar of

PROHIBITIONS APPLICABLE TO EXTERNAL ACTORS 295

External actors involved in TG in these countries have thus been exposed to criticism because they artificially accelerated the process. States can, however, legitimately insist on a timely closure if the transition agenda was appropriately defined domestically. TA can then be encouraged to execute their agenda *in tempore utile* and to administer the country *ad interim*. Diplomatic insistence is different from the scenario of external actors imposing their agenda. Nothing prevents an external actor from reminding, even with insistence, TA of their own limits *ratione temporis*. Such 'procedural influence'[50] was for example exercised in Burundi,[51] the DRC[52] and Tunisia.[53] External actors may indeed place confidence in domestically agreed-on or self-imposed time limits, and can exercise non-coercive pressure to remind domestic actors of their own schedule.[54]

21 and 22 September 2015, EUI. Hammady noted that TG could 'be meaningful only to the extent it reflects local needs and realities. The supposed achievements of the Yemeni process *rushed* under international pressure are unlikely to be lasting'. Own emphasis.

[50] P. Dann, Z. Al-Ali, 'The Internationalised Pouvoir Constituant', op. cit., p. 463.

[51] In the case of the Burundi transition, the 'South African mediation applied sustained pressure to move the process forward'. K. Papagianni, 'Power Sharing, Transitional Governments and the Role of Mediation', op. cit., p. 46. With a reference to ICG, 'Elections in Burundi: the Peace Wager', ICG Africa Briefing, 9 December 2004.

[52] In the DRC, CIAT 'made an effort to make the former belligerents feel responsible for the successful implementation of the transitional agenda and the consequences of spoiling it'. M. de Goede and C. van der Borgh, 'A Role for Diplomats in Postwar Transitions?', op. cit. CIAT also made clear that there was no alternative to the agreed transition. *Communiqué du Comité International d'Accompagnement de la Transition* of 1 December 2004: 'il n'existe *aucune alternative* au processus de transition qui doit déboucher sur la tenue d'élections libres et transparentes en juin 2005. A cet égard, le CIAT condamne toute action, de l'intérieur ou de l'extérieur, visant à déstabiliser ce processus et l'instauration d'une paix durable dans la région'. Own emphasis and translation : 'there is *no alternative* to the transition process that will lead to the holding of free and fair elections in June 2005. In this respect, the CIAT condemns any action, internal or external, aimed at destabilising this process and the establishment of a lasting peace in the region'.

[53] As regards Tunisia, in September 2013 the then Italian minister of foreign affairs for example insisted on a swift end to the transition in Tunisia, as Italy has commercial interests (and a considerable number of citizens) in Tunisia. Interview with Emma Bonino in *Le Temps* of 7 September 2013.

[54] Thus, Akashi writes that "the time-frame specified by the [Paris] Agreements and implemented by UNTAC served to exert a form of pressure on the parties to maintain progress on the path towards democratic elections and a comprehensive peace". Y. Akashi, 'The Limits of UN Diplomacy and the Future of Conflict Mediation', *Global Politics and Strategy*, 37:4, 2008, p. 88.

3 *Prohibition on Violating Limits* Ratione Materiae

External actors must respect the fiduciary nature of TG. Their discretion is limited in a way which mirrors the commitments increasingly undertaken by TA. Emerging custom indicates that TA do not have unbridled freedom in foreshadowing the future, affecting rights acquired in the past, or managing the present.[55] These limits *ratione materiae* entail obligations for external actors who must not entrench the future constitutional order (3.1), and must respect the body of past laws and treaties (3.2).

3.1 Prohibition on Leaving Post-Transition Imprint through Transition Instruments

External actors are barred from influencing TG with a view to leaving a definitive imprint on the post-transition stage. This prohibition concerns the third function of constituent TI, that is constitutional reconfiguration (via the constituent TI as a tertiary norm and indirect *regulator of the post-transition order*). Youssef notes:

> certaines règles de droit, malgré leur intégration dans des instruments provisoires ou intérimaires, sont porteuses d'un caractère permanent qui dépasse le cadre transitoire de l'instrument intérimaire où elles ont été adoptées. C'est le cas des règles constituant les fondements juridiques du nouvel ordre juridique et constitutionnel.[56]

In line with the fiduciary nature of TG, substantive questions are to be deferred to the legislature set up in accordance with the post-transition constitution: 'no final decisions are being made on elemental matters'.[57] For the same reason, external actors must not impose long-term institutional arrangements; 'they should certainly not impose substantive outcomes on the parties to a constitutional process'.[58] In Libya, for instance, one was well aware of the danger that external actors might abuse the weakness of the state to pre-define the post-transition order: 'the Interim Constitutional Declaration drafters were instructed not to allow the

---

[55] Chapter 6, Section B.

[56] N. Youssef, *La Transition démocratique et la garantie des droits fondamentaux*, op. cit., p. 125. Own translation : 'certain legal rules, despite their inclusion into provisional or interim instruments, carry a permanent character which goes beyond the transitional framework of the interim instrument in which they were adopted. This is the case of the rules constituting the legal foundations of the new legal and constitutional order'.

[57] H. Ludsin, 'Peacemaking and Constitution-Drafting: A Dysfunctional Marriage', op. cit., p. 288.

[58] P. Dann, Z. Al-Ali, 'The Internationalised Pouvoir Constituant', op. cit., p. 460.

PROHIBITIONS APPLICABLE TO EXTERNAL ACTORS   297

transitional authority to undertake any long-term institutional arrangement. This was explained by the fear that international actors might use the relative weakness of Libyan rebels to obtain commitments on political agendas'.[59]

In the past, the influence of external actors on constituent TI as regulators of the post-transition order has triggered questions in a number of cases. To what extent did external actors influence the constitutional order in Iraq and Bosnia-Herzegovina through TI?

External actors have left an indelible imprimatur on the Iraqi post-transition order. It is not seriously contested that the US administration did so. The US administration wanted the transition to 'turn out in the right way, i.e., that the enemies of the United States, whether successors to the old Baath or the friends of Iran, [would] not inherit political power in the country'.[60] A controversial point in this regard is not only the de-Baathification programme but also the 2004 TAL. This TI was promulgated during US occupation, and is widely regarded as a product of US administrator Paul Bremer.[61] It *anticipated* a number of crucial issues which should have been left to a legitimate elected assembly.[62] Given the fiduciary nature of TG, the question of division of power between the constituencies of Iraq, for example, should have been deferred to the post-transition stage. Nevertheless, the TAL included a provision enshrining the so-called Kurdish veto,[63] which, in spite of the wide criticism, was eventually adopted.[64] The Kurdish veto is perceived as the direct result of an external actor's intention to leave a permanent imprimatur on a post-transition constitutional order.

Turning finally to a transition *sensu lato*, the 1995 Dayton Agreement, 'drafted by a group of lawyers while the conflict was still underway',[65]

---

[59] O. Hammady, 'International support to legal and constitutional reforms in the MENA transitional processes', presentation during International Expert Seminar of 21 and 22 September 2015.

[60] A. Arato, 'Post-Sovereign Constitution-Making and Its Pathology in Iraq', op. cit., p. 545.

[61] L. Brahimi, 'State-Building in Crisis and Post-Conflict Countries', op. cit., p. 8.

[62] J. Benomar, 'Constitution-Making after Conflict: Lessons for Iraq', op. cit., pp. 92–3. See also E. De Groof, 'The Features of Transitional Governance Today', op. cit. See 'Practice 4'.

[63] TAL, art. 61: '[t]he general referendum will be successful and the draft constitution ratified if a majority of the voters in Iraq approve and if two-thirds of the voters in three or more governorates do not reject it'. Because three governorates are led by the Kurdish, this provision resulted in the so-called Kurdish veto.

[64] This raises the question whether the issue was acquiesced by the Iraqi TA or population. S. Wheatly, 'The Security Council, Democratic Legitimacy and Regime Change in Iraq', op. cit., p. 550.

[65] IDEA, 'Interim Constitutions in Post-Conflict Settings', op. cit., p. 12.

included a long-term power-sharing arrangement with effects going well beyond the transition. Several commentators criticised this, not least because the 'Dayton Accords saw the creation of a fictional state that was recognised by powerful elements of the international community'.[66] The external influence on the constitution-making process in Bosnia-Herzegovina was not marginal or even partial but *total*. The National Congress of Bosnia-Herzegovina even considered the Dayton Agreement to be unlawful under international law.[67] This position is not uncontested but it confirms that subjecting a TI or the way it was adopted to an international law assessment is not something unseen.[68]

3.2   Respect for State Continuity

External actors involved in the transition must respect a state's constitutional and institutional identity insofar it was not validly altered by the TI. As with belligerent occupation, external actors must respect the laws in force as a state renaissance is not premised on a *tabula rasa* with the past. In addition, external actors must uphold their international (investment) treaties with the transition state even when it may not be in their interest to do so.[69]

4   *Prohibition on Undermining Inclusivity*

External actors are not supposed to prevent groups from being involved in TG, especially as 'bolster[ing] the power of unrepresentative leaders, or empower[ing] one group at the expense of another, can exacerbate the causes of conflict or create new sources of tension'.[70] This is not only a policy matter. The lowest common denominator of nascent custom in relation to TG is protective of the progressive realisation of internal self-determination. External actors thus 'increasingly face international pressure to help build governance structures and institutions that advance self-

---

[66] Id., p. 13. Cf. also K. Papagianni, 'Power Sharing, Transitional Governments and the Role of Mediation', op. cit., p. 51.

[67] 'Bosnians Want the Constitution of the Republic of Bosnia-Herzegovina Back', Online Newsletter of 24 February 2006 available on http://republic-bosnia-herzegovina.com /arhiva/?p=329 (last accessed 29 March 2020).

[68] For a fine analysis, cf. P. C. Szasz, 'The Dayton Accord: The Balkan Peace Agreement', *Cornell International Law Journal*, Vol. 30, no. 3, Art. 8, 1997.

[69] See the very restrictive conditions under VCLT, art. 62, by virtue of which a fundamental change of circumstances mostly *cannot* be invoked as a ground for terminating a treaty.

[70] Report of the Secretary-General on peacebuilding in the immediate aftermath of conflict of 11 June 2009, A/63/881-S/2009/304, §§ 11 and 12.

determination'.[71] They must not impede inclusive TG nor assist TA in pursuing exclusive TG. This negative obligation in law is complemented by a positive deontological obligation to promote inclusion.

First, while external actors are not in a position to *guarantee* inclusive TG elsewhere and are even less under an obligation to do so, they should neither hinder TA pursuing inclusive TG nor assist TA undermining inclusivity. Like under IHL, transitions 'should not be distorted to promote transformations that undercut self-determination'.[72] In principle, the prohibition to impede inclusive TG or to assist TA in pursuing exclusive/unrepresentative TG also protects the position of representatives from the (outgoing) incumbent power.[73]

External actors in any event must *not* be tempted to 'favour the participation of certain political groups and leaders over others based on their own interests and understanding of a country's political realities';[74] or, worse, exclude a country's entire population from a transition. If they do one or the other, they risk violating the principle of self-determination as further specified by recent custom. This would clearly be at odds with the widespread idea that progressive inclusion serves either to redress transitions which kicked off as oppositional, unrepresentative or elite-based, or to prevent TG from moving in that direction.

In short, impeding inclusive TG will increasingly be considered unlawful. How would this prohibition apply to external assistance to TG in Iraq, the DRC, Yemen, Libya and Syria? External actors favoured an exclusive transition in Iraq and have been heavily criticised for that reason.[75] The inclusivity of the transition was undermined from the outset. This was further reinforced by a lack of transparency. Even the constituent TI, the TAL, was elaborated in secrecy.[76] In other countries, by contrast, more

---

[71] J. Stromseth, *Can Might Make Rights?*, Cambridge University Press, 2006, p. 19.

[72] K. E. Boon, 'Obligations of the New Occupier: The Contours of Jus Post Bellum', op. cit., p. 75.

[73] E. De Groof, 'First Things First: R2P Starts with Direct Negotiations', *The International Spectator*, Vol. 51, no. 2, 2016.

[74] M. Saul, *Popular Governance of Post-Conflict Reconstruction*, op. cit., p. 29.

[75] D. H. Ucko, 'Militias, Tribes and Insurgents – The Challenge of Political Reintegration in Iraq' in M. Berdal, D. H. Ucko (eds.), *Reintegrating Armed Groups after Conflict*, op. cit.: 'the process of political reintegration [of armed groups] was perhaps most fatally undermined by the dearth of attention paid, by both the Coalition Provisional Authority (CPA) in Iraq and the Bush administration in Washington, to this critical component of state building' as the 'Shia and Kurdish were . . . not integrated'.

[76] J. Benomar, 'Constitution-Making after Conflict: Lessons for Iraq', op. cit., pp. 92–3. Benomar adds that this law 'should have been at least presented as a draft to an inclusive national dialogue before being finalised'.

300 LIMITS TO EXTERNAL INVOLVEMENT WITH TG

efforts were made to make TG inclusive. This was arguably the case in the DRC,[77] and perhaps, but to little avail, in Yemen where 'the international community played an important role in keeping the sides at the table'.[78] In yet other countries, results were (very) mixed. In Libya, external attempts at promoting an inclusive transition rapidly deteriorated when the political exclusion law was adopted in 2013, and even more so when political power was split in 2014 between two competing governments. In Syria, finally, at least one state affirmed, yet in vain, that there should be 'no attempt to exclude any group from the [transitional] process'[79] while other states clearly tried to sideline the incumbent.[80]

In addition, external actors are more and more assumed to promote inclusive TG as a deontological positive obligation. The deontological obligation goes beyond the legal prohibition on undermining inclusivity. The UN, for instance, is expected to support processes 'that help governments to "broaden ownership" to as wide an array of domestic stakeholders as possible'.[81] In line with this, Samuels argues that 'the international community should [also] commit sufficient aid to supporting inclusive and participatory processes',[82] while Papagianni remarks that 'political engagement by third parties is often needed . . . to allow . . . the wider public to participate meaningfully in the transitional process'.[83] Such deontological obligations have not entered the realm of law. But, clearly, external actors may encourage TA to increase the number of parties engaged in TG:

---

[77] In 2010, Papagianni writes: 'the war continued in the east of the country following the establishment of the transitional government in 2003, and efforts to bring rebel groups into the political process continue to this day . . . the role of third parties in mediating between the transitional governments and the nonsignatories has been indispensable'. K. Papagianni, 'Mediation, Political Engagement, and Peacebuilding', *Global Governance: A Review of Multilateralism and International Organisations*, Vol. 16, no.2, 2010, pp. 243–63.

[78] P. B. Holzapfel, 'Yemen's Transition Process: Between Fragmentation and Transformation', op. cit., p. 16. See also the efforts of UN Special Envoy Martin Griffith and the conclusion of the 2018 Stockholm ceasefire agreement.

[79] 'Talks come up with plan for Syria, but not for Assad's exit', *NYT*, 30 June 2012.

[80] E. De Groof, 'First Things First: R2P Starts with Direct Negotiations', op. cit.

[81] Balfour explains that 'the aim of supporting "deep democracy" through the Civil Society Facility and the European Endowment for Democracy, for instance, raises questions about *which groups to support . . .*'. R. Balfour, 'Changes and Continuities in EU-Mediterranean Relations after the Arab Spring' in S. Biscop, R. Balfour, M. Emerson (eds.), An Arab Spring for EU Foreign Policy?, op. cit., p. 38.

[82] K. Samuels, 'Postwar Constitution Building' in R. Paris and T. D. Sisk, *The Dilemmas of Statebuilding – Confronting the Contradictions of Postwar Peace Operations*, op. cit., p. 175.

[83] K. Papagianni, 'Power Sharing, Transitional Governments and the Role of Mediation', op. cit., p. 44. Own emphasis.

the role of external actors during the transitional periods is to encourage –
and when necessary pressure – national leaders to engage in inclusive
political processes at the national level, to implement joint agreements
with their former enemies, and to reach out to non-signatories of the
peace settlement; [i]t is therefore important that national leaders are in the
driving seat of transitional politics with external actors, when necessary,
pushing for inclusive political processes and for the expansion of political
participation.[84]

External actors may thus have a constructive role 'in advocating for
wide participation in constitutional discussion'.[85] The presence and
involvement of third parties can be instrumental to expanding popular representation and participation.[86] Thus, for one observer, 'the
support provided to certain civil society organisations in the
[MENA] region turned out to be decisive in terms of enhancing
popular participation in legal and constitutional reforms',[87] for
example with regard to a national dialogue in Tunisia.[88] Actually,
nothing prevents external actors from exercising even diplomatic
influence or pressure (short of coercion) to boost the inclusivity of
the transition.

[84] K. Papagianni, 'Political Transitions after Peace Agreements: The Importance of
Consultative and Inclusive Political Processes', op. cit., pp. 53–4. See also P. Dann,
Z. Al-Ali, 'The Internationalised Pouvoir Constituant', op. cit., p. 453, and pp.
459–60: 'external actors have generally tried to ensure that the constitutionmaking
processes are as inclusive as possible in order to enhance the society's ownership over
the new constitution. However, such external attempts often fail. ... Nevertheless,
the failure does not diminish the value of such attempts to provide channels for more
participation'.

[85] K. Papagianni, 'Power Sharing, Transitional Governments and the Role of Mediation', op.
cit., p. 52.

[86] Id., p. 44. Own emphasis.

[87] O. Hammady, 'International support to legal and constitutional reforms in the MENA
transitional processes', presentation during International Expert Seminar of 21 and
22 September 2015.

[88] See, for example, the interview by Ennouri with a vice president of l'UTICA, Slim
Ghorbal: '[t]he national dialogue was launched by the UGTT but the external foreign assistance helped the real implementation and advancement of the national
dialogue. Cited in B. Ennouri, 'The National Dialogue in Tunisia', on file with
author. See also the 'sanctions and embargoes to be used in attempts to persuade
Syrian President Bashar al-Assad first to go to a negotiating table with the
opposition'. R. Balfour, 'EU Conditionality after the Arab Spring', European
Institute of the Mediterranean, June 2012.

302   LIMITS TO EXTERNAL INVOLVEMENT WITH TG

5   Prohibition on Externally Imposed Constitution-Making 'Tout Court'

Some consider external assistance to constitution-making to symptomise a renewed *'mission civilisatrice'*.[89] External assistance to constitution-making *tout court* is not entirely a new question in international law. In 1758, already, Vattel accepted that outside states may act as mediators of constitutional affairs, if they were requested to do so.[90] In 1858, von Martens confirmed that states may assist each other in their constitutional transformation processes.[91] The article 'Into the Heart of the State: Intervention through Constitution-Making' includes examples of the twentieth century.[92] This phenomenon does not contradict the fact that, over the centuries, 'the traditional view has always been that the State does not suffer limitations ... regarding its own organisation of government.[93] Especially its constitution remains at the heart of its *domaine réservé*.

Today, we witness how the balance between external assistance and the preservation of the *domaine réservé* is more under pressure as external actors are increasingly engaged in state-building *cum* constitution-making enterprises. A state's post-conflict constitutional transformation nigh-systematically becomes an international project. Assistance to constitution-making is explicitly part of the mission and policy statements of several states and IO.[94] Since the end of the Cold War, at least thirty reconstitutionalisation processes have been influenced by the UNSC, UN missions and/or UNDP, regional IO or contact groups.[95] The internationalisation of constitution-making is the epitome of the internationalisation of the interregnum. The growing interconnectedness between international peace and

---

[89] R. Paris, 'International Peacebuilding and the "Mission Civilatrice"', op. cit., pp. 637–56.

[90] E. de Vattel, *Le Droit Des Gens, Ou, Principes de La Loi Naturelle, Appliqués À La Conduite et Aux Affaires Des Nations et Des Souverains*, op. cit., p. 37 (§§ 36-37) : 'les lois fondamentales ... n'intéressent que la Nation, aucune Puissance Etrangère n'est en droit de se mêler, ni ne doit y intervenir autrement que par ses bons offices, à moins qu'elle n'en soit requise, ou que des raisons particulières ne l'y appellent'. Own translation: 'the fundamental laws ... are of interest only to the nation. No foreign power has the right to interfere, nor to intervene otherwise than by its good offices, unless it is invited to do so, or specific reasons push him to do so'.

[91] G. F. von Martens, *Précis du droit des gens moderne de l'Europe. Tome premier*, Guillaumin, 1858, pp. 211 and 220.

[92] V. Mayer-Schönberger, 'Into the Heart of the State: Intervention Through Constitution-Making', op. cit.

[93] B. Conforti, *The Law and Practice of the United Nations*, op. cit., p. 136.

[94] Cf. references under Chapter 1, Section B.

[95] Chapter 1, Section B.1.1.

PROHIBITIONS APPLICABLE TO EXTERNAL ACTORS 303

security and domestic reconstruction and TG,[96] and the emphasis on a legal-regulatory vision of international peace and security, sharply resonate with constitution-making during the interregnum.

Whether deplorable or not, this evolution merits international legal analysis. I challenge the assumption that 'there is no *general* legal regime that regulates external influence on constitution-making processes'.[97] General international law – with a refined understanding of the principle of self-determination – does. The prohibition on *internally* imposed constitution-making[98] is mirrored in the prohibition on *externally* imposed constitutionalism.[99] This prohibition builds on the limits *ratione materiae* to TG, and can also be associated with the prohibition on external actors to entrench the post-transition era through a constituent TI. It echoes the conservation principle which also applies to post-conflict constitution-making,[100] and is in line with the inclusivity requirement, which privileges contracted over unilateral constitution-making processes.

Constitution-making *tout court* must therefore not be externally imposed. This is true from a deontological perspective.[101] Ensuring national ownership is one of the UN's guiding principles on assistance to constitution-making processes. These principles emphasise that TA must explicitly consent to any assistance in the constitution-making process.[102] Further, practitioners involved in transitions are required to

[96] Y. Daudet, 'L'exercice de compétences territoriales par les Nations Unies', op. cit.: 'les aspects internationaux et internes sont fréquemment mêlés et l'assistance à la reconstruction de l'État, question interne, devient partie intégrante du maintien et de la construction de la paix, question internationale'. Own translation: 'international and internal aspects are frequently intertwined. Assistance to state reconstruction, an internal issue, becomes an integral part of the maintenance and construction of peace, an international issue'.

[97] P. Dann, Z. Al-Ali, 'The Internationalised Pouvoir Constituant', op. cit., p. 460.

[98] Chapter 7, Section B.2.

[99] This has also been called 'external constitutionalisation by imposition'. U. K. Preuss, 'Perspectives on Post-Conflict Constitutionalism: Reflections on Regime Change through External Constitutionalisation', op. cit., p. 467.

[100] J. L. Cohen, 'The Role of International Law in Post-Conflict Constitution-Making: Toward a Jus Post Bellum for "Interim Occupations"', op. cit., pp. 498–532.

[101] K. Papagianni, 'Political Transitions after Peace Agreements: The Importance of Consultative and Inclusive Political Processes', op. cit., p. 53: 'international and comparative "constitutional engineers" should be humble and accept the limitations of their influence on the building or reform of institutions in post-conflict countries as these processes are ultimately influenced by indigenous political forces. In most cases, constitutions cannot be imposed from the outside'.

[102] 'Guidance note of the Secretary-General on UN assistance to constitution-making processes', op. cit., p. 4: '[t]he UN should recognise that constitution-making is a *sovereign national process*, and that to be successful the process must be *nationally owned and led*. The UN should be particularly sensitive to the need to provide advice and

cultivate inclusivity by 'protect[ing] the mediation process from the undue influence of other external actors'.[103] For the same reason, deontology requires a systematic emphasis on (domestic) 'ownership', and international mediators operating in post-conflict contexts are expected to 'cultivate consent'.[104] TA can thus be encouraged to involve the population in constitution-making.

Beyond mere deontology, legally speaking the prohibition on impeding the progressive realisation of internal self-determination during the interregnum surely applies to constitution-making. Consent to the internationalisation of constitution-making *tout court* must be valid. Nascent custom requires that valid consent may only emanate from TA that are at least credibly and meaningfully committed to inclusivity (as detailed under Part III) by including 'the people' according to its new, multi-faceted definition. External actors searching to assist TA should also verify this and 'refus[e] to initiate involvement on the basis of a request from a government with little claim to be an embodiment of the will of the people'.[105]

The conditions for valid consent were already discussed.[106] In cases of internationally assisted transitions, the analysis of the state's consent to the partial or complete 'internationalisation of constituent powers'[107] is sometimes difficult to make. Ensuring consent-based and domestically-led transformative constitutionalism is not merely a theoretical issue. If 'external influence consists only of advice from external experts, which is sought voluntarily by the domestic actors while control over the process and substance of the constitution remains clearly in hands of the nation at hand',[108] assistance is only marginal and hence unproblematic under *ius in interregno*. In some cases, however, one doubts whether the consent to the internationalisation of constituent powers was real or fictitious.

---

options without causing national actors to fear that UN or other international assistance could lead to a *foreign imposed constitution*. Any assistance will need to *stem from national and transitional authorities' 'requests'*. Own emphasis.

[103] Id., p. 15.

[104] 2012 UN Guidance for Effective Mediation, op. cit., p. 9.

[105] M. Saul, 'Local Ownership of Post-Conflict Reconstruction in International Law: The Initiation of International Involvement', op. cit., p. 168.

[106] Part IV, Introduction.

[107] N. Maziau, 'L'internationalisation du pouvoir constituant. Essai de typologie : le point de vue hétérodoxe du constitutionnaliste', *R.G.D.I.P.*, 2002, pp. 549–79: 'le droit international couvre, de plus en plus, les matières touchant à l'exercice du pouvoir constituant'. Own translation: 'international law increasingly covers matters relating to the *pouvoir constituant*'.

[108] P. Dann, Z. Al-Ali, 'The Internationalised Pouvoir Constituant', op. cit., p. 429.

One case stands out as a genuinely domestically led constitution-making process. The South African constitution-making process was inspired by other constitutional systems worldwide. Yet, it was based on a domestic negotiation process: 'we don't model ourselves on any other country, but rather absorb and benefit from the experiences and techniques used in other countries'.[109] In another case and on a different continent, even if there were doubts as to the validity of the 2001 Bonn Agreement, and as to the inclusivity of Afghanistan's transition, the constitution-making process itself cannot be described as externally imposed.[110] UNAMA established a 'Constitution Commission Support Unit' to support the constitution-making process in Afghanistan, but 'the role of the Islamic Transitional Administration [was] to *lead* the process of developing the Constitution'.[111] It seems that the drafting of the new Afghan constitution was an overwhelmingly 'Afghan' process[112] despite the quasi-imposition of the Bonn Agreement itself.[113]

In other cases, however, for example the transitions in Iraq and Somalia, one can seriously doubt whether the constitution-making process was truly domestic and inclusive. In Iraq, the sequence and development of the constitution-making process was controlled by the US. The constitutional processes there 'can be safely described as constitution-making through external imposition'.[114] As indicated earlier, the imposition of the TAL, on the one hand, and the ensuing constitution-making, on the other, should be subject to separate analysis. In any event, while 'the Constitutional Committee did manage to evolve into

---

[109] A. Sachs, 'South Africa's Unconstitutional Constitution: the Transition from Power to Lawful Power', op. cit, p. 1253.

[110] C. McCool, 'The Role of Constitution-Building Processes in Democratisation', op. cit., p. 6.

[111] Islamic Transitional Administration of Afghanistan, United Nations Assistance Mission in Afghanistan, United Nations Development Programme, Support to the development of a new Constitution for Afghanistan, AFG/02/012/01/34.

[112] E. Afsah, A. Guhr, 'Afghanistan: Building a State to Keep the Peace', op. cit., pp. 424–5.

[113] E. De Groof, 'The Features of Transitional Governance Today', op. cit. See 'Practice 4'. For considerations on the effect of an imposed TI on the transition itself, see the last footnote under subsection 1 'Prohibition on externally imposing TG' above (p. 292).

[114] A. Arato, 'Post-Sovereign Constitution-Making and Its Pathology in Iraq', op. cit., p. 545. See also K. Papagianni, 'Transitional Politics in Afghanistan and Iraq: Inclusion, Consultation, and Public Participation', op. cit., p. 753: 'The appointment in June 2004 of the IIG, with the blessing of the UN, gave some managerial responsibilities to the Iraqis, but did not change the central premise of the political process, namely that the transition to elections and *constitutional drafting was to be managed by the USA* and a select political grouping. The IGC then more or less reproduced itself in the IIG'. Own emphasis.

a relatively representative body', consensus-building was subsequently sacrificed due to domestic US political reasons, and the US and other actors directly intervened in the constitution-making process.[115]

In Somalia, 'the constitutional process grew from the TFC and transitional institutions, whose legitimacy was fundamentally challenged as having been developed outside Somalia with *too much foreign influence*'; 'the *level of external oversight* of the Roadmap has *undermined Somalia's sovereignty*'.[116] Whether a constitutional process was externally imposed is always fact-dependent and should be carefully analysed on a case-by-case basis. As a matter of principle, *ius in interregno* forbids external actors to negatively impact the realisation of self-determination during the interregnum. Constitution-making is the emblem and epicentre in this regard.

6   Respect for Domestic Ownership of Transitional Justice

TA generally conceptualise a form of TJ *sensu lato* at the latest towards the end of the interregnum. We shall see that external actors must respect the domestic choice made with regard to TJ (6.1), and analyse how this choice, where relevant, impacts the jurisdiction of the International Criminal Court (6.2).

6.1   Respect for Domestic Transitional Justice Choice

TA have considerable leeway in choosing which TJ mechanism apply, within the limits of the provision that no amnesty be granted for war crimes, genocide, crimes against humanity and other serious violations of international human rights and humanitarian law ('serous crimes'). External actors may *assist* TA in designing TJ mechanisms, and for some even have an obligation to do so under 'the responsibility to rebuild'.[117] But the choice for domestic TJ ultimately lies with the TA. This is why, also in the domain of TJ, 'foreign actors must see their role as

---

[115] P. Dann, Z. Al-Ali, 'The Internationalised Pouvoir Constituant', op. cit., p. 439. Cf. also pp. 440 and 442.

[116] A. Ainte, 'Somalia – Legitimacy of the Provisional Constitution', op. cit., p. 64 and p. 60. Own emphasis. In the same vein, for Mosley there is '*pressure, largely external*, to adhere to the "Vision 2016" agenda – especially the revision, finalization and approval by referendum of the provisional constitution'. J. Mosley, 'Somalia's Federal Future – Layered Agendas, Risks and Opportunities', Chatham House, September 2015. Own emphasis.

[117] ICISS Report of the International Commission on Intervention and State Sovereignty, pp. 41–2.

PROHIBITIONS APPLICABLE TO EXTERNAL ACTORS 307

one of support and facilitation of domestic policies'.[118] For instance, 'for a truth commission to succeed ... it must be regarded by a broad cross-section of society as legitimate *and independent from extraneous political influences*'.[119] This also implies that external actors should avoid advocating a rushed approach to TJ.[120] It finally means that consultations about TJ processes should be as inclusive as possible.[121]

Whichever way is chosen to realise TJ, there is general agreement that it must be 'owned' by the population of the state in transition. The modality of TJ cannot be externally imposed. As discussed under Part III, this position is shared by several transition states as well as other states. In the same vein, a UNSG report finds that 'reconciliation cannot be imposed'.[122] UN technical assistance to TJ is thus based on national consultations, as occurred for instance in Côte d'Ivoire, Guinea, Mali and Uganda.[123] Furthermore, the ICC Office of the Prosecutor must not be intrusive when it assists transitional states.[124] The principle and policy of (positive) complementarity requires such an unobtrusive stance.

The ownership of TJ is in line with the precept that TG must be carried out inclusively, and in conformity with the principle of internal self-determination. Sriram much insists on the ownership of TJ.[125] For other scholars, too, external actors 'must facilitate instead of impose, empower the people instead of "picking the fruits of sorrow", support local initiatives instead of drowning the post-conflict society in a sea of foreign

---

[118] D. Bloomfield, T. Barnes, L. Huyse (eds.), *Reconciliation after Violent Conflict, A Handbook*, op. cit., p. 163.

[119] E. Stover, H. Megally, H. Mufti, 'Bremer's Gordian Knot: Transitional Justice and the US Occupation of Iraq', op. cit., p. 852. Own emphasis.

[120] Id., p. 164.

[121] For a counter-example, cf. TJ in Iraq: 'Iraq's transitional justice process could potentially be viewed as an American process operating under an Iraqi façade'. E. Stover, H. Megally, H. Mufti, 'Bremer's Gordian Knot: Transitional Justice and the US Occupation of Iraq', op. cit., p. 835.

[122] S/2001/394 of 20 April 2001.

[123] See A/68/213 of 29 July 2013.

[124] P. P. Soares, 'Positive Complementarity: Fine-Tuning the Transitional Justice Discourse', op. cit., p. 208: 'the OTP [Office of the Prosecutor] should not directly engage with domestic authorities in the effort to enhance their legal system ... maintaining an *advising* and pedagogical role vis-à-vis their activities'. Own emphasis.

[125] For a discussion on TJ and how it is imported or imposed, see C. L. Sriram, 'Transitional Justice and the liberal peace' in E. Newman, R. Paris, O. P. Richmond, *New Perspectives on Liberal Peacebuilding*, op. cit., pp. 121–3, noting that '[t]ransitional justice, and trials in particular, are frequently imported from the outside and occasionally externally imposed. In this they are similar to the liberal peacebuilding of which they are a part'.

projects'.[126] In sum, the prohibition on imposing externally designed or on impeding domestically conceived TJ entails that external actors, when assisting states in transition, adopt a facilitative role. When external actors impose a TJ avenue or impede a domestically conceived TJ avenue, they risk violating the principle of self-determination as TJ is instrumental to state renaissance.[127]

6.2 Complementarity and Independence of the ICC

The relation between TA and the ICC is case-dependent. The Court's jurisdiction is either actively searched for or, on the contrary, carefully avoided. Two scenarios are particularly relevant in the context of conflict-related TG. First, the transitory nature of TG may be invoked to challenge the jurisdiction of the ICC. This, then, triggers the question of how to define whether the judiciary of a state in transition is 'able' and 'willing' to discharge its duties (6.2.1). Second, the particular context of TG can be invoked for instrumentalising the ICC. This triggers the question of how one can avoid that the ICC be politicised by states in transition (6.2.2).

6.2.1 Ability and Willingness Test: Flexible Standards The commitment to organising a form of post-conflict justice is to be taken into account in three circumstances: when the Prosecutor to the ICC considers initiating investigations *proprio motu* on crimes within the jurisdiction of the Court;[128] when the UNSC considers referring a situation to the Prosecutor;[129] and when a representative of a state party to the Rome Statute considers doing this.[130] In view of the principle of complementarity that is central to the functioning of the ICC,[131] a situation should not be submitted to the Court's jurisdiction if the issue can appropriately be dealt with on the national level.

The ability test is flexible in the context of TG. True, the 'total or substantial collapse or unavailability of [a state's] national judicial system'[132] must be taken into account in the evaluation of a state's ability or inability to carry out its own proceedings. Yet, in transition states such collapse or unavailability is

---

[126] D. Bloomfield, T. Barnes, L. Huyse (eds.), *Reconciliation after Violent Conflict, A Handbook*, op. cit., p. 164.

[127] Chapter 7, Section C.2.2.

[128] Rome Statute, art. 15.1.

[129] Id., art. 13.b.

[130] Id., art. 13.a.

[131] Id., Preamble, tenth consideration; art. 17.

[132] Id., art. 17.3.

PROHIBITIONS APPLICABLE TO EXTERNAL ACTORS 309

considered to be *temporary*. Consequently, evidentiary standards for proving that a transition state's judiciary has substantially collapsed or is unavailable will be more demanding than under normal circumstances. Regarding the case of Libya, referred to the ICC by the UNSC,[133] the Prosecutor thus argued: 'in relation to "inability" . . . the Statute's complementarity provisions should *not become a tool for overly harsh structural assessments* of the judicial machinery in developing countries or *in countries in the midst of a post-conflict democratic transition* which, as Libya notes, will not possess a sophisticated or developed judicial system'.[134] In essence, the Prosecutor's argument was that the ability test should be applied with lenience for states in transition. Following this argument, the ICC accepted the challenge against the admissibility of the case *Prosecutor v. Saif Al-Islam Gaddafi*. It considered that Libya, even if in transition, would be able and willing to prosecute Al-Islam Gaddafi.[135] This is also the case, the Court confirmed, when the security situation leaves much to be desired.[136]

The assessment of a state's willingness to carry out proceedings should be made with reference to the state's own law.[137] In the context of TG, substantiating a state's unwillingness is harder than usual. The reason is that TA often announce ambitious reforms of their country's judicial system and reaffirm their commitment to combating impunity. For transition states, precisely because they are in flux the standards used for assessing their willingness to carry out proceedings are therefore flexible. This is in line with the principle and policy of positive complementarity, which allows the Office of the Prosecutor to assist TA in their

---

[133] S/RES/1970 of 26 February 2011, §§ 4–8.

[134] Decision of 11 October 2013 on the Admissibility of the case against Abdullah Al-Senussi, §187. Own emphasis. On 2 November 2011, the Prosecutor reported that '[t]he Office was informed that the new Libyan authorities are in the process of preparing a comprehensive strategy to address crimes, including the circumstances surrounding the death of Muammar Gaddafi. In accordance with the Rome Statute the International Criminal Court should not intervene if there are genuine national proceedings'. L. Moreno Ocampo, 'Statement to the United Nations Security Council on the situation in Libya, pursuant to UNSCR 1970 (2011)', 2 November 2011, § 19.

[135] Judgment of 24 July 2014 on the appeal of Mr. Abdullah Al-Senussi against the decision of Pre-Trial Chamber I of 11 October 2013 entitled 'Decision on the admissibility of the case against Abdullah Al-Senussi'.

[136] Decision of 11 October 2013 on the Admissibility of the case against Abdullah Al-Senussi, § 261: 'the Chamber is of the view that not simply any "security challenge" would amount to the unavailability or a total or substantial collapse of the national judicial system rendering a State unable to obtain the necessary evidence or testimony in relation to a specific case or otherwise unable to carry out genuine proceedings'.

[137] Id., § 221.

310   LIMITS TO EXTERNAL INVOLVEMENT WITH TG

investigations and examinations, obviating the need for the ICC's intervention.[138]

In conclusion, the temporary reconstruction of the judiciary in times of transition does not necessarily correspond to a 'total' or even 'substantial' collapse or unavailability of the judiciary. As a result, the Prosecutor and Court must take a flexible stance with regard to the ability and willingness test even when TA are only 'in the *process of preparing a comprehensive strategy to address crimes*'.[139]

6.2.2 Avoiding the Politicisation of the ICC   The danger that the Court be politicised during transitions is high. States often refer situations to the ICC during an interregnum. The attempt to politicise the ICC on such occasions is quite noticeable:

> it may be that a state's request for an investigation is chiefly motivated by the wish to expose internationally the crimes allegedly being perpetrated by the other side. By requesting ICC intervention, that state could be *using the Court as a political weapon in the hope that its intervention could assist it in achieving its domestic political and military aims.*[140]

The period of self-referral is generally handpicked, and almost systematically relates to potential wrongdoings by the former regime or the opponent.

In CAR, transitional leader Catherine Samba Panza referred the situation to the ICC, manifestly trying to target members of the pre-transition government.[141] In the DRC, a referral letter was signed on 3 March 2004, thus during the interregnum (from 16 December 2002 until 19 December 2005), whereas in Côte d'Ivoire a referral letter was signed on 14 December 2010, right after the (second) transitional period. In Mali, the transitional authorities on 13 July 2012 triggered investigations into alleged crimes committed since January 2012.[142] In Ukraine, the interim government headed by former opposition politician Yatsenyuk lodged a declaration under the Rome Statute on 17 April 2014, 'accepting the jurisdiction of the Court over alleged crimes committed on its territory

---

[138] OTP Strategy Plan 2012–15.

[139] L. Moreno Ocampo, 'Statement to the United Nations Security Council on the situation in Libya, pursuant to UNSCR 1970 (2011)', 2 November 2011, § 19. Own emphasis.

[140] P. Gaeta, 'Is the Practice of Self-Referrals a Sound Start for the ICC', *Journal of International Criminal Justice*, 2, 2004, pp. 951–2. Own emphasis.

[141] CAR, referral letter of 30 May 2014.

[142] Mali, referral letter of 13 July 2012.

from 21 November 2013 to 22 February 2014'.[143] The period under investigation runs from the beginning of the Euromaidan demonstrations on 21 November 2013 until the ousting of Yanukovych on 22 February 2014. Since exactly this period was referred to the ICC, it was fair to see the interim government's initial referral letter as an instrument for delegitimising Yanukovych' government. Subsequently, Ukraine lodged another declaration accepting ICC's jurisdiction in relation to alleged crimes committed from 20 February 2014 onwards, with no end date.[144]

For the Court and Prosecutor to preserve their independence when hearing or investigating cases associated with transitions, the period of referral should be critically examined. In the case of Ukraine, for example, which did not ratify the Rome Statute, the Court cannot exercise jurisdiction over acts preceding the referral period at the risk of acting *ultra vires*. But at the same time, the Court would have compromised its independence if it had rubber stamped the interim government's choice. In light of its limited temporal jurisdiction, this would have prevented it from investigating crimes potentially committed by both sides of what eventually evolved into a civil war. If, like on the occasion of the first Ukrainian referral letter, the Court finds itself between Scylla (acting *ultra vires*) and Charybdis (compromising its independence), the Court may decide to critically assess its own jurisdiction.

In conclusion, self-referrals by TA, be they a party to the Rome Statute or not, should be carefully examined. Declarations by the Court's Prosecutor according to which all allegations, no matter which political side, are to be examined, are therefore to be welcomed.[145] In the context of TG, the Court and its organs must critically scrutinise the situation before deciding whether and how to exercise jurisdiction, lest the Court be instrumentalised for legitimising or facilitating regime changes.

B   Legal Implications

The last section discusses two implications of the prohibitions discussed above. First, when external actors violate these prohibitions, they may

---

[143] Report on Preliminary Examination Activities 2014 of 2 December 2014. Cf. also the Draft Decree of the Parliament Amending the Declaration of Parliament dated 25 February 2014, which is explicit about the political goal of the self-referral.

[144] Ukraine, referral letter of 8 September 2015.

[145] In this sense, L. Moreno Ocampo, 'Statement to the United Nations Security Council on the situation in Libya, pursuant to UNSCR 1970 (2011)', 2 November 2011. Similarly, but in relation to the DRC, P. Gaeta, 'Is the Practice of Self-Referrals a Sound Start for the ICC', op. cit., p. 952.

312 LIMITS TO EXTERNAL INVOLVEMENT WITH TG

engage their international responsibility under international law. Second, this chapter allows us to recapitulate which kind of external pressure in relation to TG is permissible under international law.

1 Potential Engagement of International Responsibility

The emphasis on national ownership in the context of TG is certainly laudable from a policy perspective as it may contribute to fighting a culture of dependency.[146] At the same time, while tasked with bringing the transition into safe harbour, TA cannot always bear, from a legal perspective, exclusive responsibility for mismanaged TG. This is especially the case when they administer the interregnum only on the surface. Where TG is highly exposed to and even malleable by the international community, one can legitimately criticise the point of departure – that is the exclusive responsibility of TA for 'their' transitions[147] – taken by the PBC, the UNGA, the UNSC as well as international contact groups for its simplicity. Any pretence of conceptual clarity does not stand in the way of legally assessing the role, sometimes beneficial, sometimes harmful, of external actors on the occasion of TG.

In the above we discussed prohibitions for external actors on imposing TG; violating the limits *ratione temporis* and *ratione materiae* of the interregnum; favouring particular groups during the interregnum; imposing constitution-making *tout court*; and imposing modes of TJ. These prohibitions mirror the prohibitions TA must respect themselves. As noted, this reasoning is based either on the external actors' obligation to respect the principle of self-determination as further refined by *ius in interregno* directly; or, if they engage with transitional authorities representing the state (progressively or *ex post*), on the ILC's DASR, reflecting international custom,[148] which prohibit that a state *aid* or *assist* another state in violating international law.[149] The same *a fortiori* applies for

---

[146] Interview with C. Westendorp cited in Y. Daudet, 'L'exercice de compétences territoriales par les Nations Unies', op. cit., p. 30.

[147] Chapter 1, Section A.2.3.

[148] A. Pellet, 'The ILC's Articles on State Responsibility for Internationally Wrongful Acts and Related Texts' in J. Crawford, A. Pellet, S. Olleson, *The Law of International Responsibility*, Oxford University Press, 2010. For a brief discussion about the DASR being essentially a codification of customary international law, cf. A. Aust, *Handbook of International Law*, op. cit., pp. 376–7.

[149] DASR, art. 16. Note the two conditions: (a) That State does so with knowledge of the circumstances of the internationally wrongful act; and (b) The act would be internationally wrongful if committed by that State.

LEGAL IMPLICATIONS 313

states *directing* and *controlling* other states in the commission of internationally wrongful acts.[150] If, with regard to specific acts or policies, states (and IO)[151] go beyond acts of assistance by placing TA under '*de facto* international trusteeship'[152] or 'under [their] supervision',[153] the conduct of the TA can be considered the act of the supervising state(s) (or IO).[154] In such a case, the external actors directing a TA in acting *ultra vires* and violating *ius in interregno* also engage their international responsibility.

External actors are therefore not allowed to support just *any* sort of TI or form of TG. They would be well advised to adjust or even retract their support during the interregnum when it becomes clear that the (selected) TA is violating the lowest common denominator of customary rules in relation to TG. To the extent that these rules acquire legal force or specify existing principles, external actors do not have unbridled freedom in supporting TA. They must respect *ius in interregno* as anchored in the principle of self-determination, particularly when the constitutional aspects of TG are concerned.

2 Permissible Pressure

The substantive limits to the interregnum are incompatible with any form of (indirect) neo-trusteeship.[155] During the interregnum, external actors must not go beyond acts of mere assistance at the request of the TA unless they received an explicit and valid mandate to do so. Even when they enjoy international assistance, TA have the primary task of administering the country during the interregnum. The powers of transitional authorities are confined by the transition agenda, which mostly revolves around administering the country *ad interim* and consolidating security. External actors should direct their assistance accordingly, that is to realise similar aims.

---

[150] DASR, art. 17.

[151] Similar provisions apply for IO. DARIO, art. 14.

[152] F. Reyntjens, 'Briefing: Democratic Republic of Congo: Political Transition and Beyond', op. cit., 307–17.

[153] ICG Report nr. 203, 11 June 2013, 'Central African Republic: Priorities of the Transition', p. 11.

[154] DASR, art. 8. Cf. also DASR, art. 17.

[155] A. Carati, 'Intervention and Promotion of Democracy. The Paradoxes of External Democratisation and the Power-Sharing Between International Officials and Local Political Leaders', *World Political Science Review*, 9, no. 1, 2013, p 132. Carati thus argued that the 'power-sharing between international officials and local political' in Afghanistan, Bosnia-Herzegovina, East Timor, Haiti and Kosovo possibly resulted in a violation of their sovereignty.

314   LIMITS TO EXTERNAL INVOLVEMENT WITH TG

Nothing of the above however excludes diplomatic pressure (short of coercion) by appointed diplomats and mediators, especially if their role is regulated by valid TI as is sometimes the case with implementation committees.[156] External actors may lawfully exert non-coercive pressure on TA and can encourage TA to abide by their own obligations.[157] Examples were given throughout this chapter. Such encouragements are not unlawful, and sometimes actually reflect (positive) deontological obligations. External actors not only may exhort TA to abide by their own obligations, but may also condemn any action that violates *ius in interregno* or derails a transition being carried out in conformity with it.

---

[156] Table 1.1.

[157] K. Samuels, 'Postwar Constitution Building' in R. Paris and T. D. Sisk, *The Dilemmas of Statebuilding – Confronting the Contradictions of Postwar Peace Operations*, op. cit., p. 175: 'the international community, and particularly the regional actors, should take a *more proactive approach* to requiring that any new government act in accordance with its constitutional obligations'. Own emphasis.

9

The Inducement of Oppositional Transitional Governance

Increasingly, states and IO, often in group format, assess the 'legitimacy' or 'democratic potential' of a political body presenting itself as a potential alternative to a (governmental) regime within a state deemed to be 'illegitimate' or 'undemocratic'. Some actors are supposedly deemed more fit than others to lead and succeed to the interregnum: 'an *acceptable alternative government* should be readily available, one that promises to be effective, so that, ideally, all that would be involved is regime change and not regime reconstruction or nation building'; 'Regime changes will be most difficult when there is no likely successor and no coherent internal political process that can produce an effective and *acceptable candidate.*'[1]

Such parlance is not politically innocent. It is related to the question who in the pre-transition stage triggers TG, and why. 'One of the key aspects in the functioning and effects of transitional regimes involves the issue of *who initiates* . . . the transitional process'[2] because 'the interim governments that now occur in the context of post-war or post-crisis transitions tend to be *initiated and often managed by external actors*'.[3] The early involvement by external actors with embryonic or inchoate TA can substantially define, even generate, transitions. This can, whether rightly or wrongly, become a reason for political concern. Russia, for instance, voiced such concerns in 2012 with regard to a transition being considered in Syria.[4] In 2019, on a different continent, and in relation with (prospective) TG *sensu lato*, several countries voiced their 'concern

---

[1] M. Reisman, 'The Manley O. Hudson Lecture: Why Regime Change Is (Almost Always) a Bad Idea', op. cit., pp. 524–5. Own emphasis.
[2] K. Guttieri and J. Piombo, 'Issues and Debates in Transitional Rule', op. cit., p. 5. Own emphasis.
[3] Id., p. 12.
[4] Russia insisted that there be 'no attempt to impose any kind of a transition process'. Cf. 'Talks come up with plan for Syria, but not for Assad's exit', *NYT*, 30 June 2012.

about expressions of support for a transitional Government [in Venezuela]'.[5] But how should this issue be understood from a legal perspective, and in particular in relation to oppositional TG?

There is no doubt that the external imposition of any form of government is unlawful under the twin principles of self-determination and non-intervention. The right of internal self-determination, understood as the right to decide freely on a form of government, 'does not present any particular problems' for Simma: '*any outside pressure* designed to enforce the installation of a particular form of government . . . must be defined as an *internationally prohibited intervention*'.[6] In situations of TG, however, the issue becomes subtler. For states in transition, the installation of a particular (supposedly stable) government occurs after a considerable lapse of time, the interregnum. The question, then, becomes whether external states or IO may intervene before a prospective interregnum, not necessarily to install a specific form of government *but to influence the course of TG itself.*

A variety of external actors can influence the interregnum and, thus, the ensuing reconfiguration of the state order.[7] Moreover, 'international agencies are oftentimes the main agents of transition as they intervene to strengthen or even create government where internal authority is deemed too weak to run a transition'.[8] This chapter is about states triggering or supporting TG in other states. They can do so by creating or participating in contact groups that endorse oppositional TA. We will examine the legality *vel non* of indirect creation or empowerment of new regimes. Regimes are indirectly created when oppositional TA are used as intermediaries.

In the remainder of this book, the focus will be on transitions by replacement. The initial phases of replacement (stages 1 and 2) will retain our attention. Crucially, the lowest common denominator of emerging customs in relation to TG applies both to oppositional and consensual TA wielding effective power. As a result, the prohibitions derived from

---

[5] 'With Venezuela Buckling under Severe Shortages, Security Council Emergency Session Calls for Political Solution to End Crisis, as Divisions Emerge over Path Forward', SC/13680, 26 January 2019. Antigua and Barbuda, Barbados, Bolivia, China, Cuba, Dominica, Equatorial Guinea, Nicaragua, South Africa, Suriname, Turkey and Venezuela.

[6] B. Simma (ed.), *The Charter of the United Nations – a Commentary*, op. cit., p. 63. See also N. Bhuta, 'New Modes and Orders', op. cit., p. 65. Own emphasis.

[7] Chapter 1, Section B. See also E. De Groof, M. Wiebusch (eds.), *International Law and Transitional Governance: Critical Perspectives*, op. cit.

[8] J. Strasheim, H. Fjelde, 'Pre-Designing Democracy: Institutional Design of Interim Governments and Democratisation in 15 Post-Conflict Societies', op. cit., p. 338.

that lowest common denominator and identified in the previous chapter remain applicable to oppositional TA. This chapter specifically concentrates on the initial phases of TG by replacement, whereby oppositional TA are leading the interregnum, or intend to do so. Oppositional TA which were set up in Syria and Libya in the context of the so-called Arab Spring will serve as illustrations.

Which legal leeway do states have in (indirectly) initiating non-constitutional TG in other states? There was no doubt as to the legality of external support to peoples' struggle for self-determination and liberation from colonial and foreign domination.[9] Contrary to NLM, however, TA do not represent a legal category. The research problem here thus reflects a whole different context and reality. In the absence of a specific legal regime comparable to the one applicable to NLM, it seems opportune to identify the legal criteria for, or limits to, engaging with oppositional TA under general international law.

In line with this study's general focus, only the *non-forcible* aspects of external impact on opposition-based TG will be examined. I do not deal with the question as to whether unilateral armed intervention in the domestic affairs of a so-called rogue state may, under certain conditions, be justified. This question was already fiercely debated *en lien* with the doctrine of humanitarian intervention. This chapter rather deals with a factual understanding and legal assessment of non-forcible inducement of oppositional TG.

The first section describes the practice itself while focusing on the role of contact groups (A). The second section places the practice in legal context. It observes that the existing literature with regard to recognition of government or belligerency is not particularly helpful in this regard; and explains that non-forcible albeit coercive empowerment of oppositional TG is generally prohibited under international law (B).

A External Inducement of Oppositional Transitional Authorities

After observing that the influence of contact groups was central to the empowerment of the Libyan and Syrian TA (1), this practice will be given a label, 'inducing oppositional transitions' (2).

---

[9] UNGA/RES/2787 of 6 December 1971. Cf. also UNGA/RES/3103 of 12 December 1973.

1 Observing a Practice: Contact Groups Empowering Oppositional Transitional Authorities

Which legal leeway do contact groups have for triggering non-constitutional TG indirectly, that is by supporting and empowering TA? To what extent is a contact group allowed to exert influence on a state's interregnum, and eventually, on the reconfiguration of that state's political and constitutional order? The answer to these questions depends both on the type of TA that is being supported and on the manner in which such influence is being exercised.

As discussed under Chapter 4, TA are distinguishable from other realities. Oppositional TA are political/civilian (non-military) entities that have the publicly proclaimed aim of introducing a new political regime by non-constitutionally reconfiguring the constitutional order, without (at least initially) collaborating with the incumbent power. They pursue a state-order-reconfiguration aim within the existing state, without aiming for secession. Their main features thus are:

- their civilian (non-military) role or character;
- their proclaimed state-order-reconfiguration aim;
- their initial choice to reach this aim by unilateral and non-constitutional means.

These features characterised two oppositional TA created during the so-called Arab Spring: the Syrian National Council/Syrian National Coalition ('SNC') and the Libyan Transitional National Council ('TNC'). From the beginning, both the SNC and the TNC were clear about their aim: pursuing a reconfiguration of the state order within their respective states. This broad aim was publicly announced, however undetailed their plans and intentions. The very raison d'être of these oppositional TA, both in Syria and Libya, was to realise this aim.

In Syria, on 2 October 2011, seven months after the beginning of the revolution, a consensus was reached on establishing the SNC. The 'basic principles' of this oppositional umbrella organisation included the 'overthrow [of] the regime using all legal means', the 'manage[ment of] the transitional period' in order to avoid any political vacuum,[10] and the organisation of the elections of a constitutional

---

[10] www.syriancouncil.org/en/objectives.html. Now only available en cache. To the same end, the London 11 group considered setting up a 'transition coordination committee'. See 'Planning under Way for Possible Syrian Collapse', *The Wall Street Journal*, 31 August 2013.

EXTERNAL INDUCEMENT OF OPPOSITIONAL TA 319

assembly.[11] On 20 April 2013, the SNC issued a declaration in which it listed the 'basic principles' guiding its struggle. The fifth principle provided that 'the Coalition ... is aiming at a political solution and a transition in Syria on the basis that Bashar Al Assad and his close associates cannot take part in it or be part of this solution for Syria'.[12] The eighth principle clarified that this coalition will preserve but reorganise the state institutions.

In Libya, according to the unilateral Constitutional Declaration, the TNC was 'the supreme power in the State of Libya and shall undertake the works of the supreme sovereignty including legislation and laying down the general policy of the State'.[13] This TI also defined how, and in light of which standards, the permanent constitution should be drafted,[14] even though the means for achieving this end were limited:

> whilst the TNC members and the rebel groups knew what they wanted to get rid of – the Qaddafi regime and its convoluted governance/pseudo administrative framework – the question and reality they faced once the regime fell was: *did they have any constructive ideas* that transcended the demise of the Qaddafi regime to the pivot of the main grievance – a *nuanced State building agenda?*[15]

From the outset, both the Syrian and Libyan oppositional TA received explicit support from contact groups. Their politico-legal origin and institutional advancement arguably *depended* on contact groups. The circumstances in which international community actors interacted with both oppositional TA are sufficiently known.[16] The following overview summarises how both the Syrian (1.1) and Libyan TA (1.2) were

---

[11] www.syriancouncil.org/en/mission-statement.html; www.syriancouncil.org/en/about .html (not available anymore). Documents on file.

[12] 'Declaration by the national coalition for Syrian revolutionary and opposition forces', http://en.etilaf.org/coalition-documents/declaration-by-the-national-coalition-for-syr ian-revolutionary-and-opposition-forces.html, last accessed 26 February 2019.

[13] Constitutional Declaration of 3 August 2011, op. cit., art. 17.

[14] Draft Constitutional Charter for the Transitional Stage, artt. 1–16; 31–33.

[15] J. N. Maogoto, A. Coleman, 'Changing the Guard – The Price of Democracy: Lessons from the Arab Spring on Constitutionalism' in C. Panara, G. Wilson (eds.), *The Arab Spring, New Patterns for Democracy and International Law*, op. cit., p. 11. Own emphasis.

[16] For an overview of how Syrian and Libyan oppositional structures were acknowledged and endorsed by particular states, regional and global organisations, cf. S. Talmon, 'Recognition of the Libyan National Transitional Council', op. cit.; S. Talmon, 'Recognition of Opposition Groups as the Legitimate Representative of a People', op. cit., p. 219, p. 226 a.f.; cf. also P. Thielbörger, 'Die Anerkennung oppositioneller Gruppen in den Fällen Libyen (2011) und Syrien (2012)', op. cit.

320 THE INDUCEMENT OF OPPOSITIONAL TG

internationally created and endorsed following the 'disqualification' of the incumbent governments.[17]

1.1 The Creation and Endorsement of the Syrian Oppositional Transitional Authority

In the case of Syria, members of the so-called international community purported to de-legitimate the Syrian incumbent. Notwithstanding calls for an inclusive transition, they attempted and partly managed to empower the opposition-based Syrian National Council (subsequently the Syrian National Coalition).

About three months after Syria was suspended from the Arab league, the 'Group of Friends of the Syrian People' (the 'contact group') convened for the first time in February 2012, in Tunisia, with the participation of numerous countries and IO.[18] The conclusions of this meeting show how states and IO endorsed and strengthened the position of the Syrian National Council. The contact group called for accountability for the 'regime's gross human rights violations'[19] and committed to 'reduc[ing] diplomatic ties with the Syrian regime'.[20] Crucially, they 'recognise[d] the Syrian National Council as a legitimate representative of Syrians seeking peaceful democratic change',[21] and agreed to 'increase [their] engagement with and practical support for the Syrian opposition'.[22]

In April 2012, the contact group met again, in Istanbul; and in July, in Paris. The chairman's conclusions to the Paris meeting indicated that the group 'commended and encouraged the opposition efforts to present a united front as a *credible alternative* to the current regime', and 'decided to greatly increase assistance to the opposition'.[23] In November 2012, the Syrian National Council merged with the Syrian National Coalition leading to the formation of the *National Coalition for Syrian Revolutionary and Opposition Forces* (the 'Coalition'), based in Cairo.

---

[17] About the link between disqualification and legitimacy of exercise, cf. J. d'Aspremont, 'Legitimacy of Governments in the Age of Democracy', op. cit.

[18] The Chairman's Conclusions of the International Conference of the Group of Friends of the Syrian People, 24 February 2012, § 1: 'more than 60 countries and representatives from the United Nations, the League of Arab States, the European Union, the Organisation of Islamic Cooperation, the Arab Maghreb Union and the Cooperation Council for the Arab Gulf States'.

[19] Id., § 8.

[20] Id., § 10.

[21] Id., § 12.

[22] Id., § 12.

[23] See 'Group of Friends of the Syrian People: 3rd Conference', 6 July 2012. Own emphasis.

The Coalition was first recognised by the member states of the Cooperation Council for the Arab states of the Gulf, by France, then by Turkey and Qatar, and Britain.[24] It then enjoyed the support of regional organisations,[25] including the EU (also a member of the 'Group of Friends of the Syrian People') which welcomed the formation of the Coalition, and backed it as a 'credible alternative' to the incumbent.[26]

These acts of support and recognition were criticised by Iran and Syria itself, the latter calling the Coalition a '*creation of the foreign states* and ineligible to take part in any national dialogue'.[27] On 5 December 2012, the US nonetheless 'expressed fresh support for the coalition'.[28] At the same time, 'pressure [was] building on the Coalition to transform itself into a political force that could earn *formal recognition* from the United States and other countries as a viable alternative to the Syrian government'.[29] In December 2012, the contact group (again) welcomed the foundation of the Coalition.[30] In January 2013, representatives of the Coalition met envoys from more than fifty countries in Paris. Meeting in February 2013, the EU Council confirmed 'its engagement in strengthening its support to the [Coalition]'.[31]

---

[24] 'Syria criticises 3 countries for recognising opposition', *IHT*, 19 November 2012.

[25] See, about the Gulf Cooperation Council for example, 'Opposition in Syria war is urged to pick leaders; US and others want to see a political structure that could replace regime', *IHT*, 7 December 2012.

[26] EU Council conclusions of 19 November 2012. See also 'European Union Backs Syrian Opposition Coalition', *NYT*, 19 November 2012. See the conclusions of the 3199th Foreign Affairs Council meeting: 'the EU welcomes the agreement reached on 11 November in the meeting of the Syrian opposition groups gathered in Doha and in particular the formation of the National Coalition for Syrian Revolutionary and Opposition Forces. *The EU considers them legitimate representatives of the aspirations of the Syrian people. . . .* The EU looks forward to this new coalition continuing to work for full inclusiveness, subscribing to the principles of human rights and democracy and engaging with all opposition groups and all sections of Syrian civil society. The EU stands *ready to support this new Coalition* in these endeavours and its relations with the international community. The EU encourages the Coalition to engage with the UN/LAS Special Representative and to put forward its programme for a political transition with a view to *creating a credible alternative* to the current regime'. Own emphasis.

[27] 'Syria criticises 3 countries for recognising opposition', *IHT*, 19 November 2012. Own emphasis to highlight that the perception of an oppositional TA created by third states concretely existed in this case.

[28] 'Opposition in Syrian war is urged to pick leaders; US and others want to see a political structure that could replace regime', *IHT*, 7 December 2012.

[29] Id. Own emphasis.

[30] The Chairman's Conclusions of the Fourth Ministerial Meeting in Marrakech on 12 December 2012. See the section 'Recognising the National Coalition'.

[31] EU Council Conclusions of 18 February 2013, § 4.

In March 2013, the Arab League decided to transfer Syria's seat to the Coalition.[32] In April 2013, the Coalition issued a declaration with 'basic principles' of which the fourteenth 'call[ed] on the international community to accelerate its support for all Coalition institutions including the current interim government'. At its height, the Coalition had representations or liaison offices in several countries among which Germany, Turkey, France, Qatar, UK, US and Hungary. For the Coalition, this was 'one of the important indicators of withdrawal of international legitimacy from the regime of Bashar al-Assad'.[33]

On 15 May 2013, the UNGA adopted a resolution, opposed by twelve countries,[34] on the situation in Syria in which it 'welcome[d] the *establishment* of the National Coalition ... and note[d] the *wide international acknowledgement* ... of the Coalition as the *legitimate representative* of the Syrian people'.[35] On 27 May 2013, the EU Council called for a 'transitional governing body which would exercise full executive powers'[36] and for a 'stronger and more united opposition [as] a credible alternative'.[37]

In November 2013, the Joint Special Envoy of the UN and the League of Arab States confirmed that 'the National Coalition will play a very important role in forming the [opposition] delegation'.[38] On 12 January 2014, the contact group and the coalition gathered in Paris. The final communiqué stated that 'as the legitimate representative of the Syrian people, the National Coalition should establish a delegation'[39] to the Geneva II Conference of 22 January 2014. To the disappointment of the Coalition,[40] neither the UN nor the UN Special Envoy to Syria recognised the Coalition in the run-up to this conference. But the Special Envoy did nevertheless agree to deal with the Coalition's Special Representative.

---

[32] 'Opposition takes seat at Arab League Summit', *BBC News*, 26 March 2013.

[33] See for example 'Bassam Abdullah Appointed as Ambassador to Germany', media statement of the Syrian Coalition, 1 November 2013.

[34] Belarus, Bolivia, China, Cuba, Democratic People's Republic of Korea, Ecuador, Iran, Nicaragua, Russian Federation, Syria, Venezuela, Zimbabwe.

[35] A/RES/67/262 of 15 May 2013. Own emphasis. Resolution adopted with 107 yes votes, 12 no votes and 59 abstentions.

[36] EU Council Conclusions on Libya of 27 May 2013, § 2.

[37] Id., § 3.

[38] 'Geneva Conference on Syria set for January, UN Chief announces', *UN News Centre*, 25 November 2013.

[39] 'Ministerial Meeting on Syria – Paris Declaration of the Core Group' of 12 January 2014.

[40] 'Jamous to Brahimi: FSA and Syrian Coalition Represent the People of Syria', media statement of the Syrian Coalition, 7 November 2013.

EXTERNAL INDUCEMENT OF OPPOSITIONAL TA

1.2 The Creation and Endorsement of the Libyan Oppositional Transitional Authority

The Libyan pre-transition period started with civil unrest and protests in Benghazi in mid-February 2011. The Libyan Transitional National Council (the 'Council') was self-proclaimed on 5 March 2011. On 17 March 2011, the UNSC adopted resolution 1973.[41] Only twelve days later, on 29 March 2011, the International Contact Group (the 'contact group') for Libya was created in London to accompany the transition.[42]

The first meetings of the contact group took place in Doha on 13 April 2011, and Rome on 5 May 2011. On 22 May 2011, the High Representative of the EU opened the 'EU Office' in Benghazi.[43] From June 2011 onwards, various states started recognising or otherwise endorsing the Council,[44] and many Libyan embassies abroad shifted allegiance. The contact group reconvened in Abu Dhabi on 9 June 2011, and Istanbul on 15 July 2011. At the latter meeting, the 'participants agree[d] to deal with the National Transitional Council (NTC) as the legitimate governing authority in Libya'.[45]

On 3 August 2011, the Council's Constitutional Declaration was published. The contact group reconvened in Istanbul on 25 August 2011, and in Paris on 1 September 2011 where it was re-baptised as the 'Friends of Libya Group'. On 16 September 2011, the Council was granted Libya's seat at the UNGA.[46]

*

These overviews show how the very existence of the Syrian and Libyan TA was conditional on the support of contact groups. There is no doubt

---

[41] S/RES/1973 of 17 March 2011.

[42] 'Report of the chairperson of the commission on the activities of the AU High Level Ad Hoc Committee on the situation in Libya', 26 April 2011, § 12. See also The Chair's Statement of 29 March 2011.

[43] See 'Remarks by EU High Representative Catherine Ashton at the opening of the EU Office in Benghazi', of 22 May 2011.

[44] S. Talmon, 'Recognition of the Libyan National Transitional Council', op. cit. See also Wikileaks for a vast overview of diplomatic cables in this regard. On the role of non-public documents in assessing *opinio iuris*, see B. D. Lepard, *Customary International Law – A New Theory with Practical Applications*, Cambridge University Press, 2010, p. 220: 'there is no per se bar against considering nonpublic statements or documents as evidence of a belief by states that a particular rule should or should not be recognised as an authoritative legal rule'.

[45] The Chair's Statement of 15 July 2011.

[46] 'After Much Wrangling, General Assembly Seats National Transitional Council of Libya as Country's Representative for Sixty-Sixth Session', UNGA press release, 16 September 2011.

that the foundation and institutional development of the Syrian National Council ('Council')/Syrian National Coalition ('Coalition') was supported by the states and IO composing the 'Group of Friends of the Syrian People', among other actors. Events include: the establishment of the Syrian National Council in October 2011; its evolvement into the Syrian National Coalition; the suspension of Syria from the Arab League; the regular meetings of the 'Group of Friends of the Syrian People' to support or 'recognise' the Syrian National Coalition. All of this indicates that the increasing relevance and leverage of the Council/Coalition hinged on early external support by the 'Friends of Syria'.

Similarly, the creation and development of the Libyan Transitional National Council was largely conditional on the support of the contact group. The decisive influence of the contact group on the Libyan transition is evidenced by: its very creation to accompany the transition, the subsequent establishment of the Council; the Council's transformation into a transitional administration; the external representation channels it established with various states; the acts of support and recognition by the contact group, culminating in the acceptance of the Council's credentials at the UNGA. There is no doubt that the relevance and leverage of the Council largely depended on the early support of the 'Friends of Libya'.

2 Labelling a Practice: Inducing Oppositional Transitions

The contact groups for Libya and Syria, consisting of powerful members of the international community, tried to catalyse TG in these countries. They did so by assisting oppositional TA that were set up to dismantle and redefine the state apparatus. At first sight, the number and political weight of their members may give the impression that their involvement with (prospective) TG enjoyed multilateral support on a global scale. Also, their systematic but vague commitment to 'inclusivity' might give the impression that (prospective) TG in these countries would be based on a domestic consensus. In reality, neither in Syria nor in Libya there was either global or domestic consensus on the triggering of TG.

Undeniably, the involvement by the Syrian and Libyan contact groups represented collective initiatives. Their initiatives were however a form of *concerted unilateralism* given the strong presence or marked absence of some powers. These self-selected contact groups were created outside the context of the established multilateral fora. Their conclusions thus cannot be seen as the fruit of (global) multilateral diplomacy. Concerted unilateralism, the state-order-reconfiguration aim shared between contact groups and oppositional TA, and the prospect of sequenced TG constitute the factors which, when combined, lend considerable power to contact groups.

Whether or not such groups have tried to provoke a regime change in Syria or Libya through *military* intervention is less relevant here. It seems states have (also) pursued this aim, in vain or successfully, through *political* means, that is by supporting oppositional TA: 'while it is one thing for states and international actors to formally deny any intention of effecting regime change . . ., the reality is that the very actions which they have taken or supported have directly resulted in this'.[47] Through their actions, contact groups have clearly confirmed that they intended contributing to regime change in Libya and Syria.

The state-order-reconfiguration aim was publicly proclaimed both by the oppositional TA and the supporting contact groups. The fourth proclaimed aim of the Syrian Coalition was 'overthrowing the Syrian regime'[48] while the proclaimed aim of the Libyan TNC was to 'be the basis of rule in the transitional stage until a permanent Constitution is ratified in a plebiscite'.[49] The contact groups for Syria and Libya must or should have been cognisant of this. It is therefore likely that the *common* aim was to introduce a political regime by non-constitutionally reconfiguring a state's legal order, without that state's consent. The fact that the endorsing contact group can reasonably be said to be cognisant of the publicly proclaimed ambitions of the oppositional TA, indicates that these ambitions were – at least putatively – *shared*.

Contact groups have actually gone further by *empowering* oppositional TA. 'Empowerment' refers to the diplomatic, political, material and/or financial support lent by contact groups to oppositional TA to achieve the common goal of a state renaissance. This practice, and the effects it purports to generate, is here referred to as *inducing oppositional transitions*. In one breath, inducing oppositional transitions refers to the

---

[47] G. Wilson, 'The United Nations Security Council, Libya and Resolution 1973: Protection of Civilians or Tool for Regime Change?' in C. Panara, G. Wilson (eds.), *The Arab Spring, New Patterns for Democracy and International Law*, op. cit. pp. 118–19.

[48] Cf. the Principles of the Syrian National Coalition, available on www.etilaf.org/en/about-us/principles.html last consulted on 9 December 2013 (now available en cache).

[49] Constitutional Declaration of 3 August 2011, Preamble, § 3.

diplomatic, political, material and/or financial support given by contact groups to oppositional TA with a view to introducing a political regime and reconfiguring the (interim) constitutional order of a state, in a non-constitutional fashion and without the (initial) consent of that state.

As a relatively novel practice, the inducement of oppositional TG should be distinguished from directly provoking a regime change. It should furthermore be differentiated from collective support for NLM during decolonisation, for two reasons which go beyond the conspicuous observation that, contrary to NLM, oppositional TA aim at reconfiguring the constitutional order within their country rather than by liberating themselves from it. First, the OAU and its Liberation Committee were mandated to act as a broker between the UN and NLM in the specific context of decolonisation. As the criteria for recognising NLM were relatively vague, the OAU gained considerable brokering power.[50] The inducement of oppositional TG through contact groups, on the contrary, often occurs without a (clear) mandate, and on the basis of criteria possibly even vaguer. Second, contrary to the OAU Liberation Committee, contact groups assisted the Syrian and Libyan TA at quite an early stage, that is before their political allegiance or popular attachment (the principal criterion for recognising NLM) were secured.

B Inducing Oppositional Transitions under International Law

How can one qualify the inducement of oppositional TG in international legal language? On the scale of intensity ranging from verbal critique or condemnation addressed to a state; an unfriendly but lawful act ('retorsion'); sanctions applied as countermeasures; and non-forcible but coercive intervention in a state's domestic affairs; to the use of force against a government, it can be considered – depending on the modalities of the support and the larger context – either as a retorsion, a (mostly invalid) countermeasure or as a non-forcible but coercive intervention.

Although, needless to say, the Syrian and Libyan oppositional TA were founded in diverse circumstances, they raise similar legal challenges that are relevant beyond the particular contexts in which they were generated. The inducement of oppositional transitions occurs in sensitive and volatile contexts. Political scientists and international lawyers alike may be inclined to conclude that, in such contexts, the jungle makes the law. Is

---

[50] Chapter 4, Section B.2.

there any role for the law in this? Is the external support or 'recognition' of embryonic or inchoate TA *neutral* – neither allowed nor forbidden – under international law? As a *coercive* measure, the inducement of oppositional TG cannot be meaningfully assessed under the doctrine of recognition (1). It is however in principle prohibited under the principle of non-intervention (2), unless the measure is taken or allowed by the UNSC (3).

1 The Irrelevance of the Doctrine of Recognition

The doctrine of recognition is of little assistance for assessing the legality of inducing oppositional transitions. In international law, recognition refers to the 'acknowledgement of the existence of an entity or situation indicating that the full legal consequences of that existence will be respected';[51] or to 'the act by which a state confirms ... a specific legal situation or consequence'.[52] Traditionally, the doctrine of recognition applies not only to states but also to governments, belligerency and insurgency, to which the non-recognition of unlawful situations may be added.

The inducement of oppositional TA has been associated with the vernacular use of the word 'recognition', especially in the press and media. But this needs to be sharply distinguished from recognition as a legal doctrine or institution. There is vast literature concentrating on the doctrine of premature recognition and the distinction between political and legal recognition. Neither this doctrine nor this distinction however assist us in legally analysing how external actors induced oppositional transitions in Syria and Libya, or purported to do so.

When an oppositional TA is recognised *as the government*, but one or more governmental features (effective control over state territory; the capacity to enter into international relations)[53] are lacking, such recognition is traditionally seen as premature. Recognition is governed by a duty of restraint.[54] The theory of unlawful premature recognition remains relevant today, but, in the context of TG, only so when an embryonic or inchoate oppositional TA is being recognised *as the government*.

---

[51] M. J. Peterson, *Recognition of Governments: Legal Doctrine and State Practice, 1815–1995*, Macmillan Publishers Limited, 1997, p. 1.

[52] J. Frowein, 'Recognition', MPEPIL.

[53] Montevideo Convention on the Rights and Duties of States, 26 December 1933. See, generally, S. Magiera, 'Government', MPEPIL.

[54] H. Lauterpacht, *Recognition in International Law*, op. cit., p. 7 and p. 283. Cf. also N. Henry, *Les gouvernements de fait devant le juge*, op. cit., § 178.

328 THE INDUCEMENT OF OPPOSITIONAL TG

States and IO are careful when drafting official statements. They would tend to recognise an embryonic or inchoate TA as a 'valid interlocutor' or a 'legitimate representative'[55] rather than as a government.[56] Thus, the contact group for Syria recognised the Syrian National Council 'as a *legitimate representative* of Syrians seeking peaceful democratic change'.[57] The Council of the EU 'consider[ed] them *legitimate representatives* of the aspirations of the Syrian people'[58] and 'strengthen[ed] its *support* to the National Coalition'.[59] Similarly, the US 'expressed fresh *support* for the coalition',[60] without according formal recognition. In the same vein, the contact group for Libya 'agree[d] to deal with' the National Transitional Council 'as the legitimate *governing authority* in Libya',[61] without recognising it *as the government*. (In 2019, several EU states proceeded with similar caution when supporting the opposition in Venezuela.) Outright recognition of the Syrian and Libyan TA was thus generally avoided. Regarding the latter authority:

> there were several obstacles to the blunt recognition of the NTC as the democratic replacement for Gaddafi at the early stage of conflict. The NTC was not a democratically elected government that for example suffered from a military coup. Gaddafi could not be trusted with an orderly transition to democracy but neither could the NTC; it was their first appearance on the political scene and they were barely introduced to the international community. This is not to say that they were not competent or democratic per se but at that point in time they had not proven their good or bad faith to the international community.[62]

At the time they received explicit public support, neither the Syrian nor the Libyan authorities, as inchoate TA, exhibited classical governmental features. Since neither the Syrian nor the Libyan TA were recognised *as governments*, the theory of unlawful premature governmental recognition

---

[55] Amoroso observes that the vocabulary of '(sole) representative of the people' is akin to the vocabulary used in relation to NLM. D. Amoroso, 'Il ruolo del riconoscimento degli insorti nella promozione del principio di autodeterminazione interna: considerazioni alla luce della "Primavera Araba"', op. cit., p. 3. Cf. also p. 22.

[56] Id., p. 3.

[57] The Chairman's Conclusions of the International Conference of the Group of Friends of the Syrian People, 24 February 2012, § 12. Own emphasis.

[58] Cf. the conclusions of the 3199th Foreign Affairs Council meeting, op. cit. Own emphasis.

[59] Id., § 4. Own emphasis.

[60] 'Opposition in Syrian war is urged to pick leaders; U.S. and others want to see a political structure that could replace regime', *IHT*, 7 December 2012. Own emphasis.

[61] The Chair's Statement of 15 July 2011, op. cit. Own emphasis.

[62] M. A. E. Youssef, 'Security Council Resolution 1973: A New Interpretation of the Notion of Protection of Civilians?', op. cit., p. 165.

OPPOSITIONAL TRANSITIONS UNDER INTERNATIONAL LAW 329

has little relevance. It can certainly not be used for legally assessing the support these authorities received from a substantial part of the so-called international community.

Does the inducement of oppositional TG constitute a form of *political* recognition? In the legal literature, a distinction is drawn between 'legal' and 'political' recognition.[63] Recognising a group merely as 'interlocutor' would be an act of political recognition. If an organisation is recognised as the 'legal entity that will lead the Libyan people to the critical new phase of a transitional process to benefit Libya, peace and stability in the region',[64] such a recognition would be merely political, too. On the other hand, if recognition of 'belligerency', for instance, is accorded to a group whether or not it fulfills the conditions to this effect, such act of recognition constitutes a legal act. Similarly, if a political body is recognised *as* the government of a state, such recognition constitutes a legal act, even if it would be *unlawful* to the extent that this body does not have the features of a government.

Characterising recognition as 'legal' or 'political' therefore usually depends on whether the wordings used to label the recognised entity (the words following 'as') coincide with a legal category ('state', 'government', 'belligerency'). The distinction between 'legal' and 'political' recognition thus in no way indicates whether the legal act of recognition is in conformity with international law, or produces valid effects. The label used to recognise one or the other organisation *as* interlocutor, *as* belligerent party, *as* legitimate representative or *as* government, *in itself* is not even instructive in this regard (even though, in light of the theory of estoppel, the precise wordings used must be taken into consideration when conducting this analysis).[65]

In sum, the characterisation of 'legal' or 'political' bears no link with the legal basis or effects of recognition. When analysing whether a specific act

---

[63] Succinctly, for Talmon legal recognition would flow from the facts (from the facts, legal consequences follow); while political recognition would not create any legal obligations, neither for the recogniser nor for the recognised. Cf. also P. Thielbörger, 'Die Anerkennung oppositioneller Gruppen in den Fällen Libyen (2011) und Syrien (2012)', op. cit.

[64] 'Greece Recognises Libyan rebels', *The New Age*, 23 August 2011.

[65] The confines of the obligation of estoppel are proportional to and dependent on the wordings used and conduct adopted by the 'recogniser'. Under this obligation, the vocabulary used is never insignificant since any act of recognition, as a unilateral act, can create legitimate expectations protected by estoppel. In this sense, Talmon rightly emphasises that 'with regard to recognition statements wording is all important'. S. Talmon, 'Recognition of Opposition Groups as the Legitimate Representative of a People', op. cit., pp. 219 and 226 a.f.

330   THE INDUCEMENT OF OPPOSITIONAL TG

of recognition is legally justifiable, the distinction is useless: it does not provide any insight on the legality of an act of recognition or support. As qualifiers of recognition, the words 'legal' and 'political' are, slightly ironically, uninformative for such an assessment. The distinction should thus be dismissed for the purposes of the present analysis.

To avoid the confusion surrounding the distinction between political and legal recognition,[66] one could refer to (political) *acknowledgement* rather than (political) recognition. This word is also used in practice.[67] The acknowledgement of TA simply indicates the 'willingness to enter into official relations' rather than manifesting 'an opinion on legal status'.[68] This usually follows the disqualification[69] (but not necessarily the withdrawal of recognition) of the incumbent government. Disqualification can be accompanied by the freezing of assets to the advantage of the inchoate oppositional TA.[70] It is in this sense that contact groups *acknowledged* the Syrian and Libyan TA.

In sum, the acknowledgement by contact groups of the Libyan and Syrian TA does not amount to 'formal' or 'legal' recognition, be it of government or belligerency. The institution of recognition is, in any event, of no avail for examining how the inducement of oppositional TA must be legally assessed. As regional legal frameworks do not shed more light on this issue and in the absence of a *lex specialis* on the matter

---

[66] This is not to mention the various meanings ascribed to *de facto* government or recognition. Talmon distinguishes six senses in which the word *de facto* has been used, i.e. to describe '(1) an effective government, i.e. a government wielding effective control over people and territory, (2) an unconstitutional government, (3) a government fulfilling some but not all the conditions of a government under international law, (4) a partially successful government, i.e. a belligerent community or a military occupant, (5) a government without sovereign authority, and (6) an illegal government under international law'. S. Talmon, *Recognition of Governments in International Law: With Particular Reference to Governments in Exile*, Clarendon Press, 1998, p. 60.

[67] Cf. e.g. A/RES/67/262 of 15 May 2013, Preamble, § 26: 'the wide international acknowledgement, notably at the fourth Ministerial Meeting of the Group of Friends of the Syrian People, of the Coalition as the legitimate representative of the Syrian people'.

[68] S. Talmon, *Recognition of Governments in International Law: With Particular Reference to Governments in Exile*, op. cit., pp. 23–43.

[69] d'Aspremont and de Brabandere write that 'there will be an expansion of the disqualification role'. See J. d'Aspremont, E. De Brabandere, 'The Complementary Faces of Legitimacy in International Law: The Legitimacy of Origin and the Legitimacy of Exercise', op. cit., p. 214. They do not portray the legal framework for this disqualification role, but observe that an assessment of legitimacy of exercise increasingly becomes a ground for 'disqualification'.

[70] See S. Talmon, 'Recognition of the Libyan National Transitional Council', op. cit. Cf. also, for example, 'Libya Rebels Get Formal Backing, and $30 Billion', *NYT*, 15 July 2011.

OPPOSITIONAL TRANSITIONS UNDER INTERNATIONAL LAW 331

(either on non-constitutional transitions, generally, or on inducing oppositional transitions, specifically),[71] we should now turn to general international law.

2 The Relevance of the Principle of Non-Intervention

Under the principle of non-intervention, introduced in Chapter 5, no state has the right to intervene, directly or indirectly, in the internal or external affairs of any other state. How does this principle constrain external actors committed to indirectly imposing regime change?

At their inception, and given their oppositional and non-constitutional origin, oppositional TA do not (widely) embrace officials or representatives of the incumbent regime. The question as to how the non-intervention principle would regulate external involvement with oppositional TA is thus especially relevant during these early stages, that is in the pre-transition stage or when the transition is founded. By contrast, when the transition is completed, and on the assumption that a fully-fledged government results from it, matters concerning recognition, attribution, consent or representation do not pose particular theoretical or practical difficulties. Interactions by external actors would then take place *in tempore non suspecto*, so to speak. But this chapter and the following analysis focus on the early stages of TG.

We have already emphasised that the non-intervention principle also applies to areas other than the use of force.[72] Is there any legal leeway under this principle permitting the indirect imposition of regime change through inducing oppositional TG *without* using force? Note that the non-intervention principle is not absolute. It is limited in two ways, as already discussed.[73] Only when outside coercion (2.1) is exercised in the *domaine réservé* (2.2) is the principle violated.

2.1 Coercion

Is supporting a political group that intends to unilaterally reconfigure the state order an act of coercion? The absence of consent by the target state is not sufficient for concluding that there is coercion. The external actor's

---

[71] Chapter 3, Section A.2.

[72] UN Charter, art. 2, § 4. See also *Nicaragua Case*, op. cit.: there is no general right to intervene in support of an opposition group; and a distinction must be made between arming and training a rebel group (threat or use of force) vs. supplying funds (not a threat or use of force, but possibly a violation of principle of non-intervention).

[73] Chapter 5, Section A.2.2.

332 THE INDUCEMENT OF OPPOSITIONAL TG

behaviour must also be *compelling*,[74] from the perspective of the target state.[75] Not all external involvement with oppositional TA reaches the threshold of compelling behaviour. Moral support to an embryonic oppositional authority (for example to the Uganda National Transition Council or the TA of China)[76] does not automatically amount to coercion, even if it goes against the will of the incumbent.

But what about the following scenario? Several states and IO politically, diplomatically and sometimes financially support an oppositional TA. They are cognisant of its state-reconfiguration aim, and declare it to be the sole legitimate representative of the people. They may even assist it in gaining effective control. Such concerted unilateralism clearly aims at subordinating a sovereign's rights and privileges. Even when unaccompanied by armed force or making abstraction of it, the inducement of oppositional transitions is likely to be coercive under this scenario.

2.2 Domaine Réservé

In itself, coercion is not contrary to the non-intervention principle. Only where coercion is used in the *domaine réservé* can the non-intervention principle be violated.[77] In Chapter 5, we already noted that the non-constitutional reconfiguration of a state goes, in principle, to the heart of the *domaine réservé*. By endorsing an inchoate TA whose raison d'être consists in non-constitutionally reconfiguring the state order, the external actor pursues the same goal. Such involvement directly touches upon that state's *domaine réservé*.

States, whether acting individually or collectively, are however entitled to take measures towards another state committing serious and systematic breaches of fundamental and non-derogable human rights. Such human rights are valid 'towards all', *erga omnes*.[78] They

---

[74] 'Coercion in inter-State relations involves the government of one State compelling the government of another State to think or act in a certain way by applying various kinds of pressure, threats, intimidation or the use of force', C. Joyner, 'Coercion', MPEPIL; 'the application of a coercive means by the actor towards the target to achieve a distinctive external, pre-determined goal'. V. Mayer-Schönberger, 'Into the Heart of the State: Intervention through Constitution-Making', op. cit., p. 315.

[75] S. Talmon, 'Recognition of Opposition Groups as the Legitimate Representative of a People', op. cit., p. 28.

[76] Chapter 4, Section A.2.1.

[77] '[a] prohibited intervention must . . . be one bearing on matters in which each state is permitted, by the principle of state sovereignty, to decide freely', *Nicaragua Case*, op. cit., § 205.

[78] J. Frowein, 'Obligations Erga Omnes', MPEPIL: '[a]lthough *ius cogens* and obligations *erga omnes* have different legal consequences, they are related to each other in important

OPPOSITIONAL TRANSITIONS UNDER INTERNATIONAL LAW 333

concern the 'obligations of a State towards the international community as a whole' which are 'the concern of all States' and for whose protection all states have a 'legal interest'.[79] By definition, *erga omnes* norms fall outside the *domaine réservé* of any state.[80] They are no longer considered to be the internal affairs of the state. Consequently, even coercive measures taken in response to serious breaches of human rights, in principle, do not necessarily amount to unlawful intervention.

Would this imply that inducing oppositional TG escapes the *domaine réservé* when the incumbent power is violating *erga omnes* norms? In order to answer this question, a distinction must be drawn between the context and the object of such measures:

- Coercive measures may be taken in response to violations of *erga omnes* norms;
- Coercive measures may impact *acta iure gestionis* (activities of a commercial nature) or *acta iure imperii* (activities of a governmental and public nature). The constitutional (re)definition of a state clearly falls under the latter category.

There is certainly a right to engage with, or 'intervene in', the non-domestic and/or *erga omnes*-related affairs of a state. But can all means be deployed to that end? There is no unbridled freedom to intervene in a state's domestic affairs – particularly the redefinition of its constitutional order – *on the occasion of* a non-domestic issue. Inducing oppositional TG does not automatically escape the *domaine réservé* because of a context of human rights

---

aspects. A rule from which no derogation is permitted because of its fundamental nature will normally be one in whose performance all states seem to have a legal interest'. This position is confirmed by the Barcelona Traction, Light and Power Company, Limited, Judgment, ICJ Reports 1970, p. 3.

[79] ICJ, *Barcelona Traction Case*, op. cit., § 33.

[80] The category of *erga omnes* norms concerns the 'obligations of a State towards the international community as a whole' which are 'the concern of all States' and for whose protection all States have a 'legal interest'. *Barcelona Traction, Light and Power Company, Limited, Belgium v Spain*, Merits, second phase, ICJ GL No 50, [1970] ICJ Rep 3, ICGJ 152 (ICJ 1970), (1970) 9 ILM 227, (1970) 64 AJIL 653, 5th February 1970, International Court of Justice [ICJ], § 33 ('*Barcelona Traction Case*'). Cf. also IDI, 'The Protection of Human Rights and the Principle of Non-Intervention in Internal Affairs of States', Session of Santiago de Compostela, 1989, art. 2: 'a state acting in breach of its obligations in the sphere of human rights cannot evade its international responsibility by claiming that such matters are essentially within its domestic jurisdiction'. Scholarship generally agrees that this category of norms includes the prohibition of aggression, the right to self-determination, and fundamental and non-derogable human rights, notably the right to life and the prohibition of torture.

violations. It is therefore unsustainable to argue that inducing oppositional TG, even in response to violations of *erga omnes* obligations, would not *a priori* constitute a breach of the non-intervention principle.[81]

There is only one exception to this: when the context of *erga omnes* violations and the object of external endorsement coincide. Inducing oppositional TG thus only escapes the *domaine réservé* if the constitutional identity of the target state directly contradicts *erga omnes* rights. If constitutional texts and practice violate *erga omnes* obligations, the externally induced constitutional reconfiguration might escape the target state's *domaine réservé*. This is the rather unrealistic scenario of constitutional texts explicitly condoning or encouraging aggression, genocide and torture, for example – all considered violations of *erga omnes* norms.

Coercively inducing oppositional transitions consequently quasi-systematically implies an intervention in a state's domestic affairs. For this reason, this is normally prohibited under the principle of non-intervention, except under the two following circumstances: if the UNSC lawfully authorises it or if it can be justified as a countermeasure. We shall address the UNSC authorisation in the following lines. The justification for inducing oppositional TG as a countermeasure deserves separate analysis and will be critically assessed in the last chapter.

3   The UNSC Inducing Oppositional Transitions

The UNSC bears the primary responsibility for the maintenance of international peace and security.[82] It determines the existence of any threat to or breach of international peace and security,[83] and may decide on (forcible or non-forcible) measures to give effect to its decisions.[84] Although the UN must respect the principle of non-intervention, this principle shall not prejudice the application of measures by the UNSC to maintain or restore international peace and security.[85] To honour its mandate under the UN Charter, the UNSC can thus take measures directly impacting the *domaine réservé*.[86]

---

[81] For a more liberal understanding based on a right to intervene (linked to a restrictive understanding of the *domaine réservé*), see R. Quadri, *Diritto Internazionale Pubblico*, Liguori Editore, 1968, p. 277.

[82] UN Charter, art. 24.

[83] Id., art. 39.

[84] Id., art. 41.

[85] Id., art. 2.7.

[86] O. Corten, P. Klein, 'Droit D'ingérence Ou Obligation de Réaction ?', op. cit., p. 379.

OPPOSITIONAL TRANSITIONS UNDER INTERNATIONAL LAW 335

The UNSC has already imposed sanctions against 'spoilers' of TG.[87] In addition, and in light of the broad and non-exhaustive formulation of article 41 of the UN Charter, it may also decide to coercively induce oppositional TG if this is necessary for maintaining or restoring international peace and security. Under the same circumstances, the UNSC might *authorise* states to coercively induce an oppositional transition. Of course, in discharging its duties, the UNSC must act in accordance with the purposes and principles of the UN.[88] The UNSC is not *legibus solutus*,[89] in other words must respect international law. If and when the UNSC envisages inducing oppositional TG as a non-forcible but coercive measure to maintain or restore international peace and security, it must take two elements into account.

First, on the sole basis of a lack of or threat to democracy, the UNSC is not entitled to induce an oppositional transition or to authorise other actors to do so. The absence of democracy or legitimacy does not, in itself, constitute a threat to international peace and security. When authorising military interventions in internal conflicts, 'considerations of democratic legitimacy ... have hardly played a role in the Security Council's determinations'.[90] The same reasoning should apply to the UNSC's involvement in TG.[91] A *ius in interregno*-based assessment must prevail over considerations of democratic legitimacy when the UNSC envisages inducing an oppositional transition to maintain or restore international peace and security. To facilitate this assessment, it is preferable that the UNSC provide detailed reasons for its decision, especially when potentially impacting the definition of a state's legal order.[92]

Second, the *marge de manoeuvre* of the UNSC to empower an oppositional TA is limited. It should be based on a conscientious assessment of the TA's compliance with the lowest common denominator of emerging customary rules in relation to TG, or of the reasonable prospects of abiding by these obligations, mainly of conduct, as described under

---

[87] Chapter 5, Section B.2.3.

[88] UN Charter, art. 24.2.

[89] ICTY, *The Prosecutor v. Dusko Tadić*, IT-94-1-AR72, Appeals Chamber, Decision, 2 October 1995, § 28.

[90] M. Payandeh, 'The United Nations, Military Intervention, and Regime Change in Libya', *Va. J. Int'l L.*, 52, 355, 2011–12, pp. 368–9 and p. 371.

[91] Chapter 7, Section A.

[92] S. Wheatly, 'The Security Council, Democratic Legitimay and Regime Change in Iraq', *EJIL*, 17, 2006, pp. 531–51.

Part III. Otherwise the UNSC risks violating the principle of self-determination as further detailed since the turn of the millennium. The UNSC, too, must pay heed to this principle, and must respect the precepts of *ius in interregno* when it envisages inducing oppositional TG. Unless the current evolution of nascent custom is halted, it must consequently ensure and monitor that the chosen TA respects the limits *ratione temporis* and *materiae* of the interregnum and meaningfully commits to inclusivity. The (continued) legality of the UNSC inducing an oppositional transition also depends on this assessment. It is thus paramount for the UNSC to correctly, and continuously, assess the chosen oppositional TA's compliance with the core obligations under *ius in interregno*. To say it with its own jargon, it must 'remain seized' of the matter.

But what happens when the UNSC remains inactive in the face of violations of *erga omnes* norms or even of *ius cogens*? The following and final chapter analyses whether external actors can induce oppositional TG in such a context.

10

Indirect Regime Change

A Response to *Ius Cogens* Violations?

Coercively inducing oppositional TG so as to trigger a regime change is in principle prohibited under international law.[1] This final chapter examines whether this prohibition remains applicable in the most egregious circumstances, that is when the incumbent power violates a specific category of *erga omnes* norms:[2] *ius cogens* 'accepted and recognised by the international community of states *as a whole* as a norm from which no derogation is permitted'.[3] This chapter purports to frame this issue exclusively in legal terms, and therefore can also be considered a 'theorisation-within-the-law enterprise'.[4]

The aim of this chapter is not to analyse whether forcible action is permissible as a response to *ius cogens* violations. The question is rather whether, or under which concrete conditions, such violations can be countered through TG and law-abiding TA, without the use of force. Before turning to this analysis, I will give two reasons why I focus on *ius cogens*.

To verify whether inducing oppositional TG can *ever* be legally justified, the gravest context of international law violations must be envisaged. Concentrating on *ius cogens* violations facilitates drawing the lines between what is permissible for external actors engaged with

---

[1] Chapter 9, Section B.

[2] *Ius cogens* is by definition valid *erga omnes* (A. Frowein, 'Obligations erga omnes', MPEPIL: 'a rule from which no derogation is permitted because of its fundamental nature will normally be one in whose performance all states seem to have a legal interest'). But not all *erga omnes* rules – e.g. the protection of the environment – amount to *ius cogens* (F. Francioni, 'International "Soft Law": A Contemporary Assessment' in V. Lowe, M. Fitzmaurice, *Fifty Years of the International Court of Justice*, op. cit., p. 177. F. Francioni, 'Realism, Utopia and the Future of International Environmental Law', Law 2012/11, with reference to Principle 21 of the 1972 Stockholm Declaration enouncing the 'responsibility [of states] to ensure that activities within their jurisdiction or control do not cause damage to the environment of other States or of areas beyond the limits of national jurisdiction').

[3] VCLT, art. 53.

[4] Introduction, Section C.2.

oppositional TA, and what is not. If coercively inducing an oppositional transition is unlawful even in response to *ius cogens* violations, then clearly this practice is *absolutely forbidden*, no matter under which circumstances. If it is not, the question becomes *why, and under which conditions* external actors may coercively induce oppositional TG to put an end to *ius cogens* violations. This chapter will thus acquire practical relevance for anyone wishing to develop an *argumentarium* in relation to TG. The limits to state powers will be exposed and some ammunition (under the form of counter-arguments) will be provided to states that are potentially subject to indirect regime change through TG.

Second, the very succinct first section of this chapter focuses on the limits to assistance to opposition-based TG in countries where *ius cogens* violations took place, Syria and Libya. Investigations evidenced that, both in Syria[5] and Libya,[6] the Arab Spring uprisings and their subsequent repression evolved into a situation where notably the right to life and the prohibition of torture were massively violated. Did the context of *ius cogens* violations form a potential legal basis for inducing oppositional transitions in these countries?

Importantly, the obligations which would be corollaries to the 'right to legitimacy' or the 'right to democracy' – the obligation to adopt a legitimate and democratic form of government – cannot be classified as *erga omnes*, let alone *ius cogens* obligations. The very existence of legitimacy or democracy as rights or obligations is controverted.[7] On the other hand, it is now generally accepted that a number of international legal obligations or prohibitions do not fall under the *domaine réservé* of any state anymore. As a result of the progressive development of

---

[5] UNGA, Human Rights Council, 'Report of the independent international commission of inquiry on the Syrian Arab Republic', 23 November 2011; 'I wanted to die – Syria's torture survivors speak out', Amnesty International 2012; UN Human Rights Office of the High Commissioner, 'Open Wounds – Torture and ill-treatment in the Syrian Arab Republic', 14 April 2014; Sir Desmond de Silva QC, Sir Geoffrey Nice QC, Professor David Crane, 'A Report into the credibility of certain evidence with regard to torture and execution of persons incarcerated by the current Syrian regime', 2014 (Note that this report was commissioned by a law firm acting for Qatar); 'Special Advisers of the United Nations Secretary-General on the Prevention of Genocide, Francis Deng, and on the Responsibility to Protect, Edward Luck, on the situation in Syria', UN press release, 21 July 2011.

[6] UN Support Mission in Libya, UN Human Rights Office of the High Commissioner, 'Torture and deaths in detention in Libya', October 2013; Human Rights Watch, 'Libya – Country Summary', January 2015; UN Support Mission in Libya, UN Human Rights Office of the High Commissioner, Report on Human Rights Situation in Libya, 16 November 2016.

[7] Chapter 2, Section B.

INDIRECT REGIME CHANGE 339

international law since the Second World War, a number of rules have become incumbent upon all states.

Ius cogens is characterised by the absence of persistent objectors, and per definition touches upon issues of international peace and security.[8] Scholarship generally agrees[9] – some call it a truism[10] – that *ius cogens* includes the prohibition of aggression and fundamental and non-derogable human rights, notably the right to life and the prohibition of torture.[11] In many cases, there is an intrinsic link between the protection of fundamental and non-derogable human rights and the principle of internal self-determination.[12] A way to gauge whether or not this principle is conformed with, involves looking at the incumbent's human rights record.

Now that the relevance of *ius cogens* for the purposes of this final chapter has been clarified, we can ask whether, and if so how, external actors can induce oppositional TG when the UNSC remains inactive in the face of *ius cogens* violations. This depends on the legal consequences generally flowing from such violations and on the question of how this practice might be justified in law as a last resort measure. I will argue that external actors are required to follow specific procedures, in first order (general reactions to *ius cogens* violations – Section A) and subsidiary

---

[8] Cf. 1980 DASR, art. 19, and the description of 'international crime'. In the same sense, P.-M. Dupuy, 'The Deficiencies of the Law of State Responsibility Relating to Breaches of "Obligations Owed to the International Community as a Whole": Suggestions for Avoiding the Obsolescence of Aggravated Responsibility' in A. Cassese (ed.), *Realising Utopia*, Oxford University Press, 2012, p. 225; A. Garwood-Gowers, 'The Responsibility to Protect and the Arab Spring: Libya as the Exception, Syria as the Norm?', op. cit., p. 601: R2P 'bolsters the legitimacy of the broader, ongoing UNSC trend towards an expansive interpretation of the concept of "threat to the peace"'.

[9] O. Corten, P. Klein, *Droit D'ingérence Ou Obligation de Réaction ?*, op. cit., pp. 88 and 95. In the same sense, Q. D. Nguyên, P. Daillier, A. Pellet, *Droit International Public*, LGDJ, 1994, p. 440. See also B. R. Roth, *Governmental Illegitimacy in International Law*, op. cit., p. 31.

[10] A. Cassese, '*Ex iniuria ius oritur*: Are We Moving towards International Legitimation of Forcible Humanitarian Countermeasures in the World Community', *EJIL*, 10, 1999, 23–30, p. 70.

[11] *Questions relating to the Obligation to Prosecute or Extradite (Belgium v. Senegal)*, Judgment, ICJ Reports 2012, p. 422, § 99. For the IDI, there is a 'wide consensus ... to the effect that the prohibition of acts of aggression, the prohibition of genocide, obligations concerning the protection of basic human rights, obligations relating to self-determination' are examples of obligations reflecting fundamental values of the international community. IDI Krakow resolution (2005/1) on 'obligations and rights *erga omnes* on international law'.

[12] Chapter 7, Section B.2.3. A. Cassese, *Self-determination of Peoples: a Legal Reappraisal*, op. cit., p. 140.

340 INDIRECT REGIME CHANGE

order (prerequisites under the countermeasure framework – Section B) before even thinking of inducing oppositional TG.

A   Obligations of Non-Recognition, Cooperation, and Peaceful Settlement

States must cooperate on the UN level in addressing *ius cogens* violations. When a state commits serious breaches of *ius cogens*, this entails three consequences for other states under international law.

- States must not recognise as lawful a situation created by *ius cogens* breaches, nor render aid or assistance in maintaining that situation. Concretely, they must abstain from rendering any aid or assistance in prolonging these violations.
- Second, to bring an end to *ius cogens* violations, states must cooperate through the collective security system, that is, through the UNSC and, in case of inactivity of the UNSC, through the UNGA. The obligation of cooperation furthermore entails that interested states cannot be arbitrarily excluded from diplomatic processes which aim at finding a negotiated solution to a situation that is contrary to *ius cogens*.[13]
- Third, states must seek to settle disputes surrounding *ius cogens* violations peacefully.

The emphasis on prior exhaustion of non-coercive measures is even more salient when states are said to be in transition, or pushed into a situation of TG. Institutional and constitutional structures are then held in abeyance, thus rendering the state fragile, and making the threshold for outside states to violate the principles of self-determination and non-intervention easier to reach. Especially in such circumstances, states must seek to cooperate and privilege a peaceful settlement by entering into direct negotiations with the incumbent leaders, no matter how negatively they are being publicly profiled.

On another occasion, I have already considered the normative basis and practical implications of these obligations, and applied the framework to states reacting to *ius cogens* violations in Syria and Libya after the Arab Spring.[14] So we can keep this section short. In a nutshell, while UN fora were addressed in an attempt to alleviate the suffering of the population in Libya and Syria, a number of other actions or omissions were

[13] E. De Groof, 'First Things First: R2P Starts with Direct Negotiations', op. cit.
[14] Id.

NON-RECOGNITION, COOPERATION, PEACEFUL SETTLEMENT 341

rather problematic under the threefold framework summarised above. Both in relation to Syria and Libya, a number of interested states were excluded from the negotiations. Also, from the outset states should have been in contact with the incumbent leaders in both countries so as to work towards a negotiated solution where possible. Direct negotiations should have been undertaken *before* contact groups purported to endorse and empower oppositional TA.

Regardless of whether the available multilateral fora were seized, states were not exempted from entering in direct contact with the leaders, no matter how 'rogue', of countries violating *ius cogens* before considering to respond by coercive or forcible action. Under international law, there is no doubt that there should have been direct and proactive negotiations between the community of states and the incumbent leaders of Syria and Libya. But this compulsory step was deliberately omitted.

The obligation of cooperation and peaceful settlement of disputes furthermore prevents states from jeopardising negotiations. A peaceful settlement and direct negotiations were however hampered from the start both in Syria and Libya, as I have shown elsewhere.[15] Negotiations with the incumbent leaders were hindered and some states were refused the opportunity to contribute to a durable TG-based solution. Moreover, the Syrian and Libyan oppositional TA received considerable support from contact groups. Because both oppositional TA clearly had a state transformation agenda, the extensive support given to them, without (in itself) amounting to forcible intervention, arguably constituted a *coercive* measure.

But let us assume now for a moment that states did do their best to abide by the obligations of cooperation and negotiation – but that the collective reactions – non-recognition, cooperation and peaceful settlement – failed? What if a multilateral response to *ius cogens* violations and direct negotiations had been actively pursued but all initiatives turned out to be unfruitful? Could states, following such failed attempts, have legitimately induced an oppositional transition on their own initiative against Syria and Libya as they were violating *ius cogens*?

This question is largely irrelevant for the cases just mentioned in light of the conclusion I just summarised here, that is that prior compulsory steps were disregarded by the relevant contact groups.[16] For other (present or future) cases, it remains relevant however to examine whether,

---

[15] E. De Groof, 'First Things First: R2P Starts with Direct Negotiations', op. cit. See also J. Pospisil, 'Peacebuilding and Principled Pragmatism', op. cit., p. 20.
[16] E. De Groof, 'First Things First: R2P Starts with Direct Negotiations', op. cit., pp. 30–48.

342   INDIRECT REGIME CHANGE

provided all prior compulsory steps were exhausted, external actors may apply coercive measures intended to curb the state apparatus, and to facilitate a transition toward a stable and law-abiding government. This is why, in Section B, we shall ask whether, in the absence of any fruitful multilateral response to *ius cogens* violations, states may unilaterally induce oppositional TG against states persevering in violating *ius cogens*. The following Table 10.1 outlines the argument for the remainder of this final chapter.

B   As a Last Resort, Inducing Oppositional Transitions As a Non-Forcible Countermeasure?

Can states, acting individually or in group format, trigger TG as a response to *ius cogens* violations if multilateral institutions remain inactive or are paralysed? We saw in Chapter 9 that indirect regime change is, in principle, forbidden under international law because eventually it aims at reconfiguring the constitutional order of the target state through TG. This still directly affects the heart of a state's *domaine réservé*. Furthermore, in the previous section we concluded that if states wish to halt gross and persistent breaches of *ius cogens*, they must exhaust the available multilateral fora and respond through collective non-recognition; multilateral cooperation; and peaceful settlement including by directly negotiating with the regime committing these breaches.

But what if collective steps fail? Expecting the UN to swiftly react to incumbent governments violating *ius cogens* has proven to be unrealistic.[17]

---

[17] In 1987, Gaja wrote, when commenting the *Barcelona Traction Case*: '[t]he Court thus identified obligations existing towards the international community as a whole with obligations existing towards all States, which possess corresponding "rights". The lack of distinction on the part of the Court between these obligations finds some justification in the present state of (lack of) organisation in international society. Moreover, it would make little sense to say that an obligation existed if the corresponding rights could be exercised by all the other States only jointly: this would never take place in practice'. G. Gaja, 'Obligations *Erga Omnes*, International Crimes and *Jus Cogens*: A Tentative Analysis of Three Related Concepts', op. cit., p. 152. Cf. also C. Leben, 'Les contre-mesures inter-étatiques et les réactions à l'illicite dans la société internationale', *Annuaire français de droit international*, Vol. 28, 1982, p 76 : 'le caractère aléatoire de la mise en jeu du mécanisme de la responsabilité internationale, et la faiblesse des garanties offertes par les organisations internationales, ne peuvent *que* pousser les Etats à adopter par eux-mêmes les mesures assurant une certaine répression de ce qu'ils considèrent être des violations flagrantes du droit international'. Own emphasis and translation: 'the random nature of how international responsibility is applied, and the weak guarantees offered by international organisations in this regard, can *only* lead States to adopt measures by themselves to ensure a level of repression of what they consider to be flagrant

Table 10.1 *Limits to the inducement of oppositional TG in response to a* ius cogens-*violating state*

	Non-coercive steps which must precede the coercive unilateral inducement of oppositional TG		Coercive yet non-forcible unilateral inducement of oppositional TG
Level external involvement	Multilateral (preponderance UN security system) ➔ *Section A 'Obligation of cooperation and peaceful settlement'*	Unilateral (last resort) ➔ *Section B 'As a last resort, inducing oppositional transitions as a non-forcible countermeasure?'*	

Compulsory steps	Obligation of multilateral reaction:
	▪ Non-recognition & non-assistance
	▪ Cooperation
	   o UNSC/UNGA
	   o Include interested state(s)
	▪ Direct negotiations with incumbent leader
		▪ Provide hard evidence of *ius cogens* violations
		▪ Defend liberal interpretation of non-performance requirement
		▪ Abide by procedural safeguards:
		   o Responsibilisation
		   o Notification
		   o Negotiation
		▪ Choice of oppositional TA in conformity with *ius in interregno*
			Reversibility requirement: retract support to oppositional TA if:
			▪ a *ius cogens*-violating state resumes obligations
			▪ Oppositional TA does not abide by lowest common denominator under *ius in interregno*

Stage of transition process	Pre-transition		Transition following 'external empowerment' (political, diplomatic and/or economic support)

Would states have the *possibility* to react at their own discretion?[18] Can an oppositional transition be induced as a coercive measure outside the UN system, by states acting unilaterally or within contact groups? Can they coercively impose oppositional TG upon a state that is unwilling and unable to rectify *ius cogens*-violating behaviour once the multilateral system is deadlocked? The repeated inability of the multilateral collective security system to react in such contexts begs the question whether the prima facie unlawfulness of unilaterally and coercively induced oppositional TG can be *cured* by one of the so-called 'circumstances precluding the wrongfulness of conduct that would otherwise not be in conformity with the international obligations of the State concerned'. These circumstances are articulated in the ILC's DASR, which are generally accepted as customary law.[19]

Turning our attention to the DASR and the 'circumstances precluding wrongfulness' is not intended to artificially bring grist to the mill of actors trying to justify indirect regime change or to condone this practice even when it is unilaterally and coercively applied. The intention is, on the contrary, to expose the strict limits to their powers, and to provide an argumentative toolbox also for states claiming to be the *victim* of indirect regime change. The conditions curing unlawfulness indeed expose the legal constraints on indirect regime change even when it is applied in the extreme context of *ius cogens* violations. The goal of this chapter is thus to expose a formal, self-referential *argumentarium* to facilitate legal debate about indirect regime change in such contexts.

---

violations of international law'. In the same sense, J. A. Frowein, 'Die Verpflichtungen erga omnes im Völkerrecht und ihre Durchsetzung' in R. Bernhardt, W. K. Geck, G. Jaenicke, H. Steinberger (eds.), *Völkerrecht als Rechtsordnung, Internationale Gerichtsbarkeit, Menschenrechte*, op. cit., p. 253: 'in neuster Zeit [hat] die Erkenntnis, dass das Sanktionssystem der Vereinten Nationen weithin funktionsunfähig ist, dazu geführt, dass Drittstaaten bei Verstößen gegen grundlegende Normen der Völkerrechtsordnung wie der Gefährdung des Friedens auch rechtliche Reaktionen prüfen und teilweise zur Anwendung bringen'. Own translation: 'recently, the recognition that the United Nations sanctioning system is largely inoperative has led third countries to consider and, in part, apply legal responses to breaches of fundamental norms of international law such as the threat to peace'.

[18] It is assumed that the obligation of cooperation, even in the face of *ius cogens* violations, cannot *oblige* states to take countermeasures. Cf. C. Hillgruber, 'The Right of Third States to Take Countermeasures', op cit., pp. 292–3.

[19] They can also constitute a basis for a 'theorisation-within-the-law enterprise' (as introduced in Introduction, Section C.2). In a similar sense, D. J. Bederman, 'Counterintuiting Countermeasures', *The American Journal of International Law*, 96, no. 4, October 1, 2002, p. 823.

A LAST RESORT?

I shall argue that, both in theory and in practice, it is virtually impossible to cure the unlawfulness of unilaterally and coercively induced oppositional TG. Legally speaking, an extremely small but strictly regulated possibility remains however to this effect. Stringently regulated, this practice can only very seldom be applied as its legality will depend on a conscientious assessment of facts, a scrupulous abidance with procedures, and the selection of a law-abiding inchoate oppositional TA. A duty of strict restraint thus applies. Unless states and IO rigorously play by the book, lawfully inducing oppositional TG outside of the multilateral context will remain rather theoretical: the probability that all conditions and procedures to which we will turn in a moment are respected, is indeed very low.

The DASR set out six 'circumstances precluding wrongfulness'.[20] Only the third circumstance – countermeasures – is relevant.[21] Countermeasures are 'measures that would otherwise be contrary to the international obligations of an injured State vis-à-vis the responsible State, if they were not taken by the former in response to an internationally wrongful act by the latter in order to procure cessation and reparation'.[22] Only if inducing oppositional TG can be framed as a countermeasure, its unlawfulness can be cured.[23]

---

[20] The six circumstances are: consent (art. 20); self-defence (art. 21); countermeasures in respect of an internationally wrongful act (art. 22); *force majeure* (art. 23); distress (art. 24); and necessity (art. 25).

[21] A note about the irrelevance of other 'circumstances precluding wrongfulness'. The first of these circumstances – consent – is not pertinent because the inducement of oppositional TG is applied without the consent of the target state. The second circumstance – self-defence – is not relevant either because only non-forcible measures in relation to TG are analysed in this book. The fourth circumstance – *force majeure* – is incompatible with the policy of inducing oppositional TG, which is based on the premise of *deliberate* support to an oppositional TA. The fifth – distress – exonerates the state (actor) that has 'no other reasonable way, in a situation of distress, of saving its life', a scenario manifestly irrelevant for our analysis. The sixth – necessity – is very restrictive; it can only be invoked when it is 'the only way for the State to safeguard an essential interest against a grave and imminent peril', a justification that is not relevant either for this analysis.

[22] DASR, Commentaries to Chapter II.

[23] Without going into detail, P. Thielbörger just points to the fact that the countermeasure framework can be relevant in this regard: 'Befinden sich also Staaten automatisch im Bruch des Völkerrechts, wenn sie Oppositionsbewegungen als "Vertreter eines Volkes" oder gar als "neue Regierung" anerkennen, ohne dass die dafür aufgezeigten Voraussetzungen gegeben sind? Die Frage ist grundsätzlich zu bejahen. ... *Es stellt sich stets die Frage der Rechtfertigung*'. P. Thielbörger, 'Die Anerkennung oppositionneller Gruppen in den Fällen Libyen (2011) und Syrien (2012)', op. cit., p. 41. Own emphasis. Own free translation: 'are states automatically violating international law when they recognise opposition movements as "representative of the people" or even as "new

In line with the primacy of the UN security system, recourse to countermeasures constitutes a *subsidiary* means for sanctioning unlawful behaviour,[24] which should only be considered when the UNSC (or the UNGA under the Uniting for Peace resolution allowing it to act when the UNSC is deadlocked) is unable to take effective measures.[25] Moreover,

> unilateral coercive measures taken for the purpose of overthrowing foreign governments or for imposing a certain political system *must be treated with caution*. This is because states must not be given an opportunity to abuse the law on countermeasures by using them as a mechanism for imposing their values on the rest of the world. Countermeasures must then be applied only after the *most stringent conditions* are met.[26]

The verification of these strict conditions depends on two separate analyses. First, can the countermeasure framework offer a theoretical basis for this practice (1)? Second, can this practice be applied in conformity with the relevant substantive and procedural prerequisites for taking countermeasures? This includes the question whether this practice must be qualified, that is what type of oppositional TA it may envisage (2). After addressing these questions, we shall conclude that coercing indirect regime change is subject to very strict conditions, and therefore rather unlikely to be carried out lawfully (3).

1 Thin Theoretical Compatibility: Indirect Regime Change by Solidarity Countermeasure

Responding to supposed illegality potentially forms the conceptual link between applying countermeasures and coercing indirect regime change. Countermeasures aim to restore a legal relationship interrupted by

---

government" if the necessary preconditions for this are not fulfilled? Fundamentally, the question must be answered affirmatively. *But the question of the circumstance precluding wrongfulness is still there'*.

[24] J. Verhoeven, *Droit international public*, op. cit., p. 662: 'si favorable que l'on soit aux contre-mesures, celles-ci devraient être tenues pour illicites lorsqu'elles sont décidées en violation des dispositions arrêtées par les Nations unies … ou sans qu'aient été préalablement utilisés les mécanismes de sanction organisés dans ces cadres. Si "police" unilatérale il faut admettre, ce n'est jamais que lorsqu'il est établi que la sanction collective n'est pas ou ne peut pas être efficace'.

[25] In the same sense, P.-M. Dupuy, 'The Deficiencies of the Law of State Responsibility Relating to Breaches of "Obligations Owed to the International Community as a Whole": Suggestions for Avoiding the Obsolescence of Aggravated Responsibility', op. cit., p. 211.

[26] E. K. Proukaki, *Countermeasures, The Non-Injured State and the Idea of International Community*, Routledge Research in International Law, 2010, p. 178. Own emphasis.

A LAST RESORT? 347

unlawful behaviour. Similarly, inducing oppositional TG is mostly framed as a corrective measure, as a response to non-compliance. The endorsement of the Syrian and Libyan oppositional TA, for instance, was framed as such.[27] External actors have then pointed their finger at unlawful behaviour by the incumbent. These examples suggest that the rationale behind inducing oppositional TG can often be reconciled with the ratio legis of countermeasures. Whether countermeasures constitute a sound theoretical basis for inducing oppositional TG however depends not only on the occurrence of unlawful acts (*ex hypothesi* breaches of *ius cogens*) (1.1) but also on the position of the injured state (1.2).

1.1 Prior Unlawfulness: Need for Substantiation

Countermeasures can only be applied in response to prior wrongful acts. Actors seeking to induce oppositional TG as a countermeasure must *substantiate* this.[28] Without proven allegations of prior unlawful conduct, any countermeasure is out of place.[29] Anticipatory countermeasures are excluded.[30] Pre-emptively endorsing oppositional TA is thus in any event forbidden. The countermeasures framework is therefore of no avail when indirect regime change is founded exclusively on grounds unrelated to allegations of unlawful conduct. Triggering TG to secure economic advantages or to see political ideologies implemented, or as a response solely to alleged 'illegitimacy' or 'undemocratic behaviour', is insufficient. Collective responses to *ius cogens* violations cannot be framed as issues of 'legitimacy' or 'democracy', concepts which, taken in isolation, have no legal weight or consequence.[31]

---

[27] Chapter 9, Section A.

[28] 'A fundamental prerequisite for any lawful countermeasure is the existence of an internationally wrongful act which injured the state taking the countermeasure', DASR, commentary to art. 49.

[29] In these cases, the non-intervention principle would be the principal legal point of reference to interpret the practice of coercively inducing oppositional TG in legal terms.

[30] DASR, comment 4 to art. 49.1. O. Y. Elagab, *The Legality of Non-Forcible Counter-Measures in International Law*, Clarendon Press, 1988, pp. 52–3.

[31] In the same sense, in relation to Libya, J. Vidmar, 'Democracy and Regime Change in the Post-Cold War International Law', op. cit., pp. 367 and 380: 'gross and systematic violations of human rights and the grave humanitarian situation ... triggered a collective response and denial of governmental legitimacy to Gaddafi'. Also, international reactions in the cases of Southern Rhodesia (1965), the Homelands (1976–1982), Northern Cyprus (1974) and Kuwait (1990) 'were not about democracy'. J. Vidmar, 'Human Rights, Democracy and the Legitimacy of Governments in International Law: Practice of States and UN Organs', op. cit., p. 59. Similarly, the violation of human rights, fundamental freedoms and the right to self-determination were invoked against the Ian Smith government, not (just) general considerations of legitimacy. V. Gowlland-Debbas,

The substantiation of prior unlawfulness on the basis of *ius cogens* breaches provides a benchmark (and a rather solid one, for that matter, even if standards of proof are variably applied)[32] against which the inducement of oppositional TG is to be justified. On the basis of that condition alone, the possibility of lawfully inducing oppositional TG as a coercive measure is already significantly reduced. There is a conceptual but also evidentiary distinction between unlawfulness, especially when violations of *ius cogens* are concerned, and 'undemocratic' or 'illegitimate' governmental behaviour. In contrast with the indeterminate threshold for substantiating such behaviour, providing proof of *ius cogens* violations is highly demanding.

Actors resorting to countermeasures must thus prove their right to do so (*actori incumbit probatio*), and there should not be the slightest doubt about the commission of internationally wrongful acts.[33] Indeed, 'a State which resorts to countermeasures based on its unilateral assessment of the situation does so at its own risk and may incur responsibility for its own wrongful conduct in the event of an incorrect assessment'.[34] In addition, it is not sufficient for legally injured states to invoke *any* sort of unlawful behaviour. Unless they are directly injured by the 'target state', they must argue they are victims *de iure* of violations of *ius cogens* norms, which, being accepted and recognised by the international community as a whole, are valid *erga omnes*. The reason why external actors considering inducing oppositional TG would be well-advised to build their argument along these lines will be explained now.

Collective Responses to Illegal Acts in International Law: United Nations Action in the Question of Southern Rhodesia, op. cit., p. 203.

[32] The notification itself should be accompanied by the (substantiated) allegation that the responsible state is responsible indeed, and, what is more, has transgressed *erga omnes* obligations. It cannot be analysed here in light of which standards of proof, violations of *erga omnes* obligations are to be (independently and/or multilaterally?) established. The idea has already been voiced to establish an international 'Commission of Inquiry', i.e. an 'international non-judicial oversight mechanism' to monitor the respect for *ius cogens* norms on human rights. A. Cassese, 'A Plea for a Global Community Grounded in a Core of Human Rights' in A. Cassese (ed.), *Realising Utopia*, op. cit., pp. 141–2.

[33] J. A. Frowein, 'Die Verpflichtungen erga omnes im Völkerrecht und ihre Durchsetzung' in R. Bernhardt, W. K. Geck, G. Jaenicke, H. Steinberger (eds.), *Völkerrecht als Rechtsordnung, Internationale Gerichtsbarkeit, Menschenrechte*, op. cit., pp. 258–9.

[34] DASR, commentary to art. 49. Own emphasis. In the same sense, O. Y. Elagab, *The Legality of Non-Forcible Counter-Measures in International Law*, op. cit., p. 62.

A LAST RESORT? 349

1.2 The *De Iure* Injured State and Solidarity Countermeasures

> An injured State may only take countermeasures against a State which is responsible for an internationally wrongful act in order to induce that State to comply with its obligations.[35]

At first sight, this article reads as a one-on-one issue. This provision includes both an 'active identity requirement', regarding the identity of the state entitled to take countermeasures (the injured state) and a 'passive identity requirement' regarding the identity of the state against which the countermeasure is directed (the wrongdoer). The 'passive identity requirement' is linked to a self-evident but fundamental precondition for applying countermeasures: prior unlawfulness,[36] which we have just discussed.

What about the active identity requirement? Is only the directly injured state allowed to take countermeasures? This question is relevant to the extent that inducing oppositional TG (1) can be done collectively, for example by contact groups, in which case there is not always a direct (tangible) relationship between all members of the contact group and the state deemed to have committed an internationally wrongful act; (2) is framed as a response to *ius cogens* violations taking place *within* a state's territory, in which case there is no directly injured state. Without being directly and tangibly injured, a state can claim to be injured only in one scenario: when it is the victim of *erga omnes* norms, which *ius cogens* norms are per definition.[37] The community of states as a whole has an interest in their compliance.

Can a state, without being tangibly injured, then take remedial action by resorting to so-called solidarity countermeasures? The issue of solidarity countermeasures is controverted. Yet, framing indirect regime change through TG as a solidarity countermeasure seems the only way

---

[35] DASR, art. 49.1.

[36] In short, the countermeasure framework can only be invoked if the state(s) or organisation(s) seeking to legally justify the coercive inducement of oppositional TG can substantiate that they proceed as such in response to an internationally wrongful act.

[37] Because the injury resulting from violations of *erga omnes/ius cogens* obligations is only of a legal nature, the terms 'non-injured state' for designating the legally-but-not-materially-injured state do not seem to be adequate. It has therefore been argued that 'a different term for designating the state or states affected by the violation of an *erga omnes/ius cogens* obligation should be introduced'. K. Zemanek, 'New Trends in the Enforcement of *Erga Omnes* Obligations', *Max Planck UNYB*, 4, 2000, p. 29.

350 INDIRECT REGIME CHANGE

to legally justify it. By exploring this line of reasoning, I will attempt to imagine how states intending to induce oppositional TG may try to legitimise their action. This is not a more or less cynical exercise in condoning indirect regime change. Quite on the contrary, the following paragraphs allow us to detect how the endorsement of oppositional TG is to be legally limited.

1.2.1 Solidarity Countermeasures The countermeasure framework '*does not prejudice* the right of any State, entitled under article 48, § 1 [regarding *erga omnes* obligations], to invoke the responsibility of another State, to take lawful measures against that State to ensure cessation of the breach and reparation in the interest of the injured State or of the beneficiaries of the obligation breached'.[38] When referring to this 'savings clause', the ILC, in 2001, observed that 'the current state of international law on countermeasures taken in the general or collective interest is *uncertain*',[39] adding that this matter should be left to the further development of international law. In the literature, the savings clause has seldom been considered as an impediment in this regard.[40] Yet, even those who intend to justify oppositional TG as a solidarity countermeasure must recognise that such measures are controversial for two reasons:[41] a policy reason, related to a risk of abuse; and grounds related to the classical 'bilateralist' approach to international law.

From a policy perspective, solidarity countermeasures touch upon a difficult balance: the line between sheriff behaviour and anarchy.[42]

---

[38] DASR, art. 54. Own emphasis.

[39] DASR, comments 6 and 8 to art. 54. Own emphasis.

[40] Faced with the ILC's inconclusive observation, Bederman posits that, ironically, the savings clause might represent the 'most significant act of indirect progressive development among the countermeasure clauses', and continues: 'a savings clause that notionally makes no law is actually intended to induce significant state practice and is expected to tend toward the progressive development that will be achieved through time'. D. J. Bederman, 'Counterintuiting Countermeasures', op. cit., pp. 827–8. For another commentator, the savings clause must be seen as confirming the existence of solidarity countermeasures. A. Bird, 'Third State Responsibility for Human Right Violations', *EJIL*, Vol. 21, no. 4, 2011, p. 896.

[41] Cf. for a discussion, A. Orakhelashvili, *Peremptory Norms in International Law*, Oxford University Press, 2006, pp. 270–2. Against solidarity countermeasures, cf. B. Conforti, A. Labella, *An Introduction to International Law*, op. cit., pp. 127–8.

[42] P.-M. Dupuy, 'The Deficiencies of the Law of State Responsibility Relating to Breaches of "Obligations Owed to the International Community as a Whole": Suggestions for Avoiding the Obsolescence of Aggravated Responsibility' in A. Cassese (ed.), *Realising Utopia*, op. cit., pp. 210–26.

An over-use of such measures could lead to abuse, a might-makes-right context, and the 'risk that some states will use a norm violation as a pretext for engaging in predatory behaviour'.[43] At the same time, external actors envisaging to induce oppositional TG may argue that a blunt rejection of such measures creates the risk that, in a world without a central sanctioning mechanism, violations of *erga omnes* norms would go unsanctioned, leading to anarchy.

Solidarity countermeasures defy the classical, bilateralist, conception of international law. Some consider them to epitomise the evolution 'from bilateralism to community interests' in international law.[44] External actors envisaging coercing indirect regime change may agree, thus would contest that solidarity countermeasures should be ignored just because they allegedly defy classical conceptions of international law.[45] One can actually go back to the seventeenth century to find support for the application of solidarity countermeasures.[46] Moreover, whenever a directly injured state is missing, the bilateralist position would lead to the ineffectiveness of primary rules assorted with *erga omnes* effects protecting the state's citizenry,[47] so they may argue.

1.2.2 Countermeasures in Case of *Ius Cogens* Violations Since the DASR were adopted, leaving the issue of solidarity countermeasures open for further development, a wealth of scholarship, with ample reference to state practice, has confirmed their relevance. In 2005, the IDI stated that all states to which *erga omnes* obligations are owed 'are

---

[43] A. Posner, 'Erga Omnes Norms, Institutionalization, and Constitutionalism in International Law', U. of Chicago Law & Economics, Online Working Paper No. 419.

[44] B. Simma, 'From Bilateralism to Community Interest in International Law', *RdC*, 250, 1994.

[45] See also the dissenting opinion of Judge Weeramantry in the *Case Concerning East Timor*, *a contrario*: '[i]f a direct obligation-right relation existed between Australia and East Timor, there would seem to be no need for the existence of a legal interest on the part of other States in the observance of the obligation *erga omnes* to respect the right of peoples to self-determination'. Cf. also P. Picone, 'Le reazioni collettive ad un illecito *erga omnes* in assenza di uno Stato individualmente leso', *Comunità internazionale e obblighi 'erga omnes' - studi critici di diritto internazionale*, Jovene Editore, 2013, p. 627.

[46] J. I. Charney, 'Third State Remedies in International Law', op. cit., p. 61.

[47] G. Gaja, 'Obligations *Erga Omnes*, International Crimes and *Jus Cogens*: A Tentative Analysis of Three Related Concepts', Walter de Gruyter, 1989, p. 155: 'Let us assume that in the case of an infringement of human rights, no State may seek a reparation or adopt a countermeasure: does this not mean that an obligation exists, whose violation is automatically condoned? Does this not convey the impression that the term "obligation" is misused, because States are practically free to ignore the rule imposing it?'.

entitled to take non-forcible countermeasures' should a widely acknowledged grave breach of such obligations occur.[48] Scholars have argued that, according to current law, the violation of *erga omnes* rules justifies the resort to countermeasures,[49] and that, based on extensive state practice, customary law would now recognise the right to take solidarity countermeasures.[50] All of this is grist to the mill for external actors intending to induce oppositional TG in such contexts.

Several authors consider, however, that solidarity countermeasures can only be taken in response to large-scale or systematic breaches of *erga omnes* norms. In spite of the inconclusive ICJ jurisprudence,[51] states have confirmed that they accept such countermeasures 'in specific disputes involving serious breaches of obligations *erga omnes*'.[52] Simma for example defends the validity of solidarity countermeasures, at least in reaction to violations of gross and persistent breaches of human rights.[53] External actors intending to induce oppositional TG may thus argue that, especially if this threshold requirement is taken into account, the initial scepticism regarding

---

[48] Id., art. 5. It is furthermore noted that 'measures designed to ensure the collective protection of human rights are particularly justified when taken in response to especially grave violations of these rights, notably large-scale or systematic violations, as well as those infringing rights that cannot be derogated from in any circumstances'.

[49] E. K. Proukaki, *Countermeasures, The Non-Injured State and the Idea of International Community*, op. cit., pp. 204–8.

[50] Id., p. 202: 'during the discussions in the ILC there was *never a general or strong opposition to the concept [of solidarity measures]* with many states providing their support for the recognition of the right of states not directly injured to exercise unilateral coercive peaceful measures for inducing the wrongdoer to comply with its international obligations'. Own emphasis.

[51] The ICJ neither supports nor excludes solidarity countermeasures. Cf. however the rejection of the *actio popularis* in international law in the South West Africa cases (*Ethiopia v. South Africa*; *Liberia v. South Africa*), Second Phase, ICJ Reports 1966, p. 6.

[52] C. J. Tams, *Enforcing Obligations Erga Omnes in International Law*, op. cit., p. 250. Cf. also p. 230: "as regards the types of breaches prompting countermeasures, States have not responded against isolated or minor violations, but only if the previous breach had assumed considerable proportions. Although an exact threshold is difficult to establish, it seems fair to say that countermeasures were taken in response to large-scale or systematic breaches". V. Gowlland-Debbas, 'The Limits of Unilateral Enforcement of Community Objectives in the Framework of UN Peace Maintenance', *EJIL*, Vol. 11, No. 2, 2000, p. 378.

[53] B. Simma, P. Alston, 'The Sources of Human Rights Law: Custom, *Jus Cogens*, and General Principles', op. cit., p. 87: 'the existence of [a wide range of customary law obligations] would probably entitle all States – not just the parties to human rights treaties *inter se* – to apply remedies or countermeasures at least in cases of gross and persistent breaches of such obligations'.

A LAST RESORT? 353

the validity of solidarity countermeasures in response to *ius cogens* violations has been waning.

*

The above suggests that solidarity countermeasures may arguably be taken in response to *ius cogens* violations. It seems however that such measures only form a thin and fragile theoretical basis for coercing indirect regime change. Abidance by strict criteria is required as inducing oppositional TG is conditioned on the systematic, gross and persistent violations of *ius cogens* by the incumbent; the substantiation that these violations have actually occurred; and the inactivity of the UN institutional framework in the face of these violations. Respecting these pre-conditions is necessary but not sufficient for taking solidarity countermeasures so as to cease *ius cogens* violations. The question remains *under which additional conditions and procedures* they may do so, and whether executing them is practically feasible.

2 Thin Practical Compatibility: Compliance with Stringent Conditions

If states successfully argue that an oppositional TG may be imposed as *ultimum remedium*, they would still need to ensure that such a remedy be practically consistent with the relevant procedures and prerequisites. What are the concrete implications of legitimising external support to oppositional TG as a countermeasure? Countermeasure prerequisites consist of procedural and substantive conditions. Procedural conditions inform us as to specific procedures that must be followed *before* countermeasures are taken, and comprise the prerequisites of 'responsibilisation', 'notification' and 'negotiation'. Substantive conditions inform us as to what kind of countermeasures can be taken; they include the 'non-performance', 'reversibility' and 'proportionality' prerequisites. The following paragraphs explain why procedural (2.1) and substantive (2.2) prerequisites apply to solidarity countermeasures.

2.1 Procedural Prerequisites and Their Preponderance

External actors can induce oppositional TG as a last resort measure in response to *ius cogens* violations provided they respect a number of procedural prerequisites. They must 'call upon the responsible State ...

354 INDIRECT REGIME CHANGE

to fulfil its obligations'[54] and 'notify the responsible State of any decision to take countermeasures', and 'offer to negotiate with that State'. In short, they must respect the procedural prerequisites of *responsibilisation, notification* and *negotiation.*[55]

The requirement that countermeasures must be preceded by procedural safeguards has a long history. As far back as 1650, prior demand for redress was a precondition for resorting to countermeasures.[56] Throughout the eighteenth century, this continued to be the case.[57] Also for nineteenth century scholars, countermeasures 'had to be preceded by a prior demand'.[58] In 1840 Great Britain thus addressed 'a warning to Sicily that reprisals would be taken against her within a week' if Sicily would continue violating a bilateral treaty.[59] In 1850, Great Britain addressed a similar warning against Greece if demands for compensation were not met.[60] In 1934, the IDI confirmed the requirement of prior notification before taking countermeasures.[61] State practice, doctrine and jurisprudence until 1945 indicates that the resort to countermeasures had to be preceded by a demand for

[54] DASR, art. 52.1.a.
[55] DASR, art. 52.1.b. Cf. also R. Quadri, *Diritto Internazionale Pubblico*, op. cit., p. 269: 'il ricorso alla rappresaglia deve presentarsi come necessario. Dovrà normalmente essere preceduto da una protesta e, ove possibile, da negoziati diretti a stabilire il fondamento della protesta e delle richieste di riparazione e soddisfazione con essa avanzate. *Potrà dunque aver luogo solo quando la richiesta di risarcimento del danno o di soddisfazione sia rimasta infruttuosa'*. Own emphasis and free translation: 'the recourse to countermeasures must be necessary. It should be preceded by a protest and, where possible, by negotiations aimed both at remedying the situation which led to the protest and at obtaining reparation and satisfaction. *It can therefore take place only when the request for compensation or satisfaction was unsuccessful'*.
[56] O. Y. Elagab, *The Legality of Non-Forcible Counter-Measures in International Law*, op. cit., p. 10, citing R. G. Marsden, *Documents Relating to Law and Custom of the Sea, 1649–1767*, Vol. ii, 1916, pp. 7–8. Thus, the reprisals taken in 1650 by Great Britain against France were ordered after 'all fair courses have been taken and observed . . . in seeking and demanding redresse and reparation, yet none could be obteyned' (sic).
[57] Id., pp. 10–11. For a brief historical overview, see D. Gaurier, *Histoire du droit international – De l'Antiquité a la création de l'ONU*, op. cit., pp. 696–700.
[58] O. Y. Elagab, *The Legality of Non-Forcible Counter-Measures in International Law*, op. cit., p. 16.
[59] Id., p. 20.
[60] Id., p. 21.
[61] IDI resolution on the 'Régime des représailles en temps de paix', Paris 1934: 'dans l'exercise des représailles, l'Etat doit . . . [m]ettre au préalable l'Etat auteur de l'acte illicite en demeure de le faire cesser et d'accorder éventuellement les réparations requises'. Own free translation: 'when applying countermeasures the State must first notify the State author of the unlawful act and formally demand that it stop the unlawful act and grant any necessary repairs'.

A LAST RESORT?

reparation.[62] After 1945, this was confirmed in international jurisprudence[63] and state practice.[64]

Taken as a last resort measure and as a response to *ius cogens* violations, coercing indirect regime change must be reconciled with these procedural safeguards. Reflecting on the role of solidarity countermeasures in the international order, Koskenniemi suggested that such procedural safeguards are not always available: 'a legally circumscribed solidarity measure should be taken in accordance with international procedures, principles of due process, transparency, and the possibility of administrative or perhaps judicial review. *If those are not available*, the redefinition of a political process as a law-applying process presents more problems than it solves'.[65] Although less exhaustively and thoroughly than what Koskenniemi proposes, the DASR do however refer to specific procedural prerequisites which, long before their adoption in 2001, already had quite some pedigree.

Procedural prerequisites applicable to countermeasures, generally, also apply to *solidarity* countermeasures, specifically.[66] Ignoring the procedural and substantive safeguards when solidarity measures are concerned would leave the door wide open for abuse, and would be contrary to the ILC's cautious approach on the matter. As the DASR do not preclude the right of states to take lawful measures against states breaching *ius cogens*, that right surely must be exercised in accordance with the prerequisites applicable to countermeasures. To argue otherwise would be unsustainable even for actors intending to coerce indirect regime change.

Coercing a state into oppositional TG is not a practice that can be carried out in haste. The offer (and acceptance) of diplomatic, political, material and/or financial support to empower oppositional TA requires

---

[62] O. Y. Elagab, *The Legality of Non-Forcible Counter-Measures in International Law*, op. cit., p. 36.

[63] Naulilaa Incident Case, 1929, Annual Digest, Vol. 4, 1927–8, case no. 179, p. 274; RIAA, Vol. ii, 1949, p. 1013; Case Concerning the Air Service Agreement of 27 March 1946, 1978, ILR, Vol. 54, 1979, p. 304; Case Concerning United States Diplomatic and Consular Staff in Tehran (Judgment), ICJ Reports, 1980, p. 3.

[64] For a discussion, see O. Y. Elagab, *The Legality of Non-Forcible Counter-Measures in International Law*, op. cit., pp. 69–76.

[65] M. Koskenniemi, 'Solidarity Measures: State Responsibility as a New International Order?', *British Yearbook of International Law*, Vol. 72, no.1, 2001, p. 355. Own emphasis.

[66] This may be contested on a restrictive, textual interpretation. The savings clause under art. 54 about 'measures' (rather than countermeasures) 'taken by states other than an injured state' does not *explicitly* refer to the conditions applicable to countermeasures, which some may thus consider not to be applicable to solidarity countermeasures.

time and coordination. This excludes inducing oppositional TG as an urgent measure,[67] and makes the following exception redundant. The procedural prerequisites of responsibilisation, notification and (proposed) negotiation need *not* be applied in case of extreme urgency.[68] But as TG cannot unfold in haste and urgency cannot be invoked, the exception becomes irrelevant. In other words, said procedural prerequisites apply in any event. Quite surprisingly, the preponderance of procedural prerequisites has rarely been emphasised, although, as a solitary voice observes, 'the primacy thrust of these provisions is to superimpose procedural values of rectitude and transparency on states' assessments of countermeasure options'.[69]

Inducing oppositional TG may therefore only be considered after all procedural prerequisites have been duly complied with. The passage of time allows for the compliance with the requirements of responsibilisation, notification and (proposed) negotiation. The procedural requirements, applicable by default, thus gain considerable legal weight. As a result of the time-consuming nature of coercing indirect regime change, such requirements are, without exception, legally compulsory. Concretely, before even *considering* inducing oppositional TG, external actors must:

- Call upon the responsible state to fulfil its obligations;
- Notify their intention to endorse oppositional TG;
- Propose to negotiate with the responsible state.

If the responsible state resumes its obligations in response to these steps, external actors cannot proceed with inducing oppositional TG.[70] The obligatory notification functions as a last reminder. For the future, one commentator suggested that the specifics of this *mise en demeure* be

---

[67] DASR, art. 52 § 2: 'the injured state may take such urgent countermeasures as are necessary to preserve its rights', notwithstanding the requirements of notification and negotiation.

[68] Id., art. 4. Own emphasis: '*except in case of extreme urgency*, the State perpetrating the violation shall be formally requested to desist before the measures are taken'.

[69] D. J. Bederman, 'Counterintuiting Countermeasures', *The American Journal of International Law* 96, no. 4 October 1, 2002, p. 819. Bederman pertinently adds that 'the central conceptual mission of the countermeasure provisions [is] the search for a polite international society' (id., p. 819), and that these provisions are 'largely framed in terms of what might be called "international legal process"' (id., pp. 822–23) and are 'intended to marginally restrain atavistic state behavior' (id., p. 824). Throughout the article, Bederman emphasises the need for formalism in the area of countermeasures.

[70] DASR, art. 53.

A LAST RESORT?

similar to the procedure for terminating or suspending a treaty.[71] Applied to coercing indirect regime change, a notification would need to indicate why such radical measure is envisaged, and allow for a stopgap period of three months.[72] While the reason-giving requirement already exists, the introduction of a stopgap period is only a *de lege ferenda* consideration.

Under current law, the existing procedural safeguards merely aim at motivating the wrongdoer to rectify, within the briefest delays, its alleged unlawful conduct before it sees TG imposed upon itself. This confirms the *adjusting* (rather than punitive) role of external actors in the absence of a central sanction mechanism in international law.[73] The general emphasis on prior procedure is in line with the obligation to settle international disputes peacefully.[74] Inevitably, even if external actors manage to substantiate prior *ius cogens* violations and to prove the relevance and applicability of solidarity countermeasures, indirect regime change must be proceduralised. It would be difficult also for external actors who consider inducing oppositional TG to argue otherwise.

If the wrongdoer perseveres in spite of these procedural safeguards, and no commitment to a peaceful settlement can be obtained,[75] external actors could dare to argue that oppositional TG may be imposed. Such a threat should continue to pursue a law-inducement aim though.[76] In addition, mere compliance with procedural safeguards would not suffice.

---

[71] O. Y. Elagab, *The Legality of Non-Forcible Counter-Measures in International Law*, op. cit., pp. 76–7.

[72] VCLT, art. 65.1 is here paraphrased.

[73] This context explains the 'necessity for retaining non-forcible countermeasures as a means of enforcing international legal order'. O. Y. Elagab, *The Legality of Non-Forcible Counter-Measures in International Law*, op. cit., p. 214.

[74] UN Charter, art. 2.3. See also DASR, art. 50.2.a. In this sense, 'the commitment to peaceful settlement of disputes will be deemed to prevail over the right to take reprisals under customary law', O. Y. Elagab, *The Legality of Non-Forcible Counter-Measures in International Law*, op. cit., p. 165.

[75] Elagab has argued that the availability of effective international procedures for a peaceful settlement of the matter does not bar the application of countermeasures if recourse to countermeasures 'is the only feasible method for inducing the defaulting party' to accept such procedures (p. 189), 'will facilitate acceptance of third party settlement procedure' (p. 184) or is 'necessary as a means of stimulating the offending party to agree to a settlement' (p. 214). O. Y. Elagab, *The Legality of Non-Forcible Counter-Measures in International Law*, op. cit.

[76] DASR, commentary 1 to art. 49: '[c]ountermeasures are not intended as a form of punishment for wrongful conduct, but as an instrument for achieving compliance with the obligations of the responsible state'.

An intervention in a state's domestic affairs cannot be legitimised only because a number of – critical, but non-substantive – procedures are complied with. A number of substantive prerequisites must also be respected to justify indirect regime change as a last resort measure.

2.2 Substantive Prerequisites

The substantive countermeasure prerequisites are 'non-performance' (2.2.1), 'reversibility' (2.2.2) and 'proportionality' (2.2.3). We shall examine how actors intending to trigger indirect regime would argue compliance with them, and what type of TA might be endorsed (2.2.4).

2.2.1 Non-Performance

Countermeasures are limited to 'the non-performance for the time being of international obligations of the State taking the measures towards the responsible State'.[77] This 'non-performance requirement' is to be read in conjunction with the 'moderation requirement', which provides that countermeasures shall not affect obligations relating to the use of force, fundamental human rights, obligations of humanitarian character, or other peremptory norms.[78] The breach of the non-intervention principle nigh-systematically caused by indirect regime change led us to examine whether such unlawfulness could be cured by reference to countermeasures. Can the *suspension* of the non-intervention principle be justified in light of the moderation requirement? This question depends on two other parameters, namely (a) whether the principle of non-intervention is a *ius cogens* principle, in which case it would be impossible to suspend,[79] and (b) whether the 'provisional non-performance of an obligation' can be applied to the principle of non-intervention.

The non-intervention principle is not a peremptory norm *insofar as the prohibition of the use of force is not concerned*. The segment of (political, diplomatic and economic) activities relevant under the non-intervention principle, without being covered by the prohibition of the use of force, has grown over time as a result of the progressive expansion of the concept of intervention, especially since the 1970 Friendly Relations Declaration.[80]

---

[77] DASR, art. 49.2.

[78] DASR, art. 50 § 1.

[79] DASR, art. 50.

[80] 'The new and broader definition of intervention forbids not only direct military force but also indirect interference through economic, political, and diplomatic means'. P. Kunig, 'Prohibition of Intervention', MPEPIL.

A LAST RESORT?

While the prohibition of aggression is undoubtedly a *ius cogens* norm, the obligation of non-intervention, for the most part, is not. External actors intending to induce oppositional TG may thus argue that its suspension is not ruled out under the countermeasure framework, allowing them to apply solidarity countermeasures by temporarily intervening in matters within the domestic jurisdiction of a state.[81]

Can a *negative* obligation such as the principle of non-intervention be suspended? Countermeasures must indeed be 'limited to the *non-performance* for the time being of international obligations of the State taking the measures towards the responsible State'[82]? The suspension of the principle of non-intervention can only be justified if the condition of 'non-performance' ('*inexécution*') applies not only to positive obligations, for example under a bilateral treaty of commerce and friendship, but also to *proscriptions*. Granted, countermeasures are generally implemented through actions such as the freezing of assets, the suspension of trade or development relations, an embargo, the expulsion from an IO, etc. These actions relate to the non-performance of *positive* conduct. Does the countermeasure framework envisage the possibility that the execution of a negative obligation be withheld[83] or temporarily rendered inoperative?[84]

External actors intending to justify indirect regime change may think of two arguments to defend a broad interpretation of non-performance. First, the countermeasure framework is not anchored in the idea of privity or connectedness; it need not concern the suspension of the same or closely related obligations.[85] A perfect equivalence is not expected.[86] Second, the application of *solidarity* countermeasures, in particular, cannot, at the risk of becoming irrelevant, hinge on the existence of a reciprocal legal relation such as a treaty of commerce and friendship, which lends itself more easily to the termination of a positive obligation.

Although both points suggest that the non-performance requirement and the suspension of the non-intervention principle can be reconciled,

---

[81] P. Kunig, id.: '[s]elf-help against breaches of international law . . . [is] regarded as [a] valid argument[s] in favour of the admissibility of interference'.

[82] DASR, art. 49.2. Own emphasis.

[83] DASR, commentary 6 to art. 49.

[84] In this sense, cf. the Second report on State responsibility of 30 April 1999 by J. Crawford, Special Rapporteur.

[85] DASR, commentary 5 to Ch. II. Note also that in the *Gabčíkovo* case, the ICJ decided that the Czech republic had not correctly applied the countermeasure framework on the basis of a proportionality test rather than on the basis of a 'non-performance' test. Nagymaros Project, Judgment, ICJ Reports 1997, p. 7.

[86] B. Conforti, A. Labella, *An Introduction to International Law*, op. cit., p. 121.

360 INDIRECT REGIME CHANGE

this argument remains vulnerable. It is the Achilles' heel of the *argumentarium* based on the countermeasure framework. If it proves to be unsustainable, external actors cannot justify their temporary intervention in a state's domestic affairs by provoking oppositional TG as a solidarity countermeasure. This already suggests that legitimising oppositional TG under international law is far from self-evident. The legality of this practice furthermore depends on whether two other substantive prerequisites – reversibility and proportionality – can be wedded to the very idea of indirectly coercing a regime change.

2.2.2 Reversibility

The reversibility requirement is reflected in three different provisions.[87] Inducing oppositional TG must not be an irreversible step. The expectation is that 'countermeasures shall, as far as possible, be taken in such a way as to permit the resumption of performance of the obligations [of the responsible state]'.[88] Although this duty is not absolute,[89] one still wonders whether this requirement is compatible with imposing indirect regime change. Here, again, one cannot neglect the *passage of time*. Inducing oppositional TG is not a measure taken overnight.[90] Also, as was concluded above, it must be preceded by procedural safeguards. The notification procedure should leave enough time for the responsible state to adjust its behaviour. The reversibility requirement can in principle even be met *after* the wrongdoer was summoned to correct its conduct. External actors considering to induce oppositional TG may argue that this is true both from the perspective of the responsible state and external actors:

- The notification procedure or even the eminently pending endorsement of an oppositional TA does not bar the wrongdoer from resuming its obligations. On the contrary, to the extent it is applied as a deterrent or corrective rather than punitive act, it precisely instigates that state to resume its obligations.[91]
- From the moment the wrongdoer reconciles itself with the law, nothing prevents external actors from reviewing or withdrawing their

---

[87] DASR, artt. 49.3, 52.3.a, 53. The two latter provisions enshrine the obligation of termination of countermeasures when the unlawful conduct by the responsible state has ceased.

[88] DASR, art. 49.3.

[89] DASR, ILC commentary 9 to art. 49.

[90] Cf. also the overview pertaining to the support of the Syrian and Libyan oppositional TA. Chapter 9, Section A.1.

[91] J. I. Charney, 'Third State Remedies in International Law', op. cit., p. 87 a.f.

A LAST RESORT?

initial support. The often discrete representation or communication channels with oppositional TA can be suspended or closed at any time;[92] at any moment the support they received can (and sometimes must) be retracted.[93]

2.2.3 Proportionality

The proportionality requirement requires that countermeasures be 'commensurate with the injury suffered, taking into account the gravity of the internationally wrongful act and the rights in question'.[94] Proportionality concerns the legal constraints within which a certain measure is afforded.[95] Does inducing oppositional TG as a response to *ius cogens* violations withstand the proportionality test? External actors may argue that, in spite of the 'steady erosion of proportionality's indeterminacy',[96] this requirement remains quite open-ended.[97] Its application remains contingent upon two variables, one open and the other less so.

The first variable concerns the need to assess proportionality in light of the alleged unlawful conduct and of the 'importance of the issue of principle involved'.[98] The graver the unlawful conduct, the more liberty countermeasure-applying states have. There is an

> intuitive difference in the reaction to the violation of a bilateral treaty posing reciprocal rights and the reaction to a serious breach of *erga omnes* obligations. It is reasonable to suppose that in the first case the response

---

[92] For a study of discrete diplomacy on the basis of 'disguised embassies' like representative offices or front missions, special missions, and mediation, see G. Berridge, *Diplomacy: Theory and Practice*, 4th ed., Palgrave Macmillan, 2010, p. 207.

[93] This is all the more so because the inducement of oppositional TG does not amount to 'legal' governmental recognition. It is used as a flexible diplomatic tool that is not premised on permanence.

[94] DASR, art. 51.

[95] T. M. Franck, 'On Proportionality of Countermeasures in International Law', *American Journal of International Law*, Vol. 102, No. 4, October 2008, p. 765.

[96] Id.

[97] K. Zemanek, 'New Trends in the Enforcement of *Erga Omnes* Obligations', op. cit., p. 30: 'there is no mechanism for assessing the overall proportionality of conduct taken by way of "collective countermeasures"'.

[98] DASR, commentary 7 to art. 51. DASR, commentary 6 to art. 51: '[p]roportionality must be assessed taking into account not only the purely "quantitative" element of the injury suffered, but also "qualitative" factors such as the importance of the interest protected by the rule infringed and the seriousness of the breach. Article 51 relates proportionality primarily to the injury suffered but "taking into account" two further criteria: the gravity of the internationally wrongful act, and the rights in question'.

may be kept in a reciprocal withdrawal of rights, while in the second case the reaction *may pursue the aim of imposing compliance with the breached rule.*[99]

For a countermeasure to be effective there has to be a *'permissible level of escalation* in response to illegal acts'.[100] It was assumed in this chapter that the responsible state had (allegedly) engaged in *ius cogens* violations. Proportionality constraints applicable to solidarity countermeasures are then in a sense less demanding. All other things being legal, even a practice as intrusive as inducing oppositional TG, applied as *ultimum remedium* in such context, is not ruled out under the proportionality requirement, an external actor contemplating indirect regime change may contend.

The proportionality test, however, also depends on another variable, less flexible perhaps than the first, namely the nature of the oppositional TA chosen to guide the *ius cogens*-violating state through a cathartic transition. In order to withstand the proportionality test, the alternative regime must be chosen carefully and respecting the limits allowed for by *ius in interregno*, a final issue we shall consider now.

2.2.4 Qualifying the Inducement of Oppositional TG

Until now, we have not asked whether, on the assumption that all above-mentioned procedures and conditions were respected, *any sort of TG* can be externally triggered. In political speech, oppositional TA are sometimes labelled as 'legitimate partners' or 'acceptable alternatives'. But in law, criteria of legitimacy or acceptability have little weight. Can *ius in interregno* be of any assistance in framing the issue without having recourse to such concepts? For evident reasons, endorsing an oppositional transitional authority which itself is infringing *ius in interregno* is unlikely to be lawful. Would it not be absurd if, in response to *ius cogens* violations, external actors endorsed an oppositional TA which, itself, would transgress the law albeit at a lesser scale? Even if the theoretical and practical compatibility tests described above succeed, external actors could not endorse just *any* oppositional TA. In line with the obligations generally incumbent on external actors,[101] inducing oppositional TG must consist in endorsing an (oppositional) TA abiding by its own obligations.

[99] E. Cannizzaro, 'The Role of Proportionality in the Law of International Countermeasures', op. cit., p. 896. Own emphasis.

[100] D. J. Bederman, 'Counterintuiting Countermeasures', op. cit., p. 820 (citing relevant jurisprudence). Own emphasis.

[101] Chapter 8.

The acknowledgement and endorsement of oppositional TA as a coercive unilateral countermeasure must thus be qualified by virtue both of the proportionality requirement and of *ius in interregno* itself. External actors envisaging to induce oppositional TG as a coercive measure therefore have a restricted margin of manoeuvre. Their decision should be based on a conscientious assessment of the TA's compliance with the lowest common denominator of *ius in interregno*, or of reasonable prospects in this regard,[102] lest they violate the principle of self-determination.

As a result, external actors should ensure that the selected TA acts within the limits *ratione temporis* and *materiae* of the interregnum, commits to inclusivity and fulfils its fiduciary role. They should furthermore monitor the selected TA's continued abidance by its obligations, and should suspend their support if the TA, in the course of the interregnum, does not comply (anymore) with its own core obligations. Whether the endorsing state acts lawfully also depends on this assessment. More accurately, the legality of coercing oppositional TG as a response to *ius cogens* violations also hinges on a correct assessment of the selected oppositional TA's compliance with the lowest common denominator under *ius in interregno* as anchored in the principle of self-determination.

This study is concerned only with one component of self-determination: internal self-determination of the people of a state; it is neither involved with external self-determination nor with internal self-determination understood as a right to secession. We observed that this principle frames the conditions under which TG is to be pursued in conformity with international law.[103] As a multifaceted obligation mainly of conduct during the interregnum, and an obligation of result towards the end of it, it functions as an enriched reference frame for assessing whether or not TG is lawful.

External actors considering to induce oppositional TG must thus analyse whether the oppositional TA abides by the principle of internal self-determination, and embraces the idea that TG be pursued to realise this principle. If the oppositional TA does the opposite (e.g. manifestly violates the inclusivity requirement), this prevents external actors from empowering it. Indirect regime change in aid of internal self-determination bars

---

[102] When it comes to the commitment to abide by specific norms, a parallel may be drawn with the recognition of putschist governments that had pledged to organise elections. J. d'Aspremont, 'Legitimacy of Governments in the Age of Democracy', op. cit., p. 902.

[103] Part III.

external actors from installing governments which refuse to commit to a progressively inclusive transition.[104] *A fortiori*, endorsing puppet governments is out of the question.

Crucially, the temporal and substantive limitations to the interregnum entail that support to an oppositional TA should not reverberate on a long-term post-transition institutional arrangement. Emerging custom suggests that the interregnum is supposed to generate a culture of progressive inclusion, participation and representation during the process of redefining the social contract.[105] Enabling a fiduciary transition is different from defining the post-transition era.

3   Policy Implications: The Highly Restricted Possibility of Inducing Oppositional TG

If external actors strictly play by the book and are successful in empowering an oppositional TA, this practice could result in the creation of a new regime. But this should not be the *immediate* goal of inducing oppositional TG which, in order to be lawful, must envisage a transition as limited by *ius in interregno* and not a haphazard or instantaneous regime change. In principle, international law does not fully rule out the possibility of inducing oppositional TG as a last resort measure. But the chances of impeccable lawfulness are quite low in light of the stringent procedures and conditions described above.

A *duty of strict restraint* is therefore incumbent on external actors intending to induce oppositional TG. The presupposition of prior unlawfulness and the applicable prerequisites reinforce this conclusion. Checks and balances, both procedural and substantive, are to become integral part of the unilateral and coercive inducement of oppositional TG. Even when taken as a last resort, states or contact groups do not have a blank check to diplomatically, politically, materially or financially support an oppositional TA. On the contrary, it is only in specific, objectively justified and procedurally contained situations that there may be little latitude in this regard. Specific reason-giving and information-sharing

---

[104] The representative character of the Syrian coalition, for example, has been contested since its creation. See D. Amoroso, 'Il ruolo del riconoscimento degli insorti nella promozione del principio di autodeterminazione interna: considerazioni alla luce della "Primavera Araba"', op. cit., p. 12.

[105] See the practices and beliefs unveiled in Part III and in E. De Groof, 'The Features of Transitional Governance Today', op. cit.

A LAST RESORT? 365

procedures considerably restrain the possibility of indirect regime change, to such an extent that they reaffirm today's relevance of the principle of non-intervention.

As a unilateral coercive measure with direct effects on a state's *domaine réservé*, inducing oppositional TG will rarely be lawful, even in response to *ius cogens* violations. It can only be applied to endorse an oppositional government after multilateral reactions fail, and provided a series of stringent prerequisites are fulfiled. Under the principles of proportionality and non-performance, it is hard to make that case. The complexity of this argument accentuates, *a contrario*, that coercively inducing oppositional TG will only highly exceptionally be lawful. The ease with which states could argue their support to NLM during decolonisation[106] stands in stark contrast with the difficulty to abide by the rigorous conditions and procedures to justify external support even to *ius in interregno*-abiding and self-determination-promoting oppositional TA.

Given the stringency of the test, and the limited circumstances in which it applies, the theory unveiled here about inducing oppositional TG should cause little controversy, and in any event less so than four theories which imply the disruption of territorial integrity or involve the use of force: the theories of 'remedial secession';[107] of 'forcible humanitarian countermeasures';[108] of 'humanitarian intervention'[109] (to be

---

[106] D. W. Glazier, 'Wars of National Liberation', MPEIL. Cf. UNGA/RES/2621 of 12 October 1970. The UNGA 'moved from declaring that states had the right to aid national liberation movements to declaring that they had the obligation to do so'.

[107] A. Buchanan, *Justice, Legitimacy, and Self-Determination*, Oxford University Press, 2003, p. 335: 'if the state persists in serious injustices toward a group, and the group's forming its own independent political unit is a remedy of last resort for these injustices, then the group ought to be acknowledged by the international community to have the claim-right to repudiate the authority of the state and to attempt to establish its own independent political unit'. See also, J. Vidmar, 'Conceptualizing Declarations of Independence in International Law', op. cit., p. 15. Simma, for instance, writes that 'a right of secession may arise if the [minority] group concerned is exposed to extremely brutal discrimination'. B. Simma (ed.), *The Charter of the United Nations – a Commentary*, op. cit., p. 63. See also N. Bhuta, 'New Modes and Orders', op. cit., p. 8.

[108] A. Cassese, 'A Follow-Up: *Forcible Humanitarian Countermeasures* and *Opinio Necessitatis*', *European Journal of International Law*, Vol. 10, no. 4, 1999, pp. 791–800. According to this theory, the use of *forcible* countermeasures by groups of states may be legitimised under strict conditions if the UNSC does not react to serious breaches of international humanitarian law. In the same sense, P.-M. Dupuy, 'The Deficiencies of the Law of State Responsibility Relating to Breaches of "Obligations Owed to the International Community as a Whole": Suggestions for Avoiding the Obsolescence of Aggravated Responsibility', op. cit., p. 211.

[109] This theory would allow for the 'threat or use of armed force against another state that is motivated by humanitarian considerations'. V. Lowe, A. Tzanakopoulos, 'Humanitarian

distinguished from R2P);[110] or any theory defending the forcible regime change of illegitimate non-democratic systems.[111]

As a final step, let us reframe this conclusion using the concepts of 'legitimacy of origin' and 'legitimacy of exercise'.[112] On a highly exceptional basis, remedial action by non-tangibly injured states inducing oppositional TG in a state violating *ius cogens* might be valid. If multilateral options were exhausted and after obligatory reactions to *ius cogens* violations failed, external actors may, under strict – notably procedural – conditions, trigger indirect regime change through TG against the recalcitrant government. This is the case even if this government enjoyed 'legitimacy of origin' (it came to power in a democratic or legitimate way) but subsequently failed the 'legitimacy of exercise' test (it exercised its powers in violation of *ius cogens*). In other words, grave illegitimacy of exercise may exceptionally and under strict conditions lead to the disqualification of the incumbent government and justify triggering oppositional TG.

In conclusion, far from accepting that external actors have a blank check in indirectly imposing their regime preferences, the involvement with non-constitutional transitions must comply with specific conditions: the (prior) occurrence of substantiated gross and persistent

Intervention', MPEPIL. Note that Reisman contends that regime change may be imposed through foreign intervention 'in the most egregious instances of widespread human rights violations' (W. M. Reisman, 'Why Regime Change is (Almost Always) a Bad Idea', op. cit., p. 51). For a discussion of this theory, cf. J. Crawford, 'The Right of Self-Determination in International Law: Its Development and Future', op. cit., pp. 43 a.f.

[110] R2P is to be differentiated from the concept of 'humanitarian intervention' defined as 'coercive interference in the internal affairs of a state, involving the use of armed force, with the purposes of addressing massive human rights violations or preventing widespread human suffering' (J. Welsh, *Humanitarian Intervention and International Relations*, Oxford University Press, 2006, p. 3). R2P may encompass 'humanitarian intervention' authorised by the UNSC but, as the ICISS report shows, is much broader than that. 'Implementing the responsibility to protect – Report of the Secretary-General', A/63/677 of 12 January 2009, § 7. R2P 'provides for a much larger set of policy tools to forestall the need for such intervention in recognition that prevention is the best form of protection', S. Rosenberg, 'Responsibility to Protect: A Framework for Prevention' in Alex J. Bellamy, Sara E. Davies, Luke Glanville, *The Responsibility to Protect and International Law*, Martinus Nijhoff, 2010, p. 158. See also E. De Groof, 'First Things First: R2P Starts with Direct Negotiations', op. cit.

[111] For an overview of arguments in this sense, cf. G. H. Fox, 'Regime Change', MPEPIL. See also literature quoted by W. M. Reisman. J. J. Paust, 'International Law, Dignity, Democracy and the Arab Spring', *Cornell International Law Journal*, Vol. 46, no. 1, 2013.

[112] Chapter 2, Section B.1. J. d'Aspremont, 'Legitimacy of Government in the Age of Democracy', op. cit., p. 916.

CONCLUSION OF PART IV

breaches of *ius cogens* by a state may give rise to inducing oppositional TG, provided that this practice be taken as a last resort measure, follow the procedural requirements of responsibilisation, notification and negotiation, but to no avail, and select an oppositional TA which abides by its own obligations. The burden of proof to legitimise indirect regime change is consequently extremely high, and in the vast majority of cases cannot be reached to ever justify it.

Conclusion of Part IV

External influence on TG is now commonplace, and can often be felt at the very foundation of the transition already. Coercing a TI upon a state clearly infringes the prohibition on imposing TG, and violates the principle of self-determination. But in this part we unearthed duties incumbent on external actors also beyond the obvious. External actors involved in transitions must respect prohibitions extending beyond those directly related to the foundation of TG. Taking those prohibitions applicable before and following the foundation together, external actors:

- Must not impose TG;
- Must not artificially alter the limitations *ratione temporis* to the interim rule;
- Must not counteract the limitations *ratione materiae* and the fiduciary nature of TG;
- Must not undermine inclusivity during the interregnum;
- Must not impede domestic TJ efforts.

External pressure – rife in diplomatic interactions – should echo the prohibitions just enumerated. It should focus on bringing procedures in sync with emerging custom based on the lowest common denominator of TG practices: bringing the transition agenda to the attention of TA and relevant parties without imposing deadlines or jeopardising TG; reminding that TA mainly play a fiduciary role; encouraging TA to abide by the other prerequisites associated to the principle of internal self-determination. In sum, external actors may only fulfil a *facilitative role*.[113] On a more general note, the duty to align external assistance with the lowest common denominator of emerging custom calls for *moderation and restraint*. If, by contrast, external actors prevent TA

---

[113] Y. Ghai, G. Galli, *Constitution Building Processes and Democratisation*, op. cit., p. 10. In the same sense, I. S. Spears, 'Africa: The Limits of Power-Sharing', op. cit., p. 116.

from carrying out their commonly accepted core tasks, their international responsibility may be engaged at least to the extent that such tasks have contributed to custom formation and added a layer to pre-existing principles.

The coercive inducement of oppositional TG is, in principle, prohibited under international law, unless the measure was taken or allowed by the UNSC. This prohibition remains applicable in the most extreme circumstances, that is when the incumbent power violates *ius cogens*. The only exception is when support to oppositional TA can be justified ('cured') as a last-resort countermeasure, after the obligations of non-recognition, cooperation and peaceful settlement have been exhausted. In case of inactivity or failure at the multilateral level, condoning indirect regime change could only be based on the countermeasure framework.

The last chapter of this book was therefore dedicated to the question of externally imposed TG as *ultimum remedium*. The countermeasure framework arguably provides the ultimate argumentative toolbox for justifying this. It is the sole legal ground that states can possibly invoke to coerce another state into opposition-based TG – and mostly to little avail. Countermeasures can only be considered after *all* the steps described in Chapters 9 and 10 have effectively been taken. Not even in the context of systematic *ius cogens* violations can a non-constitutional transition be lightly imposed. Attempts at peaceful settlement and serious, meaningful negotiations with the incumbent (no matter how rogue) must have failed. If multilateral reactions did not bear fruit, the respect for stringent procedural and substantive prerequisites imposes difficult-to-reach standards. Inducing an oppositional transition as a unilateral countermeasure is thus a rigorously circumscribed possibility. In theory, though, a small and strictly regulated possibility remains for inducing indirect regime change through TG, *itself* also increasingly subject to regulation.

General Conclusion

TG is subject to high-voltage politics. Yet, it is not entirely immune from normativity. This book showed that the impact of international law is increasingly being felt in the field of TG, and furthermore suggested that TG norms and practices are, conversely, enriching international law, even if only modestly by adding non-negligible detail to some of its pre-existing fundamental principles. The current *emergence* of customary rules in relation to TG, testified by a perusal of practice, does not itself happen in a normative vacuum. In turn, emerging customary rules add a normative layer to their normative environment, notably the twin principles of self-determination and non-intervention, underscoring their continued relevance. The movement of this pendulum, whereby international law partly directs TG, and whereby transition practices also contribute to the law's development, carries both risks and opportunities. One swing of the pendulum is driven by the law as it currently stands; the other represents the law as it is now changing, which, in turn, is greatly influenced by culture and knowledge patterns that lie behind norm diffusion.

'European liberalism's origin myth of the state of nature is projected onto countries deemed to be in the conflict/post-conflict zone, i.e. candidates for "transitional governance"', Nesiah writes.[1] Does norm germination in relation to TG indeed echo, in yet another form, this myth? In the affirmative, is such a risk also propagated by international mediators, diplomats and facilitators emulating culture and knowledge produced in so-called developed states?[2] Without analysing in full what the drivers are behind norm diffusion in times of transition, it is safe to say that peace-through-transition, and the nexus between peace mediation and constitution-making, has become nothing less than a paradigm in international diplomacy – for the

---

[1] V. Nesiah, 'The Ambitions and Traumas of Transitional Governance: Expelling Colonialism, Replicating Colonialism', op. cit., p. 142.
[2] M. Saliternik, 'Reducing the Price of Peace: The Human Rights Responsibilities of Third-Party Facilitators', op. cit., p. 232–3.

better or for the worse.[3] Transitions have become internationalised. TG is becoming an instrument of choice at the disposal both of the collective security system, of individual (often powerful) diplomatic actors, and sometimes of the people.

In this context, and as war was outlawed as a means for resolving international disputes since the 1928 Briand-Kellogg Pact, this book investigated what international law allows for *within* the range of non-forcible measures to maintain or restore international peace and security; and hereby concentrated on TG as an instrument of choice. In spite of the often violent context of or antecedents to TG, this study thus prioritised the analysis of *non-forcible* aspects of TG. These can indeed be severed from use-of-force-related questions, including such issues as states in transition consenting to the use of force, humanitarian intervention, forcible countermeasures against so-called failing or rogue states and transformative occupation. The dynamics between external actors and TA driven by their political-diplomatic raison d'être – state renaissance – were scrutinised independently of such issues. In this vein, the last chapter examined whether it is possible to counter *ius cogens* violations by inducing TG without using force.

As an instrument at the disposal of the collective security system and of individual diplomatic actors, TG can vacillate between multilateral state transformation and unilateral constitutional geopolitics. Against the backdrop of this tension, this book has argued that international law increasingly regulates, albeit in a rudimentary fashion, the manner in which TA are to administer the interim rule, and the conditions under which external actors may engage with them. In using international law as a register of analysis, we have avoided systematic reliance on concepts such as 'democracy' and 'legitimacy'. Although these concepts are often named in relation to regime change, they are mostly relevant for the period preceding or following the transition as such. By relying on the self-regulating character of TI – and drawing on the rich practice surrounding TG[4] – this study has promoted the transition as an object of analysis *in its own right*. Bearing the functions of TG such as self-regulation and constitutional reconfiguration in mind, it thus dealt with recurrent practices *of* the interregnum while de-emphasising the transition's origin or outcome. The journey became the destination.

Slightly ironically, perhaps, this journey has resulted in the acknowledgement that, because of the rudimentary and partly changing nature of

---

[3] Berghof Foundation & UNDPPA, *Constitutions and Peace Processes – A Primer*, 2020.
[4] E. De Groof, The Features of Transitional Governance Today, op. cit.

RESERVATIONS

ius in interregno, politics continue to significantly influence TG. Law is not ubiquitous. Yet, the role of politics is not absolute either, and the discretion of TA and external actors is not unlimited: international law prescribes some rules (especially of behaviour and procedure) restricting the freedom of domestic and external actors purporting to influence TG. While one should always be sceptical about the law's pretensions, one should never be cynical about the law's possibilities. Applied to this book, this adage implies, more specifically, that in spite of a number of reservations (A) *ius in interregno* enables a marginal though meaningful scrutiny of TG (B).

A Reservations

How the international law applicable to TG evolves is not, and need not be, smooth. This has led to a number of reservations being expressed throughout the book. Rather than undermining the argument, these reservations are supposed to expose its nuances. They provide answers to three interrelated questions. First, can international law play any useful role in relation to a politico-legal phenomenon as complex and contingent as TG? Second, how is *ius in interregno* affected by the fact that TG often fails; and what if *ius in interregno* is not always complied with? Third, is *ius in interregno* too rudimentary and underdetermined to play any significant role in practice?

1 International Law's Role: A Common Frame for Debate on Transitions

As only one among many registers for analysis, international law offers a common frame for debate in an increasingly decentralised and heterarchical international society. The complexity and contingency of each instance of TG cannot be overemphasised. 'Context is everything' is a much-heard caveat – and rightly so. Yet, lest its relevance be significantly diminished, international legal doctrine also plays a role in using the existing international legal vocabulary to analyse this and other complex and contingent phenomena. This forms an invitation less to be original than creative with tools already put at our disposal by international law seen as a language and register for argumentation. In this way, debates on politically sensitive topics such as TG can gain serenity. '[T]here is a question as to whether general rules of public international law govern external influence over constitutionmaking processes. Such

372 GENERAL CONCLUSION

rules could form the basis of a more general legal regime that could govern external influence on constitution-making processes anywhere and at any time.'[5] This book goes beyond this open invitation: it has enquired not only how general rules of international law apply to external influence over constitution-making, but to TG generally – and how TG practices in turn enrich international law. Self-evidently, the recourse to international law for interpreting TG is neither an innocent choice nor is it driven by the utopian ambition of having controversies surrounding TG legally settled, 'once and for all'. On the contrary, this study fully acknowledges that power relations are internalised in the law, partly stable and partly evolving, and that the law serves as a tool for reinterpreting these relations. Law is not beyond politics but is itself an intense manifestation of political battle.[6]

A common frame for debate on TG also comes to the benefit of actors who, directly or indirectly, would be the victim of unlawful TG practices. For instance, if external actors coerce a state into a transition, or favour specific groups during the interregnum – thus undermining the transition's inclusivity – the targeted state could organise its defence beyond developing a well- or ill-conceived moral argument. It could also invoke legal standards and nascent norms which, for ease of reference, have been grouped under *ius in interregno*. By conducting *lawfare*, states unduly affected by constitutional geopolitics can elevate the political debate beyond the moral level, referring to long-standing principles and emerging customary rules.

2 Issues of Ineffectiveness or Non-Compliance: Relative Legal Impact

As a peace-through-transition measure, TG often fails. Does the accusation that TG is often ineffective in the long run, and sometimes even

---

[5] P. Dann, Z. Al-Ali, 'The Internationalised Pouvoir Constituant', op. cit., p. 451.

[6] Paraphrasis of J. Klabbers, 'The Right to be Taken Seriously: Self-Determination in International Law', op. cit., p. 199. J. Salmon, 'Le droit international à l'épreuve au tournant du XXI siècle', op. cit. Cassese remarked in the same sense that legal principles 'are the expression and result of conflicting views of States on matters of crucial importance. When States cannot agree upon definite and specific standards of behaviour because of their principled, opposing attitudes, but need, however, some sort of basic guideline for their conduct, their actions and discussions eventually lead to the formulation of principles'. A. Cassese, *Self-Determination of Peoples*, op. cit., p. 128. It is also in this sense that self-determination 'becomes a capacious architecture that accommodates the conflicting powers and fault-lines of the international order'. N. Bhuta, 'New Modes and Orders', op. cit., p. 10.

RESERVATIONS   373

incentivises immoral action (for example the scenario of armed groups continuing violence in the hope to be 'included'), prevent TG practices from forming a fertile breeding ground for the progressive development of international law? In the same vein, one can ask: does non-compliance with *ius in interregno* affect its legal relevance? I will address these questions in turn, answering both of them in the negative.

First, that TG can be ineffective has only relative impact, at least legally speaking. Is it politically or even morally desirable to pursue TG against the backdrop of conflict? Are reconstitutionalisation processes not doomed to fail unless they take into account that state transformation is a laborious process – contingent and historically determined?[7] If this truism is systemically overlooked, then practices and discourses under-girding TG, amplified by small epistemic communities through large communities of practitioners, must be reassessed. After the failures in Libya, Syria and Yemen, this reassessment has shyly started. Some argue, and probably rightly so, that concerns should be voiced louder. Should notions like 'transition', 'post-conflict', 'ownership' and 'inclusivity' be techno-political constructs which tend to ignore the domestic social and political fabric or even erode it (questions this book leaves unanswered), then scholars and practitioners alike should grow more critical towards associated practices eventually informing the law's progressive development. If it is justified, such a critique is to be conducted at the policy level first, and only then at the legal level.

This study thus readily accepts the warning against the 'cure-all view on interim governments'[8] or against high expectations – such as those which characterised the early days of the 'Arab Spring' – attached to TG generally. Yet it also cautions against the misconceived conviction that repeated and widely accepted practices would be deprived of any legal impact on the sole ground that they might not be – morally or politically – commendable. One cannot, for example, simply ignore recurrent and

---

[7] N. Bhuta, 'New Modes and Orders', op. cit., pp. 19–20: Admittedly, 'merely introducing a new constitutional law or transforming an existing basic law will be irrelevant unless it is a result of a transformation in the sources and nature of power, authority and representation in the political life of that state'. In the same sense, IDEA, 'Constitutionbuilding after Conflict: External Support to a Sovereign Process', op. cit., p. 11: Issue of failure of TG: 'any assumption that a referendum followed by the enactment of a constitution marks a conclusive transformation of conflict into a political contest within rules misunderstands the nature and difficulties of transitions and romanticizes constitutions as well as elections'.

[8] J. Strasheim, 'Interim Governments: Short-Lived Institutions for Long-Lasting Peace', *GIGA Focus*, nr. 9, 2014.

widespread commitments to 'inclusion' or 'ownership' merely because such practice ought to be subjected to a deeper, and certainly welcome, policy critique – a critique perhaps along the lines that, to be effective, state renaissance should become more politically savvy and conscious of pre-existing formal and informal power structures. If this is the case indeed, we should be wary of the 'jurisgenerative train' connecting socialised deontology, constitutional or supraconstitutional texts, and international law: 'if this connection generates norms that are out of tune with reality or even contribute to harming it, this affects the credibility of practitioners' deontology and constitutional practice, which eventually may also leave an imprint on evolving international law'.[9]

Second, the legal implications of non-compliance with *ius in interregno* are also only relative. *Ius in interregno* remains rudimentary. Even if it were a fully-fledged body of detailed obligations of result, *quod non*, occasional non-compliance would not, by itself, affect its international legal relevance. If non-compliance is treated as such, that is as the breach of a rule rather than as the recognition of a new rule, this actually confirms the rule's validity. Occasional or partial non-compliance with *ius in interregno*, difficult to prove in relation to obligations of conduct, so far has not caused states to abandon their commitment to the practices and principles (such as the limits *ratione temporis* and *ratione materiae* to a progressively inclusive transition) which they must do their best to implement.

3   The Current Maturation of Ius in Interregno: Quo Vadis?

How advanced is international law in relation to TG? International law applicable to TG is stable, yet does not stand still. While the stable part depends on well-established pre-existing fundamental principles of international law which will not easily vanish, the evolving part of *ius in interregno* may be halted at any moment. This would be the case if today's widespread TG practices and corresponding emerging customary rules were aborted, in the near or distant future.

The practice underpinning *ius in interregno* is abundant. Admittedly, the lowest common denominator of emerging custom in relation to TG is

---

[9] E. De Groof, 'The Emulation of Peace Mediation Practices: Beware of the Jurisgenerative Train', in C. Turner, M. Wählisch (eds.), *Rethinking Peace Mediation: Critical Approaches to International Peace Making*, op. cit., forthcoming. About how widely shared practices may increase scepticism about constitutions, see H. Ludsin, 'Peacemaking and Constitution-Drafting: A Dysfunctional Marriage', op. cit. p. 286.

RESERVATIONS

mainly based on the practice of 'non-Western' states,[10] themselves *nolens volens* often influenced by Western culture and knowledge production. Yet, as reactions to such practice, sometimes by acquiescence, come from around the world, it becomes clear that *ius in interregno* is not just of regional relevance. Further, while UNSC practice is not, in itself, formative of custom,[11] its resolutions are often echoed in the conclusions of contact groups, and inversely. Such resolutions and conclusions are not universal but nonetheless unveil what interested states and IO think and do in relation to TG. Their informative and normative potential should therefore not be underestimated.

Especially the array of TI is informative for the evolving part of *ius in interregno*. Whether enshrined in agreements, constitutional texts or declarations, TI share distinctive features: they have a supraconstitutional function and reflect the purposes of transformative constitutionalism: transforming conflict, regulating the interregnum and redefining the social contract as a fresh foundation for peace in a post-conflict setting. Further analysis of the broad but conceptually distinct category of TI, complemented with a continued perusal of TG practices, will reveal whether nascent customary rules will be confirmed, modified or rejected in the coming years or decades. But any prediction is risky. We are now at this tilting point.

In the meantime, *ius in interregno* remains rudimentary. At present, TA must merely respect the core requirements of what has been called *l'Etat légal intérimaire*. For a transition to be successful, these minimum requirements must, without any doubt, be complemented by domestic norms and practices. On particular points, specific procedures could be further detailed in the future. The countermeasure framework, which includes a notification procedure, could for instance inform international legal practice on information-sharing in relation to oppositional TG, and ultimately influence state behaviour. Generally speaking, however, *ius in interregno* is not overly prescriptive. It does not offer detailed one-size-fits-all solutions to the problems of transition states. A number of lines must not be crossed, but within these boundaries discretionary powers remain large.

---

[10] Note however that even 'practice followed by a very small number of states can create a rule of customary law if there is no practice which conflicts with the rule'. M. Akehurst, 'Custom as a Source of International Law' in M. Koskenniemi, op. cit., p. 268.

[11] V. Gowlland-Debbas, 'The Limits of Unilateral Enforcement of Community Objectives in the Framework of UN Peace Maintenance', op. cit., p. 377.

TG is often portrayed as techno-politics, as transferable expertise. It takes ideas and institutions resulting from a particular history and political trajectory – in our case post-Cold War transitions – 'and posit[s] them as the principal solutions to undesirable political dynamics and outcomes'.[12] The perceived transferability, catalysed by a small but powerful epistemic community (in spite of the constantly growing community of practitioners), precisely forms the breeding ground for international law to progressively develop in relation to TG. Quite ironically, 'while international organisations caution against "a blueprint approach" to their interventions, they tend to revert to blueprints as a default position'.[13] This example illustrates why *ius in interregno* is based on the *skeletonisation* of TG practices, that is rather superficial commonalities of TG.

Here, too, criticism should be relegated to other domains including critical theory of international law, to assess power relations behind practices and beliefs underpinning emerging custom. Heightened self-reflection and concrete readjustments by practitioners would also be welcome should they come to the conclusion that recurrent TG practices ought to be modified or abandoned. As long as practices based on the peace-through-transition paradigm continue to proliferate animated by the conviction that these reflect social necessity and then law, it will be difficult to contest that they may contribute to a body of norms *in statu nascendi*, no matter whether or not it will eventually be aborted.

B   Marginal Scrutiny

While international law leaves a considerable margin of appreciation to TA, a number of red lines cannot be crossed. As a final consideration, I shall pause on the finding that discretionary powers both of TA (1) and external actors (2) are limited.

1   Limits to Discretionary Powers of Transitional Authorities

To the extent they exercise effective power, TA must respect three sets of obligations. First, the powers of TA are limited *ratione temporis*: TA accept that their mandate is time-bound. They direct the transition towards permanent institutions, and then relinquish power. They

---

[12] N. Bhuta, 'Against State-Building', op. cit., p. 526.
[13] C. Bell, 'Introduction: Bargaining on Constitutions – Political Settlements and Constitutional State-Building', op. cit., p. 31.

exercise these duties temporarily, that is with the aim of being replaced on the basis of new elections or laws. This implies that they are barred from suspending or perpetuating the interim rule, and generally from re-presenting their leaders and/or members after the transition.

Second, the powers of TA are limited *ratione materiae*. TA exercise a fiduciary type of administration. This precludes them from carrying out activities that exceed their mandate. They prepare for the future but without fully predefining it, respect state continuity both internally (vis-à-vis their own citizens) and externally (vis-à-vis other international legal persons, and foreign investors), and concentrate on managing the present, especially the transition itself. In principle, they take the task of administering the transition upon themselves, even when they receive considerable external assistance.

Third, TA pursue TG in an inclusive way. The inclusivity requirement is to be dissociated from the concept of (procedural or substantive) democracy. Instead, inclusivity permits the principle of self-determination to be deployed so as to prepare for any form of government permitted by international law. As an obligation mainly of conduct during the interregnum, and an obligation of result towards the end of the interregnum, inclusive TG constitutes a mode of implementation of the principle of self-determination. In addition, practices of inclusion further extend and specify the contours of this principle (for example by the redefinition of 'the people' through the involvement of women's groups and representatives of various segments of society during the interregnum, and by confirming the domestic ownership of TJ). In combination with the limits *ratione temporis* and *ratione materiae*, inclusivity specifies the principle of internal self-determination and confirms its continuing relevance.

Together, these duties form the benchmark for assessing the activities and legality of TA. As *ius in interregno* defines the limits to the powers of TA, it also gives an indication of how to conceptually isolate TA legally pursuing TG. This then allows distinguishing them from political bodies illegally provoking a state transformation. The principle of self-determination eventually forms the overarching legal benchmark against which TG practices must be assessed. Fundamentally, *ius in interregno* requires that the interregnum become an effective medium for self-*re* determination whereby the people, in nearly all its facets, is entitled to be taken seriously. As a continuing principle, self-determination is to be realised and respected throughout the interregnum, both by TA and external actors.

2 Limits to Discretionary Powers of External Actors

The idea that domestic duties incumbent on TA should be mirrored to the international level was developed in the final Part. This mirroring is done in two ways, depending on the case. If external actors engage with TA (progressively or *ex post*) representing the state, they are bound to respect these authorities' obligations on the basis that the DASR, reflecting international custom,[14] prohibit that a state aid or assist another state in violating international law.[15] When external actors, on the other hand, do not interact with TA (progressively or *ex post*) representing the state but influence the transition otherwise, for example by dealing directly with oppositional TA, they are still bound by the twin principles of self-determination and non-intervention, which themselves are being refined through relevant emerging custom.

The level of intensity of prohibitions incumbent on external actors (and the potential engagement of their international responsibility)[16] depends on the legal force of the core obligations from which they are derived and on the extent to which said principle has effectively gained precision through them. In either case, external actors must respect duties incumbent on TA, at least to the extent these have entered the realm of law. While primarily incumbent on domestic TA, these duties also reveal their importance beyond the domestic plane: they are factors which external actors should take into account. When external actors try to leave their mark on a transition – on the interregnum generally, on constitution-making specifically – they must respect the lowest common denominator of emerging customary rules, that is the core obligations incumbent on TA. This translates into concrete prohibitions for external

---

[14] A. Pellet, 'The ILC's Articles on State Responsibility for Internationally Wrongful Acts and Related Texts' in J. Crawford, A. Pellet, S. Olleson, *The Law of International Responsibility*, Oxford University Press, 2010. About the DASR being essentially a codification of customary international law, cf. A. Aust, *Handbook of International Law*, op. cit., pp. 376–7.

[15] DASR, art. 16. Note the two conditions: (a) That State does so with knowledge of the circumstances of the internationally wrongful act; and (b) The act would be internationally wrongful if committed by that State.

[16] About this automacity, cf. S. Von Schorlemer, 'Verfahrensrechtliche Aspekte bei Ansprüchen aus Verletzungen von *Erga-omnes-Normen*', in E. Klein, *Menschenrechtsschutz durch Gewohnheitsrecht*, Kolloquium 26–28 September 2002, Potsdam, p. 241: 'internationale Verantwortlichkeit kann mit der herrschenden Ansicht als eine neue Rechtsbeziehung angesehen werden, die automatisch entsteht, wenn eine zurechenbare Völkerrechtsverletzung –sei sie ein Handeln oder ein Unterlassen– vorliegt'. Own free translation: 'the prevailing view is that international responsibility creates a new legal relationship arising automatically whenever there is a violation of international law – be it an act or an omission – that can be attributed [to a state]'.

actors who are prevented from imposing TG; altering the limitations *ratione temporis* and *ratione materiae* to the interim rule; undermining inclusivity; and impeding domestic TJ efforts. On a more general note, they have a duty of restraint and must respect the fiduciary nature of TG serving a specific goal: the progressive and inclusive realisation of self-determination.

Can aiding or assisting oppositional TA ever be justified? This was the last issue we addressed. The examination concentrated on the non-forcible support provided to oppositional TA which operated against national governments violating *ius cogens*. This approach allowed us to examine whether, in the most egregious circumstances, external actors could *indirectly* impose a regime change by supporting oppositional TA pursuing a state renaissance. We hereby focused on the possibility of a non-forcible course of action to incrementally impose regime change in extreme and often horrific contexts – those of *ius cogens* violations.

Ius cogens is, per definition, valid *erga omnes* as it concerns the international community of states as a whole. As *ius cogens* falls outside a state's *domaine réservé*, reactions to its violations, in principle, do not violate the non-intervention principle. But this logic is subject to an exception when states directly target another state's social contract even on the occasion of *ius cogens* violations. Unless the constitutional texts are, themselves, written in direct violation of *ius cogens* – a highly exceptional scenario – coercing indirect regime change, which touches upon the heart of a state's *domaine réservé* no matter how atrocious the context, is contrary to the principle of non-intervention. We therefore mentioned what the general reactions must be to *ius cogens* violations – non-recognition, cooperation and direct negotiation – and only then examined whether or not the imposition of an indirect regime change could exceptionally be justified as a last-resort countermeasure, that is after all generally required reactions would have been exhausted.

Before even thinking of inducing oppositional TG be it in such extreme contexts, external actors are required to follow specific procedures, in first order (general reactions to *ius cogens* violations), and subsidiary order (procedural and substantive prerequisites). Subsidiary procedures include the offer to negotiate with the incumbent government, and, when negotiations are unsuccessful, responsibilising and notifying, as a sort of *mise en demeure*, the defaulting state. In sum, the external instigation of TG as a reaction to *ius cogens* violations is subjected to very strict procedural requirements. In addition, the selected oppositional TA must (demonstrate a reasonable prospect of success to) act in compliance with *ius in interregno*.

As a result, at least in theory, oppositional TG could be instigated when (a) the situation could not be solved at the UN level, and (b) after a number of stringent conditions were met. Under *ius in interregno*, indirect regime change through TG can only be applied as an *ultimum remedium*. In practice, however, the stringency of the tests significantly reduces the likelihood that indirectly provoking regime change can ever be justified. (The conditions are much stricter than those advanced in theories on humanitarian intervention, remedial secession or forcible countermeasures.) At the same time, a small and strictly regulated possibility remains for indirect regime change through TG, which, *nota bene*, itself is subject to *ius in interregno*. In theory, the door is not completely closed. It is just a little ajar, which, *a contrario*, confirms the continuing relevance and validity of the non-intervention principle.

*

Supported by the peace-through-transition paradigm, state renaissance has been increasingly advocated as a measure to cope with threats to international peace and security, and to confront or respond to armed conflict. Also to address situations not reaching those thresholds, transitions *sensu lato* are increasingly being proposed. Largely replacing ITA, TG has today become an instrument of choice in the international collective security system without however assuaging the risk of instrumentalisation especially by individual states sometimes regrouped in diplomatic coalitions.

In essence, this study has shown that, except if the evolution of *ius in interregno* itself embarks upon a sea change, TA and external actors must respect rules (and thus cannot act *legibus soluti*) when realising or contributing to state renaissance. The role of the law in this field is likely to influence diplomatic culture and deontology in the coming decades. In spite of its relevance, TG and its ideological basis – the peace-through-transition paradigm – have received remarkably little attention from an international legal perspective. The rationale behind writing this book goes however beyond the simple observation that TG is recurrent today, and likely to be repeated in the future.

A refined legal model for analysing TG is overdue in two regards. First, as an argumentative toolbox *ius in interregno* can bring grist to the mill of any state feeling that the pendulum between TG as multilateral state transformation and unilateral geopolitics has swung to the wrong side. The second reason is related to the growing number of actors engaged

MARGINAL SCRUTINY

381

with TG, in spite of the associated epistemic community producing technical knowledge being rather small. As more and more practitioners and mediators engage with transitions, calls will grow louder for more coordination and a refined legal model paying attention to the complex relationship between law and political settlements in transition settings.[17] The many actors involved with transitions will benefit from a refined international legal analysis, also in light of the significant budgets allocated to assistance to TG.

By concentrating on the law applicable to TG, and pointing at the current germination of robust but clear norms both for domestic and external actors engaged with TG, this study attempted to lay the groundwork for such a refined legal model. *Ius in interregno* factors in *when* in the transition, *which* actors (purportedly) pursue or influence TG, and *how* they exercise their leverage. The core of a state's *domaine réservé* is in play. Yet, the formally domestic nature of TG does not render an international legal assessment of TG redundant, especially as fundamental legal principles are in play. Also potentially impacted by *ius in interregno*, although only indirectly and in part, is international law's traditional neutrality on non-constitutionality. If international law relating to TG progressively develops on the basis of current trends, it will engage more with the dynamics between domestic non-constitutionality and international illegality by indicating *how* a transition must be administered after a non-constitutional moment. Other issues for further analysis include the potential 'judicialisation' (through international adjudication) of TG.

Questions should also be asked outside the realm of the law and in fields about the law. The analysis of the financial repercussions and socio-economy of TG, just as a number of other issues related to TG, are food for thought for another day. The most pressing challenge is perhaps for diplomats, civil servants, and policymakers – or what one may misleadingly call the agents of the 'international community' – to assess whether the current practices and paradigm underpinning the law applicable to TG – how it currently stands, and how it is in flux – should be continued. And whether, pending a further crystallisation of the law, maintaining course is a feasible and wise choice considering that 'a quarter of a century of investment in transitions ... failed to lead to democracy

---

[17] C. Bell, 'Introduction: Bargaining on Constitutions – Political Settlements and Constitutional State-Building', op. cit., p. 14.

and peace taking hold worldwide'.[18] The law can be useful as much as it can be harmful when long-term effects on institutional resilience and collective well-being are not appropriately considered. In which direction the law on state renaissance will evolve depends on how experts, practitioners and diplomats reconcile action and reflection perhaps more than on the peoples vesting their hopes in its potential for meaningful change.

***

[18] Id., p. 15.

INDEX

Abkhazia, 14, 34
Acquiescence, 110–11, 171, 173, 291, 375
Afghanistan, 4–5, 9, 12, 19, 35–7, 41, 44, 49, 52–4, 58, 75, 82, 86, 90, 96, 107, 114, 117, 120, 125, 130, 155, 163, 167–8, 172–4, 177, 179–80, 185–6, 201–2, 205, 208–10, 218, 225, 229, 231, 234, 237–8, 244–5, 263, 269, 289–90, 294, 305, 313
African Union ('AU'), 7–8, 21, 41, 47–9, 51–2, 54, 61, 91–2, 94, 144, 178, 323
    2000 Constitutive Act, 47, 92
    2007 Governance Charter, 92
    decolonisation, 91, 145
    Lomé Declaration, 92
    OAU Liberation Committee, 326
Algeria, 5, 17, 164, 267, 380
Anocracy, 5, 33, 247
Arab Spring, xxiii, 19, 22, 47, 58, 60, 68, 74, 91, 94, 146, 206, 231, 236, 301, 319, 325, 338–40, 366, 373
    inducement of oppositional TG, 317–26
    & self-determination, 231, 236
Argument of the book, 3, 369
Assistance model, 12, 35, 38, 58, 77, 117–18, 121, 167
    external influence, 275, 277–9
Autumn of Nations, 15–16, 237

Belgium, 1, 17, 41, 333, 339
Black Spring, xxiii
Bosnia, 41, 120–1, 174, 297–8, 313
Briand-Kellogg Pact, 18, 370
Burkina Faso, xxiii, 4–5, 9, 17, 43, 47, 49, 51, 57, 82, 86, 91, 96, 107–8,
129, 132, 144, 164, 177, 201–2, 208, 214, 225, 233–4, 263
Burundi, xxiii, 4–6, 9, 12, 44, 49, 59–60, 82, 85–6, 94, 97, 107, 114, 125, 127, 130, 131–2, 155, 164, 172–4, 177, 185, 201–2, 206, 208, 213, 218, 225, 233, 237, 263, 265, 269, 289–91, 295

Cambodia, 5, 41, 44, 49, 82, 97, 108, 111, 120–2, 132, 151, 155, 174–6, 201–2, 230, 238, 245, 254, 263, 288
Catalonia, 13, 34
Central African Republic ('CAR'), xxiii, 5, 8, 40, 45–7, 49, 53–4, 60, 82, 98, 107–8, 129, 135, 165, 167–8, 177, 179–82, 185, 199, 201–2, 208, 211, 214, 225, 234, 263, 269, 310
Charter of decolonisation, 156
China, 1–2, 15, 56, 69, 126, 129, 152, 154, 175, 210, 268, 316, 322, 332
Civil society, 40, 225, 234, 237, 245, 254, 258, 301, 321, *See also* Inclusivity
Cold War, xxiii, 3–4, 13, 15, 17, 31, 43–5, 48, 67, 71, 77, 90, 108, 151, 155, 185, 188, 193, 197, 221, 224, 258, 275, 302
Colombia, 109, 245
Comoros, 5, 49, 82, 98, 107, 166, 172, 201–2, 225
Conservation principle, 217, 220–1, 303
Constituent assembly, 102, 131–3, 206, 208, 218, 228, 238, 256, 294
    involvement of the people, 252

INDEX

Constitutional geopolitics, xxii, xxxii, 58, 61, 77, 275, 370, 372
definition, 20
role of multilateralism, 277
Constitutional law, 25, 89, 93, 154, 156, 243, 373
& international law, 154–6, 172
internationalisation of, 154,
See also International law, non-constitutionality, neutrality vis-à-vis
Constitution-making
constitution-making *tout court*, 123, 237, 240, 243, 255, 259, 279, 302–6, 312
assistance to, 279
external actors, 303
inclusivity, 239
internationalisation, 304
post-sovereign constitution-making, 123, 239
& state continuity, 212
prohibition of externally imposed constitutionalism, 303
prohibition of internally imposed constitution-making, 240, 242, 251–2, 254, 259, 303
transitional constitution-making, 123, 154, 212, 218, 236, 243, 255
assistance to, 278
inclusivity, 254
internationalisation, 279
political elites, 236
representation, 237
Contact groups, 40, 48, 52, 54, 344
absence of mandate, 326
concerted unilateralism, 324, 332
countermeasures, active identity requirement, 349
critique, 54
custom formation, 178
custom, *opinio necessitatis*, 165
duty of restraint, 364
financial support to TA, 166
functions of, 52
inducement of oppositional TA, 317, 319, 323, 325

obligation of direct negotiations, 341
oppositional TA, no formal recognition, 330
peace-through-transition paradigm, 61
UN Security Council, 375
Côte d'Ivoire, 5, 8–9, 49–51, 68, 82, 86, 90, 98–9, 107, 114, 130, 132, 155, 160, 172, 175, 179–80, 182, 199, 201, 203, 208, 214, 225, 262, 307, 310
Countermeasures. *See* sanctions
Crimea, 33, 57, 70
Custom
coutume sauvage, 183
existing law, 2–3, 25, 150, 188, 193–4, 270, 369
financial and economic incentives, 168
lowest common denominator, 140, 192, 195, 276, 283, 286, 298, 313, 316–17, 335, 343, 363, 367, 374, 378
duty of restraint, 367
external actors and inclusivity, 298
external actors avoiding misalignment, 283, 286, 335
impact on indirect regime change, 363
relevance for oppositional TA, 316
& external actors, 276, 313, 367
nascent custom, 184, 191, 369
non-compliance, 186
opinio iuris, 163, 169
opinio necessitatis, 163, 168–70
opposability of emerging custom, 283
& self-determination, 150, 193
state practice, 163
evidence of, 169, 173
& treaties, 175
& UN Security Council, 176

De facto governments, 87–8, 134, 188, 212, 270, 330
De facto states, 13, 87
De iure governments, 87

INDEX

Declarations of independence, 90

Decolonisation, 2, 13, 18, 33–4, 42, 61, 91, 149, 158, 219, 229–30, 240–1, 254, 365
  internationalised constitution-making as neocolonial enterprise, 275
  renewed '*mission civilisatrice*', 302

Democracy, xxiv, 71, 338, 370
  conceptual indeterminacy, 75
  democratic peace theory, 72
  democratic transition paradigm, 4
  disassociation from TG, 228
  illiberal democracy, 73
  inconsistent practice, 74
  inclusivity, 227
  lack of, no basis for indirect regime change, 347
  legal status of, 74
  readings of, 72
  right to, 75
  too high a standard for TG, 227–8

Democratic Republic of Congo ('DRC'), 4–5, 9, 28, 40–1, 44, 50, 54–5, 59–60, 82, 99, 107–8, 110, 114, 120, 124–5, 130, 132, 135, 143, 155, 167, 173–6, 182, 185, 201, 203, 205, 208, 212–13, 225, 233, 263, 291, 295, 299, 310–11

Deontology, 22, 24, 155, 226, 277, 300
  constitution-making, domestic ownership, 303
  custom formation, 166
  inclusivity, promotion of, 299–300
  internationalisation of interim constituent power, 289
  permissible pressure, 314
  time pressure, 293
  transitional justice, 265
  women's involvement, 234

Diplomacy, xiii, xxiii, 7–8, 27, 40–1, 44, 48, 54, 76, 169, 171, 185, 253, 254, 295, 301, 314, 320, 325–6, 340, 343, 355, 358, 361, 368, 369, 380–2
  contact groups, 325
  nexus between mediation and constitution-making, 369

Track I, II, III diplomacy, 253–254

Disarmamant, demobilisation and reintegration ('DDR'), 8, 179, 209–11

Domestic ownership, xxxii, 39, 117, 192, 194, 224–6, 377
  as guiding principle, 238, 303
  of transitional justice, 264
  & external actors, 306–08

Draft Articles on State Responsibility, 276, 312, 378, *See also* responsibility regime
  circumstances precluding wrongfulness, 344–5
  countermeasures
    escalation, 362
    history of, 351, 354
    non-performance, 358
    procedural prerequisites, 353, 355
    proportionality, 361
    reversibility, 360
    substantive conditions, 353, 358
  solidarity countermeasures, 350–1, 355
    active identity requirement, 349
    controversy, 349–50
    gross and persistent human rights breaches, 352
    passive identity requirement, 349

Droit de transition, 107

Duty of conservation, xxxii, 199, 222

Duty of restraint
  applicable to external actors, 276, 345, 364, 379
  contact groups, 277, 325, 364
  See also Fiduciary role of TG

East Timor, 34–5, 44, 118–20, 122, 157, 238, 313, 351

ECCAS, 21, 47–8, 54

ECOWAS, 22, 47–9, 51, 83, 91, 94, 100, 117, 143–4, 178, 203, 214

Egypt, 17, 21, 44, 141, 143–4, 206

Epistemic community, xxiv, 154, 165, 237, 376, 381
  migration of constitutional ideas, 166

INDEX

Epistemic community (cont.)
  socialisation, 155, 183, 189, 195, 226
    & custom formation, 165
    & inclusive constitution-
      making, 238
    & transitional justice, 264
Eritrea, 13, 44, 142, 199, 201
Ethiopia, 13, 245, 352
European Union ('EU'), 22, 48, 57,
    92–3, 234, 264, 265, 268–9, 278,
    321–3, 328
  democracy, 92–3
  EU Civil Society Facility, 22
  European Endowment for
    Democracy, 22
  inclusivity and women's
    involvement, 234
  no blanket amnesty, 265
  oppositional TA, empowerment of,
    127, 321–2
  oppositional TA, no formal
    recognition, 328
  transitional justice, 264
    domestic ownership, 268

Fiduciary role of TG, 163, 192, 217,
    219–23, 270, 272, 364, 367, 377
  assessment of TA, 363
  conservation principle, 220–1, 303
  duty of restraint, 276
    external actors, 296, 367, 379
    post-transition constitution,
      296–8
  effects of violation, 215
  law of occupation, comparison, 217
France, xxvi, 14, 19, 25, 27, 52, 56, 105,
    117, 157, 174, 177, 193, 208–9,
    211, 232, 266, 354
  oppositional TA, empowerment of,
    127, 321–2
Friendly Relations Declaration (1970),
    18, 158–60, 162, 194, 358

Gambia, 44, 158, 263
Germany, 15, 56, 105, 111, 135, 164,
    266, 269, 322
  oppositional TA, empowerment
    of, 322

Ghana, 9, 17, 49, 51, 57, 201, 205
Global South, 28, 164
Greece, 17, 329, 354
Guinea, 4–5, 7, 11, 18, 25, 47, 50–1, 55,
    83, 94, 99–100, 107–8, 120, 130,
    133, 143–4, 166–7, 179–81, 201,
    203, 208, 213, 225, 234, 263, 269,
    307, 316
Guinea-Bissau, 5, 7–8, 47, 94,
    107–8, 225
Gulf Cooperation Council ('GCC'), 47,
    85–6, 321
  oppositional TA, empowerment of,
    127, 321

Haiti, 9, 12, 27, 38, 44, 48, 58, 90–1, 117,
    155, 179, 208, 215, 263, 269, 313
Hart, Herbert Lionel Adolphus, 10, 89
Human rights, 5, 64, 72, 97, 123, 133,
    151–5, 168, 177, 183, 221, 225,
    235–6, 241, 250, 261–2, 265,
    267, 306, 320–1, 333, 335, 339,
    347–8, 351–2, 358, 366
  droit-de-l'hommisme, 64, 183
  gross and persistent breaches,
    solidarity countermeasures, 352
  nonderogable rights
    erga omnes character, 332
    ius cogens, 339
    link with self-determination, 339
  peace agreements, 153
  ticking-the-box exercise, 247
  transitional justice, 262, 268
Humanitarian intervention, 19, 317,
    365–6, 370, 380, See also
    'Responsibility to
    Protect' ('R2P')
Hungary, 93
  oppositional TA, empowerment
    of, 322

ICCPR, 72, 156, 239–42, 266
ICESCR, 156
Inclusivity
  aim of, 224
  compensatory function, 229
  continuous obligation, 258
  definition, 224

INDEX

democracy, 227
deontological obligation, 299–300
diaspora, 225, 235, 252
discretionary powers of TA, 259
downstream constraints, 242
elite involvement, 224, 244, 247, 249,
253–5
epistemological challenge, 247
guiding principle, 238
horizontal inclusion, 234
human rights, 241
interim rule, 240
minority involvement, 225, 245
negative criticism, 245, 373
overestimation societal
malleability, 248
participation, 224, 258
positive criticism, 244
power-sharing, 246
precursor of democracy, 229
private sector, 225, 236, 245, 252
progressive inclusion, 251, 253, 255
recognition, 241
representation, 224, 258
self-determination, 227, 229, 249
expansion *ratione materiae*,
236, 252
expansion *ratione personae*,
232, 249
expansion *ratione temporis*,
243, 254
socialisation, 226
territorial cleavages, 246
transformative
constitutionalism, 224
UN and socialisation, 227
upstream constraints, 238, 253
vertical inclusion, 238
women's involvement, 225, 234, 245,
258–9, 272, 377
beyond socialised practice, 235
& re-definition of people, 249
& UN Security Council, 234–5
youth involvement, 245
Indirect regime change, 114, 337, 342,
353, 358, 365–6, 368, 379
argumentarium, 338, 344
countermeasures, 346

prior proof unlawfulness, 347
distinction direct regime change, 326
high burden of proof, 367
inducement of oppositional TG,
326
legitimacy, 362
obligatory notification, 356,
360
oppositional TA, qualification of,
362–4
perspective external actors, 351–2,
355, 359
procedural safeguards, 355, 357
reversibility, 360
thin chance of lawfullness, 346,
353, 360
time-consuming nature, 356
ultimum remedium, 353, 362,
368, 380
Ineligibility-after-transition, 201,
205–6, 364, *See also* Limits
ratione temporis
rationale, 206
technocracy of TG, 206
Institut de droit international ('IDI'),
351, 354
Interim constitutionalism, 10
International cases (jurisprudence),
See also International Court of
Justice
Assanidze v. Georgia (ECtHR), 134
Barrios Altos v. Peru (Inter-Am.Ct.
H.R.), 266
Bazorkina v. Russia (ECtHR),
266
Diergaardt et al. v. Namibia (Human
Rights Committee), 193
Gelman v. Uruguay (Inter-Am.Ct.
H.R.), 266
Ivan Kitok v. Sweden (Human Rights
Committee), 193
Mavrommatis Palestine Concessions
(PCIJ), 174
Sahin v. Turkey (ECtHR), 266
Tinoco Claims Arbitration
(International arbitration), 216
Velasquez Rodriguez case (Inter-
Am.Ct.H.R.), 266

INDEX

International community, 30, 71, 164, 166–7, 267, 283, 312, 319–20
International Court of Justice (ICJ jurisprudence)
  Aegean Sea Continental Shelf case, 175
  Armed Activities on the Territory of the Congo (v. Rwanda) case, 177
  Barcelona Traction case, 333, 342
  East Timor case, 157, 351
  Fisheries Jurisdiction case, 291
  Frontier Dispute (Burkina Faso v. Mali), 177
  Gabčíkovo case, 359
  Genocide Convention case, 174
  LaGrand case, 134–5
  Namibia advisory opinion, 157, 215
  Nicaragua case, 77, 161, 187
  North Sea Continental Shelf case, 174, 184
  Nottebohm case, 174
  Nuclear Tests case, 174–5
  Obligation to Prosecute or Extradite case, 293
  South Africa in Namibia advisory opinion, 157, 180, 215
  Temple of Preah Vihear case, 111, 174
  Tunisia/Libya Continental Shelf case, 187
  Unilateral Declaration of Independence in Kosovo, advisory opinion, 18, 90, 254
  US Diplomatic and Consular Staff in Tehran case, 355
  Wall in occupied Palestinian territory, advisory opinion, 157
  Western Sahara, advisory opinion, 77, 157, 242
International Criminal Court ('ICC'), 266, 306, 309
  ability and willingness test, 308
  admissibility of the case against Abdullah Al-Senussi (ICC), 309
  complementarity, 307
  independence, 308
  politicisation, 310

self-referral by TA, 310
International humanitarian law, 38
  transformative occupation, 19, 370
International law,
  autonomy, 90, 248
  bilateralist conception, 351
  culture of debate, 28, 259, 273, 338, 360, 371
  language, comparison, 25
  limits of, xxv, 371
  non-constitutionality, neutrality vis-à-vis, 90, 189, 284
  role of, 25, 28, 370
  See also Internationalisation of transitional governance, legal internationalisation
International peace and security
  legal-regulatory approach, 28, 179, 303
International territorial administration ('ITA'), 12, 33–4, 36–7, 39, 41–2, 46, 76, 116–21, 163, 167, 222–3, 285, 380, See also Transitional governance, distinction ITA
Internationalisation of TG
  constitution-making tout court (history), 302
  embryonic or inchoate TA, 315
  external involvement in tempore fragili, 140, 284, 293, 340
  externally imposed constitutionalism, 303
  factual internationalisation, 44
  inclusivity, 298–300
  interim constituent power, consent to internationalisation, 288
  law abidance beyond consent, 284, 292
  legal internationalisation, 44, 151
  limitations ratione temporis, 293
  permissible influence, 313
  post-transition order, 296
  respect for state continuity, 298
  time pressure, 292, 294–5
  transitional justice, 306
Internationalised intrastate agreements, 106, 172–3

INDEX

Interregnum, *See also* Transitional
governance
definition, 3
factual internationalisation, 12
historic examples, 1
legal internationalisation, 12
Iran, 57, 297, 321
Iraq, 3, 5, 9, 19, 33, 40–1, 44, 50, 55,
83, 100, 107–8, 111–12, 117,
125, 130–1, 133, 135, 154–5,
163, 165, 185–6, 200–1, 203,
205–6, 208, 210–12, 214,
217–18, 221–3, 225, 228–9,
231, 234, 236, 239, 245, 253–4,
263, 268–9, 271, 278–9,
289–92, 294, 297, 299, 305,
307, 335
Irrelevance of origin, 94
Irrelevance of outcome, 77, 94, 191
Ius ad bellum, 19
Ius ad interregnum, 193, 261, *See also*
Self-determination,
right-holder perspective
Ius cogens
absence of multilateral response,
341–2
consequences, 340
definition, 337
international peace and security, 339
non-recognition, 340
obligation of cooperation, 340–3
obligation of direct negotiations,
340–3, 356
obligation of peaceful settlement,
340–3
Ius in bello, 19, *See also* International
humanitarian law
Ius in interregno
definition, xxiii, 2–3, 27, 107, 150
in transition (itself), 184, *See also*
Custom, nascent custom
marginal scrutiny, 273, 376–80
non-compliance, 185
scope *ratione personae*, 135, 137
Ius post bellum, xxxii, 63, 65–6, 77, 124,
217–18

Japan, 15, 94, 111, 212, 265, 268

Kosovo, 13, 18, 34–5, 37, 41, 44, 55, 90,
119–20, 254, 268, 313
Kyrgyzstan, 5, 52, 83, 100, 107–8, 114,
130, 132, 201, 203, 225,
233–4, 237

League of Arab states, 320
oppositional TA, empowerment of,
322, 324
Legal globalisation, 196
Legitimacy, xxiv, 68, 338, 370
conceptual indeterminacy, 69
custom formation, 166
external legitimacy, 70
indirect regime change, 362, 347
internal legitimacy, 70
readings of, 68
Legitimacy of exercise/origin, 70, 189,
269, 320, 330
& indirect regime change, 366
Lex pacificatoria, 66
Liberia, 4–5, 44, 47, 50, 83, 101, 107,
114, 120, 125, 130, 155, 172, 177,
201, 203, 206, 214–15, 219, 225,
233, 246, 251, 263, 269, 352
Libya, xxxii, 4–5, 7–8, 10–11, 19, 28,
44–6, 51, 55, 60–1, 69, 83, 85, 91,
101, 107–8, 110, 112, 114–15,
124–6, 129, 132–3, 137, 142, 146,
152–3, 171, 179, 185–7, 199, 201,
204, 206, 208, 213, 216, 219, 225,
233, 236–7, 263, 296–7, 299,
309–11, 317, 319, 322–30, 335,
338–41, 347, 360, 373
oppositional TA, empowerment
of, 323
Transitional National Council, 318
Light footprint approach, xxxii, 33,
35–6, 42, 58, *See also* Assistance
model
Limits *ratione materiae*, 207
concessions to investors, 220
consequences, 207
exploitation of natural resources, 220
law of occupation, comparison,
221
supraconstitutional principles,
219

Limits *ratione temporis*, 199
  limitations legal capacity, 206
  link with limits *ratione materiae*, 201, 205
  prolonged interregnum, 199

Madagascar, 17
Mali, xxiii, 5, 8, 11, 19, 47, 51, 83, 101, 107, 114, 117, 129, 135, 172, 177, 179, 201, 204, 280, 307, 310

National dialogues, 104, 123, 209, 224, 228, 237–8, 255–6, 299, 301
  & democracy, 228
National liberation movements ('NLM'), xxxii, 18, 137, 140, 142, 145–9, 188, 229–30, 328, 365
  analogies with TA, 148
  effectiveness criterion, 146
  external self-determination, 148
  external support to, 147, 317
    contrast with inducement of oppositional TG, 317, 326
  Goodwill Mission Report, 146
  inclusivity, 230
  legal category, 149
  political allegiance, 326
  regional organisations, 148
  territorial control, 146
  variety, 147
Nepal, 5, 9, 44, 51, 58, 84, 102, 107–8, 130, 132–3, 172, 201, 204, 208, 219, 228
Nexus peacemaking and constitution-making, 8–9, 369
Non-compliance, xxxii, 38, 183, 186, 205, 271, 372–3
  & impact on law, 186
Non-constitutionality, 81
  association with violence, 16
  definition, 11, 81
  distinction constitutional reforms, 85
  interim constitutionalism, 87
  non-indifference, 93
  praeter constitutionem, 11, 93, 95

regional frameworks, 91
rupture, 11, 85
unconstitutionality, 11
unconstitutional constitutional amendments, 85, 93
Non-international armed conflicts, 2
Non-intervention
  See Principle of non-intervention
Norm entrepreneurship, 28, 183, 195
Northern Cyprus, 14, 70, 347

Obligations of means or conduct, 186, 191–2, 206, 211, 220, 232, 250, 252, 255, 259
  inclusivity, 227, 258
Obligations of result, 186, 191–2, 201, 232, 239, 242, 250, 250, 259, 261, 363, 377
  closure of transition, 242, 258, 273
  generated by obligations of means, 252, 254
  human rights and self-determination, 242
  people's involvement (constitution-making), 238, 259
  women's involvement, 251, 259
Oppositional transitional authorities, definition, 20, 114, 318
  no formal recognition, 328
  See also Transitional governance

Palestine, 131–2, 174
Paris Declaration on Aid Effectiveness, 39
Peace-through-transition paradigm, xxxii, 6–7, 9, 18, 22, 28, 39, 43–4, 46–7, 56, 61, 67, 77, 109, 116, 163–5, 168, 171, 179, 187–8, 380
  contingency of state transformation, 373
  custom formation, 376
  definition, 5
  inclusivity, 248
  international influence, 275

INDEX 391

panacea, 42, 61
UN Security Council, 8, 22
Pelt, Adriaan, 219, 222
Poland, 56, 93
Pound, Roscoe, 2, 270
Power of modification, xxxii, 199, 222
Power-sharing, xxiii, 20, 22, 81, 115,
153, 207, 235, 240, 243–4, 246,
257, 290, 313
  beyond the transition, 298
  inclusivity, 246
  time-finite or permanent, 246
  women's involvement, 235
Principle of non-intervention
  coercion, 161–2, 331,
    358
    acta iure gestionis/imperii, 333
  conditions of application, 161, 331
  definition, 160
  diplomatic pressure/influence, 161
  domaine réservé, 161–2
    & nonderogable rights, 332
  non-forcible aspects, 160, 317, 331,
    337, 358
  oppositional TG, 331
Principle of self-determination. *See*
  Self-determination
Proxy governance, 41, 55, 59, 62

Qatar, 338
  oppositional TA, empowerment of,
    127, 321–2

Responsibility to protect ('R2P'), 18,
  299–300, 339–41, 366
  no blanket amnesty, 266
  See also humanitarian intervention
Recognition
  alternatives to, 328
  definition, 327
  distinction political and legal
    recognition, 327, 329
  distinction acknowledgement, 330
  duty of restraint, 327
  oppositional TG, inducement of, 327
  premature recognition, 327
  TA as recognised governments, 115

Regime change
  See Indirect regime change
Reconstitutionalisation, 11, 44, 46, 56,
  76–7, 87, 109–10, 129, 134, 155,
  188, 209, 222, 258–9, 261, 302
  closure of transition, 242
  consent to, 279
  contact groups, role of, 275
  self-determination, 227
  UN, role of, 44, 275
Referenda, xxxii, 20, 87, 98, 100, 103,
  111, 125–6, 132, 157, 159,
  194–5, 209, 218, 224, 228, 236,
  240, 242, 244, 250, 252, 256, 259,
  271, 297, 306, 373
  & inclusivity, 242
Replacement, xxxii, 19–20, 85, 88, 92,
  187, 201, 251, 316, 328
Responsibility regime
  aiding *ius in interregno*
    violations, 276
  circumstances precluding
    wrongfulness, 344
  countermeasures, 345
    definition, 345
    prior proof unlawfulness, 347
  division of responsibility, 39,
    276, 312
  domestic responsibility despite
    internationalisation, 39–41, 209
  investors' protection, 216
  legal personality, 134
  perspective UN & contact groups,
    39–40, 312
Rome Statute, 266–7, 308–11
Rule of law, 24, 46, 73, 92–3, 264, 269,
  270, 277
Rwanda, 5, 44, 54, 84, 102, 107, 114,
  120, 127, 133, 155, 172, 178, 185,
  214, 218, 263, 265, 268

Sanctions, 9, 144, 156, 178–82, 301, 326
  confirming nascent custom, 248
  countermeasures, 345–62
  external actors, adjusting role, 357
  solidarity countermeasures, 350–3, 355
  See also spoilers

392 INDEX

Secession, 2, 13, 42, 61, 159, 318,
  363, 365
  remedial secession, 19, 365, 380
  self-determination, 258
Secondary norms, 6, 25, 77, 89, 253
  See also Tertiary norms
Self-determination
  after decolonisation, 158, 258
  constitution-making as heart of
    domaine réservé, 162
  continuing character, 254, 292
  democracy, 272
  detailed through custom, 232, 251,
    259, 271
    esp. obligations of means, 272
  expansion *ratione materiae*, 194, 236,
    236, 252, 272
  expansion *ratione personae*, 233, 245,
    249, 272
  expansion *ratione temporis*, 195, 243,
    255, 272
  further detailed by custom,
    150, 194
  human rights, 241, 339
  implementation through TG,
    194, 252
  inclusivity, 227, 249
  internal self-determination, 145,
    158, 363
  International Court of Justice, 157
  proceduralised conception, 259
  right to be taken seriously, 233, 249,
    258, 377
  right-holder perspective, 157, 193,
    233, 239
  self-*re*determination, 163, 193, 210,
    222, 249, 276, 377
  & the people, 232, 249
    beyond territoriality, 234, 271
  umbrella principle for TG, 231
  wide scope, 160
Sierra Leone, 4–5, 36, 44, 51, 84, 90, 103,
    107, 121, 172, 211, 246, 251, 263,
    265, 269
Somalia, 5, 8, 12, 27, 38, 44–6, 48, 51, 58,
    84, 86, 103, 107–8, 114, 117,
    120–1, 132, 155, 179–81, 201,

204, 209, 215, 225, 233, 263,
    289–91, 294, 305–6
Somaliland, 14
South Africa, xxiii, xxvi, 4, 6, 10, 27, 35,
    41, 47, 70, 84, 86–7, 103, 107–8,
    111, 142, 147, 155, 157, 166, 180,
    208, 210, 213, 215, 220, 225, 231,
    263, 291, 294–5, 305, 316, 352
South Ossetia, 14, 34
South Sudan, 13, 56, 60, 159, 164
Sovereignty
  co-governance, 122
  co-sovereignty, 59
  & international territorial
    administration ('ITA'), 37
Spoilers, 9, 43, 180–2, 248, 335
Sri Lanka, 56, 62
State continuity, 211–13
  investors' protection, 215
  Namibia principle, 215
  odious debts, 216
  private interests, 214
  third states, 214
State dissolution, 2, 13, 33–4, 42, 61, 83,
    126, 128, 134
State succession, 1, 13, 45, 188, 216
Statebuilding, 36, 39, 122, 131, 151, 175,
    196, 200, 219, 237, 239, 277, 300,
    302, 314
  New York Consensus, 163
Sudan, xxiii, 5–6, 8, 13, 17, 44, 52, 56,
    60–1, 84, 86, 104, 107, 114, 129,
    143, 159, 164, 172–3, 179, 185,
    204, 211, 231, 253, 263, 269, 380
Supraconstitutionality, 11–12, 81, 85–7,
    95–113, 123, 155, 172–3, 188,
    212, 214, 219, 243, 278, 374–5
  definition, 95
Syria, xxiii, xxxii, 6, 21, 33, 51, 55, 57,
    60–1, 69, 84, 103–4, 107–8,
    127–9, 142, 146, 153, 164, 201,
    204, 225, 299–301, 315, 317–28,
    330, 338–41, 347, 360, 364, 373
  oppositional TA, empowerment
    of, 320
  National Council, National
    Coalition, 318

INDEX

Tajikistan, 52, 114
Tertiary norms, 89, 110, 115–16, 123, 172, 220, 275, 296
Thailand, 94, 111, 174, 245, 268
Theorisation-within-the-law, 27, 344
  ius cogens and indirect regime change, 337
Tobar doctrine, 90
Transformations, 19–20, 187
Transformative constitutionalism, xxxii, 11, 95, 109, 111–13, 172
  broad understanding, 111
  external actors, powers of, 113
  pacification, 109
  reconstitutionalisation, 110
  self-limitation, 110
  tensions inherent to, 222
  variety of instruments, 278
Transition, *See* Transitional governance
  definition, 3
Transition instruments
  categories, 95
  definition, 81
  ex post validation, 110
  invalidation, effects of, 291–292
  purpose, 109, 172, 188
  supraconstitutional function, 95, 108
  treaties, 175
  unilateral declarations, 173
  variety, 171, 187
Transition paradigm, *See* Peace-through-transition paradigm
Transitional authorities ('TA')
  aspirational TA, 126
  assistance to, seen as obligation, 167
  attribution of conduct, 170
  civilian nature, 142
  common conceptualisation, 115, 187
  core tasks, 211
  definition, 114
  distinction *de facto* governments and states, 128
  distinction military or armed groups, 140
  diverse politico-legal reality, 115
  effective control, 115

embryonic/inchoate TA, 115, 126, 128, 137
  contact groups, 166
  & external actors, 287, 315
  external empowerment, international law, 327
  moral support to, 332
  recognition, 327
ex post attribution of conduct, 170
functionality, criterion of, 143
human rights, 241
inclusivity,
  effect on consent, 304
  obligation of verification, 304
international legal personality, 134, 188
  & distinction international lawmaking power, 170
procedural duties, 218
self-imposed obligations, 175, 285
separate structure and hierarchy, 142
transitional justice, 271
validity of consent, 279
Transitional governance ('TG')
  budgets allocated to, 167
  conflict-related, 16
  contested utility, 185, 197, 372
  core tasks, 207
  democracy, disassociation from, 228
  distinction ITA, 12, 117
  domestic nature, 13, 116
  end of, 132
  external assistance,
    consent, 279
    definition, 277
    degrees, 278
    forms, 277
    timing, 278
  fiduciary role, *see* Fiduciary role of transitional governance
  foreign occupation, 117
  foundation, 127
  inducement oppositional TG, as *coercive* measure, 327
  inducement oppositional TG international law, 325–26
  irrelevance of origin, 94

INDEX

Transitional governance ('TG') (cont.)
irrelevance of outcome, 75
jurisdiction of ICC, 308
length, 131
non-forcible aspects, 18
normative underpinnings, 196
panacea, 186, 188
path-dependency, 196
people, limited direct powers, 240
pre-transition, 126
preventive measure, 8, 60, 111
regional organisations, 21
responsibility, 22
retroactive attribution to state, 115
rudimentary practices, 195
Transitional justice ('TJ'), 4, 63–5, 77,
109, 132, 178, 206, 210–11, 220,
260, 263, 268, 286–7, 306–7, 377
broad finality, 260
categories, 260
closure of transition, 264
contested utility, 263
contribution to *ius in interregno*, 260
definition, 4, 63, 260
discretionary powers, limits to,
262, 264
domestic ownership, 260, 268
consequences for external
actors, 307
opinio iuris, 268
effective remedy, 266
expansion, 262
external actors and states, 267,
367, 379
facilitative role, 308
self-determination, 308
time pressure, 307
external assistance, 306
fact-finding missions, 260
generalised practice, 262
inclusivity, 267, 307
jurisdiction of the ICC, 308
no blanket amnesty, 265
jurisprudence, 266
opinio iuris, 265
normative underpinnings, 196,
264
overstretch, 64

self-determination, 267
sensu stricto, 260
socialisation, 264
state practice, 263
transitional criminal justice,
260
UN Security Council, 263
women's involvement, 235
Transitional period. *See* Interregnum
Transitions *sensu lato*,
definition, 16
instances of, 111, 121, 141, 143, 164,
297, 315, 380
Transplacement, xxxii, 19–20, 85,
187, 251
Trusteeship, 34, 42, 217, 223
Turkey, 15, 21, 109, 164, 210,
264–5, 316
oppositional TA, empowerment of,
127, 321–2

Überconstitutions, 108–9
Uganda, 114, 126, 129, 307, 332
Ukraine, 5, 28, 33, 52, 56–7, 85, 105,
107–8, 129, 172, 175, 201, 205,
208, 225, 245, 263, 310–11
Ulysses, 10, 110, 253
UN Charter, 7–8, 18, 45, 48, 74, 157,
159–60, 175, 178–9, 182, 241,
286, 331, 334–5, 357
responsibilities UN Security
Council, 334
UN Constitutional Focal Point, 22,
47
UN General Assembly
accreditation, 90
oppositional TA, empowerment of,
322–3
Uniting for Peace resolution, 346
UN Guidance for Effective Mediation, 53,
56, 155, 235, 260, 267, 293, 304
UN Mediation Support Unit, 22,
46, 166
UN Peacebuilding Commission, 22,
39–40, 53, 86, 182
UN Security Council
custom formation, 177
domaine réservé, 334

INDEX

oppositional TG, inducement of,
334–5
ius in interregno abidance, 335
ius cogens violations, inactivity,
340
resolutions, binding nature of,
179–82
socialisation, 375
spoilers, 335, *See also* Spoilers
subject to international law,
335
TG, increased involvement with, 183
threat to peace, definition, 179
transitional justice, 263
women's inclusion, 234–5
United Kingdom ('UK'), 164, 265,
269, 354
oppositional TA, empowerment of,
127, 321–2
United States of America ('US'), 19, 49,
56–7, 61–2, 117, 144, 164, 167,
210, 216, 268, 289–90, 294, 297,
305–7
oppositional TA, empowerment of,
321–2
no formal recognition, 328

Use of force, 16, 19, 145, 160, 162, 326,
331–2, 358, 370
consent to, 279

Vattel, Emer de, 1, 302
Venezuela, xxiii, 5–6, 17, 48, 94, 128,
245, 316, 322, 328, 380
Venice Commission, 100, 213, 277,
285
Vienna Convention on the Law of
Treaties ('VCLT'), 89–90, 97,
162, 172, 175–6, 213, 288, 291,
298, 337, 357
coercion into TG, 291
state continuity, 213

Weber, Max, 26, 183, 208

Yemen, xxiii, 5, 7–8, 47, 52, 54, 57,
60–1, 66, 85–6, 105–8, 135, 153,
167, 172–3, 177, 179–80, 185,
201, 205, 208, 225, 233, 233,
235–6, 238, 246, 263, 278, 294,
299–300, 373

Zimbabwe, xxiii, 18, 45, 322